Visual J++™ 6 Secrets®

Visual J++™ 6 Secrets®

Chuck Wood

IDG Books Worldwide, Inc.
An International Data Group Company

Foster City, CA ♦ Chicago, IL ♦ Indianapolis, IN ♦ New York, NY

Visual J++™ 6 Secrets®

Published by
IDG Books Worldwide, Inc.
An International Data Group Company
919 E. Hillsdale Blvd., Suite 400
Foster City, CA 94404
www.idgbooks.com (IDG Books Worldwide Web site)

Library of Congress Catalog Card Number: 98-70267

ISBN: 0-7645-3138-7

Printed in the United States of America

10 9 8 7 6 5 4 3 2 1

1B/RU/QZ/ZY/FC

Distributed in the United States by IDG Books Worldwide, Inc.

Distributed by Macmillan Canada for Canada; by Transworld Publishers Limited in the United Kingdom; by IDG Norge Books for Norway; by IDG Sweden Books for Sweden; by Woodslane Pty. Ltd. for Australia; by Woodslane (NZ) Ltd. for New Zealand; by Addison Wesley Longman Singapore Pte Ltd. for Singapore, Malaysia, Thailand, Indonesia, and Korea; by Norma Comunicaciones S.A. for Colombia; by Intersoft for South Africa; by International Thomson Publishing for Germany, Austria, and Switzerland; by Toppan Company Ltd. for Japan; by Distribuidora Cuspide for Argentina; by Livraria Cultura for Brazil; by Ediciencia S.A. for Ecuador; by Ediciones ZETA S.C.R. Ltda. for Peru; by WS Computer Publishing Corporation, Inc., for the Philippines; by Unalis Corporation for Taiwan; by Contemporanea de Ediciones for Venezuela; by Computer Book & Magazine Store for Puerto Rico; by Express Computer Distributors for the Caribbean and West Indies. Authorized Sales Agent: Anthony Rudkin Associates for the Middle East and North Africa.

For general information on IDG Books Worldwide's books in the U.S., please call our Consumer Customer Service department at 800-762-2974. For reseller information, including discounts and premium sales, please call our Reseller Customer Service department at 800-434-3422.

For information on where to purchase IDG Books Worldwide's books outside the U.S., please contact our International Sales department at 650-655-3200 or fax 650-655-3297.

For information on foreign language translations, please contact our Foreign & Subsidiary Rights department at 650-655-3021 or fax 650-655-3281.

For sales inquiries and special prices for bulk quantities, please contact our Sales department at 650-655-3200 or write to the address above.

For information on using IDG Books Worldwide's books in the classroom or for ordering examination copies, please contact our Educational Sales department at 800-434-2086 or fax 317-596-5499.

For press review copies, author interviews, or other publicity information, please contact our Public Relations department at 650-655-3000 or fax 650-655-3299.

For authorization to photocopy items for corporate, personal, or educational use, please contact Copyright Clearance Center, 222 Rosewood Drive, Danvers, MA 01923, or fax 978-750-4470.

is a trademark under exclusive license to IDG Books Worldwide, Inc., from International Data Group, Inc.

ABOUT IDG BOOKS WORLDWIDE

Welcome to the world of IDG Books Worldwide.

IDG Books Worldwide, Inc., is a subsidiary of International Data Group, the world's largest publisher of computer-related information and the leading global provider of information services on information technology. IDG was founded more than 25 years ago and now employs more than 8,500 people worldwide. IDG publishes more than 275 computer publications in over 75 countries (see listing below). More than 90 million people read one or more IDG publications each month.

Launched in 1990, IDG Books Worldwide is today the #1 publisher of best-selling computer books in the United States. We are proud to have received eight awards from the Computer Press Association in recognition of editorial excellence and three from *Computer Currents'* First Annual Readers' Choice Awards. Our best-selling *...For Dummies®* series has more than 50 million copies in print with translations in 38 languages. IDG Books Worldwide, through a joint venture with IDG's Hi-Tech Beijing, became the first U.S. publisher to publish a computer book in the People's Republic of China. In record time, IDG Books Worldwide has become the first choice for millions of readers around the world who want to learn how to better manage their businesses.

Our mission is simple: Every one of our books is designed to bring extra value and skill-building instructions to the reader. Our books are written by experts who understand and care about our readers. The knowledge base of our editorial staff comes from years of experience in publishing, education, and journalism — experience we use to produce books for the '90s. In short, we care about books, so we attract the best people. We devote special attention to details such as audience, interior design, use of icons, and illustrations. And because we use an efficient process of authoring, editing, and desktop publishing our books electronically, we can spend more time ensuring superior content and spend less time on the technicalities of making books.

You can count on our commitment to deliver high-quality books at competitive prices on topics you want to read about. At IDG Books Worldwide, we continue in the IDG tradition of delivering quality for more than 25 years. You'll find no better book on a subject than one from IDG Books Worldwide.

John Kilcullen
CEO
IDG Books Worldwide, Inc.

Steven Berkowitz
President and Publisher
IDG Books Worldwide, Inc.

IDG Books Worldwide, Inc., is a subsidiary of International Data Group, the world's largest publisher of computer-related information and the leading global provider of information services on information technology. International Data Group publishes over 275 computer publications in over 75 countries. More than 90 million people read one or more International Data Group publications each month. International Data Group's publications include: **ARGENTINA:** Buyer's Guide, Computerworld Argentina; PC World Argentina; **AUSTRALIA:** Australian Macworld, Australian PC World, Australian Reseller News, Computerworld, IT Casebook, Network World, Publish, Webmaster; **AUSTRIA:** Computerwelt Osterreich, Networks Austria, PC Tip Austria; **BANGLADESH:** PC World Bangladesh; **BELARUS:** PC World Belarus; **BELGIUM:** Data News; **BRAZIL:** Annuário de Informática, Computerworld, Connections, Macworld, PC Player, PC World, Publish, Reseller News, Supergamepower; **BULGARIA:** Computerworld Bulgaria, Network World Bulgaria, PC & MacWorld Bulgaria; **CANADA:** CIO Canada, Client/Server World, ComputerWorld Canada, InfoWorld Canada, NetworkWorld Canada, WebWorld; **CHILE:** Computerworld Chile, PC World Chile; **COLOMBIA:** Computerworld Colombia, PC World Colombia; **COSTA RICA:** PC World Centro America; **THE CZECH AND SLOVAK REPUBLICS:** Computerworld Czechoslovakia, Macworld Czech Republic, PC World Czechoslovakia; **DENMARK:** Communications World Danmark, Computerworld Danmark, Macworld Danmark, PC World Danmark, Techworld Denmark; **DOMINICAN REPUBLIC:** PC World Republica Dominicana; **ECUADOR:** PC World Ecuador; **EGYPT:** Computerworld Middle East, PC World Middle East; **EL SALVADOR:** PC World Centro America; **FINLAND:** MikroPC, Tietoverkko, Tietoviikko; **FRANCE:** Distributique, Hebdo, Info PC, Le Monde Informatique, Macworld, Reseaux & Telecoms, WebMaster France; **GERMANY:** Computer Partner, Computerwoche, Computerwoche Extra, Computerwoche FOCUS, Global Online, Macwelt, PC Welt; **GREECE:** Amiga Computing, GamePro Greece, Multimedia World; **GUATEMALA:** PC World Centro America; **HONDURAS:** PC World Centro America; **HONG KONG:** Computerworld Hong Kong, PC World Hong Kong, Publish in Asia; **HUNGARY:** ABCD CD-ROM, Computerworld Szamitastechnika, Internetto online Magazine, PC World Hungary, PC-X Magazin Hungary; **ICELAND:** Tolvuheimur PC World Island; **INDIA:** Information Communications World, Information Systems Computerworld, PC World India, Publish in Asia; **INDONESIA:** InfoKomputer PC World, Komputek Computerworld, Publish in Asia; **IRELAND:** ComputerScope, PC Live!; **ISRAEL:** Macworld Israel, People & Computers/Computerworld; **ITALY:** Computerworld Italia, Macworld Italia, Networking Italia, PC World Italia; **JAPAN:** DTP World, Macworld Japan, Nikkei Personal Computing, OS/2 World Japan, SunWorld Japan, Windows NT World, Windows World Japan; **KENYA:** PC World East African; **KOREA:** Hi-Tech Information, Macworld Korea, PC World Korea; **MACEDONIA:** PC World Macedonia; **MALAYSIA:** Computerworld Malaysia, PC World Malaysia, Publish in Asia; **MALTA:** PC World Malta; **MEXICO:** Computerworld Mexico, PC World Mexico; **MYANMAR:** PC World Myanmar; **NETHERLANDS:** Computer! Totaal, LAN Internetworking Magazine, LAN World Buyers Guide, Macworld Netherlands, Net, WebWereld; **NEW ZEALAND:** Absolute Beginners Guide and Plain & Simple Series, Computer Buyer, Computer Industry Directory, Computerworld New Zealand, MTB, Network World, PC World New Zealand; **NICARAGUA:** PC World Centro America; **NORWAY:** Computerworld Norge, CW Rapport, Datamagasinet, Financial Rapport, Kursguide Norge, Macworld Norge, Multimediaworld Norge, PC World Ekspress Norge, PC World Nettverk, PC World Norge, PC World ProduktGuide Norge; **PAKISTAN:** Computerworld Pakistan; **PANAMA:** PC World Panama; **PEOPLE'S REPUBLIC OF CHINA:** China Computer Users, China Computerworld, China InfoWorld, China Telecom World Weekly, Computer & Communication, Electronic Design China, Electronics Today, Electronics Weekly, Game Software, PC World China, Popular Computer Week, Software Weekly, Software World, Telecom World; **PERU:** Computerworld Peru, PC World Profesional Peru, PC World SoHo Peru; **PHILIPPINES:** Click!, Computerworld Philippines, PC World Philippines, Publish in Asia; **POLAND:** Computerworld Poland, Computerworld Special Report Poland, Cyber, Macworld Poland, Networld Poland, PC World Komputer; **PORTUGAL:** Cerebro/PC World, Computerworld/Correio Informático, Dealer World Portugal, Mac*In/PC*In Portugal, Multimedia World; **PUERTO RICO:** PC World Puerto Rico; **ROMANIA:** Computerworld Romania, PC World Romania, Telecom Romania; **RUSSIA:** Computerworld Russia, Mir PK, Publish, Seti; **SINGAPORE:** Computerworld Singapore, PC World Singapore, Publish in Asia; **SLOVENIA:** Monitor; **SOUTH AFRICA:** Computing SA, Network World SA, Software World SA; **SPAIN:** Communicaciones World España, Computerworld España, Dealer World España, Macworld España, PC World España; **SRI LANKA:** Infolink PC World; **SWEDEN:** CAP&Design, Computer Sweden, Corporate Computing Sweden, Internetworld Sweden, it.branschen, Macworld Sweden, MaxiData Sweden, MikroDatorn, Nätverk & Kommunikation, PC World Sweden, PCaktiv, Windows World Sweden; **SWITZERLAND:** Computerworld Schweiz, Macworld Schweiz, PCtip; **TAIWAN:** Computerworld Taiwan, Macworld Taiwan, NEW ViSiON/Publish, PC World Taiwan, Windows World Taiwan; **THAILAND:** Publish in Asia, Thai Computerworld; **TURKEY:** Computerworld Turkiye, Macworld Turkiye, Network World Turkiye, PC World Turkiye; **UKRAINE:** Computerworld Kiev, Multimedia World Ukraine, PC World Ukraine; **UNITED KINGDOM:** Acorn User UK, Amiga Action UK, Amiga Computing UK, Apple Talk UK, Computing, Macworld, Parents and Computers UK, PC Advisor, PC Home, PSX Pro, The WEB; **UNITED STATES:** Cable in the Classroom, CIO Magazine, Computerworld, DOS World, Federal Computer Week, GamePro Magazine, InfoWorld, I-Way, Macworld, Network World, PC Games, PC World, Publish, Video Event, THE WEB Magazine, and WebMaster; online webzines: JavaWorld, NetscapeWorld, and SunWorld Online; **URUGUAY:** InfoWorld Uruguay; **VENEZUELA:** Computerworld Venezuela, PC World Venezuela; and **VIETNAM:** PC World Vietnam. 5/7/98

Credits

Acquisitions Editor
John Osborn

Development Editor
Laura E. Brown

Technical Editor
Gene Olafsen

Copy Editors
Pamela Clark
Barry Childs-Helton
Marcia Baker

Project Coordinator
Tom Debolski

Quality Control Specialists
Constance Petros
Mark Schumann
Mick Arellano

Graphics and Production Specialists
Stephanie Hollier
Linda Marousek
Hector Mendoza
Mary Penn
Christopher Pimentel
Jude Levinson

Proofreader
David Wise

Indexer
Sharon Hilgenberg

Cover Photo
Mark Johann/Photonica

Cover Coordinator
Andreas Schueller

About the Author

Chuck Wood is a systems consultant, instructor, and author. He has over 10 years experience developing software in Java, PowerBuilder, C++, Visual Basic, and other languages.

Chuck is the author of *Visual J++*, *Using PowerBuilder*, and *Using Watcom SQL*. He contributed to *PowerBuilder 4*, *Client/Server Unleashed,* and *Special Edition Using Turbo C++ for Windows*.

Chuck has spoken internationally on database design, object-oriented design, Java programming, and PowerBuilder development, and has taught classes in Advanced System Development in Java at the University of Minnesota as well as C and C++ courses at Indiana Vocational Technical College. Chuck has bachelor's degrees in corporate finance and computer science, and a master's degree in business administration. He is currently pursuing a Ph.D. in information and decision sciences at the University of Minnesota.

I would like to dedicate this book to the three girls in my life. Lyn, Kelly, and Kailyn, thanks for putting up with me as I write yet another book. My life would be empty without you.

Preface

Visual J++ 6 Secrets takes the Visual J++ 6.0 environment and *rips it apart* to find out how to make Visual J++ work the way you want. This book is more advanced than other Java and Visual J++ books. It starts where most other Java books end. It covers areas that other books don't (unless the authors of those other books read this one first!). Instead of repeating documentation, the entire Visual J++ package is delved into, picked apart, tested, reviewed, and documented. *Visual J++ 6 Secrets* is more than just a rehash of Visual J++ 1.0 documentation with a couple of added features (as many other Visual J++ books are). Visual J++ 6.0 is vastly different from Visual J++ 1.0 and 1.1 — and this book lets you know all the differences.

Just because this book is advanced doesn't mean it's hard to read. It has tons of code inside, often as many as four fully functional, fully commented Java programs per chapter! ADO and JDBC class libraries, WFC coding techniques that go beyond how to paint a window, Dynamic HTML with database access, and advanced Java AWT and networking are just some of the really technical areas covered. You also get examples, step-by-step instructions, screen shots, and, best of all, you get *secrets!*

Who This Book Is For

This book is definitely for Java programmers who want to learn Visual J++ or want to take their development to the next highest step. This book contains advanced code samples, database techniques, client/server development, and many new code examples to help developer efforts.

This book is *not* for new programmers. Although it's not intended for those first starting to learn Java — with the possible exception of current C++ developers — if you fall into this category, check out Appendix D (which compares and contrasts Java with C++) before you get into the Java code.

What This Book Covers

Visual J++6 Secrets is divided into five parts.

Part I: Dealing with Visual Studio

Part I discusses debugging, Visual Studio tools, and Visual Studio sources. Here I describe Visual Studio solutions, Visual Studio projects, painters, and other neat features. If you're a Java developer who has just started using the Visual Studio 6.0 environment, this part is for you. Also, if you have been a Visual J++ 1.1 user and are upgrading to the new version, you should review this part to get a handle on the new environment.

Part II: Visual J++: Java with Cream and Sugar

There's Java, and then there's Visual J++ Java. Visual J++ comes with tools and methods for accessing some of the Windows environment directly:

- Tools such as the Windows Foundation Class (WFC), ActiveX, COM, Internet Explorer and ActiveX security, and delegates are discussed. Many of these methods only work within a Windows environment.

- Certain tools covered in this part, such as JavaBeans, can work in the standard Java environments. (Incidentally, JavaBeans can be used to contain ActiveX components).

- Dynamic HTML is discussed; it runs on Microsoft servers but can deliver runtime HTML for ultimate compatibility, even if the Web browser in use is not Java-enabled.

- You'll learn about Microsoft's enterprise-wide tools. Visual SourceSafe employs a check-in, check-out process that allows you to develop new code while constantly keeping older versions of the code in an archive. (This is a wonderful feature for group development.)

- Microsoft Transaction Server Development is also discussed as an enterprise-wide development tool.

- Finally, Microsoft has packaging and deployment options that are hard to match anywhere else. Remote deployment, self-extracting setup files, Windows Executable development, ZIP and CAB file development, and digital signatures are all discussed.

Part III: Developing 100% Pure Java with Visual J++

Microsoft has included a wide variety of Windows development tools, but Visual J++ can also be used to deliver standard, 100% pure Java. This part shows how standard Java can be accomplished using Visual J++. Here are some of the topics covered in this part:

- The Advanced Window Toolkit (AWT) is discussed. You can see how to make business forms that use standard Java, and how to program for events.

- Graphics can spice up any Web page. There are some advanced programs that show how to inherit a component, how to draw using the XOR mode, and how to handle animation.

- File IO is also discussed. Sometimes, it's quicker and easier to store information in a file. Printing is also discussed in this part.

- This part shows how Java interfaces are supposed to be implemented. Java interfaces can be used to implement *safe* multiple inheritance.

- Java data structures such as arrays, vectors, pointers, linked lists, and binary trees are discussed.

- Threads, advanced threads, and multithreading are the key to making a Java program efficient. You'll need to understand threads to make a graphical Java program.

- Finally, Web programming is discussed. You'll need to understand Web programming to implement your Java applets over the Web. Advanced topics such as networking, sockets, and HTML interfacing are also discussed.

Part IV: Database Development in Visual J++

Talk about alphabet soup! Unlike standard Java, there are many different ways to access a database inside Visual J++:

- Microsoft's new standard, ActiveX Data Objects (ADO), is discussed. A new database application is painted to show you how Microsoft can quickly deliver a database application.

- For those of you ready to leave the painter behind, an ADO class library is developed that can increase your productivity and standard interfaces in a way the ADO painter never could.

- Just to add equal time, a JDBC (Java Database Connectivity) class library is also developed. JDBC is the Java standard for database access. By using JDBC you can ensure that your applications work on all Java-enabled machines.

- Older standards such as DAO (Data Access Objects) and RDO (Remote Data Objects) are also discussed. DAO has been somewhat superseded by ADO, but there's a lot of DAO code still out there, and you can still use it if you need to. RDO is still in use as a fast interface to ODBC.

- What would database access be without the Standard Query Language (SQL)? A chapter that briefly covers some of the more common and more standard SQL statements is introduced.

Oh, and if you want more database stuff, don't forget Part I. Dynamic HTML can also access ODBC database. In Part I, I show you how.

Appendixes

Some topics are important, but didn't fit within the book's chapter structure. That's why the following appendixes are included:

- Appendix A is a Java language reference for quick reviews and reminders on standard Java syntax and operators.

- Appendix B is a reserved-word reference to make sure you don't use reserved words incorrectly or as part of a variable name.

- Appendix C is an HTML reference so you can review your HTML code.

- For you C++ developers who don't want to start from scratch, Appendix D compares and contrasts Java with C++. This appendix gets C++ developers up to speed without having to start over.

- Java is an international standard, and uses Unicode rather than ASCII for character strings. Appendix E discusses Unicode.

What Are Visual J++ Secrets?

Secret

Secrets are denoted with the Secret icon. A secret can be any one of the following:

- Features that are deliberately hidden

- Features that are poorly documented or not documented at all

- Complex techniques that require a deep understanding of Visual J++ and Java

- Industry observations that may have affected (or will affect) Visual J++ production development but are beyond the scope of pure Visual J++ use

The goal of any Secrets book is to not only give you an advanced reference and tutorial, but also to include those topics that may be too difficult for other authors to discover, understand, or convey.

What's a Sidebar?

This is a sidebar. If a secret is outside the normal scope of the book and is pretty lengthy, it may be included in a sidebar. Sidebars separate out the lengthy information so that the reader is not distracted when trying to learn the Visual J++ advanced procedures.

Comments from the Author

Currently, Microsoft and Sun are both trying to establish standards that enable developers to write code that can run over the Internet and is accessible in any environment. Their competition has resulted in products that can help you develop and deploy solutions that were unthinkable five years ago.

This book is designed to help you on your journey to be come a world-class Windows and Internet developer. The result is a fantastic book that can really help you. I hope you enjoy this book.

Acknowledgments

An author never writes a book by himself. Any book is impossible without the combined efforts of several hard-working individuals. I would like to take a moment to acknowledge them.

Special thanks to Laura Brown and John Osborn. Their tireless efforts, reviews, comments, and encouragement made this book possible. Also, special thanks to Gene Olafsen for technically reviewing the book and writing the much needed chapter on Java Beans. Special thanks to Chris "Deal Maker" van Buren of Waterside, Inc. for putting me in contact with the wonderful people at IDG Books Worldwide. Thanks to all the people at IDG Books who helped get this book out, including Pamela Clark, Barry Childs-Helton, Marcia Baker, and Tom Debolski.

Finally, a special thanks to my wife, Lyn, and my daughters, Kelly and Kailyn, who have to put up with me while I exist on a diet of coffee and no sleep while I write.

Contents at a Glance

Contents

Introduction

Java is, by almost any measure, the most successful new language ever. Because Sun Microsystems developed Java on the basis of C++, the Java language is designed for object-oriented, network-intensive programming. However, Java surpasses C++ by including many features such as automatic garbage collection, interfaces, exception handling, and inherent multithread support. These additions allow developers to write high-quality code more rapidly, in ways C++ developers have only dreamed of.

Java has also become the top Internet development tool. Java applets are easily incorporated into Web pages to allow sophisticated Web pages that are not possible with traditional HTML.

Although Java has become something of an immediate standard, traditional Windows programming was often forgotten in Java environments. Windows includes years of development and several tools built directly into the operating system. In addition, many current packages and software cannot be interfaced into the Java Virtual Machine. Often, the resulting choice of developers is to develop *either* Java applications *or* Windows applications. Even some environments that offered to compile Windows executables forced developers to abandon advanced and robust Windows tools in favor of Java libraries.

Visual J++ is the first tool that combines a fully functional Windows development environment with a fully functional Java development environment to give you the best of both worlds. Unlike other Java development environments, Visual J++ allows you to:

- Write pure Java and deliver it as both a .Class file or an .EXE file

- Write Java code that directly accesses the Windows environment and be run on any Windows Web client

- Write in Visual Studio, which is also the environment for Visual C++ and Visual Basic

- Write database calls directly into your Java code using ODBC, OLE DB, JDBC, DAO, DHTML, or RDO

With a system full of such features, Visual J++ is destined to become the premier Java development platform. Microsoft has enabled Java to be more productive than any other Java development tool, and more versatile than any other Windows development tool. People may gravitate toward Visual J++ for this reason alone.

Sun developed Java to work a certain way; Microsoft wants to implement Java another way. The tension between the owners of a language and the licensers of a language has led to two developments:

- Microsoft has tried extremely hard to give you the best Java development environment possible. Visual J++ surpasses other development environments to deliver a truly professional and enterprise-wide Java development *and* Windows development environment.

- In an effort to convince you to code Java for Windows, Microsoft has not fully endorsed some pure Java development methods, such as JDBC or JavaBeans. (They prefer that you use Windows calls rather than Java routines.) However, contrary to some popular press articles, Visual J++ is more than capable of compiling pure Java 1.1 (as are JavaBeans and JDBC) and delivering standard .class files to the Web. Delving into how Java is implemented in the Visual J++ environment is the source of many of this book's secrets.

By including such strong Windows support, Visual J++ has opened the door for concurrent Java and Windows development. This book shows that if you're coding in pure Java, you can deliver Java classes that run on any Java-aware machine and Windows executables that install automatically from a CD or disk *without changing a line of code*! You'll even see how to deploy the output from your files, to specific remote locations with a click of the mouse.

What's New with Visual J++ 6.0

It would help if you thought of Visual J++ 6.0 as a completely new product, and not as an extension of Visual J++ 1.1. Consider some of these features:

- A totally new environment. Visual Studio has a completely different look and feel from Developer Studio (used in Visual J++ 1.1).

- The Java 1.1 specification is supported, instead of the Java 1.0 specification supported in Visual Studio 1.1. (The Java 1.1 specification is much more advanced and complicated.)

- Microsoft Developers Network (MSDN) is used for the help system. The Infoviewer used in Visual J++ 1.1 is gone.

- Microsoft has added a screen painter for Windows Foundation Class (WFC) applications that can access remote databases using ActiveX Data Objects (ADO). The WFC encapsulates J-Direct Windows API and Dynamic HTML object model in a unified class package, easily accessible from Java. Although not painter-enabled, the Java 1.1 AWT classes and the JDBC classes are also supported.

- You can develop COM modules or access COM modules from within your Visual J++ environment. (You could also use and develop COM modules in Visual J++ 1.1, but that was a lot harder.)

- Dynamic HTML is supported. You can create HTML on the fly for remote viewers.

- You get tons of database support, including ADO, DHTML, JDBC, DAO, and RDO. All of these can access ODBC data sources.

- You get an on-the-fly syntax checker and popup, as-you-type class and parameter information.

- You can package and deploy your applications as Java classes, Windows executables, COM components, Web pages, ZIP files, CAB files, or even self-extracting setup files. These deployment options also support digital signatures for enhanced security.

- You can build enterprise-wide systems that use Active Server Page or Microsoft Transaction Server and DCOM components.

Moving on

In Chapter 1, you delve into Visual J++ and Visual Studio, examining Visual J++ environment fundamentals and mastering the functions of Visual Studio. So let's get started.

Part I

Dealing with Visual Studio

Chapter 1

Delving into Visual J++ and Visual Studio

In This Chapter

▶ Examining Visual J++ environment fundamentals

▶ Using Projects and Solutions

▶ Mastering the functions of the Visual Studio

Visual Studio is the Microsoft environment for both their Visual C++ and Visual J++ languages. An understanding of the environment and the tools that are included with Visual J++ is necessary to master Java development.

Visual Studio is relatively new. Visual J++ 1.0 and 1.1 came with Developer's Studio, which was the precursor to Visual Studio. Developer's Studio did not include many of the features that are included in Visual Studio (such as Visual Basic and Visual FoxPro). In addition, the integration of the products was almost nonexistent. Visual Studio not only integrates the help files but also includes such features as the Microsoft Developers Network (MSDN) and Windows Foundation Class (WFC) support.

Understanding Projects and Solutions

Traditional Java development is done at the file level. That is, you edit a single Java file, compile it, then move on to the next Java file. For Java developers, this is cumbersome, especially if there are several Java files and packages to keep track of, as is the case in multiuser environments where you may be working on someone else's code or project.

Microsoft has introduced a hierarchical structure to help Java development. All Java files that relate to a package (including HTML files) are placed inside a *Project*. Several projects, then, can be placed inside a *Solution*. This is shown graphically in Figure 1-1.

This section shows you how to use Visual J++ Projects and Visual J++ Solutions to manage your Java development efforts.

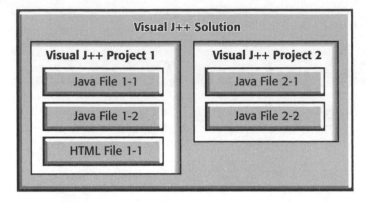

Figure 1-1: Java files are placed inside a Visual J++ Project. Several projects are placed inside a Visual J++ Solution.

Creating a new project

Projects in Visual J++ are a common-sense approach to the traditional Java package. Like packages, Projects enable you to group several Java files together in a single directory. Projects contain all the information needed to compile and execute a program. Usually, you create a Project on the first compile and then use the Project to retrieve a program, rather than opening the Java program without a Project. This is helpful because you only need to define your environment once. You can then pull up the same environment for later work without having to reset everything (such as how to execute the system, what files are contained in the project, and so on).

When you first enter the Visual J++ environment, the New Project window pops up (Figure 1-2). (This can also be opened by clicking File, New from the Visual J++ menu.)

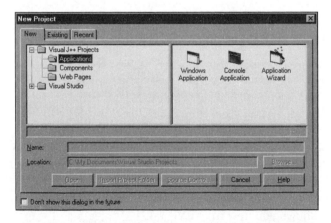

Figure 1-2: Visual J++ Projects and Solutions can be created by using the New Project window.

In the New Project window, you can do the following:

- Create a Java application by clicking the Console Application or the Windows Application icon. Normally the Console Application icon is used. Console applications have an advantage over Windows applications for straight Java because console applications display any untrapped error messages in the MS-DOS window created by the JVIEW application.

- Create a Windows application by clicking the Console Application or the Windows Application icon. Usually the Windows Application icon is used. Windows applications take advantage of Microsoft's Windows Foundation Class (WFC), although you can replace the generated code with your own Java 1.1-compliant code. Windows applications use the WJVIEW application to run the Java code.

- Create COM (Common Object Model) Components from Java by clicking Components. These components can be called by any ActiveX-compliant program.

- Click on Web Pages (Figure 1-3) to create Java Applets that run on the Web.

- Create Dynamic HTML applications that can run on any Web page or Web server. Dynamic HTML is a WFC-based program that can create HTML dynamically. Dynamic HTML can be used if you want to use WFC, and also want to allow non-Microsoft developers to access your Web site.

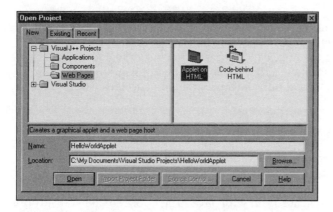

Figure 1-3: Projects can contain all the files necessary to create HTML documents or Dynamic HTML documents that create the necessary HTML at runtime.

After choosing a Java application type, click OK, and a Project is created for you. As shown in Figure 1-4, Visual J++ automatically generates a skeleton program for you. This makes development easier and eliminates some syntactical errors (like forgetting to import the proper files or forgetting to code an `init()` method).

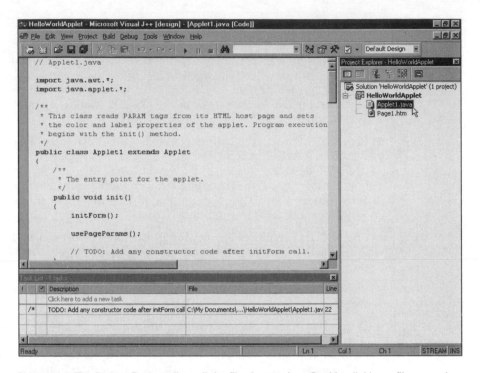

Figure 1-4: The Project Explorer lists all the files in a project. Double-clicking a file opens it in the Visual Studio environment.

Secret

The Application Wizard is a type of project that builds a Java/Windows program using WFC. This topic is covered in Chapters 4 and 23. Be careful when using the Application Wizard, because the code it generates is strictly for Windows and Internet Explorer. The Application Wizard, WFC programming, and pure Java programming are discussed in more detail later.

Renaming projects and project files

You can enter the name of your project in the New Project window shown in Figures 1-2 and 1-3. However, the names of the Java programs created are meaningless (for example Applet1.java, Page1.htm, and so on). You can delete existing files from your Java Project or rename your programs by right-clicking the file and choosing your action from the pop-up menu, as shown in Figure 1-5.

Secret

Be sure that all your Java programs have a .java extension or they won't compile. Compiling and syntax checking are discussed in a later section of this chapter. If you rename a Java Web-based program, you need to go into the HTML file and change the name of the program that is run from `Applet1.class` **to** `yournewname.class`.

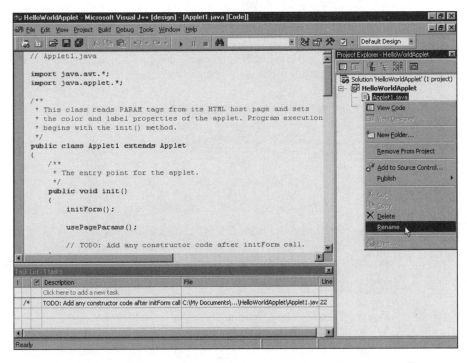

Figure 1-5: You can delete existing files from your Java project or rename your programs by right-clicking the file and choosing your action from the pop-up menu.

Opening existing projects

By choosing File, Open Project on the Visual Studio menu bar, you open the New Project window shown in Figure 1-2. By clicking the Existing tab (Figure 1-6), you can see folders that contain Project files.

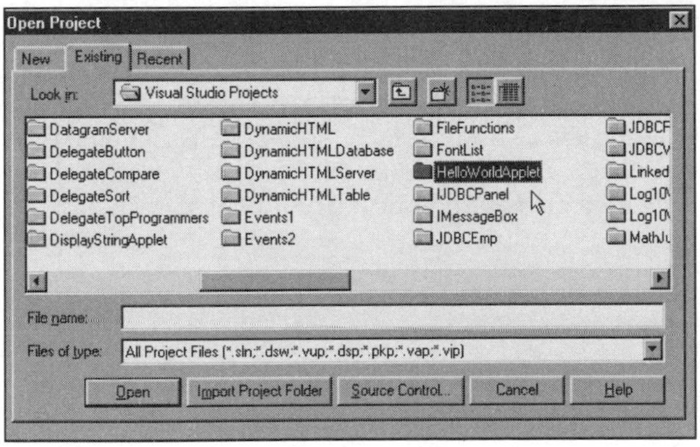

Figure 1-6: Every existing project has its own folder.

By double-clicking a folder, you can see all Project or Solution files that exist in that folder (Figure 1-7). A *.sln* file is a Solution file that was created by Visual J++ to contain Projects. A *.vjp* file is a Project file that contains references to Java files. If you open a Project file where no Solution file exists, a Solution file is automatically created.

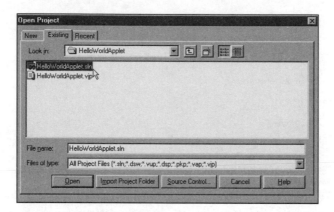

Figure 1-7: You can open Projects by opening Solution files or by opening Project files.

Creating new classes in your project

A Project can contain many classes. To insert a new Java file containing a public Java class into a folder, click Project, Add Class from the Visual Studio menu or right-click the Project and click Add ⇨ Add Class as shown in Figure 1-8.

Figure 1-8: One of the ways to insert a new class into a Visual J++ Project is to right-click Add ⇨ Add Class.

This opens the Add Item window as shown in Figure 1-9. This window enables you to add a class, an interface, an HTML Web page, or a WFC class. Click the type of class you want to insert and then type the class name to add a completely new class into your current project.

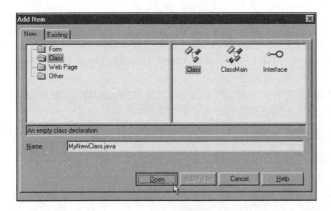

Figure 1-9: The Add Item window enables you to add several different types of classes to your Visual J++ Project.

Opening existing Java files

New files can also be created using the Open File window. The Open File window is also used to add existing files to your Visual J++ Project (Figure 1-10). The Open File window can be reached by choosing File, Open File or File, New File from your Visual Studio environment.

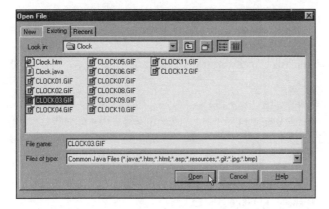

Figure 1-10: You can add files to a Miscellaneous Files section of your Visual J++ Solution using the Open File window.

In Figure 1-10, a .gif file was added to a project. This .gif file can now be displayed under a Miscellaneous Files project, as shown in Figure 1-11. Double-clicking the filename opens the file using the appropriate application. (In this case, Internet Explorer usually opens .gif files.)

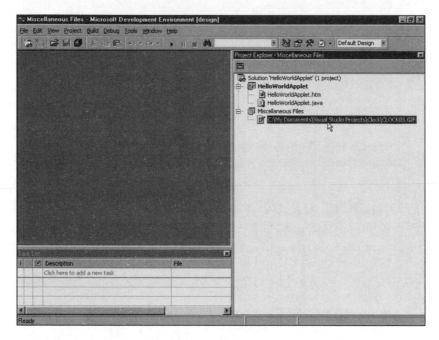

Figure 1-11: The files you open or create in the Open File window are added to the Miscellaneous Files Project under the current Solution.

Secret

If you'd rather have the new file as part of the existing Project, then move the file to the Project's directory. Once that is done, Visual J++ detects it and adds it to your project file list.

Looking at the Toolbox and HTML inside Visual Studio

Visual Studio is good not only for creating Java applications, but also for editing HTML. When you double-click an HTML file, Design, Source, and Quick View tabs are displayed along the bottom of your editor window. The Toolbox (which is activated using Ctrl+Alt+X and closed by using the Destroy button on the Toolbox window) lists HTML controls that can be added to an HTML document. The toolbox enables you to actually paint your HTML document.

Figure 1-12 shows how a Submit button, a Reset button, and a file opener were all added to the HTML document using the Visual J++ Toolbox.

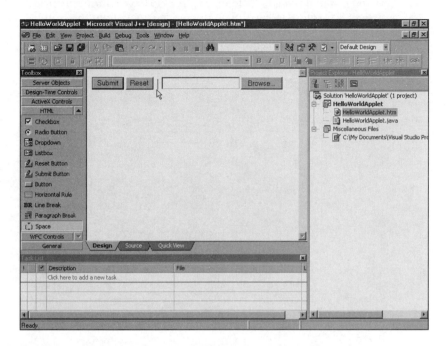

Figure 1-12: Visual J++ has a great HTML painter.

Listing 1-1 shows the HTML source code that was generated after the Visual J++ screen painter was activated.

Listing 1-1: HelloWorldApplet.htm

```html
<HTML>
<HEAD>
<META NAME="GENERATOR" Content="Microsoft Visual Studio 98">
<META HTTP-EQUIV="Content-Type" content="text/html">
<TITLE>Document Title</TITLE>
</HEAD>
<BODY><!-- Insert HTML here -->
  <INPUT id=submit1 name=submit1 type=submit value=Submit>
  <INPUT id=reset1 name=reset1 type=reset alue=Reset>
     
<INPUT id=file1 name=file1 type=file>
<APPLET code=HelloWorldApplet.class
codeBase="file://C:\My Documents\Visual Studio Projects\HelloWorldApplet\"
height=248 name=Applet1 style="HEIGHT: 248px; WIDTH: 393px" width=393>
  <PARAM NAME="foreground" VALUE="FFFFFF">
  <PARAM NAME="background" VALUE="008080">
  <PARAM NAME="label" VALUE="This string was passed from the HTML host.">
  </APPLET>
  </BODY>
</HTML>
```

In the preceding code, the Submit, Reset, and File buttons were added with `<INPUT. . .>` tags, and five spaces were added with an ` ` tag. Although the generated code is a little messy, it's code you didn't need to write yourself. The Quick View tag enables you to see how the buttons look in relation to your Java class file placement. The Browse button even works and pulls up files under the HTML document, as shown in Figure 1-13.

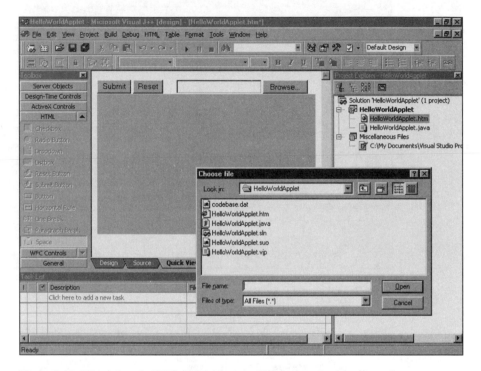

Figure 1-13: Visual J++'s HTML Quick View enables you to check out your Java program inside your Visual J++ environment.

The Toolbox is also used when painting WFC controls. Unfortunately, the Toolbox cannot be used when coding 100 percent pure Java, although you can type in pure Java and make class files from it using Visual J++.

Secret

Sometimes, you want to quickly get into an HTML file, make some easy text changes, and get out again. This is easily accomplished by right-clicking the HTML file, choosing Open With, and clicking the Source Code (Text) Editor, as shown in Figure 1-14. This enables you to quickly open your file, make some changes, and quickly close it again without waiting for Visual Studio to try to paint your Web page and run your applet.

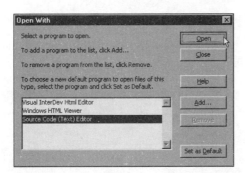

Figure 1-14: The Open With dialog box enables you to open HTML with a simple text editor.

Adding projects to solutions

Many Projects can be contained inside one Solution. Projects are a neat way to have Java code from two different directories "talk" to each other without adding an entry to your class path in your registry. To add a Project to a Solution, right-click the Solution and choose Add Project from the popup menu, as shown in Figure 1-15.

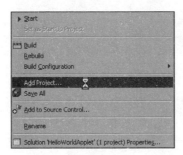

Figure 1-15: You can add a Project to a Solution by using the popup menu.

This pulls up the Add Project window (Figure 1-16). From this window, you can create a new Project for this Solution, or you can choose any other Project or Solution to add to your current Solution.

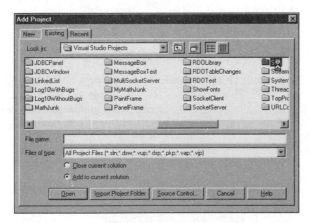

Figure 1-16: The Add Project window can be used to add a new, recent, or existing Java Project to an existing Java Solution.

Once you've added a Project or Solution to your current Solution, it displays in the Project Explorer. In Figure 1-17, the Sort Project is added to the HelloWorldApplet Project. Now code from HelloWorldApplet can call public variables from the Sort Project.

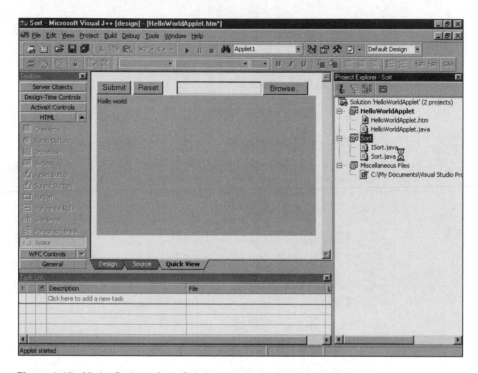

Figure 1-17: All the Projects for a Solution are displayed in the Project Explorer.

Building and Running a System

After you've written your Java code, you can run it from the Visual Studio environment. This section discusses Project settings and compiling and running your Java program.

Using the Visual J++ environment

Compared to how most developers build Java systems, the Visual J++ environment is a marvel. Visual J++ has features that are not found in any other Java development environment. Three of these features are tokenized comments, as-you-type programming help, and Microsoft Word-like syntax-error highlighting.

Tokenized comments

Microsoft enables you to embed messages inside comments that can be displayed in the task list at the bottom of the Visual J++ environment. This is done by typing in TODO after a comment, as shown in Figure 1-18.

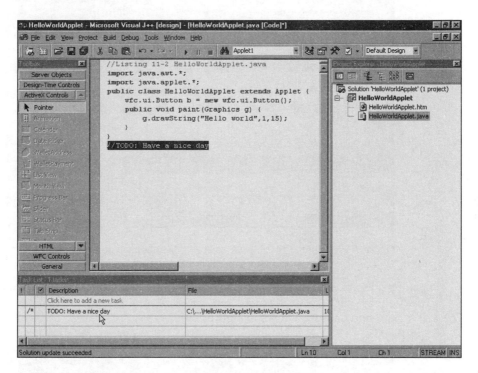

Figure 1-18: TODO lists can make development easier by giving a developer the capability to leave messages.

Figure 1-18 shows the message, "Have a nice day," left inside the Visual J++ code. Using TODO comments, a developer can leave comments (such as "Delete this line after Christmas" or "Talk to Joe before deleting this code") that can make the development and maintenance process easier.

Help while you type

One of the neatest new features in Visual J++ 6 occurs while you are typing. To help you remember which methods belong to a class or which classes belong to a package, Visual J++ generates a popup list of possible expression completions. As you type, the list shrinks until the proper method or class is displayed. (See Figure 1-19.) The method parameters are also displayed as you type.

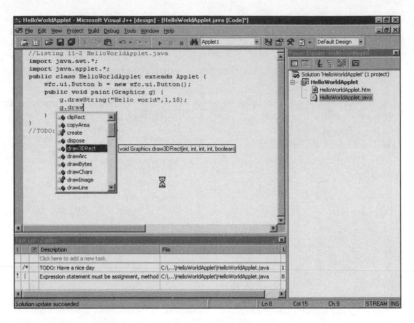

Figure 1-19: Both the possible methods and the method parameters display as you type.

If a method has more than one polymorphic method prototype, a multiple-choice list is created where you can click to toggle between accepted method calls, as shown in Figure 1-20.

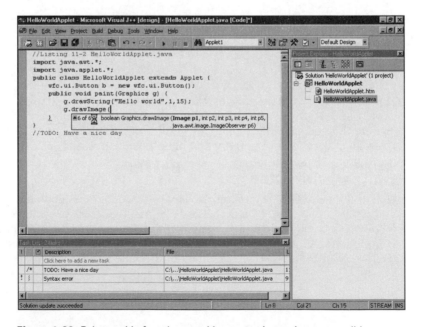

Figure 1-20: Polymorphic functions enable you to choose between valid parameters for a method call.

No other development environment offers so much support so easily.

Errors while you type

Visual Studio highlights errors while you type with the same red curvy lines as those used in Microsoft Word to indicate spelling errors. Many errors appear as they are typed, avoiding the need for a formal compilation. If you see a red curvy line, like the one in Figure 1-21, position the cursor over it to display the detected error.

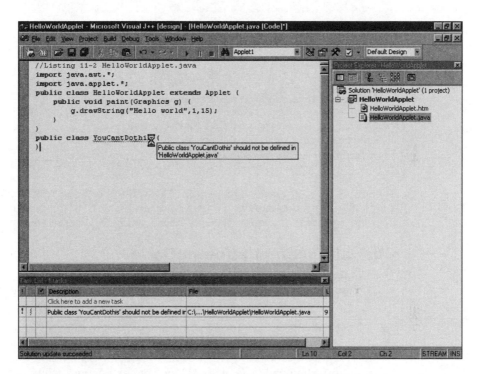

Figure 1-21: Errors, such as two public classes in one Java source file, are detected as you type.

Changing project properties

Visual J++ developers need to change the default project settings too often. Although Visual J++ tries to determine how you want to run your program, you may not agree with the assumptions it makes (such as automatically generating an .exe file), and your programs may have dramatically increased compile times. To change the Project settings, choose Project ⇨ Properties or press Alt+F7. The Properties window appears, as shown in Figure 1-22. From here you can choose different compile options and which Web browser file is opened at run time.

Figure 1-22: You can change the default compile and runtime settings in your Project by using the Properties window.

You see the Launch tab in Figure 1-22. The Launch tab controls which Java or HTML program is launched at run time, and which program is used to launch it. Many more properties can be set using the Properties window.

Changing compilation options

The Compile tab gives you control over some compilation options (Figure 1-23). This is especially useful if you are working in a multiuser environment. The following options can be checked:

- Disable Microsoft Language Extensions — This feature helps to ensure a 100 percent Java environment. Do this if you are using different Java development tools. However, be careful, because Microsoft packages still function when called. Only their language extensions, such as delegate and multicast, are disabled.

- Optimize compiled code — This feature enables your code to run more quickly. However, if you have runtime errors that don't seem to be caused by your code, disable this option and see if they go away.

- Generate Debugging Information — This feature provides information during development. Turn this feature off during deployment. With no debugging information, your Java code is smaller, runs faster, and has less chance of being hacked into.

- Recompile only changed files — This speeds up your compilation. Check it, and if you run into problems during run time, you can always turn it off.

Figure 1-23: You can change the compile options by using the Compile tab in the Properties window.

Changing your classpath

The Classpath tab (Figure 1-24) is useful when you want to add other Java class libraries to existing code. It can be used to include Sun's default libraries or other vendor-specific Java class libraries.

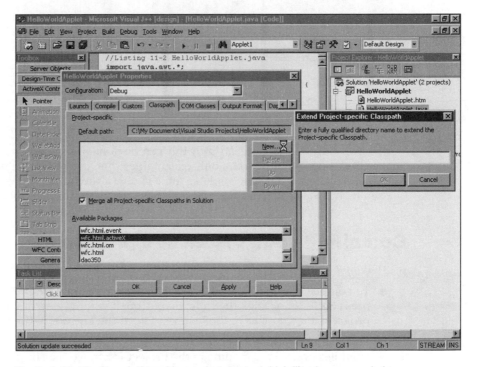

Figure 1-24: The Classpath enables you to choose which libraries are needed to run your program.

Generating a Windows executable

When you are developing a stand-alone Java application, Visual J++ defaults to creating a Windows executable as well. While this is not necessarily a bad thing, generating an executable takes longer than compiling a Java class library, especially if you consider that Microsoft has one of the fastest (if not the fastest) Java compilers available.

To change your compilation output, click the Output Format tab, as shown in Figure 1-25. Here, you can check Enable Packaging and deliver a Windows executable from your Java source code.

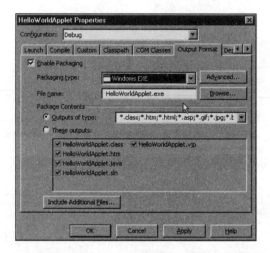

Figure 1-25: You can deliver a Windows executable from any stand-alone Java application.

Secret

I just enabled an executable to be generated for a Web page for display purposes only. Although *technically* this can be done, it usually is just not possible using Visual J++. The only executables that can be generated are Java applications, not Java Applets. You can check the option to generate an .exe file, but Visual J++ returns an error message when it tries to build it.

Compiling your Visual J++ program

Compiling a Visual J++ program is straightforward. Remember these points:

■ To compile your new Visual J++ program, choose Build from the menu, press Shift+F8, or click the Compile button. If you have errors in your program, they appear in the task window at the bottom of the screen.

■ Visual J++ supports project builds. When building a project, Visual J++ compiles every Java module in the Project (or those that haven't already been compiled or that have been modified since the last compile, depending on your compile options).

■ If you have set options that don't force a recompile on certain modules that you want recompiled, you need to rebuild the entire project. This can be necessary if some called class methods have changed or if your project no longer seems to function. To recompile every module in a project, select Build, Rebuild from the menu.

■ You may notice or remember some errors in your Project after starting a build. You *could* stop a build by choosing Build, Cancel from the Visual J++ menu (Figure 1-26). This menu option is only available during a build. However, Visual J++ compiles code at such an extremely fast rate that I don't think you ever get the chance to actually stop a build.

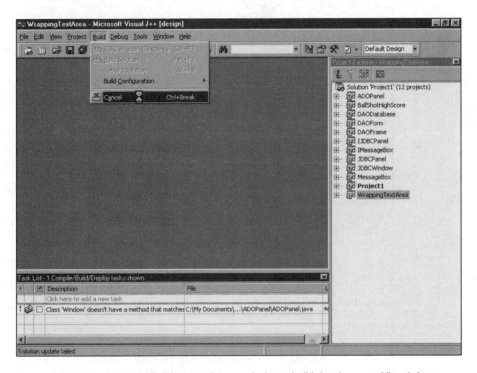

Figure 1-26: Visual J++'s Build menu changes during a build, but because Visual J++ compiles so quickly, most developers never notice.

Running your Visual J++ program

When you're finished compiling, you can run your Visual J++ program by choosing Debug, Start Without Debugging, or press Ctrl+ F5. Visual J++ automatically issues a build and saves all files. Visual J++ then uses the appropriate tool (for example, JVIEW.EXE, WJVIEW.EXE, or Internet Explorer) to run your application.

Customizing Your Toolbars

Before you learn which buttons perform which functions, you should know how to add buttons to toolbars and how to view other toolbars on your system. When you right-click a toolbar, a pop-up menu appears (see Figure 1-27). The same menu can be shown by clicking View, Toolbars from the menu.

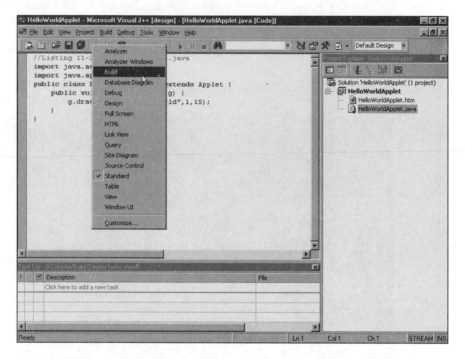

Figure 1-27: You can choose which toolbars to display, or choose to customize your toolbars by right-clicking any toolbar.

Choose Customize from the menu to open the Customize dialog box (see Figure 1-28).

Figure 1-28: The Customize dialog box enables you to choose which toolbars should be shown and to set options about your toolbar buttons.

The Customize dialog box gives the developer several options:

- The Toolbars Tab enables you to choose, once more, which toolbars to show.

- By clicking the Commands tab, you can drag-and-drop icons to and from a toolbar (Figure 1-29).

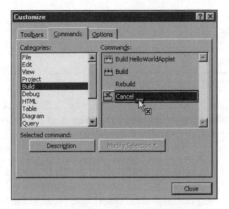

Figure 1-29: The Commands tab of the Customize dialog box give you an easy way to drag and drop icons to and from a toolbar.

- Using the Options tab (Figure 1-30) on the Customize dialog box, you can choose to show or disable ToolTips, and you can disable showing the shortcut key combination that can perform the same task. You can also display larger icons if you wish.

Figure 1-30: The Options tab of the Customize dialog box enables you to display icons the way you want them displayed.

ToolTips are yellow boxes that appear if you keep your mouse over a button for a second or two. They're really helpful, especially when you're in a new environment.

Secret

I really wouldn't disable ToolTips. They're pretty useful, especially with the scores of buttons included in the multiple toolbars inside the Visual Studio.

Examining Other Visual Studio Functions

Table 1-1 shows some popular Visual J++ functionality — the icons that can be used for some of the more popular Windows functionality.

Secret

Some of the buttons shown in this section are not available by default, but can be added to any toolbar.

Table 1-1	Visual Studio Functions	
Icon	Function	Description
	Add Item	Adds an item to the existing Project list
	Copy	Copies any selected text (leaving the text on the file) and places the text on the Clipboard. Pressing Ctrl+C or choosing Edit, Copy also copies selected text to the Clipboard.
	Cut	Cuts any selected text (deleting the text from the file) and places the text on the Clipboard. Pressing Ctrl+X or choosing Edit, Cut also cuts selected text to the Clipboard.
	Delete	Deletes any selected text from the current file. Pressing the Del key when text is selected has the same effect.
	New Project	Opens a new Visual J++ Project
	Paste	Pastes any text from the Clipboard to the current cursor location in the Studio. Pressing Ctrl+V or choosing Edit, Paste also pastes text from the Clipboard to your current Studio document.
	Print	You can print your Java files by clicking the Print button, or by choosing File, Print. The Print dialog box appears, and enables you to choose the printer and the number of copies.
	Redo	The Redo button repeats actions that were undone. Clicking the Redo button (or pressing Ctrl+Y or choosing Edit, Redo) redoes one action. You can also redo several undone actions using the multilevel Redo button.
	Save	Saves the current open document
	Save All	Saves all open documents

Icon	Function	Description
	Find and Replace	Visual J++ supports the standard find and replace functions. Click the Find button (or press Ctrl+F or choose Edit, Find) to open the Find dialog box (see Figure 1-14). Here you can specify the usual find criteria, such as case, whole word, or whether to search up or down. F3 finds the next entry in a document. Search and Replace enables you to specify the search and replace string as well as the search criteria and whether you want the whole file searched or just a selection.
	Tile Horizontal	Horizontally tiles all open windows
	Tile Vertical	Vertically tiles all open windows
	Undo	The Visual Studio supports multilevel undos. To undo the last action you performed, click the Undo button, press Ctrl+Z, or choose Edit, Undo. You can also redo several undone actions using the multilevel Redo button.
	Window Cascade	Cascades all open windows
	Window Split	Splits the current window into panes so you can view part of a file while keeping another part always in view

Summary

- The Visual Studio, with tokenized comments, standard Windows functionality, integrated debugging, and customizable toolbars, is arguably the best Java development environment available.

- Visual J++ Solutions contain Visual J++ projects.

- Visual J++ Projects contain Java programs, HTML files, graphics, and any other files that are implemented in a Java development environment.

- Visual J++ includes a toolbox that can be used to paint HTML, WFC, ActiveX, and Dynamic HTML.

Chapter 2

Mastering the Visual J++ Debugger

In This Chapter

▶ Viewing variables currently in scope

▶ Discovering watches and learning to set them

▶ Examining breakpoints and learning to set them

▶ Stepping through a program in the debugger

Visual J++ makes debugging, a reasonably sophisticated task in Java, simple. With a completely visual integrated debugger built into the Visual J++ compiler, Java development has never been easier. This section introduces you to the Visual J++ debugger in which a log10 function is developed.

Mastering the log10 Method

Java's `java.lang.Math` class contains a natural log function. You, however, may be used to working with base-10 logarithms, if you work with logarithms at all. (On a calculator, natural logs use the ln function while base-10 logs use the log button.)

Java does not contain a base-10 logarithm function, so I have written one to show you how to debug, and it may also be useful to some of you in your day-to-day work environment.

The Logs class you are about to debug contains one method: `log10`. Listing 2-1 shows the reasonably easy, buggy `Log10WithBugs` module, which compiles cleanly. Listing 2-2 shows the final code.

Listing 2-1: Log10WithBugs

```java
import java.awt.*;
import java.awt.event.*;
public class Log10WithBugs extends Frame implements WindowListener{
int x;              //Number to take the Log 10 of
  int i_lineNumber = 0;     //Current line number
  String sa_lines[] = new String [10];  //Number of lines
  public static void main (String args[]) {
    //Construct a new Log10WithBugs entry
    Log10WithBugs log10 = new Log10WithBugs();
  }
  public Log10WithBugs () {  //Log10WithBugs constructor
    addWindowListener(this);  //Add the window listener
    setTitle("Log10 With Bugs");  //Set the frame title
    setSize(300,200);     //Set the frame size
    show();        //Show the frame
    printLog10 (1000);     //Print the log-10 of 1000
    printLog10 (100);     //Print the log-10 of 100
    printLog10 (50);     //Print the log-10 of 50
    printLog10 (-1);     //Print the log-10 of -1
  }
  public void paint (Graphics g) {
    //Display all the lines of output
    for (int loop = 0; loop < sa_lines.length; loop++) {
      g.drawString(sa_lines[loop], 10, loop * 20);
    }
  }
  public void printLog10 (double a) {
  //Add an answer to the log 10 display array
    int answer = (int) Logs.log10(x);
    sa_lines[i_lineNumber++] = "The log (base 10) of "
                + Double.toString (a)
                + " is "
                + Double.toString(answer);
    repaint();
  }
  public void windowClosing(WindowEvent e) {   //User closed window
    dispose();
    System.exit(0);
  }
  public void windowActivated(WindowEvent e) { }  //Window got focus
  public void windowDeactivated(WindowEvent e) { }  //Window lost focus
  public void windowDeiconified(WindowEvent e) { }  //Window expanded
  public void windowClosed(WindowEvent e) { }  //Window is done closing
  public void windowIconified(WindowEvent e) { }  //Window is turned
                                             //into an icon
  public void windowOpened(WindowEvent e) { }  //Window is first opened
}
class Logs {  //This class contains a function that returns a log 10
  public static double log10(double x) throws ArithmeticException {
    double answer = Math.log(x) / Math.log(10);
    return answer;
  }
}
```

Let's briefly discuss the two classes in `Log10WithBugs.java`:

■ The `Log10WithBugs` class contains the code for the user interface. It calls the `Logs.log10()` method to take the base-10 log of 1000, 100, 50, and -1. It then displays the results.

■ The `Logs` class contains only the `log10()` method. The `log10()` method returns the base-10 logarithm of a number.

It compiles, so it should work, right? (Don't laugh too hard. On the other hand, you should be laughing a little!)

Secret

For you math wizards, you can derive the log10 of a number by dividing the natural log of the number by the natural log of 10:

`log10(x) = ln(x) / ln(10)`

This formula is derived by the code in the `Logs.log10` method:

`double answer = Math.log(x) / Math.log(10);`

Although this program has bugs, the preceding line is not one of them.

Entering the Debugger

View the output of the program in Figure 2-1. Notice that only the log of two numbers is displayed, when four were requested, and that the log returned is incorrect.

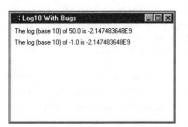

Figure 2-1: The output of Log10WithBugs isn't quite correct. Clearly some debugging is required.

You must debug the program, and the easiest way to debug a Visual J++ program is by using the Visual J++ debugger. You can enter the Visual J++ debugger in several ways:

■ Choose Debug, Start, as shown in Figure 2-2, to start your program. Your program won't stop until it finishes or it encounters a breakpoint. You can also press F5 or click the Go button.

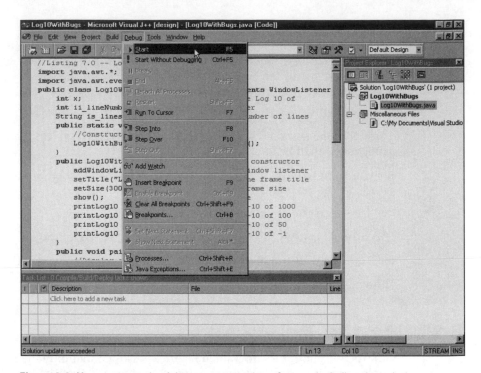

Figure 2-2: You can enter the debugger any number of ways, including through the menu.

Secret

The Restart button starts the program and the debugging process from the beginning of the program. Therefore you can use it to start a program in the debugger. This button is also handy if you need to restart after finding some errors, but are not yet ready to leave the debugger.

■ Choose Debug, Step Into. This steps you into the next deepest method, or, in this case, into the main method, which is the first method of this system. You can also press F8 or click the Step Into button.

■ Choose Debug, Run to Cursor to execute until the current line of code (where the cursor sits) is reached. You can also press F7 or click the Run to Cursor button.

Secret

To terminate the program immediately, leave the debugger, and then enter the usual Visual J++ environment, click the End button, or press Alt+F5.

Using the Debugger

Now you're in the debugger. As you see in Figure 2-3, your Visual J++ environment has changed.

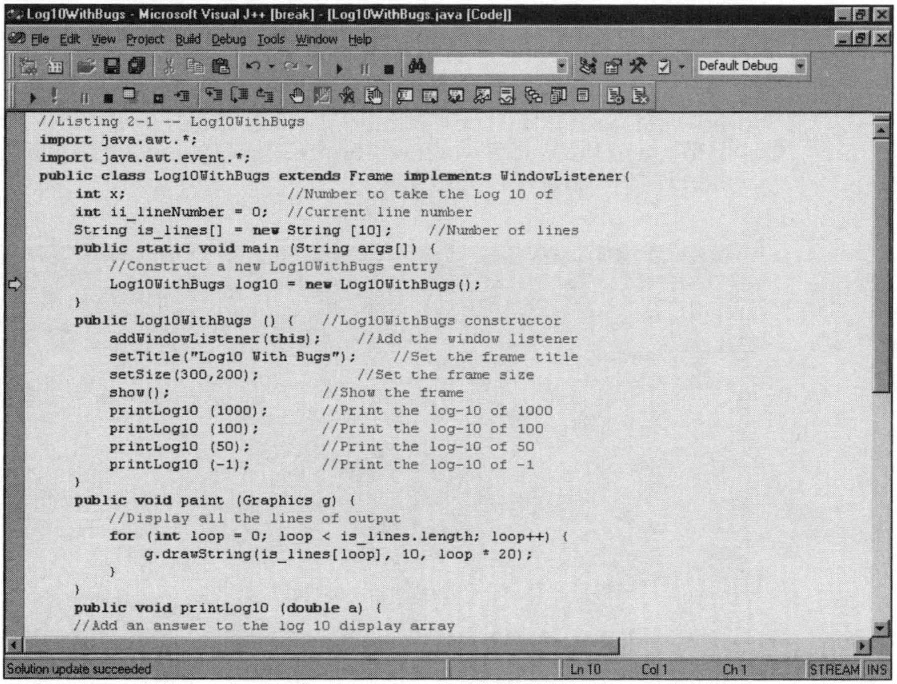

Figure 2-3: The debugger environment is similar to the Visual J++ development environment.

Your Visual J++ program is still running in a window, while the debugger traces through your code.

Stepping through a program

To step through your program a line, or set of lines, at a time in the debugger, choose one of the following options:

- Click the Step Over button or press F10 to step to the next line in your method.

- Click the Step Into button or press F8 to step into the code of the method about to be called.

- Click the Run to Cursor button or press F7 to execute your program until reaching the current line of code (where the cursor sits).

Secret

Sometimes, you may accidentally step into methods when you meant to step over them. Click the Step Out button, press Shift+F11, or choose Debug, Step Out. This executes the current method outside the debugger until you're back in the calling module.

Viewing information in the Debug windows

In Debug mode you can view the Debug windows. The two most commonly used windows are the Locals window, which shows you all the Locals window, and the Watch window. Choose View, Debug, to display all debug windows, as shown in Figure 2-4.

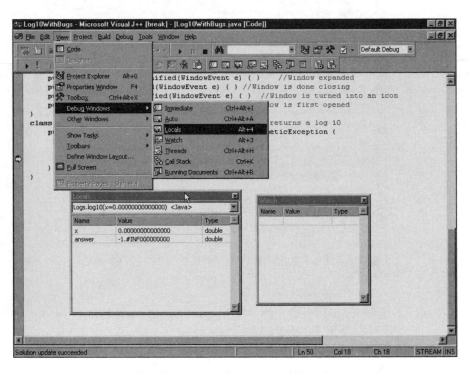

Figure 2-4: Visual J++ menu options enable you to control which debug windows are displayed.

Using the Locals window

As you see in Figure 2-4, the Locals window shows all local variables of the current method you're stepping through. Showing the Locals window is handy during debugging for two reasons:

- Because it shows the local variables of the current method, you can effortlessly step through a program and see how the local variables change without trying to view each variable separately.

- Often, bugs are hidden. You may see some errors in the Locals window that you wouldn't have caught during debugging if the Locals window was not displayed.

Using the Watch window

The Watch window can be seen on the bottom right of the window in Figure 2-4. A *watch* is a variable that you constantly monitor during debugging. Often you want to trace a class attribute through several methods. The Watch window excels at this. In Figure 2-5, you can see the Locals and the Watch windows. In the first row, *x* was dragged from the Locals window instead of typing it in the Watch window.

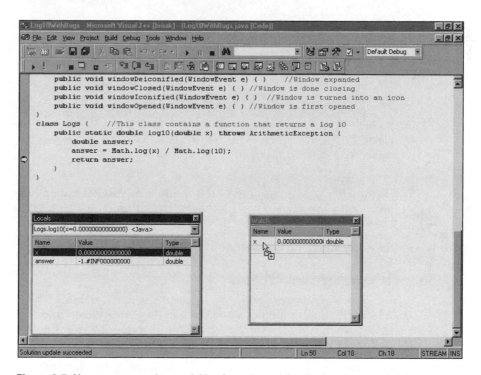

Figure 2-5: You can type or drag variables from the variable list into the watch list.

You can also enter variables into the list by highlighting a variable and then either dragging it to the Watch window or choosing Debug, Add Watch, as shown in Figure 2-6.

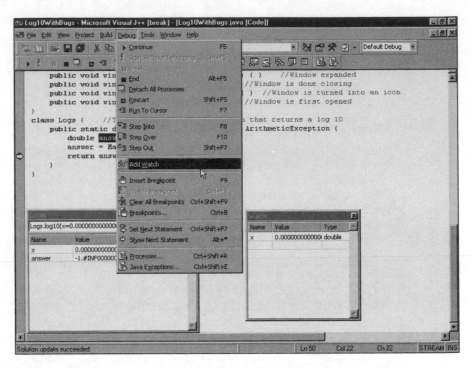

Figure 2-6: The Add Watch choice is an easy way to enter a variable from the source to the watch list.

Secret

If you don't want to use the Watch window, or you have already turned it off and want to reactivate it, click the Watch button. The Watch button hides or shows the Watch window.

Similarly, click the Locals button to toggle the Locals window on and off.

Viewing the Stack

One advanced feature of the debugger is the Stack window. The Stack shows a list of the called methods and the line they were called from. This comes in handy when trying to trace a Visual J++ program. To view the Stack, click the Call Stack button. You should see something similar to Figure 2-7.

The Stack is an important window if you want to see the called methods and the values that have been sent to those methods. Press F9 to set a breakpoint on any method that is currently highlighted in the stack window.

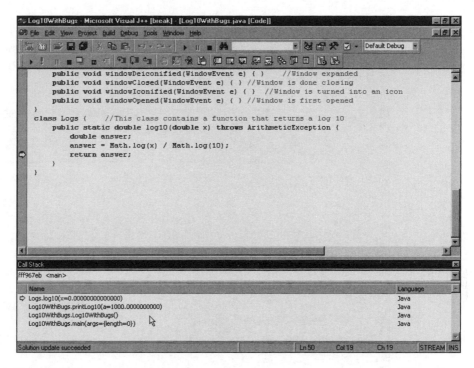

Figure 2-7: The stack provides a history of the called methods and the location of the calls.

Examining breakpoints

One of the obvious bugs is calling `printLog10` four times:

```
printLog10 (1000);    //Print the log-10 of 1000
printLog10 (100);     //Print the log-10 of 100
printLog10 (50);      //Print the log-10 of 50
printLog10 (-1);      //Print the log-10 of -1
```

Yet, as shown in Figure 2-1, only two lines are displayed instead of four. When you finally step through your program, you find that the `paint` method goes through the loop ten times to display four lines:

```
public void paint (Graphics g) {
  //Display all the lines of output
  for (int loop = 0; loop < sa_lines.length; loop++) {
    g.drawString(sa_lines[loop], 10, loop * 20);
  }
}
```

Clearly, the `paint` module needs more investigation.

Tracing all the way through a program can take a lot of time. Breakpoints were designed to enable the developer to signify a line of code to stop on. With the cursor on line 25 (which is a line inside the loop), click the Insert/Remove Breakpoint button to toggle a breakpoint off and on that line, as shown in Figure 2-8.

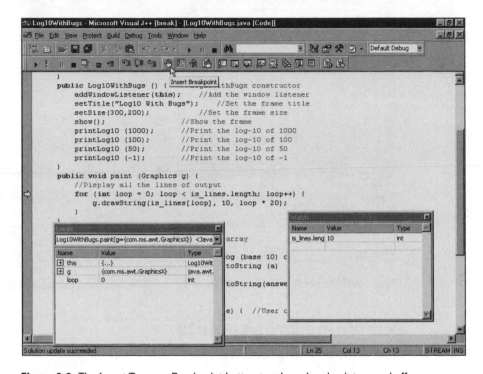

Figure 2-8: The Insert/Remove Breakpoint button toggles a breakpoint on and off.

A red dot to the far left indicates that the line has a breakpoint assigned to it, as shown in Figure 2-9.

Secret

Click the Remove All Breakpoints button to remove or disable all breakpoints.

Choose Debug, Breakpoints or press Ctrl+B to open the Breakpoints dialog box. Use the Breakpoints dialog box to specify exact lines to break on. Click the arrow next to the Break At text box to display the current line of code (see Figure 2-10). You can also use the Breakpoints dialog box to remove certain breakpoints.

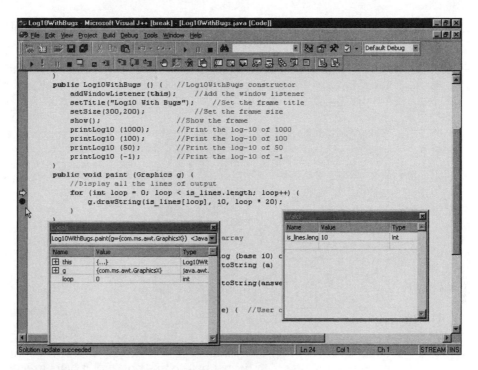

Figure 2-9: A red dot indicates a breakpoint.

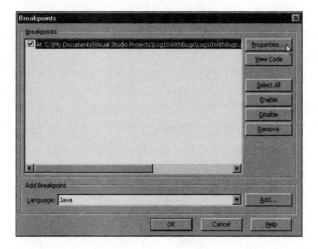

Figure 2-10: You can display the current line of code in the Breakpoints dialog box.

Secret

The Breakpoints dialog box is also the only way to set conditional breakpoints. A conditional breakpoint is one that doesn't halt the program until meeting a certain condition. Highlight the breakpoint you want to be conditional and click the Properties button in the Breakpoints dialog box (see Figure 2-10) to open the Java Breakpoint Properties dialog box (see Figure 2-11).

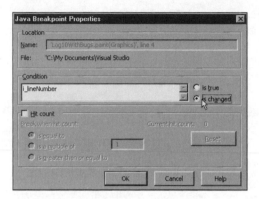

Figure 2-11: The Java Breakpoint Properties dialog box enables you to skip a breakpoint a number of times before breaking or to set a conditional breakpoint.

Using the Java Breakpoint Properties dialog box, you can either enter a hit count to specify how many times you want to skip this breakpoint, or enter a condition that needs to be met before this breakpoint halts execution. In Figure 2-12, the breakpoint takes effect when i_lineNumber changes value.

Finishing Debugging

As you step through the paint() method, as seen in Figure 2-12, you notice that the value of loop goes from zero to four and that the value of the String, sa_lines[loop], seems to be valid. After pouring over the three lines of code, you may notice that the line

```
g.drawString(sa_lines[loop], 1, loop * 12);
```

should be expanded to make more room for lines at the top and on the right:

```
g.drawString(sa_lines[loop], 10, loop * 12 + 40);
```

This gives enough room to display all four Log10 messages.

Well, that wasn't too hard (you think), but then when you run your program, you get the output shown in Figure 2-13. Notice that now you are displaying four lines, as you wanted — but you are getting the same value for all four lines.

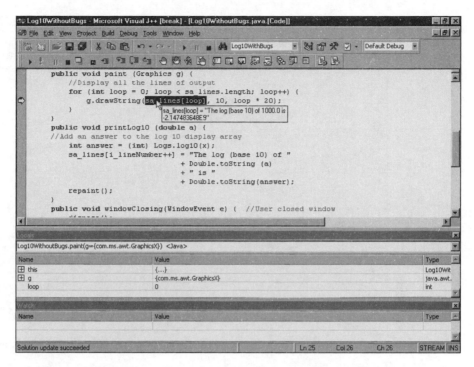

Figure 2-12: In the debugger, placing the cursor on top of a variable shows its value.

Figure 2-13: Clearly the Log10WithoutBugs program still needs some work.

After setting even more breakpoints in the paint() method and adding the current sa_lines[loop] to your Watch window (see Figure 2-14), you can eventually see that you are trying to display a null! This causes the null pointer exception and prevents the Graphics.drawString() method from functioning.

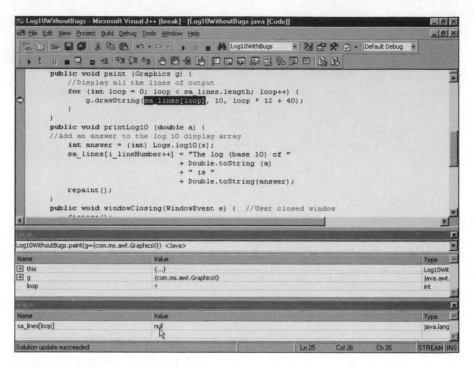

Figure 2-14: Oops. You can't display a null value.

This null occurred because you allocate 10 array elements, but only use 4. Instead, change the `paint()` method to test for null values before using the `Graphics.drawString()` method and then start the loop at zero instead of one:

```
public void paint (Graphics g) {
  //Display all the lines of output
  for (int loop = 0; loop < sa_lines.length; loop++) {
    if (sa_lines[loop] != null) {
      g.drawString(sa_lines[loop], 10, loop * 20 + 40);
    }
  }
}
```

Now the code doesn't try to display the null errors, but the results of the log are still not correct. Something must be wrong with the `Logs.log10()` method, right? However, when you step into the `log10` method as shown in Figure 2-15, you notice that the argument *x* is zero. Somehow zero was passed to the `log10` method instead of 1000.

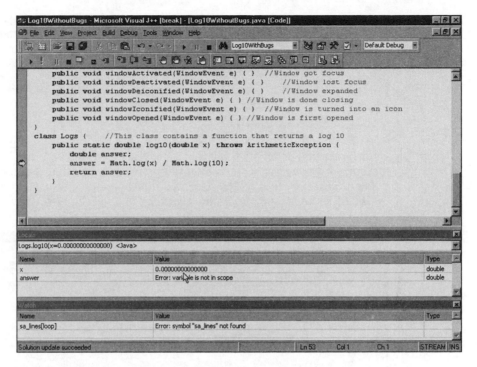

```
Log10WithoutBugs - Microsoft Visual J++ [break] - [Log10WithoutBugs.java [Code]]
File  Edit  View  Project  Build  Debug  Tools  Window  Help
                                    Log10WithBugs              Default Debug

        public void windowActivated(WindowEvent e) { } //Window got focus
        public void windowDeactivated(WindowEvent e) { }    //Window lost focus
        public void windowDeiconified(WindowEvent e) { }    //Window expanded
        public void windowClosed(WindowEvent e) { } //Window is done closing
        public void windowIconified(WindowEvent e) { } //Window is turned into an icon
        public void windowOpened(WindowEvent e) { } //Window is first opened
    }
    class Logs {    //This class contains a function that returns a log 10
        public static double log10(double x) throws ArithmeticException {
            double answer;
            answer = Math.log(x) / Math.log(10);
            return answer;
        }
    }
```

```
Logs.log10(x=0.00000000000000) <Java>
Name            Value                                   Type
x               0.00000000000000                        double
answer          Error: variable is not in scope         double
```

```
Name            Value                                   Type
sa_lines[loop]  Error: symbol "sa_lines" not found
```

```
Solution update succeeded                    Ln 53    Col 1    Ch 1    STREAM INS
```

Figure 2-15: Somehow the wrong value was passed to log10.

After stepping back through to the calling module and viewing the log10 call in the printLog10() method (see Figure 2-15), you'll soon notice that it is sending *x* to log10 when you want to send *a* because *a* has the value 1000 and *x* has a zero value. You need to change

```
int answer = (int) Logs.log10(x);
```

to:

```
int answer = (int) Logs.log10(a);
```

At last you should see valid results, but when you review the output from Log10WithoutBugs (Figure 2-16), you still see some problems. You know the log10 of 100 is 2 and the log10 of 10 is 1, so the log10 of 50 must be between the two. Also, the log10 of -1 is undefined, not 0, and the log10 of 1000 is 3.

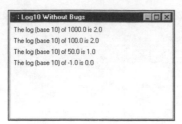

Figure 2-16: Although Log10WithoutBugs is much better than before, there is still some bug affecting one of the log10(1000), log10(50), and log10(-1) output values.

Once more, you probably think that something is wrong with the log10() method. However, when you step into the method, you find that the value being returned for log10(1000) is 3, and the value being returned for log10(50) is about 1.69, not 1 (see Figure 2-17). (See? I *told* you it worked.)

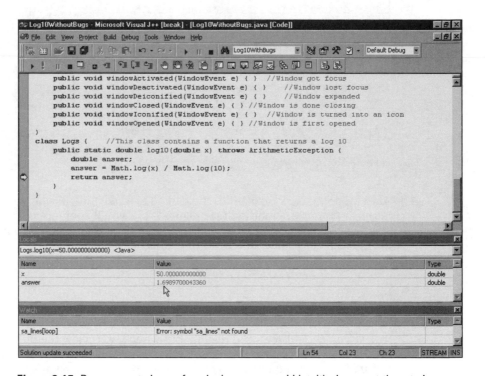

Figure 2-17: Bugs are not always found where you would intuitively expect them to be.

As soon as you step through to the printLog10 method, however, you see that *answer* is truncated from 1.67 to 1, as shown in Figure 2-18.

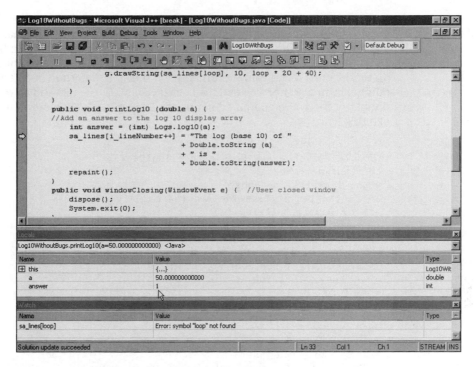

Figure 2-18: The correct answer is being truncated.

After some review, you find that, for some reason, *answer* is declared as an integer and the double return value of the log10 method is being cast into an integer. You need to change answer to a double and remove the integer type casting. Change the answer declaration from:

```
int answer = (int) Logs.log10(a);
```

to

```
double answer = Logs.log10(a);
```

As you step further through the program, you may notice that the *answer* variable in the log10 method contains an invalid number (Figure 2-19). You should test variables before trying to display them.

Figure 2-19: It looks like answer contains an invalid value when trying to take the log of a negative number.

You need to change the `printLog10` method again to handle numerical errors. Although you changed *answer* to a double, you need to change it again to use the Double class, which is a double wrapper found in the `java.lang` package. Then you can use the `Double.isNaN` (is not a number) method to test if the value returned from the `log10` method is an actual number. You also need to use the `Double.doubleValue` method to return a double of the value contained in *answer*. The `printLog10` method now looks like this:

```
public void printLog10 (double a) {
  Double answer = new Double(Logs.log10(a));
  if (answer.isNaN()) {
    sa_lines[i_lineNumber++] =
      "You cannot take the log (base 10) of "
      + Double.toString (a)
      + ".  The result is undefined.";
  }
  else {
    sa_lines[i_lineNumber++] = "The log (base 10) of "
    + Double.toString (a)
    + " is "
    + Double.toString(answer.doubleValue());
  }
  repaint();
}
```

Finally, `Log10WithBugs` works the way it was intended, as shown in Figure 2-20.

Figure 2-20: After much debugging, the result is a working program.

Finding only five bugs in a module is actually pretty good. Here's a rundown again of what was found:

1. Trying to display off the Frame. Make sure that when you place an object or text on a Frame that the area is within the viewable area of the Frame.

2. Displaying a null value. Trying to use uninitialized values is a common source of bugs in a Java program.

3. Passing the wrong argument to a method. This often happens in large systems with lots of variables.

4. Casting a variable to the wrong type. Although this is easier to do by accident in C++, it still happens in Java.

5. Failing to trap invalid arguments and results. This not only happens with math functions, but also with database calls.

Every programmer makes errors, and these errors are by no means unusual. The trick is to catch the errors during testing, to repeat your testing after the fix, and to use the debugger to help you find those hard-to-find errors that occur.

Secret

Remember that when running Console programs, the JVIEW window displays any untrapped errors that occur in your program. Listing 2-2 shows the working Log10WithoutBugs module.

Listing 2-2: Log10WithoutBugs

```java
import java.awt.*;
import java.awt.event.*;
public class Log10WithoutBugs extends Frame implements WindowListener{
    int x;              //Number to take the Log 10 of
    int i_lineNumber = 0;   //Current line number
    String sa_lines[] = new String [10];   //Number of lines
    public static void main (String args[]) {
    //Construct a new Log10WithoutBugs entry
        Log10WithoutBugs log10 = new Log10WithoutBugs();
    }
    public Log10WithoutBugs () {   //Log10WithoutBugs constructor
    addWindowListener(this);   //Add the window listener
        setTitle("Log10 Without Bugs");   //Set the frame title
        setSize(300,200);         //Set the frame size
        show();                //Show the frame
    printLog10 (1000);     //Print the log-10 of 1000
        printLog10 (100);      //Print the log-10 of 100
        printLog10 (50);      //Print the log-10 of 50
        printLog10 (-1);     //Print the log-10 of -1
    }
    public void paint (Graphics g) {
    //Display all the lines of output
        for (int loop = 0; loop < sa_lines.length; loop++) {
      if (sa_lines[loop] != null) {
        g.drawString(sa_lines[loop], 10, loop * 20 + 40);
      }
        }
    }
    public void printLog10 (double a) {
   //Add an answer to the log 10 display array
      Double answer = new Double(Logs.log10(a));
      if (answer.isNaN()) {
        sa_lines[i_lineNumber++] =
          "You cannot take the log (base 10) of "
          + Double.toString (a)
          + ".  The result is undefined.";
      }
      else {
        sa_lines[i_lineNumber++] = "The log (base 10) of "
```

```
                    + Double.toString (a)
                    + " is "
                    + Double.toString(answer.doubleValue());
            }
                repaint();
            }
        public void windowClosing(WindowEvent e) {   //User closed window
            dispose();
            System.exit(0);
        }
        public void windowActivated(WindowEvent e) { }  //Window got focus
        public void windowDeactivated(WindowEvent e) { }  //Window lost focus
        public void windowDeiconified(WindowEvent e) { }  //Window expanded
        public void windowClosed(WindowEvent e) { }  //Window is done closing
        public void windowIconified(WindowEvent e) { }  //Window turned into
                                                         //an icon
        public void windowOpened(WindowEvent e) { }   //Window is first opened
}
class Logs {   //This class contains a function that returns a log 10
        public static double log10(double x) throws ArithmeticException {
            double answer;
            answer = Math.log(x) / Math.log(10);
            return answer;
        }
}
```

Summary

The Visual J++ debugger is an important part of the Visual J++ environment. Typically, debugging is extremely difficult in Java, but Visual J++ makes it a lot easier by including an integrated, intuitive debugger.

- The debugger can view current variables in scope.

- The debugger can set watches to view variables across methods.

- The debugger can set breakpoints to stop execution at a given point with a given condition.

- The debugger can step through a program and either over or through called methods.

Chapter 3

Using Visual J++ Tools

Visual Studio is the Microsoft environment for both the C++ and Visual J++ languages. An understanding of the environment and the tools that are included with Visual J++ is necessary to master Java development.

Getting Help with Microsoft Developers Network

The Microsoft Developers Network (MSDN) has won awards for comprehensive help coverage. Inside MSDN, you find a plethora of help topics that not only span Visual J++ but also cover every other Visual Studio topic.

To invoke MSDN, type the word you want help with, position the cursor over the word, and press F1. MSDN opens with the index on the topic.

I Only Want a Little Help

The Microsoft Developers Network is Visual J++'s answer to a comprehensive help system. In fact, one might argue that it's too comprehensive. Because Visual Studio comes with several products, help on every topic is displayed. There is little communication between the tool you're currently using and the help you're currently getting. You may wind up with a glut of topics when, in Java-specific development, a specific topic would suffice. There also seems to be a tendency to generate help with primarily Microsoft-specific topics and ignore Java-specific topics, in an attempt to persuade you to code Microsoft's way rather than choosing the way that's right for you.

For instance, try to find help on the `Graphics.drawString()` method. As per normal procedures, click `drawString()` in your Java code and then press F1. MSDN is invoked, and several `drawString()` methods are returned, including a Java/ActiveX method that can paint text on a form, but none of them include a 100-percent-pure-Java solution, as shown in the following figure.

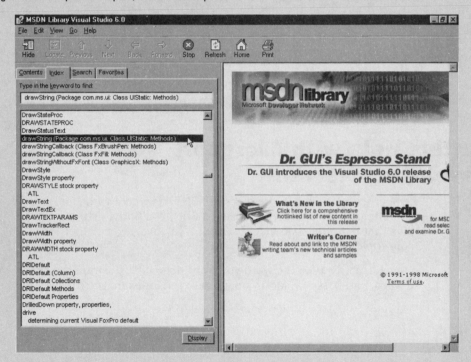

All is not lost, however. If what you're searching for is not found or is buried in a sea of references, click the Search tab and search for `drawString()`. You find that the Visual J++ documentation containing the `Graphics.drawString()` method arrives near the top of the list, as shown in the following figure. If you still can't find what you're looking for, try clicking Location so that all references to Visual J++ are grouped together. Try to remember that MSDN is *huge*, and the help reference you need is in there, somewhere. It may take a little effort to find it.

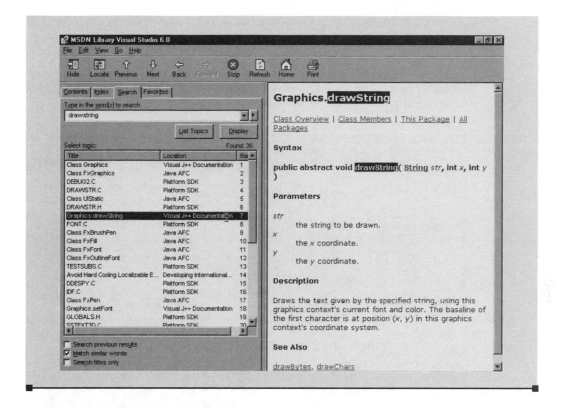

Using Visual Modeler

Visual Studio is a subset of the Rational Rose tool that was developed by Rational Software. It is included with the Visual Studio Enterprise version only. Visual Modeler is a graphical object-oriented modeling tool. It enables you to create applications quickly using a painter. Code can be generated in Visual C++ or Visual Basic. Sorry, it does not support Visual J++. However, you can still use the graphical capabilities to generate object diagrams.

Visual Modeler enables you to use a tree structure to organize your code. The following three capabilities are provided by Visual Modeler:

■ Object modeling with class diagrams enables you to design your system as an object model. Visual Modeler defines a subset of the modeling constructs of the Unified Modeling Language (UML), which is a method of object modeling.

■ Visual Basic and Visual C++ code can be generated from the design model you create with Visual Modeler. Usually some modification of the generated code is needed for a full application.

■ Reverse engineering can be done to create or update the model. Changes can then be made to the model and a new program can be automatically generated. Only Visual Basic currently supports reverse engineering.

Hopefully, Visual J++ will be supported in future releases, but for now, there seems to be a heavy bias toward Visual Basic. Figure 3-1 shows a class model of Microsoft's RDO components.

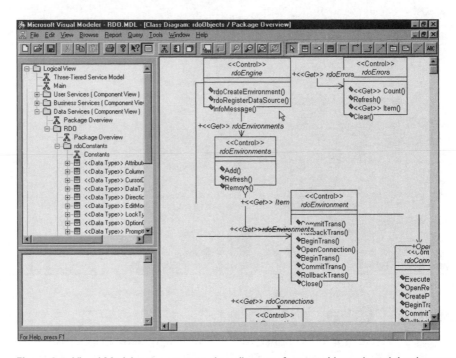

Figure 3-1: Visual Modeler can generate class diagrams for your object-oriented development.

Handling Stress

The life of a developer can be stressful, but personal stress is not the kind of stress that the Microsoft Stress Utility (Stress) tries to measure. Stress is a program that measures the system resources used by your computer. As shown in Figure 3-2, Stress shows how much of the system resources you are currently using. (Personal stress reduction is still unresolved.)

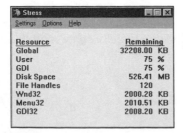

Figure 3-2: The Stress Utility enables you to monitor machine stress.

Using AVIEdit

Movies can be placed on the Internet using AVI files or MOV files. The MOV and AVI file formats are universally accepted movie files. Visual Studio includes an AVIEdit program that enables you to edit your AVI slides. By using AVIEdit, you can put slides into an AVI file or remove them. Figure 3-3 shows a countdown AVI that is included with Visual Studio.

Figure 3-3: You can edit movie files using AVIEdit.

Using the Visual J++ Command Line Compiler

Visual J++ comes with many tools that are essential to testing and development. The first of these is the Visual J++ Command Line Compiler (JVC.EXE). Instead of using the Visual J++ environment, you can use JVC to compile your code. Its syntax is:

```
JVC [options] <Visual J++ program>
```

The Visual J++ program must be included unless the /? option is used. Table 3-1 is a list of valid options for Visual J++.

Table 3-1   JVC Options

Option	Description
/?	Displays help for JVC.
/cp <classpath>	Sets the class path for compilation.
/cp:p <path>	Prepends the system path to the class path for compilation.
/cp:o	Prints the class path.
/cp:o-	Does not print the class path.
/d <directory>	Sets the directory for the compile class file. (The default is the current directory.)

(continued)

Table 3-1   *(Continued)*

Option	Description
/D <symbol>	Defines a conditional compilation symbol.
/g	Generates full debug information (g:1, g:d).
/g-	Does not generate debug information (default).
/g:1	Generates line number debug information.
/g:1-	Does not generate line number debug information (default).
/g:t	Generates debug tables.
/g:t-	Does not generate debug tables (default).
/nologo	Doesn't display the copyright banner. (The default is to display the copyright banner.)
/nowarn	Turns warnings off. (The default is to display warnings.)
/nowrite	Compiles but does not generate class files. (The default is to generate a class file.)
/O	Performs full optimization (O:I, O:J).
/O-	Does not perform optimization (default).
/O:I	Optimizes by inlining.
/O:I-	Does not optimize by inlining (default).
/O:J	Optimizes bytecode jumps.
/O:J-	Does not optimize bytecode jumps (default).
/verbose	Prints messages about the compilation progress. (The default is not to print compilation messages.)
/w{0-4}	Sets the warning level. (The default warning level is /w2.)
/wx	Treats warnings as errors.
/wx-	Does not treat warnings as errors (default).
/x	Disables extensions.
/x-	Enables extensions (default).

The JVC shouldn't be used in place of the Visual J++ environment, but it's a nice tool for generating batch compiles if needed.

Using the Visual J++ Application Viewers

WJView and JVIEW are tools for running Java applications without a Web browser. Standalone Java applications need some type of Java Virtual Machine environment to run. WJView and JVIEW are included with Visual J++ to run Java applications. Although you usually access JView (to run Console applications) and WJView (to run Windows applications) from inside the Visual J++ environment, you can also access them as standalone programs using the following syntax:

```
JView [options] <classname> [arguments]
WJView [options] <classname> [arguments]
```

Secret

If an argument contains spaces, place it in quotes.

The classname is the name of the Java class you want to run. The classname is always needed unless /? is specified. Arguments are arguments that the Java class needs to run (if any). Table 3-2 lists the JView and WJView options you can define.

Table 3-2   JView and WJView Options

Option	Description
/?	Displays help for JView
/a	Runs <classname> as an Applet using the AppletViewer
/cp <classpath>	Sets the class path for compilation
/cp:p <path>	Prepends the system path to the class path for compilation
/cp:a <path>	Appends the system path to the class path for compilation
/d <name> = <value>	Defines system property
/n <namespace>	Defines the namespace in which to run
/p	Adds a pause before terminating if an error occurs
/v	Verifies all classes

Secret

When using these Java viewers, the default is to run the class as an application if it contains a main method and run it as an Applet if not. However, if you're running an Applet, use Internet Explorer (or, if you prefer, Netscape). JView and WJView simply aren't as full-featured as Internet Explorer, and Internet Explorer supports all the standard debugging features that are supported in WJView and JView.

As command-line programs, JView and WJView typically won't be used with Visual J++ applications, and probably never should be used with Applets unless debugging is necessary. However, you could use JView or WJView, if you received a Java application class without the Java source code and wanted to view it immediately.

Examining Internet Explorer

When running an Applet, you should probably use Internet Explorer. Internet Explorer has a Java Virtual Machine that is centered around Visual J++. You won't find a faster Web browser, or one that's easier to use. It also has the following benefits:

- It's free — not just shareware.

- It's Visual J++-aware and includes ActiveX support, WFC support, Dynamic HTML support, and all the other support you need to implement Windows solutions in your Java environment.

- It's a fully-featured Web browser.

Figure 3-4 shows Internet Explorer running the `HelloWorldApplet`.

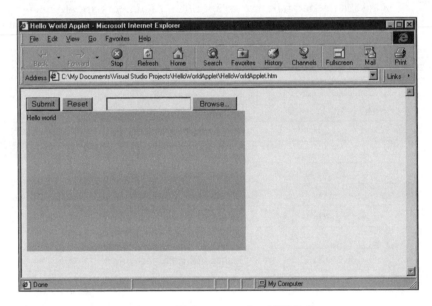

Figure 3-4: You can use Internet Explorer to run local HTML files.

I wouldn't feel right writing an entire book without a `HelloWorld` program in it. Listing 3-1 is the `HelloWorldApplet` program that is displayed in Figure 3-4.

Listing 3-1 HelloWorldApplet.java

```
import java.awt.*;
import java.applet.*;
public class HelloWorldApplet extends Applet {
  public void paint(Graphics g) {
    g.drawString("Hello world",1,15);
  }
}
```

Of course, Internet Explorer is an excellent Internet Web browser. In Figure 3-5, you can see how the Visual J++ Web site looks on Internet Explorer. (The Web site, by the way, is `http://www.microsoft.com/visualj/`.

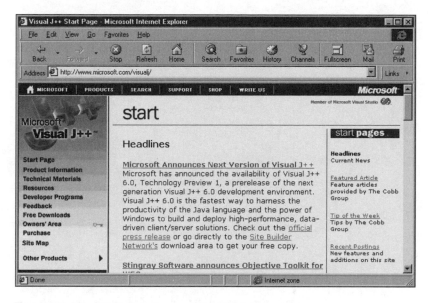

Figure 3-5: Internet Explorer is an excellent Web browser.

Summary

This chapter briefly explains most of the features found in Visual J++:

- The Visual Studio is arguably the best Java development environment available.

- Visual J++ Solutions contain Visual J++ projects which contain Java programs, HTML files, graphics, and any other files that are implemented in a Java development environment.

- Visual Studio uses the Microsoft Developers Network for its help function.

- Visual J++ includes several standalone programs, including Internet Explorer, which is arguably the best browser available.

Part II

Visual J++: Java with Cream and Sugar

Chapter 4: Mastering JDirect with
the Windows Foundation Class

Chapter 5: Digging into COM, DCOM, OLE, and ActiveX

Chapter 6: Mastering ActiveX Programming

Chapter 7: Making Your Own ActiveX and COM Components

Chapter 8: Better Security Over the Web

Chapter 9: JavaBeans

Chapter 10: Packaging and Deploying Your Application

Chapter 11: Programming Dynamic HTML with Visual J++

Chapter 12: Using Delegates

Chapter 13: Enterprise-Wide Development

Chapter 4

Mastering J/Direct with the Windows Foundation Class

In This Chapter

▶ What is the Windows Foundation Class (WFC)?

▶ Why the WFC has caused such a stir

▶ How to make WFC Forms

▶ How to use WFC Components

▶ Graphical development with the WFC

One of the more controversial additions to Visual J++ is the Windows Foundation Class (WFC). The WFC is an object-oriented class library written in Java that enables Visual J++ applets and applications to access Windows ActiveX routines directly via J/Direct. This chapter deals with how and when to use the WFC.

Understanding the WFC

The WFC simplifies and enhances Windows development in Java by using J/Direct calls to integrate the Windows platform with the Java language. The WFC library provides classes for user-interface routines and Windows system-level routines. Visual J++ includes tools that can quickly generate applications and components for the Windows platform using the WFC.

The WFC streamlines your Windows calls using Microsoft's J/Direct calls. (The J/Direct calls are hidden from you inside the WFC package.) Figure 4-1 shows how Visual J++ WFC calls stack up against pure Java programming.

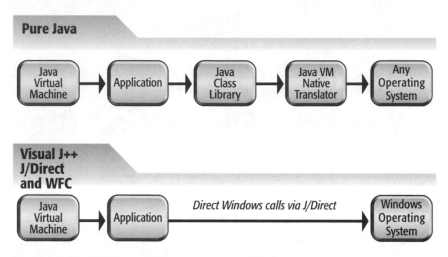

Figure 4-1: The WFC uses J/Direct to streamline Windows calls.

When dealing with only Windows clients, the WFC can increase the efficiency of your Java programs.

Is the WFC Good or Evil?

Java purists say that the WFC violates the claim of "write once, run anywhere" that Sun originally promised when it developed the Java language. Some even claim that Visual J++ is not a true Java compiler, or that you can't run Visual J++ classes on any non-Microsoft Java VM. Microsoft has "fueled the fire" by making statements that it will optimize for the WFC and not for Java. On the other hand, Windows developers claim that the WFC provides functionality that is not available in pure Java. Who's right?

As seen in this book, Visual J++ *can* deliver pure Java. Visual J++ is a great tool for programming, debugging, and deploying pure Java code - even for those that have no wish to embrace nonstandard Java. In other words, you don't have to use the WFC to use Visual J++.

The WFC, by definition, is *always* more efficient than Java. This is because with the WFC, programmers make direct calls to native

Windows programs using J/Direct. When using non-WFC programs, programs go through the additional layer of the Java VM and a Java interpreter. Statements such as "Microsoft is optimizing for the WFC and not for Java" simply mean that Microsoft has made an efficient native Windows-based library that can be accessed by Java. Figure 4-1 shows graphically that *any native library is more efficient than a Java library.* By accessing a native library, Microsoft is making Java a more viable Windows development tool.

Microsoft has put a lot of effort into the WFC, thereby making it incredibly easy to develop J/Direct-based applications by delivering tools that greatly enhance Windows programming. In contrast, Microsoft has made hardly any effort to deliver pure Java other than allowing pure Java to compile. This is because Microsoft would like to tie Java more closely with the Windows operating system.

If you are deploying on multiple platforms or don't know which platforms users may have when they access your Web page or Java application, then you should avoid the WFC. On the other hand, if you have no intention of supporting non-Windows environments (for example, an Intranet or Windows application), or wish to deploy .exe files rather than Java .class files, then go ahead and use the WFC. It delivers great functionality for development and execution speeds that are hard to match in other environments.

Although developing a library takes significant effort, any well-developed library can approach or exceed the "paint-and-deliver" development time of the WFC. I am not belittling the efficiency or ease of use of the WFC, but I am pointing out that

if you don't want to use the WFC, you have other options.

Any prepackaged language vendor, such as Microsoft, Sun, PowerSoft, Borland, and Symantec, tries to enhance a language to separate themselves in the market. For example, Borland's JBuilder contains an XYLayout class that enables you to set a component at an *(x, y)* coordinate on a frame or an applet. No one complained about their "nonstandard" Java because people like to complain about market leaders, such as Microsoft, more than they like to complain about "regular" market competitors. However, far from being a bad thing, language enhancements help users become more productive.

Secret

The WFC is *not* a replacement for standard Java, but rather a supplement. The WFC helps you manipulate Windows databases, controls, and events, but many times, you still need Java for advanced techniques such as socket communication or Web access.

Mastering WFC Java Packages

Instead of using the normal Java packages included in the Java language specification (for example, java.awt.*, java.net.*), Microsoft has replaced much of the functionality with the new packages listed in Table 4-1.

Table 4-1   WFC Packages

Package import	Package Description
wfc.core.*	Contains core WFC functionality and should be included with every WFC Visual J++ program.
wfc.app.*	Contains application classes, thread wrapper, and access to Clipboard and Registry.
wfc.data.*	Contains data access classes for ActiveX Data Objects (ADO). The wfc.data package is used in Visual J++ 6.0 to access databases via ADO.
wfc.html.*	Contains HTML classes that can process dynamic HTML.
wfc.ui.*	Contains user interface classes, including components (such as Buttons and Checkboxes).

Using the Visual J++ Designer and the WFC Toolbox

Microsoft enables you to graphically paint your windows by using the
Visual J++ Designer. Select View ➪ Designer, as shown in Figure 4-2, to
access the Designer.

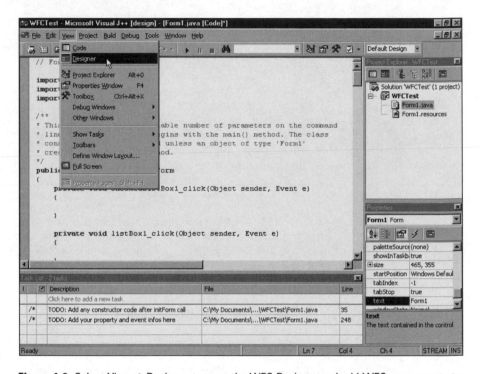

Figure 4-2: Select View ➪ Designer to open the WFC Designer and add WFC components to
your Web page.

Secret

In an almost insidious move to force WFC development, Microsoft only
enables you to add WFC controls when in the Visual J++ Designer. If you use
the Designer, you are forcing your application to run on Windows
environments *only*. If you want standard Java applications and applets,
you're going to have to code them the hard way.

Digging into the Designer Drawing Environment

Click WFC Controls in the toolbox to see the many controls that you can add to your form. Figure 4-3 shows some popular controls that are placed on a window.

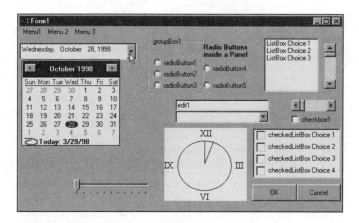

Figure 4-3: The WFC supports many controls.

Using the toolbox and the Designer, a developer can create graphical applications in a fraction of the time it normally takes to code an application from scratch. Table 4-2 lists several components that you can add to your WFC Form.

Table 4-2   WFC Components

Component	Component Description
Button	The same construct as in the Java specification. A user clicks a Button to perform some action.
Checkbox	Allows the user to have a yes or no choice.
CheckedListBox	Lists several Checkboxes for you to click.
ComboBox	A ListBox that is displayed when a down arrow is clicked. ComboBoxes are also called DropDownListBoxes.
ContextMenu	A menu that appears in the middle of a window, usually in response to a right-click.
DataBinder	Binds SQL statements to a database.
DataNavigator	Navigates through a DataSource.

(continued)

Table 4-2 *(Continued)*

Component	Component Description
DataSource	Stores information about a database source.
DateTimePicker	Enables you to pick a date from a popup calendar.
Edit	A text box that enables you to enter data in single or multiple lines.
GroupBox	A GroupBox contains components. Each radio button in a group box is joined to act as one component.
HScrollBar	Horizontal scroll bar, used to scroll up and down. Use is uncommon because components often automatically implement their own scroll bars.
Label	Uneditable text that shows the name of fields or displays messages to the user.
ListBox	Lists choices in a box. Usually only one choice may be made, although a ListBox can be configured to give multiple choices.
MainMenu	A menu at the top of your window.
Panel	Divides your window into partitions.
PictureBox	Enables display of various types of pictures on your window. Unlike standard Java, PictureBoxes can display many popular forms of graphical files, such as .tif, .bmp, and .pcx (in addition to the .gif and .jpg formats supported by standard Java.) The only caveat here is that .jpg and .gif files are compressed and load quickly, while .bmp, .pcx, and .tif can take quite a while to load over a modem.
RadioButton	Enables you to choose one among many choices. The current choice is checked similar to a checkbox.
Splitter	Often used to split a window into two partitions.
TabStrip	Enables you to make tab forms on your Java window. Java has no equivalent.
ToolTip	Displays a brief explanation when your mouse rests on it for a while.
TrackBar	Tracks the percentage completion of a process.
VScrollBar	A vertical scroll bar, used to scroll up and down. Use is uncommon because components often automatically implement their own scroll bars.

When you're done painting the form and adding all the events, you still need to add the events code behind the Components.

Examining WFC Forms and Applications

The WFC Form class contains all the functionality needed to paint a
Window. The Form class should be extended into a subclass to take
advantage of all the WFC Form functionality:

```
//import WFC Packages
import wfc.app.*;
import wfc.core.*;
import wfc.ui.*;
public class WFCForm extends Form {  // Extends the WFC Form
```

WFC applications can't be instantiated like "normal" Java applications. To
instantiate a WFC application, you need to create a new Applications class in
your main method:

```
public static void main(String args[]) {
  // use the Application.run method instead of the new command
  Application.run(new WFCForm());  //Define a new WFC Application
}
public WFCForm() {  // WFCForm Constructor run by the
                    //Application.run method . . .
```

The `Application.run` method sets up the application and invokes the class
constructor. When using WFC applications, you must always use the
`Application.run` method. Normal instantiation in the main method does not
work properly.

Forms have functionality that can change color, size, shape, auto scale,
resizing, formatting, and the size of the Windows client area, as shown by
the following method:

```
private void formatForm() {      // do Form settings
  setBackColor(Color.CONTROL);  // set the Form color
  setLocation(new Point(0, 0));    // set the Form location
  setSize(new Point(300, 300));  // set the Form dimensions
  setTabIndex(-1);         // Forms don't need a tab stop
  setTabStop(false);
  setText("WFCTest");       // set the Form title
  setAutoScaleBaseSize(13);    // sets the resize formatting
  setClientSize(new Point(292, 273));  // sets the Windows client
area
}
```

The preceding method sets the shape, size, and color of the window.
Adding controls (such as buttons and labels) to a form is discussed later
in this chapter.

Whenever you define a component location or size, you must pass a Point
class to the `setSize` or `setLocation` methods. The Point class is defined by
passing an *x* and a *y* component:

```
Point(int x, int y)
```

Usually, you don't actually define a Point variable, but rather construct a new Point as a parameter, as shown in the `setSize` and `setLocation` methods:

```
setSize(new Point(300, 300));  // set the Form dimensions
```

The auto scale base size is used for sizing components during Form construction or Form resizing. The `setAutoScaleBaseSize` method is used for this. Microsoft suggests 13 for the base size:

```
setAutoScaleBaseSize(13);      // sets the resize formatting
```

The window client size is the area within the window where objects can be located. Figure 4-4 shows the areas defined in the Window. The window client area is the area left after the border (also known as Insets) and the title bar are painted.

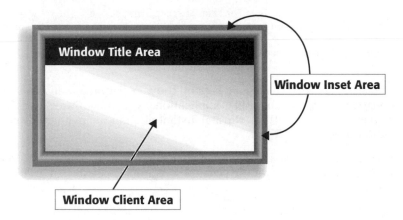

Figure 4-4: Windows are divided into title area, inset area, and client area.

The size of the client area is determined by the `setClientSize` method:

```
setClientSize(new Point(292, 273));  // sets the Windows client area
```

Exploring WFC Components

The WFC comes with several components, such as labels or edit boxes, that can be added to your Visual J++ window via WFC program calls. This section delves into several different WFC components.

Using the WFC Label Class

Labels are WFC Form components that display text and messages. Usually labels have no events associated with them. (For example, if you click a Label, nothing happens.) In addition, labels never receive focus. The following method forms a red label called statusLabel:

```
private void makeStatusLabel() {
  Label lbl_status = new Label();
  lbl_status.setLocation(new Point(10, 230));  // set the Label
location on the form
  lbl_status.setSize(new Point(220, 30));  // set the Label size
  lbl_status.setTabIndex(-1);  // Labels usually don't have tab stops
  lbl_status.setTabStop(false);
  lbl_status.setForeColor(Color.RED);  // Red makes a Label stand out
}
```

Labels use the setText method to display a message, as shown by the following method:

```
// method to display a message inside the lbl_status label.
private void showStatus(String message) {
  lbl_status.setText(message);          // Place message in label
}
```

Secret

Unlike a Java Label, a WFC label can wrap and enable you to display multiple lines. By setting a label height to 30 (by using the setSize method), you can usually display two text lines in a Label. Java's standard Label class only handles single line Labels and truncates when the end of the Label has been reached. (Remember, the actual number of lines depends on your Java default font.)

Using the WFC Button Class

Buttons are WFC components that are clicked by the user to perform some function. To make a button on a window, you need code similar to the makeOKButton method:

```
private void makeOKButton() {     // Make the WFC OK button
  bu_OK.setLocation(new Point(10, 10));  // set the button location
                                         //on the form
  bu_OK.setSize(new Point(60, 20));  // set the button size
  bu_OK.setTabIndex(1);      // set the tab position
  bu_OK.setTabStop(true);       //set tab to stop on the position
  bu_OK.setText("OK");       // set the text of the button
}
```

The preceding code places a 60 × 20 button at position (10, 10) on your window. The button's tab stops are enabled so that tabs stop on the button. Finally, the button shows an "OK" string when it is displayed.

Secret

In Windows, a Cancel button is automatically clicked when the ESC key is pressed. You can use the setCancelButton to establish a button as a Cancel button. The following code sets up a button named bu_exit to be the Cancel button:

```
// make this button execute when the ESC key is hit
setCancelButton(bu_exit);
```

Understanding WFC Events

Most components, such as Buttons, require some event processing. This is accomplished using an EventHandler. You must pass a method to the EventHandler class:EventHandler eh = new EventHandler(method);

Usually, you don't instantiate an EventHandler but rather use the EventHandler class in conjunction with a component method. For example, the Button class has an `addOnClick` method that enables you to pass an EventHandler to a button:

```
// tell which event to use when you click the button
bu_OK.addOnClick(new EventHandler(bu_OKClick));
```

The preceding code tells the WFC to invoke the `bu_OKClick` method when the button is clicked. The `bu_OKClick` method then has code that is executed every time it is clicked:

```
// method for OK button
private void bu_OKClick(Object sender, Event e) {
  showStatus("bu_OK was clicked");  // call method to send message
}
```

In the preceding code, the sender is a Java object (*not* necessarily a WFC object) that invoked the method, and the event is a WFC Event that is used to define what event took place. Usually, these parameters are unnecessary because you know that the `bu_OKClick` method is executed only when a specific button (`bu_OK`) is clicked.

Adding WFC Components to a WFC form

After defining all your components and events, you need to add the components to your form. Use the `Form.setNewControls` method to do this. The following code adds the `lbl_status` label and the `bu_OK` and `bu_exit` buttons to the current form:

```
// Now add all the controls to the form
setNewControls(new Control[] {  lbl_status,
        bu_OK,
      by_exit});
```

All the previous code examples can be combined into a simple WFC application. Listing 4-1 shows how you can use the WFC to integrate Forms, Buttons, and Labels.

Listing 4-1: WFCButtonForm.java

```
//import WFC Packages
import wfc.app.*;
import wfc.core.*;
import wfc.ui.*;
public class WFCButtonForm extends Form {
  Label lbl_status = new Label();
  Button bu_OK = new Button();
  Button bu_exit = new Button();
```

```
public static void main(String args[]) {
  Application.run(new WFCButtonForm());  //Define a new WFC Application
}
public WFCButtonForm() {     // WFCButtonForm Constructor
  makeStatusLabel();     // Call the makeStatusLabel method in this
class
  makeOKButton();      // Call the makeOKButton method in this class
  makeExitButton();     // Call the makeExitButton method in this class
  formatForm();        // Format the form
}
private void formatForm() {        // do Form settings
  setBackColor(Color.CONTROL);  // set the Form color
  setLocation(new Point(0, 0));    // set the Form location
  setSize(new Point(300, 300));  // set the Form dimentions
  setTabIndex(-1);        // Forms don't need a tab stop
  setTabStop(false);
  setText("WFCTest");        // set the Form title
  setAutoScaleBaseSize(13);     // sets the resize formatting
  setClientSize(new Point(292, 273));  // sets the Windows client area
  // Now add all the controls to the form
  setNewControls(new Control[] {  lbl_status,
              bu_OK,
              bu_exit });
}
private void makeStatusLabel() {
  lbl_status.setLocation(new Point(10, 250));  // set the Label
                          //location on the form
  lbl_status.setSize(new Point(220, 20));  // set the Label size
  lbl_status.setTabIndex(-1);     // Labels usually don't have tab stops
  lbl_status.setTabStop(false);
  lbl_status.setForeColor(Color.RED);     // Red makes a Label stand out
}
private void makeOKButton() {        // Make the WFC OK button
  bu_OK.setLocation(new Point(10, 10));  // set the button location on
                          //the form
  bu_OK.setSize(new Point(60, 20));     // set the button size
  bu_OK.setTabIndex(1);         // set the tab position
  bu_OK.setTabStop(true);        //set tab to stop on the position
  bu_OK.setText("OK");        // set the text of the button
  // tell which event to use when you click the button
  bu_OK.addOnClick(new EventHandler(bu_OKClick));
}
private void makeExitButton() {        // Make the WFC Exit button
  bu_exit.setLocation(new Point(70, 10));  // set the button location
                          //on the form
  bu_exit.setSize(new Point(60, 20));     // set the button size
  bu_exit.setTabIndex(2);        // set the tab position
  bu_exit.setTabStop(true);         //set tab to stop on the position
  bu_exit.setText("Exit");        // set the text of the button
  // tell which event to use when you click the button
  bu_exit.addOnClick(new EventHandler(bu_exitClick));
  // make this button execute when the ESC key is hit
  setCancelButton(bu_exit);
}
```

```
    private void bu_OKClick(Object sender, Event e) {   // method for OK
button clicks
      showStatus("bu_OK was clicked");     // call method to send message
    }
    private void bu_exitClick(Object sender, Event e) {   // method for Exit
                                                          //button clicks
      showStatus("bu_exit was clicked");    // call method to send message
    }
    // method to display a message inside the lbl_status label.
    private void showStatus(String message) {
      lbl_status.setText(message);        // Place message in label
    }
}
```

Figure 4-5 shows the results of Listing 4-1. Every button click sends a
message to a label describing what happened.

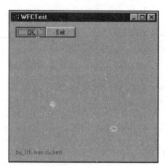

Figure 4-5: WFCButtonForm.java
displays messages in a WFC Label
when a WFC button is clicked.

Using WFC Checkboxes and Push Buttons

One good thing about the WFC is that coding for different components is
similar. Therefore, when you learn to code for one component (such as
Buttons), you are close to learning to code for other components (such as
Checkboxes). Table 4-3 shows some methods unique to Checkboxes.

Table 4-3   Checkbox Methods

Checkbox Method	Description
addOnCheckStateChanged	Called whenever a checkbox state changes. This method is similar to the `Button.addOnClicked` method.
getChecked	Returns a true or false depending on whether the checkbox is checked.
setChecked	Allows you to pass a true or false to toggle a checkbox on or off.
setPushLike	Changes a checkbox into a push button. A push button looks like a Button component, except that when a push button is clicked, it stays pushed until clicked again.

Listing 4-2 is a modification of Listing 4-1. The lines of code in bold are needed for checkbox and push button functionality.

Listing 4-2: WFCCheckboxForm.java

```
//import WFC Packages
import wfc.app.*;
import wfc.core.*;
import wfc.ui.*;
public class WFCCheckboxForm extends Form {
  Label lbl_status = new Label();
  Checkbox cb_yesOrNo = new Checkbox();
  Checkbox cb_pushButton = new Checkbox();
  public static void main(String args[]) {
    Application.run(new WFCCheckboxForm()); //Define a new WFC Application
  }
  public WFCCheckboxForm() {  // WFCCheckboxForm Constructor
    makeStatusLabel();    // Call the makeStatusLabel method in this class
    makeCBYesOrNo();     // Call the makeCBYesOrNo method in this class
    makePushButton();     // Call the makePushButton method in this class
    formatForm();      // Format the form
  }
  private void formatForm() {       // do Form settings
    setBackColor(Color.CONTROL);  // set the Form color
    setLocation(new Point(0, 0));    // set the Form location
    setSize(new Point(300, 300));  // set the Form dimentions
    setTabIndex(-1);      // Forms don't need a tab stop
    setTabStop(false);
    setText("WFCTest");       // set the Form title
    setAutoScaleBaseSize(13);    // sets the resize formatting
    setClientSize(new Point(292, 273));  // sets the Windows client area
    // Now add all the controls to the form
    setNewControls(new Control[] {  lbl_status,
            cb_yesOrNo,
            cb_pushButton });
  }
  private void makeStatusLabel() {
    lbl_status.setLocation(new Point(10, 250));  // set the Label location
                       //on the form
    lbl_status.setSize(new Point(220, 20));  // set the Label size
    lbl_status.setTabIndex(-1);     // Labels usually don't have tab stops
    lbl_status.setTabStop(false);
    lbl_status.setForeColor(Color.RED);    // Red makes a Label stand out
  }
  private void makeCBYesOrNo() {     // Make the WFC yesOrNo checkbox
    cb_yesOrNo.setText("Checkbox");    // set the text of the checkbox
    cb_yesOrNo.setLocation(new Point(10, 10)); // set the location on the
                        //form
    cb_yesOrNo.setTabIndex(1);     // set the tab position
    cb_yesOrNo.setTabStop(true);   //set tab to stop on the position
    cb_yesOrNo.setChecked(true);  // Default checkbox to true
    // tell which event to use when you click the checkbox
    cb_yesOrNo.addOnCheckStateChanged(new
EventHandler(cb_yesOrNoChanged));
  }
```

```
private void makePushButton() {        // Make a WFC push button
  cb_pushButton.setLocation(new Point(10, 50));  // set the button
                                          //location
  cb_pushButton.setSize(new Point(70, 20));  // Set the size of the Push
                                          //Button
  cb_pushButton.setTabIndex(2);     // set the tab position
  cb_pushButton.setTabStop(true);     //set tab to stop on the position
  cb_pushButton.setText("Push Button");  // set the text of the button
  cb_pushButton.setPushLike(true);   // Turn the checkbox into a push
                                          //button
  cb_pushButton.setChecked(false);    // Default to not pushed in
  // tell which event to use when you click the button
  cb_pushButton.addOnCheckStateChanged(
          new EventHandler(cb_pushChanged));
}
// method for cb_yesOrNo state changes
private void cb_yesOrNoChanged(Object sender, Event e) {
  // send a message if cb_yesOrNo is clicked or not
  showStatus("cb_yesOrNO was clicked to " +
String.valueOf(cb_yesOrNo.getChecked()));
}
// method for cb_pushButton state changes
private void cb_pushChanged(Object sender, Event e) {
  // send a message if cb_pushButton is pressed or out
  String inout = (cb_pushButton.getChecked()) ? "In" : "Out";
  showStatus("cb_pushButton was clicked to " + inout);
}
// method to display a message inside the lbl_status label.
private void showStatus(String message) {
  lbl_status.setText(message);        // Place message in label
}
}
```

As you see in Listing 4-2, coding for checkboxes and push buttons is not much different than coding for buttons. However, Figure 4-6 shows how differently the checkbox components look and function as compared with button components.

Figure 4-6: Checkboxes can be either in the form of a standard checkbox or in the form of a push button.

Using Radio Buttons and GroupBoxes

Radio buttons are a special type of checkbox. Radio buttons always exist in a group of two or more. In each radio button group, only one radio button can be turned on at a time. Furthermore, once a radio button is turned on in a group, a user can't turn off all the radio buttons.

To assign radio buttons to a group, you need a Form, Panel, or GroupBox. All radio buttons in each of these containers belong to a single group. Figure 4-7 shows how two radio buttons are added directly to a frame, while three others are added to a GroupBox.

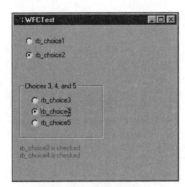

Figure 4-7: Radio buttons can exist inside or outside of a GroupBox.

Listing 4-3 shows the code to generate the radio buttons in Figure 4-7.

Listing 4-3: WFCRadioButton.java

```
//import WFC Packages
import wfc.app.*;
import wfc.core.*;
import wfc.ui.*;
public class WFCRadioButton extends Form {
  Label lbl_status = new Label();
  GroupBox gb_choices = new GroupBox();
  RadioButton rb_choice1 = new RadioButton();
  RadioButton rb_choice2 = new RadioButton();
  RadioButton rb_choice3 = new RadioButton();
  RadioButton rb_choice4 = new RadioButton();
  RadioButton rb_choice5 = new RadioButton();
  public static void main(String args[]) {
    Application.run(new WFCRadioButton()); //Define a new WFC Application
  }
  public WFCRadioButton() {  // WFCRadioButton Constructor
    makeStatusLabel();   // Call the makeStatusLabel method in this class
    makeRadioButtons();  // Call the makeRadioButtons method in this class
    makeGroupBox();    // Call the makeGroupBox method in this class
    formatForm();       // Format the form
  }
  private void formatForm() {       // do Form settings
```

```
        setBackColor(Color.CONTROL);  // set the Form color
        setLocation(new Point(0, 0));    // set the Form location
        setSize(new Point(300, 300));  // set the Form dimentions
        setTabIndex(-1);        // Forms don't need a tab stop
        setTabStop(false);
        setText("WFCTest");        // set the Form title
        setAutoScaleBaseSize(13);     // sets the resize formatting
        setClientSize(new Point(292, 273));  // sets the Windows client area
        setNewControls(new Control[] {  lbl_status,
                rb_choice1,
                rb_choice2,
                gb_choices });
    }
    private void makeStatusLabel() {
        lbl_status.setLocation(new Point(10, 210));  // set the Label location
                                                     //on the form
        lbl_status.setSize(new Point(210, 30));  // set the Label size
        lbl_status.setTabIndex(-1);    // Labels usually don't have tab stops
        lbl_status.setTabStop(false);
        lbl_status.setForeColor(Color.RED);     // Red makes a Label stand out
    }
    private void makeRadioButtons() {        // Make 5 radio buttons
//Set the location, size, tab order, text, and events for Radio Button 1
    rb_choice1.setLocation(new Point(20, 20));  // Set position
    rb_choice1.setSize(new Point(80, 15));  // Set size
    rb_choice1.setTabIndex(1);        // Set tab order
    rb_choice1.setTabStop(true);        //set tab stops
    rb_choice1.setText("rb_choice1");     // Set text
    rb_choice1.addOnCheckedChanged(     // Set event
            new EventHandler(radioButtonClicked));
//Set the location, size, tab order, text, and events for Radio Button 2
    rb_choice2.setLocation(new Point(20, 40));  // Set position
    rb_choice1.setSize(new Point(80, 15));  // Set size
    rb_choice2.setTabIndex(2);        // Set tab order
    rb_choice2.setTabStop(true);        //set tab stops
    rb_choice2.setText("rb_choice2");     // Set text
    rb_choice2.addOnCheckedChanged(     // Set event
            new EventHandler(radioButtonClicked));
//Set the location, size, tab order, text, and events for Radio Button 3
    rb_choice3.setLocation(new Point(20, 20));  // Set position
    rb_choice1.setSize(new Point(80, 15));  // Set size
    rb_choice3.setTabIndex(3);        // Set tab order
    rb_choice3.setTabStop(true);        //set tab stops
    rb_choice3.setText("rb_choice3");     // Set text
    rb_choice3.addOnCheckedChanged(     // Set event
            new EventHandler(radioButtonClicked));
//Set the location, size, tab order, text, and events for Radio Button 4
    rb_choice4.setLocation(new Point(20, 40));  // Set position
    rb_choice1.setSize(new Point(80, 15));  // Set size
    rb_choice4.setTabIndex(4);        // Set tab order
    rb_choice4.setTabStop(true);        //set tab stops
    rb_choice4.setText("rb_choice4");     // Set text
    rb_choice4.addOnCheckedChanged(     // Set event
```

```
                      new EventHandler(radioButtonClicked));
    //Set the location, size, tab order, text, and events for Radio Button 5
      rb_choice5.setLocation(new Point(20, 60));  // Set position
      rb_choice1.setSize(new Point(80, 15));  // Set size
      rb_choice5.setTabIndex(5);        // Set tab order
      rb_choice5.setTabStop(true);        //set tab stops
      rb_choice5.setText("rb_choice5");     // Set text
      rb_choice5.addOnCheckedChanged(     // Set event
                new EventHandler(radioButtonClicked));
    }
   private void makeGroupBox() {       // Make a WFC push button
      gb_choices.setLocation(new Point(10, 100));// Set the group box
location
      gb_choices.setSize(new Point(150, 100));  // Set the group box size
      gb_choices.setTabIndex(-1);         // Don't tab stop here
      gb_choices.setTabStop(false);
      gb_choices.setText("Choices 3, 4, and 5");  // label the group box
      // Now add all the controls to the form
      gb_choices.setNewControls(new Control[] {  // Add controls to the
group box
        rb_choice3,
        rb_choice4,
        rb_choice5});
   }
   // method for radio button clicks
   private void radioButtonClicked(Object sender, Event e) {
      String message = "";            // Initialize message
      if (rb_choice1.getChecked()) {     // is rb_choice1 checked?
        message += "\nrb_choice1 is checked";
      }
      if (rb_choice2.getChecked()) {     // is rb_choice2 checked?
        message += "\nrb_choice2 is checked";
      }
      if (rb_choice3.getChecked()) {     // is rb_choice3 checked?
        message += "\nrb_choice3 is checked";
      }
      if (rb_choice4.getChecked()) {     // is rb_choice4 checked?
        message += "\nrb_choice4 is checked";
      }
      if (rb_choice5.getChecked()) {     // is rb_choice5 checked?
        message += "\nrb_choice5 is checked";
      }
      if (message.length() > 0) {       // is anything checked?
        message = message.substring(1);  //Strip the first character
        showStatus(message);        // Display the message
      }
   }
   // method to display a message inside the lbl_status label.
   private void showStatus(String message) {
      lbl_status.setText(message);       // Place message in label
   }
}
```

As you can see in Listing 4-3, there is little difference between the creation of a radio button and the creation of a checkbox. However, due to the special nature of radio buttons, a GroupBox is usually created to contain the radio buttons. In Listing 4-3, two radio buttons are added directly to the Form (to form one group) and three radio buttons are added to the Group Box (to form the other group).

Secret

Please note that the positions of all components are in relation to the container (whether it is a Form, GroupBox, or Panel) as opposed to the form. With radio buttons, this is particularly important because radio buttons are usually associated with a GroupBox rather than placed directly on a form.

Using WFC Edit Controls

WFC Edit is probably the simplest, but most commonly used, WFC component. The Edit component is used to display and enter text. Figure 4-8 shows an edit control.

Figure 4-8: Edit controls are the simplest WFC components and the most often used.

The main methods for edit controls are getText() and setText(String). Listing 4-4 shows the code needed to generate the program in Figure 4-8.

Listing 4-4: WFCEdit.java

```
//import WFC Packages
import wfc.app.*;
import wfc.core.*;
import wfc.ui.*;
public class WFCEdit extends Form {
  Label lb_status = new Label();
  Edit ed_field = new Edit();
  public static void main(String args[]) {
    Application.run(new WFCEdit()); //Define a new WFC Application
  }
  public WFCEdit() {    // WFCEdit Constructor
    makeStatusLabel();  // Call the makeStatusLabel method in this class
    makeEdit();    // Call the makeEdit method in this class
```

```
      formatForm();        // Format the form
   }
   private void formatForm() {        // do Form settings
     setBackColor(Color.CONTROL);  // set the Form color
     setLocation(new Point(0, 0));     // set the Form location
     setSize(new Point(300, 300));  // set the Form dimentions
     setTabIndex(-1);         // Forms don't need a tab stop
     setTabStop(false);
     setText("WFCTest");         // set the Form title
     setAutoScaleBaseSize(13);      // sets the resize formatting
     setClientSize(new Point(292, 273));  // sets the Windows client area
     // Now add all the controls to the form
     setNewControls(new Control[] {  lb_status,
             ed_field});
   }
   private void makeStatusLabel() {
     lb_status.setLocation(new Point(10, 230));  // set the Label
                                          //location on the form
     lb_status.setSize(new Point(220, 30));  // set the Label size
     lb_status.setTabIndex(-1);      // Labels usually don't have tab stops
     lb_status.setTabStop(false);
     lb_status.setForeColor(Color.RED);      // Red makes a Label stand out
   }
   private void makeEdit() {        // Make the WFC DateTimePicker
     ed_field.setLocation(new Point(10, 10));
     ed_field.setSize(new Point(210, 30));
     ed_field.setTabIndex(1);
     ed_field.setTabStop(true);
   // tell which event to use when you click the listbox
     ed_field.addOnChange(new EventHandler(ed_fieldChange));
   }
   private void ed_fieldChange(Object sender, Event e) {
     // send a message if ed_field is clicked or not
     showStatus("ed_field value changed to " + ed_field.getText());
   }
   // method to display a message inside the lb_status label.
   private void showStatus(String message) {
     lb_status.setText(message);        // Place message in label
   }
}
```

Using WFC List Boxes and ComboBoxes

List boxes are boxes with choices inside that enable the user to make one or more choices from a list. ComboBoxes are list boxes that can be "pulled down" by clicking a down arrow and limit selection to a single choice. Additionally, ComboBoxes may be configured to enable a user to enter a choice that is not on the list. Figure 4-9 shows examples of both components.

Figure 4-9: List boxes enable you to choose from a list.

Table 4-4 shows methods that are vital when using list boxes and ComboBoxes.

Table 4-4   ComboBox Methods

ComboBox Method	Description
addOnSelectedItemChanged	Invokes a method whenever the selected item in a list box changes.
getText	Returns the current contents of a ComboBox, although not used in this example. (ComboBox only) .
setIntegralHeight	(ListBox only) Accepts true or false as a parameter to specify whether a list box should display. If true, only full items are displayed, and the list box is resized to prevent partial items from being shown. Otherwise, all items are shown. (ListBox only)
setItemHeight	Sets the height of each of the items in a list box.
setItems	Specifies the items in a list box.
getSelectedItem	Returns the item currently selected in a list box.

Listing 4-5 is a modification of Listing 4-1. Listing 4-5 is the source code for Figure 4-9.

Listing 4-5: WFCListBox.java

```
//import WFC Packages
import wfc.app.*;
import wfc.core.*;
import wfc.ui.*;
public class WFCListBox extends Form {
  Label lb_status = new Label();
  ListBox lb_choices = new ListBox();
  ComboBox cb_choices = new ComboBox();
  public static void main(String args[]) {
    Application.run(new WFCListBox()); //Define a new WFC Application
```

```
    }
  public WFCListBox() {      // WFCListBox Constructor
    makeStatusLabel();        // Call the makeStatusLabel method in this
                              //class
    makeListBox();      // Call the makeListBox method in this class
    makeComboBox();       // Call the makeComboBox method in this class
    formatForm();         // Format the form
  }
  private void formatForm() {       // do Form settings
    setBackColor(Color.CONTROL);   // set the Form color
    setLocation(new Point(0, 0));    // set the Form location
    setSize(new Point(300, 300));   // set the Form dimentions
    setTabIndex(-1);        // Forms don't need a tab stop
    setTabStop(false);
    setText("WFCTest");        // set the Form title
    setAutoScaleBaseSize(13);      // sets the resize formatting
    setClientSize(new Point(292, 273));  // sets the Windows client
                                         //area
    // Now add all the controls to the form
    setNewControls(new Control[] {  lb_status,
              lb_choices,
              cb_choices});
  }
  private void makeStatusLabel() {
    lb_status.setLocation(new Point(10, 230));  // set the Label
                                                //location on the
                                                //form
    lb_status.setSize(new Point(220, 30));  // set the Label size
    lb_status.setTabIndex(-1);       // Labels usually don't have tab
                                     //stops
    lb_status.setTabStop(false);
    lb_status.setForeColor(Color.RED);    // Red makes a Label stand
                                          //out
  }
  private void makeListBox() {       // Make the WFC yesOrNo checkbox
    lb_choices.setLocation(new Point(10, 10)); // set the location
                                               //on the form
    lb_choices.setTabIndex(1);     // set the tab position
    lb_choices.setTabStop(true);      //set tab to stop on the
                                      //position
    lb_choices.setSize(new Point(100, 100));  // Set the listbox
                                              //size
    lb_choices.setIntegralHeight(true);  // Show partial items
    lb_choices.setItemHeight(13);  // Set the height of the items
    lb_choices.setItems(new Object[] {  // Add items to the list
      "ListBox Choice 1",
      "ListBox Choice 2",
      "ListBox Choice 3"});
    // tell which event to use when you click the listbox
    lb_choices.addOnSelectedItemChanged(
            new EventHandler(lb_choicesClick));
  }
  private void makeComboBox() {    // Make the WFC Combo
    cb_choices.setLocation(new Point(120, 10)); // set the location
on the form
    cb_choices.setTabIndex(2);     // set the tab position
```

```
      cb_choices.setTabStop(true);   //set tab to stop on the position
      cb_choices.setSize(new Point(150, 100));   // Set the combo box
                                               //size
      cb_choices.setItemHeight(13);   // Set the height of the items
      cb_choices.setItems(new Object[] {  // Add items to the list
        "ComboBox Choice 1",
        "ComboBox Choice 2",
        "ComboBox Choice 3"});
      // tell which event to use when you click the combo box
      cb_choices.addOnSelectedItemChanged(
              new EventHandler(cb_choicesClick));
    }
    // method for lb_choices state changes
    private void lb_choicesClick(Object sender, Event e) {
      // send a message if lb_choices is clicked or not
      showStatus("lb_choices was clicked to choose: " +
                  (String) lb_choices.getSelectedItem());
    }
    // method for cb_choices state changes
    private void cb_choicesClick(Object sender, Event e) {
      // send a message if cb_choices is clicked or not
      showStatus("cb_choices was clicked to choose: " +
              (String) cb_choices.getSelectedItem());
    }
    // method to display a message inside the lb_status label.
    private void showStatus(String message) {
      lb_status.setText(message);          // Place message in label
    }
}
```

Secret

Unlike the Java list box component, the WFC ListBox and ComboBox components enable any object to serve as a list box item. You can also add pictures or other objects when using a WFC ListBox or ComboBox.

Using a CheckedListBox

A checked listbox is similar to a list box except that the choices have checkboxes. Usually with list boxes (though not always), you only select one choice at a time. With checked list boxes, you can select multiple entries at a time, as seen in Figure 4-10.

Figure 4-10: CheckedListBoxes enable you to choose several items from a list.

Listing 4-6 is a modification of Listing 4-5. The modification produces a checked list box. Notice that the formation of the checked list box is identical to the formation of a list box. However, the events that are coded to retrieve information for a checked list box are different from those coded for a "normal" list box. (See the code in bold in Listing 4-6.)

Listing 4-6: **WFCCheckedListBox.java**

```java
//import WFC Packages
import wfc.app.*;
import wfc.core.*;
import wfc.ui.*;
public class WFCCheckedListBox extends Form {
  Label lbl_status = new Label();
  CheckedListBox clb_choices = new CheckedListBox();
  public static void main(String args[]) {
    Application.run(new WFCCheckedListBox()); //Define a new WFC
                                              //Application
  }
  public WFCCheckedListBox() {  // WFCCheckedListBox Constructor
    makeStatusLabel();    // Call the makeStatusLabel method in this class
    makeCheckedListBox();  // Call the makeListBox method in this class
    formatForm();          // Format the form
  }
  private void formatForm() {        // do Form settings
    setBackColor(Color.CONTROL);  // set the Form color
    setLocation(new Point(0, 0));    // set the Form location
    setSize(new Point(300, 300));   // set the Form dimentions
    setTabIndex(-1);         // Forms don't need a tab stop
    setTabStop(false);
    setText("WFCTest");        // set the Form title
    setAutoScaleBaseSize(13);    // sets the resize formatting
    setClientSize(new Point(292, 273));  // sets the Windows client area
    // Now add all the controls to the form
    setNewControls(new Control[] {  lbl_status,
              clb_choices });
  }
  private void makeStatusLabel() {
    lbl_status.setLocation(new Point(10, 230));  // set the Label
                                                 //location on the form
    lbl_status.setSize(new Point(220, 50));  // set the Label size
    lbl_status.setTabIndex(-1);      // Labels usually don't have tab stops
    lbl_status.setTabStop(false);
    lbl_status.setForeColor(Color.RED);      // Red makes a Label stand out
  }
  private void makeCheckedListBox() {     // Make the WFC list box
    clb_choices.setLocation(new Point(10, 10)); // set the location on
                                                //the form
    clb_choices.setTabIndex(1);         // set the tab position
    clb_choices.setTabStop(true);       //set tab to stop on the position
    clb_choices.setSize(new Point(200, 97));  // Set the listbox size
    clb_choices.setIntegralHeight(true);     // Show partial items
    clb_choices.setItemHeight(13);       // Set the height of the items
    clb_choices.setItems(new Object[] {     // Add items to the list
```

```
                "CheckedListBox Choice 1",
                "CheckedListBox Choice 2",
                "CheckedListBox Choice 3",
                "CheckedListBox Choice 4"});
      // tell which event to use when you click the listbox
      clb_choices.addOnSelectedItemChanged(
              new EventHandler(clb_choicesClick));
    }
    // method for clb_choices state changes
    private void clb_choicesClick(Object sender, Event e) {
      // send a message if lb_choices is clicked or not
      String message;     // Hold the message to be displayed
      // Retrieve an array of checked items
      int checkedItems[] = clb_choices.getCheckedIndices();
      if (checkedItems.length > 0) {  // Are any checked?
        message = "clb_choices was clicked. ";
        if (checkedItems.length == 1) {
          message += "The only current choice is ";
        }
        else {
          message += "Current choices are ";
        }
        // loop through the choices and add to the message String
        for (int loop = 0; loop < checkedItems.length; loop++) {
          if (loop == 0) {  // First item checked
            message += clb_choices.getItem(checkedItems[loop]);
          }
          // Last item checked
          else if (loop == checkedItems.length - 1) {
            // More than two items checked
            if (checkedItems.length > 2) {
              message += ",";
            }
            message += " and " +
              clb_choices.getItem(checkedItems[loop]);
          }
          else {    // Other items checked
            message += ", " +
clb_choices.getItem(checkedItems[loop]);
          }
        }
      }
      else {  //There were no items checked
        message = "clb_choices was clicked.  There are no current
choices.";
      }
      showStatus(message);
    }
    // method to display a message inside the lbl_status label.
    private void showStatus(String message) {
      lbl_status.setText(message);       // Place message in label
    }
  }
```

In Listing 4-6, the `getCheckedIndices` method is called to retrieve an array of checked item indexes. Then `getItem` is called to return the string associated with the index of the checked items. Then a String is built describing which items are checked.

Using a DateTimePicker

One of the more interesting controls inside the WFC is the DateTimePicker control. This control is a combination of an edit box and a calendar. Using the DateTimePicker, you can choose a valid date from a calendar that is displayed inside a text box, as shown in Figure 4-11.

Figure 4-11: DateTimePickers combines a calendar with an edit control.

Listing 4-7 contains the code to show the DateTimePicker in Figure 4-11.

Listing 4-7: WFCDatePicker.java

```java
//import WFC Packages
import wfc.app.*;
import wfc.core.*;
import wfc.ui.*;
public class WFCDatePicker extends Form {
  Label lb_status = new Label();
  ComboBox cb_choices = new ComboBox();
  DateTimePicker dtp_date = new DateTimePicker();
  public static void main(String args[]) {
    Application.run(new WFCDatePicker()); //Define a new WFC Application
  }
  public WFCDatePicker() {     // WFCDatePicker Constructor
    makeStatusLabel();  // Call the makeStatusLabel method in this class
    makeDatePicker();    // Call the makeDatePicker method in this class
    formatForm();        // Format the form
  }
```

```
      private void formatForm() {          // do Form settings
        setBackColor(Color.CONTROL);  // set the Form color
        setLocation(new Point(0, 0));    // set the Form location
        setSize(new Point(300, 300));  // set the Form dimentions
        setTabIndex(-1);            // Forms don't need a tab stop
        setTabStop(false);
        setText("WFCTest");         // set the Form title
        setAutoScaleBaseSize(13);      // sets the resize formatting
        setClientSize(new Point(292, 273));  // sets the Windows client area
        // Now add all the controls to the form
        setNewControls(new Control[] {  lb_status,
              dtp_date});
      }
      private void makeStatusLabel() {
        lb_status.setLocation(new Point(10, 230));  // set the Label
                                    //location on the form
        lb_status.setSize(new Point(220, 30));  // set the Label size
        lb_status.setTabIndex(-1);     // Labels usually don't have tab stops
        lb_status.setTabStop(false);
        lb_status.setForeColor(Color.RED);     // Red makes a Label stand out
      }
      private void makeDatePicker() {        // Make the WFC DateTimePicker
        dtp_date.setLocation(new Point(10, 10));
        dtp_date.setSize(new Point(210, 30));
        dtp_date.setTabIndex(1);
        dtp_date.setTabStop(true);
        dtp_date.setCalendarBackColor(Color.WINDOW);
        dtp_date.setCalendarForeColor(Color.WINDOWTEXT);
        dtp_date.setCalendarFont(Font.DEFAULT_GUI);
        dtp_date.setCalendarTitleBackColor(Color.ACTIVECAPTION);
        dtp_date.setCalendarTitleForeColor(Color.ACTIVECAPTIONTEXT);
        dtp_date.setCalendarTrailingForeColor(Color.GRAYTEXT);
        dtp_date.setCalendarMonthBackground(Color.WINDOW);
        dtp_date.setMaxDate(-1l);
        dtp_date.setMinDate(-1l);
      // tell which event to use when you click the listbox
        dtp_date.addOnValueChange(new
              DateTimeChangeEventHandler(dtp_dateClick));
      }
      private void dtp_dateClick(Object sender, DateTimeChangeEvent e) {
        java.util.Date date = new java.util.Date(dtp_date.getValue());
        // send a message if dtp_date is clicked or not
        showStatus("dtp_date value changed to " + dtp_date.getText());
      }
      // method to display a message inside the lb_status label.
      private void showStatus(String message) {
        lb_status.setText(message);        // Place message in label
      }
    }
```

As you can see by the lines in bold in Listing 4-7, a number of options can be used for calendar formatting.

Impressing Everyone with WFC TabStrips and Panels

Tab controls are recent within GUI interfaces (compared to other controls such as buttons and edits). Tab controls can make efficient use of window space while delivering an easy-to-use, friendly user interface. The TabStrip is the WFC's tab control. Figure 4-12 shows how a tab control is supposed to look.

Figure 4-12: Tab controls make user interfaces friendly while conserving window space.

Pushing one tab displays certain components, and pushing another tab displays different components. In Figure 4-12, Tab1 was clicked. In Figure 4-13, Tab2 was clicked. Notice how the components on the window change.

Figure 4-13: Clicking different tabs changes the display.

The fastest and easiest way to create this functionality is to use WFC Panels. Panels are containers, just like Forms, but Panels need to be place on a Form to be visible. Listing 4-8 shows how Panels and TabStrips can be used together to deliver a fantastic user interface.

Listing 4-8: WFCTab.java

```java
//import WFC Packages
import wfc.app.*;
import wfc.core.*;
import wfc.ui.*;
public class WFCTab extends Form {
  Label lb_status = new Label();
  TabStrip tab_stuff = new TabStrip();
  Panel panel1 = new Panel();
  Panel panel2 = new Panel();
  public static void main(String args[]) {
    Application.run(new WFCTab()); //Define a new WFC Application
  }
  public WFCTab() {     // WFCTab Constructor
    makeStatusLabel();    // Call the makeStatusLabel method in this
                             //class
    makeTab();     // Call the makeTab method in this class
    makePanel1();     // Call the makePanel1 method in this class
    makePanel2();     // Call the makePanel2 method in this class
    formatForm();        // Format the form
  }
  private void formatForm() {        // do Form settings
    setBackColor(Color.CONTROL);  // set the Form color
    setLocation(new Point(0, 0));     // set the Form location
    setSize(new Point(300, 300));   // set the Form dimentions
    setTabIndex(-1);        // Forms don't need a tab stop
    setTabStop(false);
    setText("WFCTest");        // set the Form title
    setAutoScaleBaseSize(13);      // sets the resize formatting
    setClientSize(new Point(292, 273));  // sets the Windows client
                                     //area
    // Now add all the controls to the form
    setNewControls(new Control[] {  lb_status,
               panel1,
               panel2,
               tab_stuff});
  }
  private void makeStatusLabel() {
    lb_status.setLocation(new Point(10, 230));  // set the Label
                                          //location on the
                                          //form
    lb_status.setSize(new Point(220, 30));  // set the Label size
    lb_status.setTabIndex(-1);       // Labels usually don't have tab
                                   //stops
    lb_status.setTabStop(false);
    lb_status.setForeColor(Color.RED);  // Red makes a Label stand
                                     //out
  }
  private void makeTab() {        // Make the WFC DateTimePicker
    tab_stuff.setLocation(new Point(10, 10));
    tab_stuff.setSize(new Point(280, 220));
    tab_stuff.setTabIndex(1);
    tab_stuff.setTabStop(true);
    tab_stuff.setItemSize(new Point(100, 20));
    tab_stuff.setTabs(new Object[] {
```

```
                    "Tab1",
                    "Tab2"});
      // tell which event to use when you click the listbox
         tab_stuff.addOnClick(new EventHandler(tab_stuffClick));
      }
      private void makePanel1() {         // Make a panel for tab control
         makePanels(panel1);           // Format a standard Tab panel
         Label l = new Label();          // Add a label to the panel
         l.setText("This is Panel 1");
         l.setSize(new Point(220, 30));
         l.setLocation(new Point(10,10));
         Button b = new Button();      // Add a button to the panel
         b.setText("Panel 1 button");
         b.setLocation(new Point(10,40));
         panel1.setNewControls(new Control[] {l, b});
      }
      private void makePanel2() {         // Make a panel for tab control
         makePanels(panel2);
         Label l = new Label();          // Add a label to the panel
         l.setText("This is Panel 2");
         l.setSize(new Point(220, 30));
         l.setLocation(new Point(10,10));
         Edit e = new Edit();          // Add an Edit control to the panel
         e.setText("Panel 2 Edit Control");
         e.setLocation(new Point(10,40));
         e.setSize(new Point(220, 30));
         panel2.setNewControls(new Control[] {l, e});
      }
      private void makePanels(Panel p) {  // Make a standard panel for
                                          //tab control
         p.setLocation(new Point(30, 40));  //Set panel location
         p.setSize(new Point(240, 180));    //Set panel size
         p.setTabIndex(1);            //set tabs
         p.setTabStop(true);
         p.setBorderStyle(BorderStyle.FIXED_3D);  // 3-d Lowered
      }
      private void tab_stuffClick(Object sender, Event e) {
         // send a message about the tab click
         if (tab_stuff.getSelectedIndex()== 0) {
           showStatus("Tab 1 selected");
           panel1.setVisible(true);     // Make panel visible
           panel2.setVisible(false);    // Make panel invisible
         }
         else {
           showStatus("Tab 2 selected");
           panel1.setVisible(false);    // Make panel invisible
           panel2.setVisible(true);     // Make panel visible
         }
      }
      // method to display a message inside the lb_status label.
      private void showStatus(String message) {
         lb_status.setText(message);       // Place message in label
      }
   }
```

Listing 4-8 creates two Panels. Different components populate each Panel. Depending on which tab is selected, one Panel is hidden, and one is shown. This method of implementing tab controls is quick to develop, *somewhat* painless, and fast when running.

Secret

Panels in standard Java are useful for separating the Frame into components. When using the WFC, Panels lose some of their importance because the WFC is so good at placing components at a specific location.

Summary

- The WFC is great for Windows development, delivering fast executables in minimal time.

- The WFC toolbox and the Designer enable a developer to create graphical applications in a fraction of the time it normally takes to code an application from scratch.

- The WFC has replaced much of the functionality of the "normal" Java packages included in the Java language specification with wfc.core.*, wfc.app.*, wfc.data.*, wfc.html.*, and wfc.ui.*.

- The WFC offers many components and tools such as the Label and Button Classes, List Boxes, and ComboBoxes. The WFC makes Windows development a breeze.

- The WFC is a source of great controversy in the Java development community. Microsoft and Sun fight over the WFC and how it violates Java's promise of "write once, run anywhere." However, standard Java has nothing as powerful and easy as the WFC.

Chapter 5

Digging into COM, DCOM, OLE, and ActiveX

Microsoft added the Developer Studio to Visual J++ to aid in Java development. However, with the actual Visual J++, they only made one enhancement over the original Java specifications. Microsoft has added ActiveX controls to the Java language.

ActiveX is based on the Component Object Model (COM) specified by Microsoft. This COM model is designed to be open and to run on *every* major system.

Examining the COM Specification

The computer industry has *always* grown at a phenomenal rate. Such growth has lead to several developments in computer software:

- Software is large and complex. As the complexity continues to increase, the cost and time needed to develop the software also increases. Many small software developers have been "frozen out" of retail prepackaged software due to the entry costs associated with developing a product.

- Software has reached the point where much of the same functionality is duplicated in several applications on each user's system. This duplication not only wastes disk space, but also causes some tasks to behave inconsistently with similar tasks in other applications. When you have programs performing the same routines differently, you end up with not only more need for maintenance, but also more need for training.

- Although software packages have grown large, you typically cannot update a portion of the software with other interchangeable components. In fact, even modification of these software packages is difficult.

- Packages cannot "talk" to each other. Transferring information from one application to another (for example, from a database to a spreadsheet) can take inordinate amounts of time and involve export functions with potential loss of data or formatting.

Microsoft developed the COM specification to answer these issues. With COM software, Microsoft provides:

- Encapsulated modules to perform functions that are isolated from other modules. You can easily replace and upgrade these encapsulated modules.

- A cross-platform-supported implementation of common system components.

- Easy replacement of modules that don't affect older systems that access previous versions of these same modules.

Traditional systems don't provide for all three of these features:

- Rarely is a system truly encapsulated. Exceptions to this are Dynamic Link Libraries (DLLs) and, to a lesser degree, function libraries that can be accessed and then compiled.

- Few cross-platform development products exist. Java is one of the few exceptions. C++ may be considered somewhat cross-platform-oriented, but this language has "mutated" into several flavors with the advent of Windows. This has caused a rift between operating systems.

- You can't upgrade most component systems without affecting other systems that call the components. This is because systems were forced to allocate storage for each class they called. COM uses a pointer and lets the called class allocate its own storage.

Learning What Component Software Delivers

Component software enables you to talk to current interfaces, and to develop upgraded software that can evolve over time *without the need to update other existing software*! Component software delivers three main functions:

1. Components enable you to update part of your system. For instance, if you develop a new user interface, you can issue an update that affects just the user interface component.

2. Components enable you to choose between commercial components when developing your application. For instance, if you need a sorting algorithm for an average of 50 records, you might try a binary sorting algorithm. Later, if you find a bubble-sort algorithm from a different vendor, you may use that algorithm instead. Finally, if you come across software that provides several different algorithms based on the condition of the sort

data, you can try that. Each time, you never need to update your system other than to call a different module. The writers of these components can sell them as a package to various development companies.

3. Users can replace components that you have delivered with your system with other components. These other components might actually improve your original system.

Ultimately, component software delivers the concept of "interchangeable software parts" for software developers to deliver quality applications built using components rather than writing each software package from the ground up. Components can benefit software development in many ways:

■ Component software techniques decrease development time. If component software is accepted by corporate America, those three-to-five-year backlogs for new development may evaporate, not only making IS departments look good, but also easing their scheduling burden.

■ Integration and implementation costs decrease because components are designed to work together with existing components. Implementation run-time errors are drastically reduced.

■ Maintenance is easier because it is at the modular level rather than the system level. Also, because many modules will be "bulletproof" due to their wide use, you may find that the number of errors is reduced.

Discovering What COM Delivers

COM's implementation of component software is quickly becoming accepted by the corporate world and soon will cause developers to gravitate toward it. COM establishes a link between the "server" where the component module resides, and the "client" that is calling the component module, as shown by Figure 5-1.

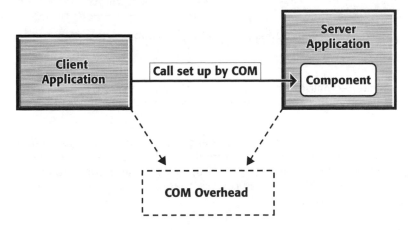

Figure 5-1: COM components have little overhead.

COM provides linkage services between two applications. After the COM link is established, *all COM overhead is dropped* and the client module can call the server module without any overhead. Therefore, the performance cost of using COM software is small. COM defines a binary standard for operation. Unlike traditional object-oriented programming environments, these mechanisms are independent of the applications that use object services and of the programming languages used to create the objects. This standard originated in the Windows environment, but because COM is defined with a binary standard, it can and has been duplicated on other operating systems.

COM functions a lot like DDE (Windows Dynamic Data Exchange) and DLL (Dynamic Link Library) components, with some important differences:

- Microsoft's DDE interface and (usually) DLLs are not standard and can be implemented in any fashion an application wanted. Conversely, COM has a set of guidelines that must be used.

- COM is not language- or compiler-dependent. In Microsoft's own words, "COM therefore defines a *binary interoperability standard* rather than a language-based interoperability." Often, you can't call DLLs (except new ActiveX DLLs) from other DLLs using the same language compiled by different compilers without writing an assembly language layer to handle the interface.

- COM is location independent. You can even distribute ActiveX controls over Web servers or run ActiveX controls on the user's own machine, passing it data from your Visual J++ application.

As shown by Figure 5-2, ActiveX and COM are a great way for two (or more) applications to "talk" to each other and assist each other in using building blocks already in place for good software development.

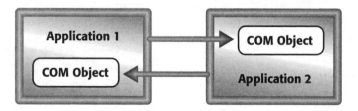

Figure 5-2: ActiveX (and therefore COM) objects are methods within applications that can be called from other applications.

The best part of the COM interface is that the applications *talk directly to each other* via memory pointers that are set up internally. The COM layer between the two applications drops as soon as a connection is made. Therefore, little overhead (except that of two programs running concurrently) is needed.

Discerning How ActiveX and COM Relate

ActiveX controls are a necessary component to a strongly Internet-influenced language such as Java. ActiveX controls used to be known as OLE (Object Linking and Embedding) Automation, because by using ActiveX, one program could be "automated" with another. However, the term *OLE Automation* is now obsolete and replaced by the term *ActiveX*.

ActiveX is a major part of COM controls (Component Object Modules). COM enables a developer to write components. These components can then be pieced together to form a new system or part of a new system. Although developed independently, Visual J++ (and Java) and the COM specification seem made for each other. Visual J++'s automatic garbage collection and use of multiple interfaces make it a natural candidate for COM implementation.

Digging into Cross-Platform Development

ActiveX controls are designed to be cross-platform. In fact, several companies are designing ActiveX support for multiple platforms:

- Metrowerks has announced that it will develop cross-platform ActiveX controls that are compatible with the Macintosh in the Internet Explorer for Macintosh.

- Sun Microsystems has a free license to ActiveX from Microsoft.

- Software AG has a DCOM (Distributed Common Object Model) implementation available for the Sun Solaris platform. Software versions are also available for the Digital UNIX and Linux platforms.

- Software AG is also developing versions of ActiveX for Hewlett Packard HP/UX, IBM AIX, SCO UnixWare, IBM OS/400, Digital Open VMS, and Siemens Nixdorf SINIX.

Clearly, Microsoft is dedicated to standardizing ActiveX across platforms. Indeed, itis in their best interest.

Using the DCOM Specification

COM modules are location-independent. This means COM modules can run on remote machines if that is where they reside. This part of COM is called *Distributed Component Object Model* or DCOM. By being distributed, Microsoft has "raised the bar," enabling component software to run over the Internet. ActiveX implements the DCOM specification.

DCOM is simply "COM with a longer wire." DCOM uses the COM specification to implement component software from remote locations. Like COM, DCOM is available on multiple platforms such as Windows, Unix, and Macintosh. DCOM has the broadest possible industry support of any distributed component software. Over 1,000 commercial software components exist already that work with DCOM and are available for use by developers.

Secret

What's one of the biggest problems with Java? It's that Java programs and applets *have a hard time communicating*! Internet Explorer, however, can expose Java classes as ActiveX components, and therefore ActiveX *enables you to call one Java Application from another*!

With the largest installed base, native support for Internet protocols, and open support for multiple platforms, developers and businesses can immediately make DCOM work in their environment.

Summary

- Visual J++ is well suited to ActiveX/COM development. This is because, just as all Java classes are COM objects, all COM objects appear to Visual J++ as Visual J++ classes. Because ActiveX is used with the tools included with Visual J++, it's important for Visual J++ developers to understand ActiveX development.

- ActiveX uses COM and DCOM to enable your Visual J++ application to use Window controls.

- COM software is extremely efficient. COM software enables you to write small components that can be used with both Java software over the Internet as well as with standard Windows programs.

- ActiveX programs look like regular classes inside Visual J++. This makes ActiveX programming easier using Visual J++ than by using *any other language*.

Chapter 6

Mastering ActiveX Programming

In This Chapter

▶ Calling ActiveX programs within Visual J++

▶ Using the ActiveX Toolbox

▶ Using the OLE/COM Object Viewer included with Visual J++

▶ Writing a Web page that uses ActiveX components

Microsoft has spent much time developing ActiveX programs to fit within the Java framework. ActiveX modules are easily developed in Visual C++ and Visual Basic. These modules can then be called from Java programs. This chapter shows how to incorporate ActiveX calls inside your Visual J++ program.

Examining ActiveX

ActiveX uses Common Object Module (COM) technology to enable developers to write small modules that can be linked together. Unlike the WFC, ActiveX can be used in environments other than Windows. In fact, several flavors of UNIX and Macintosh computers can run ActiveX modules with some additional software sold by third-party vendors. Figure 6-1 shows how a Microsoft Wallet ActiveX component can be added to a Java window:

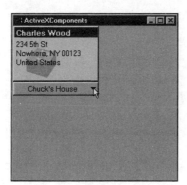

Figure 6-1: ActiveX components can be used to give you access to prewritten powerful constructs, such as Microsoft Wallet.

Secret

Microsoft placed Visual J++ within the Visual Studio to aid in Java development. However, when you compare Visual J++ with Sun's Java, you see only one major enhancement over the original Java specifications. Microsoft has added ActiveX controls to the Java language. All other enhancements, including WFC, delegates, multicast, and J/Direct-based calls stem from ActiveX support.

ActiveX (COM) objects work seamlessly in Visual J++. Visual J++ looks at an ActiveX object as a Java class. This makes implementing ActiveX easier in Java than almost any other language. You'll be amazed at how easily Visual J++ handles ActiveX integration.

Using ActiveX and the Toolbox

When first viewing the Visual Studio Toolbox, you see that you can drag ActiveX components to your Visual J++ Form. Figure 6-2 shows how a Microsoft Wallet component is added to a form.

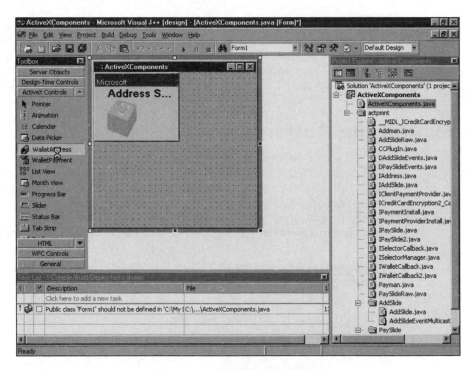

Figure 6-2: The Toolbox can be used to drag Visual ActiveX controls to your form.

ActiveX components are easy to use. The Microsoft Wallet commands (designated by the `actpmnt` "package") are indistinguishable from standard Java.

Listing 6-1: ActiveXComponents.java

```java
import wfc.app.*;
import wfc.core.*;
import wfc.ui.*;
import com.ms.com.*;

/**
* This class can take a variable number of parameters on the command
* line. Program execution begins with the main() method. The class
* constructor is not invoked unless an object of type 'ActiveXComponents'
* created in the main() method.
*/
public class ActiveXComponents extends Form
{
  public ActiveXComponents()
  {
    // Required for Visual J++ Form Designer support
    initForm();
  try {
      actpmnt.Addman a = new actpmnt.Addman();
      String s = a.GetFriendlyName(1);
      MessageBox.show(s);
    }
    catch (Throwable t) {
      handleError(t);
    }
  }
  void handleError(Throwable t) {
    t.printStackTrace();
    MessageBox.show(t.toString(),
                       "Error in ActiveXComponents");
  }

  /**
   * The main entry point for the application.
   *
   * @param args Array of parameters passed to the application
   * via the command line.
   */
  public static void main(String args[])
  {
    Application.run(new ActiveXComponents());
  }


  /**
   * NOTE: The following code is required by the Visual J++ form
   * designer. It can be modified using the form editor. Do not
   * modify it using the code editor.
   */

  Container components = new Container();
  actpmnt.AddSlide.AddSlide addSlide1 = new actpmnt.AddSlide.AddSlide();
```

```
     private void initForm()
     {
       ResourceManager resources = new ResourceManager(
               this, "ActiveXComponents");
       this.setBackColor(Color.CONTROL);
       this.setLocation(new Point(0, 0));
       this.setSize(new Point(300, 300));
       this.setTabIndex(-1);
       this.setTabStop(true);
       this.setText("ActiveXComponents");
       this.setAutoScaleBaseSize(13);
       this.setClientSize(new Point(292, 273));
       addSlide1.setLocation(new Point(0, 0));
       addSlide1.setSize(new Point(154, 123));
       addSlide1.setTabIndex(1);
       addSlide1.setTabStop(false);
       addSlide1.setOcxState((AxHost.State)resources.getObject(
               "addSlide1_ocxState"));
       this.setNewControls(new Control[] {
         addSlide1});
     }
     // NOTE: End of form designer support code

   }
```

Secret

Visual J++ also generates Java code that is used to document the ActiveX calls to the new ActiveX Components. (These Java programs can be viewed in the Project Explorer shown in Figure 6-2.) Because you can call ActiveX modules directly from Visual J++, this code isn't needed, and is only used so that the Visual J++ programmer has some documentation on what calls can be made. Listing 6-2 shows the AddSlide class generated by the Visual J++ Toolbox. As you can see by the listing, the methods generated in the AddSlide class are simple wrappers to COM calls. You can make these calls yourself without the (albeit slight) overhead of a wrapper class. (Later in this chapter, you learn how.)

Listing 6-2: AddSlide.java

```
// Auto-generated using JActiveX.EXE 4.79.2611
//  ("C:\PROGRAM FILES\MICROSOFT VISUAL STUDIO\VJ98\jactivex.exe" /wfc /w
/X:rkc /l "c:\windows\TEMP\jvcA351.TMP" /nologo /d "C:\My Documents\Visual
Studio Projects\ActiveXComponents" "C:\WINDOWS\SYSTEM\ACTPMNT.OCX")
//
// WARNING: Do not remove the comments that include "@com" directives.
// This source file must be compiled by a @com-aware compiler.
// If you are using the Microsoft Visual J++ compiler, you must use
// version 1.02.3920 or later. Previous versionsdo not issue an error
// butdo not generate COM-enabled class files.
//

package actpmnt.AddSlide;

import com.ms.com.*;
import com.ms.com.IUnknown;
import com.ms.com.Variant;
```

```java
public class AddSlide extends wfc.ui.AxHost
{
 private actpmnt.IAddSlide _jcommem_ocx;
 private actpmnt.AddSlide.AddSlideEventMulticaster
_jcommem_eventmulticaster1;
 private com.ms.com.ConnectionPointCookie _jcommem_cookie1;


 //----------------------------------------------------------------------
 // Constructors
 //----------------------------------------------------------------------

 public AddSlide()
 {
    super( "{87D3CB63-BA2E-11CF-B9D6-00A0C9083362}" );
    _jcommem_ocx = (actpmnt.IAddSlide)(getOcx());
    _jcommem_eventmulticaster1 = new
actpmnt.AddSlide.AddSlideEventMulticaster( this );
 }

 //----------------------------------------------------------------------
 // These methods override wfc.ui.AxHost methods.
 //----------------------------------------------------------------------

 public synchronized void createSink()
 {
    try
    {
      _jcommem_cookie1 = new com.ms.com.ConnectionPointCookie(_jcommem_ocx,
_jcommem_eventmulticaster1, actpmnt.DAddSlideEvents.class);
    } catch(Throwable _jcom_t) {
    }
 }

 //----------------------------------------------------------------------
 // These methods invoke methods directly on the ActiveX Control.
 //----------------------------------------------------------------------

 public synchronized String getHilight3D() {
    return _jcommem_ocx.getHilight3D();
 }


 public synchronized void setHilight3D(String pbstrColor) {
    _jcommem_ocx.setHilight3D(pbstrColor);
 }


 public synchronized String getLight3D() {
    return _jcommem_ocx.getLight3D();
 }


 public synchronized void setLight3D(String pbstrColor) {
    _jcommem_ocx.setLight3D(pbstrColor);
 }
```

```java
public synchronized String getFace3D() {
   return _jcommem_ocx.getFace3D();
}


public synchronized void setFace3D(String pbstrColor) {
   _jcommem_ocx.setFace3D(pbstrColor);
}


public synchronized String getShadow3D() {
   return _jcommem_ocx.getShadow3D();
}


public synchronized void setShadow3D(String pbstrColor) {
   _jcommem_ocx.setShadow3D(pbstrColor);
}


public synchronized String getDarkShadow3D() {
   return _jcommem_ocx.getDarkShadow3D();
}


public synchronized void setDarkShadow3D(String pbstrColor) {
   _jcommem_ocx.setDarkShadow3D(pbstrColor);
}


public synchronized String getTextColor() {
   return _jcommem_ocx.getTextColor();
}


public synchronized void setTextColor(String pbstrColor) {
   _jcommem_ocx.setTextColor(pbstrColor);
}


public synchronized String getGrayTextColor() {
   return _jcommem_ocx.getGrayTextColor();
}


public synchronized void setGrayTextColor(String pbstrColor) {
   _jcommem_ocx.setGrayTextColor(pbstrColor);
}


public synchronized String getCtlFont() {
   return _jcommem_ocx.getFont();
}
```

```
public synchronized void setCtlFont(String pbstrFont) {
  _jcommem_ocx.setFont(pbstrFont);
}


public synchronized String getProgID() {
  return _jcommem_ocx.getProgID();
}


public synchronized void setProgID(String pbstrProgID) {
  _jcommem_ocx.setProgID(pbstrProgID);
}


public synchronized boolean getAutoAdd() {
  return _jcommem_ocx.getAutoAdd();
}


public synchronized void setAutoAdd(boolean pbAutoAdd) {
  _jcommem_ocx.setAutoAdd(pbAutoAdd);
}


public synchronized String getAutoAddText() {
  return _jcommem_ocx.getAutoAddText();
}


public synchronized void setAutoAddText(String pbstrAutoAddText) {
  _jcommem_ocx.setAutoAddText(pbstrAutoAddText);
}


public synchronized boolean getNoDefault() {
  return _jcommem_ocx.getNoDefault();
}


public synchronized void setNoDefault(boolean pbNoDefault) {
  _jcommem_ocx.setNoDefault(pbNoDefault);
}


public synchronized String getNoDefaultText() {
  return _jcommem_ocx.getNoDefaultText();
}


public synchronized void setNoDefaultText(String pbstrNoDefaultText) {
  _jcommem_ocx.setNoDefaultText(pbstrNoDefaultText);
}
```

```java
public synchronized boolean getUseComboBox() {
  return _jcommem_ocx.getUseComboBox();
}


public synchronized void setUseComboBox(boolean pbUseComboBox) {
  _jcommem_ocx.setUseComboBox(pbUseComboBox);
}


public synchronized void Manage() {
  _jcommem_ocx.Manage();
}


public synchronized int GetLastError() {
  return _jcommem_ocx.GetLastError();
}


public synchronized Variant GetValues() {
  return _jcommem_ocx.GetValues();
}


public synchronized Variant GetShipToValues() {
  return _jcommem_ocx.GetShipToValues();
}


 public synchronized String GetValue(Variant nameValuePairsArray, String
fieldName, int reportErrorsFlag) {
   return _jcommem_ocx.GetValue(nameValuePairsArray, fieldName,
reportErrorsFlag);
 }



 //-------------------------------------------------------------------
 // These methods add and remove event handlers.
 //-------------------------------------------------------------------

 //-------------------------------------------------------------------
 // This class provides information about the control's events and
 // properties.
 //-------------------------------------------------------------------

 public static class ClassInfo extends wfc.ui.AxHost.ClassInfo
 {
   public static final wfc.core.PropertyInfo Hilight3DPropertyInfo = new
wfc.core.PropertyInfo (
     actpmnt.AddSlide.AddSlide.class, "hilight3D", String.class, new
wfc.core.NonPersistableAttribute() );

   public static final wfc.core.PropertyInfo Light3DPropertyInfo = new
wfc.core.PropertyInfo (
```

```
    actpmnt.AddSlide.AddSlide.class, "light3D", String.class, new
wfc.core.NonPersistableAttribute() );

    public static final wfc.core.PropertyInfo Face3DPropertyInfo = new
wfc.core.PropertyInfo (
    actpmnt.AddSlide.AddSlide.class, "face3D", String.class, new
wfc.core.NonPersistableAttribute() );

    public static final wfc.core.PropertyInfo Shadow3DPropertyInfo = new
wfc.core.PropertyInfo (
    actpmnt.AddSlide.AddSlide.class, "shadow3D", String.class, new
wfc.core.NonPersistableAttribute() );

    public static final wfc.core.PropertyInfo DarkShadow3DPropertyInfo =
new wfc.core.PropertyInfo (
    actpmnt.AddSlide.AddSlide.class, "darkShadow3D", String.class, new
wfc.core.NonPersistableAttribute() );

    public static final wfc.core.PropertyInfo TextColorPropertyInfo = new
wfc.core.PropertyInfo (
    actpmnt.AddSlide.AddSlide.class, "textColor", String.class, new
wfc.core.NonPersistableAttribute() );

    public static final wfc.core.PropertyInfo GrayTextColorPropertyInfo =
new wfc.core.PropertyInfo (
    actpmnt.AddSlide.AddSlide.class, "grayTextColor", String.class, new
wfc.core.NonPersistableAttribute() );

    public static final wfc.core.PropertyInfo ctlFontPropertyInfo = new
wfc.core.PropertyInfo (
    actpmnt.AddSlide.AddSlide.class, "ctlFont", String.class, new
wfc.core.NonPersistableAttribute() );

    public static final wfc.core.PropertyInfo ProgIDPropertyInfo = new
wfc.core.PropertyInfo (
    actpmnt.AddSlide.AddSlide.class, "progID", String.class, new
wfc.core.NonPersistableAttribute() );

    public static final wfc.core.PropertyInfo AutoAddPropertyInfo = new
wfc.core.PropertyInfo (
    actpmnt.AddSlide.AddSlide.class, "autoAdd", boolean.class, new
wfc.core.NonPersistableAttribute() );

    public static final wfc.core.PropertyInfo AutoAddTextPropertyInfo = new
wfc.core.PropertyInfo (
    actpmnt.AddSlide.AddSlide.class, "autoAddText", String.class, new
wfc.core.NonPersistableAttribute() );

    public static final wfc.core.PropertyInfo NoDefaultPropertyInfo = new
wfc.core.PropertyInfo (
    actpmnt.AddSlide.AddSlide.class, "noDefault", boolean.class, new
wfc.core.NonPersistableAttribute() );

    public static final wfc.core.PropertyInfo NoDefaultTextPropertyInfo =
new wfc.core.PropertyInfo (
```

```
         actpmnt.AddSlide.AddSlide.class, "noDefaultText", String.class, new
wfc.core.NonPersistableAttribute() );

     public static final wfc.core.PropertyInfo UseComboBoxPropertyInfo = new
wfc.core.PropertyInfo (
         actpmnt.AddSlide.AddSlide.class, "useComboBox", boolean.class, new
wfc.core.NonPersistableAttribute() );

     public void getProperties( wfc.core.IProperties props )
     {
      super.getProperties( props );
      props.add( Hilight3DPropertyInfo );
      props.add( Light3DPropertyInfo );
      props.add( Face3DPropertyInfo );
      props.add( Shadow3DPropertyInfo );
      props.add( DarkShadow3DPropertyInfo );
      props.add( TextColorPropertyInfo );
      props.add( GrayTextColorPropertyInfo );
      props.add( ctlFontPropertyInfo );
      props.add( ProgIDPropertyInfo );
      props.add( AutoAddPropertyInfo );
      props.add( AutoAddTextPropertyInfo );
      props.add( NoDefaultPropertyInfo );
      props.add( NoDefaultTextPropertyInfo );
      props.add( UseComboBoxPropertyInfo );
     }

     public void getEvents( wfc.core.IEvents events )
     {
      super.getEvents( events );
     }
    }
}
```

Using the OLE/COM Object Viewer

Use the OLE/COM Object Viewer to view what's inside a registered ActiveX control. To open the Object Viewer, choose Tools ➪ OLE/COM Object Viewer. Then select View ➪ Expert Mode to view the Type Libraries that can be called by Java programs. Refer to Figure 6-3.

Double-clicking Type Libraries expands the tree view to show the ActiveX modules you can call from your Visual J++ program or Applet. To view the specifications for a specific ActiveX module, double-click that module. This can be seen in Figure 6-4, where Microsoft Wallet is double-clicked.

Secret

If you don't see Microsoft Wallet in your list of ActiveX controls, you didn't install it when you installed Internet Explorer. If you don't want to install it now, you can choose any ActiveX type library currently installed on your system.

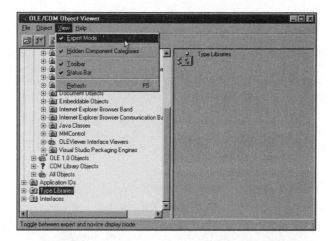

Figure 6-3: View the ActiveX Type Libraries using Expert Mode in the OLE/COM Object Viewer.

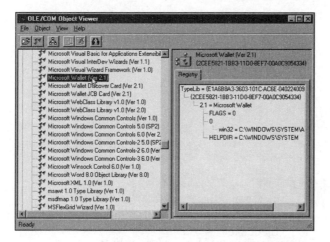

Figure 6-4: Microsoft Wallet is listed as an ActiveX control in the OLE/COM Object Viewer window.

Now you should see the ITypeLib Viewer shown in Figure 6-5. Use the ITypeLib Viewer to view several different types of OLE constructs:

■ *Enums* contain constants that you can use when calling other ActiveX methods.

■ *Structs* contain any data structures present in an ActiveX module. Often this is empty.

■ *Modules* contain any submodules contained inside an ActiveX module. Usually this is empty.

- *Interfaces* contain function prototypes you can use when you call ActiveX classes.

- *Dispinterfaces* are the most used ActiveX modules. They contain the classes inside the package, and the methods inside those classes. If you spend much time in the ITypeLib Viewer, you'll probably be using Dispinterfaces almost exclusively.

- *Coclasses* are classes inside the ActiveX module. Unlike Modules, which can be entire ActiveX modules, Coclasses can contain only classes that were defined in the Dispinterfaces section.

- *Typedefs* are type definitions. Although used in C++ quite extensively, type definitions are not implemented in Java.

- *Unions* include ActiveX modules that can be used in conjunction with the current ActiveX module. Unlike Modules, Unions point to ActiveX modules that exist outside the current ActiveX module.

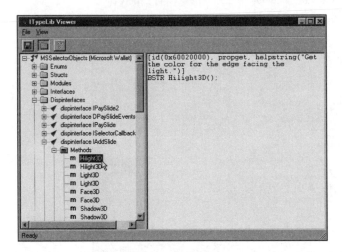

Figure 6-5: A help string and a function prototype are displayed in the ITypeLib Viewer for each method inside a Dispinterface.

Secret

Don't confuse ActiveX Dispinterfaces with Java interfaces. They are different. Java interfaces contain no functionality and are used to tie two classes together. ActiveX Dispinterfaces contain functionality and are functional software components that can be added to a program.

Using ActiveX Inside a Java Program

The Visual Studio environment automatically generates Java wrappers for your ActiveX modules. When you develop functions inside your Java program for ActiveX modules not found in the Toolbox, you need to develop your own ActiveX calls without the benefit of the automatically generated ActiveX wrappers.

Microsoft Word Programming

This section shows how to create and open a Microsoft Word document inside a Web page using a Visual J++ program. Although every ActiveX program is different, Microsoft seems to format most of their ActiveX programs similarly.

Microsoft applications usually have a master class that needs to be instantiated. (In Word's case, that master class is called Application.) Then Microsoft applications usually place "container classes" inside that master class. For instance, the Application class inside Microsoft Word contains a Documents container class that contains all the documents and a FontNames container class where all the Font names are stored. These two containers are only two of many different containers found in Microsoft Word's ActiveX module.

Finally, an "array" of classes exists inside each container class. They can be retrieved by using a ( ) or ( ) method and an array number as a parameter. (This can be seen later in this section.) Microsoft Word's setup can be seen in the following figure.

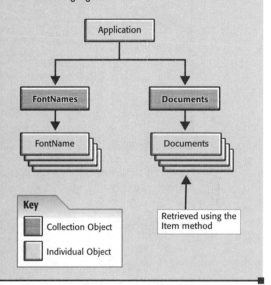

This is not as difficult as it seems. Java and ActiveX share many of the same structures, and can be used interchangeably inside an ActiveX module. Accessing ActiveX modules inside Visual J++ is *easier than with any other language!* If you've ever tried ActiveX programming inside another language, I'm sure you'll agree, especially after reading this section.

Using ActiveX controls inside your program

To write your ActiveX module, you need to find the name of the ActiveX Type Library. The Type Library is analogous to a Java package. In fact, Visual J++ treats ActiveX Type Libraries as if they were Java packages. Look for a filename with an OLB extension, and that's the name of your package.

As you see in Figure 6-6, the ITypeLib Viewer shows that Microsoft Word 8 (Word 97) uses an MSWORD8.OLB file.

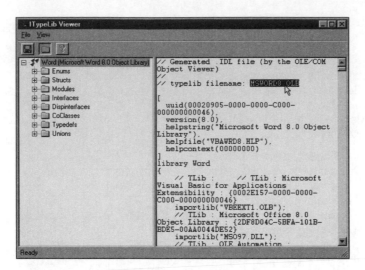

Figure 6-6: The ITypeLib Viewer displays the OLB file used for ActiveX. You import this file.

Write the `import` command for your Visual J++ module as follows:

```
//Now Import routines to remotely access Microsoft Word
import msword8.*;
```

After importing the `msword8` type library, you can declare classes for it. The following lines of code declare a Word Application interface and use it to retrieve a Word application from the ActiveX modules:

```
//Declare a new Application and assign it to your _Application
variable.
_Application app = new Application();
```

Secret

Notice how an Application interface is used to contain the new application. ActiveX interfaces contain all the methods needed to run an ActiveX module.

Usually classes need to be constructed outside of the Java environment and inside the ActiveX modules themselves. This means that you rarely use the new operator to construct a new class, have the ActiveX module return a preconstructed class instead. The following line of code creates a Documents container class from the Application class:

```
//Retrieve the Documents container from the Application
Documents docs = app.getDocuments();
```

ActiveX modules have methods that can be used for manipulation. Code needs to be developed to do the following:

■ Define Variants that can be used for parameters to create a new document.

■ Use the `Documents.Add()` method to create a new document.

- Use the `Documents.Item()` method to return the newly created document.

- Use the `Document.activate()` method to activate the newly created document inside the Word environment.

- Place the Word environment inside a window, resize it, make it visible, and activate it.

The following code accomplishes these tasks:

```
//Define three variants that are used for parameters
      com.ms.com.Variant v1 = new com.ms.com.Variant();
      com.ms.com.Variant v2 = new com.ms.com.Variant();
      com.ms.com.Variant v3 = new com.ms.com.Variant();
    //Put a 1 integer in variant 1
      v1.putInt(1);
    //Use a default template and a new template
      v2.putString("");
      v3.putBoolean(true);
    //Add a new Document to the Documents container
      docs.Add(v2, v3);
    //Retrieve the first (and only) Document from
    //the Documents container
      _Document doc = docs.Item(v1);
    //Activate the document with the application
      doc.Activate();
    //Activate the Word window
      app.NewWindow();
    //Resize the Word window so you can see it
      app.Resize(400, 400);
    //Make the word window visible
      app.putVisible(true);
    //Active the Word application
      app.Activate();
```

So What's a Variant?

Microsoft ActiveX modules often use a `com.ms.com.Variant` class. A Variant is a class developed by Microsoft that can store almost any data type and pass it to an ActiveX module or another Java module.

Variants have `put()` methods (for example, `putBoolean()`, `putString()`, `putInt()`) that can place a variable inside a variant. Similarly, Variants have `get()` methods (for example, `getBoolean()`, `getString()`, `getInt()`) that return the values to Java type classes.

Variants are used whenever coding for Microsoft ActiveX modules.

Catching errors in ActiveX modules

Often an ActiveX call ends in an error. Unlike standard Java errors, most ActiveX calls do not abnormally terminate your Java program and wait for you to handle the error. ActiveX errors can be caught using a com.ms.com.ComException. A ComException is an error that occurs during a COM or ActiveX call:

```
//. . .
  catch(com.ms.com.ComException e) {
    handleThrowable((Throwable) e);
    // Handle all ms.com.ms.ComException errors
  }
//. . .
void handleThrowable(Throwable t) {
  //Print what happened inside the Throwable
    t.printStackTrace();
  //Do a WFC message box to show the error
    wfc.ui.MessageBox.show(t.toString(), "ActiveXWord error" );
}
```

In the preceding code, the ComException is caught and handled by a handleThrowable() method.

Writing an ActiveX Java program

Writing an ActiveX program using Visual J++ is easier than implementing ActiveX in any other language. Using the examples shown earlier in this section, Listing 6-3 was developed. Listing 6-3 is an ActiveXWord program that opens a Microsoft Word document.

Listing 6-3: ActiveXWord.java

```
//Import Java stuff
import java.awt.*;
import java.applet.*;
//Now Import routines to remotely access Microsoft Word
import msword8.*;
//Make a Web page
public class ActiveXWord extends Applet {
  //Init is run automatically when an Applet starts.
  public void init() {
    //Declare an MSword _Application interface
    _Application app;
    try {
    //Define three variants that are used for parameters
      com.ms.com.Variant v1 = new com.ms.com.Variant();
      com.ms.com.Variant v2 = new com.ms.com.Variant();
      com.ms.com.Variant v3 = new com.ms.com.Variant();
    //Put a 1 integer in variant 1
      v1.putInt(1);
    //Declare a new Application and assign it to your
```

```
        //_Application variable.
          app = new Application();
        //Retrieve Documents container from the Application
          Documents docs = app.getDocuments();
        //Use a default template and a new template
          v2.putString("");
          v3.putBoolean(true);
        //Add a new Document to the Documents container
          docs.Add(v2, v3);
        //Retrieve the first (and only) Document from
        //the Documents container
          _Document doc = docs.Item(v1);
        //Activate the document with the application
          doc.Activate();
        //Activate the Word window
          app.NewWindow();
        //Resize the Word window so you can see it
          app.Resize(400, 400);
        //Make the word window visible
          app.putVisible(true);
        //Active the Word application
          app.Activate();
        }
    //Catch all errors, especially ms.com.ms.ComException
    //errors
      catch (Throwable t) {
        handleThrowable(t);
        app = null;  //garbage collect
      }
    }
    // Handle all errors, especially ms.com.ms.ComException
    //errors
    void handleThrowable(Throwable t) {
    //Print what happened inside the Throwable
      t.printStackTrace();
    //Do a WFC message box to show the error
      wfc.ui.MessageBox.show(t.toString(),"ActiveXWord error" );
    }
}
```

If you didn't already know that msword8 was an ActiveX module, you sure wouldn't find it out by looking at Listing 6-3. ActiveX modules *seamlessly integrate* with Java code. (That's why I say ActiveX is easier to use with Visual J++ than with any other language.) Output from Listing 6-3 can be viewed in Figure 6-7.

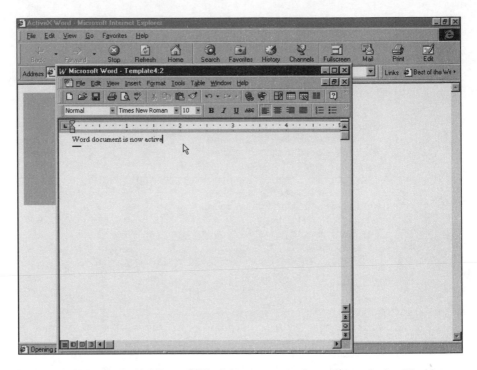

Figure 6-7: Using ActiveX, Microsoft Word documents can be easily manipulated inside a Web page.

Secret

The `com.ms.com.*` package was not imported so you could see where the classes that were used in Listing 6-3 come from. However, you would probably want to import Microsoft's `com.ms.com` library because `com.ms.com` contains all the error routines needed to detect any errors generated by an ActiveX module as well as all the Variant code.

Summary

ActiveX enables you to share modules with your Windows applications as well as your Java applications. Microsoft is doing more than any other vendor in enabling your Java applications to call Windows modules.

- Microsoft enables you to call ActiveX modules within Visual J++.

- The OLE/COM Object Viewer included with Visual J++ can be a great help when developing ActiveX applications.

- ActiveX *is not* WFC. ActiveX has limited support in other environments, including UNIX and Macintosh. WFC consists of specially designed ActiveX modules that only function in a Windows environment.

- Microsoft includes COM support for ActiveX modules.

Chapter 7

Making Your Own ActiveX and COM Components

All Visual J++ classes (and all Java classes, for that matter) are exposed as ActiveX controls through the Microsoft Java Virtual Machine, which runs under Internet Explorer. If you have a Java class running under Internet Explorer, you can make ActiveX calls to your Java program through the Java Virtual Machine running under Internet Explorer.

Generating COM

Visual J++ enables you to import and use any existing COM object. This enables developers to reuse any Windows component regardless of the language they were written in.

With the delivery of Visual Studio, Microsoft enables developers to write and deploy COM components in their language of choice that can be used by any other Windows development tool. Using Visual J++, all Java objects can be accessed as COM objects from several development environments — such as Visual Basic, PowerBuilder, Delphi, or even Microsoft Word and Microsoft Excel. Visual J++ creates COM components that are indiscernible from those created with other Windows development tools, thus enabling developers to write applications for other Windows tools using Java.

You can start writing a COM component by clicking COM DLL or COM Control, as shown in the New Project window in Figure 7-1.

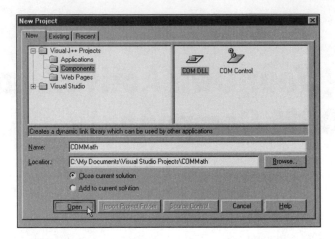

Figure 7-1: COM development is an option in the New Project window.

However, when you click these windows, you end up with an empty class and a list of TODO instructions, as shown by Listing 7-1.

Listing 7-1: Generated COM code

```
// Class1.java
/**
 * This class is designed to be packaged with a COM DLL output
format.
 * The class has no standard entry points, other than the
constructor.
 * Public methods  are exposed as COM interfaces.
 *
 */
// TODO: Modify the Project Properties and make this class a COM
Class.
// 1. From the 'Project' menu, select the 'Project
Properties...'item.
// 2. Choose the 'COM Classes' tab.
// 3. Check the checkbox for Class1.
public class Class1
{
    // TODO: Add initialization code here
}
```

Although Visual J++ is a great tool for COM development, this generated code leaves out some of the more powerful implications of COM development. The rest of this chapter shows how you can use Visual J++ as your premier COM development tool.

Looking at COM Development

Listing 7-2 and 7-3 show a Visual J++ project containing two classes. Each class contains mathematical functions. In Listing 7-2, the class MathFuncts contains algebraic methods to square, to find prime numbers, to find the greatest common denominator, and to factor a number into its prime denominators.

Listing 7-2: MathFuncts.java

```java
import java.util.*;
/**
 * @com.register ( clsid=5AF0E62D-F21F-11D1-9949-B728CAC61C6F,
typelib=5AF0E62C-F21F-11D1-9949-B728CAC61C6F )
 */
public class MathFuncts {
//Square a number
  public double square(double number) {
    return number*number;
  }
//Take the factorial of a number
  public double factorial(int number) {
    double answer = 1;
    for (int loop = number; loop > 1; loop--) {
      answer *= number--;
    }
    return answer;
  }
//Get all prime numbers up to 10,000
  public long[] getPrimes() {
    return getPrimes(10000);
  }
//Get all prime numbers up to a given number
  public long[] getPrimes(long untilNumber) {
    if (untilNumber < 2) {   //minimum until 2
      return null;
    }
    Vector v = new Vector();
    Enumeration e;
    //loop through, but skip the even numbers
    for (long start = 3; start < untilNumber; start+=2) {
      e = v.elements();
      boolean isPrime = true;
      while (e.hasMoreElements()) {
      //A long prime in a Long wrapper
        Long primeWrapper = (Long) e.nextElement();
        long prime = primeWrapper.longValue();
        if (prime > start / 3) {
      //This is a prime. Break out of the while loop
```

```
                break;
            }
        //take the modulus of the the test & prime
          if (start % prime == 0) {
        //Not a prime. Break out of the while loop
             isPrime = false;
             break;
          }
      }
      if (isPrime) {   //Add primes to the Vector
        v.addElement((Object) new Long(start));
      }
    }
    v.trimToSize();
    long[] returnValue = new long[v.size()+1];
    returnValue[0] = 2;
    for (int loop = 0; loop < v.size(); loop++) {
      Long arrayElement = (Long) v.elementAt(loop);
      returnValue[loop+1] = arrayElement.longValue();
    }
    return returnValue;
  }
//The la_PCPRimes array goes with the primeDenominators static
//method
  private long [] la_PCPrimes;
//Get the prime factors of a number
  public int[] primeDenominators(int number) {
    if (la_PCPrimes == null) {
      la_PCPrimes = getPrimes((long) number/3);
    }
    int denom = 0;
    int[] returnValue;
    int loop;
    for (loop = 0; la_PCPrimes[loop] < number / 2; loop++) {
      //take the modulus of the the parameter & prime
      if (number % la_PCPrimes[loop] == 0) {
      //Found a denominator
        denom = (int) la_PCPrimes[loop];
        break;   //Found lower denominator
      }
    }
    if (denom > 0) {   //Found a denominator
    // A little recursion goes a long way with this method.
      int[] otherDenoms = primeDenominators(number / denom);
    // Add the denom to the list of other denoms
      returnValue = new int[otherDenoms.length + 1];
      for (loop = 0; loop < otherDenoms.length; loop++) {
        returnValue[loop] = otherDenoms[loop];
      }
```

```
      returnValue[otherDenoms.length] = denom;
    }
    else {   //There is no lower denominator
      returnValue = new int[1];
      returnValue[0] = number;
    }
    return returnValue;
  }
//Return the greatest common denominator of two numbers
  public int greatestCommonDenominator(int a, int b) {
    while (a > 0) {     //Go until b has the GCD
      if (a < b) {   //Switch
        int holder = a;
        a = b;
        b = holder;
      }
      a-=b;   //Set a = a - b
    }
    return b;   //When a is zero, b contains the GCD
  }
}
```

In Listing 7-3, the class `TrigFuncts` contains trigonometric methods that take the trigonometric SINE and COSINE of a number.

Listing 7-3:   TrigFuncts.java

```
/**
 * @com.register ( clsid=5AF0E62E-F21F-11D1-9949-B728CAC61C6F,
typelib=5AF0E62C-F21F-11D1-9949-B728CAC61C6F )
 */
public class TrigFuncts {
//Take the SINE of a number
  public double sin(double number) {
    return java.lang.Math.sin(number);
  }
//Take the COSINE of a number
  public double cos(double number) {
    return java.lang.Math.cos(number);
  }
}
```

In traditional languages, these methods would have to be rewritten if the development environment was changed. COM changes all this, enabling you to share your Java code between applications. You can easily create a COM component in Visual J++ by going to the COM Classes tab in the Project Properties window and selecting those classes in the project you want to be exported as COM objects. In Figure 7-2, I chose the `MathFuncts` and the `TrigFuncts` classes. (The other class is used for testing the Java methods.)

Figure 7-2: You can select classes to generate a COM ActiveX module.

Secret

You can change COM options by clicking the Options button in the MathFuncts Properties window (Figure 7-2). This opens the Type Library Options window shown in Figure 7-3. The Type Library Options window enables you to specify the TLB name and the library name inside the TLB, as well as any help filename and its associated help context ID. Most importantly, however, is the description. The description defaults to the filename, but your code is easier to use if you add a one-line description that tells others exactly what your module does.

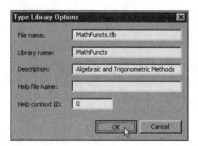

Figure 7-3: Enter a description of your Java COM module on the Type Library Options window.

After building, you notice that each class has some strange-looking COM comments in front of them:

```
/**
 * @com.register ( clsid=5AF0E62E-F21F-11D1-9949-B728CAC61C6F,
typelib=5AF0E62C-F21F-11D1-9949-B728CAC61C6F )
 */
```

All classes selected automatically obtain a class ID and are registered when the project is built. The COM register comments, like those that follow, are automatically generated by Visual J++ during build time. Visual J++ also generates the necessary Type Library information and registry entries. Figure 7-4 shows the generated comments for each class id that is used. (Other not-so-COM-friendly languages, like C++, may require the class id of the COM component.) You can see the Type Library file (.tlb) and the generated comments in Visual J++'s environment in Figure 7-4.

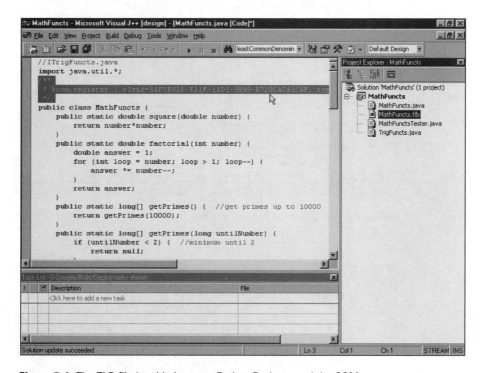

Figure 7-4: The TLB file is added to your Project Explorer, and the COM comments are added to your source code when developing COM modules from Java code.

When you open the OLE Viewer and double-click Java Classes, you can see all the Java classes that you have compiled as COM modules. In Figure 7-5, the MathFuncts class and the TrigFuncts class are shown as COM modules. Here, you can also find their associated TLB file name that is used in the import command.

Secret

The description you entered in Figure 7-3 is more than a simple comment. The OLE Viewer uses the description when listing your COM modules. Figure 7-6 shows how the OLE Viewer shows the Java module as "Algebraic and Trigonometric Methods" rather than "MathFuncts." Because the "MathFuncts" label is somewhat ambiguous, other developers may be better off using the "Algebraic and Trigonometric Methods" label instead.

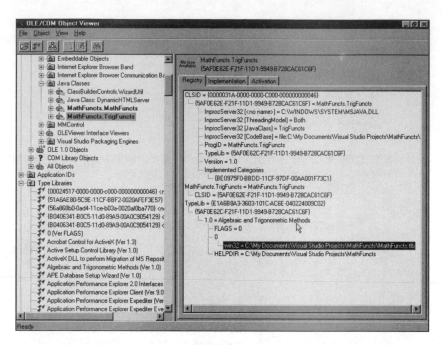

Figure 7-5: The OLE viewer shows you the Java classes you have compiled into ActiveX modules.

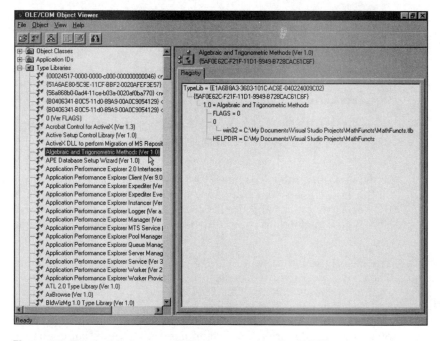

Figure 7-6: The description name is the name used by the OLE Viewer to describe your new TLB file.

As you can see in the OLE Viewer shown in Figure 7-7, the methods of the compiled class (MathFuncts), as well as the ancestor class (Object), are now callable as a COM module.

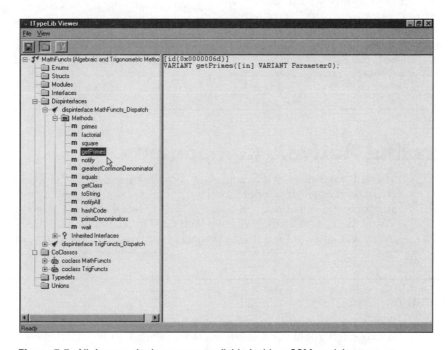

Figure 7-7: All Java methods are now available inside a COM module.

Thanks to Visual J++'s COM support, developers can write components in the language most suited for them and distribute them as objects to other languages.

Sun Versus Microsoft on COM

Sun promotes Java by promising that a developer can "write once, run anywhere." ActiveX, especially over the Web, is a response to that. Microsoft would rather control the standards than be subjected to them, and has created COM, which is a fully-functional component specification promising, at least, to "write once, run anywhere on Windows." Most Windows development environments use and support COM components.

Although Sun and Microsoft are still arguing about who's right and who's wrong, we definitely know who's winning — YOU ARE! As with many fights in a competitive environment, the customer usually wins.

As a developer, you are "doubly blessed" with the latest release of Visual J++. By using Visual J++, you can write standard, pure Java to run

(continued)

(continued)

on almost any Web browser. You can also write COM components or libraries that not only can be used on *any* environment *but also* can be used by other languages such as PowerBuilder, Delphi, Visual C++, Visual Basic, or even by Microsoft Word and Microsoft Excel — *using the SAME Java code!*

Thanks to the war to control standards, Visual J++ developers are poised to develop both Windows and Web functionality using a streamlined development process that no other Windows development tool — and no other Java development tool — can deliver.

Creating ActiveX Components

Visual J++ 6.0 enables developers to compile their own ActiveX controls to share with other developers working in Visual J++ 6.0 or any other tool that supports the use of ActiveX controls. The ActiveX controls generated by Visual J++ can be hosted within a Web page for easy and safe distribution to users. Visual J++ allows the packaging of ActiveX components from Java code.

Summary

With COM, Microsoft has upped the ante on component software. COM is extremely robust and is supported in almost all Windows development platforms.

- The Project Properties window has a COM tab that enables you to generate COM components.

- The OLE Viewer can show you where your Java COM modules are located.

- As in all things, Sun and Microsoft fight about whether COM is a viable standard. However, this competition has poised Visual J++ to be a viable development tool for both pure Java and Windows COM development.

Chapter 8

Better Security Over the Web

With the addition of ActiveX, many Java developers feel that Visual J++ Web pages don't have enough security. Microsoft, however, points out that ActiveX has its own security protocol. This chapter discusses Java and ActiveX security issues.

Reviewing Web Security Issues

When computer information is sent from a Web site to a personal computer, it passes several other computers along the way. This gives an opportunity for those computers to view your sensitive information.

Say you run an online software shop. You require a credit card number, but you're honest and don't abuse the trust your clients have given you. Unfortunately, a hacker is viewing one of the computers that some of your customer's credit card information passes through. As more of your customers have their credit card numbers stolen, you get the reputation as someone who is either selling credit card numbers or is not too careful with the information sent to you — when neither is true.

Theft of credit card information and other security problems don't happen often, but they are technically possible, and therefore a potential problem. As the Internet becomes more popular, technically savvy criminals could become more active. Internet Explorer (IE) has put in security measures that can help:

■ You can assign any files you can open or download, even those files on your own computer, to "security zones." You can set different levels of security depending on where the Web information comes from and how much you trust the Web site.

- You can send data to a secure site only if you have the proper security protocols. If you are viewing a page from a secure site, Internet Explorer displays a lock icon on the status bar.

- IE notifies you when you are about to do something that might pose a security risk — such as sending your credit card number to an unsecured site. Even if the site claims to be secure but its security credentials are suspect, IE warns you that the site might have been tampered with or the site might be misrepresenting itself.

- IE supports *personal certificates*, which guarantee that you are who you say you are. Using personal certificates, you can specify information about yourself, such as your username and password. Certificate information is used when you send personal information over the Internet to a Web site that requires a certificate verifying your identity.

- IE supports *Web site certificates* that guarantee that a Web site is secure and genuine. Web site certificates ensure that no other Web site can assume the identity of the original secure site. Web site certificates are also dated when they are issued. If you try to open an invalid site, IE displays a warning.

- IE contains Content Advisor, which is a way to help you control the types of content that your computer can access on the Internet. After you turn on Content Advisor, only rated content that meets or exceeds your criteria can be displayed. You can adjust the settings to allow only viewing of appropriate Web sites; the four content areas are language, nudity, sex, and violence.

Downloading software

Web surfers should understand the consequences of downloading the latest software from a Web site. Hopefully, software such as ActiveX controls improves and enriches their Web viewing experience. However, if users haven't interacted with a Web site before, it's not clear if they should trust and download the software because there's no way to make sure the new downloads are secure.

Initially, people thought it would be difficult to provide a secure Web system. HTML-based Web pages were considered extremely secure because of their text-only content, but downloads from the Web were considered risky due to the potential for viruses and Trojan horses.

Secret

A virus is a program that attaches itself to the existing programs or disk boot sector. The virus then goes through an "incubation period" where it propagates itself onto other programs and possibly escapes your hard disk onto a floppy disk where it can install itself on another computer. After the incubation period, some viruses perform tasks that are annoying or destructive. A Trojan horse is a program that is immediately destructive. The user thinks he or she is downloading a useful piece of software when, in fact, a destructive program is being downloaded.

In truth, the majority of viruses have been spread with commercial software, and Trojan horses never last long on the Web.

The use of Java raises additional questions of security. If a program is run on a Web page that the user doesn't even need to download, does that cause a problem? When it developed Java, Sun Microsystems tried to minimize its security risk. However, this tight security caused Java programs to have a hard time accessing the local machine's environment variables and databases.

Microsoft's distribution of an ActiveX-aware Java development tool caused quite a stir, because ActiveX can access *all* system resources, and therefore has the potential to become destructive.

Digging into Java's sandbox

Java Applets are probably more secure than any other system ever devised. Java Applets run inside a Java Virtual Machine that is isolated from the main machine. A Java Applet can only access the directory where it resides and can't access a system's environment variables.

Java's security is based on a *sandbox* methodology. The sandbox methodology states that Java programs have a predefined area on the machine, for both disk space and memory allocation, which can be accessed by the Java program. Java programs can't access any disk area or memory outside of that area.

What a Java Applet can do to a system

Even while "playing in the sandbox," Java Applets *still* have the capability to misbehave:

- Java programs can fill a server's hard drive by writing huge amounts of information to the same directory. This not only fills your disk space, but can also wreak havoc on machines that rely on virtual memory, such as the Microsoft Windows family of operating systems.

- Java programs can take control of your processor by issuing CPU-intensive commands, such as loops. This makes any other tasks difficult to run, execute, or close.

- Java Applets can "offload processing" onto your computer, thereby reducing the load of their own computer. While you are attached to a Web site, your CPU and disk may be running to help the Java Applet accomplish its tasks.

The first two problems in the previous list are often the result of programmer error, rather than programmer maliciousness. Still, the result is that your current working environment is corrupted.

These three issues, while annoying, are hardly *that* destructive. Java has done a good job with security implementation. When compared to other programs running on your machine, Java is one of the safest environments from which to run a program.

When there is too much security

Java's sandbox is sufficient for many programming tasks. However, the Java Virtual Machine may be *too* secure. Because of Java security restrictions, programmers are limited in what they can accomplish:

- Java programs can't access environment variables. Consequently, Java programs can't set environment variables either.

- Java programs can't call other Java programs outside of their own packages.

- Java programs can't analyze a system to see what else is running.

Java's many security restrictions have forced the corporate world to largely ignore Java in favor of traditional program development tools.

Incorporating ActiveX

Companies found that they couldn't develop in such a secure, yet restrictive, environment. Microsoft answered this dilemma by incorporating ActiveX into Visual J++, thereby giving developers the capability to call modules that run outside the Java Virtual Machine. This caused an uproar in the Java community, where security is considered very important. On the other hand, many companies have welcomed the change. Now they can develop Java applications that access their databases, environment variables, and other Java Applets.

Secret

In truth, Microsoft did not violate the Java security system. Microsoft uses native programs to drive its ActiveX programs. Native programs are written in system-specific code, but are accessible by the Java Virtual Machine. Any Java program can still run native programs. What Microsoft did was provide an efficient way to exploit the power of system-specific code by making Visual J++ ActiveX-aware.

Examining Internet Explorer Security

The potential security problems, coupled with the uproar caused by the potential security risk of ActiveX, caused Microsoft to develop several measures to help users screen out unwanted code, and to help Web masters inspire trust in their Web site.

By default, Internet Explorer has two levels of security:

- Certificate Security
- ActiveX Content

To get to the Internet Explorer security settings, click View, Internet Options, as shown in Figure 8-1.

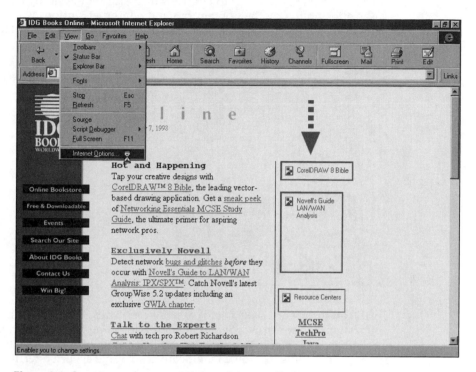

Figure 8-1: Security can be accessed through Internet Explorer.

When the Internet Options window opens, click the Content tab, as shown in Figure 8-2.

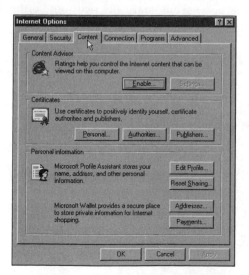

Figure 8-2: The Content tab in the Options window enables you to view and choose security settings.

Certificate security

Certificate Security is a way to control which sites you visit. By clicking the Authorities button on the Content tab in the Internet Options window in Figure 8-2, you open the Certificate Authorities window shown in Figure 8-3.

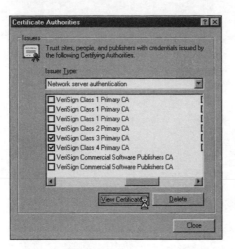

Figure 8-3: The Certificate Authorities window enables you to choose certificate providers.

Certificate providers issue certificates for Web sites. When a company applies for a software certificate, the certifying company grants them a public/private key combination that verifies the identity of the company releasing the software. You can indicate acceptable security certificate providers on your list.

You can also treat commercial software publisher sites as safe sites by clicking the Publishers button on the Security tab in the Options window. This opens the Authenticode Security Technology window, as seen in Figure 8-4. Here, you can list those software publishers and certificate providers that you trust. You can now access, automatically (without verification), those Web sites you have authorized.

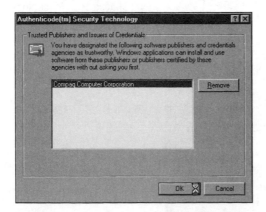

Figure 8-4: The Authenticode Security Technology enables you to list certificate providers and commercial software publisher sites as automatically accessible.

Authenticode

The backlash against ActiveX security began almost immediately. Web masters complained about the possible spread of viruses, Trojan horses, or poorly written systems that execute *automatically* when a Web page opens. Meanwhile, several Trojan horses were disguised as popular programs (such as PKZIP or McAfee Scan) for downloading.

In response, Microsoft developed *Authenticode*. Authenticode enables a digital signature to be added to files and programs. A software publisher signs their code by attaching a unique digital signature. Authenticode provides two functions:

- It enables the author to "sign" his uploads, thereby enabling any user who downloads the software to contact the point of upload.

- Authenticode catches code that has been tampered with. By knowing that the code has been tampered with, the user can avoid downloading a potentially malicious or virus-infected piece of code.

Secret

Netscape Communicator also supports code-signing methodologies, and Sun has committed to support code-signing in the future. Furthermore, Sun has proposed a competing standard to Authenticode.

The Purpose of Authenticode

On June 17, 1996, a man named Fred McLain posted an ActiveX control on his Web site. This control was called Exploder. Exploder was a Trojan horse that caused some machines to shut down Windows 95 and turn off the PC if the PC had a power conservation BIOS. On August 23, McLain had his control authenticated from VeriSign and posted it to his public Web site.

This illustrates the limitations of Authenticode. Authenticode is used to describe where the ActiveX control, Java Applet, or downloadable file came from. It *does not* mean that the new code is completely tested before upload and is free of bugs or that it is free of malicious intent. Authenticode simply gives you a way to identify the software publisher. Now that software publishers are accountable for their code, they are motivated to provide code on the Internet that has the same quality and trustworthiness as retail software.

Microsoft Wallet and Microsoft Profile Assistant

Microsoft Profile Assistant enables you to store personal information about yourself for transmission to Web sites supporting Microsoft Profile. Similarly, Microsoft Wallet enables you to store address and payment method information on a personal computer for use in online shopping transactions.

Microsoft Profile Assistant and Microsoft Wallet provide convenience and security:

■ They enable you to enter personal and payment information once. When you shop if Wallet-enabled Internet stores prompt you for your shipping address or credit card data, you can transmit the information without retyping it every time, as you would with stores that use traditional forms.

■ They provide versatility. You can specify multiple shipping addresses and multiple credit cards. Then you are prompted for them when you shop.

■ Most importantly, they are more secure than just typing in information. The information you enter is encrypted and then decrypted using a password that you type in while at a site. This makes it difficult for any nonauthorized site to access your credit card information.

Using Microsoft Profile Assistant

To edit your user profile, click the Edit Profile button shown in the Personal Information GroupBox in the Content tab of the Options dialog box (Figure 8-2). This opens your personal profile properties as shown in Figure 8-5. Here you can enter (or leave blank) any information you wish to convey.

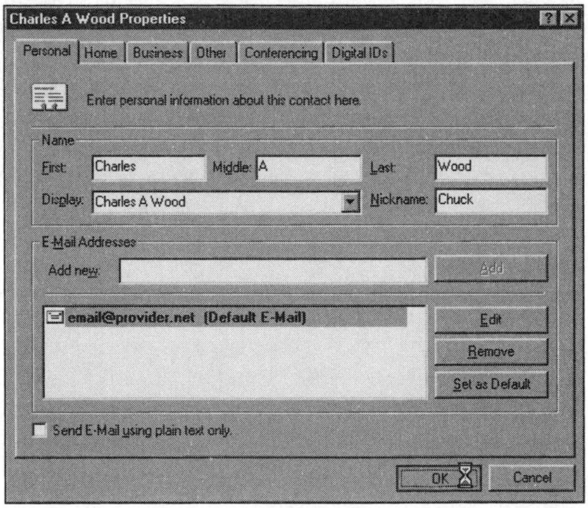

Figure 8-5: The Properties window enables you to add or remove properties.

Using Microsoft Wallet

Information contained in Microsoft Wallet can be found in the Personal Information GroupBox in the Content tab of the Options dialog box (Figure 8-2). Clicking the Addresses command button opens the Address Options list box, as shown in Figure 8-6.

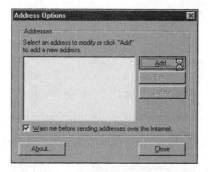

Figure 8-6: The Address Options list box

To add a new address to the address list, Click the Add command button. This opens the Add a New Address dialog box as shown in Figure 8-7.

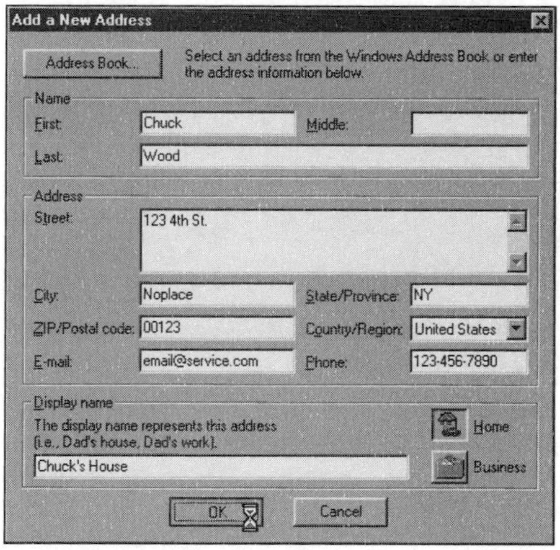

Figure 8-7: The Add a New Address dialog box

When you finish entering information, the name of your new address appears in the Address Options list box, as seen in Figure 8-8.

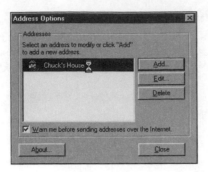

Figure 8-8: Any address added with the Add a New Address dialog box appears in the Address Options list box.

Follow these steps to add a credit card to your Microsoft Wallet:

1. Click the Payments command button in the Personal Information group box in the Content tab of the Options dialog box (Figure 8-2). This opens the Payment Options dialog box.

2. Click the Add command button to display a list of credit cards that you can add to Microsoft Wallet as seen in Figure 8-9.

Figure 8-9: Click Add on the Payment Options dialog box to add a new credit card to Microsoft Wallet.

3. After choosing a charge card, a wizard pops up for adding a charge card to your wallet. Click Next to open the Credit Card Information dialog box.

4. Enter the name on the card, the expiration date, and the card number, as shown in Figure 8-10. (No, that's not my publisher's credit card number. In case you try, this isn't a valid Visa number. In fact, the Add a New Credit Card Wizard won't let you continue with this number.) Click Next, when you're finished, to open the Credit Card Billing Address dialog box. (Shown in Figure 8-11)

Figure 8-10: The Credit Card Information dialog box

5. Assign a billing address to the credit card. This can be an address you have already entered, or you can click New address to add a new address. Click Next when you're finished.

Figure 8-11: The Credit Card Billing Address dialog box

6. Enter a credit card password in the Credit Card Password dialog box. You must enter it twice to make sure there are no typing errors. When you are done, click Finished as shown in Figure 8-12. The name of your credit card appears in the Payment Options list box.

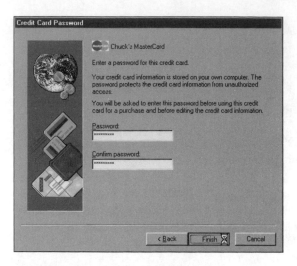

Figure 8-12: The Credit Card Password dialog box

Internet zones and security levels

Internet Explorer also provides security for downloads and ActiveX modules. This security can be accessed by clicking View ⇨ Internet Options in Internet Explorer and then clicking the Security tab. Figure 8-13 shows the Security tab.

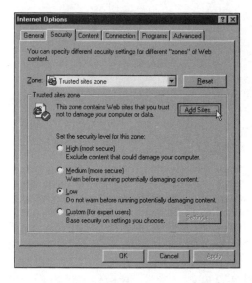

Figure 8-13: The Security tab enables you to assign security by category or individual Web site.

Internet Explorer has three security levels that you can assign to Web pages. These are described in Table 8-1.

Table 8-1 Security Levels	
Security Level	*Description*
High	High security level prevents any code from running in your IE environment that has not been signed. It's the safest of all security levels.
Medium	Medium security level will prompt you for verification if you are about to run an unsigned program.
Low	Low security disables all security, but should never be used, except with the most trusted of sites.

Using the security levels in Table 8-1, Internet Explorer enables you to divide your Web sites into security zones. There are four security zones defined as shown in Table 8-2.

Table 8-2 Security Zones	
Zone	*Description*
Local Intranet	Any address that doesn't require a proxy server is part of the Local Intranet zone. The addresses included in this zone are defined by the system administrator in the Internet Explorer Administrator's Kit (IEAK). The default security level for the Local Intranet zone is Medium.
Trusted Sites	These are Web sites that you assign to be trusted. The default security level for the Trusted Sites zone is Low.
Restricted Sites	If you don't trust a site, you can restrict it so that no downloads can occur from the site. The default security level for the Restricted Sites zone is High.
Internet	Anything that is not on your computer, an intranet, or assigned to any other zone is in the Internet zone. Most Web site access is in this security level. The default security level for the Internet zone is Medium.

In addition to assigning security levels to a security zone, you can also assign specific Web sites to your restricted sites list or to your trusted sites list. For example, by choosing Trusted Sites as the security zone and clicking the Add Sites command button, you can add specific Web sites to your list of trusted sites, as shown in Figure 8-14.

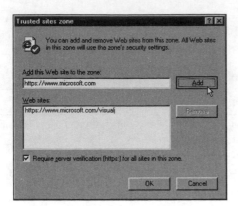

Figure 8-14: You can add specific Web sites to the Trusted Sites zone or the Restricted Sites zone.

Summary

Security is an important issue for all Web surfers. You should be aware of security when distributing and running ActiveX modules. To recap:

- Web security issues include access to the client computer and the level of security.

- Java VM Security enables minimal access to the server computer and no access to the client computer.

- Internet Explorer Security Zones enable you to configure your Internet Explorer security.

- Authenticode for ActiveX enables you to determine who has published the ActiveX control and verifies that the code hasn't changed.

Chapter 9

JavaBeans

In This Chapter

▶ Implementing JavaBeans

▶ Converting JavaBeans to ActiveX components

▶ Converting ActiveX components to JavaBeans

Even though this book is called Visual J++ Secrets it is still important to provide information regarding *pure-Java* initiatives because in many cases Microsoft gives us tools to integrate, extend, and enhance these technologies. The area of JavaBeans is no exception. Visual J++ enables you to develop JavaBeans as easily as you can ActiveX controls. As you will see, JavaBeans is a component technology like ActiveX, and Microsoft provides tools to migrate from ActiveX to JavaBeans and vice versa. When you use Visual J++ to convert JavaBeans to ActiveX components, you are then free to use these controls with other development languages, such as Visual Basic. The Visual J++ capability to import ActiveX controls for use in Java programs opens the door to hundreds, if not thousands, of existing components.

What Are JavaBeans?

JavaBeans are a platform-neutral component architecture. They are written in Java and are distributed in a file called a JAR. This should have a familiar ring to anyone who's created ActiveX components. While ActiveX components can be written in any language (including Java), they are distributed in a file called a CAB. Like Microsoft's CAB (short for *cabinet*) format, the JAR file contains all of the code and resources for the component.

Beans were conceived to be friendly to visual design tools as well. Microsoft's Visual Basic is the classic example of a visual-programming environment. ActiveX controls (OCXs and formerly VBXs) are available from a tool palette when creating applications. The programmer can drag these components from the palette and place them on a form or other such container. The act of clicking the positioned Bean then generally displays its properties in a Property Editor window.

Figure 9-1: A JavaBeans property sheet.

A Bean generally has the following distinguishing characteristics: Introspection, Customization, Persistence, Methods, Events, and Properties. Each of these traits is discussed in more detail in the following sections.

Introspection

A Bean provides external identification of its methods, events, and properties. This enables visual-development tools to present the component's properties to a programmer. Even other programs can exploit this characteristic by exploring other Beans at runtime. The *design patterns*, discussed later in this chapter, play a big part in enabling a Bean's structure to be exposed and interpreted.

Customization

While writing a program, a developer needs to tailor each Bean to perform its required function. A Bean that performs socket communication may expose many properties that enable it to be configured to connect to a specified host, on a specified port number, and so on. A Bean that provides a visual indication of engine temperature for a race car must be properly sized and positioned within its container. Customization is provided to the design tool in two ways. The first involves discovering Bean properties through *introspection* as described in the preceding section. The second mechanism provides a more sophisticated level of customization that is implemented by the Bean. This is accomplished by exposing a *Customizer* class.

Persistence

When a Bean is customized using a visual development tool, its properties must be stored and retrieved when needed. Usually a Bean provides storage for all of its exposed properties. Additionally a Bean may contain other Beans, so the properties of these Beans should be stored as well. JavaBeans provide such capability using Java's object serialization mechanism.

Events, properties, and methods

Events provide a mechanism for a Bean to notify objects that something has changed. *Properties* represent characteristics of a Bean. These may include the background color or font to use, or it may be a nonvisual attribute. *Methods* expose functionality to Beans and other objects.

Component Issues

The JavaBean specification competes with ActiveX technologies for component creation and distribution by offering a pure Java solution. ActiveX is based on COM and other proven technologies. This section identifies functionality that is important to component developers and compares JavaBeans to the ActiveX equivalent.

Portability

JavaBeans are written in Java, so they are portable and can run on any platform, or in any application that provides a Java Virtual Machine (VM). This is the major difference from ActiveX components that are compiled to binaries, which can only be executed on Intel machines hosting Microsoft operating systems.

Secret

Although ActiveX controls can be written in Java, their activation requires the Microsoft VM to be present to execute. If Microsoft offers VMs on other platforms with COM support, then ActiveX components written in Java can be platform independent.

Activation

JavaBeans run in the same address space (Java VM) as their container. If the Bean's container is not written in Java, a VM is started in which the Bean runs. ActiveX components run in the same address space as their container.

Local/remote transparency

As Java is used to solve larger and more complex problems, processing is distributed among client and server machines. Communication between client and server may offer considerable bandwidth, in the case of a private network or intranet, or it may take place using a modem over the Internet. It is important, therefore, to carefully design interfaces to bridge components executing in different address spaces. The Beans specification makes no special provision for distributed-system Bean communication. However, there are technologies that make such development possible. These include:

- Java Interface Definition Language (IDL) — This system implements the industry standard OMG CORBA distributed object model.

- Java Remote Method Invocation (RMI) — A Java equivalent of Remote Procedural Call (RPC) technology.

- Java Database API (JDBC) — Provides a means to access server databases.

ActiveX technology, because it's based on COM, is inherently remoteable. Microsoft's Distributed-COM offers seamless communication between COM-based objects. In fact, Microsoft will soon be releasing a COM-over-HTTP wrapper that enables components to communicate with a Web server, even through firewalls.

Visual representation

Although it's common to think of JavaBeans as having a user interface, there are times when this isn't appropriate. In fact, the Enterprise JavaBeans initiative is pushing to encapsulate many "back-office" operations with Bean wrappers. Many of these functions involve data management and transaction processing, whose visual representation is provided by other systems or different Beans.

Visible JavaBeans

A *visible* JavaBean provides a user interface for a person to interact with at run time. Such a Bean might draw itself to represent a thermostat for adjusting the temperature of an air conditioning system, or a calendar control from which a user selects a date, as shown in Figure 9-2.

Figure 9-2: Selecting a date with a calendar control

Invisible JavaBeans

An *invisible* Bean provides no runtime user interface (it is invisible at runtime). A common example of an invisible Bean is a timer control. The Component provides methods allowing the programmer to define the interval between triggers. The Component may also provide a visual design-time representation that includes an icon for the tool palette and Property Sheets for configuration control. The icon also appears on the form when the control is "dragged" from the tool palette. The Bean's properties can then be displayed by clicking on this image.

User interface

JavaBeans, like ActiveX components, can provide a user interface that is different at design time and runtime.

Design time

The JavaBean specification makes it easy for design tools to expose the methods and properties of a Bean. Using introspection techniques, simple tools can provide a *property editor* window that enables a programmer to customize a Bean. However, more advanced development systems may access the Bean's *customizer* classes. Such classes enable the Bean to have complete control over the graphical user interface that is used to modify the Bean. A customizer might be so advanced as to take the appearance of a *wizard*, which leads the developer through a series of configuration panels.

Runtime

A Bean can be visible at runtime. However, it is just as likely that the Bean is invisible. If the Bean is visible and accepts input directly from the user, either via mouse clicks or keystrokes, it is programmed in Java using any of the visual Component-derived objects necessary to represent itself. A visual Bean does not have to be simple, such as a picture button; in fact, it can be a number of controls on a Panel or an entire dialog box.

Security

JavaBeans are implemented using Java. As such, they are no more secure (or less secure, depending on your view of Java security) than any other Java class.

Java Applets normally operate in a *sandbox*. They are restricted in many ways—they cannot access the machine on which they are running and can only communicate with the server from which they were pulled. Beans, which are part of such an Applet, have the same restrictions.

Java Applets can also have their code *signed*. The signing process assures a user that the code has not been tampered with since it was created. The user may *trust* the signed Applet, thereby freeing it from the sandbox restrictions. This relaxes security on any Beans as well.

Java applications are a different animal altogether. They have complete access to any system running on the VM. Beans that are part of an application are free to use the entire Java API as well.

ActiveX components can have access to all system resources. Microsoft's code distribution format, the CAB file, may contain both ActiveX controls and Java code. ActiveX controls must be fully trusted to run; therefore they are treated differently from pure Java code. Internet Explorer provides the concept of Security Zones. Configuring these options in your browser determines whether an ActiveX control can be downloaded and executed. This security mechanism is covered in more detail in Chapter 8.

Minimum requirements

What does it take to be a Bean? Not much, actually. For an object to qualify as a Bean, it requires only two properties:

- *Null Constructor* — A Bean must be able to be constructed by both a visual development environment and as part of a persistence mechanism "rehydration" process.

- *Persistence Support* — To be reconstructed at run time (its properties must be restored, and so on), a Bean must support a persistence mechanism.

The Transitional Bean Specification

The transitional Bean specification was published at the time the JDK 1.1 was still under development. Its purpose was to provide a migration path for JDK 1.0.2 developers to "wrap" their objects in a Bean. I can't imagine that many people are programming to the JDK 1.0.2 release, but in case you are and you want to create JavaBeans, it can be done.

Marker classes

Marker classes are provided so that those programming for JDK 1.0.2 can begin to take advantage of the Bean architecture and create components that are compatible with the release specification. The following classes are provided:

- `sunw.util.EventObject` — The Bean event model requires that objects *listening* to a Bean receive objects derived from `EventObject` as part of the notification process.

- `sunw.util.EventListener` — Objects that register themselves with Beans must implement an interface derived from `EventListener` on which methods are called.

- sunw.io.Serializable — The Serializable interface allows a 1.1-compliant virtual machine to store and retrieve the variables associated with a Bean.

Dos and don'ts of Bean development

A transitional Bean developer must follow a small number of rules. Following these rules assures that your component is available to visual development environments and operates under 1.1-compliant VMs:

- Do not use JDK 1.1 interfaces. Because a transitional Bean is developed using the JDK 1.0.2 and can run under this VM, it is not permitted to use any JDK 1.1 extensions.

- Package the Bean in a JAR file. JAR files are analogous to Microsoft's CAB file format. Their creation is covered later in this chapter.

- Provide a default constructor — one without any arguments.

- Use the Bean *design patterns* to name the accessor and mutator methods for get and set properties. The following section details the format used to name these Bean methods.

- Use the Bean event model to implement notification. This model requires that those objects listening for events from Beans implement the EventListener interfaces. Additionally, the events delivered to these objects should be derived from EventObject. This interface and base-class are provided as marker classes.

- If a Bean wishes to use the automatic serialization mechanism provided by a 1.1-compliant VM, it must implement the Serializable interface. A stub for this interface is provided in the marker classes.

Sample transitional Bean

The examples in this section demonstrate a transitional Bean that is derived from the AWT Checkbox component. This component provides the methods necessary for registering and notifying listeners. Listing 9-1 defines an event object used for a transitional Bean.

Listing 9-1: TransitionalBeanEvent.java

```
// this class defines an event object which is compliant
// with the transitional Bean specification
public class TransitionalBeanEvent extends sunw.util.EventObject
{
    public TransitionalBeanEvent(java.awt.Component eventSource)
    {
        super(eventSource);
    }
}
```

Listing 9-2 defines an interface that is used with the Bean event defined in Listing 9-1.

Listing 9-2: TransitionalBeanListener.java

```
// This interface defines a method definition that is
// named "SomethingHappened"
// The transitional Bean calls this method on objects
// that are registered event listeners.
public interface TransitionalBeanListener extends
sunw.util.EventListener
{
    public void SomethingHappened(TransitionalBeanEvent e);
}
```

Listing 9-3 incorporates the Bean listener defined by the interface in Listing 9-2 to develop a Checkbox Bean.

Listing 9-3: TransitionalBean.java

```
import java.util.*;
import java.awt.*;
 // This class defines a transitional Bean which derives
// from the
// AWT Checkbox component. If a user "clicks" the
// mouse over the checkbox
// a new-style event is passed to all listeners.
public class TransitionalBean extends java.awt.Checkbox implements
sunw.io.Serializable
{
    private Vector m_vListeners = new Vector();

    // default constructor
    public TransitionalBean()
    {
        super("Default Checkbox Text");
    }

    // constructor which takes the label's text as an
    // argument
    public TransitionalBean(String sLabelText)
    {
        super(sLabelText);
    }

    // Register an Event Listener.
    public synchronized void
addTransitionalBeanListener(TransitionalBeanListener tbl)
    {
        if (m_vListeners.contains(tbl))
            return;
```

```
            m_vListeners.addElement(tbl);
    }

    // Remove an Event Listener.
    public synchronized void
removeTransitionalBeanListener(TransitionalBeanListener tbl)
    {
            m_vListeners.removeElement(tbl);
    }

    // Since this is a transitional Bean, it must acquire
    // events using the old-style AWT event model.
    // However it notifies registered listeners using
    // the new event listener model.
    public boolean handleEvent(Event evt)
    {
        if (evt.id == Event.ACTION_EVENT)
        {
            Vector vListClone;

            // create a Bean-style event object
            TransitionalBeanEvent tbe = new
TransitionalBeanEvent(this);

            // create a copy of the current registered
            // listener vector
            synchronized(this)
            {
                vListClone = (Vector) m_vListeners.clone();
            }

            // notify all registered listeners by calling
            // their "SomethingHappened"
            // method on the TransitionalBeanListener
            // interface they implement
            for (int i = 0; i < vListClone.size(); i++)
            {
                TransitionalBeanListener tbl =
(TransitionalBeanListener)vListClone.elementAt(i);
                tbl.SomethingHappened(tbe);
            }
        }
        return super.handleEvent(evt);
    }
}
```

The `TransitionalBean` **is instantiated and used in the** `TransBeanApp`
**application shown in Listing 9-4. Notice that the frame registers itself as the
Bean's listener and displays text in the console when it is notified by an
event.**

Listing 9-4: TransBeanApp.java

```java
import java.awt.*;
public class TransBeanApp
{
  public static void main(String[] args)
  {
      TransBeanFrame frame = new TransBeanFrame("TransBeanApp");
    frame.setupBean();
    frame.resize(200,100);
    frame.setVisible(true);
  }
}

class TransBeanFrame extends Frame implements
TransitionalBeanListener
{
  public TransBeanFrame(String s)
  {
    super(s);
  }

  public void setupBean()
  {
    setLayout(new BorderLayout());
    TransitionalBean tb = new TransitionalBean();
    add("Center", tb);
    tb.addTransitionalBeanListener(this);
  }

  public void SomethingHappened(TransitionalBeanEvent e)
  {
    System.out.println("I felt a click");
  }
  public boolean handleEvent(Event evt)
  {
      if (evt.id == Event.WINDOW_DESTROY)
      {
        dispose();
        java.lang.System.exit(0);
      }
      return super.handleEvent(evt);
  }
}
```

Design patterns

One of the secrets that enables a visual development environment to identify a JavaBean's methods and properties is the naming convention that is required when creating the Bean. The name of a method, its argument list, and return value constitute the method's signature. The JavaBean specification refers to a naming convention it calls *design patterns,* which defines a process for identifying Bean components by defining the signature.

Secret

A more recent trend in building object-oriented systems is to implement behavior using *design patterns*. A design pattern defines a general way to solve a common programming problem. Some common design patterns are *Adapter, Singleton,* and *Observer.* An Adapter converts the interface of a class to one that is compatible with a client. In this manner, the two classes can work together despite incompatible interfaces. A Singleton is a class that has a "single" instance. Finally, an Observer defines a one-to-many relationship that notifies all dependents of a change of state.

As powerful as these design patterns are, they are not the *design patterns* that are described in the JavaBeans specification. When the JavaBean specification talks about *design patterns,* it is referring to a *naming convention* that is applied to methods, classes, and interfaces.

Suppose you are designing a Bean which controls pricing in a beverage machine. This component certainly has as a property the cost of a soda. You also probably expose this property so that you can read the current price of a soda and update (read increase) the price when necessary.

The JavaBean specification defines a *design pattern* for exposing a property with get/set attributes. This definition looks like this:

```
public <data-type>get<property-name>();
public void set<property-name>(<data-type> value);
```

A pair of methods are defined for setting and getting the property's value. Notice also that the methods are public. The <data-type> tag is replaced with any scalar or object that is to be changed. The <property-tag> is a name that you give the property. Since the name is preceded by a lowercase get or set, the property name usually begins with an uppercase character.

Now you are ready to apply the naming convention to the beverage cost object. The name of the cost property is BeverageCost and it is represented by an int. The following methods are created using this information and applying it to the property template:

```
public int getBeverageCost();
public void setBeverageCost(int nCost);
```

Components that wish to obtain "Beanification" must implement some interfaces and provide methods that adhere to the design patterns previously described.

Events

Events are messages sent between objects. The originator of the event can be referred to as the *source,* and the receiver can be identified as the *listener.* If a JavaBean is designed to provide timer functionality, an *event* may be issued when the specified time has elapsed. Events are used throughout Java to represent such occurrences as keyboard strokes and mouse clicks.

JavaBeans rely on an event-handling mechanism based on the event-source/event-listener model used throughout the JDK 1.1 release. Using this listener-event model, objects or other Beans subscribe to receive notification when a specified action is taken by the source. Event objects are created by the event source and passed to all listeners.

Event object

A Bean that wishes to notify interested *listeners* of an action must distribute an event object. Events generated by Beans should extend the `java.util.EventObject` base class. The definition of this base object follows:

```
public class EventObject
{
    public EventObject(Object source);
    public Object getSource();
    public String toString();
}
```

Listing 9-5 shows an event object that is created by a Bean that interfaces with hardware that senses an obstacle encountered by an autonomous pool cleaning machine. The resulting event object identifies the direction of the obstacle and the speed of the machine when it was blocked.

Listing 9-5: PoolObstacleEvent.java

```
public class PoolObstacleEvent extends java.util.EventObject
{
    int m_nSpeed;
    String m_sObstacleDirection;

    PoolObstacleEvent(Object source, String sBlock, int nFast)
    {
        super(source);
        m_nSpeed = nFast;
        m_sObstacleDirection = sBlock;
    }

    int getSpeed()
    {
        return m_nSpeed;
    }

    String getDirection()
    {
        return m_sObstacleDirection;
    }
}
```

Secret

The JavaBeans specification does not provide a design pattern (naming convention) for event objects.

The preceding class defines an object named `PoolObstacle` that is derived from `EventObject`. The constructor requires that source, speed, and direction information be provided. The listener also provides two accessor methods to retrieve the speed and direction values.

Event listeners

JavaBeans use a mechanism to distribute events that is much more efficient than the event model provided in the original JDK release. The Bean event model requires those objects that are interested in receiving notification to register with the event source. The event source calls a method on the listening object that is defined by the event listener interface that it implements. The best way to understand this relationship is to illustrate it with an example.

Continuing with the autonomous pool cleaning machine example, I now demonstrate the code necessary to receive `PoolObstacle` objects. Any object that wishes to register itself as a listener must implement an interface based upon `java.util.EventListener`. This interface has the following definition:

```
public interface EventListener
{
}
```

That's right, it's empty. This interface is simply a tagging interface and is present to aid in introspection. Using this interface as a base, you can derive your own interface whose methods are called when pool obstacles are encountered. This interface is named `ObstacleListener` and is shown in Listing 9-6.

Listing 9-6: ObstacleListener.java

```
public interface ObstacleListener extends java.util.EventListener
{
    void obstacleEncountered(PoolObstacleEvent poe);
}
```

Now that you have an interface, which defines a method that is called when an obstacle is encountered, you have to create a class to implement this interface. Such a class is generally referred to as an *event adapter*.

Event Adapter

The role of the Event Adapter class is to implement the `EventListener` interface (or an interface derived from `EventListener`) and decouple these notifications from the listener.

Adapters can be thought of as the wiring between an event source and a listener. Common implementations of adapters perform the following functions:

- Accept events from multiple listeners and issue them to a single source.
- Provide a queuing mechanism between sources and listeners.
- Filter source events for a destination object.

Listing 9-7 shows a simple adapter implementing the ObstacleListener interface. The constructor that is responsible for identifying collisions and generating PoolObstacleEvents passes an ObstacleSensor object to the class.

Listing 9-7: ObstacleAdapter.java

```
public class ObstacleAdapter implements ObstacleListener
{
    // constructor
    public ObstacleAdapter(ObstacleSensor os)
    {
        os.addObstacleSensorListener((ObstacleListener)this);
    }

    // ObstacleListener method
    public void obstacleEncountered(PoolObstacleEvent poe)
    {
        System.out.println (
"An obstacle was encountered in the "+poe.getDirection()+
" direction, when traveling "+poe.getSpeed());
    }
}
```

The adapter registers itself with the ObstacleSensor object. When an obstacle is encountered, it prints a line to the system console indicating the speed and direction it was heading when the collision took place. The code for the ObstacleSensor class can be seen in Listing 9-8.

Listing 9-8: ObstacleSensor.java

```
import java.util.*;
// this class responds to collisions by creating
// PoolObstacleEvent objects and sending them to
// registered listeners
public class ObstacleSensor
{
    Vector m_vObstacleListener;
    String m_sDirection;
    int m_nSpeed;

    // constructor
    public ObstacleSensor(String sDir)
    {
        m_vObstacleListener = new Vector(10);
        m_sDirection = sDir;
    }

    public synchronized void
addObstacleSensorListener(ObstacleListener ol)
    {
        if (m_vObstacleListener.contains(ol))
            return;
```

```
            m_vObstacleListener.addElement(ol);
        }


    // retrieve the machine's speed
    public int getSpeed()
    {
// let's suspend our disbelief for a minute and pretend
// that this method interfaces with some hardware and
// returns the speed of the machine.
        m_nSpeed = 5;
        return(m_nSpeed);
    }


    public synchronized void
removeObstacleSensorListener(ObstacleListener ol)
    {
        m_vObstacleListener.removeElement(ol);
    }


    // loop through all registered listeners and call
    // their obstacleEncountered methods
    protected void NotifyObstacleSensorListeners()
    {
    Vector vListClone;
    PoolObstacleEvent poe = new PoolObstacleEvent(this, m_sDirection,
getSpeed());

// create a copy of the current registered listener
    synchronized(this)
            {
                vListClone = (Vector) m_vObstacleListener.clone();
            }

    for (int i=0; i< vListClone.size(); ++i)
        ((ObstacleListener)
vListClone.elementAt(i)).obstacleEncountered(poe);
    }
}
```

Properties

A property represents a characteristic of a Bean. It may define the Bean's position in a container, the color of its background, or something specific to its implementation. Each property implements two methods. One for setting the value of the property, called the set() method, and another for acquiring the value of a property, called the get() method.

Visual design tools usually display the component's characteristics in a "Property Editor" window. This window identifies the current setting of the property as well as offering a selection of available choices.

General properties

In a simple timer Bean, a property might be exposed that identifies the interval to wait before signaling its container. Suppose this Bean is called `TimerBean`, the property name is `Interval`, and the interval property is stored in a Java variable whose type is `int`. Following the design pattern for simple properties, the methods that `get` and `set` this value are defined as follows:

```
public <type>get<property>();
public void set<name>(<type> value);

// set the time interval between triggers
public void setInterval(int nValue)
{
    m_nInternalIntervalValue = nValue;
}

// retrieve the current trigger interval value
public int getInterval()
{
    return(m_nINternalIntervalValue);
}
```

Secret

Sometimes you want a property to be read-only or write-only. Read-only properties can be defined by *not* creating a `set` property method. Similarly, write-only properties can be defined by *not* providing a `get` property method.

Boolean properties

The JavaBean specification introduces a special design pattern for exposing *Boolean* properties. The `set()` method's naming convention is identical to those used by general properties. However, the `get()` method is prefixed by the word *is*, as shown:

```
public void set<property>(boolean b);
public boolean is<property>();
```

The following methods expose a Boolean property that indicates if the `TimerBean` is active or not:

```
// turn the timer on
public void setTimerActive(boolean bState)
{
    m_bInternalState = bState;
}

// retrieve the timer's active state
public boolean isTimerActive()
{
    return(m_bInternalState);
}
```

Index properties

The JavaBeans specification also makes provisions for properties, which are not simply represented by a single value. Properties that are stored in an array are called *Index Properties*. The Bean exposes Index Properties when you define their method signatures according to the following design patterns.

For a single indexed property:

```
public <type>get<property>(int index);
public void set<name>(int index, <type> value);
```

For the entire property array:

```
public <type>[] get<property>();
public void set<property>(<type>[] value);
```

Okay, enough with the fancy syntax — let's implement indexed properties for a concrete example. Suppose you are creating a Bean that defines the color of the sprinkles to be applied to the top of donuts by a custom donut-sprinkling machine. The Bean can instruct the machine to put any number of colored sprinkles on the top of the donut, and the more indices that contain a particular color, the more prevalent that color is on the top of the donut.

The sprinkle-control Bean is called `Topper`, and the methods that access the sprinkle property array are tagged with the word `Sprinkle`. The array contains Java Color objects. Methods to `get` and `retrieve` a particular color indexed in the array, as well as methods that provide access to the entire array, are shown in the following code sample:

```
// retrieve the color assigned to a specified
// sprinkle color property index
public Color getSprinkle(int nIndex)
{
    return(m_InternalSprinkleColorArray[nIndex]);
}

// set the color associated with a particular
// sprinkle color index
public void setSprinkle(int nIndex, Color argColor) throws
ArrayIndexOutOfBoundsException
{
    m_InternalSprinkleColorArray[nIndex] = argColor;
}

// acquire the entire sprinkle color property array
public Color[] getSprinkle()
{
    return(m_InternalSprinkleColorArray);
}

// assign the entire sprinkle color property array
public void setSprinkle(Color[] arrayColor)
{
    m_InternalSprinkleColorArray = arrayColor;
}
```

Property Change Notification

So far you have seen how to create and name methods that adhere to the JavaBean property design patterns, thus exposing them to tools that can parse a Bean's class for such signatures and enable a visual design tool to expose these properties and aid program development.

It is common for a program to require notification of a Property change. This may occur because the user has changed the computer's system time or date and each program must reflect the change in whatever way is appropriate. A drawing program may have to change the color of a selected element when the user selects a different color from a palette. The Bean specification provides a mechanism for just such notification. In fact, it supports two modes of notification, *bound properties* and *constrained properties*.

Bound properties

If a Java object wishes to be informed when a property in your Bean changes, it can *subscribe* to a property event notification system. This system requires you to implement two methods and generate an event object when a change occurs.

Getting a Bean to talk

Notifying an object of a property change in your Bean requires you to manage a list of objects that are interested in your changes. You must create two methods that are responsible for managing this connection, as shown here:

```
public void addPropertyChangeListener(PropertyChangeListener pcl);
public void removePropertyChangeListener(PropertyChangeListener pcl);
```

The code that fleshes out these methods is quite boilerplate and appears in the following section.

Secret

When you implement listener methods, you should synchronize access to the notification array. This is accomplished by placing the `synchronized` keyword in the method definition.

```
// adds the specified object to the managed list of
// objects that require change notification
public synchronized void
addPropertyChangeListener(PropertyChangeListener pcl)
{
    // check to see if this object is already receiving notification
    if (m_vPropertyListener.contains(pcl))
```

```
            return;
      m_vPropertyListener.addElement(pcl);
}

// remove the specified object from change notification list
public synchronized void
removePropertyChangeListener(PropertyChangeListener pcl)
{
      m_vPropertyListener.removeElement(pcl);
}
```

The vector containing the objects to be notified must be defined and allocated inside the class:

```
Vector m_vPropertyListener = new Vector();
```

You must add code to your set<property> method that runs through the list of property listeners and notifies them of the change. Again, this code is rather generic, so I created a method that accepts the property name as a string and the new value of the property as an object. Both are required by the PropertyChangeEvent object. The PropertyChangeEvent is then sent to the interested parties.

```
private void notifyBoundPropertyListeners(String sPropertyName,
Object oNewValue)
{
      Vector vListClone;
      PropertyChangeEvent pce = new PropertyChangeEvent(this,
sPropertyName, null, oNewValue);

// create a copy of the current registered listener vector
            synchronized(this)
            {
                  vListClone = (Vector) m_vPropertyListener.clone();
            }

      for (int i=0; i< vListClone.size(); ++i)
          ((PropertyChangeListener) vListClone).propertyChange(pce);
}
```

Secret

Notification must take place after the Bean's property has been set.

Well, that's certainly a lot of bits and pieces. Listing 9-9 puts all this together and adds it to the Topper Bean. The Bean provides notification to interested listeners anytime a sprinkle color is changed, or if the entire sprinkle color array is replaced.

Listing 9-9: Topper.java

```java
import java.util.*;
import java.awt.*;
import java.Beans.*;
public class Topper
{
    Vector m_vPropertyListener = null;
    Color m_InternalSprinkleColorArray[] = null;

    // Constructor
    public Topper()
    {
        // initialize member variables
        m_vPropertyListener = new Vector(10);
        m_InternalSprinkleColorArray = new Color[3];
        m_InternalSprinkleColorArray[0] = Color.red;
        m_InternalSprinkleColorArray[1] = Color.white;
        m_InternalSprinkleColorArray[2] = Color.blue;
    }

    // retrieve the color assigned to a specified
    // sprinkle color property index
    public Color getSprinkle(int nIndex)
    {
        return(m_InternalSprinkleColorArray[nIndex]);
    }

    // set the color associated with a particular
    // sprinkle color index
    public void setSprinkle(int nIndex, Color argColor) throws
ArrayIndexOutOfBoundsException
    {
        // set the color at the specified index
        m_InternalSprinkleColorArray[nIndex] = argColor;

        // notify our listeners of the change
        notifyBoundPropertyListeners("SingleColor", (Object)argColor);
    }

    // acquire the entire sprinkle color property array
    public Color[] getSprinkle()
    {
        return(m_InternalSprinkleColorArray);
    }

    // assign the entire sprinkle color property array
    public void setSprinkle(Color[] arrayColor)
    {
        m_InternalSprinkleColorArray = arrayColor;

        // notify our listeners of the change
        notifyBoundPropertyListeners("AllColors", (Object)arrayColor);
```

```
        }

        // add an object to our managed list that receive
        // notification when a property change occurs
        public synchronized void
addPropertyChangeListener(PropertyChangeListener pcl)
        {
            // check to see if this object is already
            // receiving notification
            if (m_vPropertyListener.contains(pcl))
                return;
            m_vPropertyListener.addElement(pcl);
        }

        // remove an object from our managed list
        public synchronized void
removePropertyChangeListener(PropertyChangeListener pcl)
        {
            m_vPropertyListener.removeElement(pcl);
        }

        // this method is called by property "set" functions
        private void notifyBoundPropertyListeners(String sPropertyName,
Object oNewValue)
        {
            Vector vListClone;
            // construct a new event object
            PropertyChangeEvent pce = new PropertyChangeEvent(this,
sPropertyName, null, oNewValue);

            synchronized(this)
                {
                    vListClone = (Vector) m_vPropertyListener.clone();
                }

        // iterate through our managed list of object to
        //notify and call the "propertyChange" method on each
            for (int i=0; i< vListClone.size(); ++i)
                ((PropertyChangeListener)
vListClone.elementAt(i)).propertyChange(pce);
        }
}
```

Well, that's not so bad. To review, here are the methods provided:

- A default constructor to initialize the Bean's member variables.

- Access to *Index Properties*. Four methods are required: getSprinkle(), setSprinkle(), getSprinkle(), and setSprinkle() with index notation.

- Two methods to manage listeners: addPropertyChangeListener() and removePropertyChangeListener().

- One private method that is called by set methods to notify registered listeners: notifyBoundPropertyListeners().

Listening to a Bean

If you want your Bean (or nonBean object) to *listen* to bound properties you must implement the `java.Beans.PropertyChangeListener` interface. This interface contains a single method:

```
public void propertyChange(PropertyChangeEvent pce);
```

Suppose you want to construct an object that represents a person's preference for donuts with a particular color sprinkle. Also, these people (objects) want to be notified each time the donut machine is configured to produce donuts with certain color sprinkles. This new object is called `DonutPreference` and its code appears in Listing 9-10.

Listing 9-10: DonutPreference.java

```java
import java.awt.*;
import java.Beans.*;
public class DonutPreference implements PropertyChangeListener
{
    Color m_colorILike = Color.blue;
    Topper m_topMachine = null;

    public DonutPreference(Topper topMachine)
    {
        m_topMachine = topMachine;
        topMachine.addPropertyChangeListener(this);
    }

    public void propertyChange(PropertyChangeEvent pce)
    {
        if (pce.getSource() instanceof Topper)
        {
            if (pce.getPropertyName() == "SingleColor")
            {
                Color colorSprinkle = (Color)pce.getNewValue();
                if (colorSprinkle == m_colorILike)
                {
                    System.out.println(
"Ah, my favorite\n");
                    return;
                }
            }
            else if (pce.getPropertyName() == "AllColors")
            {
                Color colorArray[] = (Color[])pce.getNewValue();
        for (int i=0; i<colorArray.length; ++i)
        {
                    if (colorArray[i] == m_colorILike)
                    {
                        System.out.println(
"Ah, my favorite\n");
                        return;
                    }
```

```
            }
          }
          System.out.println(
"Can't say I like these\n");
        }
      }
}
```

If a single sprinkle color is changed by the machine represented by the object Topper, the DonutPreference object checks to see whether it's a favorite — it responds with "Ah, my favorite" in the console. If the Topper object's entire *sprinkle array* is modified, DonutPreference loops through all of the colors and looks for one it prefers. If the donut machine isn't configured in any way that pleases the DonutPreference object, it responds with displeasure in the console window.

Listing 9-11 demonstrates how the Topper and DonutPreference objects are used in a program.

Listing 9-11: BeanProperty.java

```
import java.awt.*;

public class BeanProperty
{
  public static void main(String[] args)
  {
      BeanPropertyFrame frame = new
BeanPropertyFrame("BeanProperty");
    frame.setupBean();
    frame.setSize(100,100);
    frame.setVisible(true);
  }
}

class BeanPropertyFrame extends Frame
{
  public BeanPropertyFrame(String s)
  {
    super(s);
  }

  public void setupBean()
  {
   //Add window listener to listen for the Frame to close
      addWindowListener(new WindowAdapter(){
          public void windowClosing(WindowEvent e) {
          dispose();
          System.exit(0);
        }});
    Topper topper = new Topper();
    DonutPreference dp = new DonutPreference(topper);
```

```
        // ok, we know that the default for the DonutPreference
        // is that it prefers blue sprinkles.
        // The default for the machine is red, white and blue.
        // We'll change blue to green. (something dp doesn't like)
        topper.setSprinkle(2, Color.green);

        // now we'll make dp happy with a blue topping!
        topper.setSprinkle(2, Color.blue);
    }
}
```

Constrained properties

As you saw in the preceding section, objects can be notified after a property has been changed. However, what if an object doesn't approve of the change made to a property. Well, listening to bound properties won't suffice, because the change has already been made — so enter constrained properties.

Constrained properties are a variation on the bound-property theme. Their big difference is that objects that listen for property changes get to *vote* on whether a property change value is acceptable or not.

The design pattern for naming constrained properties appears like this:

```
public <type> get<property>();
public void set<property>(<type> value) throws
java.Beans.PropertyVetoException;
```

As with bound properties, a Bean that wishes to implement constraints must manage a list of objects to notify when a property changes. This is achieved by providing the following two methods:

```
public void addVetoableChangeListener(VetoableChangeListener vcl);
public void removeVetoableChangeListener(VetoableChangeListener vcl);
```

The boilerplate code that implements the necessary functionality looks like this:

```
// adds the specified object to the managed list of
// objects that require change notification
public synchronized void
addVetoableChangeListener(VetoableChangeListener vcl)
{
    // check to see if this object is already receiving notification
    if (m_vPropertyListener.contains(vcl))
        return;
    m_vBoundPropertyListener.addElement(vcl);
}

// remove the specified object from change notification list
public synchronized void
removeVetoableChangeListener(VetoableChangeListener vcl);
{
    m_vBoundPropertyListener.removeElement(vcl);
}
```

Objects that wish to be notified of property changes in a Bean must implement the `java.Beans.VetoableChangeListener` interface. This interface defines a single method:

```
public void vetoableChange(PropertyChangeEvent pce) throws
PropertyVetoException;
```

Secret

The `vetoableChange()` method must be called on all registered listeners *before* the Bean sets the property. In this manner, any objection to the property change can be raised prior to setting the property. The following code demonstrates a method that notifies all registered listeners of a property change before it is applied to the Bean.

```
public void setConstrainedProperty(String sNewValue)
{
    Vector vListClone;
    PropertyChangeEvent pce = new PropertyChangeEvent(this, "Some
Property", null, (Object)sNewValue);

    synchronized(this)
    {
        vListClone = (Vector) m_vPropertyListener.clone();
    }

    try {
    for (int i=0; i< vListClone.size(); ++i)

((VetoableChangeListener)vListClone.elementAt(i)).vetoableChange(pce);
    }
    catch(PropertyVetoException e)
    {
        return;
    }

    // if we got this far, no one must have rejected the change
    m_sConstrainedProperty = sNewValue;
}
```

The preceding code looks like it will perform the steps necessary to notify registered listeners of a property change and bow out gracefully if any of them raise an exception. However, one problem hasn't been addressed. What if your Bean registers three `vetoableChangeListeners`, a property is changed, and the first two objects accept the change and the third raises an exception? Well, your Bean ignores the property change, but the first two listeners (who accepted the change) may start using information present in the `PropertyChangeEvent` object, without knowing the property change was rejected.

The JavaBean specification identifies such a condition and provides a class that is helpful in dealing with such a situation. In fact, the class even manages the list of objects that are interested in constrained property changes. This helper class is called `VetoableChangeSupport`, and it appears in Table 9-1.

Table 9-1   VetoableChangeSupport

Method	Description
`public VetoableChangeSupport (Object sourceBean)`	Constructor
`public synchronized void addVetoableChangeListener (VetoableChangeListener listener)`	Listener management function
`public synchronized void removeVetoableChangeListener (VetoableChangeListener listener)`	Listener management function
`public void fireVetoableChange (String propertyName, Object oldValue, Object newValue) throws PropertyVetoException`	Reports property changes to registered listeners

Persistence

The JavaBean specification identifies *serialization* as the persistence model for a component. This model provides the following advantages:

- The component uses existing data formats.

- A mechanism that is compatible with COM and OpenDoc component architectures.

- Allows a component complete control over writing its state.

These advantages are provided by a solution that enables a Bean to choose to use either an automatic Java serialization mechanism or an *externalization* stream mechanism. The latter provides full data layout control.

Implementing persistence in a Bean is as simple as implementing the `Serializable` interface. Because this interface is a "tagging interface" that has no methods, providing this functionality takes little effort.

```
public class SimpleBean implements java.io.Serializable
{
    protected java.awt.Label labelComponent;
    protected int nNumber;
    protected Float dFloat;

    // constructor
    public SimpleBean()
    {
    }
}
```

The preceding example defines a class with three variables — an integer, a string, and a label component. The serialization mechanism manages the primitive data types — `integer` and `float`. Because `java.awt.Label` is derived from `java.awt.Component`, which implements `java.io.Serializable`, this variable's storage is managed as well.

There is much more to JavaBean serialization, which is beyond the scope of this chapter. However, this brief introduction identifies a feature that is similar to COM's IPersist storage interface.

JavaBean Customization

The Bean architecture, similar to ActiveX components, supports two modes of operation — design time and run time. Users running your program are familiar with the run-time mode. If the Bean or ActiveX component is visible, then this mode displays the component and process user interaction. Design-time operation is a state that only developers are familiar with. In this state, the component may provide assistance, usually in the form of property editors, to customize the look and behavior of the control.

BeanInfo

A Bean can specifically identify the methods, events, and properties it wishes to expose by providing a class that implements the `BeanInfo` interface.

Secret

There is a design pattern for exposing a `BeanInfo` class for a Bean. This pattern requires placing `BeanInfo` after the name of the Bean when defining the class. For example, if the Bean's name is `ThirdStage`, the BeanInfo class is named `ThirdStageBeanInfo`.

Customizing

Visual development environments commonly place components available to the programmer in a tool palette window. The icons associated with these tool buttons can be controlled by the represented component. Additionally, the component may provide more advanced property editors to assign values to properties than the droplists that are usually provided by default. The `BeanInfo` interface specifies a number of methods, which enable a Bean to expose design-time functionality.

```
public interface java.Beans.BeanInfo
{
    public final static int ICON_COLOR_16x16;
    public final static int ICON_COLOR_32x32;
    public final static int ICON_MONO_16x16;
    public final static int ICON_MONO_32x32;
```

```
public BeanInfo[] getAdditionalBeanInfo();
public BeanDescriptor getBeanDescriptor();
public int getDefaultEventIndex();
public int getDefaultPropertyIndex();
public EventSetDescriptor[] getEventSetDescriptors();
public Image getIcon(int iconKind);
public MethodDescriptor[] getMethodDescriptors();
public PropertyDescriptor[] getPropertyDescriptors();
}
```

Secret

The `java.Beans.SimpleBeanInfo` class implements the `BeanInfo` interface for you. It is a support class whose implementation provides no information. Therefore, your `BeanInfo` class can extend this class and only provide the methods that you want. This class provides a default implementation for all the other methods of the interface.

Icons

Your Bean may specify an icon to represent it when it appears in a palette of Beans in a visual development tool. The icon can be specified as either a monochrome or color bitmap — of either 16 ×1 6 or 32 × 32 pixels. Generally the images provided are in GIF format with the transparency color set for the area surrounding the image. Icon processing is shown in Listing 9-12.

Listing 9-12: ThirdStageBeanInfo.java

```
import java.Beans.*;
import java.awt.*;
public class ThirdStageBeanInfo extends SimpleBeanInfo
{
    public Image getIcon(int nType)
    {
        if (nType == BeanInfo.ICON_COLOR_16x16)
        {
            Image image=loadImage("ThirdStage16.gif");
            return image;
        }
        else if (nType == BeanInfo.ICON_COLOR_32x32)
        {
            Image image=loadImage("ThirdStage32.gif");
            return image;
        }
        return null;
    }
}
```

The preceding example overrides the `getIcon()` method, which returns an image of the specified type.

PropertyDescriptor

The `BeanInfo` class provides a mechanism for specifying the values that are to be displayed for a given property and which properties are available for editing. The class that gathers this information is called `PropertyDescriptor` and it can be retrieved by making a `getPropertyDescriptors` call on the `BeanInfo` class.

The `BeanInfo` class can create the `PropertyDescriptor` objects that describe the properties and methods supported by the Bean. Additionally, this class can specify that another object should be created to gather the information from the developer when the property is edited.

The `PropertyDescriptor` class is shown in Table 9-2. Because describing every detail of this class could be a whole book in itself, I present a small example detailing its use.

Table 9-2   PropertyDescriptor

Method	*Description*
`public PropertyDescriptor(String propertyName, Class BeanClass) throws IntrospectionException`	Constructor used to support normal `set`/`get` design pattern.
`public PropertyDescriptor(String propertyName, Class BeanClass, String getterName, String setterName) throws Introspection Exception`	Constructor that enables `get`/`set` method name definition.
`public PropertyDescriptor (String propertyName, Method getter, Method setter) throws IntrospectionException`	Constructor using reflection mechanism to identify property methods.
`public Class getPropertyEditor Class()`	Retrieve editor's class.
`public Class getPropertyType()`	Retrieve property type.
`public Method getReadMethod()`	Retrieve `get` method.
`public Method getWriteMethod()`	Retrieve `set` method.
`public boolean isBound()`	Identify bound property.
`public boolean isConstrained()`	Identify constrained property.
`public void setBound(boolean bound)`	Sets the bound specifier.
`public void setConstrained (boolean constrained)`	Sets the constrained specifier.
`public void setPropertyEditor Class(Class propertyEditorClass)`	Sets the editor's class.

As you can see by the class definition there are methods to define each of the characteristics of a property, including bound and constrained attributes. The class also has three constructors. These constructors define the following property types:

■ PropertyDescriptor(String propertyName, Class BeanClass) **defines properties that support the common** getPropertyName() / setPropertyName() **design pattern.**

■ PropertyDescriptor(String propertyName, Class BeanClass, String getterName, String setterName) **specifies method names for the** get() **and** set() **methods as strings. In this manner you can name the accessor and mutator functions anything you like. Therefore, instead of having** getEngineTemp() **and** setEngineTemp() **methods, you can define** acquireStage3Temperature() **and** modifyStage3Temperature() **methods. Also, if you want either the** get() **or** set() **method to be write-only or read-only, respectively, you supply a** null **for that constructor argument.**

■ PropertyDescriptor(String propertyName, Method getter, Method setter) **is similar to the last constructor. However, instead of passing method names as strings, instances of** java.lang.reflect.Method **are passed.**

The following code defines the get() and set() methods for two properties. As you see, the names do not have to follow the design pattern represented by getPropertyName(), setPropertyName().

```
public PropertyDescriptor[] getPropertyDescriptors()
{
    try{
        // describe get/set for stage3
        PropertyDescriptor stage3 = new PropertyDescriptor("Stage 3
Temp", Stages.class, "acquireStage3Temperature",
"modifyStage3Temperature");

        // describe read-only for stage2
        PropertyDescriptor stage2 = new PropertyDescriptor("Stage 2
Temp", Stages.class, "readStage2Temp", null);

        PropertyDescriptor result[]={stage3, stage2};
        return result;
    }
    catch (IntrospectionException e){
        System.out.println("Exception in BeanInfo : "+e);
        return null;
    }
}
```

Ok, the preceding code fragment is contrived, but the gist of it is to describe two properties in a class named Stages. The first property's name is displayed in a visual development environment as Stage 3 Temp. Its set() method is modifyStage3Temperature and its get() method is acquireStage3Temperature. The second property is called Stage 2 Temp and it is read-only with its get() method defined as readStage2Temp. Notice that the PropertyeDescriptor constructors can throw an IntrospectionException that must be caught.

Property editors

Property editors provide the most sophisticated mechanism that a Bean can give a developer for design-time customization. By providing a special property-editor object, a Bean can supply its own user interface to a programmer using a visual development tool.

Secret

The `PropertyEditorSupport` class is a helper class for defining property editors. The class provides a default value for all methods that you don't override.

The class definition for `PropertyEditorSupport` appears in Table 9-3.

Table 9-3   PropertyEditorSupport

Method	Description
`protected PropertyEditorSupport()`	Constructor
`protected PropertyEditorSupport (Object source)`	Constructor with a source object
`public synchronized void addPropertyChangeListener (PropertyChangeListener listener)`	Listener management method
`public synchronized void removePropertyChangeListener (PropertyChangeListener listener)`	Listener management method
`public void firePropertyChange()`	Notifies registered listeners
`public String getAsText()`	Retrieves the property as text
`public Component getCustomEditor()`	Retrieves the custom editor associated with this property
`public String getJavaInitializationString()`	Used by property editors that support code generation
`public String[] getTags()`	Retrieves an array of property string values, usually used to populate a drop list.
`public Object getValue()`	Retrieves the property as an Object
`public boolean isPaintable()`	Identifies if the property can be painted
`public void paintValue(Graphics gfx, Rectangle box)`	Used in displaying customizing the property's representation in an editor
`public void setAsText(String text) throws IllegalArgument Exception`	Sets the property as a String
`public void setValue(Object value)`	Sets the value of the property as an Object
`public boolean supportsCustomEditor()`	Identifies this property's support of custom editor features

While a complete discussion of this class is beyond the scope of this book, a simple example is shown that enables a development tool to display a number of string choices for a property.

Before an object derived from PropertyEditorSupport can be used, you must instruct the development tool to load your custom editor. This is done using a PropertyDescriptor described in the previous section.

```
public PropertyDescriptor[] getPropertyDescriptors()
{
    try{
        PropertyDescriptor thrustSetting = new
PropertyDescriptor("BurnRate", BurnRateLabel.class);
        thrustSetting.setPropertyEditorClass(BurnRateEditor.class);
        PropertyDescriptor result[]={thrustSetting};
        return result;
    }
    catch (IntrospectionException e){
        System.out.println("Exception in BeanInfo : "+e);
        return null;
    }
}
```

Here you define a PropertyDescriptor named BurnRate. The property editor for this property is set by the setPropertyEditorClass() method. In this case, it is set to a class named BurnRateEditor. This property editor class is shown here:

```
public class BurnRateEditor extends PropertyEditorSupport
{
    public String[] getTags()
    {
        String tags[]={"Warp","Moderate","Low"};
        return tags;
    }
}
```

The BurnRateEditor class extends the helper class PropertyEditorSupport and overrides a single method, getTags(). This method returns three strings that populate a combo box, which is provided for this property by a Bean development tool.

JAR Files

JavaBeans are distributed in JAR files, as stated at the beginning of this chapter. The JAR file is analogous to Microsoft's CAB file format, which is used to distribute ActiveX components and Java classes. A JAR file may contain more than one Bean. It may also contain a *manifest* file. This file describes the contents of the JAR.

Secret

JAR files are compressed using the ZIP file compression format. You may view the contents of a JAR file using any ZIP-compliant utility.

The JAR utility

The `jar` program has been available since version 1.1 of the JDK. It is a command-line utility and is used to create, extract, and view the contents of JAR files.

The `jar` command-line argument syntax is shown here:

```
jar (ctx) [vfmOM] [jar-output-file] [manifest-file] file-list
```

Table 9-4 summarizes the `jar` utility options.

Table 9-4   Jar Utility Options

Option	Description
c	Creates new archive
f	Files archive name
m	Includes specified manifest
M	Does not create a manifest file
t	Views archive's table of contents
x	Extracts the specified file(s)
v	Specifies verbose output
0	Turns compression off

Table 9-5 lists the descriptions of the input and output files that can be specified.

Table 9-5   Specified Input and Output Files

File	Description
jar-output-file	Defines the name of the archive file (optional)
manifest-file	Identifies the name of the manifest file to include (optional)
file-list	Specifies the files to be included in the JAR. Wildcards are supported. Full and relative directories are supported. If a directory is specified, all files in that directory and all subdirectories are recursively added to the JAR.

Secret

Files can not be individually added or removed from a JAR file. The JAR must be recreated each time you want to make such a change. All JAR files containing Beans must have a manifest file. A JAR file may contain more than one Bean.

A simple example that packages a class named `ABean.class` in a JAR file named `AJar.jar` requires the following command:

```
jar cf AJar.jar ABean.class
```

The jar program automatically generates a manifest file.

Manifest file

A JAR file that contains JavaBeans must also contain a manifest file. This file identifies which of the entries in the archive are Beans. The manifest file must be named `META-INF/MANIFEST.MF`. That is, the manifest file is named MANIFEST.MF and resides in the META-INF subdirectory. Class files that represent Beans must provide a ".class" extension, while a ".ser" extension indicates that the entry holds a serialized Bean. A sample manifest file follows:

```
Manifest-Version: 1.0

Name: MyBean.class
Digest-Algorithms: MD5 SHA
MD5-Digest: cxY3YKGH+E2UVBSnTc3jaK==
SHA-Digest: S7Bjxe2ABXdRsbWaxr9bFEaV8vB=
```

For more information regarding the use and syntax of the manifest file refer to the JavaBean specification.

JavaBeans as ActiveX

If you are comfortable developing ActiveX controls in your Java projects and a JavaBean comes along that provides functionality not offered as an ActiveX component, you are in luck. The Microsoft VM provides the necessary bridge for hosting a JavaBean in an ActiveX container. The Bean is exposed as an ActiveX control whose `IDispatch` interface is generated using discovery mechanisms such as design patterns and introspection to examine the component. Once a Bean has made the transformation to ActiveX control, you can use the Visual J++ unparalleled visual environment to exploit application development using components. Visual J++ enables you to drag and drop ActiveX components from the toolbox palette to your form — something that Visual J++ does not support for JavaBeans.

Turning a JavaBean into an ActiveX component doesn't require changing the Bean in any way. The magic is performed by a utility called `javareg`.

Wrapping a Bean

So how does Microsoft work its magic and transform a JavaBean to an ActiveX control without touching the source? Well, it's a rather straightforward task. Because both technologies strive to perform basically the same function, they solve the problem with mechanisms that closely map from one to the other.

Methods and general properties

The first characteristic exploited by Microsoft in identifying the elements of a JavaBean is the naming conventions identified by design patterns. The `get()` and `set()` methods used to identify `accessor()` and `mutator()` methods of a property are easily identified. Additionally, introspection is employed to enumerate the public methods of a Bean. These methods and the methods defined for property access are exposed by the ActiveX control through the `IDispatch` interface. JavaBeans can also provide outgoing event notification. This mechanism maps well to the ActiveX `IConnectionPointContainer` model.

Events

ActiveX controls support what are called *default event interfaces*. A COM object can expose one or more interfaces. A tag named `Default` may be applied to one source (outgoing) and one sink (incoming) interface. These interfaces are identified to handle events for the object. If an interface is specified as default, the first interface listed as part of the type information is given this distinction. Unless the JavaBean that is being "wrapped" provides its own `BeanInfo` class, all outgoing events are put in the default event interface. This is a good thing, because generally the ActiveX container only connects to the default event interface. Because Microsoft's component architecture only supports one default-outgoing interface, all of your Beans' listener interfaces are combined into a single interface exposed by the ActiveX control. To attach an event sink to the Java control, the Microsoft VM calls any `listener` methods of the outgoing event sources and passes the instance of an object, which implements the appropriate interface.

Secret

Microsoft recommends defining listener event methods for defining parameters that are not event objects because it can improve the performance in passing events in and out of the Bean. This *free-form* method is supported by the JavaBean specification.

```
interface mouseListener
{
    public void mouseEvent(int Click, int x, int y);
}
```

Mapping bound and constrained properties

The ActiveX migration for property change events is quite seamless. There are two types of property notification, bound and constrained, both of which are covered in detail in this chapter.

Bound properties require the Bean to support the `addPropertyChangeListener` and `removePropertyChangeListener()` methods that accept the `propertyChangeListener` interface as a parameter. This is the functional equivalent to ActiveX OnChange events.

Constrained properties require the Bean to support the `addVetoableChangeListener()` and `removeVetoableChangeListener()` methods that accept the `vetoableChangeListener` interface as a parameter. The property change event sources are handled properly by the Microsoft VM. For ActiveX clients, these events map to `IPropertySinkNotify` and `IPropertySinkNotify::OnRequrestEdit`.

Using the javareg utility

The `javareg` tool examines the Bean and gathers information on its methods, events, and properties. This information is used to build a *type library*. A type library is a standardized description of the interfaces that an OLE object presents. The second thing the `javareg` utility does is register the Bean as an ActiveX component.

Creating the necessary entries in the Registry enables any ActiveX container to locate and instantiate the control. This is important for end-user applications, which require the Bean-derived control at run time, but it is also a necessary step to use at design time. Most development environments — such as Visual J++, Visual Basic, and Borland Delphi — are ActiveX containers themselves. They must be properly registered to present your component in a tool palette.

Secret

The `javareg` utility doesn't change the code of your JavaBean in any way. The utility builds a standard OLE type library for the Bean, with which ActiveX containers can discover the Bean's properties. When the Bean is to be instantiated as a control, the Microsoft VM is loaded and performs the necessary mappings between events, properties, and methods.

The `javareg` utility has the following command-line format:

```
javareg [options]
```

The options are summarized in Table 9-6.

Table 9-6 Javareg Utility Options

Option	Description
/?	Displays help and usage information.
/register	Registers the command line's *class* argument with the specified class identifier provided by classid. You can also use javareg to create a CLSID and register it for you. Simply use the /register and /class parameters, but don't provide a CLASSID.
/codebase: [filename | URL]	Specifies the base location used in obtaining the Java class, either from a filename or a URL.
/control	Adds the necessary Registry information for containers to treat the Java class as an ActiveX component.
/typelib: [filename]	Creates the type library that is discovered using introspection mechanisms for the specified Java class and writes it to the specified filename location. To register a typelib without generating a new one, this option must be combined with the /nomktyplib argument.
/nomktyplib	Registers an existing typelib as specified in the filename argument of the /typelib parameter, without creating a new one.
/unregister	Unregisters the class specified by the class parameter. This requires the /class:classname argument.
/class:classname	Used to specify the name of the class to be registered with the specified classid, if provided. Otherwise, a CLSID is generated.
/clsid:CLSID	Specifies the class identifier to be used to register the class.
/surrogate	Supports remote access to COM classes. Creates the necessary Registry entries to enable the Java class to be activated out-of-process.
/progid:PROGID	Identifies the ProgId for the class being registered. A ProgId is a human-readable synonym for a CLSID.
/remote: RemoteServerName	Activates the class on a remote server using DCOM.
/q	Quiet mode. No message boxes are displayed.

The following example shows a typical `javareg` command line registering a Bean called MyBean:

```
javareg /register /control /class:MyBean /codebase:.
/clsid:{177cfa20-e8e0-1230-b8a5-0000fffeee13} /typelib:MyBean.tlb
```

ActiveX as a JavaBean Component

This sections covers hosting an ActiveX control within a Java component.

You can use the `jactivex` tool to expose an ActiveX control as a JavaBean component (a Bean). This tool also generates listener interfaces for subscribing to events.

Wrapping ActiveX

Using ActiveX controls in a Java application is more important than being able to wrap JavaBeans in an ActiveX control. This is good, because there are more ActiveX components available than Beans. Using an ActiveX control is not difficult. The following steps demonstrate the process:

1. Run the `jactivex` program on the ActiveX control or its type library (usually denoted by a .tlb extension). The appropriate Java code is generated supporting the control's methods, properties, and events. Those familiar with COM should be happy to know that the appropriate reference counting code is also generated, to manage the components' *lifetime*.

2. The source code contains compiler directives, such as /** @COM */, which can only be interpreted by the Microsoft Java compiler, jvc.

3. To use the control, these classes must be imported into your program, as you would for any other Bean.

The following example instantiates the ietimer.ocx control. The class implements the ActiveXControlListener, which exposes a single method that indicates that the control has been created.

```
public interface ActiveXControlListener extends
java.util.EventListener
{
  // Methods
  public void controlCreated(Object target);
}
```

The example code follows:

```
import java.awt.*;
import com.ms.activex.*;
import ietimer.*;  // Classes from JActiveX when run on
                   // ietimer.ocx

public class InstantiateTimer extends Frame implements
ActiveXControlListener
```

```
{
  IeTimer oTimer;
  public InstantiateTimer()
  {
    oTimer = new IeTimer();

    oTimer.addActiveXControlListener(this);
    add(oTimer);
  }

  // Implementation of ActiveXControlListener interface method
  public void controlCreated(Object obj);
  {
    if (obj instanceof IeTimer)
    {
      System.out.prinln("Timer control was created"\n);
    }
  }
}
```

Notice that the control is manipulated like any other Bean. The constructor code creates the Bean, registers a listener (in this case, one defined by the ActiveXControlListener interface), and then adds itself to the layout. The single method of the ActiveXControlListener interface is controlCreated(). When the control is created, the Microsoft VM fires an event defined by the ActiveXControlListener interface and, if the ActiveX control supports events as this example does, the corresponding listener method on the Bean is called. The code necessary to sink the event to the corresponding listener is provided automatically by the Microsoft VM.

The jactivex utility

The `jactivex` program is a command-line utility and has the following syntax:

`jactivex [options] filename`

This utility generates JavaBean-compatible Java code from either ActiveX control files or type library files. This utility's default operation is to create a JavaBean wrapper for an ActiveX Control. It creates `IDispatch` wrappers for the ActiveX object that are compatible with the JavaBean specification to add and remove listeners for the ActiveX event interfaces.

Secret

The `jactivex` utility provides all of the capabilities of the `jcom` utility, which was released in previous versions of the Microsoft SDK for Java. This utility is also used to generate Java source files from type libraries. These operations are performed with an additional switch, `/javatlb`, but are otherwise identical to the `jcom` utility.

Table 9-7 summarizes the options that are supported by the `jactivex` utility. It is important to note that the `/javatlb` option must be present when any additional options are selected.

Table 9-7 jactivex Utility Options

Option	Description
/javatlb	Accesses COM integration features not available in default mode used to generate Java source from type libraries **NOTE:** This switch must be used in combination with the following switches to create a JavaBean wrapper.
/b	Identifies properties using the JavaBean design patterns
/cj	Creates a template for implementing a *coclass* in Java. A coclass is an IDL statement that enables COM to determine the component's incoming and outgoing interfaces.
/d directory	Sets the output director for controls — by default, the directory is set as default=%WINDIR%\java\trustlib
/e	Suppresses output for typelibs not on the command line
/G3.1	Targets 3.1 Microsoft VM for Java (default=/G4)
/G4	Targets 4.0 Microsoft VM for Java (default)
/j	Generates undecorated Java source
/l listfile	Creates a list of all output files (default=none)
/n jnffile	Identifies a JNF file (default=none)
/nologo	Suppresses the Microsoft copyright message
/p packagename	Sets the root package; the default does not set the package name
/p:b-	Indicates that the type library name is not included in the package
/r	Registers the type libraries
/w	Suppresses all warnings
/WX	Elevates warnings to error status
/x2	Represents two-byte integers as a char
/xc	Ignores coclasses in the typelib
/xd-	Does not generate Default interfaces
/xh	Does not map S_FLASE to ComSuccessException
/X:m-	Disables auto-marshaling (default is auto-marshaling=enabled)
/xi	Exposes the default interface methods directly on *coclass*
/?	Displays command-line help and usage information

Secret

Do not use Visual J++ compilers earlier than version 1.02.3920 to compile the files generated by this utility.

A simple way to understand the functions that the `jactivex` utility performs is to view the output files it generates. In the following example, the `jactivex` utility operates on the `ietimer.ocx`. This common component provides simple timing functions.

The following command is issued to generate the `DIeTimerEvents.java`, `enumBoolType.java`, `IeTimer.java`, and `IIeTimer.java` files:

```
jactivex ietimer.ocx
```

DIeTimerEvents.java

This file defines the event interface for the timer control.

```
//
// Auto-generated using JActiveX.EXE 4.79.2611
//    (D:\VJ__SA~1\VJ6WEB\VJ98\JACTIVEX.EXE ietimer.ocx)
//
// WARNING: Do not remove the comments that include "@com"
directives.
// This source file must be compiled by a @com-aware compiler.
// If you are using the Microsoft Visual J++ compiler, you must use
// version 1.02.3920 or later. Previous versions do not issue an
error
// but do not generate COM-enabled class files.
//

package ietimer;

import com.ms.com.*;
import com.ms.com.IUnknown;
import com.ms.com.Variant;

// Dispatch-only interface DIeTimerEvents
/** @com.interface(iid=588DCC00-727D-11CF-AC36-00AA00A47DD2,
thread=AUTO, type=DISPATCH) */
public interface DIeTimerEvents extends IUnknown
{
  /** @com.method(dispid=1, type=METHOD, name="Timer",
returntype=VOID)
      @com.parameters() */
  public void Timer();


  public static final com.ms.com._Guid iid = new
com.ms.com._Guid((int)0x588dcc00, (short)0x727d, (short)0x11cf,
(byte)0xac, (byte)0x36, (byte)0x0, (byte)0xaa, (byte)0x0, (byte)0xa4,
(byte)0x7d, (byte)0xd2);
}
```

enumBoolType.java

This support file maps a boolean type between the ActiveX component and Java.

```
//
// Auto-generated using JActiveX.EXE 4.79.2611
//    (D:\VJ__SA~1\VJ6WEB\VJ98\JACTIVEX.EXE ietimer.ocx)
//
// WARNING: Do not remove the comments that include "@com"
directives.
// This source file must be compiled by a @com-aware compiler.
// If you are using the Microsoft Visual J++ compiler, you must use
// version 1.02.3920 or later. Previous versions do not issue an
error
// but do not generate COM-enabled class files.
//

package ietimer;

import com.ms.com.*;
import com.ms.com.IUnknown;
import com.ms.com.Variant;

// Enum: enumBoolType

public interface enumBoolType
{
  public static final int ValFalse = 0;
  public static final int ValTrue = -1;
}
```

IeTimer.java

This file identifies the public properties and methods for the control. Notice that the property values are accessed and changed using methods whose names begin with get and set. This adheres to the JavaBean design patterns.

```
//
// Auto-generated using JActiveX.EXE 4.79.2611
//    (D:\VJ__SA~1\VJ6WEB\VJ98\JACTIVEX.EXE ietimer.ocx)
//
// WARNING: Do not remove the comments that include "@com"
directives.
// This source file must be compiled by a @com-aware compiler.
// If you are using the Microsoft Visual J++ compiler, you must use
// version 1.02.3920 or later. Previous versions do not issue an
error
// but do not generate COM-enabled class files.
//

package ietimer;

import com.ms.com.*;
import com.ms.com.IUnknown;
import com.ms.com.Variant;
```

```
/** @com.class(classid=59CCB4A0-727D-11CF-AC36-
00AA00A47DD2,DynamicCasts)
*/
public class IeTimer implements
IUnknown,com.ms.com.NoAutoScripting,ietimer.IIeTimer
{
    /** @com.method() */
    public native int getInterval();

    /** @com.method() */
    public native void setInterval(int plInterval);

    /** @com.method() */
    public native int getEnabled();

    /** @com.method() */
    public native void setEnabled(int plInterval);

    /** @com.method() */
    public native void AboutBox();


    public static final com.ms.com._Guid clsid = new
com.ms.com._Guid((int)0x59ccb4a0, (short)0x727d, (short)0x11cf,
(byte)0xac, (byte)0x36, (byte)0x0, (byte)0xaa, (byte)0x0, (byte)0xa4,
(byte)0x7d, (byte)0xd2);
}
```

IIeTimer.java

This file defines the interface IIeTimer. The /** @com compiler directives are used to access the IDispatch interface exposed by the control.

```
//
// Auto-generated using JActiveX.EXE 4.79.2611
//    (D:\VJ__SA~1\VJ6WEB\VJ98\JACTIVEX.EXE ietimer.ocx)
//
// WARNING: Do not remove the comments that include "@com"
directives.
// This source file must be compiled by a @com-aware compiler.
// If you are using the Microsoft Visual J++ compiler, you must use
// version 1.02.3920 or later. Previous versions  do not issue an
error
// but do not generate COM-enabled class files.
//

package ietimer;

import com.ms.com.*;
import com.ms.com.IUnknown;
import com.ms.com.Variant;

// Dual interface IIeTimer
/** @com.interface(iid=574EE360-727D-11CF-AC36-00AA00A47DD2,
thread=AUTO, type=DUAL) */
```

```java
public interface IIeTimer extends IUnknown
{
  /** @com.method(vtoffset=4, dispid=100, type=PROPGET,
name="Interval", addFlagsVtable=4)
      @com.parameters([type=I4] return) */
  public int getInterval();

  /** @com.method(vtoffset=5, dispid=100, type=PROPPUT,
name="Interval", addFlagsVtable=4)
      @com.parameters([in,type=I4] plInterval) */
  public void setInterval(int plInterval);

  /** @com.method(vtoffset=6, dispid=101, type=PROPGET,
name="Enabled", addFlagsVtable=4)
      @com.parameters([type=I4] return) */
  public int getEnabled();

  /** @com.method(vtoffset=7, dispid=101, type=PROPPUT,
name="Enabled", addFlagsVtable=4)
      @com.parameters([in,type=I4] plInterval) */
  public void setEnabled(int plInterval);

  /** @com.method(vtoffset=8, dispid=4294966744, type=METHOD,
name="AboutBox", returntype=VOID)
      @com.parameters() */
  public void AboutBox();


  public static final com.ms.com._Guid iid = new
com.ms.com._Guid((int)0x574ee360, (short)0x727d, (short)0x11cf,
(byte)0xac, (byte)0x36, (byte)0x0, (byte)0xaa, (byte)0x0, (byte)0xa4,
(byte)0x7d, (byte)0xd2);
}
```

Summary

This chapter introduced the JavaBean component architecture, which is similar to Microsoft's ActiveX technology. Visual J++ provides a versatile design environment for ActiveX controls. Thankfully, Microsoft has provided the tools to expose JavaBeans to ActiveX containers.

- JavaBeans are pure-Java code that provide a platform-independent component architecture.

- Visual J++ provides a utility named javareg that can expose a JavaBean as an ActiveX control. This utility does not change the Java code in any way to perform this magic.

- Visual J++ can wrap an ActiveX component with Java classes, so that any ActiveX control can be easily accessed through Java.

Chapter 10

Packaging and Deploying Your Application

In This Chapter

▶ Packaging options included with Visual J++

▶ Multiproject packaging and deploying

▶ Deploying to Web sites directly from Visual J++ using the Deployment Explorer

After the monumental work of application development is finished, you still need a way to get your application to your users. You could be a corporate developer trying to keep all your users up to date, or a Web developer trying to make sure the Web site is intact, or a prepackaged software supplier trying to make sure that the setup on your application works. One of the biggest challenges facing developers is deploying an application to its ultimate destination. Well, you're in luck! Visual J++ 6.0 includes a host of innovative features designed to make the deployment of applications easy.

Wrapping with the Right Package

Visual J++ not only supports CLASS packaging but also EXE files or even self-extracting Setup files using the Output Format tab on the Properties window, as seen in Figure 10-1.

Figure 10-1: Visual J++ enables you to compile into several different formats when compiling your CLASS file.

Table 10-1 gives a brief description of the different package types.

Table 10-1 Typical Java Packaging

Package	Description
.class	Although it isn't shown in the package types, a CLASS file is the standard Java format (as you hopefully already know), and is automatically generated before these packages. In a sense, you get two packages every time you compile. One package is the standard Java CLASS file, and the other is the package you choose in the Output Format tab.
.exe	Visual J++ can compile Windows-executable files. These files are not pure binary executables, but rather contain a "mini" Java Virtual Machine that runs and interprets the rest of the Java code. Now Java developers have the capability to deliver Windows-executable programs in a Visual environment.
.cab	CAB files are Microsoft Cabinet files. Cabinets are file holders that contain both compressed files and digital signatures for security.
.zip	ZIP files contain compressed files. Although some security may be present when using a ZIP format, usually ZIP files decompress directly onto the hard drive.
.jar	JAR files are not an option with Visual J++, but are used by other Java development tools. JAR files are a CAB-competing standard from Sun Microsystems. Essentially, they behave the same as CAB files.
Self-Extracting Setup	Although a self-extracting setup is compiled into an EXE file, inside is a package that directs where and how the files inside your EXE file are placed on the hard drive of the target machine. Self-extracting executables are necessary for disk and download distributables.

You can choose the types of files you want to place in your package by choosing the proper Package Contents in the Output Format tab. You can also control file types used in deployment by clicking the Deployment tab, as shown in Figure 10-2. The Deployment tab enables you to choose from a list of standard file combinations.

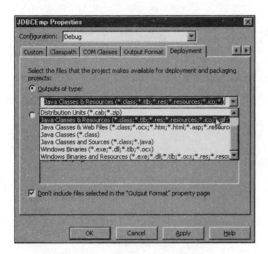

Figure 10-2: You can choose the file types you want to deploy using the Deployment tab of the Properties window.

After compiling with the EXE package turned on, both a CLASS file and an EXE file are created in the target directory as shown in Figure 10-3.

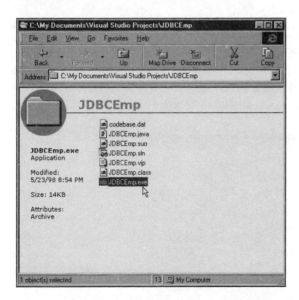

Figure 10-3: EXE packaging enables both a CLASS file and an EXE file to be created.

Self-Extracting Setup

The Self-Extracting Setup package is fully featured for complete system packaging and deployment. Figure 10-4 shows the `JDBCEmp` folder that contains a self-extracting executable, automatically created when this package is enabled.

Figure 10-4: A self-extracting executable is automatically created in the target folder when a project is built with the self-extracting executable option turned on.

When the self-extracting executable is run, it starts a professional installation program, as shown in Figure 10-5.

Figure 10-5: The self-extracting executable created by Visual J++ starts a professional installation program.

The files you indicate for inclusion in the self-extracting executable are then placed in a target directory. Figure 10-6 shows how a new folder is created automatically with the target files placed inside.

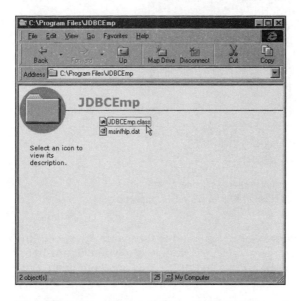

Figure 10-6: Target files and folders are created automatically during the installation process.

As you can see by Figure 10-6, little work is needed (and no additional software packages) to create a fully functional system.

Advanced properties

Each package (except ZIP) has a different set of advanced properties. Click Output Format ⇨ Advanced, as shown in Figure 10-1, to set advanced options for each package type.

EXE and COM DLL Advanced Properties

The EXE and COM DLL options enable you to set properties for your EXE and DLL, TLB, or COM file. As shown in Figure 10-7, you can enter comments, copyright and trademark information, and other useful information.

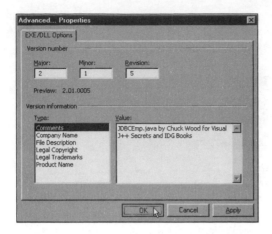

Figure 10-7: You can enter properties in the Advanced Properties window when using EXE or COM DLL packaging.

You can see the information you entered into your Advanced Properties box on the final executable properties window, shown in Figure 10-8. The CLASS files have no method for inserting properties and comments (and Microsoft *loves* to point it out whenever possible).

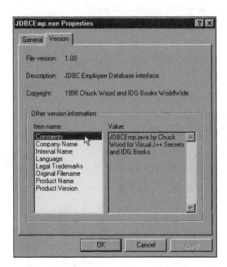

Figure 10-8: Properties you enter in the Advanced Properties window can be viewed by right-clicking the EXE file and choosing properties.

CAB Advanced Properties

If you use CAB packaging, the Advanced Properties window enables you to apply digital signatures to your CAB file. Because many browsers can be set up to stop CAB downloads without a digital signature (especially when using ActiveX); you may want to use one when distributing CAB files.

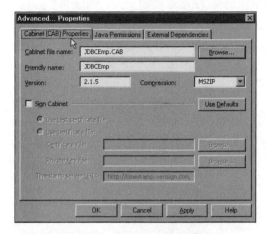

Figure 10-9: You can choose a digital signature and a compression type when using CAB files and the Advanced Properties window.

The Java Permissions tab (Figure 10-10) enables you to assign Cabinet permissions to be identical to the Java security sandbox. This technique enables you to avoid the headache of digital signing and, instead, use default Java security for your CAB files.

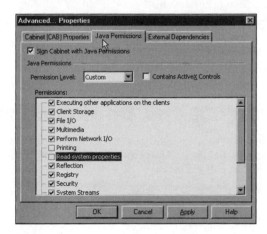

Figure 10-10: You can assign Java security to your CAB files.

Advanced properties of the Self-Extracting Setup (Figure 10-11) enable you to do the following:

- The target tab enables you to designate the target installation folder so you can place your application where you want it.

- The target tab also enables you to place the program on the Windows start task bar at the bottom (usually) of your Windows setup.

- The signing tab enables digital signing for security.

- The Nested Setups tab enables you to place setup files within setup files. This is useful if some files in a setup are to be handled differently than other files in a setup.

- The Remote Components tab enables you to use components from other network computers or the Web.

- System Directory Installation enables you to place files in the Windows system directory.

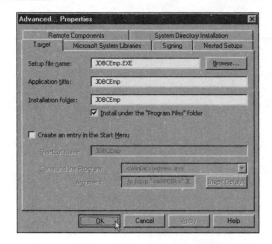

Figure 10-11: You can use Advanced Properties to deliver a fully functional installation program.

Multiproject Packaging and Deployment

Although this deployment method is light years ahead of other Java development environments, using the Output Properties tab on the Properties window does have drawbacks:

- The output methodologies are mutually exclusive. In other words, if you wanted to develop a Windows EXE *and* deploy it as a setup .EXE file, you cannot easily use the techniques defined in this chapter so far.

- Sometimes you want to include several outputs from several solutions in your package, especially when delivering entire systems to your clients. This is not possible with standard, single-project deployment methods.

Microsoft addresses these issues by enabling you to define a Setup, CAB, or ZIP project. Follow these steps:

1. Choose New ➪ Project from the Visual Studio menu.

2. Expand the choices under Visual Studio in the New Project Window.

3. Click Distribution Units.

4. Choose the package you want to use. In Figure 10-12, a Self-Extracting Setup project is chosen.

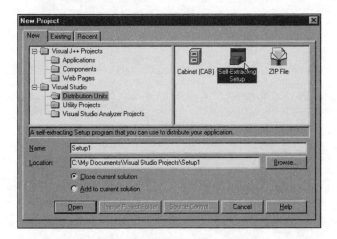

Figure 10-12: You can package the outputs of several classes by using the New Project window and choosing Distribution Units.

5. To add projects to the Setup project, right-click the project name and choose Add Project as shown in Figure 10-13.

6. Now add projects to your output. In Figure 10-14, the `JDBCEmp` project and the `HelloWorldApplet` projects are added to the Setup project.

7. Right-click the Setup project, as shown in Figure 10-14, to include output from your added projects.

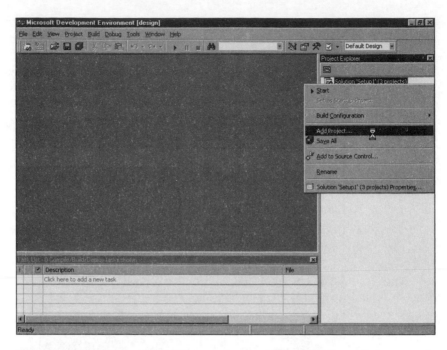

Figure 10-13: Add projects to the Setup project by right-clicking the project name and choosing Add Project.

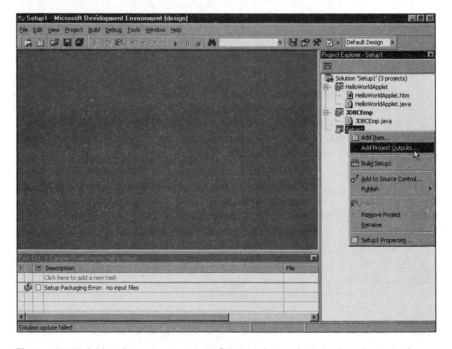

Figure 10-14: Add project outputs to your Setup project to include them in the package.

8. Choose the project outputs you wish to add to the Setup project. Normally, you choose all the projects. In Figure 10-15, outputs from the JDBCEmp and the HelloWorldApplet projects are added to the Setup project.

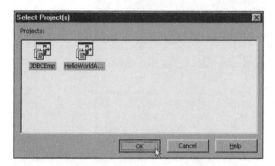

Figure 10-15: Add outputs to your Setup project in the Select Projects window.

9. After all the projects are added, right-click the Setup project and choose Build Setup (as shown in Figure 10-16) to build a self-extracting executable from the output of the projects.

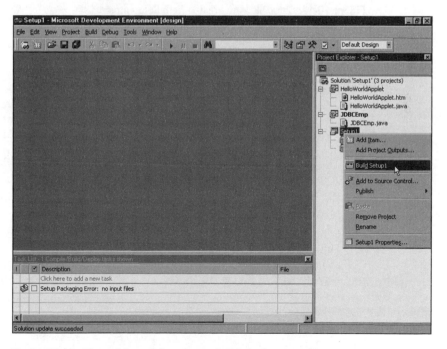

Figure 10-16: After adding all the outputs, build the Setup project.

As you can see from the folder output on Figure 10-17, a `Setup.exe` file is built containing all the compressed files from your project outputs. This setup file can be deployed on disk or CD, or downloaded from the Web.

Figure 10-17: Setup files are created from Setup projects.

Exploring the Deployment Explorer

Visual J++ makes it easy for developers to deploy their applications directly from Visual J++ to Web servers or remote sites. This deployment method ensures that the resulting application is deployed correctly and works right away. Automatic deployment can even be done using multiproject packaging.

To deploy your application, automatically, to a remote site, follow these simple steps:

1. Choose Project, New Deployment Target from the Visual Studio menu to open the New Deployment Target window.

2. Inside the Window, you see all the projects currently in your solution. In Figure 10-18, the `HelloWorldApplet` project is opened. You must choose at least one project to be deployed. Type in the location of the local or remote site. In Figure 10-18, the `www.mysite.com` is chosen as the target for the deployment.

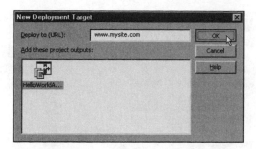

Figure 10-18: Visual J++ is ready to deploy the HelloWorldApplet project to the www.mysite.com Web site.

3. Visual J++ prompts you for the password you want to use to deploy your application by displaying the Enter Network Password dialog box, as shown in Figure 10-19. If an error occurs, Visual J++ displays the Cannot connect to network server message box.

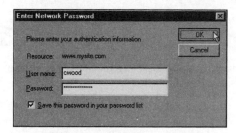

Figure 10-19: The Enter Network Password dialog box is used to help you navigate through a Web server's security.

That's all there is to it. Visual J++ is now set up to deploy your specified Project files to your remote Web site. Several different deployment options can be set using the preceding three steps.

Every time you add a deployment, the specifications for it go into the Deployment Explorer. In Figure 10-20, the deployment option to www.mysite.com, which you just added, is displayed as a choice. From the Visual J++ menu, select Project ⇨ Deploy to use one of the previously defined deployment specifications. In Figure 10-20, you are directing Visual Studio to deploy output from the current project to the specified Web site.

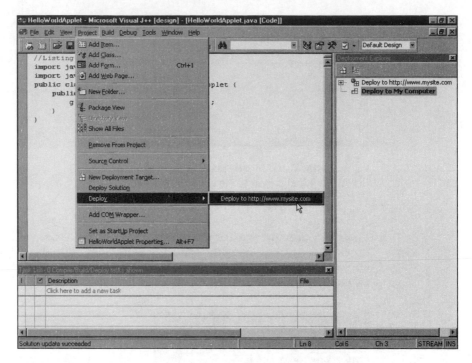

Figure 10-20: The Deployment Explorer, accessed through the Visual Studio menu, lists the possible deployment options.

The Deployment Explorer provides developers with a simple facility for browsing potential targets for deployment. By using it, developers can ensure that all files have been properly set up and deployed.

Summary

Packaging and deploying systems can be a logistics nightmare. Now, Visual J++ has streamlined the process, making it easy to package projects and ensure that the entire project is deployed. To recap:

- Visual J++ includes packaging options that enable EXE, COM DLL, ZIP, CAB, and Setup files to be created.

- Advanced properties of each packaging type enable the user to configure each package for a secure and professional packaging job.

- Multiproject solutions can be packaged and more tightly controlled by using Visual Studio's Distribution Units project option when creating a new project.

- You can add options to the Deployment Explorer and use it to automatically deploy solutions to remote servers and Web sites.

Chapter 11

Programming Dynamic HTML
with Visual J++

In This Chapter

▶ Using HTML Painter

▶ Programming Dynamic HTML

▶ Examining database DHTML programming

▶ Using Server DHTML, Client HTML, and Active Server Pages

When Microsoft came out with Internet Explorer (IE) 4.0, they introduced the concept of Dynamic HTML. Dynamic HTML (DHTML) is a revolutionary HTML object model that enables developers to manipulate HTML on the fly. Visual J++ includes a `wfc.html` package inside WFC that enables you to access IE 4.0's DHTML on a Web page directly from a Java class. This chapter documents the `wfc.html` package and shows you how to use it.

Looking at the wfc.html Package

The `wfc.html` package contains several classes. Figure 11-1 lists all the `wfc.html` classes and how they relate to each other. Table 11-1 gives a brief description of these classes.

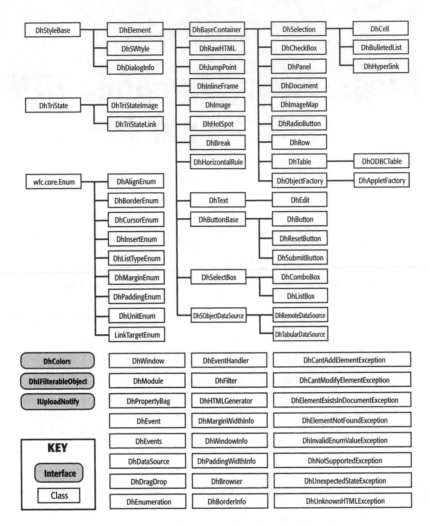

Figure 11-1: The `wfc.html` package contains a lot of functionality.

Table 11-1   The `wfc.html` package

Function: Class or Interface	Description
DhAlignEnum	Defines constants for alignment, such as TOP and TEXT_RIGHT.
DhAppletFactory	Creates an applet object and adds it to the current document. Usually, this won't be needed by the average Visual J++ dynamic HTML programmer.
DhBaseContainer	The ancestor for all container elements. DhBaseContainer is never instantiated, but its descendents are.

Function: Class or Interface	Description
DhBorderEnum	Defines constant definitions for border styles.
DhBorderInfo	Provides structured information about an element's border styles.
DhBreak	Represents an HTML line break (` `) element.
DhBrowser	Enables the developer to access information about the current browser. Currently, this functions only under Internet Explorer.
DhBulletedList	Represents an HTML unordered list of items.
DhButton	Represents an HTML button class.
DhButtonBase	This is the ancestor for all HTML buttons
DhCantAddElement Exception	Signals that a request for a named element failed, because an element with that name does not exist.
DhCantModifyElement Exception	Signals that an attempt has been made to modify a read-only element, such as one that has been sent from a server to a client.
DhCell	Creates a table cell inside an HTML table
DhCheckBox	Represents an HTML check box with a text label.
DhComboBox	Represents an HTML drop-down combo box control.
DhCursorEnum	Defines constants for controlling an element's cursor style.
DhDataSource	This forms a generic wrapper class for data sources.
DhDialogInfo	This forms dialog boxes.
DhDocument	Represents an HTML document. Although you can construct a `DhDocument`, there is usually no reason to do so. The current `DhDocument` is retrieved by the `DhModule.getDocument()` method.
DhDragDrop	Enables a drag-and-drop element.
DhEdit	Represents an HTML edit box.
DhElement	All user-interface elements are inherited from `DhElement`.
DhElementExistsIn DocumentException	Signals that a given element has already been added to the document.
DhElementNot FoundException	Signals that a request for a named element failed, because an element with that name does not exist.
DhEnumeration	Represents a collection of elements in the HTML document. Usually this is not instantiated, but rather returned by the `DhDocument.enumerate(int type)` method where the type is either `DhEnumeration.ELEMENTS`, `DhEnumeration.HLINKS`, or `DhEnumeration.IMAGES`.

(continued)

Table 11-1 *(Continued)*

Function: Class or Interface	Description
DhEvent	DhEvent is the parameter passed to the event handlers. DhEvent is almost never instantiated by itself.
DhEventHandler	DhEventHandler enables you to call a specific method when an event occurs.
DhFilter	This class is inherited to enable photographic filters and transition effects.
DhHorizontalRule	Represents an HTML horizontal rule (<HR>) element.
DhHotSpot	Represents a hotspot in an image map.
DhHTMLGenerator	Represents a base class for HTML generation.
DhHyperlink	Creates a jump in the document to another place in the current document or to a different document.
DhImage	Represents a bitmap file in the document.
DhImageMap	Represents an image map.
DhInlineFrame	Represents an inline frame (<IFRAME>) element.
DhInsertEnum	Provides constants for inserting DhElement items into container items.
DhInvalidEnum ValueException	Signals that an attempt has been made to access a value within an enumeration that doesn't have a constant for that value.
DhJumpPoint	Represents an anchor within a document (that is, a <A NAME=...> reference).
DhListBox	Represents an HTML list box control.
DhListTypeEnum	Provides constants and support for list types in a DhList control.
DhMarginEnum	Provides constant definitions for margin style manipulation.
DhMarginWidthInfo	Provides information about an element's current margin settings.
DhModule	All Dynamic HTML must be inherited from this class.
DhNotSupportedException	Signals that a request for a named element failed, because an element with that name does not exist.
DhObjectDataSource	Provides encapsulation of data source objects in the IE 4.0 <OBJECT> tags.
ObjectFactory	Creates an object and adds it to the document. Usually, this won't be needed by the average Visual J++ dynamic HTML programmer.

Function: Class or Interface	Description
DhODBCTable	Represents an HTML table that can be populated with data from any ODBC data source.
DhPaddingEnum	Provides constant definitions for padding style manipulation.
DhPaddingWidthInfo	Provides information about an element's padding width settings.
DhPanel	Represents a container for elements; uses traditional Graphical User Interface two-dimensional positioning for layout.
DhPropertyBag	Retrieves values in the <PARAM> attributes of the module's HTML tags.
DhRadioButton	Represents an HTML radio button with a text label.
DhRawHTML	Allows output of arbitrary raw HTML to the document.
DhRemoteDataSource	Encapsulates the Microsoft Remote Data Service (formerly ADC) control, which enables access to database information across an HTTP connection.
DhResetButton	Represents an HTML reset button.
DhRow	Creates a table row.
DhSection	Represents an element container that uses traditional HTML one-dimensional flow layout.
DhSelectBox	Ancestor for elements that enable selection from a list.
DhStyle	Styles enable you to create a text style (font, size, color, attributes, and so on) that can be applied to Elements. DhStyles can make programming somewhat easier.
DhStyleBase	DhStyleBase is the ancestor for DhStyle and DhElement.
DhSubmitButton	Represents an HTML submit button.
DhTable	Creates a table element that can be populated with rows and columns.
DhTabularDataSource	Encapsulates the Microsoft Tabular Data Control (TDC).
DhText	Represents HTML static text.
DhUnexpectedState Exception	Signals that a request for a named element failed, because an element with that name does not exist.
DhUnitEnum	Provides constants for various unit types in DHTML.
DhUnknownHTMLException	Signals that a request for a named element failed, because an element with that name does not exist.
DhWindow	Represents an HTML window.
DhWindowInfo	Sets the features for a new browser window.

(continued)

Table 11-1 *(Continued)*	
Function: Class or Interface	*Description*
LinkTargetEnum	Provides constants for setting the document's target window.
DhColors	This interface defines color constants.
DhIFilterableObject	This interface is for objects with filters.
IUploadNotify	This interface is for elements that use an output stream.

Programming DHTML

There are several aspects to implementing a DHTML program, as the following steps show:

1. Import the wfc.html package.

2. Inherit the DhModule class.

3. Override the documentLoad() method to place your own functionality in your class.

4. Retrieve the containing HTML DhDocument by using the DhModule.getDocument() method.

The following code depicts this framework:

```
import wfc.html.*;  //Import the wfc.html package
//Inherit DhModule
public class DynamicHTML extends DhModule {
  public void documentLoad(Object sender, DhEvent p) {
    DhDocument doc = getDocument();    //Get the HTML document
    //Put code in here that places object on your HTML document
  }
  //Put other methods here, like your event handlers
}
```

Using the DhElement Class

Elements are similar to Components in the java.awt package or Controls in the wfc.core package. All Dynamic HTML elements are inherited from DhElement. Microsoft has made programming with Elements fairly simple in two ways:

- Every element has an empty constructor. You can construct any element (for instance, a DhButton) by using a String:

```
//Place a button with "My Button" in the text
DhButton myButton = new DhButton();
```

■ You can also accomplish the same task by constructing a button, and then use the `setText()` method:

```
//Place a button with "My Button" in the text
DhButton myButton = new DhButton("My Button");
myButton.setText("My Button");
```

Secret

Elements are stateless. This means that setting properties or calling methods inside elements always works and is not conditional on some external state or circumstance. Other packages, even ADO, require that some external state be satisfied before certain classes can be used. DHTML elements are encapsulated and don't require outside conditions to be met before instantiation.

If an element is already on the page when the `documentLoad()` method is called, then you can call the document's `findElement(String name)` method and start programming to that element. You can also enumerate all the elements in the document until you find the one you want.

Handling events

All elements can fire events that you can handle in your Visual J++ program. For example, one of the events you probably want to know about in your code is when the person viewing a page clicks a button. And you want to know which button was clicked. The following code shows how to make a button call a method:

```
import wfc.html.*;   //Import the wfc.html package
//Inherit DhModule
  public class DynamicHTML extends DhModule {
    public void documentLoad(Object sender, DhEvent p) {
    DhButton button2 = new DhButton("Button 2");   //Create a button
    doc.add(button2);             //Add a button
  //Make button clicks execute the button2Click method
    button2.addOnClick(new DhEventHandler(button2Click));
    //. . .The rest of code goes here. . .
    }
//button2Click is called whenever the button2 is clicked
  public void button2Click( Object sender, DhEvent e) {
    //. . . Code for the button click goes here
    }
```

In the preceding code, a button (`button2`) is added to a `DhModule` containing HTML document. The `button2` element is then configured to execute a method (`button2Click`) every time it is clicked.

Secret

Events are fired all the way up a containment tree. This means that *not only* the button can detect events *but also* the button's container. For developers, this is a welcome addition. Java programmers usually are restricted in that a container's events won't execute if a Component has focus. Usually, this is

Okay, but sometimes some "coding gymnastics" are required to make sure the proper events are triggered. This is not a concern with DHTML.

Secret

Many different events can be fired by elements in DHTML, and you can catch them all in the same way. Most of the events are contained in the DhElement class, although some are contained in other classes. Table 11-2 lists events that you can trap.

Table 11-2   Dynamic HTML Events

Event Trapping Method	Containing Class	When the Event Occurs
addOnAfterUpdate	DhObjectFactory	After an object that is created by a factory is updated
addOnBeforeUpdate	DhObjectFactory	Before an object that is created by a factory is updated
addOnChange	DhEdit	When an edit is changed
addOnClick	DhElement	When an element is clicked
addOnDataAvailable	DhObjectFactory	When a factory has data available
addOnDataSetChanged	DhObjectFactory	When a factory changes the data set
addOnDataSetComplete	DhObjectFactory	When a factory completes loading a data set
addOnDoubleClick	DhElement	When an element is double-clicked
addOnError	DhObjectFactory	When a nonupdate error occurs inside a factory
addOnErrorUpdate	DhObjectFactory	When an update error occurs inside a factory
addOnFormReset	DhSection	When a form is reset inside a DhSection
addOnHTTPSubmit	DhSection	When a new HTTP address is submitted from a DhSection
addOnKeyDown	DhElement	When a key is pressed and released on an element
addOnKeyPress	DhElement	When a key is pressed on an element
addOnKeyUp	DhElement	When a key is released on an element
addOnMouseDown	DhElement	When a mouse button is pressed on an element

Event Trapping Method	Containing Class	When the Event Occurs
addOnMouseEnter	DhElement	When a mouse pointer enters the area of an element
addOnMouseLeave	DhElement	When a mouse pointer leaves the area of an element
addOnMouseMove	DhElement	When a mouse pointer moves in the area of an element
addOnMouseUp	DhElement	When a mouse button is released on an element
addOnReadyStateChange	DhImage	When an image state changes
addOnReadyStateChange	DhObjectFactory	When an object's ready state changes
addOnRowEnter	DhObjectFactory	When a row is entered in a DhObjectFactory
addOnRowExit	DhObjectFactory	When a row is left in a DhObjectFactory
addOnSelect	DhEdit	When text is selected in a DhEdit
addOnSelectionChange	DhSelectBox	When the current selection is changed in a DhSelectBox
addOnSetParent	DhElement	When the parent is set on this element.

Working with containers

Containers hold elements. Some examples of containers include DhPanels and DhDocuments. Every container contains an add() method that enables the developer to add the appropriate elements to it:

```
DhPanel myPanel = new DhPanel();
myPanel.add(button1);
```

Probably the most important container is the DhDocument. You normally get one DhDocument class that is created by retrieving the current HTML document:

```
DhDocument doc = getDocument();
```

All HTML controls are added to the DhDocument container.

Writing a DHTML program

To create the simplest DHTML program follow these eight basic steps:

1. Import the `wfc.html` class:

   ```
   import wfc.html.*;   //Import the wfc.html package
   ```

2. Make a new class that inherits the `DhModule` class:

   ```
   public class DynamicHTML extends DhModule {
   ```

3. Override the loader method:

   ```
   public void documentLoad(Object sender, DhEvent p) {
   ```

4. Get the containing HTML document using the `getDocument()` method:

   ```
   DhDocument doc = getDocument();
   ```

5. Create any elements that you want to use:

   ```
   DhButton button1 = new DhButton();
   DhText text1 = new DhText("DynamicHTML");
   ```

6. Add elements to the document, with proper formatting:

   ```
   doc.add(text1);    // Add a text
   doc.add(button1);    // Add a button
   ```

7. Add any event handlers to the elements:

   ```
   button1.addOnClick(new DhEventHandler(button1Click));
   ```

8. Write the method that you've declared in Step 7:

   ```
   //button1Click is called whenever the button2 is clicked
   public void button1Click( Object sender, DhEvent e) {
   }
   ```

These steps can be seen in Listing 11-1.

Listing 11-1: DynamicHTML.java

```
//Step 1: import the wfc.html class
import wfc.html.*;  //Import the wfc.html package
// Step 2: Make a new class that inherits DhModule
public class DynamicHTML extends DhModule {
// Step 3: override the loader method
  public void documentLoad(Object sender, DhEvent p) {
  // Step 4: get the containing document
    DhDocument doc = getDocument();
  //Step 5: Create any elements
    DhButton button1 = new DhButton();
    DhButton button2 = new DhButton("Button 2");
    DhText text1 = new DhText("DynamicHTML");
  // Step 6: Add elements to the document
    button1.setText("Button 1");
    text1.setColor(DhColors.DARKMAGENTA);
    text1.setFont( "arial", 14 );
    doc.add(text1);    // Add a text
    doc.newLine();    // Go to the next line
```

```
      doc.newLine();    // Go to the next line
      doc.add(button1);  // Add a button
      doc.add(button2);  // Add a button
   // Step 7: Add any event handlers to the elements
      button1.addOnClick(new DhEventHandler(button1Click));
      button2.addOnClick(new DhEventHandler(button2Click));
   }
   // Step 8: Code the event handler
//button1Click is called whenever the button2 is clicked
   public void button1Click( Object sender, DhEvent e) {
   // Get the containing document
      DhDocument doc = getDocument();
   // Make a new text element
      DhText t = new DhText("Button 1 was clicked");
   // Add a new line to the containing document
      doc.newLine();
   // Add the text to the document
      doc.add(t);
   }
//button2Click is called whenever the button2 is clicked
   public void button2Click( Object sender, DhEvent e) {
   // Get the containing document
      DhDocument doc = getDocument();
   // Make a new text element
      DhText t = new DhText("Button 2 was clicked");
   // Add a new line to the containing document
      doc.newLine();
   // Add the text to the document
      doc.add(t);
   }
}
```

The output for Listing 11-1 can be viewed in Figure 11-2.

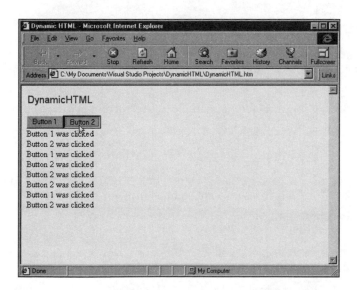

Figure 11-2: Dynamic HTML can be used to place items directly on the HTML page.

Working with Styles

In Listing 11-1, a heading was formed for the dynamic HTML Web page. That code looked like this:

```
text1.setColor(DhColors.DARKMAGENTA);
text1.setFont( "arial", 14 );
doc.add(text1);    // Add a text
```

While that's fine for one heading, say you wanted to add 15 headings. A large number of headings would dramatically increase your code size as well as your maintenance costs to change the heading color, size, or font.

Styles were introduced to capture all the text formatting options and place them in an encapsulated container. To accomplish the same task as the preceding code using the DhStyle class, you could do the following.

```
DhStyle s = new DhStyle();
s. setColor(DhColors.DARKMAGENTA);
s.setFont( "arial", 14 );
text1.setStyle(s);
doc.add(text1);    // Add a text
```

Secret

The power of a style is that when you make a change to a DhStyle during runtime, *all elements that use that style are automatically updated.* This enables you to change the color of several elements at once.

Secret

Styles are sometimes called "Cascading Styles" due to the way they behave. To determine which font to display, the program looks at the element it is displaying, the element's container, and then the container of the container (and so on). Finally, if no Style is set, DHTML displays the default font for the browser.

Working with Dynamic HTML Tables

Tables are often used inside HTML documents. These tables can be dynamically created using the DhTable, DhRow, and DhCell objects and the following steps:

1. Create a DhTable object and add it to the current HTML document:

   ```
   DhDocument doc = getDocument();  //Get the HTML document
   DhTable table = new DhTable();   //Make a new HTML table
   doc.add(table);              //Add the table to the document
   ```

2. Create a DhRow object that goes on your DhTable and add it to the table. Do this for each row you want to have on your table:

   ```
   DhRow dhr = new DhRow();     //Make a new row
   table.add(dhr);              //Add the row to the table
   ```

3. Create a DhCell object that goes on your DhRow. Do this for each cell you want per row:

   ```
   DhCell cell = new DhCell();    // Make a new cell
   dhr.add(cell);              //Add the cell to the row
   ```

4. Add an Element to each `DhCell`:

```
DhButton button = new DhButton(text);     //Make a new button
cell.add(button);             //Add the button to the cell
```

Listing 11-2 shows how you can make a table using DHTML.

Listing 11-2: **DynamicHTMLTable.java**

```
import wfc.html.*;
public class DynamicHTMLTable extends DhModule {
  public void documentLoad(Object sender, DhEvent p) {
    DhDocument doc = getDocument();  //Get the HTML document
  //Make a 3x5 Table
    DhTable table = new DhTable();  //Make a new HTML table
    for (int row = 0; row < 3; row++) {
      DhRow dhr = new DhRow();       //Make a new row
      for (int column = 0; column < 5; column++) {
      DhCell cell = new DhCell();     // Make a new cell
        String text = "Cell ("
          + Integer.toString(row+1)
          + ","
          + Integer.toString(column+1)
          + ")";
        DhButton button = new DhButton(text);  //Make a new button
        cell.add(button);         //Add the button to the cell
        dhr.add(cell);           //Add the cell to the row

      }
      table.add(dhr);            //Add the row to the table

    }
    doc.add(table);          //Add the table to the document
  }
}
```

Figure 11-3 shows the output from Listing 11-2.

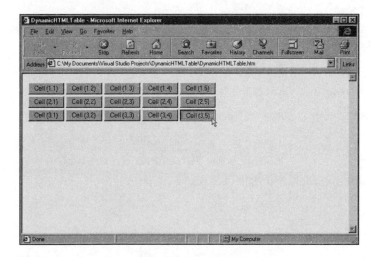

Figure 11-3: Tables can spice up any HTML page.

Examining Database DHTML Programming

What would Web programming be without databases (other than a lot easier)? Databases are a way of life, and they are necessary to stay even with competing Web pages. DHTML is one of the easiest ways to write database applications.

Secret

Like most DHTML constructs, you can write your own DHTML ODBC database application by following some simple steps:

1. Make a DHTML program that extends `DhModule`, **overrides** `documentLoad`, and retrieves the current HTML document using the `getDocument()` method:

```
public class DynamicHTMLDatabase extends DhModule {
  public void documentLoad(Object sender, DhEvent p) {
    try {
    //Get the current HTML document
      DhDocument doc = getDocument();
//. . .
```

2. Make a new instance of the `DhODBCTable`. A `DhODBCTable` is an extension of a table that facilitates ODBC access:

```
DhODBCTable db = new DhODBCTable();
```

3. Set the titles on. This provides some ease of programming.

```
db.setAutoHeader(true);
```

4. Define a repeater row. A repeater row is a `DhRow` instance that is passed to the database so it can contain all the values and repeat as needed:

```
DhRow dataRow = new DhRow();
```

5. Make new elements and bind them to the ODBC database:

```
DhEdit Name = new DhEdit();
Name.setDataField("Name");
```

6. Make `DhCells` to hold the new database-bound elements and add these cells to the repeater row:

```
DhCell NameCell = new DhCell();
NameCell.add(Name);
dataRow.add(NameCell);
```

7. Make your `DhODBCTable` connect to your database:

```
db.setConnectionString("UID=admin;PWD=;DSN=EmpDB");
```

8. Send your `DhODBCTable` some SQL and send it the repeater row:

```
//Do the SQL from the table
  db.setSQL("Select  "Name "
    + "From  Employee ",
//Don't forget the repeater row
    dataRow);
```

9. Finally, add the dhODBCTable to your DhModule HTML:

```
doc.add(db);
```

Listing 11-3 shows these steps, and Figure 11-4 shows the output.

Listing 11-3: DynamicHTMLDatabase.java

```java
import wfc.html.*;
public class DynamicHTMLDatabase extends DhModule {
  public void documentLoad(Object sender, DhEvent p) {
    try {
    //Get the current HTML document
      DhDocument doc = getDocument();
    //Make a new ODBC Table
      DhODBCTable db = new DhODBCTable();
    //Turn the titles on
      db.setAutoHeader(true);
    //Make a repeater row containing all the column formats
      DhRow dataRow = new DhRow();
    //Make Elements to bind to the database
      DhText EmployeeID = new DhText();
      DhEdit Name = new DhEdit();
      DhEdit SSN = new DhEdit();
      DhEdit Supervisor = new DhEdit();
      DhCheckBox Probation = new DhCheckBox();
      DhCheckBox Flextime = new DhCheckBox();
      DhCheckBox Benefits = new DhCheckBox();
    //Bind new elements to the database
      EmployeeID.setDataField("EmployeeID");
      Name.setDataField("Name");
      SSN.setDataField("SSN");
      Supervisor.setDataField("Supervisor");
      Probation.setDataField("Probation");
      Flextime.setDataField("Flextime");
      Benefits.setDataField("Benefits");
    //Make cells for the id
      DhCell EmployeeIDCell = new DhCell();
      EmployeeIDCell.add(EmployeeID);
      dataRow.add(EmployeeIDCell);
      DhCell NameCell = new DhCell();
      NameCell.add(Name);
      dataRow.add(NameCell);
      DhCell SSNCell = new DhCell();
      SSNCell.add(SSN);
      dataRow.add(SSNCell);
      DhCell SupervisorCell = new DhCell();
      SupervisorCell.add(Supervisor);
      dataRow.add(SupervisorCell);
      DhCell ProbationCell = new DhCell();
      ProbationCell.add(Probation);
      dataRow.add(ProbationCell);
      DhCell FlextimeCell = new DhCell();
      FlextimeCell.add(Flextime);
```

```
        dataRow.add(FlextimeCell);
        DhCell BenefitsCell = new DhCell();
        BenefitsCell.add(Benefits);
        dataRow.add(BenefitsCell);
    //Set the ODBC Connection String
        db.setConnectionString("UID=admin;PWD=;DSN=EmpDB");
    //Do the SQL from the table
        db.setSQL("Select  EmployeeID, "
            + "Name, "
            + "SSN, "
            + "Supervisor, "
            + "Probation, "
            + "Flextime, "
            + "Benefits "
          + "From  Employee ",
      //Don't forget the repeater row
        dataRow);
      doc.add(db);
    }
  catch (Throwable t) {
    handleThrowable(t);
    }
  }

  void handleThrowable(Throwable t) {  //Print an error message
      t.printStackTrace();
      wfc.ui.MessageBox.show(t.toString());
    }
}
```

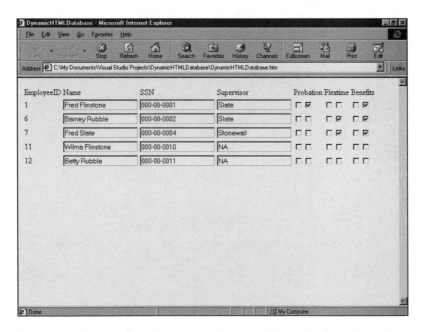

Figure 11-4: Databases used to separate the average Java developers from the truly great Java developers until Visual J++ made it easy.

Using Server DHTML, Client HTML, and Active Server Pages

Let's do a recap of the Visual J++ environment. First, Sun developed Java. Microsoft was not satisfied with Java's interface with Windows, and added WFC support to their Visual J++ tool. Now I have just described *yet another, entirely different,* way to code, this time *only supporting Internet Explorer.* Ordinarily, I would say that Microsoft has gone too far giving a developer three different ways to develop on the same environment.

However, DHTML is different when implemented in a client-server fashion using an Active Server Page (ASP). Instead of using ActiveX objects to execute dynamic HTML (as was done thus far), ASPs enable you to set up a DHTML server. This provides straight HTML to the client browser, enabling any Web browser to access your DHTML files.

To make your Java program ASP-compliant, follow these steps:

1. Register the class using the `javareg` utility. For example, to register a `DynamicHTMLServer` class, type:

   ```
   "C:\Program Files\Microsoft Visual Studio\VJ98\ JAVAREG.EXE "
   /register /class:DynamicHTMLServer /prodid:DynamicHTMLServer
   ```

   The results of this program can be seen in a message box that tells about your new OLE class ID, as seen in Figure 11-5.

   Figure 11-5: When run correctly, the javareg.exe program returns the class ID for your Java class.

2. Copy your .htm or .html file into an .asp file.

3. Change your HTML file. The current HTML file looks like this:

   ```
   <HTML>
   <HEAD>
   <TITLE>DynamicHTMLServer</TITLE>
   </HEAD>
   <BODY>
   <OBJECT classid="java:DynamicHTMLServer" height=0
   width=0></OBJECT>
   </BODY>
   </HTML>
   ```

Change it to call the ASP `Server.CreateObject()` method:

```
<HTML>
<HEAD>
<TITLE>DynamicHTMLServer</TITLE>
</HEAD>
<BODY>
<%Server.CreateObject("DynamicHTMLServer")%>
</BODY>
</HTML>
```

At run time, the framework recognizes that your wfc.html-based class is running on a server and acts accordingly. Once instantiated, all the sending of HTML is performed when you call the `DhModule.write()` method in your inherited class. The `write()` method in a server class is similar to the `add()` method in a client class; however, instead of adding the element to the document, it is sent to the client in a serial stream. If you happen to be running a client machine, the `write()` method is automatically converted to an `add()` method. Listing 11-4 shows how easily the `DynamicHTMLTable` class is converted to a `DynamicHTMLServer` class.

Listing 11-4: DynamicHTMLServer.java

```java
import wfc.html.*;
public class DynamicHTMLServer extends DhModule {
  public void documentLoad(Object sender, DhEvent p) {
    DhDocument doc = getDocument();
        DhSection section = new DhSection();
    DhText title = new DhText();
        if (getServerMode()) {
      title.setText( "Dynamic HTML running on the server" );
        }
    else {
      title.setText( "Dynamic HTML running on the  client" );
        }
  //Make a 3x5 Table
    section.add(title);
    section.newLine();
    DhTable table = new DhTable();
    for (int row = 0; row < 3; row++) {
      DhRow dhr = new DhRow();
      for (int column = 0; column < 5; column++) {
        DhCell cell = new DhCell();
        String text = "Cell ("
          + Integer.toString(row+1)
          + ","
          + Integer.toString(column+1)
          + ")";
        DhButton button = new DhButton(text);
        cell.add(button);
        dhr.add(cell);
      }
      table.add(dhr);
    }
    section.add(table);  // Add the table
  // Write will send the section down to the client
```

```
    // If this is running on the server, it will be added to the
document.
    write(section);
  }
}
```

Figure 11-6 shows the output of Listing 11-4.

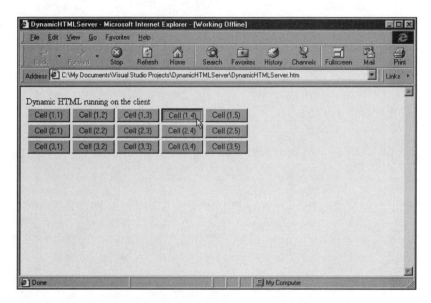

Figure 11-6: Server-side ASP programming makes it transparent to the user how the Visual J++ program is being executed.

Summary

The real power of dynamic HTML is the capability to send straight HTML to the client machine while running dynamic HTML on the server machine. This gives the server-machine developer the freedom to develop — using any tool he or she wants to use.

- Microsoft provides Visual J++ with an innovative method for calling IE 4.0's Dynamic HTML.

- Dynamic HTML Visual J++ programs are written using the wfc.html package, which is quite complex.

- Always extend `DhModule` and use the `getDocument()` method to retrieve the containing HTML document.

- Dynamic HTML can do some pretty neat stuff, including dynamic tables and ODBC database access.

Chapter 12

Using Delegates

Many languages use function pointers in programs to pass the address of a function or method. Microsoft Visual J++ 6 includes *delegates*, which are a powerful new language feature that passes a method as a parameter. Unlike function pointers found in languages such as C, C++, and Pascal, delegates are object-oriented, type-safe, and secure.

Secret

Sun has already criticized Microsoft for adding low-level constructs to the Java language specification without their approval. Although Sun has developed ways — through interfaces, adapter classes, and nested classes — to address all of the functionality found in delegates, delegates are, for the most part, *easier to use, more powerful,* and *more efficient* than Sun's constructs. However, Sun has claimed that it will *never* (which is a long time for such a promise) support delegates (time will tell), so any code you write using delegates needs to run on the IE 4.0 Java Virtual Machine.

What Are Delegates?

Delegates are simply wrappers that enable a developer to pass a method to another method. A delegate instance encapsulates a method. If you have a delegate instance and an appropriate set of arguments, you can invoke the delegate with the arguments. You've already used delegates if you've done any WFC or ADO programming. Listing 12-1 is a dynamic HTML program that uses delegates to pass the event handlers for the `addOnClick()` methods:

Listing 12-1: DelegateButton.java

```
import wfc.html.*;
public class DelegateButton extends DhModule {
DhButton bu_OK = new DhButton();     //Create a DHTML button
  DhButton bu_cancel = new DhButton(); //Create a DHTML button
  public void documentLoad(Object sender, DhEvent p) {
    bu_OK.setText("OK");       //Set the button text
    bu_OK.setLocation(10,10);     //Set the button location
    bu_cancel.setText("Cancel");     //Set the button text
    bu_cancel.setLocation(100,10);  //Set the button location
  //Use delgates to pass the bu_OKClick method
    bu_OK.addOnClick(new DhEventHandler(bu_OKClick));
  //Use delgates to pass the bu_cancelClick method
    bu_cancel.addOnClick(new DhEventHandler(bu_cancelClick));
  // Get the containing document
    DhDocument doc = getDocument();
  //Add the WFC buttons to the HTML documment
    doc.add(bu_OK);          // Add a button
    doc.add(bu_cancel);         // Add a button
    doc.newLine();
  }
  void bu_OKClick(Object sender, DhEvent e) {
    buttonMessage("Clicked OK");
  }
  void bu_cancelClick(Object sender, DhEvent e) {
    buttonMessage("Clicked Cancel");
  }
  void buttonMessage(String message) {
  // Get the containing document
    DhDocument doc = getDocument();
  // Make a new text element
    DhText t = new DhText(message);
  // Add a new line to the containing document
    doc.newLine();
  // Add the text to the document
    doc.add(t);
  }
}
```

Microsoft has written a method, addOnClick(), that requires a delegate to be passed to it. In the code above, the addresses of methods, bu_OKClick and bu_cancelClick, are passed to the addOnClick() method using delegates. As seen by the code above, WFC events require the use of delegates.

How to Program Delegates

An interesting and useful property of a delegate is that it is not sensitive to the class of the object that it references. A delegate can reference any object as long as the method's signature matches the delegate's signature. This makes delegates perfectly suited for "anonymous" invocation—a powerful capability.

Like Java interfaces, delegates are used to communicate with other classes so that these other classes can execute methods from the calling class. However, delegates are declared at the method level. This can be contrasted with Java interfaces, which work at the class level. A complete comparison between Java interfaces and Visual J++ delegates can be found later on in this chapter.

Defining and using delegates has three steps:

- declaration of the delegate
- instantiation of the delegate
- invocation of the delegate

Declaring a delegate

You declare delegates using Visual J++ delegate declaration syntax, which can appear in the same places in code as class declarations. The syntax looks like this:

```
modifier delegate returnType delegateName(parameter list);
```

As an example, consider this delegate declaration:

```
public delegate boolean DelegateCompare(Object o1, Object o2);
```

Delegates are types of classes that consist of one method. In the preceding example, a public delegate, named DelegateCompare, is declared that returns a Boolean type and takes two object parameters.

Instantiating a delegate

After declaring a delegate, you must instantiate it. An example shows this best. Place the following code, which continues to use DelegateCompare, inside a class to instantiate the delegate and bind it to a method:

```
public boolean isGreaterThan (Object string1, Object string2) {
   String s1 = (String) string 1;
   String s2 = (String) string 2;
   if (s1.compareTo(s2) < 1) {
     return false;
   }
   return true;
}
public void method ( ) {
//In some other method, a delegate is declared
   DelegateCompare dc = new DelegateCompare(isGreaterThan);
   DelegateSort ds = new DelegateSort(dc, (Object[ ]) programmers);
//. . .
}
```

The preceding code defines a method called isGreaterThan that contains two Object parameters. These objects are converted to Strings and then compared to see which one is greater. A false is returned if string1 is not greater than string2. Later a method uses the isGreaterThan() method as a parameter to construct a DelegateCompare delegate that was declared in the previous section. Then a new instance of a DelegateSort class is declared which takes the delegate and an Object array as parameters.

Invoking a delegate

Consider the following DelegateSort class. The DelegateSort class takes the DelegateCompare variable as a parameter. When needed, the calling module is invoked using the delegate.invoke() method, as shown in bold:

```
public class DelegateSort {
  public DelegateSort(DelegateCompare dc, Object object_array [ ]) {
// Go through the array several times
    for (int loop1 = 0;
      loop1 < object_array.length;
      loop1++) {
      for (int loop2 = 0;
        loop2 < object_array.length - loop1 - 1;
        loop2++) {
// Swap array elements if they aren't in the right order
        if (dc.invoke(object_array[loop2], object_array[loop2 + 1])) {
          Object holder;
          holder = object_array[loop2];
          object_array[loop2] = object_array[loop2 + 1];
          object_array[loop2 + 1] = holder;
        }
      }
    }
  }
}
```

Writing a Delegate System

Delegates act as a bridge between two classes. The preceding example uses CompareDelegate to bridge the DelegateSort and the DelegateTopProgrammers classes, as shown in Figure 12-1.

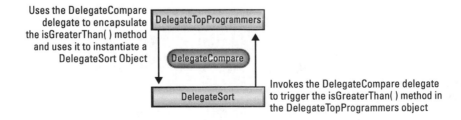

Uses the DelegateCompare delegate to encapsulate the isGreaterThan( ) method and uses it to instantiate a DelegateSort Object

Invokes the DelegateCompare delegate to trigger the isGreaterThan( ) method in the DelegateTopProgrammers object

Figure 12-1: Like Java interfaces, delegates act as a bridge between two different classes.

Listing 12-2 shows a variant of the preceding code examples. The
`DelegateTopProgrammers` class, shown in Listing 12-4, differs by having its
own sort mechanisms for sorting by lines of code, but always places
supervisors last. Listings 12-2 through 12-4 show all the code for the
`DelegateTopProgrammers` class, the `DelegateSort` class, and the
`DelegateCompare` delegate.

Listing 12-2: DelegateCompare.java

```
public delegate boolean DelegateCompare(Object o1, Object o2);
```

Listing 12-3: DelegateSort.java

```
public class DelegateSort {
    public DelegateSort(DelegateCompare dc, Object object_array [ ])
{
// Go through the array several times
        for (int loop1 = 0;
                loop1 < object_array.length;
                loop1++) {
            for (int loop2 = 0;
                    loop2 < object_array.length - loop1 - 1;
                    loop2++) {
// Swap array elements if they aren't in the right order
                if (dc.invoke(object_array[loop2],
                                object_array[loop2 + 1])) {
                    Object holder;
                    holder = object_array[loop2];
                    object_array[loop2] =
                                        object_array[loop2 + 1];
                    object_array[loop2 + 1] = holder;
                }
            }
        }
    }
}
```

Listing 12-4: DelegateTopProgrammers.java

```
import wfc.html.*;
public class DelegateTopProgrammers extends DhModule {
  private final int NUMBERPROGRAMMERS = 12;
  public void documentLoad(Object sender, DhEvent p) {
      Programmer programmers[] = new Programmer[NUMBERPROGRAMMERS];
//Create the programmers
    programmers[0] = new Programmer("Sally Gatti",     65123);
    programmers[1] = new Programmer("Craig Johnson",   75123);
    programmers[2] = new Programmer("Michelle Lehman", 62123);
    programmers[3] = new Programmer("Susan Neeves",    37564);
    programmers[4] = new Programmer("Dave O'Hearn",    64345);
    programmers[5] = new Programmer("Charles Oliva",   92365);
    programmers[6] = new Programmer("Jim Rang",        61123);
    programmers[7] = new Programmer("Jeff Rhoad",      65345);
    programmers[8] = new Programmer("Rajinder Sondhe", 54345);
    programmers[9] = new Programmer("Lance Tillman",   89573);
    programmers[10] = new Programmer("Kent Wisco",     46454);
//Create the supervisor
```

```
        int sectionTotal = 0;
        for (int loop = 0; loop < NUMBERPROGRAMMERS - 1; loop++) {
          sectionTotal += programmers[loop].getLines();
        }
        programmers[NUMBERPROGRAMMERS - 1] = new Programmer("Marv
Taylor", sectionTotal, true);
        DelegateCompare dc = new DelegateCompare(isGreaterThan);
        DelegateSort ds = new DelegateSort(dc, (Object[ ]) programmers);
        DhDocument doc = getDocument();
        DhStyle titleStyle = new DhStyle();
        DhStyle colHeadStyle = new DhStyle();
        DhStyle columnStyle = new DhStyle();
        DhText title = new DhText("This Year's Top Programmers ");
        titleStyle.setColor(DhColors.DARKMAGENTA);
        titleStyle.setFont( "Times New Roman", 18, DhStyleBase.BOLD);
        title.setStyle(titleStyle);
        title.setLocation(30, 10);
        doc.add(title);
        DhText colHead1 = new DhText("Programmer");
        DhText colHead2 = new DhText("Lines of Code");
        colHeadStyle.setColor(DhColors.BLACK);
        colHeadStyle.setFont("Times New Roman", 14, DhStyleBase.BOLD);
        colHead1.setLocation(50, 40);
        colHead2.setLocation(205,40);
        colHead1.setStyle(colHeadStyle);
        colHead2.setStyle(colHeadStyle);
        doc.add(colHead1);
        doc.add(colHead2);
        columnStyle.setColor(DhColors.BLACK);
        columnStyle.setFont("Times New Roman", 12);
        doc.setStyle(columnStyle);
        for (int loop = 0; loop < NUMBERPROGRAMMERS; loop++) {
          DhText name = new DhText(programmers[loop].getName());
          DhText lines = new DhText();
          name.setStyle(columnStyle);
          lines.setStyle(columnStyle);
          String sup = "";
          int x = 250;
          if (programmers[loop].getSupervisor()) {
            sup = " (Supervisor)";
            x -= 7;
          }
          name.setLocation(50, 15*loop+60);
          lines.setText(Integer.toString(programmers[loop].getLines()) +
sup);
          lines.setLocation(x, 15*loop+60);
          doc.add(name);
          doc.add(lines);
        }
        }

// Because you want high programmers on top IN DESCENDING ORDER,
// "greater than" means having a lower lines of code.  The low
```

```
// number of lines is at the bottom of the array and the high
// number of lines is in the first array of elements.
// Supervisors are always at the bottom of the sort.
    public boolean isGreaterThan (Object o1, Object o2) {
        Programmer c1 = (Programmer) o1;
        Programmer c2 = (Programmer) o2;
    if (c1.getSupervisor() && !c2.getSupervisor()) {
      return true;
    }
    else if (!c1.getSupervisor() && c2.getSupervisor()) {
      return false;
    }
    else if (c1.getLines() < c2.getLines()) {
      return true;
    }
    String s;
    s.compareTo
    return false;
    }
}

final class Programmer {
  private boolean ib_supervisor;
  private String is_programmerName;
  private int ii_linesOfCode;
  public Programmer(String name, int amount) {
    is_programmerName = new String(name);
    ii_linesOfCode = amount;
    ib_supervisor = false;
  }
  public Programmer(String name, int amount, boolean supervisor) {
    is_programmerName = new String(name);
    ii_linesOfCode = amount;
    ib_supervisor = supervisor;
  }
  public int getLines() {
    return ii_linesOfCode;
  }
  public String getName() {
    return is_programmerName;
  }
  public boolean getSupervisor() {
    return ib_supervisor;
  }
}
```

Listing 12-2 through Listing 12-4 show how a special sort can be achieved by using a delegate to a compare method. By using delegates in a sort, a developer is free to sort any Object since the calling class also defines the comparison routine. The DelegateTopProgrammers.Java program defines the isGreaterThan routine to place the supervisors at the bottom of the list and then to sort the lowest amount of lines of code at the bottom. The output for Listing 12-2 through Listing 12-4 is shown in Figure 12-2.

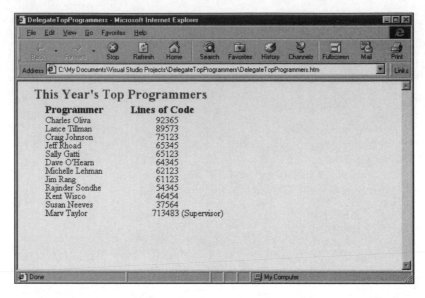

Figure 12-2: Delegates can be used for powerful, yet elegant, programming techniques.

Multicast Delegates

In addition to "normal" delegates, Visual J++ provides support for "multicast" delegates. Whereas normal delegates may invoke one method per use, multicast delegates may invoke a list of methods to be executed. The set of methods called by a multicast delegate is called the *invocation list*.

To declare a multicast delegate, add the keyword, multicast, in front of the keyword, delegate:

```
public multicast delegate boolean methodName(Object parameters);
```

Multicast delegates are different from regular delegates in several ways:

Secret

- Multicast delegates must have a void return type. Because multiple methods can be executed from a single delegate, it makes no sense to try to capture a single result.

- When a multicast delegate is invoked, the methods in the invocation list are invoked synchronously, in the order in which they appear in the list.

- If a method raises an exception, then the multicast ceases and the exception is propagated to the class that invoked the delegate.

Java has no multicast equivalent, although you can mimic multicast delegates by using a combination of adapter classes and inner classes (as shown in the next section).

Delegates Under the Hood

Although Microsoft added two key words, multicast and delegate, to their Java syntax, the compiler converts all delegate entries into `com.ms.com.Delegate` and `com.ms.com.` `MulticastDelegate` classes. This means you can deploy delegates to any machine whose Java Virtual Machine supports COM and ActiveX Java interfaces.

Delegates Versus Inner Classes and Adapter Classes

Inner classes are new to Java 1.1 and Visual J++ 6. Inner classes enable you to construct a class within another class. Although this class does not have a name per se, it can contain methods that can be used not only as parameters, but also as delegates:

```
class ButtonApplet extends Applet {
  private Button bu_OK = new Button("OK");    //new OK button
  public void bu_OKClick(ActionEvent e) {     //bu_OK was clicked
    //code for the OK clicked event
  }
  public void init() {              //Set up the Web page
    setLayout(new BorderLayout());
    // add a listener to bu_OK
  //ActionListener is an adapter class
    bu_OK.addActionListener(new ActionListener()
  //Here's the nested class
      {    //Make a new action listener
        public void actionPerformed(ActionEvent e) {
          bu_OKClick(e);
        }
      }
    );
    //Add the button to the north of the applet
    this.add("North", bu_OK);
  }
}
```

The following WFC delegate version can be contrasted with the preceding nested class adapter class version:

```
class SimpleForm extends Form {
  private Button bu_OK = new Button();
  public void bu_OKClick(ActionEvent e) {     //bu_OK was clicked
    //code for the OK clicked event
  }
  void initForm() {
    bu_OK.setText("OK");
```

```
//Use a delegate to pass an event handler
  bu_OK.addOnClick(new EventHandler(bu_OKClick));
  //Add the button to the north of the applet
  setNewControls(new Control[] {bu_OK});
}
}
```

As you can see by the preceding code, delegates and inner classes are comparable, and inner classes, in combination with listeners, give the user method-level control (as opposed to class-level control) over their programs and easily mimic the functionality found in delegates.

Delegates Versus Interfaces

Visual J++ delegates and Java interfaces are similar:

- Both exist as constructs separate from classes.

- Both act as a bridge between two classes.

- Both enable the called class to execute methods in the calling class.

You might ask why Microsoft came up with delegates at all. It's a good question, and one that has embroiled people in a hot debate. Microsoft's answer is that interfaces have shortcomings that limit their usefulness:

- A class can only implement an interface once. The Visual J++ multicast modifier enables you to implement a delegate to invoke more than one method, and a regular delegate can be implemented in a single class using many different methods as long as the parameter and return types agree.

- If two interfaces have the same name for methods contained in the interface, name collisions between interface members can occur. This might make it impossible for a class to implement certain multiple interface combinations.

- A class that implements an interface must expose the implemented members publicly. Delegates enable the developer to keep member methods private.

Delegates Versus Traditional Function Pointers

There has been much talk about delegates being function pointers like those found in C and C++. Delegates are, after all, a type of function pointer, but delegates address many issues that traditional function pointers ignore:

- Delegates are object-oriented. Function pointers are addresses to methods and actually violate the object-oriented paradigm of encapsulation. By contrast, delegate declarations are compiled into classes, are instantiated, and behave just like other instances.

- Delegates are type safe, whereas C++ pointers can be cast arbitrarily. The Visual J++ compiler and the Microsoft Java Virtual Machine enforce delegate type. To be encapsulated by a delegate, a method must meet the following conditions:

  - It must contain the same number and type of parameters as the method.

  - The return type of the method must match the return type of the delegate.

  - The method must throw the same exceptions as the delegate.

- Delegates are secure. The Microsoft Virtual Machine ensures that delegates interact well with the security system: less trusted code can't create a delegate onto more trusted code and thus gain illicit access to additional capabilities.

Sun Versus Microsoft

Sun has raised these issues about interfaces:

- Adapter classes, interfaces, and nested classes enable you to address all of the functionality that delegates introduce.

- Interfaces follow the Java standard and are supported on every Java Virtual Machine. Delegates aren't.

- Sun's main point is that Microsoft is adding a feature that doesn't work on standard Java Virtual Machines. Sun also claims that interfaces are better than delegates.

So who is right?

Sun makes some valid points. However, Sun currently controls and dictates Java development. Microsoft may be strong enough to steal that control from them, especially if other companies start putting Microsoft concepts inside their Java code. When other companies such as Borland and Sybase make additions to their Java offerings, Sun doesn't comment. When Microsoft makes changes, Sun gets worried.

Microsoft raises three main points:

- Delegates are better than interfaces because the code needed to manipulate delegates is easier than interface coding. (I think they may have a point.)

- Competition helps the user by providing choices of development environments and techniques.

- Microsoft needs to differentiate Visual J++ from other products if they are to have people buy it for their Java development.

Microsoft makes some valid points. However, Java program development may stray from the Windows standard toward the Java standard. If Java gets enough support to become a true standard like Windows, Windows may then lose control of the market. Java could, to Microsoft's detriment, begin leveling the prepackaged-software playing field. (Sure, this will probably never happen, but when you're Microsoft, what else would you have to worry about?)

All that being said, delegates are, frequently, an easier, more useful implementation than interfaces. If interfaces were as easy to use, as easy to understand, or as powerful, Microsoft would not have challenged the Java standard on that point.

If you intend to develop for Microsoft machines or intend to use ADO, DHTML, and WFC, use delegates. They are easier to code and easier to understand. However, if you intend to develop for multiple browsers and multiple operating systems, stay away from delegates and stick with interfaces.

Summary

Delegates are a way to encapsulate method pointers and use them as parameter types. By introducing a new keyword to the Java language, Microsoft has created quite a stir — especially with Sun.

- Multicast delegates enable you to invoke more than one method with each delegate call. Java's only real equivalent requires writing a lot of code.

- Standard Java can easily and completely mimic Delegate functionality by using interfaces in conjunction with inner classes.

- If you want to deploy your solution to non-Microsoft Virtual Machines, avoid delegates.

- If you are developing EXE files or writing over an intranet where the only virtual machines in use are Microsoft Virtual Machines, go ahead and use delegates. They are easy to use and a nice addition to the language.

Chapter 13

Enterprise-Wide Development

Get ready to be impressed. Traditionally, Java development consisted of deploying a class or set of classes to a Web site to be run in isolation. Even data access was severely limited in the earlier versions of Java. Now, Visual J++ Enterprise Edition delivers a secure way to have multiple developers on a single project and ways to use multi-tier architecture in a way traditional Java developers can only dream of.

Mastering DNA and Enterprise-wide Development

As with all buzzwords, *enterprise development* is often used and misused in different contexts. In the context of this book, enterprise-wide development has at least one of two components:

■ Multiple people working on the same project

■ Multiple levels of applications (for example, server and client). Figure 13-1 shows a traditional three-tier architecture.

Microsoft has coined their own term to describe client-server development over the Internet. They call it Windows Distributed interNet Applications (DNA). The DNA framework enables developers to build scalable, multi-tier applications that can be delivered over any Windows server network. Even non-Windows applications can access a DNA framework. The Visual Studio Enterprise Edition comes with a development tool suite that addresses all aspects of enterprise application development based on the DNA framework. Visual J++ Enterprise Edition includes support for the Microsoft Transaction Server (MTS) so that developers can use components inside the MTS for multi-tier development.

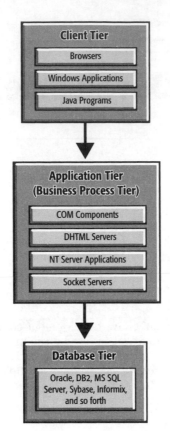

Figure 13-1: Traditional three-tier architecture

In addition to multi-tier support, Microsoft includes a myriad of team development features, including Microsoft Visual SourceSafe, the Microsoft Repository, and the Microsoft Visual Component Manager. All of these features are documented in this chapter.

Using Microsoft Visual SourceSafe

Initially, Java was used for small Applet development over the Web. Individual programmers developed small classes that Java-aware browsers could take advantage of. Now, it's a different story. You can find major corporations doing huge Java development efforts, lured by the promise of "write once, run anywhere" and of complex Web page development. Team development efforts have complicated the simple single-developer environments found when Java was in its infancy.

Microsoft Visual SourceSafe (VSS) is a tool, included with Visual J++ Enterprise Edition, that provides version control of source code. When using SourceSafe, a team of developers can manage projects, regardless of the file type (text files, graphics files, binary files, sound files, or video files), by saving them to a VSS database. When you need to share files between two or more projects, you can share them quickly and efficiently.

VSS gives several advantages to group members:

- Files in the VSS repository are backed up on the VSS database.

- All files are made available to other developers.

- Files can be "checked out" by a developer and only be available through read-only control to other developers. Other developers cannot update checked-out files until the files are "checked in" by the current developer. This control stops one developer from writing over another developer's changes. (If you've ever worked in a team environment, you know what a nightmare "overwrites" can be.)

- File changes are saved so you can recover an old version of a file at any time, even if that old version has been replaced by a newer version. (How often have you wished that you had the old source code back because you've long since overwritten it with unworkable code?)

- Developers on a team can see the latest version of any file, make changes, and save a new version of the file in the VSS database.

VSS is a separate, standalone system that is used for version control. However, VSS functions can be accessed directly from Visual J++. VSS is automatically integrated into your Visual J++ development environment, and you do not need to run VSS separately to realize the advantages of VSS source code control.

Traditionally, version control software has required tremendous overhead. Learning curves were steep, maintenance was a nightmare, and, usually, a full-time (and expensive) developer was needed simply to manage the version control. VSS may change all of that:

- Although there is a lot to VSS, it is so easy to use and intuitive that little training, if any, is necessary. (You still may want to take a class or review the documentation because it contains many features that may help your team development.)

- Because it is integrated with Visual Studio, you don't have to worry about multiple environments.

- It's stable and doesn't require much time to use. It also almost works automatically, thereby providing the developer more time to develop.

There are three major steps to VSS:

1. You must add users to your VSS environment.

2. You must add projects to your VSS repository.

3. Your developers must check these files out to make modifications, and check them back in when the modifications are done before others can check them out.

Secret

Before you begin, if you don't see a Project, Source Control choice in your Visual J++ menu, you have not installed Source Safe from your Installation CDs, or you are not running Visual J++ Enterprise Edition. (You are running Visual J++ Professional Edition.) If you are on a team, you will probably want to buy the Enterprise Edition for this tool alone, although it costs more. Otherwise, you may spend thousands of dollars in lost code, version-control problems, and overwrites.

Adding a VSS User using the VSS Administrator

To add a new user, you must leave the "normal" set of Visual Studio programs and run the Visual SourceSafe Administrator. Whenever you start to use VSS or the VSS Administrator, you need to log in to the system. VSS comes with an Admin and a Guest user IDs with no passwords. Log in as Admin, using the default database repository, as shown in Figure 13-2.

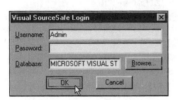

Figure 13-2: You log in to the VSS database before using the version control.

The VSS Administrator opens and lists all current users for VSS, as shown in Figure 13-3.

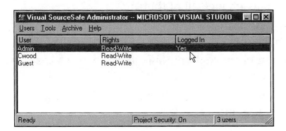

Figure 13-3: Use the VSS Administrator to add and remove users from the VSS environment.

The VSS Administrator can add or remove users, change passwords, or assign security to specific projects. Choose Users, Add Users from the VSS Administrator menu to open the Add User dialog box, as shown in Figure 13-4.

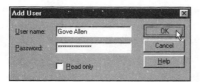

Figure 13-4: The Add User dialog box enables you to add developers to the Visual SourceSafe repository so that they can check in and check out entries.

Adding a user is one of the few times a developer needs to leave the Visual J++ environment and go to the SourceSafe environment. (However, if you want to, you can enter the SourceSafe environment through the Visual J++ menu by choosing Project, Source Control, SourceSafe.)

Adding a Project to VSS

If you want VSS to control a project, you must list that project with VSS. To do this, choose Project, Source Control, Add to Source Control from the Visual J++ menu (Figure 13-5).

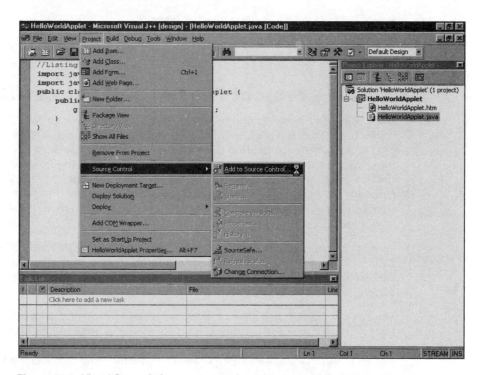

Figure 13-5: Visual SourceSafe source control can be managed through the Visual J++ environment.

The Add to Source Control dialog box appears. Click to add elements to the VSS repository. In Figure 13-6, the Java and HTML files are added to the VSS repository, but the Visual J++ project and Visual J++ Solution files are not.

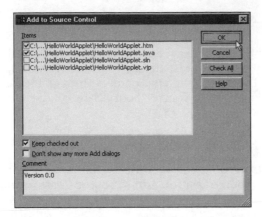

Figure 13-6: Use the Add to Source Control dialog box to choose which elements of your project that you want to add to the VSS source control repository.

Checking Project Files In and Out of VSS

Depending on the options you choose when you add your project to the VSS repository, your project files must be checked out before modification and checked in after modification. When you want to modify a Java program, you must check it out of the VSS database. VSS then copies the file from the VSS database into your working folder. If anyone else attempts to check out the same file for editing, VSS generates a message stating the file is already checked out. Checkouts ensure that one user does not overwrite another user's work.

Secret

You can change the project properties to allow multiple checkouts of the same text file to different users. The multiuser checkout mode automatically merges code or provides a manual merge mode. However, multiple users can't check out binary files (such as EXE files).

To check out a specific file in a database, choose Project, Source Control, Check Out *filename*, where filename is the name of your highlighted file in the Project Explorer. This opens The Check out item(s) dialog box shown in Figure 13-7. Here you can agree to check out a file from the VSS database.

After you finish editing the document, you check it into VSS. This copies the modified document from your folder into the VSS database, making your changes accessible to other users. VSS stores all the changes that have been made to the document; the most recent copy is always available, but earlier versions can be retrieved as well.

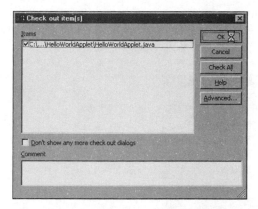

Figure 13-7: The Check out item(s) dialog box enables you to start modifying VSS project code.

After a project has been added to VSS, the current lock status of the files is displayed in the Project Explorer; see Figure 13-8. If you have a file checked out, a check appears next to the filename. If you have not checked out the file, a padlock appears next to the filename.

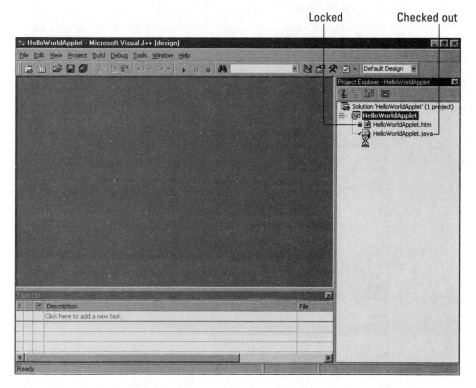

Figure 13-8: Visual Studio shows you which files have been checked out and which files are locked.

You are allowed to open a file that is not checked out, but if you try to work on it, you get a message telling you the file is not currently checked out and that it needs to be checked out for modifications (Figure 13-9).

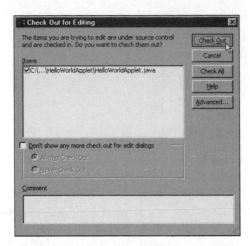

Figure 13-9: Visual J++, in conjunction with VSS, does not allow modifications to a file that has not been checked out.

When you are finished with a file, you can check it in by choosing Projects, Source Control, Check in *filename,* where *filename* is the name of the file you have highlighted in the Project Explorer. You can highlight more than one file in the Project Explorer, and the Check In window asks which items you want checked back in (Figure 13-10).

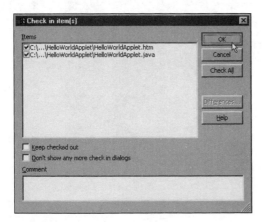

Figure 13-10: The Check in item(s) dialog box enables you to let others modify VSS project code.

HEY! I Only Have So Much Disk Space!

You may wonder how you are going to fit all your previous file versions if VSS stores all the previous versions of your files. VSS doesn't store entire copies of files, but rather uses a process called "reverse delta technology." The reverse delta process is a way of logically ANDing and ORing two files together to capture the differences between the two files. Then the result is compressed. Reverse delta technology ensures that all versions of a file are available, but a minimum of disk space is used.

Coding for the Microsoft Transaction Server

Microsoft Transaction Server (MTS) is a component-based transaction processing system for managing Internet and intranet server applications. MTS uses Microsoft's Distributed Common Object Module (DCOM) standard so all applications can access MTS with quick and scalable ActiveX components. Visual J++ enables developers to build MTS objects. Visual J++ automatically generates all of the associated type library and MTS information needed to register the Java object as a COM-callable MTS object.

Writing MTS Server Components

MTS component development is controlled through the Visual J++ Class Builder. To open the Class Builder, select the JAVA file from the Project Explorer that contains the class you want to modify. On the View menu, point to Other Windows and click Class Builder. This opens the class builder as shown in Figure 13-11. Be sure to indicate that MTS support is enabled. You can also specify to what degree it will participate in transactions, but I wouldn't require it unless needed (to maintain cross-server compatibility).

The Class Builder automatically inserts the OLE class id for the `@com` code and initializes the `@com.transaction` code with the specified field (supported) inside Java comments:

```
/**
 * @com.register ( clsid=BDFAFCD4-F354-11D1-9949-94B57FCAE66F,
typelib=BDFAFCD3-F354-11D1-9949-94B57FCAE66F )
 * @com.transaction (supported)
*/
```

To code an MTS component, you need to make the component aware of the MTS environment. This is done by importing the `com.ms.mtx.*` package used to access the MTS functionality:

```
import com.ms.mtx.*;
```

and by declaring an MTS context:

```
IObjectContext ioc_context = null;
```

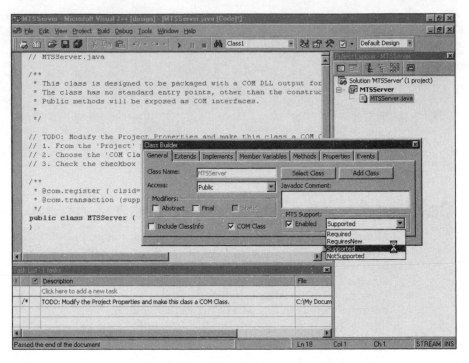

Figure 13-11: The Class Builder is required to indicate MTS support.

When MTS is accessed, an MTS context is returned. This is captured using the `com.ms.mtx.IObjectContext.GetObjectContext()` method:

```
ioc_context = (IObjectContext) MTx.GetObjectContext();
```

When the MTS method is finished, the MTS client is signaled using the `com.ms.mtx.IObjectContext.setComplete()` method:

```
ioc_context.SetComplete();
```

If an error occurs during processing, the `SetAbort()` method is called:

```
ioc_context.SetAbort();
```

Listing 13-1 shows how a factorial routine can reside on an MTS server.

Listing 13-1: MTSServer.java

```
/**
 * @com.register ( clsid=BDFAFCD4-F354-11D1-9949-94B57FCAE66F,
typelib=BDFAFCD3-F354-11D1-9949-94B57FCAE66F )
 * @com.transaction (supported)
 */
import com.ms.mtx.*;
```

```
public class MTSServer {
  IObjectContext ioc_context = null;
  public String factorial(int num) {
    try {
// Get MTS context and set the return data
      ioc_context = (IObjectContext) MTx.GetObjectContext();
// Form the return string
      long answer = 1;
      for (int loop = num; loop > 1; loop--) {
        answer *= num;
      }
      String returnString  = "The factorial of "
          + String.valueOf(num)
          + " is "
          + String.valueOf(answer)
          + ".";
// Complete transaction and return the string.
      ioc_context.SetComplete();
      return returnString;
    }
    catch(Throwable t) {
// An error has occurred so abort the transaction and return
nothing.
      ioc_context.SetAbort();
      return "";
    }
  }
}
```

Visual J++ 6.0 can automatically deploy the MTSServer program to the proper MTS server, as seen in Figure 13-12.

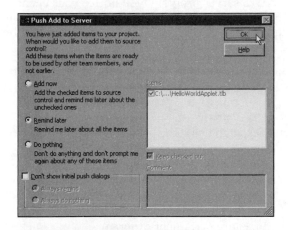

Figure 13-12: Visual J++ automatically tries to deploy MTS server applications.

Writing an MTS Client

Although both the component and the client are written in Java, the client must access the component through COM rather than a direct Java call. In other words, once you've written the MTS server, you need to add a COM wrapper to access it like any Microsoft ActiveX module. To add a COM wrapper to an MTS component, choose Project, Add COM Wrapper from the Visual J++ Menu. This opens the Com Wrapper dialog box shown in Figure 13-13.

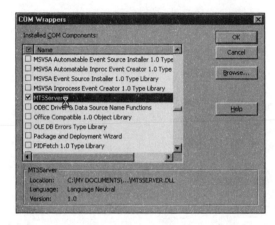

Figure 13-13: The Com Wrapper dialog box enables you to set up an MTS server component for your MTS client.

After you select your MTS server program, you notice your client area has added both the MTSServer program and an MTSServer_Dispatch program (Figure 13-14). All calls to the MTSServer must be made through the MTSServer_Dispatch.

To code the MTS client to access MTS server methods, you need two statements. First, you import the COM library:

```
import mtsserver.*;
```

Next, you construct a Dispatch using the server constructor:

```
MTSServer_Dispatch server = (MTSServer_Dispatch) new MTSServer();
```

After that, call any server method:

```
    label1.setText(server.factorial(5));
```

Listing 13-2 contains the entire MTSClient program.

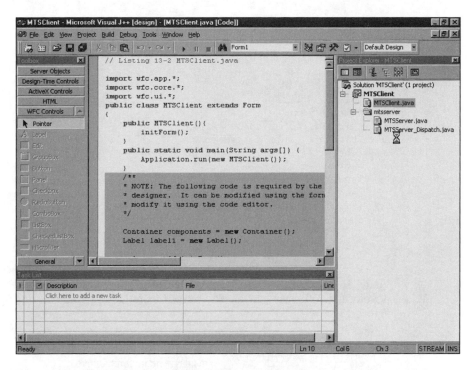

Figure 13-14: The MTSServer.java and MTSServer_Dispatch.java programs are added to your MTSClient project after using the COM wrapper.

Listing 13-2: MTSClient.java

```java
import wfc.app.*;
import wfc.core.*;
import wfc.ui.*;
import mtsserver.*;
public class MTSClient extends Form {
  public MTSClient() {
    initForm();
    MTSServer_Dispatch server = (MTSServer_Dispatch) new MTSServer();
  //Display the factorial of 5
    label1.setText(server.factorial(5));
  }
  public static void main(String args[]) {
    Application.run(new MTSClient());
  }
  /**
  * NOTE: The following code is required by the Visual J++ form
  * designer.  It can be modified using the form editor.  Do not
  * modify it using the code editor.
  */

  Container components = new Container();
  Label label1 = new Label();

  private void initForm()
```

```
{
    this.setBackColor(Color.CONTROL);
    this.setLocation(new Point(0, 0));
    this.setSize(new Point(300, 300));
    this.setTabIndex(-1);
    this.setTabStop(true);
    this.setText("MTSClient");
    this.setAutoScaleBaseSize(13);
    this.setClientSize(new Point(292, 273));
    label1.setLocation(new Point(20, 0));
    label1.setSize(new Point(250, 20));
    label1.setText("label1");
    label1.setTabIndex(1);
    this.setNewControls(new Control[] {
        label1});
}
// NOTE: End of form designer support code
}
```

Visual J++'s capability to deliver three-tier performance raises Visual J++ development to a new level. The output from Listing 13-2 can be viewed in Figure 13-15.

Figure 13-15: The MTSClient program displays the factorial of five.

Summary

Visual J++ Enterprise Edition contains programs and utilities that aid in the client-server and team development effort.

■ Three-tier architecture consists of a client tier, an application server tier, and a database tier.

■ Visual J++ delivers three-tier DNA development by utilizing Microsoft Transaction Server (MTS) functionality.

■ Visual SourceSafe is a great tool for managing team projects.

Part III

Developing 100% Pure Java with Visual J++

Chapter 14

Why Pure Java?

In This Chapter

▶ Why Java is needed with WFC

▶ When to use pure Java

▶ When not to use pure Java

Visual J++ is a fantastic tool for Windows development. However, for those of you who want standard Java without committing to the Windows platform, Visual J++ delivers there as well. With online help, easy debugging, and automatic deployment of both Java applications and Java Applets, Visual J++ is an extremely popular tool, even for those who like pure Java.

This is a short chapter that describes when Visual J++ developers need to use pure Java instead of WFC and ActiveX for their software development.

When to Use Pure Java

WFC is a robust tool. However, sometimes coding with pure Java makes more sense:

- If you are coding for the Web, you almost certainly need to avoid the use of WFC. Only Windows 32-bit applications can run your WFC applet. Any browser can run your pure Java applet.

- If your software needs to run on multiple platforms, such as Macintosh or Unix machines, you need to stick with pure Java. Again, WFC doesn't run on machines that are not running 32-bit Windows.

- WFC takes training. If your staff is currently trained in Java, you may not want the additional expense of training for WFC as well.

- If you have an extensive class library that contains business rules on screen layouts or database access, you may want developers to avoid the easy Java WFC screen painter that is included with Visual J++. By not enabling WFC and forcing pure Java, you can force the use of your Java library.

- Finally, a lot of Java development tools are available (for example, Sun's JDK, Borland's JBuilder, PowerSoft's PowerJ, and Symantec's Café). Using WFC forces every developer to use only Visual J++ when working on your programs. This may not be acceptable to certain organizations.

This part of the book is dedicated to showing how to code in pure Java with Visual J++. Remember that Visual J++ is a Java development tool that also enables Java programs and applets to call WFC classes. If you code in pure Java, you don't need to call those classes. Sun's Java specification and promise of "write once, run anywhere" have great appeal to many developers and many organizations.

Secret

One final reason to stay with pure Java is Java's formatting capability. WFC concentrates on placing objects at *a specific pixel position* on the window. For users that use different resolutions or window sizes, this may be a problem. Java, on the other hand, concentrates on patterns of placement on a window (called Layouts). These Layouts enable your components to display properly at various resolutions and window sizes.

When Not to Use Pure Java

Pure Java has a lot going for it. However, there are reasons that pure Java is not needed:

- If you are doing Windows-only applications or applets over an intranet, you might be wise to use WFC. It runs faster than straight Java.

- If you or your coworkers are new to Java, it has a steep learning curve. WFC, by contrast, is a lot easier to learn and use. WFC enables fast Windows development with the power of the Java language behind it.

- WFC runs faster than pure Java. WFC gives Java an extra boost that enables WFC developers to make applications that not only run a little faster, but also have features, such as tab support and multiline labels, which are not found in the Java specification. WFC can make your applications more robust and easier to use.

Why Java Is Still Needed with WFC

Don't think you can throw away the rest of Java if you decide to use WFC. Java contains some advanced functionality that you need to understand to become an accomplished Visual J++ developer, even if you tend toward using WFC:

- Interfaces add to the object-oriented paradigm by enabling the called class to access functionality in the calling class.

- Java offers network support that enables you to access URL files or even talk to other Java programs.

- Although supplanted by databases, file I/O with text files or flat files is still beneficial at times. Java offers a wide range of file support.

- Java offers advanced data structures such as vectors and enumerations. These structures make using internal variable storage easier than traditional programming languages.

- Java has a lot of built-in functionality that enables multitasking. The Thread class and the Runnable interface enable you to multitask your Windows applications.

In short, don't throw away your pure Java class library knowledge just yet. WFC is meant to interact with Java, not replace it.

Summary

Java offers functionality not duplicated in WFC — sometimes you need pure Java.

- If you are going to place Applets on the Web, you probably want to use pure Java. That way, you are not limited to only Windows users.

- If you are developing for Windows users only, you don't need to stick with pure Java. WFC is a robust, easy-to-use, fast tool.

- Even with WFC, you need to understand some Java constructs to make complete programs.

Chapter 15

Advanced Event Programming and Graphical Development

In This Chapter

▶ Using keyboard Listeners

▶ Examining mouse Listeners

▶ Mastering window Listeners

▶ Using component action Listeners

▶ Exploring special keys

▶ Mastering graphical programming

The concept of event-driven programming is part of most modern development tools. While traditional programming methods concentrate on program flow, event-driven languages concentrate on user actions, or events, to make the program function. Event-driven languages such as Java make graphical systems development much easier.

Java 1.1 and Visual J++ 6.0 handle events differently from previous versions of Java. The handleEvent() method and action() method are now considered obsolete and you probably shouldn't use them anymore. These two methods, which were the keystone of event handling in previous versions of Visual J++, have been replaced with *Listeners*. In this chapter, you learn how to capture keyboard and mouse events and how to use Listeners.

Note

All the Applets and applications listed in this chapter use 100 percent pure Java and conform to the Java 1.1 standard. Although Microsoft has written WFC tools that can help with graphical development, those tools are not discussed in this chapter — the WFC tools are discussed later in Chapter 4.

Examining Events

Traditional programming languages like C++ involve a single entry point, as shown in Figure 15-1. Programs written in these languages control a program and don't yield control back to the operating system (or in Java's and Visual J++'s case, the Virtual Machine) until the programs are completely finished. Even Visual C++ for Windows requires a single entry point to test for events and complete a program as soon as possible.

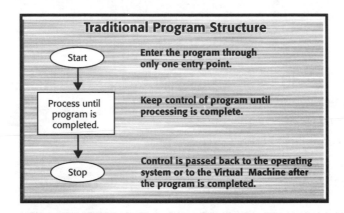

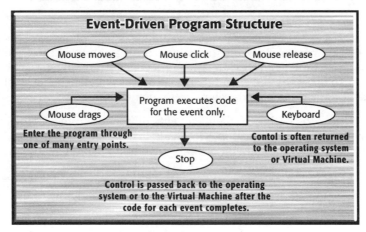

Figure 15-1: Event-driven programs leave a lot more control to the operating system and have many entry and exit points.

Programs written using event-driven languages, on the other hand, have a different entry point for every user action, such as clicking a mouse button or pressing a key on the keyboard. User actions are called events, and they yield control back to the operating system or virtual machine as often as possible.

Java uses *Listeners* to test for events — they can be used to test for both keyboard and mouse events.

Trapping keyboard events

Pressing a key on your computer keyboard triggers an event. Use the KeyListener interface to implement a keyboard Listener. After a class implements the KeyListener interface, it calls the addKeyListener() method, usually in the constructor (for stand-alone applications) or in the init() method (for Applets) as follows:

```
public class Events extends Applet implements KeyListener {
//…
  public void init() {
    addKeyListener(this);
```

The following methods are required when implementing the KeyListener interface:

- Pressing a key triggers the keyPressed(KeyEvent e) method.

- Releasing a key triggers the keyReleased(KeyEvent e) method.

- Pressing and then releasing a key triggers the keyTyped(KeyEvent e) method.

The following code displays which key is pressed:

```
public void keyPressed(KeyEvent e){
  int keyCode = e.getKeyCode();
  showStatus(e.getKeyText(keyCode));
}
```

The KeyEvent.getKeyCode() method is used to return the key that was pressed. The KeyEvent.getKeyText() method is used to return strings that describe which keys are pressed.

Secret

In the KeyTyped() method, you use the KeyEvent.getKeyChar() method rather than the KeyEvent.getKeyCode() method because the KeyTyped() method does not capture a scan code.

Trapping keyboard modifiers

Keyboard modifiers are keys that are typically combined with other keys. There are three modifiers: Alt, Shift, and Ctrl.

Secret

In addition to these three modifiers, some operating systems (such as UNIX) support a fourth keyboard modifier named Meta. Meta is not used on Windows keyboards and usually should be avoided as a keyboard modifier.

The KeyEvent parameter that is passed to all KeyListener() methods is inherited from the InputEvent() method. In this method, four methods can test for keyboard modifiers:

- The InputEvent.isShiftDown() method returns a True if the Shift key is pressed and a False if the Shift button is not pressed.

- The InputEvent.isControlDown() method returns a True if the Ctrl key is pressed and a False if the Ctrl button is not pressed.

- The InputEvent.isAltDown() method returns a True if the Alt key is pressed and a False if it is not pressed.

- Although it is hardly ever used as a keyboard modifier, the InputEvent.isMetaDown() method returns a True if the Meta key is pressed and a False if the Meta button is not pressed.

The following code tests for Alt, Ctrl, and Shift modifiers and returns a string containing a description of the current modifiers that are pressed:

```
public String getModifiersText(InputEvent e) {
  String returnString = "";
  if (e.isControlDown()) {
    returnString += "CTRL + ";
  }
  if (e.isAltDown()) {
    returnString += "ALT + ";
  }
  if (e.isShiftDown()) {
    returnString += "SHIFT + ";
  }
  return returnString;
}
```

In the preceding code, an InputEvent modifier is passed to the getModifiersText() method. InputEvent is the super class of both KeyEvent() and MouseEvent(). (MouseEvent is described in detail later in this chapter.) The keyPressed() method written in the last section could be modified to include any modifiers that may be pressed, as well as the normal key that is being pressed:

```
public void keyPressed(KeyEvent e){
  int keyCode = e.getKeyCode();
  showStatus(getModifiersText(e) + e.getKeyText(keyCode));
}
```

In the preceding code, a KeyEvent parameter is passed to the keyPressed() method by the Java Virtual Machine (VM) whenever a key is pressed. Because the KeyEvent parameter is, through inheritance, also an InputEvent parameter, the KeyEvent parameter can be passed to the getModifiersText() method. The getModifiersText() method returns a string containing a description of which keyboard modifiers are pressed.

Keyboard events in older versions of Java

Older Java VMs (like those used in IE 3.0 and Netscape 2.0 and 3.0) did not implement KeyListeners. On these machines, when you press a key on the keyboard, the keyDown event is called from the parent component class or subclass. (Applet and Frame are both inherited from Component.) Using the keyDown event and the static constants KEY_PRESS and KEY_ACTION in the Event class, you can test the event ID to see whether a regular (nonfunction) or function key was pressed. A special keys function is called to test whether the Shift, Alt, Ctrl, or Meta keys were pressed at the same time:

```java
public boolean keyDown(Event event, int key) {
    String before = "";
    String after = "";
    if (event.metaDown()) {  // Meta key pressed
        after += "META + ";
    }
    if (event.controlDown()) {  //Ctrl key pressed
        after += "CTRL + ";
    }
    if ((event.modifiers != 0) &&
        ((event.modifiers & Event.ALT_MASK) != 0)) {  // Alt key
                                                       // pressed
        after += "ALT + ";
    }
if (event.shiftDown()) {  // Shift key pressed
        after += "SHIFT + ";
    }
    switch(event.id) {
        case Event.KEY_PRESS ://  "Regular" Key
            before = "";
            after += String.valueOf(key);
            break;
        case Event.KEY_ACTION ://  Function Key
            before = "Function";
            // test key equal to Event.F1 through Event.F12
            // test key equal to Event.HOME, Event.PGDN, Event.LEFT,
            // and so on.
            after += testKey(key);
            break;
    }
    showStatus(before + "Key Down: " + after);
    return true;
}
```

Secret

The special_keys() method returns Shift+, Alt+, Ctrl+, or Meta+, or any combination of the four based on which special keys are being pressed when an event occurs. There is no real equivalent of a "Meta" key on most Windows machines. However, several UNIX boxes have them. Because Java and Visual J++ code works on *all* Java Virtual Machines, Meta keys can be tested for even though there's no real equivalent in the Windows/DOS world.

I don't know why Sun didn't define an altDown() method in the original Java 1.0 specification, but the Alt key has no testing method. However, there is a static Event constant called ALT_MASK. When ALT_MASK is logically ANDed with the Event modifiers attribute, if a nonzero value is returned, then the Alt key is being pressed. Figure 15-2 shows that a bitwise AND between ALT_MASK and modifiers yields a nonzero value.

	Meta	Alt	Ctrl	Shift
modifiers	0	1	1	1
ALT_MASK	0	1	0	0
AND value	0	1	0	0

Figure 15-2: The ALT_MASK Event constant ANDed with the modifiers Event attribute yields a nonzero value if the Alt key is currently pressed.

In later versions of Java, the keyDown functionality is still available, but the keyDown event has been deprecated in favor of KeyListeners.

Trapping mouse clicks

An event is triggered when you click your mouse button or move your mouse. A mouse listener can be implemented by using the MouseListener interface. After a class implements the MouseListener interface, it must call the addMouseListener() method, usually in the constructor (for stand-alone applications) or in the init() method (for Applets) as follows:

```
public class Events extends Applet implements MouseListener {
//...
  public void init() {
    addMouseListener(this);
```

The following methods are required when implementing the MouseListener interface:

- The mouseClicked(MouseEvent e) method is triggered when a mouse button is clicked.

- The mousePressed(MouseEvent e) method is triggered when a mouse button is pressed.

- The mouseReleased(MouseEvent e) method is triggered when a mouse button is released.

- The mouseEntered(MouseEvent e) method is triggered when the mouse pointer enters the Java Applet or Frame area.

- The mouseExited(MouseEvent e) method is triggered when the mouse pointer exits the Java Applet or Frame area.

Secret

Although the Meta keyboard modifier is not used for keyboards in Windows, window environments use it to indicate that the right mouse button is being pressed rather than the left mouse button in the `mouseClicked()`, `mousePressed()`, and `mouseReleased()` methods.

The following code tests for a left or right mouse click:

```java
public void mouseClicked(MouseEvent e) {
  if (e.isMetaDown()) {
    showStatus ("Right Mouse Clicked");
  }
  else {
    showStatus ("Left Mouse Clicked");
  }
}
```

Secret

Any mouse clicks or mouse drags that occur *outside* the Applet area are not considered Applet events. The mouse pointer must be in the Applet area to trigger a mouse event.

Trapping mouse movement

Listeners can also detect mouse movement events. A mouse listener can trap mouse movements by using the MouseMotionListener interface. After a class implements the MouseMotionListener interface, it must call the `addMouseMotionListener()` method, usually in the constructor (for stand-alone applications) or in the `init()` method (for Applets) as follows:

```java
public class Events extends Applet implements MouseMotionListener {
//…
  public void init() {
    addMouseMotionListener(this);
```

The following methods are required when implementing the MouseMotionListener interface:

- The `mouseDragged(MouseEvent)` is triggered when a mouse button is pressed while the mouse pointer moves. This is also known as dragging, as in a "Drag-and-Drop" application.

- The `mouseMoved(MouseEvent)` method is triggered when the mouse pointer is moved while no buttons are pressed.

The following code tests for a mouse drag and displays the (x, y) coordinates in the status bar using the `MouseEvent.getX()` and `MouseEvent.getY()` methods:

```java
public void mouseDragged(MouseEvent e) {
  showStatus ("Mouse dragged to ("+String.valueOf(e.getX())+",
"+String.valueOf(e.getY())+")");
}
```

Mouse events in older versions of Java

Just as with KeyListeners, older Java VMs (like those used in IE 3.0 and Netscape 2.0 and 3.0) did not implement MouseListeners. On these machines, mouse events are called from the parent component class or subclass. (Applet and Frame are both inherited from Component.) The following mouse events can be called:

- The `mouseDown()` method is triggered when the left or right mouse button is pressed.

- The `mouseDrag()` method is triggered when the left or right mouse button is dragged, which means that a button was held down while the mouse moved. (Right button drags are indicated by a Meta key modifier.)

- The `mouseUp()` method is triggered when the left or right mouse button is released. (There is no indicator to tell whether the left or right mouse button was released.)

- The `mouseEnter()` method is triggered when the mouse pointer has entered the Applet area. If the mouse pointer is outside the Applet area, then no mouse movements are recorded.

- The `mouseExit()` method is triggered when the mouse pointer has left the Applet area.

The following code can be called using earlier versions of Java to trap a mouse click using the `mouseDown` event:

```
public boolean mouseDown(Event event, int x, int y) {
    showStatus("Mouse Click: ("+ x + "," + y + ")");
    return true;
}
```

In the preceding code, the mouse position is displayed at the bottom of the browser in the status bar. However, like the `keyDown()` method, the `mouseDown()` method has been deprecated and probably shouldn't be used anymore.

Programming for events

Listing 15-1 tests for all keyboard and mouse events in a Java Web page. This program not only captures all keyboard and mouse events, but also shows that the keyboard and mouse events can be combined. The results are displayed in the results status bar at the bottom of the browser.

Listing 15-1: Events.java

```
import java.applet.*;
import java.awt.*;
import java.awt.event.*;

public class Events extends Applet
    implements KeyListener, MouseListener, MouseMotionListener {
```

```java
    public void init() {
      addMouseMotionListener(this);
      addMouseListener(this);
      addKeyListener(this);
    }
    public String getModifiersText(InputEvent e) {
      //Test for Keyboard Modifiers
      String returnString = "";
      if (e.isControlDown()) {
        returnString += "CTRL + ";
      }
      if (e.isAltDown()) {
        returnString += "ALT + ";
      }
      if (e.isShiftDown()) {
        returnString += "SHIFT + ";
      }
      return returnString;
    }
    public void displayMouseInfo(String eventName, MouseEvent e) {
      //Display the mouse event that's passed along with the x,y
coordinates
      showStatus(getModifiersText(e)
            + eventName
            + "("
            + String.valueOf(e.getX())
            + ", "
            + String.valueOf(e.getY())
            + ")");
    }
// Keyboard methods required by the KeyListener interface
    public void keyTyped(KeyEvent e){
      //Test for a key that's typed
      showStatus(getModifiersText(e) + e.getKeyChar());
    }
    public void keyPressed(KeyEvent e){ }  // A key was pressed
    public void keyReleased(KeyEvent e) { }  // A key was released
// Mouse methods required by the MouseMotionListener interface
    public void mouseMoved(MouseEvent e) { }  // Mouse was moved
    public void mouseDragged(MouseEvent e) {   // Mouse was dragged
      showStatus ("Mouse dragged to ("
            + String.valueOf(e.getX())
            + ", "
            + String.valueOf(e.getY())
            +")");
    }
   // Mouse methods required by the MouseListener interface
    public void mouseClicked(MouseEvent e) {      // A mouse button was
                                                  // clicked
      if (e.isMetaDown()) {    // Right Click
        displayMouseInfo("Right Mouse Clicked", e);
      }
      else {         // Left Click
        displayMouseInfo("Left Mouse Clicked", e);
      }
    }
```

```java
public void mousePressed(MouseEvent e) {      // A mouse button was
                                              // pressed
  if (e.isMetaDown()) {     // Right Click
    displayMouseInfo("Right Mouse Pressed", e);
  }
  else {          // Left Click
    displayMouseInfo("Left Mouse Pressed", e);
  }
}
public void mouseReleased(MouseEvent e) {  // A mouse button was
                                           // released
  if (e.isMetaDown()) {     // Right Click
    displayMouseInfo("Right Mouse Released", e);
  }
  else {          // Left Click
    displayMouseInfo("Left Mouse Released", e);
  }
}
public void mouseEntered(MouseEvent e) {   // The mouse entered
                                           // the area
  displayMouseInfo("Mouse Entered", e);
}
public void mouseExited(MouseEvent e) {    // The mouse left the
                                           // area
  displayMouseInfo("Mouse Exited", e);
}
}
```

In Figure 15-3, Events.java was run and the right mouse button was clicked while holding Ctrl, Alt, and Shift. The results show that you can trap for specific keyboard and mouse combinations.

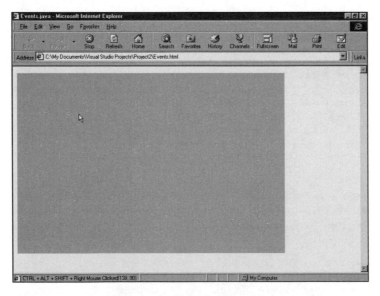

Figure 15-3: Using Events.java, you can trap for right mouse clicks as well as keyboard-mouse combinations.

Mastering Graphical Program Design

Events play an important role in graphical program design. Every mouse click on a button or checkbox creates an event for a program to interpret. In this section, the following topics are discussed:

- Window listeners and window events
- Components
- Panels and layouts
- Action listeners and Component events
- Writing your own graphical program

Trapping window events

Some events occur without specific user interaction. Frames can open, close, minimize, or maximize. These events are trapped using the `WindowListener` interface. The `WindowListener` interface is usually implemented in stand-alone programs. To use a WindowListener, you must call the `addWindowListener()` method, usually in the constructor, as follows:

```
import java.awt.*;
import java.awt.event.*;

public class PanelFrame extends Frame implements WindowListener {
//Add the following line to the PanelFrame constructor
  addKeyListener(this);
```

The following methods are required when implementing the `KeyListener` interface:

- The `windowActivated(WindowEvent e)` method is triggered when a Window or Frame receives focus.

- The `windowDeactivated(WindowEvent e)` method is triggered when a Window or Frame loses focus.

- The `windowIconified(WindowEvent e)` method is triggered when a Window or Frame is minimized to an icon.

- The `windowDeiconified(WindowEvent e)` method is triggered when a Window or Frame is expanded from an icon.

- The `windowClosed(WindowEvent e)` method is triggered when a user indicates that a Window or Frame should be closed. This is usually done by clicking the Close Window icon in the upper-right corner of the Window or Frame or by double-clicking the icon in the upper-left corner of the Window or Frame.

- The `windowOpened(WindowEvent e)` method is triggered when a Window or Frame first opens.

The following code is triggered when the user presses the Close Window button in the upper-right corner of the window:

```
public void windowClosing(WindowEvent e) {
  this.dispose();
  System.exit(0);
}
```

Using components

The Component class is inherited by every window and window control. A list of all components and their inheritance hierarchy can be seen in Figure 15-4.

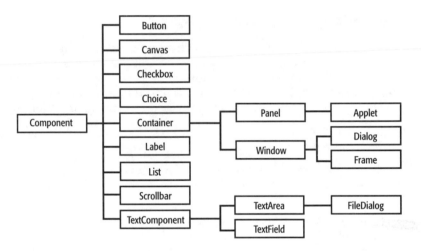

Figure 15-4: The Component class is the base class for all windows and window controls.

Table 15-1 briefly reviews all classes inherited from the Component class.

Table 15-1	Component Classes
Component Class	**Description**
Applet	Applets are the basis for all Internet software. To run on a Web browser, your class must be inherited from Applet.
Button	The Button class creates a command button to use on a window or Panel.

Component Class	Description
Canvas	Although not often used, a Canvas class enables you to paint on a component without actually painting on a class inherited from the Container class.
Checkbox	A Checkbox is a box that is checked to indicate a true or false value. Checkboxes can be grouped together in a CheckboxGroup class to form radio buttons.
Choice	The Choice class enables you to create a drop-down list box. A drop-down list box is a list of choices that appears when a down-arrow button is pressed.
Container	The Container class is the parent class for all Components that can contain other Components. Applet, Window, Dialog, Frame, and Panel are Container classes.
Dialog	The Dialog class is a special type of Window that can be modal to the application.
FileDialog	The FileDialog class is a special type of dialog box used to list files.
Frame	The Frame class is used to define top-level windows. You can also open Frames within an Applet
Label	A Label is static text that appears on your Window. Although you can still test for other events like mouse clicks on a Label, usually Labels are used for informational text.
List	The List class creates a box containing a list of choices.
Panel	A Panel is a "window within a window." Panels are used to segment your Frame or Applet into separate sections.
Scrollbar	The Scrollbar class creates a scrollbar Component. Usually, this is not used because Lists, TextAreas, and Windows all automatically generate scrollbars when needed.
TextArea	A TextArea is a multiline text field. Unlike Labels, TextAreas can be used for input as well as output.
TextComponent	The TextComponent class is the parent class for the TextArea and TextField classes. Many of the functions used in the TextArea and TextField classes can be found in the TextComponent class.
TextField	The TextField class is a single-line text field. Like TextAreas, TextFields can be used for input and output.
Window	The Window class is the parent class for all Frames and Dialogs. Usually Windows are not themselves instantiated, but rather Frames are used.

Examining panels

Panels are an important part of graphical design in Java. Panels enable you to segment your window's viewing area and format window segments differently, including different background colors, component positioning, and window placement. You can have many Panels per window. Additionally, you can place Panels within Panels.

Although both Panel and Frame are Containers, they are both also Components. Therefore, you can add Panels to any Container by using the add() method, just as you would add buttons to a Panel:

```
add("Center", myPanel);
```

Exploring layouts

Layouts enable you to control how components are placed on your Panel. You can choose from five different layouts, all inherited from the LayoutManager class. These five are as follows:

- *FlowLayout* is the default layout. It is used to place components on a window or Panel in a left-to-right flow and starts a new row when it runs out of space (like a paragraph).

- *GridLayout* is used to place items in a grid. GridLayouts also expand the size of each component to fill the space of the grid.

- *BorderLayout* is used to place items around a Panel or other Container in border fashion. You could use BorderLayout to divide your Panel into north, south, east, west, and center subsegments.

- *CardLayout* shows only one component on the window at a time. Functions contained within the CardLayout class enable you to scroll forward and backward through your components.

- *GridBagLayout* is a lot like GridLayout, except the grid cell sizes can vary in length and width independently of other cells contained in the layout.

Secret

Every Frame or Applet uses a default layout. (Frames use BorderLayout, while Applets use FlowLayout.) You can turn off the layout by passing a null as the setLayout parameter (for example, setLayout(null)). When you turn off all layouts, you must use the setLocation(x, y) method to move your component to the desired location.

Using FlowLayout

FlowLayout is one of the most popular layouts. By placing components on a window from left to right without resizing, the FlowLayout class is the most intuitive of all classes for placement on a window. Listing 15-2 shows how a FlowLayout (in bold) LayoutManager can work.

Listing 15-2: PanelFrame.java

```java
import java.awt.*;
import java.awt.event.*;

public class PanelFrame extends Frame implements WindowListener {
  // Create 5 buttons for panel demo
  private Button Button1 = new Button("Hello");
  private Button Button2 = new Button("World!");
  private Button Button3 = new Button("This");
  private Button Button4 = new Button("is");
  private Button Button5 = new Button("Chuck!");
  public static void main (String args[]) {
    // Construct a PanelFrame
    PanelFrame pf = new PanelFrame();
  }
  public PanelFrame() {  //PanelFrame Constructor
  //Add the WindowListener for Window events
    addWindowListener(this);
  //Set the layout of the frame
    setLayout(new BorderLayout());
    Panel myPanel = new Panel ();  // Create Panel
    myPanel.setBackground(Color.lightGray);
  // Set Panel Layout for demo
    myPanel.setLayout(new FlowLayout());
  //Add Buttons to panel
    myPanel.add(Button1);
    myPanel.add(Button2);
    myPanel.add(Button3);
    myPanel.add(Button4);
    myPanel.add(Button5);
  // Add Panel to Frame
    add("Center", myPanel);
    setTitle("PanelFrame.java");
    setSize (300,200);
    show();
  }
// The following are required by the WindowListener interface
  public void windowClosing(WindowEvent e) {
    this.dispose();
    System.exit(0);
  }
  public void windowActivated(WindowEvent e) { }
  public void windowDeactivated(WindowEvent e) { }
  public void windowDeiconified(WindowEvent e) { }
  public void windowClosed(WindowEvent e) { }
  public void windowIconified(WindowEvent e) { }
  public void windowOpened(WindowEvent e) { }
}
```

Figure 15-5 shows the results of running this program.

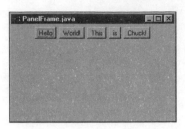

Figure 15-5: The FlowLayout LayoutManager class places objects on a Container class from left to right.

Using GridLayout

The GridLayout class lays out your Container in a grid and then places components inside the grid. Unlike the FlowLayout class, the GridLayout class constructor requires two arguments — rows and columns. The following is a prototype for creating a new GridLayout instance:

```
GridLayout gl = new GridLayout(rows, columns);
```

If you replace the boldface line in Listing 15-2 with the following line:

```
myPanel.setLayout(new GridLayout(5, 1));
```

you see the results pictured in Figure 15-6.

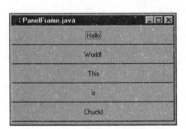

Figure 15-6: Here, buttons are arranged in a five, one grid.

Buttons are arranged in Figure 15-6 five rows down and one column across. Conversely, the following line of code:

```
myPanel.setLayout(new GridLayout(1, 5));
```

produces the results shown in Figure 15-7.

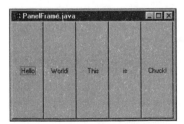

Figure 15-7: Here, buttons are arranged in a one, five grid.

In Figure 15-7, there is only one row down and five columns across. Finally, consider the following line of code:

```
myPanel.setLayout(new GridLayout(3, 2));
```

It produces three rows down and two columns across, as seen in Figure 15-8.

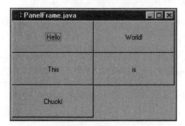

Figure 15-8: Here, buttons are arranged in a three, two grid.

Using CardLayout

The CardLayout class shows only one component at a time. If you replaced the boldface line in Listing 15-2 with the following lines:

```
//CardLayout needs to be separately declared so
//you can use the first, last, next, previous,
//and show methods contained within the CardLayout
//class.
CardLayout cl = new CardLayout();
myPanel.setLayout(cl);
```

you get one button shown at a time, as shown in Figure 15-9.

Figure 15-9: A CardLayout only shows one Component at a time, like an address card catalog.

To scroll through your components, the CardLayout class includes five methods not found in other classes. Table 15-2 lists these classes.

Table 15-2   CardLayout methods

Card Layout Method	Description
first(Container parent)	Shows the first component added to the CardLayout.
last(Container parent)	Shows the final component added to the CardLayout.
next(Container parent)	Shows the following component added to the CardLayout.
previous(Container parent)	Shows the preceding component added to the CardLayout.
show(Container parent, String name)	Shows the specific component added to the CardLayout using the addLayoutComponent() method.

To show the next button in the PanelFrame class, you need to add the following line of code:

```
cl.next(myPanel);
```

Secret

Although all classes define an addLayoutComponent() method, it is used most often with the CardLayout class. After you add a component to your layout, you can use the addLayoutComponent() method and the show() method to display the component by name. Use the following lines of code:

```
CardLayout cl = new CardLayout();
myPanel.setLayout(cl);
myPanel.add(Button5);
cl.addLayoutComponent("Button5", Button5);
cl.show(myPanel, "Button5");
```

The preceding code accomplishes the following:

1. Declares a new CardLayout instance.

2. Sets a Panel instance to use the new CardLayout instance.

3. Adds a button to the Panel using the Container.add() method. This can be done since Panel is inherited from Container.

4. Names the button you added using the CardLayout.addLayoutComponent() method.

5. Shows the button by using the CardLayout.show() method.

Notice that you *still* need to use the Container.add method when you use the CardLayout.addLayoutComponent method. The Component must be added to the Container before it can be named as an added Component.

Using BorderLayout

The BorderLayout class breaks a Container class down into north, south, east, west, and center components, as shown in Figure 15-10.

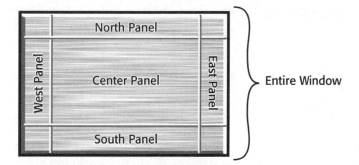

Figure 15-10: BorderLayout Panels enable you to partition your window into five different segments.

To use a BorderLayout with Listing 15-2, you must replace the boldface line *and* the myPanel.add commands that immediately follow with the following block of code:

```
myPanel.setLayout(new BorderLayout());
//Add Buttons to Panel WITH DIRECTIONS
myPanel.add("North", Button1);
myPanel.add("West", Button2);
myPanel.add("Center", Button3);
myPanel.add("East", Button4);
myPanel.add("South", Button5);
```

This displays the buttons in the format shown in Figure 15-11.

Figure 15-11: The BorderLayout class enables you to have north, south, east, west, and center components.

Secret

You can place the direction (for example, North, West, Center, East, or South) on the add() method of a Panel anytime without causing a syntax or run-time error. However, it is ignored unless the Panel uses the BorderLayout.

Using GridBagLayout

GridBagLayouts are the most versatile of all layouts, and the hardest to use. GridBagLayouts enable you to make grids that look like Figure 15-12.

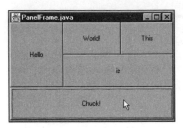

Figure 15-12: GridBagLayouts provide versatile placement of Components on a Container.

In Figure 15-13, the buttons and their desired position are laid out. As you can see, the GridBagLayout still forces you to use a grid to lay out your components, but unlike the GridLayout class, the GridBagLayout class enables each component to occupy more than one cell.

May occupy 2 spaces

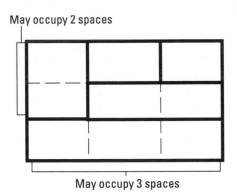

Figure 15-13: You still must lay out components in a grid using a GridBagLayout, but each component can occupy more than one cell.

May occupy 3 spaces

Secret

GridBagLayouts are extremely complicated. Follow these steps to use a GridBagLayout:

1. Declare GridBagLayout and GridBagConstraints variables.

2. Set the layout of your table to the GridBagLayout.

3. Set default GridBagConstraint values.

4. Set unique GridBagConstraint values for each component.

5. Use the `GridBagLayout.setConstraints()` method to set the constraints for each component.

6. Add the Component to the Container.

The code to use a GridBagLayout is much more complex than the code for any other layout. Listing 15-2's `PanelFrame()` method implements a GridBagLayout (indicated by the lines in boldface type):

```
public PanelFrame() {
//Add the WindowListener for Window events
  addWindowListener(this);
//Set the layout of the frame
  setLayout(new BorderLayout());
  Panel myPanel = new Panel();
  myPanel.setBackground(Color.lightGray);
//Initialize the GridBagLayout and declare GridBagLayout
//and GridBagConstraints Variables
  GridBagLayout gbl = new GridBagLayout();
  GridBagConstraints gbc = new GridBagConstraints();
//Set the layout of your table to the GridBagLayout
  myPanel.setLayout(gbl);
//Set Default GridBagConstraints values
  gbc.fill = GridBagConstraints.BOTH;
  gbc.weightx = 0.0;
  gbc.weighty = 0.0;
//Add Button1
  gbc.gridwidth = 1;
  gbc.gridheight = 2;
  gbl.setConstraints(Button1, gbc);
  myPanel.add(Button1);
//Add Button2
  gbc.gridheight = 1;
  gbc.gridwidth = GridBagConstraints.RELATIVE;
  gbl.setConstraints(Button2, gbc);
  myPanel.add(Button2);
//Add Button3
  gbc.gridwidth = GridBagConstraints.REMAINDER;
  gbl.setConstraints(Button3, gbc);
  myPanel.add(Button3);
//Add Button4
  gbl.setConstraints(Button4, gbc);
  myPanel.add(Button4);
//Add Button5
  gbl.setConstraints(Button5, gbc);
  myPanel.add(Button5);
// Add Panel to Frame
  add("Center", myPanel);
  setTitle("PanelFrame.java");
  setSize (300,200);
  show();
}
```

In Listing 15-2, `GridBagConstraints.fill` is set to `BOTH` to indicate that the grid being defined fills both horizontal and vertical dimensions of the Container. `GridBagConstraints.weightx` and `GridBagConstraints.weighty` are set to one, indicating that the components inside the container grow or shrink as the window is resized.

The `GridBagConstraints.gridwidth` and `GridBagConstraints.gridheight` specify the width and height of your Component (in number of cells). Setting `GridBagConstraints.gridwidth` to REMAINDER tells Java that this is the last cell on the row and to continue a new row with the next Component. Setting GridBagConstraints.gridwidth to `RELATIVE` places your next Component following your current component.

Secret

Many times, you can accomplish the look provided by GridBagLayout by creating Panels within Panels, which use simpler layout managers such as FlowLayout and BorderLayout. This *Panel-in-Panel* technique is demonstrated in the next example.

Writing Your Own Graphical Program

The challenging part of this is to take what you learn in this chapter (plus a little more that I show in this example) and write a program. Say you needed to develop an application that enabled the user to paint graphical masterpieces like the Frame pictured in Figure 15-14.

Figure 15-14: Another "Hello World!" program

Secret

Most business-based applications contain window controls such as list boxes, command buttons, checkboxes, and radio buttons. The application pictured in Figure 15-14 also contains a graphical painting area, which could be fun to add to your Web site.

Listing 15-3 shows the code for this application and is discussed throughout the remainder of the chapter.

Listing 15-3: PaintFrame.java

```java
import java.awt.*;
import java.awt.event.*;
public class PaintFrame extends Frame
   implements  WindowListener, MouseListener,
      MouseMotionListener, ActionListener,
      IColorPanel {
  int i_lastX;
  int i_lastY;
  int i_lastObjectX;
  int i_lastObjectY;
  private boolean isSettingColor = false;
// Define CheckboxGroups for choices for drawing
  private CheckboxGroup cbg = new CheckboxGroup();
// Choices for drawing
  private Checkbox rb_draw = new Checkbox("Draw", cbg, true);
  private Checkbox rb_line = new Checkbox("Line", cbg, false);
  private Checkbox rb_box = new Checkbox("Box", cbg, false);
  private Checkbox rb_circle = new Checkbox("Circle", cbg, false);
//Buttons on Window
  private Button bu_clear = new Button("Clear");
  private Button bu_exit = new Button("Exit");
//Color choices
  private ColorPanel cp_black = new ColorPanel(this, Color.black);
  private ColorPanel cp_blue = new ColorPanel(this, Color.blue);
  private ColorPanel cp_lightGray = new ColorPanel(this,
Color.lightGray);
  private ColorPanel cp_magenta = new ColorPanel(this,
Color.magenta);
  private ColorPanel cp_red = new ColorPanel(this, Color.red);
  private ColorPanel cp_yellow = new ColorPanel(this, Color.yellow);
  private ColorPanel cp_green = new ColorPanel(this, Color.green);
  private ColorPanel cp_white = new ColorPanel(this, Color.white);
  private Color col_currentForeground = Color.black;
  private Color col_currentBackground = Color.white;
  private ColorPanel cp_currentForeground = new ColorPanel(this,
col_currentForeground);
  private ColorPanel cp_currentBackground = new ColorPanel(this,
col_currentBackground);
// Main method for starting the PaintFrame
  public static void main (String args[]) {
    PaintFrame pf = new PaintFrame();
  }
  public PaintFrame () {
  //Add the WindowListener, MouseListener, and MouseMotionListener
  //for Window and Mouse events
    addWindowListener(this);
    addMouseListener(this);
    addMouseMotionListener(this);
```

```java
//Define Panels and the layouts they use
  Panel myNorthPanel = new Panel();
  Panel myWestPanel = new Panel();
  Panel mySouthPanel = new Panel();
  myNorthPanel.setBackground(Color.lightGray);
  mySouthPanel.setBackground(Color.lightGray);
  myWestPanel.setBackground(Color.lightGray);
  myNorthPanel.setLayout(new GridLayout(1, 8));
  myWestPanel.setLayout(new GridLayout(4, 1));
  mySouthPanel.setLayout(new FlowLayout());
//Add the clear and exit command buttons.
  mySouthPanel.add(new Label("Foreground:"));
  mySouthPanel.add(cp_currentForeground);
  mySouthPanel.add(new Label("Background:"));
  mySouthPanel.add(cp_currentBackground);
  cp_currentBackground.disableMouse();  // Disable Mouse Clicks
  cp_currentForeground.disableMouse();  // Disable Mouse Clicks
  mySouthPanel.add(bu_clear);
  mySouthPanel.add(bu_exit);
//Add ActionListeners for all buttons
  bu_clear.addActionListener(this);
  bu_exit.addActionListener(this);
//Add color panels
  myNorthPanel.add(cp_black);
  myNorthPanel.add(cp_blue);
  myNorthPanel.add(cp_lightGray);
  myNorthPanel.add(cp_magenta);
  myNorthPanel.add(cp_red);
  myNorthPanel.add(cp_yellow);
  myNorthPanel.add(cp_green);
  myNorthPanel.add(cp_white);
  myWestPanel.add(rb_draw);
  myWestPanel.add(rb_line);
  myWestPanel.add(rb_box);
  myWestPanel.add(rb_circle);
// Add the panels to the frame
  add("West", myWestPanel);
  add("South", mySouthPanel);
  add("North", myNorthPanel);
  setTitle("PaintFrame.java");
  setSize (600,400);
  show();
}
public void clear(Graphics g) {
  Rectangle r = getBounds();
  g.setColor(Color.white);
  g.fillRect(0, 0, r.width-1, r.height-1);
}
public void paintClick(int x, int y) {
  isSettingColor = false;
  i_lastX = x;
  i_lastY = y;
  i_lastObjectX = 0;
  i_lastObjectY = 0;
}
public void draw(int x, int y) {
```

```
        draw(x, y, false);
    }
    public void draw(int x, int y, boolean xor) {
        int lastX;
        int lastY;
        Graphics g = getGraphics();
        if (xor) {
          if (col_currentForeground == Color.black) {
            g.setXORMode(Color.white);
          }
          else {
            g.setXORMode(col_currentForeground);
          }
          if (i_lastObjectX > 0) {
            int fromX = Math.min(i_lastObjectX, i_lastX);
            int fromY = Math.min(i_lastObjectY, i_lastY);
            int toX = Math.max(i_lastObjectX, i_lastX);
            int toY = Math.max(i_lastObjectY, i_lastY);
            if (rb_line.getState()) {
              g.drawLine(i_lastX, i_lastY, i_lastObjectX,
i_lastObjectY);
            }
            else if (rb_box.getState()) {
              g.drawRect(fromX, fromY, toX - fromX, toY - fromY);
            }
            else if (rb_circle.getState()) {
              g.drawOval(fromX, fromY, toX - fromX, toY - fromY);
            }
          }
        }
        else {
          g.setColor(col_currentForeground);
        }
        i_lastObjectX = x;
        i_lastObjectY = y;
        lastX = Math.min(i_lastX, x);
        lastY = Math.min(i_lastY, y);
        int toX = Math.max(i_lastX, x);
        int toY = Math.max(i_lastY, y);
        if(rb_draw.getState() || rb_line.getState()) {
          g.drawLine(i_lastX, i_lastY, x, y);
        }
        else if(rb_box.getState()) {
          g.drawRect(lastX, lastY, toX - lastX, toY - lastY);
          if (xor == false) {
            g.setColor(col_currentBackground);
            g.fillRect(lastX + 1, lastY + 1, toX - lastX - 1, toY -
lastY - 1);
          }
        }
        else if(rb_circle.getState()) {
          if (xor == false) {
            g.setColor(col_currentBackground);
            g.fillOval(lastX, lastY, toX - lastX, toY - lastY);
            g.setColor(col_currentForeground);
          }
```

```java
          g.drawOval(lastX, lastY, toX - lastX, toY - lastY);
        }
      }
    public void newForeground(Color foreground) {
      col_currentForeground = foreground;
      cp_currentForeground.newColor(foreground);
    }
    public void newBackground(Color background) {
      col_currentBackground = background;
      cp_currentBackground.newColor(background);
    }
// The handleColorPanel() is required by the IColorPanel interface
    public void handleColorPanel(MouseEvent e, Color c) {
      isSettingColor = true;
      if (e.isMetaDown()) {   //Right button clicked
        newBackground(c);
      }
      else {                 //Left button clicked
        newForeground(c);
      }
    }
//The actionPerformed method is required
//by the ActionListener interface
    public void actionPerformed(ActionEvent e) {
      // Get the text of the button
      String buttonText = e.getActionCommand();
      //First test for buttons
      if (buttonText.equals("Clear")) {
        i_lastX = 0;
        i_lastY = 0;
        clear(getGraphics());
      }
      else if (buttonText.equals("Exit")) {
        dispose();
        java.lang.System.exit(0);
      }
    }
// The following are required by the WindowListener interface
    public void windowClosing(WindowEvent e) {
      this.dispose();
      System.exit(0);
    }
    public void windowActivated(WindowEvent e) { }
    public void windowDeactivated(WindowEvent e) { }
    public void windowDeiconified(WindowEvent e) { }
    public void windowClosed(WindowEvent e) { }
    public void windowIconified(WindowEvent e) { }
    public void windowOpened(WindowEvent e) { }
// Mouse methods required by the MouseMotionListener interface
    public void mouseMoved(MouseEvent e) { }   // Mouse was moved
    public void mouseDragged(MouseEvent e) {    // Mouse was dragged
      if (isSettingColor == false) {
        if (rb_draw.getState()) {
          draw(e.getX(), e.getY());
          i_lastX = e.getX();
          i_lastY = e.getY();
```

```
        }
        else {
          draw(e.getX(), e.getY(), true);
        }
      }
    }
  // The following are required by the MouseListener interface
    public void mouseClicked(MouseEvent e) { }
    public void mousePressed(MouseEvent e) {   //A mouse button was
pressed
      paintClick(e.getX(), e.getY());
    }
    public void mouseReleased(MouseEvent e) {   // A mouse button was
released
      if (isSettingColor == false && rb_draw.getState() == false) {
        draw(e.getX(), e.getY());
      }
    }
    public void mouseEntered(MouseEvent e) { }
    public void mouseExited(MouseEvent e) { }
}
interface IColorPanel {
  public void handleColorPanel(MouseEvent e, Color c);
}
class ColorPanel extends Panel implements MouseListener{
  private boolean b_enabled = true;   // Mouse Clicks are enabled
  private Color col_background;
  private IColorPanel icp_callingModule;
  public ColorPanel(IColorPanel cm, Color bg) {
    super();
    addMouseListener(this);
    icp_callingModule = cm;
    newColor(bg);
  }
  public void newColor(Color bg) {
    col_background = bg;
    setBackground(col_background);
    repaint();
  }
  public void disableMouse() {   // Disable clicks
    b_enabled = false;
  }
  public void enableMouse() {   // Enable clicks
    b_enabled = true;
  }
  public void paint(Graphics g) {
    Rectangle r = getBounds();
    setForeground(Color.black);
    g.drawRect(0, 0, r.width-1, r.height-1);
  }
// The following are required by the MouseListener interface
  public void mouseClicked(MouseEvent e) {
    if (b_enabled) {
      icp_callingModule.handleColorPanel(e, col_background);
    }
  }
```

```
    public void mousePressed(MouseEvent e) { }  //A mouse button was
pressed
    public void mouseReleased(MouseEvent e) { }  // A mouse button was
released
    public void mouseEntered(MouseEvent e) { }
    public void mouseExited(MouseEvent e) { }
}
```

Declaring Listeners in a graphical Java program

As you can see, the class declaration gets quite long when using several Listeners. Listing 15-3 has the following class declaration:

```
public class PaintFrame extends Frame
    implements  WindowListener, MouseListener,
        MouseMotionListener, ActionListener,
        IColorPanel {
```

The WindowListener, MouseListener, MouseMotionListener, ActionListener, and a customized IColorPanel interface are all implemented inside PaintFrame. Most business graphical applications require at least a WindowListener and an ActionListener to handle functions such as data entry and Frame-Window navigation.

Using constructors in a graphical Java program

In the constructor of Listing 15-3, much of the window is built. This section discusses radio buttons, command buttons, and Panels.

Using panels

1. Declare all the Panels and set their background colors to light gray, as shown by the following:

   ```
   Panel myNorthPanel = new Panel();
   myNorthPanel.setBackground(Color.lightGray);
   ```

2. Choose layouts for each panel. Choose a GridLayout to enable the top panel to display the different colors and a side panel to display radio buttons. Components placed on those panels take up enough space in the window to be viewable. Choose a FlowLayout for the bottom of the window because the South panel just has informational displays and command buttons, which work well in a FlowLayout pattern:

   ```
   myNorthPanel.setLayout(new GridLayout(1, 8));
   myWestPanel.setLayout(new GridLayout(4, 1));
   mySouthPanel.setLayout(new FlowLayout());
   ```

3. Add Components, such as Buttons, Checkboxes, and Panels to the North, West, and South panels. The following line adds the `bu_exit` Button to `mySouthPanel`:

```
Button bu_exit = new Button("Exit");
//…
mySouthPanel.add(bu_exit);
```

4. Finally, add the Panel to the Frame. And then resize, title, and show the Frame:

```
add("North", myNorthPanel);
setTitle("PaintFrame.java");
setSize (600,400);
show();
```

Creating customized components

The easiest way to create a component is to inherit the component from an existing component. In Listing 15-3, `ColorPanel` was created by inheriting it from Panel:

```
class ColorPanel extends Panel implements MouseListener{
```

On the North Panel, the programmer chooses which background color is needed for a Component:

```
Panel cp_black = new ColorPanel(Color.black);
///…
myNorthPanel.add();
```

The current background and foreground colors display on the South Panel:

```
ColorPanel cp_currentForeground = new ColorPanel(this,
col_currentForeground)
mySouthPanel.add(cp_currentForeground);
```

`ColorPanel` has all the functionality of a panel, plus four other features:

■ The ColorPanel constructor receives both a background color and the calling module as arguments. A MouseListener is then added to determine when a user clicks the panel. Finally, the `newColor()` method is called to set the background color to the color specified by the programmer.

```
public ColorPanel(IColorPanel cm, Color bg) {
  super();
  addMouseListener(this);
  icp_callingModule = cm;
  newColor(bg);
}
public void newColor(Color bg) {
  col_background = bg;
  setBackground(col_background);
  repaint();
}
```

■ A flag is set to disable or enable the mouse depending on whether or not the calling program wants ColorPanel to send messages about mouse control.

```
public void disableMouse() {  // Disable clicks
  b_enabled = false;
}
public void enableMouse() {  // Enable clicks
  b_enabled = true;
}
```

■ When a mouse button is clicked on a Panel, the handleColorPanel() method from the calling program handles the event:

```
// The following are required by the MouseListener interface
public void mouseClicked(MouseEvent e) {
  if (b_enabled) {
    icp_callingModule.handleColorPanel(e, col_background);
  }
}
```

■ Finally, when the window is painted, a rectangular border is placed around the Panel.

Customized components show the power of inheritance. When you need a component to have more functionality, inherit the component and add the functionality yourself *without* rewriting an entire Component.

Using the paint() method

The paint() method is part of the Container class. It is executed every time an Applet, Frame, or Panel is painted, and it can be triggered by calling the repaint() method. In the ColorPanel() method, a black rectangle is drawn as a border around every () method.

```
public void paint(Graphics g) {
    Rectangle r = bounds();
    setForeground(Color.black);
    g.drawRect(0, 0, r.width-1, r.height-1);
}
```

Secret

The paint() method is used often in Java because it is executed every time a Container repaints itself. However, changing the background color does not ensure that a component repaints itself. For this, you need to use the repaint() method. The paint() method is executed every time a repaint() method is called.

Using Checkboxes and radio buttons

Checkboxes in a graphical program enable the user to toggle them on and off by clicking them with a mouse. A special form of Checkbox is a *radio button*. Radio buttons are a series of Checkboxes that have only one choice selected at a time.

In Figure 15-14, the Line, Draw, Box, and Circle choices are radio buttons. Only one drawing construct can be chosen at a time. For instance, if you want to draw a line, click Line and then draw the line with your mouse. When you click Line, the default choice, Draw, is turned off automatically.

In Java, radio buttons are actually a set of Checkboxes placed in a CheckboxGroup. To make a radio button in Java, you must first declare a CheckboxGroup, and then create a Checkbox using the CheckboxGroup:

```
// Define CheckboxGroups for choices for drawing
  private CheckboxGroup cbg = new CheckboxGroup();
// Choices for drawing
  private Checkbox rb_draw = new Checkbox("Draw", cbg, true);
  private Checkbox rb_line = new Checkbox("Line", cbg, false);
  private Checkbox rb_box = new Checkbox("Box", cbg, false);
  private Checkbox rb_circle = new Checkbox("Circle", cbg, false);
```

All Checkboxes inside a CheckboxGroup act as radio buttons.

Secret

The constructor for Checkbox is overloaded. In Java, you can construct a Checkbox in two ways:

- A Checkbox that is not a radio button can be created using a string argument in the constructor:

  ```
  Checkbox yesOrNo = new Checkbox("Yes or No");
  ```

- A Checkbox that is part of a radio button needs to pass the CheckboxGroup and the boolean state (true for clicked, false for not clicked) of the Checkbox. The following code creates a radio button of Choice A and Choice B and makes Choice A the default:

  ```
  CheckboxGroup AorB = new CheckboxGroup();
  Checkbox choiceA = new Checkbox("Choice A", cbg_choices, true);
  Checkbox choiceB = new Checkbox("Choice B", cbg_choices, false);
  ```

Examining components and ActionListeners

When any Button is clicked, an action event occurs. This can be trapped with an ActionListener. First, the containing class has to implement an ActionListener interface:

```
public class PaintFrame extends Frame
   implements  WindowListener, MouseListener,
      MouseMotionListener, ActionListener,
      IColorPanel {
```

Next, the ActionListener needs to be added to each button that needs to trap the action event. This is done by using the addActionListener() method:

```
//Add ActionListeners for all buttons
bu_clear.addActionListener(this);
  bu_exit.addActionListener(this);
```

Finally, the action event is handled by the `actionPerformed()` method:

```
//The actionPerformed method is required
//by the ActionListener interface
  public void actionPerformed(ActionEvent e) {
     // Get the text of the button
     String buttonText = e.getActionCommand();
     //First test for buttons
     if (buttonText.equals("Clear")) {
       i_lastX = 0;
       i_lastY = 0;
       clear(getGraphics());
     }
     else if (buttonText.equals("Exit")) {
       dispose();
       java.lang.System.exit(0);
     }
  }
```

As you can see in the preceding code, the `ActionEvent.getActionCommand()` method is used to return the text of the Button. The returned String can be used to test which button has been pressed.

Using mouse events

Rather than testing for a mouse click using the `mouseClicked()` method, as shown earlier in this chapter, a graphical paint program needs to test for a click, a drag, and a release. This is done using methods from the MouseListener and the MouseMovementListener interfaces and the following steps:

1. When a click is first detected, the `mousePressed()` method calls the `paintClick()` method to determine the chosen options and the next program action:

```
public void mousePressed(MouseEvent e) {       //A mouse button was
pressed
 paintClick(e.getX(), e.getY());
 }
```

2. If the mouse is dragged, the `mouseDragged()` method tests to see if a color is being set. If not, then if the Draw radio button is chosen, a *small* line is drawn between two adjacent points. This has the equivalent effect of "scribbling" on the Frame. Otherwise, the `draw()` method is called with an optional parameter that asks to test for XOR graphics mode. (This is described later.)

```
public void mouseDragged(MouseEvent e) {     // Mouse was dragged
   if (isSettingColor == false) {
     if (rb_draw.getState()) {
       draw(e.getX(), e.getY());
       i_lastX = e.getX();
```

```
        i_lastY = e.getY();
      }
    else {
      draw(e.getX(), e.getY(), true);
      }
    }
  }
```

3. Finally, if a mouse button is released and the Draw option is not chosen, the `draw()` method is called to finish the drawing:

```
  public void mouseReleased(MouseEvent e) {  // A mouse button
was released
    if (isSettingColor == false && rb_draw.getState() == false) {
      draw(e.getX(), e.getY());
      }
    }
```

Mastering drawing functions and XOR graphics mode

The easiest drawing method written in Listing 15-3 is the `clear()` method. The `clear()` method fills a white rectangle around the drawing area, giving the user a new, clean, white area to start a new drawing:

```
  public void clear(Graphics g) {
      Rectangle r = bounds();
      g.setColor(Color.white);
      g.fillRect(0, 0, r.width-1, r.height-1);
  }
```

Two drawing modes are supported: permanent and temporary. The `draw()` method is overloaded to enable an (x, y) argument to be passed for a permanent drawing or an (x, y, *true*) to be passed for a temporary drawing. The argument (x, y, *false*) also creates a permanent drawing:

```
  public void draw(int x, int y) {
      draw(x, y, false);
  }
  public void draw(int x, int y, boolean xor) {
//...
```

Delving into the XOR graphics mode

If the Boolean XOR value is set to true, the drawing is "temporary." This means that the line that is drawn is erased with the next mouse action. This is done by using the XOR graphics mode and the `SetXORMode()` method.

If you use the `setXORMode()` method to set the color rather than the `setColor()` method:

```
if (xor) {
    if (col_currentForeground == Color.black) {
        g.setXORMode(Color.white);
    }
    else {
        g.setXORMode(col_currentForeground);
    }
//...
```

all drawings *are not* in the color you chose, but rather are logically ORed with the existing color that is being drawn over. The result is that a color is never the same as the background over which it is drawn. However, if you draw over the same area with the exact same color twice, the *original* picture is restored. In this way, you can make a "temporary" line:

1. Set the drawing color using `setXORMode()` rather than the `setColor()` method:

   ```
   if (xor) {
   g.setXORMode(col_currentForeground);
   ```

2. Draw *over* the last line or shape you drew in XOR mode. This restores the color to the original color before you drew your first XOR line or shape.

   ```
   g.drawLine(i_lastX, i_lastY, i_lastObjectX, i_lastObjectY);
   ```

3. Calculate the new line or shape dimensions:

   ```
   i_lastObjectX = x;
   i_lastObjectY = y;
   lastX = Math.min(i_lastX, x);
   lastY = Math.min(i_lastY, y);
   int toX = Math.max(i_lastX, x);
   int toY = Math.max(i_lastY, y);
   ```

4. Draw your new line or shape. If the new line is the final shape, use the `setColor()` method to set the color. Otherwise, continue to use the `setXORMode()` method to set color.

The XOR mode enables you to make lines that are erased without erasing the picture underneath the line. This is handy for moving graphics around the window.

Using drawing methods

Whether you use the `setColor()` method or the `setXORMode()` method to set your color, Java provides drawing methods that you can use with the color and drawing mode you have selected. The most popular ones are shown in Listing 15-3 and are described in Table 15-3.

Table 15-3   Drawing Methods

Method Prototype	Description
`drawLine(int x1, int y1, int x2, int y2)`	Draws a line between the coordinates (*x1,y1*) and (*x2,y2*). The `drawLine()` method is used not only for drawing lines between two distant points, but also for drawing lines between two adjacent points — in the Draw option.
`drawOval(int x, int y, int width, int height)`	Draws an oval inside a rectangle defined by *x, y*, width, and height using the current color.
`drawRect(int x, int y, int width, int height)`	Draws the outline of a rectangle identified by *x, y*, width, and height using the current color.
`fillOval(int x, int y, int width, int height)`	Fills an oval inside a rectangle defined by *x, y*, width, and height using the current color.
`fillRect(int x, int y, int width, int height)`	Fills a rectangle (identified by *x, y*, width, and height) with the current color.

Summary

- Mouse, window, keyboard, and action events are captured by using Listener interfaces. These interfaces need to be implemented, then the Frame, Applet, or Component needs to add itself to the Listener.

- Graphical programming can be easily achieved through Components. If a Component doesn't quite meet your needs, it's easy to inherit the component and add the needed functionality.

- Java includes a host of graphical draw functions. These functions can draw lines, ovals, and rectangles.

- The `paint()` method is executed every time a Container such as a Frame or Applet is drawn, moved, or resized. Often, drawing functionality exists in the `paint()` method so that any window movement causes the necessary repainting to take place.

- If you need to draw a "temporary" line, as many graphical packages require, try using the XOR mode to draw rather than normal mode. By drawing the identical object twice in XOR mode, you restore your image to its original appearance.

Chapter 16

Advanced Graphics

In This Chapter

▶ Displaying bitmaps in your Java application

▶ Using drawn objects, as well as bitmaps, for animation

▶ Manipulating fonts

▶ Using the elusive ImageObserver and ImageProducer interfaces

▶ Using threads for graphical manipulation

▶ Using Canvases effectively

In the last chapter, I discussed graphics and graphical constructs, including drawing functions, menus, Components, and Panels. This chapter delves into graphics at a higher level and shows how easy advanced graphics can be in Java.

Writing a Picture Button Component

Java provides no picture button construct. A picture button is a button with a picture on it instead of text. Writing a picture button, however, is easily accomplished. Listing 16-1 shows how a picture button class can be written.

Listing 16-1: PictureButton.java

```
import java.awt.*;
import java.awt.event.*;
Public class PictureButton extends Canvas implements MouseListener {
    public final static int DEFAULT_WIDTH = 70;
    public final static int DEFAULT_HEIGHT = 70;
    public final static int BUTTON_BORDER = 10;
// Color of the upper left corner
    private Color ico_leftUp = Color.white;
    // Color of the lower right corner
    private Color ico_rightDown = Color.black;
    private Image im_image;      // Image on the PictureButton
    // True if the button is to stay pushed
    private boolean b_stayPushed = false;
      // Currently, the button is not pushed
    private boolean b_pushed = false;
    // The module that called this module
```

```java
    private IPictureButton ipb_callingModule;
    public PictureButton(IPictureButton cm, String filename) {
        super();            // Call the constructor
    // Make a 70x70 picture button
        afterConstructor(cm, filename, 70, 70);
    }
    public PictureButton(IPictureButton cm, String filename, int width,
int length) {
        super();            // Call the constructor
        afterConstructor(cm, filename, width, length);
    }
    private void afterConstructor(IPictureButton cm, String filename,
int width, int length) {
    // Assign the calling module program
        ipb_callingModule = cm;
    // Get a image Toolkit to handle the image on the
    // PictureButton
        im_image = Toolkit.getDefaultToolkit().getImage(filename);
        setSize (width, length);    // resize
        addMouseListener(this);     // Capture mouse events
    }
    // Change the PictureButton so
    // that it stays pushed when clicked.
    public void setStayPushed(boolean stayPushed) {
        b_stayPushed = true;
    }
    public boolean getPushed() {        // See if the button is
    //currently pushed
        return b_pushed;
    }
    public void paint(Graphics g) {     // Draw picture and button
        int b = BUTTON_BORDER;
        Rectangle r = getBounds();
        g.drawImage(im_image, b, b, r.width-2*b - 1, r.height-2*b - 1,
this);
        g.setColor(ico_leftUp);
        g.drawLine(0,0,0,r.height);
        g.drawLine(0,0,r.width,0);
        g.setColor(ico_rightDown);
        g.drawLine(r.width-1,r.height-1,1, r.height-1);
        g.drawLine(r.width-1,r.height-1,r.width-1, 1);
    }
    public void pushButton() {          // Push button in
        ico_leftUp = Color.black;
        ico_rightDown = Color.white;
        repaint();
        b_pushed = true;
    }
    public void popButton() {       // Pop button back up
        ico_leftUp = Color.white;
        ico_rightDown = Color.black;
        b_pushed = false;
        repaint();
    }
```

```
// The following are required by the MouseListener interface
// This component was clicked
  public void mouseClicked(MouseEvent e) { }
// mouse button was pressed
  public void mousePressed(MouseEvent e) {
    if (ipb_callingModule.beforeClick()) {
      pushButton();
    }
  }
  // A mouse button was released
  public void mouseReleased(MouseEvent e) {
    ipb_callingModule.afterClick();
    if (!b_stayPushed) {
      popButton();
    }
  }
  public void mouseEntered(MouseEvent e) { }
  public void mouseExited(MouseEvent e) { }
}
```

An interface is needed so the button knows what calling program method to call when it has been clicked. This interface, shown in Listing 16-2, enables the `PictureButton` class to call a method before and after the button click.

Listing 16-2: IPictureButton.java for the IPictureButton interface

```
// Interface so that the Picture Button can call routines from the
calling module.
public interface IPictureButton {
  public boolean beforeClick();
  public void afterClick();
}
```

Figure 16-1 shows how to implement picture buttons in a graphical environment.

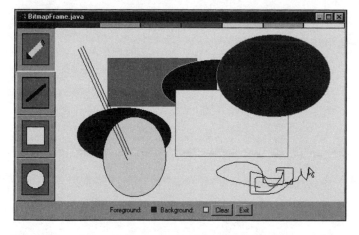

Figure 16-1: Notice the new picture buttons on the left side of the window.

There are several concepts you must grasp before discussing graphics:

■ The Toolkit class is an abstract class that contains code for a platform-dependent implementation of the Java VM. The Toolkit class contains the `getDefaultToolkit()` method, which returns the Toolkit that is in use for a Frame or Dialog. Also, the `getImage()` method is used to store an image file as an instance of the Image class.

■ The Toolkit class is only used for retrieving information into Frames or DialogBox classes. If you are using a Web Applet, you need to use the `Applet.getImage()` method, which retrieves images from URLs.

■ All images need to be stored in an Image class instance. However, the Image class *is not* descendent from Component, and therefore does not trigger events when clicked.

Using images

The `java.awt.Image` class is needed when using a bitmap in your Java Applet or program. Images can be retrieved by using the `getDefaultToolkit()` method to return the current Toolkit, and then using the `Toolkit.getImage()` method to retrieve an image from a file. This is done from the following line found in the PictureButton constructor:

```
im_image = Toolkit.getDefaultToolkit().getImage(filename);
```

In the PictureButton constructors, the parent class constructor is called with the super method. Then the image is retrieved from a passed filename. Finally, PictureButton is resized to a default 70×70 or, if they passed length and width, to a specified length and width:

```
public PictureButton(IPictureButton cm, String filename) {
   super();          // Call the constructor
   afterConstructor(cm, filename, 70, 70);  // Make a 70x70 picture
button
}
public PictureButton(IPictureButton cm, String filename, int width,
int length) {
   super();          // Call the constructor
   afterConstructor(cm, filename, width, length);
}
private void afterConstructor(IPictureButton cm, String filename, int
width, int length) {
   ipb_callingModule = cm;       // Assign the calling module program
// Get a image Toolkit to handle the image on the PictureButton
   im_image = Toolkit.getDefaultToolkit().getImage(filename);
   setSize (width, length);      // resize
   addMouseListener(this);       // Capture mouse events
}
```

Don't confuse the `java.awt.Image` class with the `java.awt.image` package. Strangely enough, the Image class is in the `java.awt` package. The `java.awt.image` package contains classes and interfaces that control or observe facts about images being processed in your Java program.

Images can then be drawn using the `Graphics.drawImage` class. This is often done when using the `paint()` method, as shown by the following example:

```
public void paint(Graphics g) {
    g.drawImage(im_image, 0, 0, this);
}
```

The PictureButton class first assigns the BUTTON_BORDER constant to a local integer. Then, the length and width of the PictureButton are determined using the `bounds()` method. The image is drawn in the middle of the PictureButton, and black and white lines are drawn to simulate a 3D button effect:

```
public void paint(Graphics g) {
    int b = BUTTON_BORDER;
    Rectangle r = bounds();
    g.drawImage(im_image, b, b, r.width-2*b - 1, r.height-2*b - 1,
this);
    g.setColor(ico_leftUp);
    g.drawLine(0,0,0,r.height);
    g.drawLine(0,0,r.width,0);
    g.setColor(ico_rightDown);
    g.drawLine(r.width-1,r.height-1,1, r.height-1);
    g.drawLine(r.width-1,r.height-1,r.width-1, 1);
}
```

Exploring the Canvas Class

The previous section states that Images are not Components, and therefore don't have events. To create a picture that has events, you must place it on a Component. This is often done using the Canvas class.

Although the Canvas class is not abstract and can be instantiated, it usually isn't. Rather, it is inherited to make individual Components. By using a class inherited from the Canvas class, you not only get Images that can have events, but also get Components that can process Images.

Some books tell you to use the Canvas class to paint on so you don't have to paint directly on the Applet or Frame. Unless you're animating, this is ludicrous, because there's nothing wrong with painting directly on an Applet or Frame. (These books never tell you why they think it's bad to paint directly on an Applet or Frame, and their examples outside of the Canvas discussion *never* use a Canvas.)

Canvases are great for making your own Components. Although Panels can be used in the same manner, a Panel carries with it Container overhead that a Canvas does not. Because Canvas is the only non-Container Component that has a paint() method, it is the only non-Container method that can truly support additional graphics.

Because Canvas is a Component, it supports the standard mouse events. These events are used to call the pushButton() and popButton() methods. These methods change the 3D appearance of the PictureButton to give a "pushed-down" or "pushed-up" look:

```
public void pushButton() {       // Push button in
  ico_leftUp = Color.black;
  ico_rightDown = Color.white;
  repaint();
  b_pushed = true;
}
public void popButton() {         // Pop button back up
  ico_leftUp = Color.white;
  ico_rightDown = Color.black;
  b_pushed = false;
  repaint();
}
```

Retrieving an image from a URL or disk

Retrieving an image from a disk has already been discussed. Using the getImage() method in the Toolkit class, you can retrieve an image from a disk, and store it into an Image class:

```
//Inside a Frame or DialogBox
im_image = Toolkit.getDefaultToolkit().getImage("DRAWICON.GIF");
```

You can also retrieve an image from a URL using the Applet getImage() method. There are several ways to do this. The most intuitive (and the worst) way to retrieve an image is to hard-code the path into your getImage() method:

```
//Inside an Applet
im_image = getImage(new URL "http://www.mywebpage.com/logo.jpg");
```

A better way to retrieve an image is by using a relative URL rather than an absolute URL. The getImage() method also supports a URL with a filename inside that URL:

```
//Inside an Applet
im_image = getImage(new URL "http://www.primapublishing.com/",
"logo.jpg");
```

Secret

The preceding code is not much different from the full hard-coded pathname, except you can then replace the hard-coded URL with a `getDocumentBase` call. The `getDocumentBase()` method returns the URL of the HTML page on which the current Applet resides.

```
//Inside an Applet
im_image = getImage(getDocumentBase( ), "logo.jpg");
```

Secret

Sometimes, you need to keep your Java class files in a separate directory from your graphical files. In this case, you can use the `<APPLET CODEBASE=url>` HTML tag to define a CODEBASE variable for your Java Applet. You can then use the `getCodeBase()` method like the `getDocumentBase()` method to retrieve a relative URL call for an image:

```
//Inside an Applet
im_image = getImage(getCodeBase( ), "logo.jpg");
```

Currently, Java Virtual Machines support only JPEG and GIF files. Microsoft has added the popular BMP format, although BMP file sizes are large compared to JPEG and GIF. Other popular formats, such as TIF and PCX are not yet supported. For now, JPEG and GIF image formats are best, especially inside a Web page. GIF files have the added advantage of supporting a transparency bit that enables the background on which they are painted to show through.

Using the new PictureButton component

The `PaintFrame()` program (from the last chapter) can be modified to use the new PictureButton class, as shown in Figure 16-1. Listing 16-3 shows, in boldface, the lines you need to change in the `PaintFrame` program to use a picture button rather than radio buttons.

Listing 16-3: IPictureButton.java for the IPictureButton interface

```
import java.awt.*;
import java.awt.event.*;
public class BitmapFrame extends Frame
   implements  WindowListener, MouseListener,
      MouseMotionListener, ActionListener,
      IColorPanel, IPictureButton {
   int i_lastX;
   int i_lastY;
   int i_lastObjectX;
   int i_lastObjectY;
   private boolean isSettingColor = false;
// Choices for drawing
   private PictureButton pb_draw = new PictureButton(this,
"DRAWICON.GIF");
   private PictureButton pb_line = new PictureButton(this,
"LINEICON.GIF");
```

```java
  private PictureButton pb_box = new PictureButton(this,
"BOXICON.GIF");
  private PictureButton pb_circle = new PictureButton(this,
"CIRCLEIC.GIF");
//Buttons on Window
  private Button bu_clear = new Button("Clear");
  private Button bu_exit = new Button("Exit");
//Color choices
  private ColorPanel cp_black = new ColorPanel(this, Color.black);
  private ColorPanel cp_blue = new ColorPanel(this, Color.blue);
  private ColorPanel cp_lightGray = new ColorPanel(this,
Color.lightGray);
  private ColorPanel cp_magenta = new ColorPanel(this,
Color.magenta);
  private ColorPanel cp_red = new ColorPanel(this, Color.red);
  private ColorPanel cp_yellow = new ColorPanel(this, Color.yellow);
  private ColorPanel cp_green = new ColorPanel(this, Color.green);
  private ColorPanel cp_white = new ColorPanel(this, Color.white);
  private Color col_currentForeground = Color.black;
  private Color col_currentBackground = Color.white;
  private ColorPanel cp_currentForeground = new ColorPanel(this,
col_currentForeground);
  private ColorPanel cp_currentBackground = new ColorPanel(this,
col_currentBackground);
// Main method for starting the BitmapFrame
  public static void main (String args[]) {
    BitmapFrame bf = new BitmapFrame();
  }
  public BitmapFrame () {
//Add the WindowListener, MouseListener, and MouseMotionListener
//for Window and Mouse events
    addWindowListener(this);
    addMouseListener(this);
    addMouseMotionListener(this);
//Define Panels and the layouts they use
    Panel myNorthPanel = new Panel();
    Panel myWestPanel = new Panel();
    Panel mySouthPanel = new Panel();
    myNorthPanel.setBackground(Color.lightGray);
    mySouthPanel.setBackground(Color.lightGray);
    myWestPanel.setBackground(Color.lightGray);
    myNorthPanel.setLayout(new GridLayout(1, 8));
    myWestPanel.setLayout(new GridLayout(4, 1));
    mySouthPanel.setLayout(new FlowLayout());
  //Add color panels
    myNorthPanel.add(cp_black);
    myNorthPanel.add(cp_blue);
    myNorthPanel.add(cp_lightGray);
    myNorthPanel.add(cp_magenta);
    myNorthPanel.add(cp_red);
    myNorthPanel.add(cp_yellow);
    myNorthPanel.add(cp_green);
    myNorthPanel.add(cp_white);
  //Add the clear and exit command buttons.
    mySouthPanel.add(new Label("Foreground:"));
    mySouthPanel.add(cp_currentForeground);
```

```java
    mySouthPanel.add(new Label("Background:"));
    mySouthPanel.add(cp_currentBackground);
    cp_currentBackground.disableMouse();  // Disable Mouse Clicks
    cp_currentForeground.disableMouse();  // Disable Mouse Clicks
    mySouthPanel.add(bu_clear);
    mySouthPanel.add(bu_exit);
//Add ActionListeners for all buttons
    bu_clear.addActionListener(this);
    bu_exit.addActionListener(this);
//Add buttons andhave them stay pushed
    pb_draw.setStayPushed(true);
    pb_line.setStayPushed(true);
    pb_box.setStayPushed(true);
    pb_circle.setStayPushed(true);
    pb_draw.pushButton();  // Default to draw
    myWestPanel.add(pb_draw);
    myWestPanel.add(pb_line);
    myWestPanel.add(pb_box);
    myWestPanel.add(pb_circle);
// Add the panels to the frame
    add("North", myNorthPanel);
    add("West", myWestPanel);
    add("South", mySouthPanel);
    setTitle("BitmapFrame.java");
    setSize (600,400);
    show();
}
public void clear(Graphics g) {
    Rectangle r = getBounds();
    g.setColor(Color.white);
    g.fillRect(0, 0, r.width-1, r.height-1);
}
public void paintClick(int x, int y) {
    isSettingColor = false;
    i_lastX = x;
    i_lastY = y;
    i_lastObjectX = 0;
    i_lastObjectY = 0;
}
public void draw(int x, int y) {
    draw(x, y, false);
}
public void draw(int x, int y, boolean xor) {
    int lastX;
    int lastY;
    Graphics g = getGraphics();
    if (xor) {
        if (col_currentForeground == Color.black) {
            g.setXORMode(Color.white);
        }
        else {
            g.setXORMode(col_currentForeground);
        }
        if (i_lastObjectX > 0) {
            int fromX = Math.min(i_lastObjectX, i_lastX);
            int fromY = Math.min(i_lastObjectY, i_lastY);
```

```
                    int toX = Math.max(i_lastObjectX, i_lastX);
                    int toY = Math.max(i_lastObjectY, i_lastY);
                    if (pb_line.getPushed()) {
                        g.drawLine(i_lastX, i_lastY, i_lastObjectX,
i_lastObjectY);
                    }
                    else if (pb_box.getPushed()) {
                        g.drawRect(fromX, fromY, toX - fromX, toY - fromY);
                    }
                    else if (pb_circle.getPushed()) {
                        g.drawOval(fromX, fromY, toX - fromX, toY - fromY);
                    }
                }
            }
            else {
                g.setColor(col_currentForeground);
            }
            i_lastObjectX = x;
            i_lastObjectY = y;
            lastX = Math.min(i_lastX, x);
            lastY = Math.min(i_lastY, y);
            int toX = Math.max(i_lastX, x);
            int toY = Math.max(i_lastY, y);
            if(pb_draw.getPushed() || pb_line.getPushed()) {
                g.drawLine(i_lastX, i_lastY, x, y);
            }
            else if(pb_box.getPushed()) {
                g.drawRect(lastX, lastY, toX - lastX, toY - lastY);
                if (xor == false) {
                    g.setColor(col_currentBackground);
                    g.fillRect(lastX + 1, lastY + 1, toX - lastX - 1, toY -
lastY - 1);
                }
            }
            else if(pb_circle.getPushed()) {
                if (xor == false) {
                    g.setColor(col_currentBackground);
                    g.fillOval(lastX, lastY, toX - lastX, toY - lastY);
                    g.setColor(col_currentForeground);
                }
                g.drawOval(lastX, lastY, toX - lastX, toY - lastY);
            }
        }
    public void newForeground(Color foreground) {
        col_currentForeground = foreground;
        cp_currentForeground.newColor(foreground);
    }
    public void newBackground(Color background) {
        col_currentBackground = background;
        cp_currentBackground.newColor(background);
    }
// The handleColorPanel() is required by the IColorPanel interface
    public void handleColorPanel(MouseEvent e, Color c) {
        isSettingColor = true;
        if (e.isMetaDown()) {   //Right button clicked
            newBackground(c);
```

```
      }
      else {              //Left button clicked
        newForeground(c);
      }
    }
//The actionPerformed method is required
//by the ActionListener interface
    public void actionPerformed(ActionEvent e) {
      // Get the text of the button
      String buttonText = e.getActionCommand();
      //First test for buttons
      if (buttonText.equals("Clear")) {
        i_lastX = 0;
        i_lastY = 0;
        clear(getGraphics());
      }
      else if (buttonText.equals("Exit")) {
        dispose();
        java.lang.System.exit(0);
      }
    }
// The following are required by the WindowListener interface
    public void windowClosing(WindowEvent e) {
      this.dispose();
      System.exit(0);
    }
    public void windowActivated(WindowEvent e) { }
    public void windowDeactivated(WindowEvent e) { }
    public void windowDeiconified(WindowEvent e) { }
    public void windowClosed(WindowEvent e) { }
    public void windowIconified(WindowEvent e) { }
    public void windowOpened(WindowEvent e) { }
// Methods required by the IPictureButton interface
    public boolean beforeClick() {
      pb_draw.popButton();   //Pop all the buttons back up
      pb_line.popButton();
      pb_box.popButton();
      pb_circle.popButton();
      return true;
    }
    public void afterClick() { }
// Mouse methods required by the MouseMotionListener interface
    public void mouseMoved(MouseEvent e) { }  // Mouse was moved
    public void mouseDragged(MouseEvent e) {   // Mouse was dragged
      if (isSettingColor == false) {
        if (pb_draw.getPushed()) {
          draw(e.getX(), e.getY());
          i_lastX = e.getX();
          i_lastY = e.getY();
        }
        else {
          draw(e.getX(), e.getY(), true);
        }
      }
    }
// The following are required by the MouseListener interface
```

```java
      public void mouseClicked(MouseEvent e) { }
      public void mousePressed(MouseEvent e) {   //A mouse button was
      //pressed
        paintClick(e.getX(), e.getY());
      }
      public void mouseReleased(MouseEvent e) {   // A mouse button was
      //released
        if (isSettingColor == false && pb_draw.getPushed() == false) {
          draw(e.getX(), e.getY());
        }
      }
      public void mouseEntered(MouseEvent e) { }
      public void mouseExited(MouseEvent e) { }
}
interface IColorPanel {
      public void handleColorPanel(MouseEvent e, Color c);
}
class ColorPanel extends Panel implements MouseListener{
      private boolean b_enabled = true;  // Mouse Clicks are enabled
      private Color col_background;
      private IColorPanel icp_callingModule;
      public ColorPanel(IColorPanel cm, Color bg) {
        super();
        addMouseListener(this);
        icp_callingModule = cm;
        newColor(bg);
      }
      public void disableMouse() {   // Disable clicks
        b_enabled = false;
      }
      public void enableMouse() {   // Enable clicks
        b_enabled = true;
      }
      public void paint(Graphics g) {
        Rectangle r = getBounds();
        setForeground(Color.black);
        g.drawRect(0, 0, r.width-1, r.height-1);
      }
      public void newColor(Color bg) {
        col_background = bg;
        setBackground(col_background);
        repaint();
      }
   // The following are required by the MouseListener interface
      public void mouseClicked(MouseEvent e) {
        if (b_enabled) {
          icp_callingModule.handleColorPanel(e, col_background);
        }
      }
      public void mousePressed(MouseEvent e) { }  //A mouse button was
      //pressed
      public void mouseReleased(MouseEvent e) { }  // A mouse button was
      //released
      public void mouseEntered(MouseEvent e) { }
      public void mouseExited(MouseEvent e) { }
   }
```

Secret

If you want to, you can use adapter classes instead of implementing Listeners. Adapter classes enable you to add listeners without implementing a listener interface and leaving empty method bodies. For instance, MouseAdapter and WindowAdapter can be subclassed instead of implementing empty method bodies for MouseListener and WindowListener.

```
addMouseListener(new MouseAdapter()
  public void mouseClicked(MouseEvent e) {
    if (b_enabled) {
      icp_callingModule.handleColorPanel(e, col_background);
    }
  }
    });
```

As you can see, not many changes are needed once the new component is created.

Manipulating Fonts

You can change the font associated with any Graphics or Component object. To use a new font, create a Font instance with the following code:

```
Font myFont = Font(String name, int style, int size)
```

This prototype creates a new font with the specified name, style, and point size. The name can be any font supported by Java or by the operating system. Examples are Helvetica, TimesRoman, and Courier. The style argument specifies the sum of the constants Font.PLAIN, Font.BOLD, and/or Font.ITALIC. For instance, if you wanted a Font to be boldface and italics, define the Font's style to be Font.ITALIC + Font.BOLD.

Listing 16-3 uses these commands to add clear and exit buttons to the `BitmapFrame` **Frame:**

```
// Create the clear and exit command buttons.
mySouthPanel.add(bu_clear);
mySouthPanel.add(bu_exit);
```

The following code uses an 18-point boldface italics TimesRoman font, instead of the default 8-point normal Helvetica font:

```
// Create the clear and exit command buttons.
  Font timesFont = new Font("TimesRoman", Font.ITALIC + Font.BOLD,
18);
  bu_clear.setFont(timesFont);
  bu_exit.setFont(timesFont);
  mySouthPanel.add(bu_clear);
  mySouthPanel.add(bu_exit);
```

Your buttons would look like those pictured in Figure 16-2.

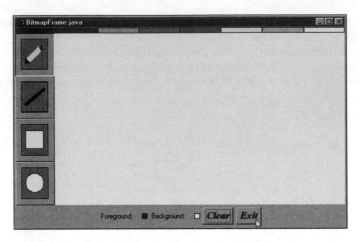

Figure 16-2: Different fonts can enhance a program's appearance.

Notice that even though TimesRoman font was specified in the previous paragraph, it looks like the Times New Roman true type font is used instead. This is because Java's TimesRoman font maps to the Times New Roman font. Table 16-1 shows the fonts specified by the Java standard.

Table 16-1	Windows Fonts Supported by Java
Standard Java Font	*Corresponding Windows Font*
Courier	Courier New
Dialog	MS Sans Serif
DialogInput	MS Sans Serif
Helvetica (default)	Arial
TimesRoman	Times New Roman
ZapfDingbats	WingDings

Currently, most Java developers don't change Fonts too often because of poor platform font-mapping support. However, this will change as Java programs become more sophisticated and end users demand a professional look and feel from their Java applications.

Getting a list of available fonts

All Java Virtual Machines are required to support the six fonts. If you try to use a font that is not specified by the Java standard, some browsers will not be capable of using it. This may cause your text to display in some other font or not at all.

You can, however, get a list of all fonts that are supported by a given virtual machine, because some virtual machines may support fonts not available on other virtual machines. Listing 16-4 is a short program that lists all the fonts on any Java VM.

Listing 16-4: FontList.java

```java
import java.awt.*;
import java.awt.event.*;
public class FontList extends Frame implements WindowListener {
  private TextArea ta_fonts = new TextArea();  // Area to hold
  //display
  public static void main(String args[]) {
    FontList f = new FontList();       // Construct FontList class
  }
  public FontList() {             //FontList constructor
    //Add the WindowListener for Window events
    addWindowListener(this);
    setLayout(new GridLayout(1,1));
    add(ta_fonts);          // Add a text area for output
  // Get the font names from the Toolkit
    String fonts[] = Toolkit.getDefaultToolkit().getFontList();
    ta_fonts.append("The following fonts are avaiable:\n\n");
  // Display the fonts
    for (int loop = 0; loop < fonts.length; loop++) {
      ta_fonts.append("\t" + fonts[loop] + "\n");
    }
    setSize(300, 220);          // resize
    setTitle("FontList.java");      // set the title
    show();          // show the frame
  }
// The following are required by the WindowListener interface
  public void windowClosing(WindowEvent e) {  // User wants the
  //window to close
    this.dispose();
    System.exit(0);
  }
  public void windowActivated(WindowEvent e) { }  // Window got
  //focus
   public void windowDeactivated(WindowEvent e){}  // Window lost
   //focus
  public void windowIconified(WindowEvent e) { }  // Window is
  //reduced
  public void windowDeiconified(WindowEvent e){}  // Window is
  //expanded from an icon
  public void windowClosed(WindowEvent e) { }  // Window is finished
  //closing
  public void windowOpened(WindowEvent e) { }  // Window is finished
  //opening
}
```

This short list is compiled using the `Toolkit.getFontList()` method:

```
String fonts[] = Toolkit.getDefaultToolkit().getFontList();
```

The `getFontList()` method returns a String array containing all the names of the Fonts supported at the current installation. That list is then displayed by a loop in the `paint()` method, as shown in Figure 16-3.

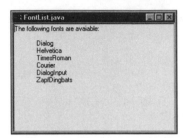

Figure 16-3: FontList.java returns a list of all available fonts for a given Java Virtual Machine.

Examining FontMetrics

Often, you want to know how much space is used by a string or character using a certain font. Listing 16-5 lists all the fonts (the same as Listing 16-4), and then displays them with Font.BOLD and Font.ITALIC style modifiers. Then the FontMetrics class is used to get the size of the "Hello World" string used in the program. Figure 16-4 shows the output of the program.

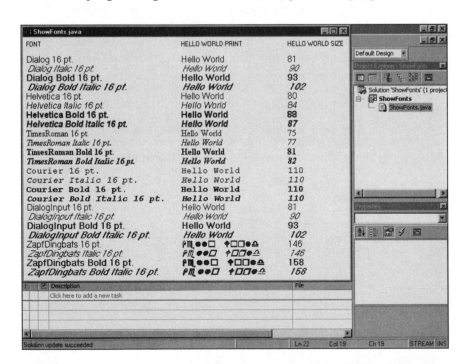

Figure 16-4: FontInfo.java uses the FontMetrics class to return information about a font.

Listing 16-5: ShowFonts.java

```java
import java.awt.*;
import java.awt.event.*;
public class ShowFonts extends Frame implements WindowListener{
  String isa_fonts[];           // Array containing font names
  Font fa_allfonts[][];          // Array containing fonts
  public static void main(String args[]) {
    ShowFonts f = new ShowFonts();  // Construct the ShowFonts class
  }
  public ShowFonts() {            // Constructor
    addWindowListener(this);     // Enable window events
  // Get the font names from the Toolkit
    isa_fonts = Toolkit.getDefaultToolkit().getFontList();
    fa_allfonts = new Font[4][isa_fonts.length];
  // Build the fa_allfonts for normal, italic, bold, and italic-bold
    for (int loop = 0; loop < isa_fonts.length; loop++) {
      fa_allfonts[0][loop] = new Font(isa_fonts[loop], Font.PLAIN,
16);
      fa_allfonts[1][loop] = new Font(isa_fonts[loop], Font.ITALIC,
16);
      fa_allfonts[2][loop] = new Font(isa_fonts[loop], Font.BOLD,
16);
      fa_allfonts[3][loop] = new Font(isa_fonts[loop], Font.ITALIC +
                Font.BOLD, 16);
    }
    setSize(620, 475);          //resize
    setTitle("ShowFonts.java");     // set the title
    show();           // show the Frame
  }
  public void paint(Graphics g) {
    // Draw the headings
    g.drawString ("FONT", 10, 40);
    g.drawString ("HELLO WORLD PRINT", 300, 40);
    g.drawString ("HELLO WORLD SIZE", 500, 40);
    for (int loop2 = 0; loop2 < fa_allfonts[0].length; loop2++) {
      for (int loop1 = 0; loop1 < 4; loop1++) {
        String display = fa_allfonts[loop1][loop2].getName();
        // Set string font
        if (display.equals("ZapfDingbats")) {
          g.setFont(fa_allfonts[loop1][0]);
        }
        else {
          g.setFont(fa_allfonts[loop1][loop2]);
        }
        if (fa_allfonts[loop1][loop2].isBold()) {
          display += " Bold";
        }
        if (fa_allfonts[loop1][loop2].isItalic()) {
          display += " Italic";
        }
        display += " 16 pt.";    // Display string and "Hello
                       // World"
        g.drawString(display, 10, 17*((loop2)*4 + loop1)+70);
        if
(fa_allfonts[loop1][loop2].getName().equals("ZapfDingbats")) {
```

```
            g.setFont(fa_allfonts[loop1][loop2]);
        }
        g.drawString("Hello World", 300, 17*((loop2)*4 + loop1)+70);
        FontMetrics fm = g.getFontMetrics();
        if
(fa_allfonts[loop1][loop2].getName().equals("ZapfDingbats")) {
            g.setFont(fa_allfonts[loop1][0]);
        }
        g.drawString( Integer.toString(
            fm.stringWidth("Hello World")),
            500, 17*((loop2)*4 + loop1)+70);
        }
    }
}
// The following are required by the WindowListener interface
  public void windowClosing(WindowEvent e) {   // User wants the
// window to close
    this.dispose();
    System.exit(0);
  }
  public void windowActivated(WindowEvent e) { }   // Window got
  //focus
  public void windowDeactivated(WindowEvent e){}   // Window lost
  //focus
  public void windowIconified(WindowEvent e) { }   // Window is
  //reduced
  public void windowDeiconified(WindowEvent e){}   // Window is
  //expanded from an icon
  public void windowClosed(WindowEvent e) { }   // Window is finished
  //closing
  public void windowOpened(WindowEvent e) { }   // Window is finished
  //opening
}
```

In Listing 16-5, all the fonts are loaded at 16 points with all possibilities of
BOLD and ITALIC. To retrieve the size, you must first retrieve the
FontMetrics used for the Graphics Component in the `paint()` method:

```
FontMetrics fm = g.getFontMetrics();
```

Tip

The FontMetrics class is abstract, and therefore cannot be instantiated
without generating a compiler error. However, the `getFontMetrics()` method
can be used to return a FontMetrics class.

You can then use the `stringWidth()` method of the FontMetrics class to
determine the length of a String before or after displaying it:

```
g.drawString( Integer.toString(
    fm.stringWidth("Hello World")),
    500, 17*((loop2)*4 + loop1)+70);
```

Mastering Animation

Animation was discussed in the last chapter in the description of using XOR mode to enable a user to draw a line. That line would begin to grow or shrink depending on how and where the end user dragged the mouse.

Secret

The XOR mode and the setXORMode() method are useful in animation. They are quick to use, and they don't involve too much programming.

This section deals with more animation techniques:

- Drawn animation
- An introduction to threads
- Bitmap animation

Examining drawn animation

Now you are going to see how to build a bouncing ball program and how to make it into a game using drawn animation. First, let's discuss the bouncing ball program. Listing 16-6 draws a ball on a frame and animates it so that it bounces around, as shown in Figure 16-5.

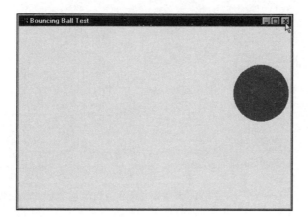

Figure 16-5: A simple bouncing ball program

Listing 16-6: BouncingBallA.java

```java
import java.awt.*;
import java.awt.event.*;
public class BouncingBallA extends Frame implements WindowListener {
// The corner of the rectangle containing the circle
  private int ii_x;
  private int ii_y;
//ballDiameter is used to determine ball size
  private int ballDiameter = 100;
  private int incrementX = 1;
```

```java
    private int incrementY = 1;
    public static void main (String args[]) {
      BouncingBallA bb = new BouncingBallA();
    }
    public BouncingBallA () {
      addWindowListener(this);     //Enable Window Objects
//Initialize Variables
      ii_x = 1;
      ii_y = 1;
      setTitle("Bouncing Ball Test");
      setSize(500,350);
      show();
    }
    public void paint(Graphics g) {
//Now animate
      Rectangle r = getBounds();
      while (true) {
//Erase old ball
        g.setColor(Color.white);
        g.fillOval(ii_x, ii_y,
                ballDiameter, ballDiameter);
//Calculate new ball
        ii_x += incrementX;
// Boooiiinng (Bounce)
        if (ii_x > r.width - ballDiameter || ii_x < 1) {
//Change horizontal direction
          incrementX *= -1;
          ii_x += (2 * incrementX);
        }
        ii_y += incrementY;
// Boooiiinng (Bounce)
        if (ii_y > r.height - ballDiameter || ii_y < 1) {
          incrementY *= -1;   //Change vertical direction
          ii_y += (2 * incrementY);
        }
        g.setColor(Color.red);
        g.fillOval(ii_x, ii_y, ballDiameter, ballDiameter);
      }
    }
// The following are required by the WindowListener interface
  public void windowClosing(WindowEvent e) {   // User wants the window
// to close
    this.dispose();
    System.exit(0);
  }
  public void windowActivated(WindowEvent e) { }  // Window got focus
  public void windowDeactivated(WindowEvent e){}  // Window lost focus
  public void windowIconified(WindowEvent e) { }  // Window is reduced
  public void windowDeiconified(WindowEvent e){}  // Window is expanded
// from an icon
  public void windowClosed(WindowEvent e) { }  // Window is finished
// closing
  public void windowOpened(WindowEvent e) { }  // Window is finished
// opening
}
```

There are two problems with this program:

- The ball flickers as it moves instead of having continuous movement.

- The exit button doesn't seem to work, although the code seems airtight.

The ball flickers because the ball is constantly being redrawn and erased. This section discusses several ways to reduce or eliminate flickering.

The exit button doesn't work because the `paint()` method never stops executing, and therefore the WindowListener methods never get control. This is resolved using Threads, which is also discussed in this section.

Understanding system resources and Threads

Threads enable several routines to run concurrently. If you had methods A, B, and C that could run independently of each other, traditional programs would still force you to run A, then B, and then C. Java and Visual J++ are multithreaded. This means that methods A, B, and C can run concurrently, and we hope finish in a lot less time (or at least offer functionality that couldn't be provided otherwise), as seen in Figure 16-6.

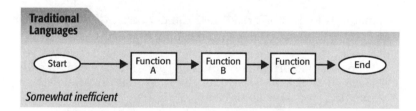

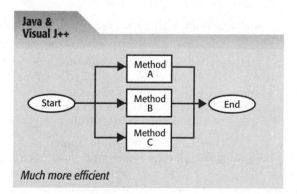

Figure 16-6: Threads enable several methods to run concurrently.

The processor often waits for Components to finish their tasks before it continues. For example, if a Pentium is doing floating point arithmetic, it funnels that request to a built-in math coprocessor and *waits* for a result.

With multithreading, your program takes advantage of a processor's waiting time to execute other functions. The end result is a faster program (or better response time). Also, on machines with Pentium chips, whose architecture encourages multithreaded environments, the percentage increases in speed can be high.

Discovering Thread Subclasses and Methods

To implement Threads, you extend the Thread class. The following class declaration declares a new Thread class called MyThread with methodA, methodB, and methodC:

```
public class MyThread extends Thread {
    public void methodA { ... }
    public void methodB { ... }
    public void methodC { ... }
    public void run ( ) { ... }
}
```

All methods in the MyThread class run concurrently with all other methods.

There are several Thread methods you should know:

- The most important is run(). The run() method contains the body of Java code that the Thread executes. Without overriding the run() method, you have no thread.

- The start() method invokes a Thread's run() method. Without start(), your thread never begins.

- The stop() method stops a Thread. This is used when the Thread is finished running.

- The wait() method causes a thread to wait until notified, while the notify() and notifyAll() methods are called within a synchronized method to notify any waiting methods to start again. The notify() method notifies all waiting methods within its containing class, while notifyAll() notifies all waiting methods from any class.

- The suspend() method causes a thread to immediately halt, while the resume() method starts all the classes that have been suspended. These are similar to the wait() and notify() methods, but are defined within the Thread class rather than the Object class.

- Finally, sleep() enables your program to wait for a given number of milliseconds:

```
// I don't care if my sleep is interrupted
try {Thread.sleep(10); }
catch (InterruptedException e) { }
```

Notice that you had to use a `try-catch` block when using the `sleep()` method. This is in the Java specifications, and the Visual J++ compiler forces you to at least acknowledge that you don't care if an `InterruptedException` is thrown from within the `sleep()` method.

Dissecting the Runnable Interface

Often, your classes are inherited from another Class. You *could* go to a lot of trouble and create another class that inherits Thread, then instantiate that class in your object. However, that's usually unnecessary. You often use a Thread so that you don't monopolize a machine. This can also be achieved with the `Runnable` interface.

The Thread class implements the `Runnable` interface. The `Runnable` interface provides a means of using Threads without actually extending the Thread class. To do this, create an instance of a thread and pass itself as the target.

Secret

Always implement a Runnable interface, rather than extend a Thread, if all you need is to multithread one method. It's more efficient.

To implement a Runnable interface, perform these five steps:

1. Add `implements Runnable` to your class declaration:

   ```
   public class MyClass extends Frame implements Runnable {...
   ```

2. Add a `Thread` attribute to your class.

   ```
   Thread myThread;
   ```

3. Move all of your `start()` method code and infinite loops to a `run()` method:

   ```
   public void run() {
   // All your thread code goes in here.
   }
   ```

4. In your `start()` method, instantiate your Thread and pass yourself as a parameter. Testing for null first ensures that the `myThread` variable has not already been instantiated:

   ```
   public void start() {
       if (myThread == null) {
           myThread = new Thread(this);
           myThread.start();
       }
   }
   ```

5. Code a `stop()` event. The `stop()` event overrides the `Applet.stop` event, and also is called from your program if you're using a Frame instead of an Applet:

   ```
   public void stop() {
       if (myThread != null) {
           myThread.stop();
           myThread = null;
       }
   }
   ```

The synchronous modifier added to a modifier *does not* force a method to run independently of all other methods, but disables any modification of the containing instance of the class until it is finished running. (However, static variables can still change.) For example, consider the following changes to the MyThread class:

```
public class MyThread extends Thread {
    public void methodA ( ) { ... }
    public synchronous void methodB ( ) { ... }
    public void methodC ( ) { ... }
    // Overrides the Thread run method.
    public void run( ) { ... }
}
```

Once methodB has started, changes can't be made to the current instance of the MyThread class, except from methodB, until methodB finishes. (methodA and methodC *can still run*, but can't change the contents of the MyThread class until methodB is finished.) The synchronous modifier is handy to keep certain methods waiting until other methods are finished running.

Making BouncingBall multithreaded

Now, to make the BouncingBall class multithreaded, you must first change the class declaration to implement the Runable interface. You should also declare a Thread instance class variable.

```
    public class BouncingBallB extends Frame implements WindowListener,
Runnable {
    Thread ith_thread;
```

Then, change the following line:

```
public void paint(Graphics g) {
```

to the following set of lines:

```
public void run() {
    Graphics g = getGraphics();
```

This enables the run() method to be called from the Thread class. Next, add these two lines to the bottom of your constructor:

```
    ith_thread = new Thread(this);
    ith_thread.start();
```

This starts your thread and automatically invokes the run() method. Finally, to make your thread stop, be sure to add the following line to your windowClosing() method:

```
    ith_thread.stop();
```

Resolving flickering

Now it's time to resolve the awful flickering that the BouncingBall class has. This section reviews different methods you can use to resolve flickering.

Comprehending delayed clearing

One way to reduce flickering is to use the Thread.sleep() method to make the painted ball appear for a little longer than the "white ball" that is used to erase the old ball for animation, as shown by the boldface lines at the end of the following run() method:

```
public void run() {        // Needed for multithreading
    Graphics g = getGraphics();  // Get the Graphics class for this
Frame
//Now animate
    Rectangle r = getBounds();
    while (true) {
//Erase old ball
    g.setColor(Color.white);
    g.fillOval(ii_x, ii_y,  ballDiameter, ballDiameter);
//Calculate new ball
    ii_x += incrementX;
// Boooiiinng (Bounce)
    if (ii_x > r.width - ballDiameter || ii_x < 1) {
//Change horizontal direction
        incrementX *= -1;
        ii_x += (2 * incrementX);
    }
    ii_y += incrementY;
// Boooiiinng (Bounce)
    if (ii_y > r.height - ballDiameter || ii_y < 1) {
        incrementY *= -1;  //Change vertical direction
        ii_y += (2 * incrementY);
    }
    g.setColor(Color.red);
    g.fillOval(ii_x, ii_y, ballDiameter, ballDiameter);
// I don't care if my sleep is interrupted
    try {Thread.sleep(10); }
    catch (InterruptedException e) { }
  }
}
```

I call this technique delayed clearing, because you delay clearing the old image so that the image flickers less. You still have some flickering with this method, just not as much as doing nothing at all.

Exploring clipping areas

When the `paint()` method is invoked, the entire window is repainted. This can cause problems for static graphics, which constantly need to be refreshed, and can also cause delays when the whole window is repainted to refresh only a small section. This smaller area is called the clipping area.

A way around this dilemma is to set the clipping area before the `paint()` method. To do this, you must understand the paint dynamics. When a `repaint()` method is issued, first the `update()` method is executed and then the `paint()` method. You must change the clipping area *before* executing the `paint()` method inside the `update()` method.

However, by using the `repaint()` and the `drawing()` method inside the `paint()` method, you run into some problems. The `repaint()` method detects that no changes have been made to the drawing area and does *not* call the `update()` method. To get around this, a `drawBall()` method is added:

```
public void drawBall(Color c) {
    Graphics g = getGraphics();
    g.clipRect(ii_x, ii_y, ballDiameter+1, ballDiameter+1);
    g.setColor(c);
    g.fillOval(ii_x, ii_y, ballDiameter, ballDiameter);
}
```

Secret

Sometimes you have to play with the clipping area to get an entire area. The `fillOval()` method didn't reach the far ends of the rectangle that bounds the circle until the clipping area was increased by one pixel width and height.

All of the Graphics class processing is removed from the `run()` method and placed in `drawBall`. Then a call to `drawBall` is made when the program erases or draws the bouncing ball:

```
public void run() {
//Now animate
    Rectangle r = bounds();
    while (true) {
//Erase old ball
        drawBall(Color.white);
//Calculate new ball
        ii_x += incrementX;
// Boooiiinng (Bounce)
        if (ii_x > r.width - ballDiameter || ii_x < 1) {
//Change horizontal direction
            incrementX *= -1;
            ii_x += (2 * incrementX);
        }
        ii_y += incrementY;
// Boooiiinng (Bounce)
        if (ii_y > r.height - ballDiameter || ii_y < 1) {
            incrementY *= -1;    //Chg vertial direction
            ii_y += (2 * incrementY);
        }
        drawBall(Color.red);
// I don't care if my sleep is interrupted
```

```
        try {Thread.sleep(10); }
        catch (InterruptedException e) { }
    }
}
```

Although a clipping area still causes the ball to flicker, the rest of the graphics on the window stop flickering. A clipping area is also more efficient because only a small area of the window is redrawn.

Repainting only what's needed

In the drawCircle class, you repaint the entire circle. Because the ball is moving one pixel away at a time, most of the area does not need to be blanked out with white and then redrawn with red, as shown by Figure 16-7. Blanking out the entire circle with white is the main cause of the flickering.

Figure 16-7: Only a portion of the outer area of the circle needs to be cleared.

You would think that because only a pixel at a time is cleared, an oval could be drawn, instead of filled, to clear the old area:

```
public void drawBall(Color c) {
    Graphics g = getGraphics();
    g.clipRect(ii_x, ii_y, ballDiameter+1, ballDiameter+1);
    g.setColor(c);
    if (c.equals(Color.white)) {
        g.drawOval(ii_x, ii_y, ballDiameter, ballDiameter);
    }
    else {
        g.fillOval(ii_x, ii_y, ballDiameter, ballDiameter);
    }
}
```

However, while logically this is correct, physically the inefficiencies of a VGA monitor (however slight) cause some "bleeding" to occur from the last oval, as seen in Figure 16-8.

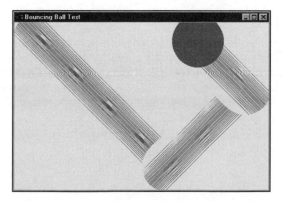

Figure 16-8: By trying to clear out precisely the area that is affected, some bleeding of the colors can occur.

You *can*, however, try something like a rectangle behind the ball to clear out any remaining bleeding:

```
public void drawBall(Color c) {
    Graphics g = getGraphics();
    g.clipRect(ii_x, ii_y, ballDiameter+1, ballDiameter+1);
    g.setColor(c);
    if (c.equals(Color.white)) {
        g.drawOval(ii_x, ii_y, ballDiameter, ballDiameter);
        g.drawRect(ii_x, ii_y, ballDiameter, ballDiameter);
    }
    else {
        g.fillOval(ii_x, ii_y, ballDiameter, ballDiameter);
    }
}
```

The results of this are shown in Figure 16-9. As you can see, all the bleeding is caught by the rectangle that follows the oval, but it still leaves a triangular-shaped trail following the ball.

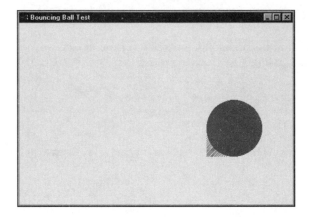

Figure 16-9: A circle followed by a rectangle leaves a triangular bleed.

You should make every attempt to eliminate or drastically reduce both bleeding and flickering from your Applets.

Using a Canvas

Using a Canvas is usually the best way to animate drawings. Remember that a Canvas Component can be used to make a new Component. Now you can use a Canvas class, again, to make a Component containing a drawing. This time, however, instead of testing for events, move the Canvas around and have Java take care of the rest. Listing 16-7 shows the BouncingBall program using a Canvas.

Listing 16-7: BouncingBallC.java

```java
// Multithreaded BouncingBall with Customized Canvas Component
import java.awt.*;
import java.awt.event.*;
public class BouncingBallC extends Frame implements WindowListener,
Runnable {
   Thread ith_thread;           // Thread used for Multi-threading
   public static void main (String args[]) {
     BouncingBallC bb = new BouncingBallC();
   }
   public BouncingBallC () {
     addWindowListener(this);      //Enable Window Objects
//Initialize Variables
     setTitle("Bouncing Ball Test");
     setSize(500,350);
     show();
     // Make a new thread and start it.  This  triggers the run
     //method
     if (ith_thread == null) {
       ith_thread = new Thread(this);
       ith_thread.start();
     }
   }
   public void run() {            // Needed for multithreading
     add("Center", new BouncingBallCanvas(50)); // Add the new BB
     //Canvas class
   }
// The following are required by the WindowListener interface
   public void windowClosing(WindowEvent e) {  // User wants the
// window to close
     ith_thread.stop();
     this.dispose();
     System.exit(0);
   }
   public void windowActivated(WindowEvent e) { }  // Window got
// focus
   public void windowDeactivated(WindowEvent e){}  // Window lost
   //focus
   public void windowIconified(WindowEvent e) { }  // Window is
   //reduced
   public void windowDeiconified(WindowEvent e){}  // Window is
   //expanded from an icon
   public void windowClosed(WindowEvent e) { }  // Window is finished
   //closing
   public void windowOpened(WindowEvent e) { }  // Window is finished
   //opening
}
class BouncingBallCanvas extends Canvas implements Runnable {
   Thread ith_thread;
//ii_ballDiameter is used to determine ball size
   private int ii_ballDiameter = 100;
// (x,y) for the corner of the rectangle containing the circle
```

```
     private int ii_x = 1;
     private int ii_y = 1;
     private int ii_incrementX = 3;
     private int ii_incrementY = 3;
     public BouncingBallCanvas () {
       this(100);
     }
     public BouncingBallCanvas (int size) {
//Initialize Variables
       ii_ballDiameter = size;
       setSize(ii_ballDiameter, ii_ballDiameter);
       ith_thread = new Thread(this);
       ith_thread.start();
     }
     public void paint (Graphics g) {
       g.setColor(Color.red);
       g.fillOval(0, 0, ii_ballDiameter, ii_ballDiameter);
     }
     public void run() {
//Now animate move
       Rectangle r = getParent().getBounds();
       while (true) {
         ii_x += ii_incrementX;
// Boooiiinng (Bounce)
         if (ii_x > r.width - ii_ballDiameter || ii_x < 1) {
           ii_incrementX *= -1; //Chg horizontal direction
           ii_x += (2 * ii_incrementX);
         }
         ii_y += ii_incrementY;
// Boooiiinng (Bounce)
         if (ii_y > r.height - ii_ballDiameter || ii_y < 1) {
           ii_incrementY *= -1; //Chg vertical direction
           ii_y += (2 * ii_incrementY);
         }
         setLocation(ii_x, ii_y);
         Toolkit.getDefaultToolkit().sync();
         ith_thread.yield();
       }
     }
   }
```

There are two commands at the end of the `BouncingBall.run()` method that you may not have seen:

```
         Toolkit.getDefaultToolkit().sync();
         ith_thread.yield();
```

The `Toolkit.sync()` method flushes the graphical buffers. A Toolkit is a machine-dependent class that handles graphical interfaces. Some Toolkits buffer graphical images and don't display them right away. This is disastrous in an arcade-style game if your "person" is not really where it appears on the window.

The `Thread.yield()` method yields control back to another method. This enables other methods to execute when you finish moving.

The BouncingBall then bounces with *minimal flicker and no trail.* This is vastly superior to other methods. Furthermore, by making the bouncing ball a separate class, you can add as many balls to the window as you wish, as seen in Figure 16-10.

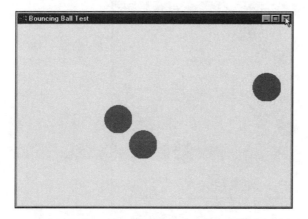

Figure 16-10: You can add more bouncing balls to the Frame by instantiating a new BouncingBall Canvas class.

Do this by adding new balls to the bouncing ball class after a time delay:

```
public void run() {
    add(new BouncingBallCanvas());
    Thread.sleep(10);
    add(new BouncingBallCanvas());
    Thread.sleep(10);
    add(new BouncingBallCanvas());
    Thread.sleep(10);
    add(new BouncingBallCanvas());
}
```

Canvases are great for nonbleeding, nonflickering animation. However, you may have some difficulty if your image is not in a square, because all Canvases are rectangular.

Tip

The Canvas technique described in this section works identically for Panels. Panels, being Containers, also enable you to add multiple Components (such as Buttons, Labels, or Checkboxes) inside the Panel.

I only use Panels if I am going to add Components. Otherwise, I use Canvases for animation whenever possible.

Looking at arcade-style games

One of the neatest things to put on a Web site is an arcade-style game. The program detailed later, in Listing 16-10, called BallShot.java, uses bouncing balls that try to crash into a rectangular player (Figure 16-11). The object is to avoid the bouncing balls for as long as possible.

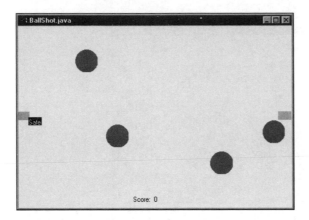

Figure 16-11: Arcade-style games can ensure frequent visits to your Web site.

Secret

First and foremost, make sure your game is playable. For instance, a restart button is needed for the BallShot class so that the user can replay the game without restarting the program. (This feature is added, along with a high score screen, in a later chapter.) Be sure to play your game before putting it on your Web site. If you think part of your game is slightly annoying, you can bet your users will *hate* it.

Movement

Arcade-style games have two types of movement:

■ Purposeful movement, or action, is movement that the end user controls. Moving a man across the screen, firing a laser, and so on, are all examples of action.

■ Random movement is movement that is generated by the computer in a random fashion. New balls appearing, speed, and direction are all random movement.

Some games, such as Tetris, have little random movement and leave the playing up to the end user. Others, such as the Super Mario games, have lots of random movement. Objects on the window that fire at you or move toward you are examples of random movement.

Player definition

In the BallShot program, the player is represented by a simple black rectangle on a Canvas subclass. This can be accomplished in the Canvas subclass `paint()` method:

```
// Paint the moving person, and indicate if it's safe
   public void paint (Graphics g) {
        if (i_x == 0 && i_y == 0) {          // Define location for the
        //first time
            Rectangle r = getParent().getBounds();
            i_x = 2;
            i_y = r.height / 2;
            setLocation(i_x, i_y);
            getParent().repaint();
        }
        g.setColor(Color.black);
        g.fillRect(0, 0, i_width-1, i_height-1);
        if (b_safeArea) {              // Is the player at a safe area?
            g.setColor(Color.white);
            g.drawString("Safe",0, i_height-2);

        }
        if (b_blowedUpRealGood == false) {  // Is the player dead
        //yet?
            requestFocus();
        }
}
```

If you want a more developed graphical program, use a Canvas subclass with a bitmap or changing bitmaps.

Action

Movement is handled by the `move()` method in the Canvas subclass (called MovingPerson). Depending on what direction you request, the `move()` method moves the player around the parent Container. Instead of moving one pixel at a time, movement is controlled by a SPEED constant, which tells how many pixels the `MovingPerson` Canvas should move:

```
// Constants tell which arrow key has been pressed.
public final static int UP = 1;
public final static int DOWN = 2;
public final static int LEFT = 3;
public final static int RIGHT = 4;
public final static int SPEED = 10;        // Speed of the player
//...
// Move and check for safe areas
  public void move(int direction) {
  Rectangle r = getParent().getBounds();
  switch (direction) {     // Move in the right direction
    case UP :    // Use the same speed as the game balls
      i_y = Math.max(i_y - SPEED, 2);
```

```
        break;
      case DOWN :
        i_y = Math.min(i_y + SPEED, r.height - i_height - 1);
        break;
      case LEFT :
        i_x = Math.max(i_x - SPEED, 2);
        break;
      case RIGHT :
        i_x = Math.min(i_x + SPEED, r.width - i_width - 1);
        break;
  }
  setLocation(i_x, i_y);
  Toolkit.getDefaultToolkit().sync();
}
```

The `keyPressed` event is used to move the player around the Frame. First, the `keyDown()` method tests to see if the MovingPerson class has been blown up yet. Then it calls the `MovingPerson.move()` method to move the MovingPerson class in the direction that was pressed:

```
// Keyboard methods required by the KeyListener interface
  public void keyTyped(KeyEvent e){ }     // A key was typed
  public void keyPressed(KeyEvent e){     // A key was pressed
    if (isBlowedUpRealGood() == false) {  // Has the player blown up
      switch (e.getKeyCode()) {    // Get the key and check it
        case e.VK_UP :
          move(UP);
          break;
        case e.VK_DOWN :
          move(DOWN);
          break;
        case e.VK_LEFT :
          move(LEFT);
          break;
        case e.VK_RIGHT :
          move(RIGHT);
          break;
      }
    }
  }
  public void keyReleased(KeyEvent e) { }  // A key was released
}
```

Safe areas

The calling module of the MovingPerson class needs to have a way to establish safe areas. The `setSafeArea()` method enables the calling program to pass an (x, y) coordinate to set a safe area:

```
// Enable the calling module to set safe areas
public void setSafeArea(int x, int y) {
  i_safeX[i_numberSafeAreas] = x;
  i_safeY[i_numberSafeAreas++] = y;
}
```

The `isSafe()` method can be used to determine if the player is currently in a safe area:

```
public boolean isSafe() {
  return b_safeArea;      // Return if player is safe
}
```

Scores

With arcade-style games, a means of scoring is necessary. The `move()` method could be augmented so that a player makes 20 points for each move and is awarded 1,000 points for making it to a new safe area (different than the previous safe area):

```
// Add this code to the move method
for (int loop = 0; loop < i_numberSafeAreas; loop++) {
  if (i_x >= i_safeX[loop] - i_width  // Check to see if player is
safe
    && i_x <= i_safeX[loop] + i_width
    && i_y >= i_safeY[loop] - i_height
    && i_y <= i_safeY[loop] + i_height)  {
    if (!b_safeArea) {
      b_safeArea = true;
      repaint();
      if (i_lastSafeArea != loop) {
        l_score += 1000;
        i_lastSafeArea = loop;
      }
    }
    break;
  }
  else {
    l_score += 20;      // Increment score fore every move
    if (b_safeArea) {
      b_safeArea = false;
      repaint();
    }
  }
}
```

A routine needs to be added to retrieve the score from the MovingPerson class:

```
public long getScore() {          // Return the score
  return l_score;
}
```

Bad Moves

Most arcade-style games define methods in which the player dies a horrible death. (The more horrible, the better.) The MovingPerson has methods that enable you to flag when a player has died and return a boolean variable to test whether or not a player is dead.

```
public void blowedUpRealGood () {      // Arrrggghh...
  b_blowedUpRealGood = true;   // You've been blown up (real good)
  getParent().repaint();       // Paint the blow up
}
public boolean isBlowedUpRealGood() {
  return b_blowedUpRealGood;  // Return true if the player has
  //blown up
}
```

Obviously, the horrible death is outside the scope and capabilities of this class. Later in this section, you use the `blowedUpRealGood()` and the `isBlowedUpRealGood()` methods from the calling class.

The MovingPerson class

Listing 16-8 shows the entire MovingPerson class that incorporates movement, score, "death," and safe areas.

Listing 16-8: MovingPerson.java

```
import java.awt.*;
import java.awt.event.*;

public class MovingPerson extends Canvas implements KeyListener {
  // Constants tell which arrow key has been pressed.
  public final static int UP = 1;
  public final static int DOWN = 2;
  public final static int LEFT = 3;
  public final static int RIGHT = 4;
  public final static int SPEED = 10;        // Speed of the ball
  private boolean b_blowedUpRealGood = false;  // Has the player
  //been "Blowed Up Real Good"
  private boolean b_safeArea = true;   // Is the player in a safe
// area
  private long l_score = 0;        // Current player score
// x,y corner of the rectangle
  private int i_x = 0;          // Current X
  private int i_y = 0;          // Current Y
  private int i_lastSafeArea = 0;     // Keep track of which safe
  //areas
  private static int i_width = 25;   // The width of the player
  private static int i_height = 15;  // The height of the player
  private int i_numberSafeAreas = 0;  // The current count of safe
  //areas
  private int i_safeX[] = new int[2];  // Array of safe area X
  private int i_safeY[] = new int[2];  // Array of safe area Y
  public MovingPerson() {          // Constructor
    // Add window listener for window events
    addKeyListener(this);
    setSize(i_width, i_height);       // Resize
  }
  public long getScore() {          // Return the score
    return l_score;
  }
  public void blowedUpRealGood () {      // Arrrggghh...
    b_blowedUpRealGood = true;        // You've been blown up
```

```
        getParent().repaint();          // Paint the blow up
}
public boolean isBlowedUpRealGood() {
  return b_blowedUpRealGood;   // Return if the player has blown up
}
public boolean isSafe() {
  return b_safeArea;      // Return if player is safe
}
// Enable the calling module to set safe areas
public void setSafeArea(int x, int y) {
  i_safeX[i_numberSafeAreas] = x;
  i_safeY[i_numberSafeAreas++] = y;
}
// Paint the moving person, and indicate if it's safe
public void paint (Graphics g) {
  if (i_x == 0 && i_y == 0) {        // Define location for the
  //first time
    Rectangle r = getParent().getBounds();
    i_x = 2;
    i_y = r.height / 2;
    setLocation(i_x, i_y);
    getParent().repaint();
  }
  g.setColor(Color.black);
  g.fillRect(0, 0, i_width-1, i_height-1);
  if (b_safeArea) {          // Is the player at a safe area?
    g.setColor(Color.white);
    g.drawString("Safe",0, i_height-2);

  }
  if (b_blowedUpRealGood == false) {   // Is the player dead yet?
    requestFocus();
  }
}
// Move and check for safe areas
public void move(int direction) {
  Rectangle r = getParent().getBounds();
  switch (direction) {     // Move in the right direction
    case UP :     // Use the same speed as the game balls
      i_y = Math.max(i_y - SPEED, 2);
      break;
    case DOWN :
      i_y = Math.min(i_y + SPEED, r.height - i_height - 1);
      break;
    case LEFT :
      i_x = Math.max(i_x - SPEED, 2);
      break;
    case RIGHT :
      i_x = Math.min(i_x + SPEED, r.width - i_width - 1);
      break;
  }
  setLocation(i_x, i_y);
  for (int loop = 0; loop < i_numberSafeAreas; loop++) {
    if (i_x >= i_safeX[loop] - i_width  // Check to see if player
    //is safe
        && i_x <= i_safeX[loop] + i_width
```

```
              && i_y >= i_safeY[loop] - i_height
              && i_y <= i_safeY[loop] + i_height)  {
            if (!b_safeArea) {
              b_safeArea = true;
              repaint();
              if (i_lastSafeArea != loop) {
                l_score += 1000;
                i_lastSafeArea = loop;
              }
            }
            break;
          }
          else {
            l_score += 20;      // Increment score for every move
            if (b_safeArea) {
              b_safeArea = false;
              repaint();
            }
          }
        }
      Toolkit.getDefaultToolkit().sync();
    }
// Keyboard methods required by the KeyListener interface
    public void keyTyped(KeyEvent e){ }      // A key was typed
    public void keyPressed(KeyEvent e){      // A key was pressed
      if (isBlowedUpRealGood() == false) {   // Has the player blown up
        switch (e.getKeyCode()) {     // Get the key and check it
          case e.VK_UP :
            move(UP);
            break;
          case e.VK_DOWN :
            move(DOWN);
            break;
          case e.VK_LEFT :
            move(LEFT);
            break;
          case e.VK_RIGHT :
            move(RIGHT);
            break;
        }
      }
    }
    public void keyReleased(KeyEvent e) { }   // A key was released
}
```

The BouncingBall class

The BouncingBall class needs to be modified to test for a collision between a ball and a MovingPerson. The following additions need to be made:

■ Pass a MovingPerson object to the constructor. That way, the GameBall class can interact with the MovingPerson class.

- Multiple ball support is needed so that the balls have random starting positions, angles, and speeds.

- When the player blows up, the ball should stop bouncing.

- Add a `testForDestruction()` method to test whether or not the ball has run into the moving person.

Random movement

Random movement makes an arcade game challenging. The bouncing balls are the random element in BallShot. First, each ball has a default increment of one pixel right and one pixel down using the `i_incrementX` and `i_incrementY` variables:

```
//Initialize speed and angle
  private int i_incrementX = 1;    // The current horizontal
  //direction of the ball
  private int i_incrementY = 1;    // The current vertical direction
  //of the ball
```

However, the increment is soon changed. Using the modulus operator (% - also known as the remainder operator), you can test if the number of the ball is odd or even. If even, change `i_incrementX` so that the ball is moving left. Also test if the ball is the third or fourth ball, and if so then move the ball up instead of down:

```
            if (i_ballNumber % 2 == 0) {
                i_incrementX = -1;
            }
            if (i_ballNumber % 4 > 1) {
                i_incrementY = -1;
            }
```

Secret

The modulus operator is used so that many more balls can be added, each ball going a different direction. Modulus is a good way to force different starting positions based on different instances of a class.

The ball's position is multiplied by a random number by using the `Math.random()` method. This causes the balls to vary in both angle and speed. The ball is also randomly placed in the rectangle retrieved by the Container's `bounds()` method:

```
//Initialize starting position
        ii_x = (int) (Math.random() * (r.width - ii_ballDiameter -
1) + 1);
        ii_y = (int) (Math.random() * (r.height - ii_ballDiameter -
1) + 1);
        move(ii_x, ii_y);
        repaint();
```

Collision detection and handling

Testing needs to be done to detect collisions between a GameBall object and a MovingPerson object. Change the GameBall constructor to accept the MovingPerson class into a class instance variable:

```
public GameBall (MovingPerson mp) {
    super();
    mp_player = mp;
```

Write a GameBall.testForDestruction() method to test if the current GameBall's rectangle intersects the MovingPerson's rectangle. If an intersection is detected, call the MovingPerson.blowedUpRealGood() method to blow up the MovingPerson object:

```
public void testForDestruction () {
    if (MovingPerson.ib_blowedUpRealGood) {
        return;
    }
    Rectangle r = imp_mp.bounds();
    if (r.x + r.width > ii_x + 3
        && r.x < ii_x + ii_ballDiameter - 3
        && r.y + r.height > ii_y + 3
        && r.y < ii_y + ii_ballDiameter - 3) {
        ib_done = true;
        imp_mp.blowedUpRealGood();
    }
}
```

Listing 16-9 shows these modifications.

Listing 16-9: GameBall.java

```
import java.awt.*;
class GameBall extends Canvas implements Runnable {
    private static int i_numberOfBalls = 0;  // Counts the current number
of balls
    private static boolean b_done = false;  // Is the game over?
//i_ballDiameter is used to determine ball size
    private int i_ballDiameter = 40;  // Pixels of ball diameter
    private int i_x = 0;       // Used for the center of circle
    private int i_y = 0;       // Used for the center of circle
    private int i_ballNumber;    // This ball number -- Used for initial
    //placement
    private int i_incrementX = 1;    // The current horizontal direction
    //of the ball
    private int i_incrementY = 1;    // The current vertical direction of
    //the ball
    Thread th_thread;       // Thread used for the Runnable interface
    MovingPerson mp_player;    // Player that's passed for collision
checking
    public GameBall (MovingPerson mp) {
        super();
        mp_player = mp;
//Initialize Variables
        i_ballNumber = ++i_numberOfBalls;
        b_done = false;
```

```java
      if (i_ballNumber % 2 == 0) {
        i_incrementX = -1;
      }
      if (i_ballNumber % 4 > 1) {
        i_incrementY = -1;
      }
      setSize(i_ballDiameter, i_ballDiameter);
      th_thread = new Thread(this);
      th_thread.start();
    }
    public void finalize () throws Throwable {
      try {
        if (th_thread != null) {
          th_thread.stop();
          th_thread = null;
        }
        super.finalize();
      }
      catch (Throwable t) {
        throw t;
      }
    }
    public void paint (Graphics g) {
      if (i_x > 0 && i_y > 0
        && (b_done == false || mp_player == null)) {
        g.setColor(Color.red);
        g.fillOval(0, 0, i_ballDiameter, i_ballDiameter);
      }
    }
    public void run() {
//Now animate move
      Component c = getParent();
      if (c == null) {
        setVisible(false);
        try { finalize(); }
        catch (Throwable t) {}
        return;
      }
      Rectangle r = c.getBounds();
//Initialize speed and angle
      i_incrementX *= (int) ((Math.random() * mp_player.SPEED) + 1);
      i_incrementY *= (int) ((Math.random() * mp_player.SPEED) + 1);
//Initialize starting position
      i_x = (int) (Math.random() * (r.width - i_ballDiameter - 1) + 1);
      i_y = (int) (Math.random() * (r.height - i_ballDiameter - 1) + 1);
      setLocation(i_x, i_y);
      repaint();
      while (b_done == false || mp_player == null) {
        i_x += i_incrementX;
        // Boooiiinng (Bounce)
        if (i_x > r.width - i_ballDiameter || i_x < 1) {
          i_incrementX *= -1; //Chg horizontal direction
          i_x += (2 * i_incrementX);
        }
        i_y += i_incrementY;
        // Boooiiinng (Bounce)
```

```
            if (i_y > r.height - i_ballDiameter || i_y < 1) {
                i_incrementY *= -1; //Chg vertical direction
                i_y += (2 * i_incrementY);
            }
            setLocation(i_x, i_y);
            if (mp_player != null) {
                testForDestruction();
            }
        }
        Graphics g = getGraphics();
        setLocation(r.width+1, r.height+1);
        g.clearRect(0, 0, i_ballDiameter, i_ballDiameter);
        try { finalize(); }
        catch (Throwable t) {}
    }
    public void testForDestruction () {
        if (mp_player.isBlowedUpRealGood()
            || mp_player.isSafe()) {
            return;
        }
        Rectangle r = mp_player.getBounds();
        if (r.x + r.width > i_x + 3
            && r.x < i_x + i_ballDiameter - 3
            && r.y + r.height > i_y + 3
            && r.y < i_y + i_ballDiameter - 3) {
            b_done = true;
            mp_player.blowedUpRealGood();
        }
    }
}
```

Stopping a Thread

When you finish a thread, call the () method in the finalize() method to stop your threads in case the program ends abnormally, as was done in the MovingPerson and GameBall classes in Listings 16-8 and 16-9:

```
public void finalize () throws Throwable {
    try {
        if (ith_thread != null) {
            ith_thread.stop();
            ith_thread = null;
        }
        super.finalize();
    }
    catch (Throwable t) {
        throw t;
    }
}
```

Notice that either `finalize()` method is called, as in the bottom line of the `run()` method in the `GameBall` class:

```
    try { finalize() };
    catch (Throwable t) {}
```

which causes the Thread to stop, or a separate `Thread.stop()` method is called,

as in the `blowedUpRealGood()` method in the `MovingPerson` class:

```
    ith_thread.stop();
    ith_thread = null;
```

This is necessary because you don't know exactly how each Java Virtual Machine handles threads. Some implementations of

threads require you to stop the thread, or system resources are consumed.

The BallShot class

Now that you have `MovingPerson` and `GameBall` classes defined, you need a "master" class to contain all the objects to make one cohesive game. Listing 16-10 includes all the code to display the `GameBalls`, `MovingPerson`, and the score. Add four `GameBalls` and one `MovingPerson` to the class:

```
// Add the player
add("Center", mp_player);
// Add the game balls.  The player must avoid these
add("Center", new GameBall(mp_player));
add("Center", new GameBall(mp_player));
add("Center", new GameBall(mp_player));
add("Center", new GameBall(mp_player));
```

Next, add a `paint()` method to draw the explosion if a collision occurs, or to draw the safe areas if the game is still in play. (Because the player and the balls are Components, they handle their own methods.) If a collision occurs, then the player dies. The `paint()` method draws a circle with a "BOOM!" painted inside the circle:

```
if (mp_player.isBlowedUpRealGood()) {
  if (i_blowedUpX == 0 && i_blowedUpY == 0) {
    i_blowedUpX = Math.max(1, rmp.x - 40);
    i_blowedUpY = Math.max(1, rmp.y - 40);
    mp_player.setLocation (r.width+1, r.height+1);
  }
  g.setColor (Color.black);
  g.fillOval(i_blowedUpX, i_blowedUpY,
    rmp.width + 80, rmp.height + 80);
  g.setColor (Color.white);
  g.drawString("BOOM!", i_blowedUpX + 35, i_blowedUpY + 45);
}
```

Figure 16-12 shows the effects of this explosion.

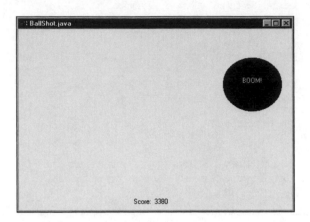

Figure 16-12: The player's life "ends" in a tragic explosion.
All arcade games eventually lead to the player's destruction.

Listing 16-10 shows the listing of the BallShot application.

Listing 16-10: BallShot.java

```
//Listing 16-10 -- BallShot.java
import java.awt.*;
import java.awt.event.*;
import java.io.*;
public class BallShot extends Frame implements WindowListener,
KeyListener {
  private Label ilb_score;        // Score at the bottom
  private int i_blowedUpX;        // The x-coord for blown up
  private int i_blowedUpY;        // The y-coord for blown up
  private int i_safeY;            // The y-coord for save
  // Declare the player
  private MovingPerson mp_player = new MovingPerson();
  public static void main (String args[]) {
    BallShot bs = new BallShot();  // Construct the BallShot game
  }
  public BallShot() {
    // Add listeners for events
    addKeyListener(this);
    addWindowListener(this);
    // Add the score
    Panel southPanel = new Panel();
    southPanel.add(ilb_score = new Label("Score:        "));
    add("South", southPanel);
    // Set the background, title, resize, and show
```

```java
          setBackground(Color.white);
          setTitle("BallShot.java");
          setSize(500,350);
          show();
          // Add the player
          add("Center", mp_player);
          // Add the game balls.  The player must avoid these
          add("Center", new GameBall(mp_player));
          add("Center", new GameBall(mp_player));
          add("Center", new GameBall(mp_player));
          add("Center", new GameBall(mp_player));
      }
   public void paint(Graphics g) {
      if (mp_player != null) {
        Rectangle rmp = mp_player.getBounds();
        Rectangle r = getBounds();
        if (mp_player.isBlowedUpRealGood()) {
          if (i_blowedUpX == 0 && i_blowedUpY == 0) {
            i_blowedUpX = Math.max(1, rmp.x - 40);
            i_blowedUpY = Math.max(1, rmp.y - 40);
            mp_player.setLocation (r.width+1, r.height+1);
          }
          g.setColor (Color.black);
          g.fillOval(i_blowedUpX, i_blowedUpY,
            rmp.width + 80, rmp.height + 80);
          g.setColor (Color.white);
          g.drawString("BOOM!", i_blowedUpX + 35, i_blowedUpY + 45);
        }
        else if (rmp.y > 0) { //Paint safe areas
          g.setColor(Color.green);
          if (i_safeY == 0) {
            i_safeY = rmp.y;
            g.fillRect(0, i_safeY, rmp.width-1, rmp.height-1);
              g.fillRect(r.width - rmp.width-4, i_safeY,
                   rmp.width-1, rmp.height-1);
            mp_player.setSafeArea(0, rmp.y);
            mp_player.setSafeArea(r.width - rmp.width, rmp.y);
          }
          else {
            g.fillRect(0, i_safeY, rmp.width-1, rmp.height);
            g.fillRect(r.width - rmp.width-4, i_safeY,
                   rmp.width-1, rmp.height);
          }
        }
        ilb_score.setText("Score:   " +
String.valueOf(mp_player.getScore()));
      }
   }
// Keyboard methods required by the KeyListener interface
   public void keyTyped(KeyEvent e){ }     // A key was typed
```

```
public void keyPressed(KeyEvent e){      // A key was pressed
  // Check for arrow movement and move player if appropriate
  if (mp_player.isBlowedUpRealGood() == false) {
    switch (e.getKeyCode()) {
      case e.VK_UP :
        mp_player.move(MovingPerson.UP);
        break;
      case e.VK_DOWN :
        mp_player.move(MovingPerson.DOWN);
        break;
      case e.VK_LEFT :
        mp_player.move(MovingPerson.LEFT);
        break;
      case e.VK_RIGHT :
        mp_player.move(MovingPerson.RIGHT);
        break;
    }
  }
}
public void keyReleased(KeyEvent e) { }  // A key was released
// The following are required by the WindowListener interface
public void windowClosing(WindowEvent e) {  // User wants the
window to close
  this.dispose();
  System.exit(0);
}
public void windowActivated(WindowEvent e) { }  // Window got
//focus
public void windowDeactivated(WindowEvent e){}  // Window lost
//focus
public void windowIconified(WindowEvent e) { }  // Window is
//reduced
public void windowDeiconified(WindowEvent e){}  // Window is
//expanded from an icon
public void windowClosed(WindowEvent e) { }  // Window is finished
//closing
public void windowOpened(WindowEvent e) { }  // Window is finished
//opening
}
```

Using Bitmaps in Animation

Sometimes, you don't want the same image to move around a window, but
you want an image to change form. This is called animation. While the
Canvas class is great for image movement, it won't help you with animiation.
One way to animate your program or Applet is to use a series of bitmaps
(usually JPG or GIF files) rather than drawing pictures. Like a movie, each
bitmap is considered a frame, and the frames are shown one after another to
simulate movement.

This section discusses the Java code needed to animate an image. Assume you have twelve bitmap pictures of clocks, as seen in Figure 16-13. These bitmaps are CLOCK01.GIF through CLOCK12.GIF in the clock project on your CD-ROM.

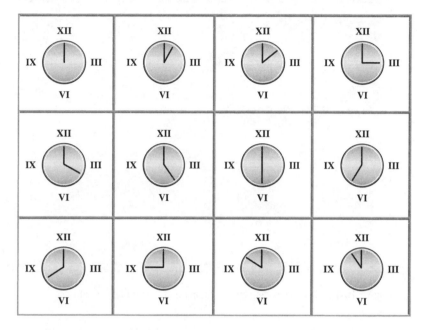

Figure 16-13: Twelve bitmaps of clocks used for animation

In Listing 16-11, you use a three-step process to display bitmaps:

1. Load the images into an Image class array. The Image class is used to store images loaded from a GIF or JPG file.

2. Loop through the images continuously, clearing out the previous Image before displaying a new Image array element.

3. Call the `Thread.stop()` method inside your finalize method. That way, if the Web browser stops, the thread also stops and does not continue unless the Web browser is started once more.

All this is done using threads for better user interaction. Figure 16-14 shows how Clock.java looks while running.

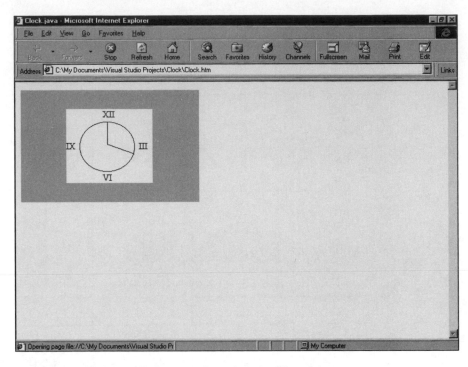

Figure 16-14: Clock.java displays an animated clock while running.

Listing 16-11 shows the code needed to display these four bitmaps sequentially to achieve an animation effect.

Listing 16-11: Clock.java

```
import java.applet.*;
import java.awt.*;
public class Clock extends Applet implements Runnable {
  private Thread th_thread;  // Thread for the runnable interface
  private Image im_images[];   // Image array for animation
  private int i_currImage;  // Current Image to display
  private int i_imageWidth  = 0;  //Width of Image
  private int i_imageHeight = 0;  // Height of Image
// Boolean set to true when all the images have loaded
  private boolean  b_allLoaded = false;  // Boolean for all loaded
  private final int i_numImages = 12;  // Number of Images
  public void init() {
    resize(320, 240);
    //Run thread, which calls the run method
    th_thread = new Thread(this);
    th_thread.start();
  }
  public void run() {  // Called for Thread support.
    i_currImage    = 0;
    String imageName;
// Array to store images
    im_images    = new Image[i_numImages];
```

```
      Graphics g = getGraphics();
      showStatus("Loading images...");
      for (int i = 1; i <= i_numImages; i++) {
        String picNum = Integer.toString(i);
        if (picNum.length() < 2) {
          picNum = "0" + picNum;
        }
        imageName = "CLOCK" + picNum + ".gif";   // Image file
        im_images[i-1] = getImage(getDocumentBase(), imageName);
        // Get width and height of one image. Assume
        // all images are same width and height
        if (i_imageWidth == 0) {
          try {
            while ((i_imageWidth =
                  im_images[i-1].getWidth(null)) < 0)
              Thread.sleep(1);
            while ((i_imageHeight =
                im_images[i-1].getHeight(null)) < 0)
              Thread.sleep(1);
          }
          catch (InterruptedException e) { }
        }
        // Force image to fully load
        g.drawImage(im_images[i-1], -1000, -1000, this);
      }
      // Wait until images are fully loaded
      while (!b_allLoaded) {
        try { Thread.sleep(10); }
        catch (InterruptedException e) { }
      }
      showStatus("Done loading images.");
      while (true) {
        try { // Draw next image in animation
          displayImage(g);
          i_currImage++;
          if (i_currImage == i_numImages)
            i_currImage = 0;
          Thread.sleep(500);
        }
        catch (InterruptedException e) {stop();}
      }
    }
    private void displayImage(Graphics g) {
      if (!b_allLoaded)
        return;
      g.drawImage(im_images[i_currImage],
          (getSize().width - i_imageWidth)   / 2,
          (getSize().height - i_imageHeight) / 2, null);
    }
    public void paint(Graphics g) {
      if (b_allLoaded) {
        Rectangle r = g.getClipBounds();
        g.clearRect(r.x, r.y, r.width, r.height);
        displayImage(g);
      }
    }
```

```
public boolean imageUpdate(Image img, int flags,
               int x, int y, int w, int h) {
  // Nothing to do if images are all loaded
  if (b_allLoaded)
    return false;
  // Want all bits to be available before painting
  if ((flags & ALLBITS) == 0)
    return true;
  // All bits are available, so increment loaded count
  // of fully loaded images, starting animation if all
  // images are loaded
  if (++i_currImage == i_numImages) {
    i_currImage = 0;
    b_allLoaded = true;
  }
  return false;
}
public void stop() {
  if (th_thread != null) {
    th_thread.stop();
    th_thread = null;
  }
}
}
```

Using Threads with Web pages

The run() method is the most complicated method in the Clock program.
The run() method is called when the Thread class is instantiated in the
init() method. Here, you show a status message saying that the images are
loading First, an array is initialized to hold the images you receive from the
hard drive:

```
im_images   = new Image[i_numImages];
```

Then, the 12 clock images are loaded. While they are loading, the for loop
used to load the images waits until the width and height of the images can
be determined. A Thread.sleep function is called to facilitate any user action,
like a mouse click. Finally, each image is drawn as it is loaded to force the
image to fully load before continuing:

```
for (int i = 1; i <= i_numImages; i++) {
  String picNum = Integer.toString(i);
  if (picNum.length() < 2) {
    picNum = "0" + picNum;
  }
  imageName = "CLOCK" + picNum + ".gif";  // Image file
  im_images[i-1] = getImage(getDocumentBase(), imageName);
  // Get width and height of one image. Assume
  // all images are same width and height
  if (i_imageWidth == 0) {
    try {
      while ((i_imageWidth =
```

```
                im_images[i-1].getWidth(null)) < 0)
            Thread.sleep(1);
            while ((i_imageHeight =
                im_images[i-1].getHeight(null)) < 0)
            Thread.sleep(1);
      }
    catch (InterruptedException e) { }
    }
    // Force image to fully load
    g.drawImage(im_images[i-1], -1000, -1000, this);
  }
}
```

Because functions called by a thread can run simultaneously, the run()
method then loops until the ib_allLoaded boolean flag is set.

```
// Wait until images are fully loaded
while (!b_allLoaded) {
  try { Thread.sleep(10); }
  catch (InterruptedException e) { }
}
showStatus("Done loading images.");
```

Finally, a loop is executed that cycles through the images and calls the
displayImage() method each time. After displaying the image, this loop then
sleeps for ½ _ second (500 milliseconds). If interrupted, the Applet.stop()
method is called.

```
while (true) {
  try { // Draw next image in animation
    displayImage(g);
    i_currImage++;
    if (i_currImage == i_numImages)
      i_currImage = 0;
    Thread.sleep(500);
  }
  catch (InterruptedException e) {stop();}
}
```

Displaying an image

The displayImage() method is called from the paint() and run() methods.
The displayImage() method displays an image in the center of the window
with the Graphics.drawImage() method:

```
private void displayImage(Graphics g) {
  if (!b_allLoaded)
    return;
  g.drawImage(im_images[i_currImage],
      (getSize().width - i_imageWidth)  / 2,
      (getSize().height - i_imageHeight) / 2, null);

}
```

Updating an image

The `imageUpdate()` method is called repeatedly by the AWT while images are being painted. The flags parameter can be bitwise ANDed with any of the `ImageObserver` attributes, like `ALLBITS`, to give information about the status of images that are currently being painted. When the last image is loaded, the boolean `ib_allLoaded` flag is set to true. The `ib_allLoaded` flag is used throughout the Clock program to make sure that all images are loaded before other processing continues or other images are painted:

```
public boolean imageUpdate(Image img, int flags,
                           int x, int y, int w, int h) {
    // Nothing to do if images are all loaded
    if (ib_allLoaded)
        return false;
    // AND flags and ALLBITS to see if
    // all bits are available before painting
    if ((flags & ALLBITS) == 0)
        return true;
    // All bits are available, so increment loaded count
    // of fully loaded images, starting animation if all
    // images are loaded
    if (++ii_currImage == ii_numImages) {
        ii_currImage = 0;
        ib_allLoaded = true;
    }
    return false;
}
```

Examining the MediaTracker class

In Listing 16-11, each image is retrieved and drawn automatically. The `getWidth()` and `getHeight()` methods are used to determine if an image is fully loaded, because these methods return a minus one if the image size is unknown. Because every image is about 2K, the images load and draw rather quickly. However, if the images are larger, your program may look slow and may run haltingly while one image is drawn and your program waits for another image.

The MediaTracker class is used to asynchronously load several images at once:

```
    MediaTracker tracker = new MediaTracker(this);
    String strImage;
// For each image in the animation, this method first constructs a
// string containing the path to the image file; then it begins
// loading the image into the m_Images array.  Note that the call to
// getImage will return before the image is completely loaded.
//-------------------------------------------------------------
    for (int i = 1; i <= NUM_IMAGES; i++) {
// Build path to next image
//-------------------------------------------------------------
        strImage = "..\\Clock" + ((i < 10) ? "0" : "") + i + ".gif";
        m_Images[i-1] = getImage(getDocumentBase(), strImage);
```

```
                    tracker.addImage(m_Images[i-1], 0);
        }
// Wait until all images are fully loaded
//--------------------------------------------------------------
    try {
        tracker.waitForAll();
        m_fAllLoaded = !tracker.isErrorAny();
    }
    catch (InterruptedException e) {
// TODO: Place exception-handling code here in case an
//       InterruptedException is thrown by Thread.sleep(),
//          meaning that another thread has interrupted this one
    }
    if (!m_fAllLoaded) {
        stop();
        m_Graphics.drawString("Error loading images!", 10, 40);
        return;
    }
//...
```

In the preceding snippet of code, a MediaTracker object is used to add images to the Image array. After starting, the `MediaTracker.waitForAll()` method is called to wait for all images to load. After all have loaded, the processing then begins.

Loading images with a MediaTracker object first is probably a better way to process images unless the images are small or the images don't require smooth animation.

Summary

The graphical capabilities of Java are astounding. They enable you to write fairly complex programs (like the `graphicsApplet` program) with a fraction of the work involved if you were to write the same program in other languages. Although Java has some advanced text-based display capabilities, most agree that text-based applications are not going to be around much longer, except perhaps in some vertical markets or in some archaic corporate legacy systems.

- Although standard Java cannot display BMP files, you can display pictures using GIF or JPG file formats.
- Java enables you to use drawn objects as well as bitmaps for animation.
- You can easily manipulate fonts in Java.
- The ImageObserver and ImageProducer interfaces are used to track image loading.
- Threads should be used for graphical manipulation.
- Canvases are an efficient way to control displays, although they are not as fully featured as Panels.

Chapter 17

Mastering File I/O

In This Chapter

▶ Getting directory and file information

▶ Using input and output streams

▶ Mastering the place and function of random access streams

▶ Using File I/O in a Java Applet

Traditional Java accomplishes its disk I/O with streams. These streams can be divided into input, output, and random access (I/O) streams.

However, while traditional file I/O has its place for simple data storage management needs, you should consider implementing Visual J++ database support for more complex applications.

Secret

Databases tend to offer greater control of stored information. Databases have abilities and features that make sorting, grouping, summation, and information retrieval more functional than simple data file retrieval.

Getting Directory and File Information

You often need to see file information. For example, you may need to know if a file is a directory, the size of a file, the read-only attribute of a file, when the file was last modified, and so on. The File class is used extensively, because you can define a File class without actually opening a file for input and output. Table 17-1 lists file methods that can be used to retrieve file and directory information.

Table 17-1   File Methods

Method	Description
File(String name)	The File constructor creates a file that references a name passed to it. You can then use File methods to obtain information about this File. Wildcards can be used to acquire the contents of a directory.
File.getName()	Returns the name of a File.
File.getParent()	Returns the name of the parent path containing the file or directory.
File.isDirectory()	Returns true or false indicating whether the file being tested is a directory.
File.length()	Returns a long? containing the length of a File.
File.list()	Returns a String array that lists the files in a directory, or a null if the File being tested is not a directory.
File.lastModified()	Returns a long date representing the last modification date of a File.
File.canRead()	Returns a true or false indicating if the File can be read from in the Java Virtual Machine.
File.canWrite()	Returns a true or false indicating if the File can be written to from the Java Virtual Machine.

Secret

The canRead() and canWrite() methods don't just return the read-only attribute. They also indicate if a file can be read from inside the Java Virtual Machine. Part of Java's security "sandbox" restricts file access inside the Java Virtual Machine to the files in the same directory as the class you are running.

In addition to the methods found in the File class, there are other file I/O methods. The most important of these is the java.lang.System.getProperty() method. Using the System.getProperty() method, you can inquire on the current working directory:

```
String cwd = System.getProperty("user.dir");   //Returns the current
    //working directory
```

Set all file information to null before assigning a new value so that the Java Virtual Machine knows to "garbage collect" the old file information:

```
//Initiate garbage collection
  if (fi_fileInfo != null) {
    for (int loop = 0; loop < fi_fileInfo.length; loop++) {
      fi_fileInfo[loop] = null;
    }
    fi_fileInfo = null;
  }
  fi_currentDir = null;
```

Garbage collection involves freeing up previously used resources. Java performs its own garbage collection, but sometimes it "cleans up" faster if you do little tricks such as assigning classes to null before reassigning them.

The best way to show how to manipulate files is with an example program written in Visual J++. In this program, called FileFunctions, you display the current directory and sort entries in the directory by name, size, or modification date, or group them by writability based on command buttons on the top of the Frame (see Figure 17-1).

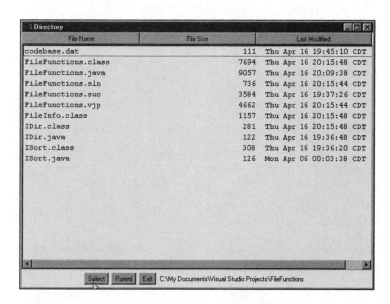

Figure 17-1: The FileFunctions class displays and sorts files.

Listing 17-1 shows the FileFunctions class listing.

Listing 17-1: FileFunctions.java

```
import java.awt.*;
import java.awt.event.*;
import java.io.*;
import java.util.*;
public class FileFunctions extends Frame implements ISort, IDir,
          WindowListener, ActionListener {
// Constant sort orders
  private final int NAME = 1;
  private final int LENGTH = 2;
  private final int MODIFIED = 3;
  private int i_sortOrder = NAME;  //Current sort order
  private IDir idir_id;        //Current Directory Interface
  private File fi_currentDir;    //Current Directory
  private List ls_fileList;    //List of files
  private Panel pa_centerPanel;  //Center Panel
//Add buttons
  private Button bu_parent = new Button ("Parent");
```

```java
  private Button bu_name = new Button ("File Name");
  private Button bu_length = new Button ("File Size");
  private Button bu_modified = new Button ("Last Modified");
  private Button bu_select = new Button ("Select");
  private Button bu_exit = new Button ("Exit");
//Add label to display the current working directory
  private Label lbl_cwd;
//Add a file information directory
  private FileInfo fi_fileInfo[];
  public static void main (String args[]) {
    FileFunctions f = new FileFunctions();
  }
  private FileFunctions() {
    idir_id = this;
    setDirectory(System.getProperty("user.dir")); //Set the current
    //working directory
    continueConstruction();   //Call rest of constructor
  }
  public FileFunctions(IDir id) {
    super();
    idir_id = id;
    setDirectory(System.getProperty("user.dir")); //Set the current
    //working directory
    continueConstruction();   //Call rest of constructor
  }
  public FileFunctions(String dir) {
    super();
    idir_id = this;
    setDirectory(dir);     //Set the current working directory
    continueConstruction();  //Call rest of constructor
  }
  public FileFunctions(IDir id, String dir) {
    super();
    idir_id = id;
    setDirectory(dir);     //Set the current working directory
    continueConstruction();  //Call rest of constructor
  }
  private void continueConstruction(){
  //Add listeners
    addWindowListener(this);
    bu_name.addActionListener(this);
    bu_length.addActionListener(this);
    bu_modified.addActionListener(this);
    bu_select.addActionListener(this);
    bu_parent.addActionListener(this);
    bu_exit.addActionListener(this);
  //Add Panels
    Panel northPanel = new Panel();
    Panel southPanel = new Panel();
    pa_centerPanel = new Panel();
  //Set the layout for the Frame and the panels
    setLayout(new BorderLayout());
    pa_centerPanel.setLayout(new GridLayout(1,3));
    northPanel.setLayout(new GridLayout(1, 3));
    southPanel.setLayout(new FlowLayout());
  //Add the buttons
```

```
        northPanel.add(bu_name);
        northPanel.add(bu_length);
        northPanel.add(bu_modified);
        southPanel.add(bu_select);
        southPanel.add(bu_parent);
        southPanel.add(bu_exit);
        southPanel.add(lbl_cwd);
    //Arrange the panels on the frame
        add("North", northPanel);
        add("South", southPanel);
        add("Center", pa_centerPanel);
    //Do frame stuff
        setTitle("Directory");
        setBounds(0,0,640,480);
        loadLists();
    }
    public boolean isGreaterThan(Object obj1, Object obj2){
        FileInfo f1 = (FileInfo) obj1;
        FileInfo f2 = (FileInfo) obj2;
        switch (i_sortOrder) {
// Sort by file name ascending
        case NAME :
            if
(f1.getName().toUpperCase().compareTo(f2.getName().toUpperCase()) > 0) {
            return true;
            }
            break;
// Sort by file length ascending
        case LENGTH :
            if (f1.getSize() > f2.getSize()) {
            return true;
            }
            break;
// Sort by modification date decending
        case MODIFIED :
            if (f1.getDate().before(f2.getDate())) {
            return true;
            }
            break;
        }
        return false;
    }
    private void loadLists() {
        Sort s = new Sort (this, fi_fileInfo);
        pa_centerPanel.removeAll();
//Set the font to a proportional Courier font
        Font f = new Font("Courier", Font.PLAIN, 14);
        String size;
        ls_fileList = null;
        ls_fileList = new List();
        ls_fileList.setFont(f);
        pa_centerPanel.add(ls_fileList);
        for (int loop=0; loop < fi_fileInfo.length; loop++) {
            if (fi_fileInfo[loop].isDirectory()) {
                size = frontPad("<DIR>", 15);
            }
```

```java
      else {
        size = frontPad(String.valueOf(fi_fileInfo[loop].getSize()),
15);
      }
      String display =
        pad(fi_fileInfo[loop].getName(), 35) +
        " " +
        size +
        " " +
        fi_fileInfo[loop].getDate().toString();
      ls_fileList.addItem(display);
    }
    show();
    repaint();
  }
  public void setDirectory(String directory) {
    if (directory == null) {
      directory = "C:";
    }
    File file = new File(directory);
    setDirectory(file);
  }
  public void setDirectory(File directory) {
//Initiate garbage collection
    if (fi_fileInfo != null) {
      for (int loop = 0; loop < fi_fileInfo.length; loop++) {
        fi_fileInfo[loop] = null;
      }
      fi_fileInfo = null;
    }
    if (lbl_cwd == null) {
      lbl_cwd = new Label (directory.getAbsolutePath());
    }
    else {
      lbl_cwd.setText(directory.getAbsolutePath());
    }
    fi_currentDir = null;
    fi_currentDir = directory;
    String fileNames[] = fi_currentDir.list();
    fi_fileInfo = new FileInfo[fileNames.length];
    for (int loop=0; loop < fileNames.length; loop++) {
      File file = new File (fileNames[loop]);
      fi_fileInfo[loop] = new FileInfo(fileNames[loop],
        file.length(),
        file.lastModified());
      fi_fileInfo[loop].setDirectory(file.isDirectory());
      file = null;      //Deallocate for garbage collection
    }
  }
  public static String pad(String inString, int length) {
    String newString = new String(inString);
    for (int x = inString.length(); x < length; x++) {
      newString = newString.concat(" ");
    }
    return newString;
  }
```

```java
// Needed for the IDir interface
  public void selectFile(File f) {
  }
  public static String frontPad(String inStr, int length) {
    String newString = new String("");
    for (int x = inStr.length(); x < length; x++) {
      newString = newString.concat(" ");
    }
    newString = newString.concat(inStr);
    return newString;
  }
//The actionPerformed method is required
//by the ActionListener interface
  public void actionPerformed(ActionEvent e) {
    // Get the text of the button
    String buttonText = e.getActionCommand();
    //Test for buttons
    if (buttonText.equals("Exit")) {
      dispose();
      java.lang.System.exit(0);
    }
    else if (buttonText.equals("Parent")) {
      setDirectory(fi_currentDir.getParent());
    }
    else if (buttonText.equals("File Name")) {
      i_sortOrder = NAME;
    }
    else if (buttonText.equals("File Size")) {
      i_sortOrder = LENGTH;
    }
    else if (buttonText.equals("Last Modified")) {
      i_sortOrder = MODIFIED;
    }
    else if (buttonText.equals("Select")) {
      int fileNumber = ls_fileList.getSelectedIndex();
      if (fileNumber >= 0) {
        String fileName = fi_fileInfo[fileNumber].getName();
        if (fi_fileInfo[fileNumber].isDirectory()) {
          setDirectory(lbl_cwd.getText() + "\\" + fileName);
        }
        else {
          File f = new File(fileName);
          idir_id.selectFile(f);
        }
      }
    }
    loadLists();
  }
  // The following are required by the WindowListener interface
  public void windowClosing(WindowEvent e) {  // User wants the window
to close
    dispose();        //Destoy this frame
    System.exit(0);     //Exit this program
  }
  public void windowActivated(WindowEvent e) { }  // Window got focus
  public void windowDeactivated(WindowEvent e){}  // Window lost focus
```

```
    public void windowIconified(WindowEvent e) { }  // Window is reduced
    public void windowDeiconified(WindowEvent e){}  // Window is expanded
      //from an icon
    public void windowClosed(WindowEvent e) { }  // Window is finished
      //closing
    public void windowOpened(WindowEvent e) { }  // Window is finished
      //opening
}
class FileInfo {
    private boolean ib_directory = false;      // Directory (yes or no)
    private String is_name;          // File name
    private long ii_length;            // File length
    private Date ida_date;            // Last Modified date
    public FileInfo(String name, long length, long date) {
        is_name = name;
        ii_length = length;
        ida_date = new Date(date);
    }
    public void setDirectory (boolean isDir) {
        ib_directory = isDir;
    }
    public boolean isDirectory () {
        return ib_directory;
    }
    public String getName () {
        return is_name;
    }
    public long getSize () {
        return ii_length;
    }
    public Date getDate () {
        return ida_date;
    }
}
```

Listing 17-2 shows the IDir interface that is used so the two Java programs can communicate with each other.

Listing 17-2: IDir.java

```
import java.io.*;
public interface IDir {
    public abstract void selectFile(File f);
}
```

The pad() and frontPad() methods were written to pad spaces to a string. That way, by using a proportional font, such as Courier, you can space your directory listing columns evenly on one string, making processing a little faster and a lot easier than synchronizing multiple lists inside a display.

The FileFunctions class implements the ISort and instantiates the Sort class to sort the file entries. The ISort interface and the Sort class are discussed in Chapter 19. All you need to know now is that the file entries are sorted by another class.

The `IDir` interface is also implemented so `FileFunctions` can use a Select button to perform actions on a file. It only requires a `selectFile()` method:

```
// Needed for the IDir interface
  public void selectFile(File f) {
  }
```

What the user does with the file after it has been selected is up to the instantiating method.

Mastering File Input and Output with Streams

Streams are how Java handles file input and output. There are various types of input, output, and random access streams that you can use inside your Java programs.

Input streams

Java uses input streams for file input. Table 17-2 shows several types of input streams.

Table 17-2   Input Streams

InputStream Class	Description
InputStream	InputStream is the ancestor of all InputStream classes. You cannot instantiate an InputStream class, but it contains some useful methods, such as read, that are present in all InputStream descendents.
StringBufferInputStream	This is an input stream that can read from a String as if it were a file. This is useful for logical files present entirely in a String in memory.
SequenceInputStream	This input stream is used to concatenate two or more input streams and treat them as if they were one file. This is handy if you're reading different files with the same file layout. This often occurs when you are trying to combine two files from two different machines.
PipedInputStream	This input stream reads data from a tempory memory table loaded by a PipedOutputStream. This is useful for writing and retrieving temporary files.
FilterInputStream	This class is the parent class for any type of stream that filters a file's data. It should not be instantiated itself.

(continued)

Table 17-2 *(Continued)*	
InputStream Class	*Description*
FileInputStream	This input stream provides low-level input from a file. Although used in Listing 17-2, you would often want some of the additional functionality found in other InputStream classes.
ByteArrayInputStream	This class is used to read from a byte array in memory as if reading from a file. This is useful for logical files present entirely in an array in memory.
BufferedInputStream	This data stream buffers input data by reading large amounts of storage into a buffer. Using a BufferedInputStream, you make repeated reads to a buffered memory area instead of to the slow disk drive.
BufferedReader	BufferedReader is the most versatile of all input streams. It can read all sorts of data types. In addition to bytes and characters, BufferedReaders can read Boolean, double, floats, integers, longs, shorts, and other formats not found in other input classes. Check out the InfoViewer to see all the methods for reading inside the BufferedReader class.
LineNumberInputStream	This input stream class keeps track of line numbers as you read a file. The `getLineNumber()` and `setLineNumber()` methods retrieve or reset (respectively) the line numbers in a LineNumberInputStream class.
PushbackInputStream	This input stream class enables you to "unread" one byte of data onto the data buffer. This is handy if you need to write a parser to parse a file.

The following `loadFile()` method uses several input streams:

```
public void loadFile() {
  String buffer = new String("");
  FileInputStream fis = null;
  ta_display.setText("");
  try {
    fis = new FileInputStream(fi_selectedFile);
  }
  catch (FileNotFoundException fnfe) {
    lbl_status.setText(fi_selectedFile + " was not found");
    return;
  }
  BufferedInputStream bis = new BufferedInputStream(fis);
  BufferedReader br = new BufferedReader(new InputStreamReader(bis));
  String holder = new String();
  try {
    holder = br.readLine();
```

```
        while (holder != null) { //run until EOF occurs
          buffer += holder + "\n";
          holder = br.readLine();
        }
        ta_display.append(buffer);
      }
    catch (IOException ioe) {
      lbl_status.setText(fi_selectedFile
          + " has an IO Exception -- "
          + ioe.getMessage());
      return;
    }
}
```

As you see, the FileInputStream is defined and then allocated with the File that was passed to the selectFile() method. This file is converted to a BufferedReader so that line processing can be used. Then the entire file is read and the input is posted in the text area.

Secret

A BufferedInputStream is used because a large buffer is needed to read a whole file in at once. If you use a large buffer to read in a file, a BufferedInputStream would "double buffer" all reads, thereby actually increasing read time.

You should not use a BufferedInputStream if you intend to read from different or random sections of a file, rather than reading sequentially. Buffering only works well with sequential input.

Table 17-3 lists some methods you may find useful to all input streams:

Table 17-3   Input Methods

InputStream Method	Description
read({byte b[]{, int offset, int length}})	The read method reads a byte of data or, if a byte array is passed, an array of bytes. An offset and? length can also be given to read characters into a subarray. A file is read until the b.length characters are read or an end of file occurs.
readLine()	Some input stream classes use the readLine method to read a line of text deliminated with a carriage-return, line feed ('\n') or the end of file.
skip(long n)	The skip method skips a number of bytes. This is helpful for nonsequential reads of a file.
close( )	The close method does not have to be called, but closing a file may speed up the recovery of resources.

(continued)

Table 17-3 *(Continued)*

InputStream Method	Description
`mark(int numberOfReads)`	The `mark` function sets a mark on the current position of a file so that a call to the `reset` method returns the file pointer to the marked position. The `numberOfReads` argument is the number of times you can read from this file before the mark becomes invalid.
`Reset`	Reset moves the file pointer to the last marked position.
`MarkSuported`	The `markSupported` function returns a true or false indicating whether or not marks are supported in the current Java implementation.

Output streams

OutputStream classes allow for easy output to a file or printer in Java. In Listing 17-2, both saving to a file and printing a file are supported. You find that the versatility of OutputStream classes makes writing to a file a little easier. Table 17-4 lists all output streams and how they're used.

Table 17-4 **Output Streams**

OutputStream Class	Description
OutputStream	OutputStream is the ancestor of all OutputStream classes. You cannot instantiate an OutputStream class, but it contains some useful methods, such as `write`, that are present in all OutputStream descendents.
PipedOutputStream	This output stream writes data to a temporary memory table to be read later by a PipedInputStream. This is useful for writing and retrieving temporary files.
FilterOutputStream	This class is the parent class for any type of stream that filters a file's output. It should not be instantiated itself.
FileOutputStream	This output stream provides low-level output from a file. Although used in Listing 17-2, you may often want some of the additional functionality found in other OutputStream classes.
ByteArrayOutputStream	This class is used to write to a byte array in memory as if writing to a file. This is useful for building logical files present entirely in an array in memory.
BufferedOutputStream	This data stream buffers output data by writing large amounts of storage into a buffer. Using a BufferedOutputStream, instead of making repeated writes to the slow disk drive, you make repeated writes to a buffered memory area.

OutputStream Class	Description
DataOutputStream	DataOutputStreams are the most versatile of all output streams. They can read many different data types. In addition to bytes and characters, DataOutputStreams can read boolean, double, floats, integers, longs, shorts, and other formats not found in other output classes. Check out the InfoViewer to see all the methods for reading inside the DataOutputStream class.
PrintWriter	A PrintWriter is useful because of the `print()` and `println()` methods that accompany a PrintWriter. PrintWriters are used to write text files or to (of course) print to a printer.

Secret

Just as buffering is not required for reading input files, it is a waste of time for writing output files. Writing occurs once from one big array — buffering output might actually run slower due to "double buffering."

The following code saves text from a text area into an output stream:

```
try {
//Open streams
  FileOutputStream fos = new FileOutputStream(fi_selectedFile);
  DataOutputStream dos = new DataOutputStream(fos);
// Write the stream from the text area
  dos.writeBytes(ta_display.getText());
// Close all files and set to null for garbage collection
  dos.close();
  dos = null;
  fos.close();
  fos = null;
}
catch (IOException e) {
  lbl_status.setText("An IOException occured while writing.");
}
```

The following steps occur in the preceding code:

1. A FileOutputStream is defined for the current selected file.

2. A DataOutputStream is formed from the new FileOutputStream. Then you can use the `writebytes` command, which is a way to write from a String rather than a byte array.

3. The selectFile ? is rewritten using a huge String and the DataOutputStream.

4. The FileOutputStream and the DataOutputStream are closed and set to null to aid in garbage collecting.

Printer output in Java

Printer output is also considered an OutputStream, but unlike other OutputStreams, printer output requires that you first define another OutputStream to be a constructor argument before a PrintWriter can be constructed. The following code forms a PrintWriter stream for output to the printer:

```
//Open streams
  FileOutputStream fos = new FileOutputStream("LPT1");
  PrintWriter pw = new PrintWriter(fos, true);
//Send the printer the information
  pw.print(ta_display.getText());
  pw.print('\f');  //Now print a form feed
// Close all files and set to null for garbage collection
  pw.close();
  fos.close();
  pw = null;
  fos = null;
```

The following list shows the steps to print a file:

1. Define a FileOutputStream as "LPT1". This is the same stream that is defined to your printer. You can also use "PRN" or you can use "LPT2" if you have a second parallel port. In the preceding code, an `fos` FileOutputStream was defined.

2. Next, you construct a PrintWriter using the `fos` FileOutputStream you just defined.

3. Print the String you need to print on the printer.

4. When you're finished, print a form feed ('\f") to eject the last page.

5. Close all OutputStream classes and set all OutputStream variables to null.

PrintWriters aren't necessary because any writes to the `fos` FileOutputStream go to the printer. However, PrintWriters come with some useful functions, such as `print()` and `println()`, which make printing to a file easier. See the Microsoft Developer's Network that comes with Visual J++ for all the print methods you can use.

Important OutputStream methods

There are three major OutputStream methods you can use, as listed in Table 17-5.

Table 17-5	Major OutputStream Methods
OutputStream Method	*Description*
`write([int b / byte b[]{, int offset, int length})`	Writes a byte to a file, or writes an array or subarray to a file

OutputStream Method	Description
PrintLine	Prints text followed by a \n to an output stream. Often, this output stream gets printed.
close()	Closes the output file, flushes all buffers, and deallocates resources used by a file
flush()	Forces any information in a buffer to be written. This is useful when exiting a class.

Unlike the InputStream methods, you often use more specialized OutputStream class methods because there is a large need for customizable output.

Stream programming

Listing 17-3 reads in and displays a text file, enables you to make changes, and prints the file or saves it.

Listing 17-3: StreamFunctions

```
import java.awt.*;
import java.awt.event.*;
import java.io.*;
import java.util.*;
public class StreamFunctions extends Frame implements IDir,
ActionListener, WindowListener {
  private FileFunctions ff;        //Call the file functions class
  private File fi_selectedFile;      //The selected file
  private Label lbl_status;        //The status message
  private Label lbl_fileName;        //The file name
  //The display area
  private TextArea ta_display = new TextArea (8,40);
  //Now add buttons
  private Button bu_print = new Button ("Print");
  private Button bu_save = new Button ("Save");
  private Button bu_exit = new Button ("Exit");
  public static void main (String args[]) {
    StreamFunctions sf = new StreamFunctions();
  }
  //Build the StreamFunctions frame, but don't show it yet.
  public StreamFunctions () {
  //Add listeners
    addWindowListener(this);
    bu_print.addActionListener(this);
    bu_save.addActionListener(this);
    bu_exit.addActionListener(this);
  //Add mySouthPanel
    Panel mySouthPanel = new Panel();
  // Set the layout of the panel and the frame
    setLayout(new BorderLayout());
    mySouthPanel.setLayout(new FlowLayout(FlowLayout.LEFT));
```

```
        //Add the components to the south panel
          mySouthPanel.add(lbl_status = new Label
(FileFunctions.pad("",70)));
          mySouthPanel.add(bu_print);
          mySouthPanel.add(bu_save);
          mySouthPanel.add(bu_exit);
          mySouthPanel.add(lbl_fileName = new Label
(FileFunctions.pad("",70)));
        //Add to the Frame
          add("South", mySouthPanel);
          add("Center", ta_display);
        //Now do frame stuff
          setTitle("File Viewer");
          setSize(640,480);
        //Show the FileFunctions frame first
          ff = new FileFunctions(this);
          ff.setTitle("File Viewer");
          ff.setSize(640,480);
          ff.show();
      }
    public void selectFile(File f) { //Method needed for IDir
        fi_selectedFile = f;
        //Load the selected File
        loadFile();
        //Show the StreamFunctions Frame.
        show();
        //Hide the FileFunctions Frame
        ff.setVisible(false);
    }
    public void loadFile() {
        String buffer = new String("");
        FileInputStream fis = null;
        ta_display.setText("");
        try {
          fis = new FileInputStream(fi_selectedFile);
        }
        catch (FileNotFoundException fnfe) {
          lbl_status.setText(fi_selectedFile + " was not found");
          return;
        }
        BufferedInputStream bis = new BufferedInputStream(fis);
        BufferedReader br = new BufferedReader(new
InputStreamReader(bis));
        String holder = new String();
        try {
          holder = br.readLine();
          while (holder != null) { //run until EOF occurs
            buffer += holder + "\n";
            holder = br.readLine();
          }
          ta_display.append(buffer);
        }
        catch (IOException ioe) {
          lbl_status.setText(fi_selectedFile
               + " has an IO Exception -- "
               + ioe.getMessage());
```

```
            return;
        }
    }
//The actionPerformed method is required
//by the ActionListener interface
    public void actionPerformed(ActionEvent e) {
        // Get the text of the button
        String buttonText = e.getActionCommand();
        //Test for buttons
        if (buttonText.equals("Exit")) {
            ff.show();
            setVisible(false);
        }
        else if (buttonText.equals("Print")) {
            try {
            //Open streams
                FileOutputStream fos = new FileOutputStream("LPT1");
                PrintWriter pw = new PrintWriter(fos, true);
            //Send the printer the information
                pw.print(ta_display.getText());
                pw.print('\f');   //Now print a form feed
            // Close all files and set to null for garbage collection
                pw.close();
                fos.close();
                pw = null;
                fos = null;
            }
            catch (IOException ioe) {
                lbl_status.setText("An IOException occured while
printing.");
            }
        }
        else if (buttonText.equals("Save")) {
            try {
            //Open streams
                FileOutputStream fos = new
FileOutputStream(fi_selectedFile);
                DataOutputStream dos = new DataOutputStream(fos);
            // Write the stream from the text area
                dos.writeBytes(ta_display.getText());
            // Close all files and set to null for garbage collection
                dos.close();
                dos = null;
                fos.close();
                fos = null;
            }
            catch (IOException ioe2) {
                lbl_status.setText("An IOException occured while
printing.");
            }
        }
    }
// The following are required by the WindowListener interface
    public void windowClosing(WindowEvent e) {  // User wants the
window to close
        ff.show();
```

```
       setVisible(false);
    }
  public void windowActivated(WindowEvent e) { }  // Window got focus
  public void windowDeactivated(WindowEvent e){}  // Window lost focus
  public void windowIconified(WindowEvent e) { }  // Window is reduced
  public void windowDeiconified(WindowEvent e){}  // Window is
    //expanded from an icon
  public void windowClosed(WindowEvent e) { }  // Window is finished
    //closing
  public void windowOpened(WindowEvent e) { }  // Window is finished
opening
}
```

Notice the flow of control in the StreamFunctions class:

1. The StreamFunctions class actually displays the FileFunctions window first using the start method.

2. When a file is selected in the FileFunctions window, the `selectFile()` method is called in the StreamFunctions class. (All this is done through the `IDir` interface.)

3. The `selectFile()` method hides the FileFunctions Frame and shows the StreamFunctions frame.

Figure 17-2 shows the resulting window for the StreamFunctions class.

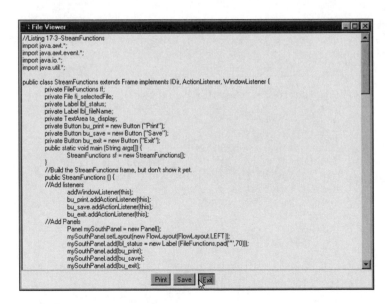

Figure 17-2: The StreamFunctions class produces output that looks like this.

Random-access I/O streams

The RandomAccessFile class handles both input and output. The methods used in the RandomAccessFile class are as versatile as the DataInputClass and DataOutputClass classes combined.

Often, you want to both read and write to a file. However, as in the StreamFunctions class, you want to do your input, close your file, and release any resources — and then later do your output. This would probably not entail using a random access file.

A RandomAccessFile object has no mark or reset methods. However, there is one method, seek(long position), which repositions the read and write pointers in a stream to a different location in a file.

Recording High Scores in BallShot

The BallShot program (shown in the last chapter) shows how graphics can be used for arcade-style games. However, one thing missing from the BallShot program is a splash screen of high scores. File I/O is often used when storing high scores from a Web-based game. Listing 17-4 shows the BallShot10.java program. Some modifications were made (in boldface) to add a RandomAccessFile to keep track of the top ten high scores.

Listing 17-4: BallShotIO.java

```
import java.awt.*;
import java.awt.event.*;
import java.io.*;
public class BallShotIO extends Frame implements WindowListener,
KeyListener {
  private boolean b_IOException = false;    //IO Error has occurred
  private boolean b_securityException = false;  //Security error has
    //occurred
  private boolean b_throwable = false;     //Throwable error has
    //occurred
  private Label lbl_score;       // Score at the bottom
  private int i_blowedUpX;       // The x-coord for blown up
  private int i_blowedUpY;       // The y-coord for blown up
  private int i_safeY;         // The y-coord for save
  private String s_name;        // The name of the player
  // Declare the player
  private MovingPerson mp_player = new MovingPerson();
  public static void main (String args[]) {
    BallShotIO bs = new BallShotIO(null);  // Construct the
BallShotIO game
  }
  public BallShotIO() {      //Constructor with no params
    super();
    continueConstruction();
  }
```

```java
public BallShotIO(String name) {   //Constructor with player name
  super();
  s_name = name;
  continueConstruction();
}
//Constructor with calling module and player name
public BallShotIO(IBallShotIO ibsio, String name) {
  super();
  ibsio_callingApplet = ibsio;
  s_name = name;
  continueConstruction();
}
public void continueConstruction() {
// Add listeners for events
  addKeyListener(this);
  addWindowListener(this);
// Add the score
  Panel southPanel = new Panel();
  southPanel.add(lbl_score = new Label("Score:          "));
  add("South", southPanel);
// Set the background, title, resize, and show
  setBackground(Color.white);
  setTitle("BallShot.java");
  setSize(500,350);
  show();
// Add the player
  add("Center", mp_player);
// Add the game balls. The player must avoid these
  add("Center", new GameBall(mp_player));
  add("Center", new GameBall(mp_player));
  add("Center", new GameBall(mp_player));
  add("Center", new GameBall(mp_player));
}
public void paint(Graphics g) {
  if (mp_player != null) {   // Draw the player
    Rectangle rmp = mp_player.getBounds();
    Rectangle r = getBounds();
    if (mp_player.isBlowedUpRealGood()) {
      if (i_blowedUpX == 0 && i_blowedUpY == 0) {
        i_blowedUpX = Math.max(1, rmp.x - 40);
        i_blowedUpY = Math.max(1, rmp.y - 40);
        mp_player.setLocation (r.width+1, r.height+1);
        writeHighScore();
      }
      g.setColor (Color.red);
      if (b_IOException) {        // Test for errors
        g.drawString("IOException has occurred", 10,10);
      }
      else if (b_securityException) {  // Test for errors
        g.drawString("SecurityException occurred", 10,10);
      }
      else if (b_throwable) {     // Test for errors
        g.drawString("Unknown error has occurred", 10,10);
      }
```

```
        g.setColor (Color.black);
          g.fillOval(i_blowedUpX, i_blowedUpY,
            rmp.width + 80, rmp.height + 80);
          g.setColor (Color.white);
          g.drawString("BOOM!", i_blowedUpX + 35, i_blowedUpY + 45);
        }
        else if (rmp.y > 0) { //Paint safe areas
          g.setColor(Color.green);
          if (i_safeY == 0) {
            i_safeY = rmp.y;
            g.fillRect(0, i_safeY, rmp.width-1, rmp.height-1);
            g.fillRect(r.width - rmp.width-4,
              i_safeY, rmp.width-1, rmp.height-1);
            mp_player.setSafeArea(0, rmp.y);
            mp_player.setSafeArea(r.width - rmp.width, rmp.y);
          }
          else {
            g.fillRect(0, i_safeY, rmp.width-1, rmp.height);
            g.fillRect(r.width - rmp.width-4,
              i_safeY, rmp.width-1, rmp.height);
          }
        }
        lbl_score.setText("Score: " +
String.valueOf(mp_player.getScore()));
      }
    }
public void writeHighScore() {
    int changeNum = -1;
    String cwd = "";
    //Get directory that I have access to
    if (ibsio_callingApplet != null) {
      cwd =
ibsio_callingApplet.getCodeBase().toString().substring(6);
    }
    String fileName = cwd + "HiScore.dat";  //Finish file name
    int loop;
    RandomAccessFile raf = null;
    long score = mp_player.getScore();
    String names[] = new String[10];
    long scores[] = new long[10];
    for(loop = 0; loop < 10; loop++) {     //Fill in zeros for score
      names[loop] = "";
      scores[loop] = 0;
    }
    try {    //Now read scores in
      raf = new RandomAccessFile(fileName, "rw");
      for(loop = 0; loop < 10; loop++) {
        names[loop] = raf.readUTF();
        scores[loop] = raf.readLong();
        if (score > scores[loop] && changeNum == -1) {
          changeNum = loop;
        }
      }
```

```java
      }
      catch (EOFException e1) {}
      catch (IOException e2) {
        b_IOException = true;
      }
      finally {
        if (loop < 10) {      //Finish filling in scores
          changeNum = loop;
          scores[loop] = 0;
          names[loop] = "";
        }
        try {
          if (raf != null) {   //Close random access file
            raf.close();
          }
        }
        catch (Throwable t) {}
      }
      if (changeNum >= 0) {   //Your score made the list!
        for (loop = 9; loop > changeNum; loop--) {
          names[loop] = names[loop-1];
          scores[loop] = scores[loop-1];
        }
        names[changeNum] = s_name;
        scores[changeNum] = score;
        try {   //Form an output stream and put the score in
          FileOutputStream fos = new FileOutputStream(fileName);
          DataOutputStream dos = new DataOutputStream(fos);
          for(loop = 0; loop < 10; loop++) {
            dos.writeUTF(names[loop]);
            dos.writeLong(scores[loop]);
          }
          dos.close();
          fos.close();
          ibsio_callingApplet.BallShotIOExit();
        }
        catch (IOException e1) {
          b_IOException = true;
        }
        catch (SecurityException e2) {
          b_securityException = true;
        }
      }
    }
  }
// Keyboard methods required by the KeyListener interface
  public void keyTyped(KeyEvent e){ }     // A key was typed
  public void keyPressed(KeyEvent e){     // A key was pressed
    // Check for arrow movement and move player if appropriate
    if (mp_player.isBlowedUpRealGood() == false) {
      switch (e.getKeyCode()) {
        case e.VK_UP :
          mp_player.move(MovingPerson.UP);
          break;
```

```
        case e.VK_DOWN :
          mp_player.move(MovingPerson.DOWN);
          break;
        case e.VK_LEFT :
          mp_player.move(MovingPerson.LEFT);
          break;
        case e.VK_RIGHT :
          mp_player.move(MovingPerson.RIGHT);
          break;
      }
    }
  }
  public void keyReleased(KeyEvent e) { }  // A key was released
// The following are required by the WindowListener interface
  public void windowClosing(WindowEvent e) {  // User wants the
    //window to close
    this.dispose();
    System.exit(0);
  }
  public void windowActivated(WindowEvent e) { }  // Window got focus
  public void windowDeactivated(WindowEvent e){}  // Window lost focus
  public void windowIconified(WindowEvent e) { }  // Window is reduced
  public void windowDeiconified(WindowEvent e){}  // Window is
    //expanded from an icon
  public void windowClosed(WindowEvent e) { }  // Window is finished
    //closing
  public void windowOpened(WindowEvent e) { }  // Window is finished
    //opening
}
```

A RandomAccessFile is used in case the file needs to be created. An InputFileStream causes an IOException if the file is not yet created. Now, when a MovingPerson object blows up, the score is compared against the top ten scores and saved.

The `DataOutputStream.writeUTF` and `RandomAccessFile.readUTF` methods read and write a variable-length name String to a file in UTF format. The `writeUTF` and `readUTF` methods are handy for String variables because you don't have to worry about string length.

The two main features missing in the BallShotIO game in Listing 17-4 are a restart button, so that you don't have to fully restart the program every time you play, and a high score listing combined with a "splash screen" as seen in Figure 17-3:

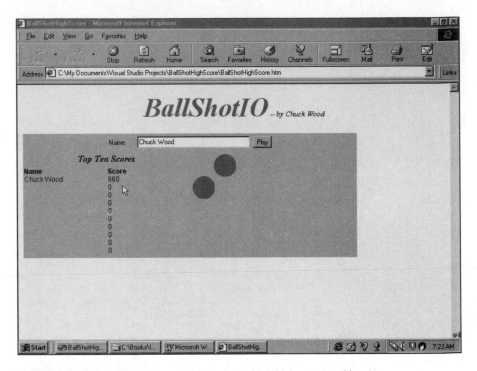

Figure 17-3: BallShotIO needs a splash screen with a high scores table.

To do this, you must read and display the `HiScore.dat` file created and maintained in the BallShotIO program. The BallShotHighScore Applet in Listing 17-5 displays file information on a Web page, and fires off the BallShotIO program.

Listing 17-5: BallShotHighScore.java

```
import java.awt.*;
import java.awt.event.*;
import java.io.*;
import java.applet.*;
public class BallShotHighScore extends Applet implements
ActionListener, IBallShotIO {
  private Button bu_play = new Button("Play");  //Play button
  private BallShotIO ibs_BallShot;  //The ball shot module
  private Label lbl_name;          //The name
  private TextField itf_name;       //The text field name
  private Label lbl_names[] = new Label[10]; //Array of high names
  private Label lbl_scores[] = new Label[10];  //Array of high
scores
  // Bouncing balls for display
  private BouncingBallPanel bbp_bouncingBalls = new
BouncingBallPanel();
  public void init() {
    bu_play.addActionListener(this);  // Listen for button click
  // Fonts for names
```

```
   Font fbi = new Font("TimesRoman", Font.BOLD + Font.ITALIC, 16);
   Font fb = new Font("Helvetica", Font.BOLD, 12);
   Font f = new Font("Helvetica", Font.PLAIN, 12);
   lbl_name = new Label("Name: ");
   itf_name = new TextField(30);
//Create labels
   Label h1 = new Label("Top Ten Scores", Label.CENTER);
   Label h2 = new Label("Name");
   Label h3 = new Label("Score");
//Set label fonts
   h2.setFont(fb);
   h3.setFont(fb);
   h1.setFont(fbi);
//Define Panels
   Panel scorePanel = new Panel();
   Panel scoreInfoPanel = new Panel();
   Panel centerPanel = new Panel();
   Panel northPanel = new Panel();
//Set layout for Applet and Panels
   setLayout(new BorderLayout());
   centerPanel.setLayout(new GridLayout(1, 2));
   scorePanel.setLayout(new GridLayout(11, 2));
   scoreInfoPanel.setLayout(new BorderLayout());
//Add components to Panels
   scoreInfoPanel.add("North", h1);
   scoreInfoPanel.add("Center",scorePanel);
   centerPanel.add(scoreInfoPanel);
   centerPanel.add(bbp_bouncingBalls);
   northPanel.add(lbl_name);
   northPanel.add(itf_name);
   northPanel.add(bu_play);
   scorePanel.add(h2);
   scorePanel.add(h3);
   add("North", northPanel);
   add("Center", centerPanel);
   for (int loop = 0; loop < 10; loop++) {
     scorePanel.add(lbl_names[loop] = new Label());
     scorePanel.add(lbl_scores[loop] = new Label());
     lbl_names[loop].setFont(f);
     lbl_scores[loop].setFont(f);
   }
}
//Show the bouncing ball splash panel
public void start() {
  bbp_bouncingBalls.showBall();
  showScores();
}
//Player ended. Redisplay high scores
public void BallShotIOExit() {
  ibs_BallShot = null;
  showScores();
}
//Display the high scores
public void showScores() {
  int loop = 0;
  try {
```

```java
//Get the current working directory and filename
  String cwd = getCodeBase().toString().substring(6);
  String fileName = cwd + "HiScore.dat";
//Open file for input
  File f = new File(fileName);
  FileInputStream fis = new FileInputStream(f);
  DataInputStream dis = new DataInputStream(fis);
//Display high scores
  for(; loop < 10; loop++) {
    lbl_names[loop].setText(dis.readUTF());
    lbl_scores[loop].setText(String.valueOf(dis.readLong()));
  }
//Close streams and garbage collect
  dis.close();
  fis.close();
  f = null;
}
catch (EOFException e) {
  showStatus("End of file has been reached.");
  for(;loop < 10; loop++) {
    lbl_names[loop].setText("");
    lbl_scores[loop].setText("0");
  }
}
catch (FileNotFoundException e) {
  showStatus("High scores file does not yet exist.");
  for(loop = 0; loop < 10; loop++) {
    lbl_names[loop].setText("");
    lbl_scores[loop].setText("0");
  }
}
catch (IOException e) {
  showStatus("An IOException occured in the loadFile method.");
}
catch (Throwable t) {
  showStatus(t.getMessage() + " -- Unknown Exception.");
}
}
//The actionPerformed method is required
//by the ActionListener interface
  public void actionPerformed(ActionEvent e) {   //Play was pressed
    if (itf_name.getText().trim().equals("")) {   //Check Name
      showStatus("You must enter a name to play!");
    }
    else {
      showStatus("");                 //Plaaayyy Ball
      ibs_BallShot = new BallShotIO(this, itf_name.getText());
    }
  }
}
```

```
class BouncingBallPanel extends Panel implements Runnable {
  public void run () {          //Multitask this stuff
    add(new GameBall(null));   //Add bouncing ball 1
    add(new GameBall(null));   //Add bouncing ball 2
    repaint();          //Repaint so adds take
  }
  public void showBall () {
    Thread t = new Thread(this);  //Start thread
    t.start();
  }
}
```

The `showScores()` method tries to access the `HiScores.dat` file created by the BallShotIO program. Then, if there's no error, the high scores are displayed.

Secret

I recommend a splash screen with every game. That way, it's easy for the end user to use your program, see how he or she did, and restart. Furthermore, separating the actual game into its own Frame often makes the game more playable.

Here's the HTML code that accompanies the Java Applet:

```
<html>
<head>
<title>BallShotHighScore</title>
</head>
<body>
<p><center>
<i><strong><big><font size=12
color="RED">BallShotIO</font></big></strong></i>
<i><small>-- by Chuck Wood</small></i>
</center>
<br>
<applet
code=BallShotHighScore
width=600
height=220>
</applet>
</p>
</body>
</html>
```

Secret

Notice that some headings were displayed in the HTML rather than all the display being done in the BallShotHighScore Applet. HTML files used for Web pages are usually more efficient and easier to develop and maintain than Java programs. Java's a great language, but if you can avoid writing Java code by letting HTML work for you, you probably should.

Summary

File I/O and directory management are important to any language, and Java makes them relatively easy with an array of predefined file-handling classes. In this chapter, you learned how to do several directory and stream functions that make file manipulation and I/O possible.

- Java has routines that enable you to retrieve directory and file information.

- File I/O is quick and frequently used to store simple information. Java uses input and output streams to control file I/O.

- Random Access files enable you to read or write from anywhere in the file.

- File I/O is often used in Java Applets, where database access may be too slow or cumbersome.

Chapter 18

More Powerful Interfaces and Multiple Inheritance

In This Chapter

▶ Mastering interfaces

▶ Mimicking multiple inheritance with interfaces

▶ Using interfaces to communicate between two classes

Interfaces are one of the hardest concepts in Java to understand and implement. However, once implemented, they are one of Java's most powerful tools. Interfaces provide a mechanism for an instantiated class to return a value to a calling procedure, and they also can act as a substitute for multiple inheritance.

Using Interfaces to Implement Multiple Inheritance

Inheritance is an object-oriented language's most powerful tool. Using inheritance, you can subtype any class into multiple classes. However, sometimes a class should be inherited from multiple parent classes. In languages that allow multiple inheritance, this can cause numerous problems, especially when a class is derived from two or more classes with a common base class.

Multiple inheritance is not allowed in Java, with good reason. This section discusses why multiple inheritance is needed, why multiple inheritance is avoided, and how to use interfaces to *safely* simulate multiple inheritance.

Why multiple inheritance is needed

Multiple inheritance often is a logical necessity. For instance, say you want to display a list of top programmers based on lines of code on an intranet Web site, as shown in Figure 18-1.

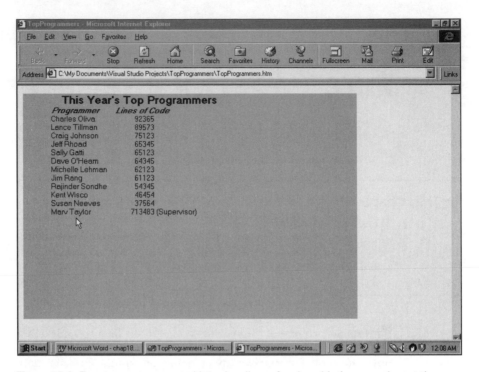

Figure 18-1: Programmers are sorted based on lines of code, with the supervisor at the bottom of the list.

You already have a class to sort objects, and you want to inherit this class. This situation can be seen in Figure 18-2.

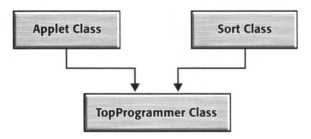

Figure 18-2: Programmers are often faced with a multiple-inheritance situation.

In Figure 18-2, the TopProgrammer class is an Applet, and therefore needs to inherit the Applet class to function. However, you also need to sort inside the TopProgrammer class, and you don't want to write a different sort routine every time a sort is needed. Multiple inheritance could resolve this issue, but multiple inheritance is tricky in any language and is not allowed in Java.

Why to avoid multiple inheritance

If TopProgrammers is inherited from both `Applet` and `Sort`, they could each have similarly named methods or attributes. TopProgrammers won't know which method or class attribute to use because of this duplication. This ambiguity causes several problems:

- A new mechanism is needed to enable TopProgrammers to access an ambiguous method or attribute.

- New public or protected methods and attributes could not be added to `Applet` or `Sort` without first making sure that the other class does not contain the same name for an attribute or method.

Such problems already affect object-oriented languages like C++ that allow multiple inheritance. In fact, many programming experts treat multiple inheritance like `goto` statements, saying that they simply should not be used. C++ does have the `virtual` keyword that, when applied to the base-class of a multiple-inherited derived class, aids the compiler in resolving function and variable references. Java doesn't support the `virtual` keyword.

Interfaces to simulate multiple inheritance

Java is different from other languages in that *every* Web page Applet is inherited from the Applet class. No Applet can be inherited from a non-Applet class because Java does not support multiple inheritance. Java gets around this limitation by using interfaces.

Interfaces are a special kind of class that act as a gateway between two classes. Interfaces have the following characteristics:

- All interfaces are `abstract` and can't be instantiated. Even if you don't use the `abstract` modifier on the class name, an interface, by definition, is still `abstract`. Interfaces are declared using the `interface` keyword and the following syntax:

```
public interface Interface1 {
```

- Interfaces can be inherited from each other using the `extends` keyword and can implement other interfaces just like classes using the `implements` keyword:

```
public interface Interface1 extends Interface2
    implements Interface3 {
```

- Interfaces do not have nonstatic class attributes. Interfaces define functionality only, not behavior. However, you can have static class attributes inside an interface.

- Unlike inheritance, using the `extends` keyword you can implement multiple interfaces on a single class using the following syntax:

```
public class ClassName extends ParentClass
    implements Interface1, Interface2, ... {
```

- Interfaces must be public and cannot be final because they are, by nature, abstract.

- Interface methods can't be declared native, static, synchronized, or final. Also, interface methods are all abstract and *cannot contain any lines of code!* All code for the interface must be written in the implementing class.

Interfaces can be used as arguments in another class's methods. Figure 18-3 restructures the multiple inheritance shown in Figure 18-2 to use interfaces:

- Instead of inheriting the TopProgrammers class from both Sort and Applet, Figure 18-3 shows that TopProgrammers is inherited from Applet, and implements the ISort interface and defines the isGreaterThan() method.

- The Sort class (the class you want to inherit from, but can't because it involves multiple inheritance) uses the ISort interface as a data type for an argument in its constructor. (A separate method could have been used instead.)

- The ISort interface requires that the TopProgrammers class, as an implementor of the ISort interface, contains the isGreaterThan method to compare itself to another object.

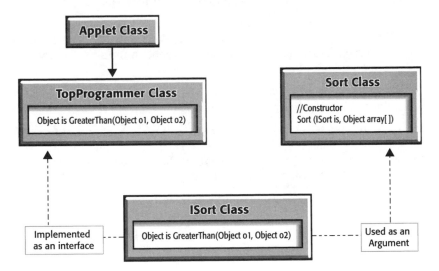

Figure 18-3: Interfaces are implemented by one class and used as the data type of a method argument in another class.

Secret

If you don't have a similar structure to the diagram in Figure 18-3, then you aren't using interfaces correctly. Don't think of an interface as a parent class. Instead, think of an interface as a gateway between two classes enabling the functionality of one class to be implemented by another class. Remember, an interface is implemented by one class and used as a method argument in another class.

Keeping this in mind, you use interfaces because one class can implement methods from another class. Usually, you end up with small interfaces (with few methods) acting as a bridge between two classes.

The modules in Listings 18-1, 18-2, and 18-3 show the code for the Sort class and the ISort interface. Listing 18-1 shows the ISort interface. This interface requires the existence of an isGreaterThan method so that the calling program can define how to sort whatever array is passed to the Sort class.

Listing 18-1: ISort.java

```
public interface ISort {
    public abstract boolean isGreaterThan (Object o1, Object o2);
}
```

The Sort class has only one method — the constructor — as shown in Listing 18-3. The constructor performs a simple bubble sort that calls the ISort.isGreaterThan method that should exist in the calling module.

Listing 18-2: Sort.java

```
public class Sort {
    public Sort(ISort is,
                Object object_array [ ]) {
// Go through the array several times
        for (int loop1 = 0;
                loop1 < object_array.length;
                loop1++) {
            for (int loop2 = 0;
                    loop2 < object_array.length - loop1 - 1;
                    loop2++) {
// Swap array elements if they aren't in the right order
                if (is.isGreaterThan(object_array[loop2],
                                    object_array[loop2 + 1])) {
                    Object holder;
                    holder = object_array[loop2];
                    object_array[loop2] =
                                    object_array[loop2 + 1];
                    object_array[loop2 + 1] = holder;
                }
            }
        }
    }
}
```

Finally, a small TopProgrammers module is provided that implements the ISort interface and constructs the Sort class, passing itself as an argument, as shown in Listing 18-3. The TopProgrammers class contains an isGreaterThan module, which is passed to the Sort class.

Listing 18-3: TopProgrammers.java

```java
import java.awt.*;
public class TopProgrammers extends java.applet.Applet   implements
ISort {
  private final int numberOfProgrammers = 12;
    Programmer programmers[] = new Programmer[numberOfProgrammers];

    public void start() {
//Create the programmers
    programmers[0] = new Programmer("Sally Gatti",      65123);
    programmers[1] = new Programmer("Craig Johnson",    75123);
    programmers[2] = new Programmer("Michelle Lehman", 62123);
    programmers[3] = new Programmer("Susan Neeves",      37564);
    programmers[4] = new Programmer("Dave O'Hearn",     64345);
    programmers[5] = new Programmer("Charles Oliva",    92365);
    programmers[6] = new Programmer("Jim Rang",          61123);
    programmers[7] = new Programmer("Jeff Rhoad",        65345);
    programmers[8] = new Programmer("Rajinder Sondhe", 54345);
    programmers[9] = new Programmer("Lance Tillman",    89573);
    programmers[10] = new Programmer("Kent Wisco",       46454);
//Create the supervisor
    int sectionTotal = 0;
    for (int loop = 0; loop < numberOfProgrammers - 1; loop++) {
      sectionTotal += programmers[loop].getLines();
    }
    programmers[numberOfProgrammers - 1] = new Programmer("Marv
Taylor", sectionTotal, true);
    Sort sa = new Sort(this, (Object[ ]) programmers);
  }
  public void paint(Graphics g) {
    Font font = new Font("Dialog", Font.BOLD, 18);
    g.setFont(font);
    g.drawString("1997 Top Programmers ", 50, 18);
    font = null;
    font = new Font("Dialog", Font.BOLD + Font.ITALIC, 14);
    g.setFont(font);
    g.drawString("Programmer", 50, 35);
    g.drawString("Lines of Code", 165, 35);
    font = null;
    font = new Font("Dialog", Font.PLAIN, 14);
    g.setFont(font);
    for (int loop = 0; loop < numberOfProgrammers; loop++) {
      g.drawString(programmers[loop].getName(),
        50, 15*loop+50);
      String sup = "";
      int y = 200;
      if (programmers[loop].getSupervisor()) {
        sup = " (Supervisor)";
        y -= 7;
      }
      g.drawString(Integer.toString(programmers[loop].getLines()) +
sup,
        y, 15*loop+50);
```

```
        }
    }

// Because you want high programmers on top IN DESCENDING ORDER,
// "greater than" means having a lower number of lines of code. The low
// number of lines are at the bottom of the array and the high
// number of lines are in the first array elements.
// Supervisors are always at the bottom of the sort.
    public boolean isGreaterThan (Object o1, Object o2) {
        Programmer c1 = (Programmer) o1;
        Programmer c2 = (Programmer) o2;
    if (c1.getSupervisor() && !c2.getSupervisor()) {
      return true;
    }
    else if (!c1.getSupervisor() && c2.getSupervisor()) {
      return false;
    }
    else if (c1.getLines() < c2.getLines()) {
      return true;
    }
    return false;
    }
}

final class Programmer {
  private boolean ib_supervisor;
  private String is_programmerName;
  private int ii_linesOfCode;
  public Programmer(String name, int amount) {
    is_programmerName = new String(name);
    ii_linesOfCode = amount;
    ib_supervisor = false;
  }
  public Programmer(String name, int amount, boolean supervisor) {
    is_programmerName = new String(name);
    ii_linesOfCode = amount;
    ib_supervisor = supervisor;
  }
  public int getLines() {
    return ii_linesOfCode;
  }
  public String getName() {
    return is_programmerName;
  }
  public boolean getSupervisor() {
    return ib_supervisor;
  }
}
```

As you see by the first line of code in Listing 18-1, interfaces are declared using the `interface` keyword rather than the `class` keyword:

```
public interface ISort {
```

Interfaces are added to a class definition using the implements keyword rather than extends as with derivation, as shown by the TopProgrammers declaration found in Listing 18-3:

```
public class TopProgrammers
    extends java.applet.Applet implements ISort {
```

Now look at the constructor for the Sort class:

```
public Sort(ISort is, Object object_array [ ]){
```

Notice that Sort requires you to pass it an ISort class. This enables the Sort class to call the isGreaterThan method (on the Applet) that it needs for testing:

```
if (is.isGreaterThan(
    object_array[loop2], object_array[loop2 + 1])) {
```

Now it's up to the class that implements the ISort class to determine the sort criteria. In this case, it is sorted on linesOfCode descending (so the highest number of lines is at the top of the array, and the lowest number of lines is at the bottom of the array):

```
// Because you want high programmers on top IN DESCENDING ORDER,
// "greater than" means having a lower number of lines of code.  The low
// number of lines is at the bottom of the array and the high
// number of lines is in the first array elements.
// Supervisors are always at the bottom of the sort.
    public boolean isGreaterThan (Object o1, Object o2) {
        Programmer c1 = (Programmer) o1;
        Programmer c2 = (Programmer) o2;
    if (c1.getSupervisor() && !c2.getSupervisor()) {
      return true;
    }
    else if (!c1.getSupervisor() && c2.getSupervisor()) {
      return false;
    }
    else if (c1.getLines() < c2.getLines()) {
      return true;
    }
    return false;
    }
```

Notice that some special criteria makes supervisors "sink" to the bottom no matter what value they have for their linesOfCode. The Sort class doesn't care how we determine which object is greater than another object, so this is OK.

Finally, you call the Sort method that uses the ISort interface as a data type for an argument (in this case, it's the Sort constructor). Of course, you still need to decide how to display this on the Web page.

```
public void displayCusts() {
    Sort sa = new Sort(
                  this, (Object[ ]) best_custs);
    // code to display customers 0 through 9 on the Web page
}
```

Here you see object-oriented programming at work:

- Bubble sorts, like the sorting algorithm found in the Sort class, work great for small sorts. However, if the number of sorted elements increases, you may need to change your sort to an insertion sort or quick sort algorithm. Your interfacing class (TopProgrammers) "doesn't care" how the records are sorted. The interfacing class needs to define what makes one object "greater" than another object.

- If you need to add further criteria to your sort order, you have to rewrite the isGreaterThan method, as you would have with multiple inheritance. The Sort class "doesn't care" how the interfacing class determines which object is greater than the other object, and sorts based on any criteria you define.

Interfaces are an important part of Java's object-oriented programming.

Using Interfaces to Return Values

Interfaces aren't always used to mimic multiple inheritance. Interfaces can also be used to "talk" (or "communicate") between two classes. Often, you would like to instantiate a class within another class, and then wait until the instantiated class is finished before continuing. You may even want to test a value in the instantiated class. A primary example of this is the MessageBox construct.

As Windows programmers know, a MessageBox stops a program while the program waits for an OK-Yes-No-Cancel button to be clicked, and then continues processing based on the button that is selected. The three main types of MessageBoxes can be seen in Figure 18-4.

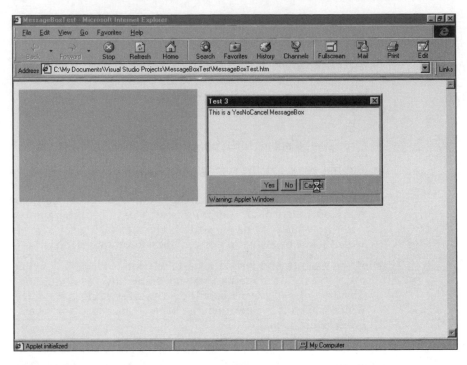

Figure 18-4: MessageBoxes can use OK for acknowledgement, and Yes/No or Yes/No/Cancel to give the end user a choice.

The processing flow needed when using a message box forces a user to answer, or at least acknowledge the MessageBox question before processing can continue, as seen graphically in Figure 18-5.

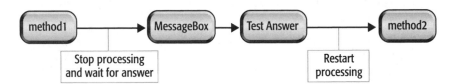

Figure 18-5: MessageBoxes are often used to halt a program and wait for a response.

In Java, this is hard to implement. Because system calls (with the exception of ActiveX modules) are hard to make and even ActiveX modules run concurrently with a Java program, interfaces are the best way to return a value from one class to another.

Listing 18-4 shows the IMessageBox interface. This interface requires that one method named "answer" be included in every class that implements a MessageBox.

Listing 18-4: IMessageBox.java

```
IMessageBox.java
public interface IMessageBox {
  public void answer(int answer);
}
```

Listing 18-4 is the MessageBox class. This class displays a dialog message box with a String that was received as a parameter. A type parameter is used to see what kind of message box (OK, Yes/No, Yes/No/Cancel) is desired. The MessageBox class opens a dialog window. When the user clicks a button, the dialog window calls the MessageBox program, which in turn calls the answer method of the calling class, as shown in boldface in Listing 18-5.

Listing 18-5: MessageBox.java

```
import java.awt.*;
import java.awt.event.*;
public class MessageBox extends Frame implements IMessageBox {
  public final static int YES = 1;
  public final static int NO = 2;
  public final static int CANCEL = 3;
  public final static int OK = 1;
  public final static int YES_NO = 2;
  public final static int YES_NO_CANCEL = 3;
  private IMessageBox imb_callingClass;
  public MessageBox (IMessageBox i,  String title, String message,
int type) {
    super();
    setTitle("");
    imb_callingClass = i;
    MessageDialog md = new MessageDialog(this, this, title,
message, type);
  }
  public void answer(int ans){
    imb_callingClass.answer(ans);
  }
}
class MessageDialog extends Dialog implements ActionListener,
WindowListener {
  public final static int OK = MessageBox.OK;
  public final static int YES_NO = MessageBox.YES_NO;
  public final static int YES_NO_CANCEL = MessageBox.YES_NO_CANCEL;
  protected Button icb_yes_ok;
  protected Button icb_no;
  protected Button icb_cancel;
  protected TextArea ita_message;
  protected Panel ipa_southPanel;
  protected Panel ipa_centerPanel;
  private IMessageBox imb_callingClass;

  public MessageDialog (IMessageBox i,  Frame parent, String title,
              String message, int type) {
    super(parent, title, true);  // Make a modal dialog box
```

```java
      addWindowListener(this);
      messageBoxSetUp(message, type);
      imb_callingClass = i;
      setSize(320, 200);
      show();
    }
  public void messageBoxSetUp (String message, int type) {
     ipa_southPanel = new Panel();
     ipa_centerPanel = new Panel();
     ipa_southPanel.setLayout(new FlowLayout());
     ipa_centerPanel.setLayout(new GridLayout(1,1));
     ipa_centerPanel.add(ita_message = new TextArea());
     switch (type) {   // Add buttons depending on type
       case YES_NO :
         ipa_southPanel.add(icb_yes_ok = new Button("Yes"));
         ipa_southPanel.add(icb_no = new Button("No"));
         break;
       case YES_NO_CANCEL :
         ipa_southPanel.add(icb_yes_ok = new Button("Yes"));
         ipa_southPanel.add(icb_no = new Button("No"));
         ipa_southPanel.add(icb_cancel = new Button("Cancel"));
         break;
       default :   // Assume OK.
         ipa_southPanel.add(icb_yes_ok = new Button("OK"));
         break;
     } // End switch
     icb_yes_ok.addActionListener(this);
     if (icb_no != null) {
       icb_no.addActionListener(this);
     }
     if (icb_cancel != null) {
       icb_cancel.addActionListener(this);
     }
     ita_message.setText(message);
     add("Center", ipa_centerPanel);
     add("South", ipa_southPanel);
   }
// actionPerformed is required by the ActionListener interface
   public void actionPerformed(ActionEvent e) {
      // Get the text of the button
      String buttonText = e.getActionCommand();
      //First test for buttons
      if (buttonText.equals("Cancel")) {
        imb_callingClass.answer(3);
      }
      else if (buttonText.equals("No")) {
        imb_callingClass.answer(2);
      }
      else {
```

```
        imb_callingClass.answer(1);
      }
      dispose();
    }
// The following are required by the WindowListener interface
  public void windowClosing(WindowEvent e) {
    dispose();
    imb_callingClass.answer(3);
  }
  public void windowActivated(WindowEvent e) { }
  public void windowDeactivated(WindowEvent e) { }
  public void windowDeiconified(WindowEvent e) { }
  public void windowClosed(WindowEvent e) { }
  public void windowIconified(WindowEvent e) { }
  public void windowOpened(WindowEvent e) { }
}


}
```

Finally, Listing 18-6 contains a MessageBoxTest class used to display three MessageBoxes.

Listing 18-6: MessageBoxText Class

```
import java.applet.*;
public class MessageBoxTest extends Applet implements IMessageBox {
  int ii_answers = 0;
  public void start() {
    MessageBox mb1 = new MessageBox(this, "Test 1",
        "This is an OK MessageBox", MessageBox.OK);
    MessageBox mb2 = new MessageBox(this, "Test 2",
        "This is an YesNo MessageBox", MessageBox.YES_NO);
    MessageBox mb3 = new MessageBox(this, "Test 3",
        "This is an YesNoCancel MessageBox",
        MessageBox.YES_NO_CANCEL);
  }
  public void answer(int ans){
    if (++ii_answers == 3) {
      System.exit(0);
    }
  }
}
```

Whenever a MessageBox is formed, the method of the parent class method finishes processing. Then, the MessageBox, being a modal dialog, does not allow any processing until a MessageBox Button is clicked. Then the answer method is called from the MessageBox class and the MessageBox terminates.

Using interfaces, you can instantiate a class and have it return a value before it deallocates itself from memory.

Summary

Interfaces are an important part of Java development; their capabilities go beyond enabling an instantiated class to return a value to a calling program.

- An interface in Java can mimic multiple inheritance without the pitfalls that multiple inheritance often brings to other languages.

- Interfaces act as a substitute for multiple inheritance.

- Interfaces enable an instantiated class to return a value to a calling procedure.

Chapter 19

Inside Information on Java Data Structures

In This Chapter

▶ Referencing data using single and multidimensional arrays

▶ Using the Enumeration class to retrieve a set of data

▶ Finding out how to use the Vector class as an adjusting array

▶ Using the Stack class to push and pop entries in storage with the Last In, First Out storage and retrieval technique

▶ Using pointers to develop stacks, linked lists, and binary trees

---

J ava has many different ways to store data in memory. This chapter discusses the many ways to keep sets of information in your Java program and the ways information can be passed to and returned from a calling program.

Mastering Arrays

Arrays are blocks of memory where similar variables are stored. An array is coded with brackets to indicate the number of variables within it. To allocate 15 integers, code the following Visual J++ statement:

```
int numbers[ ] = new int[15];
```

The best way to explain arrays is with an example. If you want to keep track of someone's bowling score (a game consists of 10 frames), you could use the following array:

```
String frames[ ] = new int[10];
```

You could also define an array without explicitly numbering the array:

```
String bowlers[ ] = {"Ollie", "Stanley", "Chuck"};
```

The bowlers array would then be stored in memory, as shown in Figure 19-1.

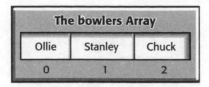

Figure 19-1: Arrays store information in contiguous blocks of memory.

Referencing array elements

You can reference arrays by using bracketed numbers as references. For example, if bowlers[2] is "Stanley" then the following line:

```
g.drawString(bowlers[2] +
    " bowled 220!", 1, 15);
```

outputs "Stanley bowled 220!" to the current window. Like C++, Java arrays begin at zero, not one.

Determining array size

Often, when you receive an array into a method, you have no idea how big it is. For instance, consider the following method prototype:

```
public void printBowlers(String names[ ]) {
```

To determine the number of elements in an array, use the length attribute. For example, to complete the printBowlers method just described, write the following method:

```
public void printBowlers(String names[ ]) {
    Graphics g = getGraphics();
    for (int loop = 0; loop < names.length; loop++) {
        g.drawString(names[loop], 50, 15*loop+50);
    }
}
```

Notice that the printBowlers method uses names.length to determine how many elements are in the names array.

Understanding multidimensional arrays

Multidimensional arrays enable you to store a "block" of information in memory as opposed to the "row" of information that is stored by a single-dimensional array. Assume the bowlers mentioned previously played a match. You can add an additional array containing the pins scored per frame:

```
String bowlers[ ] = {"Ollie", "Stanley", "Chuck"};
int frames[ ] [ ] = new int [3] [10];
```

The preceding code stores in memory the names of the three bowlers, and then declares and initializes a 3-x-10 array, as shown in Figure 19-2.

The 3 x 10 frames Array

	0	1	2	3	4	5	6	7	8	9
0										
1										
2										

Figure 19-2: While single-dimensional arrays are stored in "rows" of memory, multidimensional arrays are stored in "blocks" of memory.

Accessing a multidimensional array is similar to accessing a single-dimensional array. The following code outputs "Ollie scored 6 pins in the 3rd frame" to the current window:

```
String bowlers[ ] = {"Ollie", "Stanley", "Chuck"};
int frames[ ] [ ] = new int [3] [10];
...
// Ollie scored 6 pins in the 3rd frame
int bowler = 1;
int frame = 3;
int score = 6;
//Remember, arrays start at 0, so subtract 1
pins_scored[bowler-1][frame-1] = score;
...
g.drawString(bowlers[bowler-1]
    + " scored "
    + String.valueOf(
            pins_scored[bowler-1][frame-1])
    + " pins in the ."
    + (frame == 1) ? "1st" :
            (frame == 2) ? "2nd" :
            (frame == 3) ? "3rd" :
            String.valueOf(frame) + "th"
    + " frame"
, 1, 30);
```

Secret

The conditional operator (? :) is used to test a condition and return a true or false value. It's great for testing values inside expressions.

Using Enumerations

Enumerations return a list of items. Unlike arrays, Enumerations are accessed sequentially and each Enumeration entry is returned once. Enumeration is an interface, not a class (for more information on interfaces, see the previous chapter), and therefore cannot be instantiated. However, Enumeration interfaces are often returned by methods.

You've already seen some system properties when you used `user.dir` in Chapter 6, but the system properties in use were never documented. It would be great to have a program that lists all the system properties, as shown in Figure 19-3.

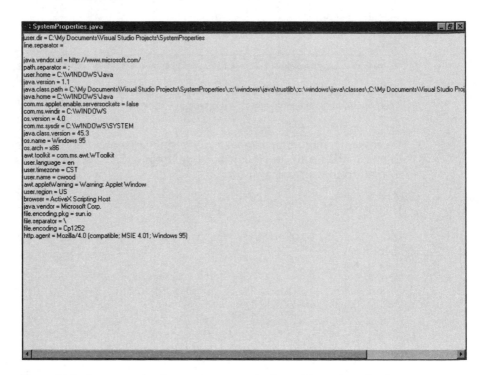

Figure 19-3: A program that lists system properties is useful to a Java developer.

As shown in Listing 19-1, system properties are listed with the aid of an Enumeration class.

Listing 19-1: SystemProperties.java

```
import java.awt.*;
import java.awt.event.*;
import java.util.*;
public class SystemProperties extends Frame implements WindowListener
{
```

```java
  private TextArea ta_properties = new TextArea();
  public static void main(String args[]) {
    SystemProperties sp = new SystemProperties();
  }
  public SystemProperties() {
  //Add the WindowListener for Window events
    addWindowListener(this);
    setLayout(new GridLayout(1,1));
    add(ta_properties);      // Add a text area for output
    // Get the System Properties
    Properties p = System.getProperties();
    // Return an Enumeration for the System Properties
    Enumeration e = p.propertyNames();
    // Loop through the Enumeration to display system properties
    for (int loop = 1; e.hasMoreElements();loop++) {
      // Get Property name
      String propName = (String) e.nextElement();
      ta_properties.append(propName + " = ");
      // Display property value
      ta_properties.append(System.getProperty(propName));
      // Don't forget the newline character
      ta_properties.append("\n");
    }
    setSize(600,450);
    setTitle("SystemProperties.java");
    show();
    }
// The following are required by the WindowListener interface
  public void windowClosing(WindowEvent e) {
    this.dispose();
    System.exit(0);
  }
  public void windowActivated(WindowEvent e) { }
  public void windowDeactivated(WindowEvent e) { }
  public void windowDeiconified(WindowEvent e) { }
  public void windowClosed(WindowEvent e) { }
  public void windowIconified(WindowEvent e) { }
  public void windowOpened(WindowEvent e) { }
}
```

Enumerations only have two methods:

- The hasMoreElements method tests to see if there are any elements in the Enumeration that have not been returned.

- The nextElement returns the next element in an Enumeration.

Using the hasMoreElements and nextElement methods, Enumerations enable you to scroll through or "enumerate" a series of objects. Each element in an Enumeration can be returned only once, and once an Enumeration is out of elements, it is no longer useful.

Understanding Vectors

The problem with arrays is that you must specify their length before populating any of the elements inside. After that, an array cannot grow or shrink. Depending on the object in the array, you could be forced to make an array obscenely big to cover every situation (which eats up system resources), or make an array somewhat smaller that does not handle every situation. Both are unacceptable.

Vectors are like arrays, except in two respects. First, they shrink and grow upon command. Vectors are a good way to keep variable length arrays. Second, while arrays are strongly typed (meaning you have to declare their class or data type), Vectors are *untyped,* meaning that Vectors can contain any number of different classes. Elements of a vector are stored and retrieved as Objects and need to be cast to their original type. To use Vectors, include an `import java.util.*;` statement in your Java program.

Secret

Vectors, unlike arrays, are untyped collections. Elements of a vector are stored and retrieved as Objects and need to be cast to their original type. You should not use Vectors unless you truly have a varying array. Arrays are more efficient than Vectors if the array size is known or determinable.

Creating a vector

For instance, suppose you are reading names from a file into an array. The name file uses UTF strings, like the HighScore table used in the `BallShot` program, so there's no way to tell how many records there are from the length of the file. You could assume there would never be more than 1,000 names and scores:

```
int MAX_RECORDS = 1000;
String names [ ] = new String [MAX_RECORDS];
int scores [ ] = new int [MAX_RECORDS];
try {
    RandomAccessFile raf = new RandomAccessFile("HiScore.dat", "rw");
    for(loop = 0; loop < MAX_RECORDS; loop++) {
        names[loop] = raf.readUTF();
        scores[loop] = raf.readLong();
    }
}
catch (EOFException e1) {}
catch (IOException e2) ib_IOException = true;
```

The preceding code has two problems:

- If there are less than 1,000 records, space is wasted in the `names` and `scores` arrays.

- If there are more than 1,000 records, the `names` and `scores` arrays can't hold the entire file.

Because Vectors can dynamically reallocate space, both problems are solved:

```
ivc_names = new Vector(10, 20);
ivc_scores = new Vector(10, 20);
try {
  RandomAccessFile raf = new RandomAccessFile("HiScore.dat", "rw");
  for(int loop = 0; ; loop++) {
    ivc_names.addElement(raf.readUTF());
    Long score = new Long(raf.readLong());
    ivc_scores.addElement(score);
  }
}
catch (EOFException e1) {
  ivc_names.trimToSize();
  ivc_scores.trimToSize();
}
catch (IOException e2) ib_IOException = true;
```

Vectors can be constructed with an initial size and an increment amount. Consider the following statement:

```
ivc_names = new Vector(10, 20);
```

A Vector is created with 10 elements and is incremented by 20 elements every time the current space is used up. You can also create a Vector by using only a size element and omit the increment:

```
ivc_names = new Vector(10);
```

However, this method *doubles* the size of the Vector every time a new addition is needed. Vector size ranges from (10, 20, 40, 80, 160, 320, 640,...). As you can see, there is a large potential for wasted space. Often, you are better off to declare an increment size. Finally, you can create a Vector with no arguments:

```
ivc_names = new Vector();
```

This creates a vector of zero size, which is incremented to one with the first addElement method call, and then doubles each time the Vector needs a new element. Vector size ranges from (0, 1, 2, 4, 8, 16, 32, 64, ...). Again, the potential for wasted space is great, but this method is often used with small Vectors.

Secret

If you are using Vectors intensively in a program, select the initial size and increment value carefully. Reallocating memory for a Vector can be time-consuming for the Java Virtual Machine.

You can find the current capacity of a Vector by using the Vector.capacity method:

```
Vector myVector = new Vector();
int canHold = myVector.capacity;
```

Secret

You can also reset the minimum capacity by using the `Vector.ensureCapacity` method. The following method sets the minimum capacity of `myVector` to 20:

```
myVector.ensureCapacity(20);
```

Adding elements to a vector

The easiest way to add an element to a Vector is to use the `Vector.addElement` method:

```
ivc_scores.addElement(score);
```

You cannot use the `addElement` method to add a primary data type, such as `int` and `long`. However, you can use the primary data type wrappers, such as `String`, `Integer`, and `Long` to add compatible objects to a Vector.

In addition to the `addElement` method, you can use the `setSize` method to ensure the exact number of elements in a Vector:

```
myVector.setSize(20);
```

Secret

There's a difference between the *size* and the *capacity* of a Vector. The capacity of a Vector indicates how many elements a Vector can hold before the amount of memory allocated for the Vector needs to be increased. The size of an array is the number of elements it contains.

Methods like `ensureCapacity` increase the minimum capacity of a Vector but don't add any elements. Methods like `setSize` actually eliminate Vector elements if the new size is smaller than the current size. If the new size is larger than the current size, null elements are added to the Vector to increase the number of elements added to the Vector.

The `size` method returns the number of elements in a Vector, and the `isEmpty` method returns a true or false to indicate if any elements have been added to a Vector. The `Vector.size` method returns the size of a Vector.

Instead of using the `addElement` method to add an element at the end of a Vector, you could use the `insertElementAt` method to insert an element in the middle of a Vector. The following command inserts a `name` Object at index four in `myVector`:

```
myVector.insertElementAt(name, 4);
```

You can also change a Vector element by using the `setElementAt` method. The following example changes the element at index four of `myVector` to `name2`:

```
myVector.setElementAt(name2, 4);
```

Secret

If you try to insert or set an element at an index that does not exist, you receive an `ArrayIndexOutOfBoundsException` error.

You can add all the elements of an array into a Vector by using the `copyInto` method. The following line of code copies all the elements of the `scoreArray` into the `ivc_score` Vector:

```
ivc_score.copyInto(scoreArray);
```

Searching through a vector

You can search for an object inside a Vector in several ways. The `contains` method tests if an object is contained within a Vector. The following line of code returns a true or false indicating if the `name` String is contained within `myVector`:

```
myVector.contains(name);
```

There are also ways to search through an array and return an object contained in a Vector. The `indexOf` method returns the index of a specific Object. The following line of code returns the index of the `name` Object in `myVector`:

```
int vectorPosition = myVector.indexOf(name);
```

Because you can add an object to a vector more than one time, you can also use an offset index to begin your search. The following line of code searches for the *next* occurrence of the name Object after index four:

```
int vectorPosition = myVector.indexOf(name, 4);
```

A minus one is always returned if the index is larger than the Vector or the object is not found.

Instead of beginning your search at the beginning of a Vector, you can also begin it at the end of a Vector by using the `lastIndexOf` method the same way you use the `indexOf` method. The following line of code searches for the *last* occurrence of the name Object:

```
int vectorPosition = myVector.lastIndexOf(name);
```

Similar to the `indexOf` method, you can specify an index to begin the search with the `lastIndexOf` method:

```
int vectorPosition = myVector.lastIndexOf(name, 4);
```

Retrieving elements from a vector

After you've searched a vector, you can return an Object from a Vector. The `elements` method returns an Enumeration containing all the Objects of a Vector:

```
Enumeration vectorElements = myVector.elements();
```

The `elementAt` method retrieves an Object at a specific index. The following line of code retrieves the element of `myVector` found at index four:

```
String name = (String) myVector.elementAt(4);
```

You can also return the first object of a Vector by using the `firstElement` method:

```
String name = (String) myVector.firstElement();
```

or the last element of a Vector by using the `lastElement` method:

```
String name = (String) myVector.lastElement();
```

Removing elements from a vector

Another advantage of Vectors over arrays is that you can remove elements from a Vector. (An array requires you to move elements around to "fill the hole" left when an Object is no longer desired in the array.) The `removeAllElements` method removes all elements from a Vector, enabling you to reuse it. The following line removes all elements from `myVector`:

```
myVector.removeAllElements();
```

To remove a specific object from a Vector, you can use the `removeElement` method. The following line removes the name Object from myVector:

```
myVector.removeElement(name);
```

The `removeElement` method returns a true if the Object was found and removed, and a false otherwise.

Secret

The `removeElement` method only removes the *first occurrence* of an Object from a Vector. If an Object is added more than once, multiple calls to the `removeElement` method are needed.

You can remove a method at a specific index with the `removeElementAt` method. The following line of code removes element number four from a Vector:

```
myVector.removeElementAt(4);
```

Delving into Stacks

Enumerations place objects in a *queue*. That is, the first object placed in the Enumeration is the first object retrieved from an Enumeration. This retrieval method is called the *FIFO*, or First In, First Out method. Sometimes, however, you want to retrieve items using a *LIFO*, or Last In, First Out method. This is done using a Stack object.

Your operating systems use stacks to manage returns to methods. The last calling method contains the first return address when the called method ends. Other areas that work well with stacks are date-sensitive material, like a mail inbox. You probably want to display in reverse-date order, so that the last mail added to your inbox is the first displayed.

The differences between a queue and a stack are shown in Figure 19-4.

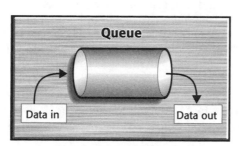

First In, First Out (FIFO)

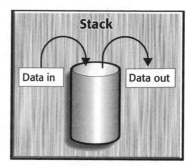

Last In, First Out (LIFO)

Figure 19-4: The difference between a queue and a stack is the order in which the data is retrieved.

The difference between a queue and a stack is that a queue places objects on the bottom and takes objects off the top, while a stack places objects on the top and takes objects off the top. The Stack class contains the methods shown in Table 19-1.

Table 19-1   Stack Class Methods

Method	*Description*
`boolean empty()`	Returns a true or false indicating if the Stack Object is empty or has elements.
`Object peek()`	Returns the object at the top of the Stack Object without actually removing the Object off the Stack Object.
`Object pop()`	Returns the object at the top of the Stack Object and removes the Object off the Stack Object.
`Object push(Object item)`	Places a new Object on top of the Stack object.
`int search(Object o)`	Returns the position from the top of the Stack of an Object. A minus one (-1) is returned if the Object is not on the Stack.

Secret

Stack is inherited from Vector, so you can also use all the Vector methods with your Stack.

Using Linked Lists and Binary Trees

Now it's time to dispel a popular misconception. You often read in trade magazines and books that Java doesn't use pointers. This is only partially true. The actual truth is that Java *hides* the use of pointers. In truth, every time you set an Object equal to another Object, you assign the pointer of that Object so that both Object variables point to the same Object in memory. For example, you might think that the following line of code:

```
Object1 = Object2;
```

actually copies `Object2` into `Object1`. In fact, it assigns an `Object1` pointer and an `Object2` pointer to the *same* Object, as shown graphically in Figure 19-5.

Your Computer Memory

Object1 pointer	
	Object in memory
Object2 pointer	

Line of Code: *Object1 = Object2;*

Figure 19-5: The equals operator (=) actually causes Object pointers to be equal rather than copying contents in memory.

Java protects you from this complexity. However, you may *want* to use pointers to form linked lists. A linked list is a class that contains a pointer to the next class, as shown in Figure 19-6.

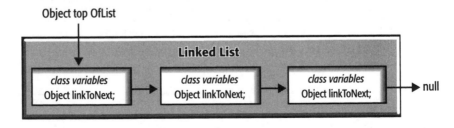

Object top OfList

Linked List

| *class variables*
Object linkToNext; | → | *class variables*
Object linkToNext; | → | *class variables*
Object linkToNext; | → null |

Figure 19-6: A linked list is easy to build in Java.

Listing 19-2 builds a linked list and displays it.

Listing 19-2 LinkedList.java

```java
import java.awt.*;
import java.awt.event.*;
//Declare a new LinkedList class with a WindowListener and an
ActionListener
public class LinkedList extends Frame implements WindowListener,
ActionListener {
  // Constant meaning to insert before selected link
  private static int BEFORE_SELECTED = 1;
  // Constant meaning to insert after selected link
  private static int SELECTED_LINK = 2;
  // Top link pointer
  private Link ili_top =  null;
  // Buttons for functionality
  private Button icb_insertBefore = new Button(
"Insert Link Before");
  private Button icb_insertAfter = new Button(
"Insert Link After");
  private Button icb_remove = new Button("Remove Link");
  private Button icb_exit = new Button("Exit");
  public static void main(String args[]) {
    LinkedList sp = new LinkedList(); // Construct Linked List
  }
  public LinkedList() {
    // Add a window listener
    addWindowListener(this);
    setLayout(new BorderLayout());
    Panel southPanel = new Panel();
    // add buttons to the south panel
    southPanel.add(icb_insertBefore);
    southPanel.add(icb_insertAfter);
    southPanel.add(icb_remove);
    southPanel.add(icb_exit);
    // Add ActionListeners for buttons
    icb_insertBefore.addActionListener(this);
    icb_insertAfter.addActionListener(this);
    icb_remove.addActionListener(this);
    icb_exit.addActionListener(this);
  // Add the panel to the frame, resize, set title, and show
    add("South", southPanel);
    setSize(500,350);
    setTitle("LinkedList.java");
    show();
  }
  public void removeLink() {
  // Code for removing a link from the linked list
    if (ili_top != null) {
      Link l;
      if (ili_top.isSelected()) {
        l = ili_top;
        ili_top = l.getNextLink();
        if (ili_top != null) {
```

```
                    ili_top.selectLink();
                }
            }
            else {
                Link before = traverseList(BEFORE_SELECTED);
                Link selected = traverseList(SELECTED_LINK);
                l =  selected;
                before.linkNext(selected.getNextLink());
                before.selectLink();
            }
            l.setVisible(false);
            l = null; //Deallocate
            rearrange();
        }
    }
    // Code for inserting a link in the linked list
    public void insertLink(boolean before) {
        Link newLink;
      if (ili_top == null) {
        newLink= new Link();
        ili_top = newLink;
      }
      else if (ili_top.isSelected() && before) {
        newLink= new Link();
        newLink.linkNext(ili_top);
        ili_top = newLink;
      }
      else {
      Link lnk;
        if (before) {   // Insert before selected
          lnk = traverseList(BEFORE_SELECTED);
      }
        else {
          lnk = traverseList(SELECTED_LINK);
      }
        newLink= new Link();
        newLink.linkNext(lnk.getNextLink());
      lnk.linkNext(newLink);
      }
      add("Center",newLink);
      rearrange();
    }
    public Link traverseList(int traverseUntil) {
        return traverseList(ili_top, traverseUntil);
    }
    // Recursive routine to go through the linked list
    public Link traverseList(Link link, int traverseUntil) {
        if (link == null) {
          return null;
        }
        else if (traverseUntil == SELECTED_LINK && link.isSelected()) {
          return link;
        }
        else if (traverseUntil == BEFORE_SELECTED &&
    link.getNextLink().isSelected()) {
          return link;
```

```
    }
    // recurse until the selected link is hit.
    return traverseList(link.getNextLink(), traverseUntil);
  }
    public void rearrange() {  // Redisplay the link
    Link currentLink = ili_top;
    for (int loop=0; currentLink != null; loop++) {
      currentLink.repaint();
      currentLink.setLocation(loop*20+1,40);
      currentLink = currentLink.getNextLink();
    }
  }
}
// actionPerformed is required by the ActionListener interface
  public void actionPerformed(ActionEvent e) {
    // Get the text of the button
    String buttonText = e.getActionCommand();
    //First test for buttons
    if (buttonText.equals("Insert Link Before")) {
      insertLink(true);
    }
    else if (buttonText.equals("Insert Link After")) {
      insertLink(false);
    }
    else if (buttonText.equals("Remove Link")) {
      removeLink();
    }
    else if (buttonText.equals("Exit")) {
      dispose();
      System.exit(0);
    }
  }
// The following are required by the WindowListener interface
  public void windowClosing(WindowEvent e) {
    dispose();
    System.exit(0);
  }
  public void windowActivated(WindowEvent e) { }
  public void windowDeactivated(WindowEvent e) { }
  public void windowDeiconified(WindowEvent e) { }
  public void windowClosed(WindowEvent e) { }
  public void windowIconified(WindowEvent e) { }
  public void windowOpened(WindowEvent e) { }
}

// Create a new component from the Canvas class that implmenets a
mouse listener
class Link extends Canvas implements MouseListener {
    // Count the number of links
  private static int ii_totalLinks=1;
        // Return the selected link
  public static int ii_selectedLink;
          // This instance's link number
  private int ii_linkNumber;
            // A pointer to the next link
  private Link ili_nextLink;
        public Link() {
```

```java
      addMouseListener(this);    // Add a mouse listener
 // Increment the number of links
    ii_linkNumber = ii_totalLinks++;
    // Assign the current link number
    ii_selectedLink = ii_linkNumber;
      setSize(20,20);        // Resize the Canvas
    setVisible(true);        // Show the Canvas
  }
  public void paint(Graphics g) {
    Rectangle r = getBounds();
    g.setColor(Color.black);
    if (ii_linkNumber == ii_selectedLink) {
      g.fillRect(0, 0, r.width-1, r.height-1);
    }
    else {
      g.drawRect(0, 0, r.width-1, r.height-1);
    }
    if (ii_linkNumber == ii_selectedLink) {
      g.setColor(Color.white);
    }
    g.drawString(String.valueOf(ii_linkNumber), 5, 15);
  }
  public Link getNextLink() {
    return ili_nextLink;
  }
  public void selectLink() {
    ii_selectedLink = ii_linkNumber;
    LinkedList ll = (LinkedList) getParent();
    ll.rearrange();
  }
  public boolean isSelected () {
    if (ii_linkNumber == ii_selectedLink) {
      return true;
    }
    return false;
  }
  public void linkNext(Link l) {
    ili_nextLink = l;
  }
  // The following are required by the MouseListener interface
  // The component was clicked
  public void mouseClicked(MouseEvent e) {
      selectLink();
  }
  //A mouse button was pressed
  public void mousePressed(MouseEvent e) { }
    // A mouse button was released
  public void mouseReleased(MouseEvent e) { }
    // The pointer left the Java area
  public void mouseEntered(MouseEvent e) { }
    // The pointer entered the Java area
  public void mouseExited(MouseEvent e) { }
    }

}
```

The output for Listing 19-2 is shown in Figure 19-7. The program enables you to select links and add links before or after the selected link, or to remove the selected link.

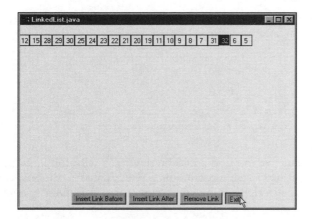

Figure 19-7: The LinkedList.java program builds a chain from a linked list.

Secret

Notice in Listing 19-2 that the `Link` class contains a `mouseDown` event. This is because the `Link` class contains the logic for selection if you click a specific `Link`. You can also select a `Link` programmatically by using the `selectLink` method in the `Link` class.

Traversing a linked list

To traverse a linked list, you need to use either a loop or recursion. The `rearrange` method uses a `for` loop to test if we hit a null in the linked list:

```
public void rearrange() {  // Redisplay the link
  Link currentLink = ili_top;
  for (int loop=0; currentLink != null; loop++) {
    currentLink.repaint();
    currentLink.setLocation(loop*20+1,40);
    currentLink = currentLink.getNextLink();
  }
}
```

Recursion is a little less efficient and conceptually harder to understand than loops. However, in many circumstances, recursion can turn a complicated loop into an easy iteration. The `traverseList` method checks if the `Link` passed to it meets the criteria of selection. If it does, the link is returned. If not, the `traverseList` method *calls itself* (making it recursive) with the next `Link` on the list:

```
// Recursive routine to go through the linked list
public Link traverseList(Link link, int traverseUntil) {
  if (link == null) {
    return null;
  }
  else if (traverseUntil == SELECTED_LINK && link.isSelected()) {
    return link;
  }
  else if (traverseUntil == BEFORE_SELECTED &&
link.getNextLink().isSelected()) {
    return link;
  }
  // recurse until the selected link is hit.
  return traverseList(link.getNextLink(), traverseUntil);
}
```

Secret

Although any recursive method could be rewritten with loops, with complicated linked lists, often recursion is used instead of loops. Once recursion is understood, it often makes the coding and maintenance of a method much easier.

Adding a node to a linked list

The insertLink method is used to add a new Link to the linked list:

```
public void insertLink(boolean before) {  // Code for inserting a
link in the linked list
  Link newLink;
  if (ili_top == null) {
    newLink= new Link();
    ili_top = newLink;
  }
  else if (ili_top.isSelected() && before) {
    newLink= new Link();
    newLink.linkNext(ili_top);
    ili_top = newLink;
  }
  else {
    Link lnk;
    if (before) {  // Insert before selected
      lnk = traverseList(BEFORE_SELECTED);
    }
    else {
      lnk = traverseList(SELECTED_LINK);
    }
    newLink= new Link();
    newLink.linkNext(lnk.getNextLink());
    lnk.linkNext(newLink);
  }
  add("Center",newLink);
  rearrange();
}
```

There are three situations that are handled in the `insertLink` method:

■ If the linked list is currently empty, a new node is added.

■ If you try to add a node to the beginning of a linked list, then the `ili_top` `Link` must be reassigned. This is done in two steps:

1. Point the top of the `nextLink` pointer to the top of the list.

2. Point the `ili_top` pointer to the new node.

This gives you a new first node, and keeps the rest of the list intact because the new first node is pointing to the old first node. These two steps are shown graphically in Figure 19-8.

Old Link List

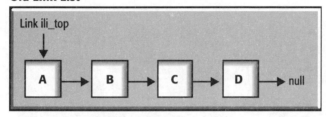

New Link List

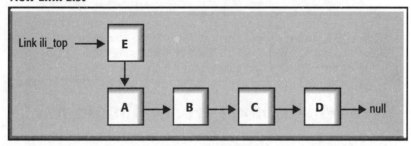

Figure 19-8: Adding a node to the beginning of a linked list requires that you point the new node (E) to the beginning of the list and then point the beginning of the list to the new node.

■ If a node is needed in the middle or end of the list, the following steps are needed:

1. Traverse the list until you get the node that exists *before* the position of the new node.

2. Point the new node's next pointer to the traversed node's next pointer.

3. Point the traversed node's next pointer to the new node.

This inserts a new node at the desired location in the linked list. These three steps are shown graphically in Figure 19-9.

Old Link List

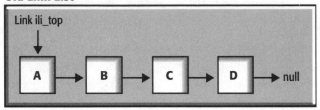

New Link List

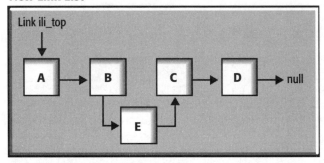

Figure 19-9: Adding a node to the middle of a linked list requires that you point the new node (E) to the node after the insertion and then point the node before the insertion to the new node.

Removing a node from a linked list

Listing 19-2 also enables you to remove a node from the linked list. Three situations must be considered when you remove a node from a linked list. The removeLink method removes a Link from a linked list and ensures all the pointers are redirected so that the linked list stays connected.

```
public void removeLink() {
  if (ili_top != null) {
    Link l;
    if (ili_top.isSelected()) {
      l = ili_top;
      ili_top = l.getNextLink();
      if (ili_top != null) {
        ili_top.selectLink();
      }
    }
```

```
    else {
      Link before = traverseList(BEFORE_SELECTED);
      Link selected = traverseList(SELECTED_LINK);
      l = selected;
      before.linkNext(selected.getNextLink());
      before.selectLink();
    }
    l.hide();
    l = null; //Deallocate
    rearrange();
  }
}
```

Examining binary trees

All this work with the linked list is to show you how a linked list can be formed in Java. There are variants of linked lists (for example, double linked lists that are linked both forward and backward) that can be used to enhance the functionality of a linked list. However, all of the linked list functionality and most of its variants are duplicated in the Vector class, and Vectors are more efficient than linked lists. Consequently, the use for *most* linked lists inside Java is slight.

A *binary tree* is a complex variant of a linked list. Binary trees can't be easily duplicated within a Vector. Binary trees are data structures that hold new objects. These structures are always just the size they need to be, and insertions can be done to the binary tree without reorganizing any other node on the tree.

Instead of one link to another node, a binary tree has two links — a left pointer and a right pointer. The left pointer points to a sub-tree containing values less than or equal to the parent tree, while the right node points to nodes that contain key values that are greater than the parent tree. A short binary tree is shown graphically in Figure 19-10.

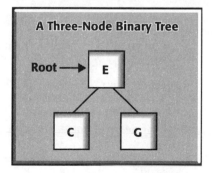

Figure 19-10: Three-node binary tree.

In Figure 19-10, the root node is the "E" node. It is the first node added to the binary tree. The "C" node is less than or equal to the "E" node, and so uses the "E"'s left pointer when it is inserted. The "G" node is greater than the "E" node, and so uses the "E"'s right pointer when it is inserted.

When more nodes are inserted on the tree, they follow the same path, as shown in Figure 19-11.

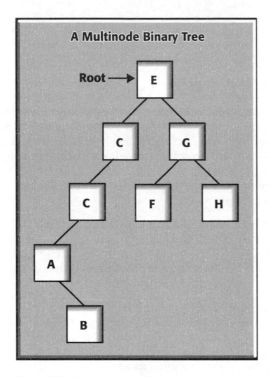

Figure 19-11: A larger multinode binary tree.

In Figure 19-11, five nodes are added to the existing binary tree started in Figure 19-10. The following steps are performed when adding the nodes in Figure 19-11:

1. Add an "H" node. Because "H" is greater than "E", it goes on "E"'s right pointer. However, the "G" node is already on "E"'s right pointer, so you must then compare "H" to "G". Because "H" is greater than "G" and "G"'s right pointer is unoccupied, the "H" node goes on "G"'s right pointer.

2. Add an "F" node. Because "F" is greater than "E", it must go on "E"'s right pointer. Again, the "G" node is already on "E"'s right pointer, so you must then compare "F" to "G". Because "F" is less than or equal to "G" and "G"'s left pointer is unoccupied, the "F" node goes on "G"'s left pointer.

3. Insert another "C" node. It is less than or equal to "E", and so goes on the left side of "E". Because the left pointer of "E" is already used, the next node down is checked. This is the other "C" node. Because "C" is less than or equal to "C", the second "C" node goes on the left pointer of the first "C" node. Notice that you can have two keys of the same value in a binary tree.

4. Insert an "A" node. It is less than or equal to "E", and so goes on the left side of "E". Because the left pointer of "E" is already used by the first "C", the "C" node must be checked. "A" is less than or equal to "C", but the first "C" node uses the left pointer for the second "C" node. Then "A" is compared to the second "C" node. Because "A" is less than or equal to "C" and there is no node occupying the second "C" node's left pointer, the "A" node goes on the left pointer of the second "C" node.

5. Insert a "B" node. It is less than or equal to "E", and so goes on the left side of "E". Because the left pointer of "E" is already used by the first "C", the "C" node must be checked. "B" is less than or equal to "C", but the first "C" node uses the left pointer for the second "C" node. Then "B" is compared to the second "C" node. "B" is less than "C", but the "A" node is already occupying the left pointer of the second "C" node. The "B" node is then compared to the "A" node. Because "B" is greater than "A" and there is no node occupying the "A" node's right pointer, the "B" node goes on the right pointer of the "A" node.

Although somewhat complex, binary trees are extremely useful in two ways:

1. Binary trees only occupy memory as needed. Because there is no need to rearrange nodes when you insert a new one, there is no need to allocate additional memory.

2. Binary trees are formed in a sort order and are easy to search. In a perfectly formed binary tree (where all the right and left pointers are filled except on the bottom level), a search through a million records takes, at most, only 20 compares.

Binary trees, or variations of them, are normally used in database indexing. Binary trees are much more efficient than many other means of sorting and storage. Listing 19-3 shows a binary tree program where an object (Node) is used to create and display a binary tree, as shown in Figure 19-12.

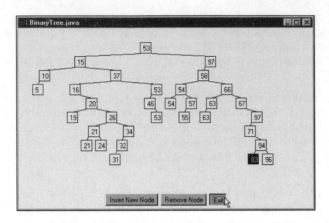

Figure 19-12: Here is the output of a large binary tree created by BinaryTree.java shown in Listing 19-3.

Listing 19-3: BinaryTree.java

```java
import java.awt.*;
import java.awt.event.*;
//Declare a new BinaryTree class with a WindowListener and an
ActionListener
public class BinaryTree extends Frame implements WindowListener,
ActionListener {
// Controls the node placement
  private float if_maxStarting = 0;
  private Panel ipa_centerPanel;      // Panel with the tree
  private Node ino_root =  null;      // Tree root pointer
  // Buttons used for functionality
  private Button icb_insert = new Button("Insert New Node");
  private Button icb_remove = new Button("Remove Node");
  private Button icb_exit = new Button("Exit");
  public static void main(String args[]) {
// Construct a new BinaryTree
    BinaryTree sp = new BinaryTree();
  }
  public BinaryTree() {              // BinaryTree constructor
    addWindowListener(this);       // Add a window listener
    setLayout(new BorderLayout());  // Set layout
    Panel southPanel = new Panel();  // Add Panels
    ipa_centerPanel = new Panel();
// Add buttons to the south panel
    southPanel.add(icb_insert);
    southPanel.add(icb_remove);
    southPanel.add(icb_exit);
  // Add Action Listeners to all the buttons
    icb_insert.addActionListener(this);
      icb_remove.addActionListener(this);
    icb_exit.addActionListener(this);
    // Add panels, set background, resize, set title, and show.
    add("South", southPanel);
    add("Center", ipa_centerPanel);
```

```java
      setBackground(Color.white);
      setSize(500,350);
      setTitle("BinaryTree.java");
      show();
  }
  public void removeNode() {   // Remove a node from the tree
     if (ino_root != null) {
        Node selected = null;
        if (ino_root.isSelected()) {
          selected = ino_root;
          ino_root = null;
        }
        else {
          Node parent = ino_root;
          int nodeNumber = Node.getSelectedNode().getNodeNumber();
          while (parent != null) {
             if (nodeNumber > parent.getNodeNumber()) {
                if (parent.getRightNode().isSelected()) {
                  selected = parent.getRightNode();
                  parent.setRightNode(null);
                  break;
                }
                else {
                  parent = parent.getRightNode();
                }
             }
             else {
                if (parent.getLeftNode().isSelected()) {
                  selected = parent.getLeftNode();
                  parent.setLeftNode(null);
                  break;
                }
                else {
                  parent = parent.getLeftNode();
                }
             }
          }
        }
        insertNode(selected.getLeftNode());
        insertNode(selected.getRightNode());
        selected.setVisible(false);
        selected = null; //Deallocate
        rearrange();
     }
  }
  // Insert a node into the tree
  public void insertNode(Node newNode) {
       if (newNode == null) {
       return;
     }
     if (ino_root == null) {
       ino_root = newNode;
     }
     else {
       Node n = ino_root;
       while (n != null) {
```

```
        if (newNode.getNodeNumber() > n.getNodeNumber()) {
          if (n.getRightNode() == null) {
            n.setRightNode(newNode);
            break;
          }
          else {
            n = n.getRightNode();
          }
        }
        else {
          if (n.getLeftNode() == null) {
            n.setLeftNode(newNode);
            break;
          }
          else {
            n = n.getLeftNode();
          }
        }
      }
    }
    newNode.selectNode();
    rearrange();
  }
    // Rearrange the nodes so they fit into a tree
    public void rearrange() {
        if_maxStarting = 0;
    Graphics g = ipa_centerPanel.getGraphics();
    Rectangle r = ipa_centerPanel.getBounds();
    g.clearRect(0, 0, r.width-1, r.height-1);
    rearrange(ino_root, 1, 1);
  }
  // Rearrange the nodes so they fit into a tree
    public float rearrange(Node currentNode, int level, float over)
{
    float starting = Math.max(over, if_maxStarting+1);
    float starting1 = starting;
    float starting2 = starting;
    if (currentNode.getLeftNode() != null) {
      starting1 = rearrange(currentNode.getLeftNode(), level+1,
starting1);
      starting2 = starting1 + 1;
    }
    if (currentNode.getRightNode() != null) {
      starting2 = starting1 + 1;
      starting2 = rearrange(currentNode.getRightNode(), level+1,
starting2);
    }
    starting = (float)((starting1 + starting2)/2);
    currentNode.repaint();
    int x = (int)(starting * 25);
    int y = (level * 25) + 1;
    currentNode.setLocation(x, y);
    if_maxStarting = Math.max(starting, if_maxStarting);
//Now draw a line between the parent and children nodes
    Graphics g = ipa_centerPanel.getGraphics();
    Rectangle r1 = currentNode.getBounds();
```

```java
      if (currentNode.getLeftNode() != null) {
        Rectangle r2 = currentNode.getLeftNode().getBounds();
        int x1 = r1.x;
        int y1 = r1.y + r1.height;
        int x2 = r2.x + (int)(r2.width / 2);
        int y2 = r2.y;
        g.drawLine(x1, y1, x2, y2);
      }
      if (currentNode.getRightNode() != null) {
        Rectangle r2 = currentNode.getRightNode().getBounds();
        int x1 = r1.x + r1.width;
        int y1 = r1.y + r1.height;
        int x2 = r2.x + (int)(r2.width / 2);
        int y2 = r2.y;
        g.drawLine(x1, y1, x2, y2);
      }
      return starting;
    }
// actionPerformed is required by the ActionListener interface
  public void actionPerformed(ActionEvent e) {
    // Get the text of the button
    String buttonText = e.getActionCommand();
    //First test for buttons
    if (buttonText.equals("Insert New Node")) {
      Node newNode = new Node();
      ipa_centerPanel.add(newNode);
      insertNode(newNode);
    }
    else if (buttonText.equals("Remove Node")) {
      removeNode();
    }
    else if (buttonText.equals("Exit")) {
      dispose();
      System.exit(0);
    }
  }
// The following are required by the WindowListener interface
  public void windowClosing(WindowEvent e) {
    dispose();
    System.exit(0);
  }
  public void windowActivated(WindowEvent e) { }
  public void windowDeactivated(WindowEvent e) { }
  public void windowDeiconified(WindowEvent e) { }
  public void windowClosed(WindowEvent e) { }
  public void windowIconified(WindowEvent e) { }
  public void windowOpened(WindowEvent e) { }
}
// Create a new component from the Canvas class that
// implmenets a mouse listener
class Node extends Canvas implements MouseListener {
  // Return the selected node
  private static Node ino_selectedNode;
    private int ii_nodeNumber;  // This instance's node number
  private Node ino_leftNode;  // A pointer to the left node
  private Node ino_rightNode;  // A pointer to the right node
```

```java
public Node() {
  addMouseListener(this);   // Add a mouse listener
// Generate a node number
  ii_nodeNumber = (int) (Math.random() * 100);
    setSize(20,20);           // Resize the Canvas
  setVisible(true);           // Show the Canvas
}
public static Node getSelectedNode() {
  return ino_selectedNode;
}
public void paint(Graphics g) {
  Rectangle r = getBounds();
  g.setColor(Color.black);
  if (isSelected()) {
    g.fillRect(0, 0, r.width-1, r.height-1);
  }
  else {
    g.drawRect(0, 0, r.width-1, r.height-1);
  }
  if (isSelected()) {
    g.setColor(Color.white);
  }
  g.drawString(String.valueOf(ii_nodeNumber), 5, 15);
}
public int getNodeNumber() {
  return ii_nodeNumber;
}
public Node getRightNode() {
  return ino_rightNode;
}
public Node getLeftNode() {
  return ino_leftNode;
}
public void selectNode() {
  ino_selectedNode = this;
  BinaryTree bt = (BinaryTree) getParent().getParent();
  bt.rearrange();
}
public boolean isSelected () {
  if (ino_selectedNode == this) {
    return true;
  }
  return false;
}
public void setRightNode(Node n) {
  ino_rightNode = n;
}
public void setLeftNode(Node n) {
  ino_leftNode = n;
}
// The following are required by the MouseListener interface
// The component was clicked
public void mouseClicked(MouseEvent e) {
    selectNode();
}
//A mouse button was pressed
```

```
public void mousePressed(MouseEvent e) { }
   // A mouse button was released
public void mouseReleased(MouseEvent e) { }
   // The pointer left the Java area
public void mouseEntered(MouseEvent e) { }
   // The pointer entered the Java area
public void mouseExited(MouseEvent e) { }
   }
```

Traversing a binary tree

Traversing an entire binary tree from start to finish is almost always a recursive task. The pseudocode to traverse a binary tree in key order is as follows:

```
Call TreeSearchMethod using the root node
...
TreeSearchMethod(node) {
   Call TreeSearchMethod using the node's left pointer
   It's now your turn to perform your operations
   Call TreeSearchMethod using the node's right pointer
}
```

Even though the code is complex, it's relatively short. To traverse a binary tree in key order, you recursively call the search method for all the nodes less than the current node. Then you do operations on your node, and recursively call the search method for all nodes greater than your node.

In Listing 19-3, you did not traverse the tree in key order, but rather in reverse level order so that the tree could be effectively painted. The pseudocode to traverse a binary tree in level order is as follows:

```
Call TreeSearchMethod using the root node
...
TreeSearchMethod(node) {
   Call TreeSearchMethod using the node's left pointer
   Call TreeSearchMethod using the node's right pointer
   It's now your turn to perform your operations
}
```

As you can see, traversing any binary tree in any order calls for recursively calling all the nodes on the left pointer and recursively calling the nodes on the right pointer, as shown by the rearrange method. The rearrange method paints the left nodes, then the right nodes, and then the parent node. It also draws a line between all parents and their children nodes. Some processing is done to make sure the positions of the nodes don't overlap with those of other nodes:

```
// Rearrange the nodes so they fit into a tree
   public float rearrange(Node currentNode, int level, float over)
{
   float starting = Math.max(over, if_maxStarting+1);
   float starting1 = starting;
   float starting2 = starting;
   if (currentNode.getLeftNode() != null) {
```

```
        starting1 = rearrange(currentNode.getLeftNode(), level+1,
starting1);
        starting2 = starting1 + 1;
    }
    if (currentNode.getRightNode() != null) {
        starting2 = starting1 + 1;
        starting2 = rearrange(currentNode.getRightNode(), level+1,
starting2);
    }
    starting = (float)((starting1 + starting2)/2);
    currentNode.repaint();
    int x = (int)(starting * 25);
    int y = (level * 25) + 1;
    currentNode.setLocation(x, y);
    if_maxStarting = Math.max(starting, if_maxStarting);
//Now draw a line between the parent and children nodes
    Graphics g = ipa_centerPanel.getGraphics();
    Rectangle r1 = currentNode.getBounds();
    if (currentNode.getLeftNode() != null) {
      Rectangle r2 = currentNode.getLeftNode().getBounds();
      int x1 = r1.x;
      int y1 = r1.y + r1.height;
      int x2 = r2.x + (int)(r2.width / 2);
      int y2 = r2.y;
      g.drawLine(x1, y1, x2, y2);
    }
    if (currentNode.getRightNode() != null) {
      Rectangle r2 = currentNode.getRightNode().getBounds();
      int x1 = r1.x + r1.width;
      int y1 = r1.y + r1.height;
      int x2 = r2.x + (int)(r2.width / 2);
      int y2 = r2.y;
      g.drawLine(x1, y1, x2, y2);
    }
    return starting;
}
```

Inserting nodes into a binary tree

When a user clicks the Insert Node button, a new node is created and the
insertNode method is called. The insertNode method uses a loop to search
through the tree for the proper insertion point. Either the setLeftNode or the
setRightNode method is used to set the proper link to the new node:

```
// Code from the action method
else if (event.target == icb_insert) {
  Node newNode = new Node();
  ipa_centerPanel.add(newNode);
  insertNode(newNode);
}
//...
public void insertNode(Node newNode) {   // Insert a node into the
tree
  if (newNode == null) {
    return;
  }
```

```
      if (ino_root == null) {
        ino_root = newNode;
      }
  else {
        Node n = ino_root;
        while (n != null) {
          if (newNode.getNodeNumber() > n.getNodeNumber()) {
            if (n.getRightNode() == null) {
              n.setRightNode(newNode);
              break;
            }
            else {
              n = n.getRightNode();
            }
          }
          else {
            if (n.getLeftNode() == null) {
              n.setLeftNode(newNode);
              break;
            }
            else {
              n = n.getLeftNode();
            }
          }
        }
      }
    newNode.selectNode();
    rearrange();
}
```

Secret

I prefer recursion when using binary trees, but I wanted to show you both looping and recursive techniques for manipulating a binary tree. Although a loop is more efficient, recursion is easier to follow once you get used to it.

Removing nodes from a binary tree

Removing a node from a binary tree involves four steps:

1. Search through the tree for the parent of the selected node you want to delete.

2. Set to null the parent's left or right pointer that points to the selected node.

3. Reinsert the left and right pointers of the selected node.

4. Set the selected node to null and remove it.

This is all done in the removeNode method shown in Listing 19-3:

```
public void removeNode() {          // Remove a node from the tree
  if (ino_root != null) {
    Node selected = null;
    if (ino_root.isSelected()) {
      selected = ino_root;
      ino_root = null;
    }
```

```
    else {
      Node parent = ino_root;
      int nodeNumber = Node.getSelectedNode().getNodeNumber();
      while (parent != null) {
        if (nodeNumber > parent.getNodeNumber()) {
          if (parent.getRightNode().isSelected()) {
            selected = parent.getRightNode();
            parent.setRightNode(null);
            break;
          }
          else {
            parent = parent.getRightNode();
          }
        }
        else {
          if (parent.getLeftNode().isSelected()) {
            selected = parent.getLeftNode();
            parent.setLeftNode(null);
            break;
          }
          else {
            parent = parent.getLeftNode();
          }
        }
      }
    }
    insertNode(selected.getLeftNode());
    insertNode(selected.getRightNode());
    selected.setVisible(false);
    selected = null; //Deallocate
    rearrange();
  }
}
```

Secret

Binary trees are often used in database engines. Instead of pointers to memory, long integer pointers to a file offset are normally used.

Summary

This chapter covers advanced programming topics dealing with Java structures. To recap:

- Single- and multi-dimensional arrays are the most efficient memory data structure you can use. They have their limitations, because they can't be resized and you must know the size of an array when you first allocate it.

- The Enumeration interface is often returned and enables you to easily scroll through a read-only list of Objects.

- If an array doesn't work for you, a Vector can be used to dynamically shrink and grow as needed. Vectors are a somewhat efficient method for storing variable-length arrays.

- The Stack class is a special kind of Vector that enables you to easily push and pop a stack.

- Linked lists are possible in Java, but most of the functionality of a linked list can be duplicated with a Vector. However, it's a good review to see some pointer manipulation in Java.

- Binary trees are a special form of a keyed linked list that enable you to store Objects in order and to quickly search through a myriad of objects. Binary trees cannot be easily duplicated with a Vector and are often used in database search engines.

Chapter 20

Better Web Programming and Networking

Web programming and networking deal with placing information on the Web and taking information from the Web. This can involve either Web sites (URLs) or users who are logged on to your program.

Mastering URLs

A URL is a name that identifies a *home* page for a Web site, an image located on an HTML page, or even a file on an FTP server. A common use of the `java.net.URL` class is to define a URL from a String:

```
import java.net.*;
//. . .
URL url_site = new URL(URLString);
```

This string must be at least parseable as a URL. It must have a protocol followed by a colon and two slashes (for example, `http://`) and then a Web site name (such as `www.microsoft.com`). If not, a `MalformedURLException` is thrown.

The URL Java class can retrieve information about the URL. Table 20-1 shows URL methods that can be used to retrieve information about the URL.

Table 20-1 URL Methods

URL Method	Description
URL.getFile()	Returns the file used within the host. This is any of the nodes after the first single slash (/) in the URL name.
URL.getHost()	Returns the host name of the URL. This is the name between the double slash (//) and first single slash (/).
URL.getPort()	Returns the port used in the URL. If no port is defined, a minus one is returned.
URL.getProtocol()	Returns the type of file being accessed. Usually, http is used for a Web site.
URL.getRef()	Returns the anchor of the Web page. Usually, this is empty.
URL.toString()	Returns a string representation of the URL.
URL.toExternalForm()	Functions identically to the URL.toString() method.

To make your browser connect to a specific URL, the AppletContext.showDocument method is used. Your Applet's AppletContext can be retrieved using the Applet.getAppletContext method. The following line of code connects to a URL defined by URLString:

```
getAppletContext().showDocument(new URL(URLString));
```

Listing 20-1 shows how a URL can be accessed in Java.

Listing 20-1: URLTest.java

```
import java.applet.*;
import java.awt.*;
import java.awt.event.*;
import java.io.*;
import java.util.*;
import java.net.*;
public class URLTest extends Applet implements ActionListener {
  private URL url_site;     // URL for connection
  // Add buttons
  private Button bu_microsoft = new Button("Microsoft");
  private Button bu_sun = new Button("Sun");
  private Button bu_connect = new Button("Connect");
  // Add text fields
  private Label lbl_file;
  private Label lbl_host;
  private Label lbl_port;
  private Label lbl_protocol;
  private Label lbl_ref;
  private Label lbl_externalForm;
  private Label lbl_string;
```

```
public void init() {     // init called when applet starts
  //Define Panels
  Panel northPanel = new Panel();
  Panel centerPanel = new Panel();
  Panel fieldPanel = new Panel();
  Panel labelPanel = new Panel();
  Panel southPanel = new Panel();
  // Set Panel and Applet layouts
  setLayout(new BorderLayout());
  centerPanel.setLayout(new BorderLayout());
  labelPanel.setLayout(new GridLayout(7,1));
  fieldPanel.setLayout(new GridLayout(7,1));
  northPanel.setLayout(new FlowLayout());
  southPanel.setLayout(new FlowLayout());
  //Add buttons to the appropriate Panels
  northPanel.add(bu_microsoft);
  northPanel.add(bu_sun);
  southPanel.add(bu_connect);
  //Add labels to the labelPanel
  labelPanel.add(new Label("File Name:  ", Label.RIGHT));
  labelPanel.add(new Label("Host:  ", Label.RIGHT));
  labelPanel.add(new Label("Port:  ", Label.RIGHT));
  labelPanel.add(new Label("Protocol:  ", Label.RIGHT));
  labelPanel.add(new Label("Reference:  ", Label.RIGHT));
  labelPanel.add(new Label("External Form:  ", Label.RIGHT));
  labelPanel.add(new Label("String:  ", Label.RIGHT));
  //Add label "fields" to the fieldPanel
  fieldPanel.add(lbl_file = new Label());
  fieldPanel.add(lbl_host = new Label());
  fieldPanel.add(lbl_port = new Label());
  fieldPanel.add(lbl_protocol = new Label());
  fieldPanel.add(lbl_ref = new Label());
  fieldPanel.add(lbl_externalForm = new Label());
  fieldPanel.add(lbl_string = new Label());
//Add ActionListeners for all buttons
  bu_connect.addActionListener(this);
  bu_microsoft.addActionListener(this);
  bu_sun.addActionListener(this);
//Arrange Panels
  centerPanel.add("West", labelPanel);
  centerPanel.add("Center", fieldPanel);
  add("North", northPanel);
  add("South", southPanel);
  add("Center", centerPanel);
}
  //Gets a new URL from a string
public void showWeb(String s) {
try {
    url_site = null; //Force garbage collection
    url_site = new URL(s);  //Define a new URL
    webInfo(); //Call webInfo method
  }
  catch (MalformedURLException mue) {
```

```
        showStatus (
"A MalformedURLException has occurred");
        url_site = null;
    }
  }
  public void webInfo() { //Displays the web info
      // URL file name
     lbl_file.setText(url_site.getFile());
   lbl_host.setText(url_site.getHost());        // URL host name
// URL port
     lbl_port.setText(String.valueOf(url_site.getPort()));
// URL protocol
     lbl_protocol.setText(url_site.getProtocol());
lbl_ref.setText(url_site.getRef());            // URL reference
// URL external form
     lbl_externalForm.setText(url_site.toExternalForm());
// URL string
     lbl_string.setText(url_site.toString());
}
//The actionPerformed method is required
//by the ActionListener interface
  public void actionPerformed(ActionEvent e) {
     // Get the text of the button
     String buttonText = e.getActionCommand();
     //Test for buttons
     if (buttonText.equals("Microsoft")) {
       showWeb("http://www.microsoft.com/visualj");
     }
     else if (buttonText.equals("Sun")) {
       showWeb("http://www.sun.com/java");
     }
     else if (buttonText.equals("Connect")) {
       showStatus("Connecting to web site...Please wait.");
       getAppletContext().showDocument(url_site);  //Connect to the URL
       showStatus("");
     }
   }
  }
}
```

In Listing 20-1, you can access either the Microsoft or Sun Web site. After you click the Sun or Microsoft button, information about the URL is displayed, as seen in Figure 20-1.

After clicking the Microsoft or Sun button, clicking the Connect button connects you to the Java sight for the selected vendor, as shown in Figure 20-2.

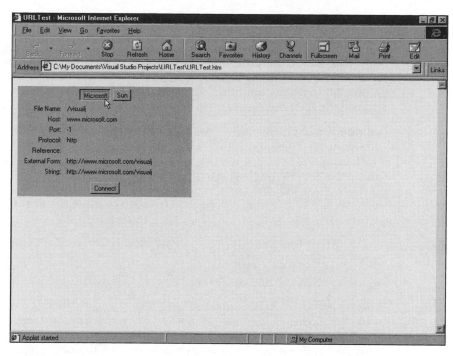

Figure 20-1: A URL can display information before a connection is made.

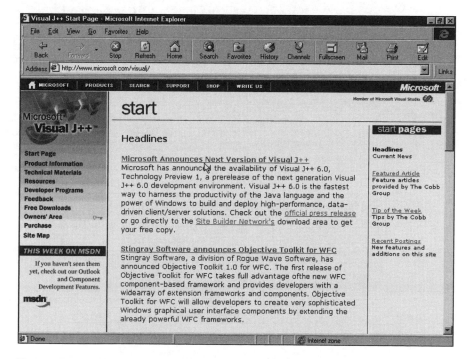

Figure 20-2: Java can be used to transfer to a specific URL.

Using the URLConnection Class

The URL class can directly access a URL, but much of the URL's information is not available to the URL class. The abstract class URLConnection is used to create a communications link between a Java application and a URL and to provide information about the URL not available with the URL class. You can also use the URLConnection class to write to, as well as read from, the URL.

Because the URLConnection class is abstract, you can't instantiate a URLConnection directly. To use a URLConnection class, you must form a URL class and then use the URL.openConnection() method to return a URLConnection for the URL. The URLConnection.openConnection() method declares a new URL and then returns the URLConnection for the URL. Then the URLConnection.connect() method is called to make the connection to the URL *without actually displaying it on the Web page*:

```
url_site = new URL(s);          // Get the URL from a String
// Define the URLConnection
uc_connection = url_site.openConnection();
iuc_uc.connect(); // Connect to URL without displaying
```

When using the connect() method, an IOException is called if the connection to the URLConnection cannot be made. URLConnections are useful if you want to know something about the URL before actually displaying it. Table 20-2 shows some methods available to the URLConnection class.

Table 20-2   Methods Available to the URLConnection Class

URLConnection Method	*Description*
getDoInput()	Returns true if input from the URL is allowed, and false if it is not.
getDoOutput()	Returns true if output to the URL is allowed, and false if it is not.
getUseCaches()	Returns true if the URLConnection is cached. Caching provides quicker access.
getContentEncoding()	Returns a string containing the value of the content encoder. Usually, this is set to null.
getContentLength()	Returns the length of the URL file.
getContentType()	Returns a string containing the value of the content type. Usually, this returns "text/html."
getDate()	Returns the value of the Date field in the URL. This is usually the creation date.
getExpiration()	Returns the expiration date of the URL. This is hopefully set far into the future.

URLConnection Method	Description
getLastModified()	Returns the LastModified date in the URL. This is the date that changes were last made to the URL.
getIfModifiedSince()	Returns the date that modifications were first made to the URL. This is often the creation date.

Listing 20-2 shows a sample of the URLConnection class.

Listing 20-2: URLConnectionTest.java

```java
import java.applet.*;
import java.awt.*;
import java.awt.event.*;
import java.io.*;
import java.util.*;
import java.net.*;
public class URLConnectionTest extends Applet implements
ActionListener {
  private URL url_site;             // URL for connection
  private URLConnection uc_connection;  // URL Connection
  // Add buttons
  private Button bu_microsoft = new Button("Microsoft");
  private Button bu_sun = new Button("Sun");
  private Button bu_connect = new Button("Connect");
  // Add Labels for fields
  private Label lbl_URLString;
  private Label lbl_DefaultAllowUserInteraction;
  private Label lbl_AllowUserInteraction;
  private Label lbl_DefaultUseCaches;
    private Label lbl_DoInput;
  private Label lbl_DoOutput;
  private Label lbl_UseCaches;
  private Label lbl_ContentEncoding;
  private Label lbl_ContentLength;
  private Label lbl_ContentType;
  private Label lbl_Date;
  private Label lbl_Expiration;
  private Label lbl_LastModified;
  private Label lbl_IfModifiedSince;
  public void init() {    // init called when applet starts
  //Define Panels
    Panel northPanel = new Panel();
    Panel centerPanel = new Panel();
    Panel southPanel = new Panel();
    Panel fieldPanel = new Panel();
    Panel labelPanel = new Panel();
  // Set Panel and Applet layouts
    setLayout(new BorderLayout());
    northPanel.setLayout(new BorderLayout());
    centerPanel.setLayout(new BorderLayout());
    labelPanel.setLayout(new GridLayout(0,1));
    fieldPanel.setLayout(new GridLayout(0,1));
    southPanel.setLayout(new FlowLayout());
```

```java
        //Add buttons to the appropriate Panels
          southPanel.add(bu_microsoft);
          southPanel.add(bu_sun);
          southPanel.add(bu_connect);
        //Add URL name to the north panel
          northPanel.add("West", new Label("URL:  ", Label.RIGHT));
          northPanel.add("Center", lbl_URLString = new Label());
        //Add labels to the labelPanel
          labelPanel.add(new Label("DefaultAllowUserInteraction:  ",
     Label.RIGHT));
          labelPanel.add(new Label("AllowUserInteraction:  ",
     Label.RIGHT));
          labelPanel.add(new Label("DefaultUseCaches: ", Label.RIGHT));
          labelPanel.add(new Label("DoInput: ", Label.RIGHT));
          labelPanel.add(new Label("DoOutput:  ", Label.RIGHT));
          labelPanel.add(new Label("UseCaches:  ", Label.RIGHT));
          labelPanel.add(new Label("ContentEncoding:  ", Label.RIGHT));
          labelPanel.add(new Label("ContentLength:  ", Label.RIGHT));
          labelPanel.add(new Label("ContentType:  ", Label.RIGHT));
          labelPanel.add(new Label("Date:  ", Label.RIGHT));
          labelPanel.add(new Label("Expiration:  ", Label.RIGHT));
          labelPanel.add(new Label("LastModified:  ", Label.RIGHT));
          labelPanel.add(new Label("IfModifiedSince:  ", Label.RIGHT));
        //Add label "fields" to the fieldPanel
          fieldPanel.add(lbl_DefaultAllowUserInteraction = new Label());
          fieldPanel.add(lbl_AllowUserInteraction = new Label());
          fieldPanel.add(lbl_DefaultUseCaches = new Label());
          fieldPanel.add(lbl_DoInput = new Label());
          fieldPanel.add(lbl_DoOutput = new Label());
          fieldPanel.add(lbl_UseCaches = new Label());
          fieldPanel.add(lbl_ContentEncoding = new Label());
          fieldPanel.add(lbl_ContentLength = new Label());
          fieldPanel.add(lbl_ContentType = new Label());
          fieldPanel.add(lbl_Date = new Label());
          fieldPanel.add(lbl_Expiration = new Label());
          fieldPanel.add(lbl_LastModified = new Label());
          fieldPanel.add(lbl_IfModifiedSince = new Label());
        //Add ActionListeners for all buttons
          bu_connect.addActionListener(this);
          bu_microsoft.addActionListener(this);
          bu_sun.addActionListener(this);
        //Arrange Panels
          centerPanel.add("West", labelPanel);
          centerPanel.add("Center", fieldPanel);
          add("North", northPanel);
          add("South", southPanel);
          add("Center", centerPanel);
        }
        public void showWeb(String s) {
          clearFields();
          try {
            uc_connection = null;
            url_site = null;
            url_site = new URL(s);          // Get the URL
          // Define URLConnection
            uc_connection = url_site.openConnection();
```

```
        // Connect to URL without displaying
          uc_connection.connect();
        webInfo();
        }
        catch (MalformedURLException mue) {
          showStatus ("A MalformedURLException has occurred");
          url_site = null;
        }
        catch (IOException ioe) {
          showStatus ("A IOException has occurred");
          uc_connection = null;
          url_site = null;
        }
    }
    public void clearFields() {      //Clear text fields
      lbl_URLString.setText("");
      lbl_DefaultAllowUserInteraction.setText("");
      lbl_AllowUserInteraction.setText("");
      lbl_DefaultUseCaches.setText("");
          lbl_DoInput.setText("");
      lbl_DoOutput.setText("");
      lbl_UseCaches.setText("");
      lbl_ContentEncoding.setText("");
      lbl_ContentLength.setText("");
      lbl_ContentType.setText("");
      lbl_Date.setText("");
      lbl_Expiration.setText("");
      lbl_LastModified.setText("");
      lbl_IfModifiedSince.setText("");
    }
    public void webInfo() {
      showStatus("Retrieving Web information.  Please wait...");
      // Available before connection
      lbl_URLString.setText(url_site.toString());
      lbl_DefaultAllowUserInteraction.setText(String.valueOf(
uc_connection.getDefaultAllowUserInteraction()));
      lbl_AllowUserInteraction.setText(String.valueOf(
uc_connection.getAllowUserInteraction()));
      lbl_DefaultUseCaches.setText(String.valueOf(
uc_connection.getDefaultUseCaches()));
      lbl_DoInput.setText(String.valueOf( uc_connection.getDoInput()));
      lbl_DoOutput.setText(String.valueOf(
uc_connection.getDoOutput()));
      lbl_UseCaches.setText(String.valueOf(
uc_connection.getUseCaches()));
     // Available after connection
      lbl_ContentEncoding.setText( uc_connection.getContentEncoding());
      lbl_ContentLength.setText(String.valueOf(
uc_connection.getContentLength()));
      lbl_ContentType.setText(uc_connection.getContentType());
      Date holdDate = new Date(uc_connection.getDate());
      lbl_Date.setText(holdDate.toString());
      holdDate = null;
      holdDate = new Date(uc_connection.getExpiration());
        lbl_Expiration.setText(holdDate.toString());
      holdDate = null;
```

```
        holdDate = new Date(uc_connection.getLastModified());
            lbl_LastModified.setText(holdDate.toString());
        holdDate = null;
        holdDate = new Date(uc_connection.getIfModifiedSince());
            lbl_IfModifiedSince.setText(holdDate.toString());
        showStatus("Retrieval is finished");
    }
//The actionPerformed method is required
//by the ActionListener interface
    public void actionPerformed(ActionEvent e) {
        // Get the text of the button
        String buttonText = e.getActionCommand();
        //Test for buttons
        if (buttonText.equals("Microsoft")) {
            showWeb("http://www.microsoft.com/visualj");
        }
        else if (buttonText.equals("Sun")) {
            showWeb("http://www.sun.com/java");
        }
        else if (buttonText.equals("Connect")) {
            showStatus("Connecting to web site...Please wait.");
        //Connect to the URL
            getAppletContext().showDocument(url_site);
        showStatus("");
        }
    }
}
```

Listing 20-2 initially displays in the Web browser, as shown in Figure 20-3.

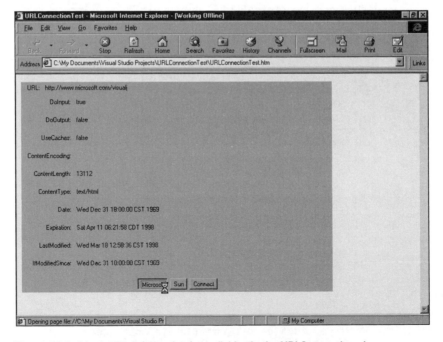

Figure 20-3: Much URL information is available via the URLConnection class.

The webInfo method uses the URLConnection class connection to retrieve information about the URL. When running Listing 20-2, you notice that some of the information fills in right away, while other URLConnection information needs to be retrieved from the Web site and is filled in only after the webInfo method can retrieve it.

Sending and Receiving Information from URL Streams

Often you may want to send or receive information from a URL. The simplist way to do this is by using a Stream. You can open a Stream from a URL or URLConnection class and use typical I/O methods to manipulate the Stream.

The displayStream() method shown in the following code sample opens a file from a URLConnection class and reads it into a text area:

```
public void displayStream() {  //Display stream contents in text area
  final int STRINGSIZE = 32766;  // buffer size
  char buffer[] = new char[STRINGSIZE];  // character buffer
  showStatus("Retrieving Web information.  Please wait...");
  lbl_URLString.setText(url_site.toString());  // Display URL
  ta_fileInfo.setText("");  //Clear text fields
  try {
    int charactersRead = 0;
    BufferedReader br =     // Set up buffer reader
      new BufferedReader(new
InputStreamReader(uc_connection.getInputStream()));
    do {  // read characters into buffer and display them
      charactersRead = br.read(buffer, 0, STRINGSIZE);
      ta_fileInfo.append(new String(buffer));
    } while (charactersRead > 1);
    showStatus("Retrieval is finished");
  }
  catch (IOException ioe) {
    showStatus(ioe.getMessage());
  }
}
```

Secret

You can also use the getOutputStream() method if the URL gives you access to write to the URL.

Listing 20-3 shows how a stream is used to read the HTML script at http://www.microsoft.com/visualj.

Listing 20-3: URLStream.java

```
import java.applet.*;
import java.awt.*;
import java.awt.event.*;
import java.io.*;
import java.util.*;
import java.net.*;
public class URLStream extends Applet implements ActionListener {
```

```
      private URL url_site;              //URL containint the site
      private URLConnection uc_connection;  //Connection for URL
// Add buttons
   private Button bu_sun = new Button("Sun");
   private Button bu_microsoft = new Button("Microsoft");
   private Button bu_connect = new Button("Connect");
   private Label lbl_URLString = new Label();  //Label containing URL
   private TextArea ta_fileInfo;  //Text area containing HTML
   public void init() {
      Panel northPanel = new Panel();
      Panel centerPanel = new Panel();
      Panel southPanel = new Panel();
   //Set layouts for Applet and Panels
      setLayout(new BorderLayout());
      northPanel.setLayout(new BorderLayout());
      centerPanel.setLayout(new GridLayout(1,1));
   //Add buttons to the south panel
      southPanel.add(bu_sun);
      southPanel.add(bu_microsoft);
      southPanel.add(bu_connect);
   //Add the current URL to the north panel
      northPanel.add("West", new Label("URL:  ", Label.RIGHT));
      northPanel.add("Center", lbl_URLString);
   //Add the text area to contain the HTML to the center panel
      centerPanel.add(ta_fileInfo = new TextArea());
   //Add ActionListeners for all buttons
      bu_connect.addActionListener(this);
      bu_microsoft.addActionListener(this);
      bu_sun.addActionListener(this);
   //Arrange panels
      add("North", northPanel);
      add("South", southPanel);
      add("Center", centerPanel);
   }
   public void showWeb(String s) {
      try {
      //Set the connection up for stream input
         uc_connection = null;
         url_site = null;
         url_site = new URL(s);
         uc_connection = url_site.openConnection();
         uc_connection.connect();
         displayStream();
      }
      catch (MalformedURLException mue) {
         showStatus ("A MalformedURLException has occurred");
         url_site = null;
      }
      catch (IOException ioe) {
         showStatus ("A IOException has occurred");
```

```
            uc_connection = null;
            url_site = null;
        }
    }
    public void displayStream() {
//Display stream contents in text area
        final int STRINGSIZE = 32766;  // buffer size
        char buffer[] = new char[STRINGSIZE];  // character buffer
        showStatus("Retrieving Web information.  Please wait...");
    //Display URL
        lbl_URLString.setText(url_site.toString());
        ta_fileInfo.setText("");  //Clear text fields
        try {
            int charactersRead = 0;
            BufferedReader br =     // Set up buffer reader
              new BufferedReader(new
InputStreamReader(uc_connection.getInputStream()));
            do {  // read characters into buffer and display them
                charactersRead = br.read(buffer, 0, STRINGSIZE);
                ta_fileInfo.append(new String(buffer));
            } while (charactersRead > 1);
            showStatus("Retrieval is finished");
        }
        catch (IOException ioe) {
            showStatus(ioe.getMessage());
        }
    }
//The actionPerformed method is required
//by the ActionListener interface
    public void actionPerformed(ActionEvent e) {
        // Get the text of the button
        String buttonText = e.getActionCommand();
        //Test for buttons
        if (buttonText.equals("Microsoft")) {
            showWeb("http://www.microsoft.com/visualj");
        }
        else if (buttonText.equals("Sun")) {
            showWeb("http://www.sun.com/java");
        }
        else if (buttonText.equals("Connect")) {
            showStatus("Connecting to web site...Please wait.");
        //Connect to the URL
            getAppletContext().showDocument(url_site);
            showStatus("");
        }
    }
}
```

The output for Listing 20-3 is shown in Figure 20-4.

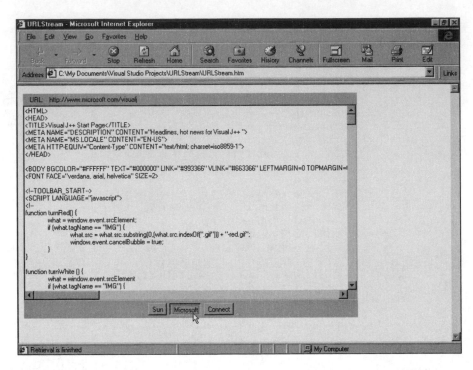

Figure 20-4: You can retrieve information from a text file and display it on your Web page without actually connecting to the URL.

Networking with Web Servers and Web Clients

A client-server architecture is the archetype used when two programs communicate or interact. In a client-server architecture, one program acts as a server while other programs connect as clients. The server handles communication received from one or more clients. This is shown graphically in Figure 20-5.

To write client software, you must first identify the IP address of your server machine. Then determine the *port* used by the server machine. A port is the number the server assigns to this communication so that the client can access a server program. By using several different port numbers, the server can communicate with different clients using different software. Although a port number is arbitrary, certain numbers are already in use. (For example, 13 is used to retrieve the date and time, and 21 is used for FTP.)

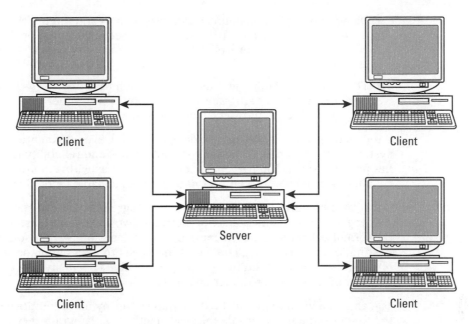

Figure 20-5: In a client-server architecture, one computer acts as a server. This server exchanges information with one or more clients.

Each client accesses a server through a host name. Usually, this host name is a URL, but it can also be an IP address. If the server exists and is listening to clients, the client passes through a port number. The port number is used to set up a link between the client and server. Remember, both the client and the server must specify the same port number for the client and the server to communicate.

In this section, you see two different ways of setting up a Web client-server construct. First, datagrams are used for an easy, low-overhead way of communicating between Web sites. For a more resilient Web client-server setup, a socket setup is used.

Using datagrams

You can use the DatagramPacket and DatagramSocket classes to send and receive information to and from a URL. Datagrams are also called UDPs, or User Datagram Protocol. Datagrams are fast and easy to use, but they have some disadvantages:

- Datagrams *are not* guaranteed to reach their destination. Although there is no reason why a datagram would not reach its destination, UDP has no error-checking protocol or handshake to ensure proper communication.

- There is no guarantee on the order in which they are received. Just because you send datagrams to a client in a given order does not ensure they reach the client or clients in the same order.

If reliability is needed, do not use datagrams. However, if you are running a system where speed is of the utmost importance, and reliability is desired but not required at 100 percent accuracy — such as with a multiuser game running over the Web — consider datagrams as a viable technology.

Datagrams use the DatagramPacket and DatagramSocket classes. A DatagramSocket is a connection between two Java programs. A DatagramPacket contains the message that is sent between a source and destination. A datagram client sends messages to a datagram server, although a program residing on a single machine can easily serve as both a datagram client and a datagram server.

You almost always implement a datagram server by using multitasking and the Runnable interface. Inside the `run()` method, a datagram server listens for any client messages using the DatagramPacket class, which defines a byte array buffer to receive information into the program, and the DatagramSocket class, which starts listening over a port:

```
//...
final int PORT = 6543;            //Constant arbitrary port number
//...
final int maxLength = 1024;       //Maximum buffer length
byte message[] = new byte[maxLength];    // Buffer
int packets = 0;            //Number of packets sent
try {
//Make packet for communication
  DatagramPacket packet = new DatagramPacket(message, maxLength);
//Declare socket with port for communication line
  DatagramSocket socket = new DatagramSocket(PORT);

//...
```

As shown by the preceding code, a DatagramPacket is formed by using a buffer and a maximum length. A DatagramSocket for a server is formed on the current machine by declaring a port.

Secret

Buffers used to transfer information over the Internet must be in the form of a byte array, because Internet communication uses bytes rather than Java characters or character strings.

After a socket and packet have been formed, a packet is received from the client machine using the `DatagramSocket.receive()` method. The `receive()` method waits until a packet is actually sent by constantly "polling" the socket to see if a message is waiting. Once a packet is received, the byte array received from the packet is converted to a string:

```
while(true) {   //Do until window closed by user
  socket.receive(packet);   //Get a packet, or wait
//Make a packet string
  String packetString = new String(message, 0, packet.getLength());
```

If the DatagramSocket message can't be formed, a SocketException is thrown, and if the DatagramSocket.receive() method fails, an IOException is thrown.

Datagram clients send messages to datagram servers. The following steps are used to send a message from a datagram client to a datagram server:

- Convert the host address string to an Internet address using the InetAddress class:

  ```
  InetAddress address = InetAddress.getByName("127.0.0.1");
  ```

- Form a DatagramPacket object from a byte array. When forming a packet to be received by the server, all you need to worry about is the message and the length. The packet to be sent by the client also needs to add the Internet address and the server port so the packet can arrive at the server location:

  ```
  DatagramPacket packet = new DatagramPacket(message, length,
  address, 6543);
  ```

- Create a new DatagramSocket class and send the packet over it. When the socket was created for the server socket example, a port was specified. Because the packet has the addressing information, including the port, the socket does not require either an address or a port number:

  ```
  DatagramSocket socket = new DatagramSocket();
  socket.send(packet);
  ```

Secret

Instead of using a URL address, such as http://www.microsoft.com, a host address of "127.0.0.1" is used for the URL string name. The "127.0.0.1" URL establishes a local loopback address that effectively enables a machine to talk to itself. It's useful for testing without waiting for your modem to catch up to your processor.

Datagrams use byte arrays rather than String objects. The information typed into a TextArea can be converted using the TextArea.getText() and the String.getBytes() methods:

```
byte message[] = ta_info.getText().getBytes();
```

Listing 20-4 shows how a datagram server can be written.

Listing 20-4: DatagramServer.java

```
import java.applet.*;
import java.awt.*;
import java.awt.event.*;
import java.io.*;
import java.net.*;
public class DatagramServer extends Frame implements Runnable,
WindowListener {
```

```java
//Constant arbitrary port number
  public final static int PORT = 6543;
  private Thread th_thread;      //Thread for Runnable multitasking
  private TextArea ta_info;      //Display area
  private Label lbl_status;      //Message Area
  public static void main(String args[]) {
  // Construct server
    DatagramServer ds = new DatagramServer();
  }
  public DatagramServer () {      //Constructor
    addWindowListener(this);  //Enable Window Listener methods
  //Declare Panels
    Panel southPanel = new Panel();
    Panel centerPanel = new Panel();
  //Set layout for Panels and Frame
    setLayout(new BorderLayout());
    centerPanel.setLayout(new GridLayout(1,1));
    southPanel.setLayout(new GridLayout(1,1));
  //Add Components
    centerPanel.add(ta_info = new TextArea());  //Add TextArea
    southPanel.add(lbl_status =      //Add Label
      new Label("                        "));
  //Arrange Panels on Frame
    add("South", southPanel);
    add("Center", centerPanel);
  //Do Frame stuff
    setTitle("DatagramServer.java");
    setSize (300, 250);
    show();
  //Make a thread for multitasking and start the run method
    th_thread = new Thread(this);  //Make a new thread
    th_thread.start();        //Multitasks the run method
  }
    public void showStatus(String message) {
   //Message at the bottom of the Frame
    lbl_status.setText(message);
  }
    public void run() {
    final int maxLength = 1024;    //Maximum buffer length
    byte message[] = new byte[maxLength];  // Buffer
    int packets = 0;          //Number of packets sent
    try {
    //Make packet for communication
      DatagramPacket packet = new DatagramPacket(message,
maxLength);
      //Declare socket with port for communication line
      DatagramSocket socket = new DatagramSocket(PORT);
      while(true) {   //Do until window closed by user
        socket.receive(packet);  //Get a packet, or wait
      //Make a packet string
        String packetString = new String(message, 0,
packet.getLength());
        ta_info.append(packetString);  //Display packet string
        ta_info.append("\n");     //carriage return, line feed
      //Display status of sends
        showStatus(String.valueOf(++packets) +
```

```
                        " Packet received");
            Thread.yield();      //Release control for waiting tasks
          }
      }
  //Something went wrong with the connection
     catch(SocketException se) {
       showStatus("SocketException occurred");
     }
//Something went wrong with the IO
     catch(IOException ioe) {
       showStatus("IOException occurred");
     }
  }
     // The following are required by the WindowListener
     // interface
  public void windowClosing(WindowEvent e) {
  // User wants the window to close
     th_thread.stop();  //Stop this thread
     dispose();         //Destoy this frame
     System.exit(0);    //Exit this program
  }
// Window got focus
  public void windowActivated(WindowEvent e) { }
// Window lost focus
  public void windowDeactivated(WindowEvent e){}
// Window is reduced
  public void windowIconified(WindowEvent e) { }
// Window is expanded from an icon
  public void windowDeiconified(WindowEvent e){}
// Window is finished closing
  public void windowClosed(WindowEvent e) { }
// Window is finished opening
  public void windowOpened(WindowEvent e) { }
}
```

Listing 20-5 shows how to write a datagram client to send information to the datagram server.

Listing 20-5: DatagramClient.java

```java
import java.applet.*;
import java.awt.*;
import java.awt.event.*;
import java.io.*;
import java.net.*;
public class DatagramClient extends Applet implements ActionListener{
  public final static String HOST = "127.0.0.1";  //Used for self-
testing
  public final static int PORT - 6543;  //Arbitrary port used in
DatagramServer
  private int i_packetSent = 0;  //Number of packet sent
  private TextArea ta_info;      //Display Area
  private Button bu_send;     //Send button
  public void init() {
  //Declare Panels
    Panel centerPanel = new Panel();
```

```java
      Panel southPanel = new Panel();
  //Set Layout for Applet and Panels
    setLayout(new BorderLayout());
    centerPanel.setLayout(new GridLayout(1,1));
    southPanel.setLayout(new BorderLayout());
  //Add input area for message to server
    centerPanel.add(ta_info = new TextArea());
  //Display host
    southPanel.add("Center", new Label("Host:   " + HOST,
Label.CENTER));
  //Add Send button
    southPanel.add("East", bu_send = new Button("Send"));
  //Add ActionListener to the Send button
    bu_send.addActionListener(this);
  //Arrange panels on Applet
    add("South", southPanel);
    add("Center", centerPanel);
  }
    public void sendDatagram() {   //Send the message
  //Get the message from the text area
    byte message[] = ta_info.getText().getBytes();
    try {
  //Get the internet address from the HOST
      InetAddress address = InetAddress.getByName(HOST);
  //Form a packet using the message, the IP address, and the port
      DatagramPacket packet = new DatagramPacket(
          message, message.length, address, PORT);
  //Form a socket connection to the server
      DatagramSocket socket = new DatagramSocket();
  //Send the message to the server
      socket.send(packet);
  //Close the socket
      socket.close();
  //Display what happened
      showStatus (String.valueOf(++i_packetSent) + " packet(s)
sent");
    }
    catch(UnknownHostException uhe) {   //Host couldn't be found
      showStatus("UnknownHostException occurred");
    }
    catch(SocketException se) {        //Something's wrong with the
connection
      showStatus("SocketException occurred");
    }
    catch(IOException ioe) {     //IO failed during send
      showStatus("IOException occurred");
    }
  }
//The actionPerformed method is required
//by the ActionListener interface
  public void actionPerformed(ActionEvent e) {  //Send button pressed
    sendDatagram();          //Send the message
    bu_send.transferFocus();        //Lose focus
  }
}
```

Figure 20-6 shows how the datagram packet and datagram server work together. Notice how the server *does not* have to reside on a Web page, but rather has to be accessible through the Web (or some other TCP/IP network). Clients are probably Applets that reside on Web pages but, again, don't need to be.

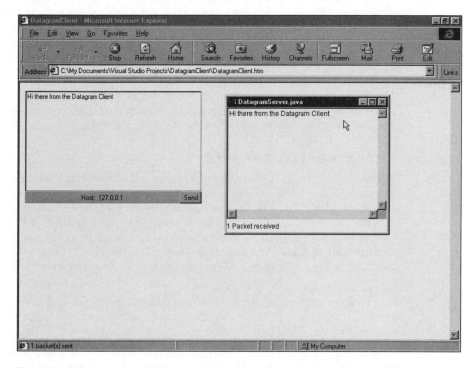

Figure 20-6: Datagrams can easily make Java Applets and a Java program "talk" to each other.

Secret

Try this. Close the datagram server and keep the datagram client running. Now click Send. If the host (127.0.0.1) can be found, the port is *assumed* to exist, and the message is sent to the host's port. *No error can be detected to show that the host did not receive the message!* The datagram client reports that the message is sent, but because the server is closed, no program ever receives the message.

Remember, datagrams are fast and easy, but have little error checking. While making communication somewhat unreliable, this lack of error checking and handshaking is the secret to datagram speed. Datagrams are excellent for Web-based games. If more reliable communication is needed, try using sockets.

Using Sockets

Sockets provide a more reliable form of network communication. Sockets are treated as streams for input and output. Any output to the socket is placed at the end of the stream, and the stream is read from the beginning. Throughout this process, the connection is tested to make sure that all packets were sent and received, making socket communication more secure and sequential than datagram communication. Finally, socket communication allows parallel information to flow both ways over a port. This differs from serial datagram communication, which typically forces a send from one port to a receive from another.

However, because of the use of streams coupled with the use of Web communication, sockets are more complicated than datagrams. Also, the overhead is greater and the processing is somewhat slower.

Using socket servers

Socket server programs are those programs that can establish one or more reliable connections to client programs. Usually socket server programs are multithreaded. This enables the SocketServer class to continuously check the port to see if any messages were sent. The run() method of the socket server program contains a nested loop. In the outer loop, the socket connection is made over a specified port, and the ServerSocket.accept() method is used to return a Socket object for the ServerSocket:

```
while (true) {
  //Create a new server socket and listen for a message here
  //. . .
}
```

Inside the outer loop, the server socket is created. Input streams and print streams are then opened and used for input and output:

```
ss_socket = new ServerSocket(PORT);   // Create new server socket
Socket socket = ss_socket.accept();   //Create a socket from the
server socket
BufferedReader br =        // Set up buffer reader
    new BufferedReader(
    new InputStreamReader(socket.getInputStream()));
//Set up the output stream to the client
PrintWriter pw = new PrintWriter(socket.getOutputStream());
pw.println("Connection Successful!!");  //Send a message to the
client
pw.flush();          // Flush the buffer to send the message
```

The inner loop reads from the input stream until the input stream is closed. And then, a message returning what was sent is echoed back to the client:

```
String line;            //Line read from client
while((line = br.readLine()) != null) {    // Test for message
  pw.println("You sent:  " + line);    //Send a message to the
client
```

```
pw.flush;              //Flush the buffer to send the message
ta_info.append(line + "\r\n");        //Display message
Thread.yield();           //Let other things run for a sec
}
```

When finished, the sockets are closed, and the outer loop begins again:

```
socket.close();        //Close the socket
ss_socket.close();        //Close the server socket
```

Listing 20-6 uses the ServerSocket class to write a socket server Java program.

Listing 20-6: SocketServer.java

```
import java.applet.*;
import java.awt.*;
import java.awt.event.*;
import java.io.*;
import java.net.*;
public class SocketServer extends Frame implements Runnable,
WindowListener {
    //Constant arbitrary port number
  public final static int PORT = 6543;
  //Thread for Runnable multitasking
  private Thread th_thread;
  private TextArea ta_info;      //Display area
  private Label lbl_status;      //Message Area
//Socket used for communication
  public ServerSocket ss_socket;
  public static void main(String args[]) {
    SocketServer ds = new SocketServer();
  }
  public SocketServer () {
    addWindowListener(this); //Enable Window Listener methods
  //Declare Panels
    Panel southPanel = new Panel();
    Panel centerPanel = new Panel();
  //Set layout for Panels and Frame
    setLayout(new BorderLayout());
    centerPanel.setLayout(new GridLayout(1,1));
    southPanel.setLayout(new GridLayout(1,1));
  //Add Components
    centerPanel.add(ta_info = new TextArea());  //Add TextArea
    southPanel.add(lbl_status =       //Add Label
      new Label("                    "));
  //Arrange Panels on Frame
    add("South", southPanel);
    add("Center", centerPanel),
  //Do Frame stuff
    setTitle("SocketServer.java");
    setSize (300, 250);
    show();
  //Make a thread for multitasking and start the run method
```

```java
      th_thread = new Thread(this);  //Make a new thread
      th_thread.start();          //Multitasks the run method
  }
    public void showStatus(String message) {
   //Message at the bottom of the Frame
    lbl_status.setText(message);
  }
    public void run() {
    try {
      while (true) {
        String line;        //Line read from client
      //Create a new server socket
        ss_socket = new ServerSocket(PORT);
      //Create a socket from the server socket
        Socket socket = ss_socket.accept();
        BufferedReader br =     // Set up buffer reader
          new BufferedReader(
          new InputStreamReader(socket.getInputStream()));
      //Set up the output stream to the client
        PrintWriter pw = new PrintWriter(socket.getOutputStream());
      //Send a message to the client
        pw.println("Connection Successful!!");
        pw.flush;  //Flush the buffer to send the message
      // Test for message
        while((line = br.readLine()) != null) {
        //Send a message to the client
          pw.println("You sent:   " + line);
          pw.flush;  //Flush the buffer to send the message
          ta_info.append(line + "\r\n");  //Display message
          Thread.yield();  //Let other things run for a sec
        }
        socket.close();        //Close the socket
        ss_socket.close();       //Close the server socket
      }
    }
    catch(IOException ioe) {        //Socket error
      showStatus(ioe.getMessage() +
           " -- IOException occurred");
    }
  }
// The following are required by the WindowListener interface
// User wants the window to close
  public void windowClosing(WindowEvent e) {
    th_thread.stop();          //Stop this thread
    try {ss_socket.close();}        //Close the socket
    catch (IOException ioe) {}    //I don't care.  I'm closing
    dispose();          //Destoy this frame
    System.exit(0);          //Exit this program
  }
// Window got focus
  public void windowActivated(WindowEvent e) { }
// Window lost focus
  public void windowDeactivated(WindowEvent e){ }
```

```
// Window is reduced
  public void windowIconified(WindowEvent e) { }
// Window is expanded from an icon
  public void windowDeiconified(WindowEvent e){}
// Window is finished closing
  public void windowClosed(WindowEvent e) { }
// Window is finished opening
  public void windowOpened(WindowEvent e) { }
}
```

Of course, when you run a socket server program, no action takes place until some socket client accesses the program.

Using socket clients

Unlike UDP clients, socket clients need to be multithreaded. This is so they can constantly listen to the server for any messages that the server may send. When you define a new socket, you must pass a host string and a port number in the constructor:

```
//Form socket from the host and the port
so_socket = new Socket(HOST, PORT);
```

If there is no server at the host and port defined in the Socket constructor, a SocketException occurs. Make sure your socket server program is running before you run your socket client program. Datagrams have no such constraints.

After defining your socket, you must set up input and output I/O streams. These streams are retrieved from the socket:

```
//Use the socket to form an output connection
  pw_output = new PrintWriter(so_socket.getOutputStream());
//Use the socket to form an input connection
  br =new BufferedReader(
    new InputStreamReader(so_socket.getInputStream()));
```

The run() method also continuously listens for any information to be sent from the server:

```
String line;          //Line that is sent from the server
//Keep polling the server
while((line = br.readLine()) != null) {
  ita_server.append(line);      //Display line
  ita_server.append("\n");      //Display new line
  Thread.yield();               //Let other stuff run
}
```

You need a way to send messages to the server. This is done through the PrintWriter class that formed from the socket.getOutputStream() method shown previously. The sendToServer() method is used to send a message to the output stream used by the socket defined in the run() method. Because the setup has been accomplished in the run() method, only a println() method is needed, followed by a buffer flush:

```
public void sendToServer() {
//Form and send message
  pw_output.println(itf_client.getText());
  pw_output.flush();          //Flush the buffered output
}
```

The socket client used to send messages back and forth to the socket server is shown in Listing 20-7.

Listing 20-7: SocketClient.java

```
import java.applet.*;
import java.awt.*;
import java.awt.event.*;
import java.io.*;
import java.net.*;
public class SocketClient extends Applet implements Runnable,
ActionListener {
  private Thread ith_thread;
  private TextField itf_client;
  private PrintWriter pw_output;
  private TextArea ita_server;
  private Button bu_send = new Button("Send");
  public static int PORT = 6543;
  public static String HOST = "127.0.0.1";
  public Socket so_socket;
  public void init() {
//Declare Panels
    Panel centerPanel = new Panel();
    Panel southPanel = new Panel();
//Set Layout for Applet and Panels
    setLayout(new BorderLayout());
    centerPanel.setLayout(new FlowLayout());
    southPanel.setLayout(new FlowLayout());
//Add text area for message to server
    centerPanel.add(new Label("Message to Server:"));
    centerPanel.add(itf_client = new TextField(30));
    centerPanel.add(new Label("Message from Server:"));
//Add input area for message from server
    centerPanel.add(ita_server = new TextArea(5,30));
//Display host
    southPanel.add(new Label("Host:   " + HOST));
//Add Send button
    southPanel.add(bu_send);
//Add ActionListeners for send button
    bu_send.addActionListener(this);
//Arrange panels on Applet
    add("South", southPanel);
    add("Center", centerPanel);
//Make a thread for multitasking and start the run method
    ith_thread = new Thread(this);
    ith_thread.start();
```

```java
      }
  public void run() {
    BufferedReader br = null;  //Declare buffered reader
    String line;    //Line that is sent from the server
    try {
    //Form socket from the host and the port
      so_socket = new Socket(HOST, PORT);
    //Use the socket to form an output connection
      pw_output = new PrintWriter(so_socket.getOutputStream());
    //Use the socket to form an input connection
      br =new BufferedReader(
        new InputStreamReader(so_socket.getInputStream()));
    //Keep pulling the server
      while((line = br.readLine()) != null) {
        ita_server.append(line);  //Display line
        ita_server.append("\n");  //Display new line
        Thread.yield();           //Let other stuff run
      }
    }
    catch(IOException ioe) { //The socket failed somehow
      showStatus(ioe.getMessage() +
              " -- Socket IOException occurred");
    }
    finally {     //Clean up
      try {
        if (pw_output != null) {
          pw_output.close();  //Close the output stream
        }
        if (br != null) {
          br.close();         //Close the buffered reader
        }
        if (so_socket != null) {
          so_socket.close();  //Close the socket
        }
      }
      catch (IOException ioe2) {}  //I don't care.
    }
  }
  public void sendToServer() {
  //Form and send message
    pw_output.println(itf_client.getText());
    pw_output.flush();  //Flush the buffered output
  }
//The actionPerformed method is required by the ActionListener
//interface
  //bu_send was pressed
  public void actionPerformed(ActionEvent e) {
    sendToServer();          //Send the message
    bu_send.transferFocus();        //Lose focus
  }
}
```

The output from Listings 20-6 and 20-7 is shown in Figure 20-7. It's similar to the datagram output seen in Figure 20-6.

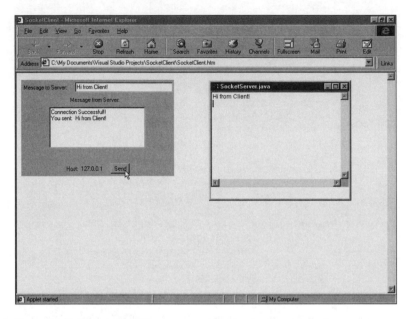

Figure 20-7: Sockets provide secure communication between a Java program and a Java Applet.

Summary

This chapter discusses Web communication with Java, with emphasis on classes, datagrams, and sockets. The following points are of particular interest:

- The URL class is often useful for retrieving disk information or transferring control of a Web page to a browser or to another URL.

- The URLConnection class can be used to retrieve information about a URL without actually transferring browser control to that URL.

- Input and output streams can be formed by using the URL or URLConnection classes. These streams can be used for I/O with Web servers.

- Datagrams and sockets can be used for communication between programs.

- Datagrams are fast and have low overhead, but can occasionally result in unreliable communication.

- Sockets are more reliable, but are also more complicated to program.

Chapter 21

Advanced Threads

In This Chapter

▶ Inheriting classes from Threads

▶ Inquiring about the state of current Threads

▶ Using the synchronized keyword

So far in this book, you've used the Runnable interface to make a class multitask. However, the Runnable interface only multitasks the run method. No other methods are considered part of the thread.

Sometimes you may want entire classes to run concurrently. In this case, you need to extend the Thread class, rather than use the Runnable interface. The Thread class enables your entire Java class to run as a separate thread.

Inheriting the Thread Class

In the last chapter, the SocketServer class enabled you to talk to one client at a time. A better design would enable the SocketServer class to handle a number of clients at one time and keep track of all of them. Listing 21-1 shows how multiple clients can access one SocketServer at the same time by the use of threads.

Listing 21-1: MultiSocketServer.java

```java
import java.applet.*;
import java.awt.*;
import java.awt.event.*;
import java.io.*;
import java.net.*;
public class MultiSocketServer extends Frame
        implements Runnable, ISingleServer, WindowListener {
// Port for Socket Service
   public static final int PORT = 6543;
private Thread th_thread;      // Thread for Runnable Interface
   private TextArea ta_info;       // Text area for Info
   private Label lbl_status;       // Status area for messages
// Socket for communications
   public ServerSocket ss_socket;
public static void main(String args[]) {
   // Instantiate MultiSocketServer
     MultiSocketServer mss = new MultiSocketServer();
```

```java
    }
  public MultiSocketServer () {
    //MultiSocketServer constructor
    Panel southPanel = new Panel();
    Panel centerPanel = new Panel();
    setLayout(new BorderLayout());
    centerPanel.setLayout(new GridLayout(1,1));
    centerPanel.add(ta_info = new TextArea());
    southPanel.setLayout(new GridLayout(1,1));
    southPanel.add(lbl_status =
      new Label(""));
    add("South", southPanel);
    add("Center", centerPanel);
    setTitle("MultiSocketServer.java");
    setSize (300, 250);
    show();
// Thread for multithreading
    th_thread = new Thread(this);
// Allow Java to end with thread running
    th_thread.setDaemon(true);
    th_thread.start();
  }
  public void run() {     // Required by the Runnable interface
    try {
      ss_socket = new ServerSocket(PORT);
      while (true) {
        SingleServer ss = new SingleServer(this,
          ss_socket.accept());
        ss.start();
      }
    }
    catch(SocketException se) {
      showStatus(se.getMessage() +
      " -- SocketException occurred");
    }
    catch(IOException ioe) {}   // WINDOW_DESTROY was pushed
  }
    public void showStatus(String message) {
    lbl_status.setText(message);
  }
  public void serverInfo(String message) {
    ta_info.append(message + "\r\n");
  }
// The following are required by the WindowListener interface
// User wants the window to close
  public void windowClosing(WindowEvent e) {
th_thread.stop();
    try {ss_socket.close();}
    catch (IOException ioe) {}   //I don't care
    dispose();
    System.exit(0);
  }
// Window got focus
  public void windowActivated(WindowEvent e) { }
// Window lost focus
public void windowDeactivated(WindowEvent e){ }
// Window is reduced
```

```java
      public void windowIconified(WindowEvent e) { }
      // Window is expanded from an icon
      public void windowDeiconified(WindowEvent e){}
      // Window is finished closing
      public void windowClosed(WindowEvent e) { }
      // Window is finished opening
      public void windowOpened(WindowEvent e) { }
    }
    class SingleServer extends Thread {
      public static int i_numberOfClients = 0;  // Number clients
      private int i_thisClientNumber;      // This client's number
    // The interfacing class
      private ISingleServer iss_callingClass;
    // Output stream for communication
    private PrintWriter pw_output;
    // Input stream for communication
    private BufferedReader br_input;
    // Constructor
    public SingleServer (ISingleServer iss, Socket s) {
    synchronized(this) {
            i_numberOfClients++;
            i_thisClientNumber = i_numberOfClients;
        }
        try {
          iss_callingClass = iss;
          br_input = new BufferedReader(
                new InputStreamReader(s.getInputStream()));
          pw_output = new PrintWriter(s.getOutputStream());
          pw_output.println(
            "Connection to client #" + i_thisClientNumber +
            " successful!!\r");
        }
        catch(IOException ioe) {
          iss_callingClass.showStatus(
                ioe.getMessage() + " -- IOException occurred");
        }
      }
        public void run() {    // Required for Thread subclasses
        try {
          String line;
          while((line = br_input.readLine()) != null) {
            pw_output.println("You sent:  " + line + "\r");
            iss_callingClass.serverInfo(line);
            Thread.yield();
          }
        }
        catch(SocketException se) {
          iss_callingClass.showStatus(
              se.getMessage() + " -- SocketException occurred");
        }
        catch(IOException ioe) {}   // WINDOW_DESTROY was pushed
      }
    }
    interface ISingleServer {  // Interface for SingleServer class
      public void serverInfo(String message);
      public void showStatus(String message);
    }
```

The `SocketServer` class handles one client at a time, as shown by Figure 21-1.

Figure 21-1: The SocketServer program handles one client.

By contrast, Listing 21-1 enables multiple clients to attach to your server by instantiating a separate `SingleServer` thread for each client, even if some of those clients aren't Java Applets.

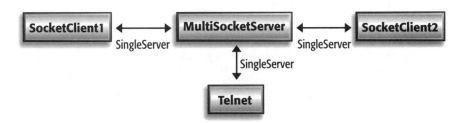

Figure 21-2: The MultiSocketServer program handles any number of clients per server.

In Listing 21-1, the `MultiSocketServer` class detects a new client only:

```
ss_socket = new ServerSocket(PORT);
while (true) {
  SingleServer ss = new SingleServer(this,
    ss_socket.accept());
  ss.start();
}
```

The `ServerSocket.accept` method is used to detect a new client. The `accept` method causes the `MultiSocketServer` program to wait until a client is detected before continuing to instantiate the `SingleServer`. Instead of handling the communications with each client, the `MultiServerSocket` program spawns a new class to handle all communication with a client, and then continues waiting for a new connection.

Each client gets its own thread for communication. The `SingleServer` class is inherited from Thread and therefore runs all its methods inside a limited amount of time determined by the Java virtual machine before yielding to other threads:

```
class SingleServer extends Thread {
```

Like the Runnable interface, a Thread subclass requires that starting logic be placed in a `run` method.

Secret

If you only need one method to multitask, use the Runnable interface — it has less overhead and is more efficient. In the `SingleServer` class, you could use the Runnable interface instead of inheriting a Thread.

Figure 21-3 shows how a Java Applet and Telnet (a Windows 95 program) can communicate with the `MultiSocketServer` program shown in Listing 21-1. The `MultiSocketServer` program handles communication with each program separately.

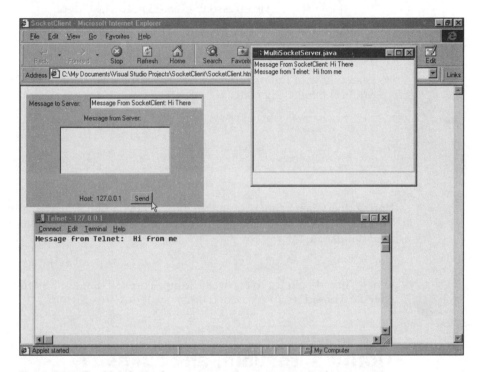

Figure 21-3: The MultiSocketServer program keeps communication separate between clients.

ThreadGroups

Every Thread class belongs to a ThreadGroup. ThreadGroups can contain other ThreadGroups or Threads. ThreadGroups enable you to configure a group of Threads identically. To add a Thread to a ThreadGroup, follow these steps:

1. Create a ThreadGroup object and give it a name. Do this by instantiating a ThreadGroup class. The following statement creates a ThreadGroup named `HighPriority`:

   ```
   ThreadGroup tg_HighPriority = new ThreadGroup ("HighPriority");
   ```

Secret

You can also create a ThreadGroup as a child of another ThreadGroup. The following statement creates a ThreadGroup named `HighPriority` as a child of the `tg_OtherThreads`:

```
ThreadGroup tg_HighPriority = new ThreadGroup(tg_OtherThreads,
"HighPriority");
```

2. When you create your Thread, you must name it and assign it to a group. The following statement creates a Thread and adds it to the `tg_HighPriority` ThreadGroup created in the last step:

```
Thread myThread = new Thread(tg_HighPriority, "myThread");
```

Threads added to a specific ThreadGroup also must be named.

Secret

You can add your Runnable interfaces to a ThreadGroup as well. This is shown in the following code:

```
public class myApplet extends Applet implements Runnable {
  private Thread myThread;
//...
    myThread = new Thread(tg_HighPriority, this);
    myThread.start( );
//...
```

Notice that when using a Runnable interface, you don't need to name your Thread. If you want to name your thread anyway, your Thread constructor would look like this:

```
myThread = new Thread(tg_HighPriority, this, "myThread");
```

Secret

Every Thread belongs to a ThreadGroup. Threads that are not added to a specific ThreadGroup are added in the system ThreadGroup.

Priorities, resume, and suspend

Every Thread has a priority. A priority states how long a Thread waits before executing. The rule is that if Threads with higher priority are waiting to execute, they take priority over Threads with lower priority.

Secret

Be careful with Thread priorities. Assume you have three Threads (A, B, and C) running at priorities 10, 6, and 5, respectively, as shown in Figure 21-4.

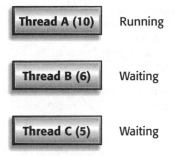

Figure 21-4: Threads waiting to run

If Thread A issues a yield, the next Thread (Thread B) runs, as shown in Figure 21-5.

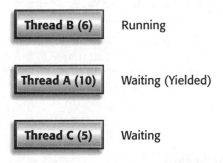

Figure 21-5: After Thread A yields, Thread B runs.

Notice that in Figure 21-5, instead of going to the bottom of the queue, Thread A "cuts" in front of Thread C because Thread A has a higher priority than Thread C. Now when Thread B yields, as shown in Figure 21-6, Thread A is running again, and Thread B "cuts" in front of Thread C.

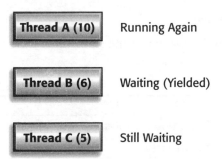

Figure 21-6: Thread C never gets a chance.

Thread C is still waiting. Many developers think that higher priorities make their programs run faster. While this may be somewhat true, for long-running programs, higher priorities can lock out other Threads — even system Threads that are needed to keep the Java Virtual Machine up and running.

If you assign higher priorities to some of your threads, you probably need to use the suspend and resume methods. These methods are available for individual Threads or entire ThreadGroups. The suspend method suspends a thread and doesn't allow it to execute until a resume method is called.

Discovering Daemons

As long as a thread is running, the Java VM cannot halt. Sometimes, you want the Java VM to stop although your thread is still running. For example, in the program shown in Listing 21-1, the Web Master may want to bring down the Java VM when all Threads are finished, and you don't want the Java VM to hold up because your Java socket server happens to be listening for a connection.

Secret

A daemon is a special type of Thread that runs like other Threads, but enables the Java VM to close while it's running. You notice in the constructor that the setDaemon method is used to set the Thread that listens for a connection to a daemon:

```
th_thread.setDaemon(true);
```

Examining Synchronization

When running classes, you are multitasking your operations. Often, you want to ensure that certain methods or sections of code run before other sections of code in the same thread or in different threads.

Earlier, in Listing 21-1, you were keeping track of the current client number by using and incrementing a static integer and assigning it to the client instance:

```
clientNumber++;
thisClientNumber = clientNumber;
```

Say you have two connections happening at the same time:

Command Sequence	Client 1	Client 2
1	clientNumber++;	
2		clientNumber++;
3	thisClientNumber = clientNumber;	
4		thisClientNumber =clientNumber;

Notice that Client 1 increments the static client number to 1. Before any further Client 1 action occurs, Client 2 also increments the static client number to 2. Then both Client 1 and Client 2 assign 2 to their client number. This causes two clients that use a 2 for a client number and no clients that use a 1 for a client number! Clearly, you need to make sure this does not happen.

To ensure the proper running order using threads, Java uses the `synchronized` keyword. This keyword ensures that no changes are made to a class's variables until the synchronized commands are finished.

To make an entire method synchronized, you can use the `synchronized` keyword as a modifier for the method:

```
public synchronized void myMethod() {
  // Synchronized commands go here
} //When the method ends, so does the synchronization
```

Sometimes, you only need to make a set of commands inside a method synchronized, as is needed to assign the previous client numbers. For this, you can use the `synchronized` keyword to build a synchronized block of statements, as is done in Listing 21-1:

```
synchronized(this) {
  clientNumber++;
  thisClientNumber = clientNumber;
}
```

To use the `synchronized` keyword, you must specify the class you want to protect until your commands are finished:

```
myClass instance = new myClass();
synchronized(instance) {
  // Synchronized commands go here
}
```

However, most often you use this keyword, as shown in Listing 21-1, to specify your own Thread class rather than a different class.

Mastering Thread Information

You can retrieve much information from classes. Listing 21-2 lists all the threads currently running on your Java VM.

Listing 21-2: ThreadInfo.java

```
import java.awt.*;
import java.awt.event.*;
import java.io.*;
public class ThreadInfo extends Frame implements Runnable,
WindowListener, ActionListener {
```

```java
private Thread th_thread;
private Button bu_exit = new Button("Exit");
private TextArea ta_info;
public static void main(String args[]) {
   ThreadInfo ti = new ThreadInfo();
}
public ThreadInfo () {
//Add window listener to listen for the Frame to close
   addWindowListener(new WindowAdapter(){
      public void windowClosing(WindowEvent e) {
         th_thread.stop();
         dispose();
         System.exit(0);
      }});
//Add ActionListeners for all buttons
   bu_exit.addActionListener(this);
   Panel southPanel = new Panel();
   Panel centerPanel = new Panel();
   setLayout(new BorderLayout());
   centerPanel.setLayout(new GridLayout(1,1));
   centerPanel.add(ta_info = new TextArea());
   ta_info.setFont(new Font("Courier", Font.PLAIN, 12));
   southPanel.setLayout(new FlowLayout());
   southPanel.add(bu_exit);
   add("South", southPanel);
   add("Center", centerPanel);
   setTitle("ThreadInfo.java");
   setSize (600, 250);
   show();
   th_thread = new Thread(this);
   th_thread.start();
}
   public void run() {
   ta_info.setText("");
   while (true) {
      int numberThreads = Thread.activeCount();
      Thread threads[] = new Thread[numberThreads];
      Thread.enumerate(threads);  // Retrieve a list of threads
      StringBuffer holder = new StringBuffer(32766);
      for (int loop = 0; loop < numberThreads; loop++) {
         Thread t = threads[loop];  // Go through each thread
         holder.append(   pad(t.getName(),20)
                  + t.getPriority() + "\t"
                  + (t.isDaemon() ? "Daemon         " : "Non-Daemon
")
                  + t.getThreadGroup() + "\r\n");
      }
      if (!holder.toString().equals(ta_info.getText())) {
         ta_info.setText(holder.toString());
      }
      holder = null;  //deallocate
      try {Thread.sleep(50);}
```

```
        catch (InterruptedException ie) {} //I don't care
      }
    }
    public static String pad (String in, int size) {
    StringBuffer sb = new StringBuffer(size);
    sb.append(in);
    while (sb.length() < size) {
      sb.append(" ");
    }
    return sb.toString();
  }
//The actionPerformed method is required
//by the ActionListener interface
  public void actionPerformed(ActionEvent e) {   // bu_exit was hit
    th_thread.stop();
    dispose();
    System.exit(0);
  }
}
```

Listing 21-2 displays the window shown in Figure 21-7. As you can see, all threads are listed with name, priority, whether or not the Thread is a daemon, and their ThreadGroup.

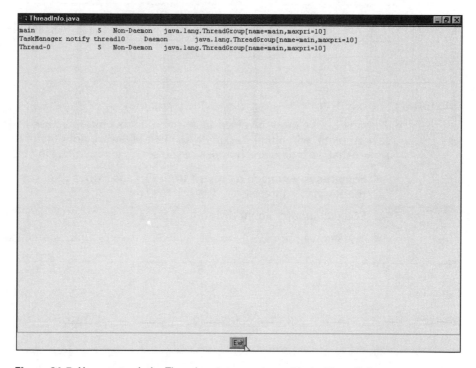

Figure 21-7: You can track the Threads on your system with the ThreadInfo program.

The methods in Table 21-1 are used to retrieve Thread information.

Table 21-1   Methods to Retrieve Thread Information

Method	Description
`Thread.activeCount()`	Returns the number of active threads currently running in the Java Virtual Machine. Because this method is static, you don't need to instantiate a thread to retrieve the active count: `int numberThreads = Thread.activeCount();`
`Thread.getName()`	Returns the name of a Thread: `holder.append(pad(t.getName(),20);`

`Thread.getPriority()`	Returns the priority of a Thread:
	`holder.append(String.valueOf`
	`(getPriority()));`

`Thread.isDaemon()`	Returns true if a Thread is a daemon, and false if the Thread is not:
	`holder.append((t.isDaemon() ? "Daemon`
	`" : "Non-Daemon    "));`

`Thread.getThreadGroup()`	Returns the ThreadGroup of a Thread: `holder.append(pad(t.getThreadGroup(),20);`

Summary

Threads can be more involved than the Runnable interface used so often in Java Applets. When multitasking, you must be aware not only of the potential power that Java delivers, but also of the problems multitasking can bring.

- Sometimes you need to inherit from threads rather than implementing the Runnable interface.

- You can inquire about the state of threads.

- You can use the `synchronized` keyword to help control multitasking.

Part IV

Database Development in Visual J++

Chapter 22

Understanding Visual J++ Database Access

In This Chapter

▶ Understanding Universal Data Access

▶ Reviewing Object Linking and Embedding Databases, and ActiveX Data Objects

▶ Manipulating Open Database Connectivity

▶ Discussing DAO and RDO, and their current place in the new database hierarchy

▶ Discussing JDBC and Visual J++

▶ Exploring visual database programming with Visual J++

Visual J++ has more ways to connect to a database than any other Java development tool on the market. Visual J++ offers the most advanced data-access capabilities for Java database developers. Using the Visual J++ data feature set, developers can quickly design and deploy data-driven applications for the Web or Windows.

Part IV of this book is dedicated to describing how to use the myriad of Visual J++ database tools. Previous versions of Visual J++ included Data Access Objects (DAO) and Remote Data Objects (RDO). Visual J++ not only adds ADO (ActiveX Data Objects) to supercede DAO, but also includes data access through Dynamic HTML (covered in Chapter 11). Finally, JDBC (Java DataBase Connectivity) is included in this version of Visual J++, whereas older versions only supported JDBC with an add-on patch. This chapter discusses mainly ADO and the database painting tools that you can use inside Visual J++.

Universal Data Access

Universal Data Access is the strategy employed by Microsoft to provide access to all types of relational *and* nonrelational information. Universal Data Access enables all Visual Studio tools to access any data source on any platform. The Universal Data Access protocol enables applications to use one set of API-class library calls to access a myriad of data sources.

Universal Data Access consists of three core technologies: Object Linking and Embedding Databases (OLE DB), ActiveX Data Objects (ADO), and Open Database Connectivity (ODBC). Visual J++ can connect to these data sources with a minimum of development time. The developer can use the Visual J++ API to connect to several different databases without having to understand the idiosyncratic differences of each database.

Object Linking and Embedding Databases (OLE DB)

OLE DB is Microsoft's newest standard for database connectivity. OLE DB consists of a set of COM interfaces that provide several database management services. OLE DB is designed to access several different kinds of data sources, as shown by Figure 22-1.

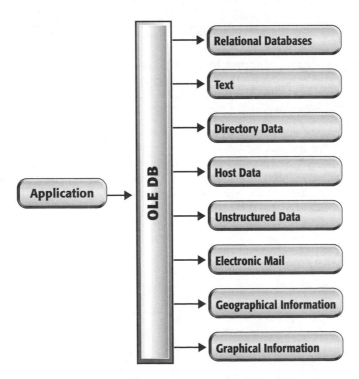

Figure 22-1: The OLE DB protocol reduces the complexity of retrieving data from a wide variety of data sources.

Many database vendors (such as Oracle, Informix, and Microsoft SQL Server) provide OLE DB drivers, as well as ODBC drivers, to access their databases.

ActiveX Data Objects (ADO)

ADO is a layer of classes designed to provide quick and easy access to OLE DB, as shown in Figure 22-2.

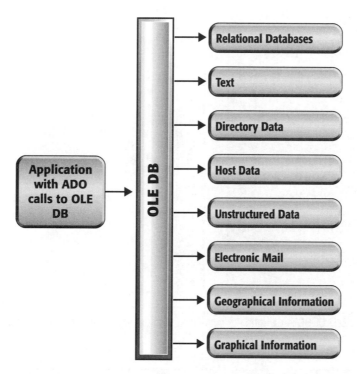

Figure 22-2: ADO is a high-level class library providing easy access to OLE DB routines.

ADO is used across platforms, enabling developers of any language, including Visual J++, to access data seamlessly. All of the Visual Studio tools can use ADO to access data. ADO drastically reduces the amount of time needed to write complex client-server and ActiveX code. ADO and Visual J++'s visual database tools are discussed later in this chapter. Calls you can make with ADO are addressed in the next chapter.

Open Database Connectivity (ODBC)

ODBC is the most open and, probably, most successful standard used to connect to a relational database. Most databases include ODBC drivers to access their database in addition to the native drivers. Some databases have even given up on native drivers and use ODBC exclusively. Even OLE DB currently uses ODBC to access most relational databases. Figure 22-3 shows how ODBC is configured.

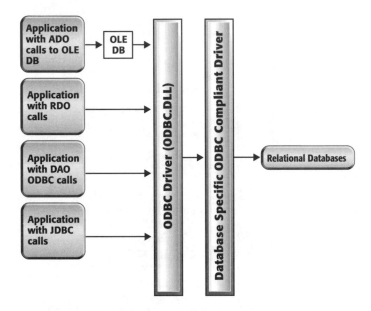

Figure 22-3: ODBC is designed to connect to a wide variety of relational databases.

OLE DB Versus ODBC

ODBC is in widespread use, whereas OLE DB is new and has only a few drivers written for it, so far. Although Microsoft currently denies it, it seems that ODBC and OLE DB are somewhat duplicative. The rumor mill has it that Microsoft is trying to phase ODBC out of the picture. With roots going back to Windows 3.0, and even before, one might understand why a new OLE DB standard is in order. However, Microsoft would make vendors angry if they announced now that ODBC is no longer desirable. These vendors have listened to Microsoft in the past and spent a lot of time and money on ODBC driver development. Still, if you had to pick a current technology to use, I would choose OLE DB and leave ODBC behind.

Using the ODBC Data Source Administrator

To get into the ODBC Data Source Administrator, click the ODBC icon in your control panel. You get to the control panel by clicking Settings, Control Panel on your Windows task bar Start button. The ODBC Data Source Administrator opens with the User DSN tab, which lists all databases currently using ODBC (Figure 22-4).

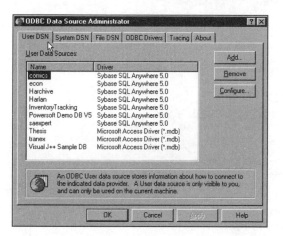

Figure 22-4: The ODBC Data Source Administrator

Secret

The User DSN tab lists the databases currently assigned to your user. If there are multiple *logged on* users in your Windows 95 system, your databases are accessible by you and no other users unless they configure them. System DSN and File DSN tabs enable you to add databases at a system-wide level.

If you click the ODBC Drivers tab, you see all the ODBC database drivers currently installed on your system, as seen in Figure 22-5. You are not allowed to delete these drivers or add new drivers through the ODBC Data Source Administrator. This must be done using your installation disk.

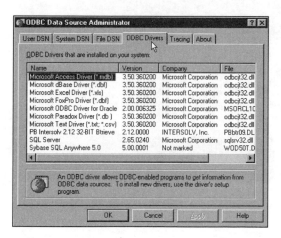

Figure 22-5: The ODBC Drivers tab of the ODBC Data Source Administrator lists all database drivers installed on your system.

Create a new ODBC data source by clicking User DSN | Add (shown in Figure 22-4) to open the Create New Data Source dialog box, as shown in Figure 22-6. Choose the type of database you want to create and then click Finish. For this sample, I used the Microsoft Access driver to access the Sample Database installed with the RDO Sample at the beginning of this chapter.

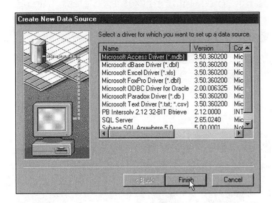

Figure 22-6: The Create New Data Source dialog box enables you to create a new database or assign an existing database to an ODBC DSN name.

If you picked Microsoft Access as your driver, the ODBC Microsoft Access 97 Setup dialog box opens, as shown in Figure 22-7. Click Select to assign an ODBC DSN name to an existing Access database.

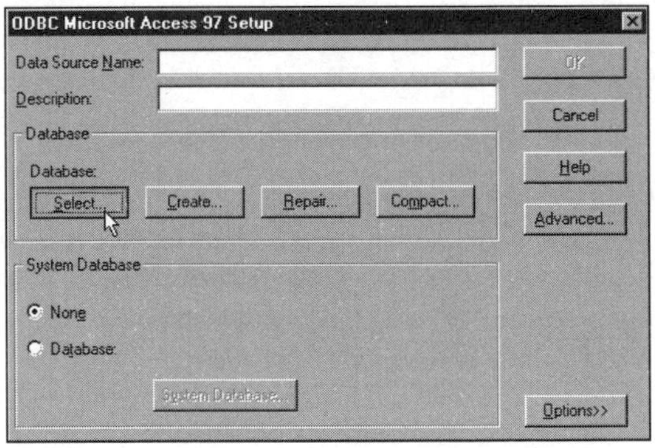

Figure 22-7: The ODBC Microsoft Access 97 Setup dialog box enables you to create or set up an Access database for ODBC.

Now use the Select Database dialog box, shown in Figure 22-7, to find the database you want to set up for ODBC. In Figure 22-8, I attached to the Sample Database found in the RDO Sample folder that I created.

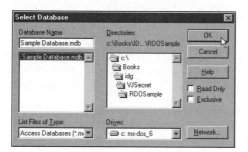

Figure 22-8: The Select Database dialog box is used to select an Access database for ODBC configuration.

When you return to the ODBC Microsoft Access 97 Setup dialog box, you see the selected database placed in the Database GroupBox—Figure 22-9. Enter a data source name, enter a description of the database, and click OK.

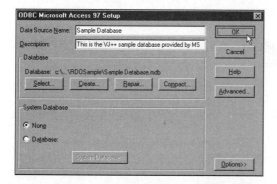

Figure 22-9: The database you selected appears in the ODBC Microsoft Access 97 Setup dialog box.

When you return to the ODBC Data Source Administrator, the database you configured is shown in the User DSN tab (Figure 22-10).

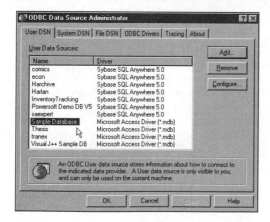

Figure 22-10: All additional databases are added to the list of databases on the User DSN tab of the ODBC Data Source Administrator.

Mastering the Registry

The Registry is a database used in Windows NT and Windows 95 to store configuration information about the programs that are currently installed on your system. When you run the ODBC administrator, the ODBC administrator updates the Registry.

You can modify the Registry to configure your ODBC database. Although this is not as easy as using the ODBC Data Source Administrator, the Registry enables you to remove database engines from your system. You can also view how ODBC is set up, from a system standpoint, by viewing the Registry.

Secret

Editing the Registry to alter your system can be dangerous. If you have never modified the Registry, you may want to pick up a Windows 95 or Windows NT book and read about it. Check out *Optimizing™ The Windows Registry*, by Kathy Ivens, published by IDG Books Worldwide.

To open the Registry editor, run `Regedit.exe` from the task bar. This opens the Registry Editor. The ODBC databases installed are listed in `HKEY_LOCAL_MACHINE\SOFTWARE\ODBC\ODBCINST.INI\ODBC DRIVERS`. This is shown in Figure 22-11. There, you can see all the ODBC drivers that various packages have installed.

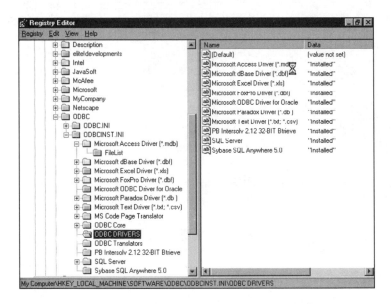

Figure 22-11: The ODBCINST.INI key contains a list of all ODBC drivers.

If you click a specific driver inside the ODBCINST.INI key, you see the drivers needed to run the database and set up a new database entry, as shown in Figure 22-12.

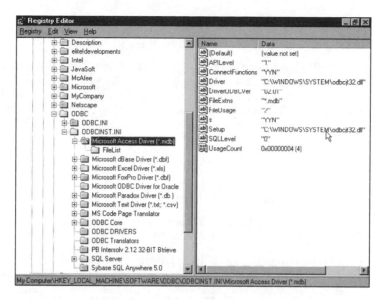

Figure 22-12: The Microsoft Access Driver key enables you to see the defaults assigned to all new Access databases.

Additionally, some drivers (such as Microsoft Access) give you a file list showing the files needed for ODBC access and which files are included, as shown in Figure 22-13.

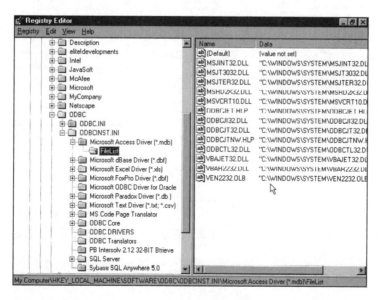

Figure 22-13: A file list is a good way for a software manufacturer to communicate to the user and user applications which files are included with a driver.

To remove a database driver by manually editing the Registry:

1. *Make a backup!* This enables you to undo what you do.

2. Delete all relevant drivers from your hard drive. These include the files listed in the Driver and Setup areas, as well as any files in the FileList. Note that some drivers can call other executables, ActiveX modules, or dynamic link libraries (DLLs); you may want to research which files are included with your driver.

3. Remove the key folder from the `ODBCINST.INI` key by clicking the folder you want to remove and pressing Delete.

4. Remove the name of the database driver from the ODBC DRIVERS key by highlighting the name of the driver and pressing Delete.

5. Search the Registry for any references to the deleted ODBC driver and either delete them or change them to an appropriate driver.

All user database information is found in the `HKEY_CURRENT_USER\Software\ODBC\ODBC.INI` key. Here you see a list of all databases currently configured in ODBC. To see all the databases configured on your system and their database type, click ODBC Data Sources, as shown in Figure 22-14.

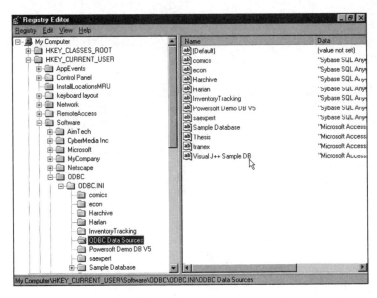

Figure 22-14: The ODBC.INI key lists all the databases installed on your system.

By clicking a database in the ODBC.INI folder, you see which drivers, directories, and files are used for that particular database, as shown in Figure 22-15.

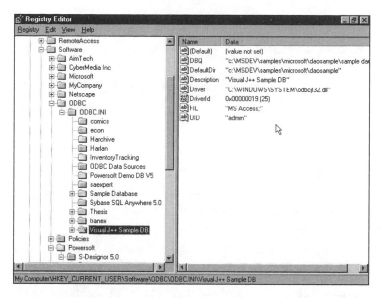

Figure 22-15: Each ODBC database has a key that describes files and drivers associated with that database.

The ODBC Registry is how programs, including the ODBC Data Source Administrator, access your ODBC database information.

Secret

Don't try to remove a database using the Registry. Use the ODBC Data Source Administrator instead. It is both safer and easier.

The Perils of Modifying the Registry

When my *extremely competent and knowledgeable* technical editor and coauthor, Gene Olafsen, read my comments on the Registry, he said, "This stuff is very dangerous." Well, he's correct. Whenever you modify the Registry, you run the risk of making one or more programs completely inoperable or causing your Windows Environment to lock up. When this happens, there is little you can do to fix your problems.

If messing around with the Windows Registry is new to you, you should pick up a copy of *Optimizing™ The Windows Registry* (by Kathy Ivens and published by IDG Books Worldwide). Read it cover to cover to find out ways you can back up your Registry, restore an old Registry if the changes you made have caused a mess, or even to discover the bad things that can happen to you if you make a mistake while updating your Registry.

Visual Database Tools

Visual Studio includes two visual database tools to help manage your database:

- Data View connects to and explores any ODBC or OLE DB database.
- SQL Query Designer designs, executes, and saves complex SQL statements.

Data View

Data View enables developers to examine all databases used in a project and to integrate database objects into an application quickly and easily. Developers can use Data View to:

- View table structures
- View database views
- View and change the actual data in a convenient database grid

SQL Query Designer

The SQL Query Designer is similar to the Microsoft Access Query designer. With the SQL Query Designer, developers can visually create, execute, and test SQL statements. The SQL Query Designer automatically recognizes database relationships and automatically generates appropriate join conditions. As with Microsoft Access, developers can work with a diagram, grid, or directly with SQL statements using SQL Query Designer.

The Application Wizard

Visual J++ contains drag-and-drop controls that enable developers to paint data sources onto a window visually. By dragging the ADO Binding Component to the Visual Form Designer, developers can customize the component's access to any available data source. Additionally, Visual J++ uses the Application Wizard to create Visual J++ database programs dynamically.

The Application Wizard provides a systematic way to create a WFC/ADO Windows application. Various features can be selected while using the wizard, which can add capabilities to the application the wizard generates. The wizard generates all code and forms needed to produce a working Notepad-style application. Once the wizard is complete, you can modify the application to fit the needs of your project. When the wizard has completed its process, a report can be displayed that provides helpful suggestions on features you can add or change in the wizard's output project.

You can use the Application Wizard to develop a full-featured database application in mere minutes. Choose File | New Project from the Visual J++ menu, as was done in Chapter 1. Then click Application Wizard | Open. This opens the VJ98 Application Wizard, as shown in Figure 22-16.

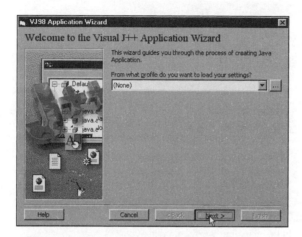

Figure 22-16: The VJ98 Application Wizard is the key to developing quick database applications.

Click Next to choose your type of application. You want database access, therefore, be sure to click Form Based Application with Data, as shown in Figure 22-17.

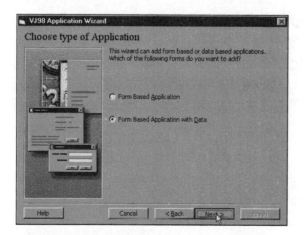

Figure 22-17: The VJ98 Application Wizard enables you to choose the type of application to build.

Next, you see a list of database types, as shown in Figure 22-18. These are the OLE DB database types defined in your Windows environment. For access to ODBC database drivers, click ODBC.

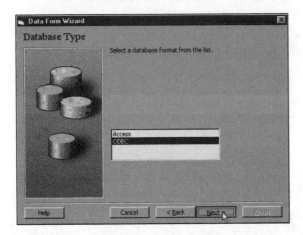

Figure 22-18: The VJ98 Application Wizard enables you to select any OLE DB driver as a data source, including all ODBC drivers.

Select your database using the Connect Information dialog box shown in Figure 22-19. In this dialog box, you also enter any other connection information that you need to connect to your data source.

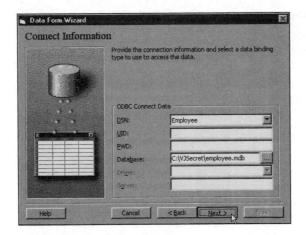

Figure 22-19: The ODBC data source name and the database table can be entered in the Connect Information dialog box.

Click Next to open the Form dialog box. This dialog box enables you to name your Java application (in the Form name text box) and also to choose which Form layout you wish to use, as shown in Figure 22-20.

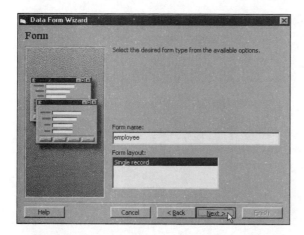

Figure 22-20: The Form dialog box enables you to name your Java application and to define the style of form you wish to use.

Click Next to open the Record Source dialog box. Here you can define the fields you want on your Form, as shown in Figure 22-21.

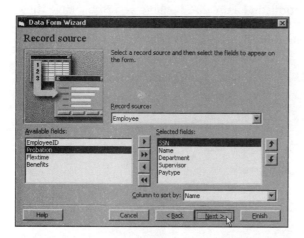

Figure 22-21: The Record Source dialog box enables you to define what columns appear in your Form window.

Click Next to open the Control Selection dialog box—Figure 22-22. Using the Control Selection dialog box, choose which controls to place on your new window.

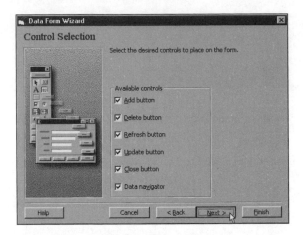

Figure 22-22: The Control Selection dialog box enables you to select the functionality of your new database window.

Secret

The Data Navigator is a scroll bar that appears at the bottom of your form that enables you to click to the next record, the previous record, the first record, or the last record.

The packaging options in Figure 22-23 enable you to package the class you have created as a normal Java class file, as a Windows EXE file, or as a compressed Cabinet file.

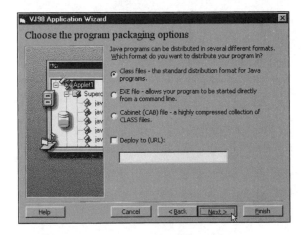

Figure 22-23: The VJ98 Application Wizard enables you to define the packaging you are using.

From here, click Finish, or click Next to view a report containing your selection before finishing. When you return to the Visual J++ development environment, you should see a form containing your fields, as shown in Figure 22-24.

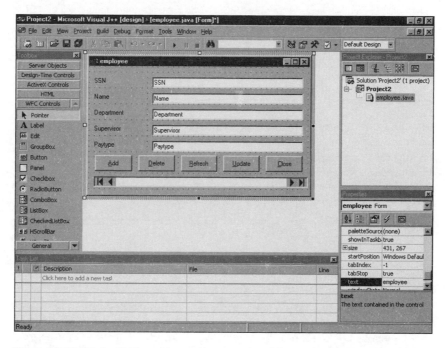

Figure 22-24: All the fields and interaction are painted for you by the VJ98 Application Wizard.

When you run this program, you see a full-featured database application that gives you complete and easy-to-use table functionality, as shown in Figure 22-25.

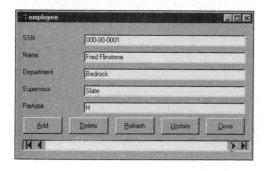

Figure 22-25: Database applications are a breeze with the VJ98 Application Wizard.

Notice that no code modification is needed. In the next chapter, you see how to code ADO to suit your programming needs.

Whatever Happened to DAO and RDO?

ADO has replaced DAO and RDO. However, some DAO and RDO code still exists. Furthermore, RDO may be more efficient than OLE DB at accessing ODBC databases and is included as an optional component in Visual Studio. Both DAO and RDO are discussed in Chapters 26 and 27 later in this part of the book.

What About JDBC?

The Visual J++ developer is faced with this dilemma: code the way Microsoft wants and run on a Windows platform, or code the way Sun wants and run on multiple platforms. For those developers who want to write for multiple platforms, Visual J++ can also access ODBC through JDBC instead of ADO. In Chapter 28, JDBC is explored.

Summary

Visual J++ has raised the bar on easy database development. The SQL Query Designer, ADO, and the visual database tools included with Visual J++ make Visual J++ an extremely powerful tool for client-server, database development.

- ADO is the Microsoft database development tool of choice.

- Microsoft includes visual database development tools that enable the developer to paint ADO functionality on the window.

- DAO and RDO can still be used to connect to a database; however, new Windows development should be done in ADO.

- If you need a pure Java implementation for multiplatform access, try JDBC instead of ADO.

Chapter 23

Complex ActiveX Data Objects

In This Chapter

▶ Programming ActiveX Data Objects (without painters)

▶ Writing a database class library

▶ Discovering why you might need to leave the painter behind someday

You learned how to write *real easy*, *real quick* database applications using Visual J++'s Application Wizard in the last chapter. This chapter describes how to code for the Visual J++ ActiveX Data Objects (ADO) library, and why you may have to leave the painter behind someday. At the end of the chapter, an ADO database library is developed that might be much easier to use than the Application Wizard.

The Importance of Database Coding

The Visual J++ Application Wizard makes simple database programming easy. However, you eventually run into two problems while developing your Visual J++ applications:

■ The application painter can't handle complex database operations. To handle these inside a Visual J++ program, you need a better understanding of ADO programming.

■ Notice how the form in Figure 23-1 differs from the form in the last chapter (Figure 22-25). Some of these features, such as radio buttons that are connected to the database, are simply unavailable without additional ADO code.

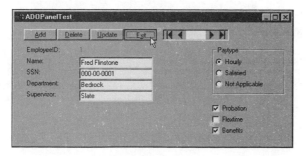

Figure 23-1: This form has features unavailable using the application painter.

Innovative screen formatting and component binding to a database are necessary for truly advanced database applications.

If a user wants *all database windows* to look similar to that in Figure 23-1, and you are using the painter exclusively, you might tell them that this cannot be done. Even if you know how to code ADO calls, you may be tempted to refuse your user on the grounds that the painter is *so* easy, and coding is so time-consuming and difficult.

The Importance of Class Libraries

Consider a different scenario. You are on a 70-person development team. Each developer is well-versed in using the Visual J++ Application Wizard. Each developer paints the windows their own way. This situation has several problems:

- Each user sees (and must learn) a new user interface for each different developer's windows. This involves a steep training curve.

- Java is an object-oriented language. Object-oriented languages stress the concept of reusable code. With the previous scenario, there is *no* reusability (other than painter reusability). The new code that is generated and run is different from all other code *that mostly does the same things*. Furthermore, each developer must repaint each window every time, even if the windows — or even the database and tables — are identical to other code.

- Managers and systems analysts have no control over standards. Standards can be defined, but cannot be enforced without viewing each program separately.

Most developers reading this book are motivated and hard-working. However, for the rest of us lazy programmers, who don't want a lot of work, developing new systems from scratch (even with an easy-to-use painter) is a real pain.

An alternative to repainting every time is the use of class libraries. Class libraries consist of a set of generalized routines that often make programming easier than using a painter. Class libraries enable reuse of existing classes, enforce standards, and standardize modules for easy training.

ADO Programming

ADO programming involves making calls to the ADO class library. The ADO library is set up in a hierarchical fashion so that you can "drill down" through the database to find the data you want. This section describes the ADO structure, ADO record sets, and ADO fields.

ADO structure

Figure 23-2 shows how ADO is configured. For Java purposes, each ADO connection has the following:

- The errors collection object collects all ADO errors. If several errors occur at once, the Errors collection can be used to track them. Usually, however, you trap ADO errors the same way you do with traditional Java: the `try-catch-finally` block.

- Each Recordset is formed by executing some SQL through the ADO modules.

- Each Recordset contains a Fields collection that, in turn, contains several Field objects. These Field objects contain information about database fields that have been retrieved — including data type, length, and stored value.

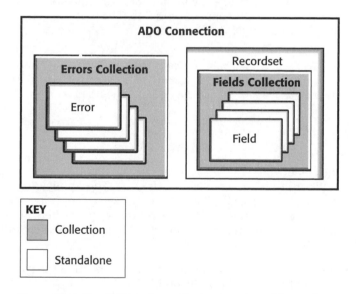

Figure 23-2: The ADO interface with Java consists of four major categories: Connections, Recordsets, Fields, and Errors.

ADO errors

In Java, you never need to worry about the Errors collection. Java's `try-catch-finally` block is all you need to handle ADO exceptions:

```
try {
  rs_records.close();        //Close the recordset
  con_dbConnection.close();     //Close the DB Connection
}
catch (Exception e) {
  handleADOException( e );
}
```

Exceptions are easier and faster than using ADO calls to see if there is an error. The following error-reporting method prints an error message using the WFC MessageBox class:

```
void handleADOException(Exception e) {   //Print an error message
  e.printStackTrace();
  MessageBox.show( e.toString());
}
```

ADO connections

Before you access an ADO database, you must first establish a connection to the database. This is done through a Connection constructor:

```
//Make a new OLE DBconnection
  Connection con_dbConnection = new Connection();
```

After a connection is constructed, you must describe the connection you wish to use. Often, an ODBC connection is fine. The following string can be used to connect to a local ODBC database:

```
//Set the connect string
  String s_database = "EmpDB";  //ODBC Database
  con_dbConnection.setConnectionString (
    "Provider=MSDASQL;"+ //Use the OLE DB provider for an ODBC
connection
    "UID=admin;" +        //Set the user id
    "PWD=;" +          //Set the password
    "DSN=" + s_database);  //Set the database name
```

Secret

If you're stuck on how to connect to your OLE DB database, try using the Application Wizard to make a connection for you. The Application Wizard builds a valid call to your OLE DB database. (However, that's not how the preceding code was developed — it was written, not generated. Some of the Application Wizard connections tied my ODBC database to Microsoft Access, which is something I didn't necessarily want.)

Microsoft recommends that you set up the cursor location for your database. Your options are shown in Table 23-1.

Table 23-1	Cursor Locations
Cursor Constant	*Description*
AdoEnums.CursorLocation.CLIENT	The database cursor is controlled from the client machine.
AdoEnums.CursorLocation.SERVER	The database cursor is controlled from the server machine.
AdoEnums.CursorLocation.NONE	Uses the default cursor control from the database.

Where Do You Get All the Constants?

With any package or library, a set of constants are required for various functions inside the package. ADO is no different. The AdoEnums package contains most of the constants you need to use throughout ADO access. You can use Visual J++'s popup tips to see the valid constant classes (such as CursorLocation, as shown in Figure 23-3) and the valid constants for each class.

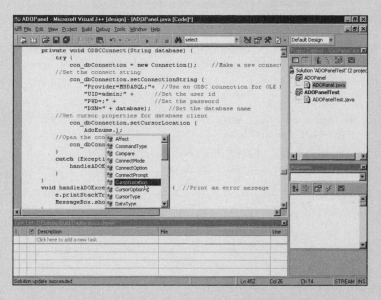

Figure 23-3: Visual J++'s popup tips can help determine the valid constant values when viewing the AdoEnums package.

For example, to control the cursor from the client machine, use the following connection option:

```
//Set cursor properties for database client
con_dbConnection.setCursorLocation
(AdoEnums.CursorLocation.CLIENT);
```

When all your connection options have been set, open the database connection:

```
con_dbConnection.open();  //Open the connection
```

Secret

Be sure to close your database connection when you finish using your database. Java can clean up after itself, but ADO runs through ActiveX and can't be garbage-collected through Java. You need to tell the ADO ActiveX routines that you want the connection closed:

```
con_dbConnection.close();  //Close the DB Connection
```

The major functionality that connections provide is to execute SQL statements against a database. To execute a single command with no return values, use the `RecordSet.execute` method:

```
con_dbConnection.execute(SQLStatement);
```

The `execute` method executes a single SQL statement. If a return value is needed, as with SELECT statements, then Recordsets must be used.

Recordsets

To return data to a program from a database, you need a Recordset. A *Recordset* is a group of records or rows that have been retrieved by accessing a database. To use a Recordset, you need to go through the following steps:

1. To create an empty Recordset, you can construct it, as you may have guessed:

   ```
   //Construct the new record set
     Recordset rs_records = new Recordset();
   ```

2. After constructing a Recordset, associate it with an open connection:

   ```
   //Attach the record set to the db connection
     rs_records.setActiveConnection(con_dbConnection);
   ```

3. Then pass a SQL statement (usually a SELECT statement) to the Recordset using the `setSource` method:

   ```
   //Tell the recordset to execute the SQL statement
     rs_records.setSource(SQLStatement);
   ```

4. Next, set all the parameters for cursor type and location, as well as locking preference:

   ```
   //Set the cursor information for the SQL
     rs_records.setCursorType(AdoEnums.CursorType.STATIC);
     rs_records.setCursorLocation(AdoEnums.CursorLocation.CLIENT);
   //Use optimistic locking so others can access the data
     rs_records.setLockType(AdoEnums.LockType.OPTIMISTIC);
   ```

5. Finally, use the `Recordset.open()` method to execute the SQL and form the Recordset from the results:

   ```
   //Now do the query and return the information into the
   recordset
     rs_records.open();
   ```

From here, you can use ADO functionality to navigate through the Recordset and update the records on the Recordset in the database.

Secret

Just as you needed to close the database connection when you were finished, you also need to tell the ADO ActiveX routines that you want the Recordset closed:

```
rs_records.close();    //Close the recordset
```

If you don't close the Recordset, the record set may remain open even after the database connection is closed.

Retrieving Recordset information

You can use two methods to determine the record count:

- The `Recordset.getRecordCount()` method returns the number of records in a query used in the connection object.

- The `Recordset.getAbsolutePosition()` method returns the current record number in a record set.

By combining the preceding features, you can display how many rows are in a Recordset, and the number of the current database cursor position.

Navigating through a Recordset

You can position the Recordset pointer to any record in the Recordset. The `moveFirst` method is needed to initialize the Recordset to the first record:

```
//Go to the first record
  rs_records.moveFirst();
```

Table 23-2 shows the methods that are available for navigating through a Recordset.

Table 23-2   Recordset Navigation Methods

Navigation Method	Description
Recordset.move(int)	Moves the Recordset pointer to a specific record in the Recordset.
Recordset.moveFirst()	Moves the Recordset pointer to the first record in the Recordset.
Recordset.moveNext()	Moves the Recordset pointer to the next record in the Recordset.
Recordset.movePrevious()	Moves the Recordset pointer to the previous record in the Recordset.
Recordset.moveLast()	Moves the Recordset pointer to the last record in the Recordset.

Secret

Most WFC/ADO developers do not bother with the Recordset navigation commands except for the initial `Recordset.moveFirst` method. Instead, a DataNavigator control is used. DataNavigators enable the user to graphically control navigation through a Recordset. The two steps for initializing a DataNavigator are as follows:

1. Construct a DataNavigator:

   ```
   private DataNavigator dn_navigator = new DataNavigator();
   ```

2. Link to the Recordset using the `setDataSource` method call:

   ```
   //Set the data navigator to be linked to the recordset
       dn_navigator.setDataSource(rs_records);
   ```

DataNavigators do a lot of work in terms of normal database row navigation (i.e., going to the first row, going to the next or previous row, or going to the last row). Used properly, DataNavigators can drastically reduce development time.

Manipulating the database with Recordset functions

A Recordset can change a database in three ways:

- New records are added to the Recordset that, in turn, are added to the database.

- Existing records are updated with new information found in a Recordset.

- Recordset records are deleted, which causes the corresponding database row to be deleted as well.

Changes are made to a Recordset by adding or changing Field values. (This is discussed later in this chapter.) To update a Recordset with the new values that you've placed in it, use the `Recordset.update()` method:

```
rs_records.update();   //Save changes to the record set.
```

To add a new row or record to a database, first add a new record to the Recordset using the `Recordset.addNew` method:

```
rs_records.addNew();   //insert a blank into the record set
```

After adding a new record and placing new values in the Recordset Fields (discussed later in this chapter), call the `Recordset.update()` method to add the new record to the database.

Deletes are trickier. If a `Recordset.addNew` method is issued and the database has not yet been updated, then cancel the `add` with the `Recordset.cancelUpdate` method. If a new record is not being updated, you probably should do three things:

1. Delete the database record corresponding to the current Recordset record.

2. Move to the next record.

3. If the move to the next record fails, move to the last record in the
   Recordset.

This process can be seen in the following code:

```
if( b_adding ) {  //Just don't add if an add is in progress
  rs_records.cancelUpdate();
  b_adding = false;
}
else {     //An add is not in progress
  rs_records.delete(AdoEnums.Affect.CURRENT);
  rs_records.moveNext();    //Go to the next or last record
  if(rs_records.getEOF()) {
    rs_records.moveLast();
  }
}
```

Fields

All the fields in a Recordset are contained in a Fields container class. This
class is retrieved using the `Recordset.getFields()` method:

```
//Get the fields of the record set
Fields fs_fields = rs_records.getFields();
```

After forming the Fields class, you can retrieve information about the fields
or retrieve individual fields. To see how many fields you have in your Fields
class, use the `Fields.getCount()` method:

```
i_numberFields = fs_fields.getCount();  //Count the fields
```

To retrieve an individual Field from the Fields class, use the
`Fields.getItem(int)` method:

```
Field f = fs_fields.getItem(0);  //Retrieve Field #0
```

Each Field in a Fields class is numbered starting from zero, just like arrays.
To scroll through the fields, use the following `for` loop:

```
for (int counter = 0; counter < i_numberFields; counter++) {
      //Retrieve Field counter+1
  Field f = fs_fields.getItem(counter);
  //Continue with processing. . .
}
```

The Field class has many methods that can be used to retrieve information
about the Field. The most common methods are shown in Table 23-3.

Table 23-3 Field Methods	
Field method	*Return value*
Field.getName()	A string containing the name of the Field.
Field.getDefinedSize()	An integer containing the size of the Field.
Field.getType()	An integer that defines the Field's data type.
Field.getAttributes()	An integer that describes all the Field's attributes.

Data types

As shown in Table 23-3, the Field.getType() method returns the data type of a field:

```
Fields fs_fields = rs_recordset.getFields();
Field fld_first = fs_fields.getItem(0);
int columnType = fld_first.getType( );
```

The columnType variable is an integer that contains the fld_first data type. It can take one of the values listed in Table 23-4.

Table 23-4 Field Data Types		
ADOEnums. DataType Value	*Retrieval Field Function*	*Description*
AdoEnums.DataType. BIGINT	Field.getLong()	BIGINT fields contain an 8-byte signed integer. BIGINT fields can be placed inside long variables.
AdoEnums.DataType. BINARY	Field.getBytes()	BINARY fields can be placed in byte arrays. Don't confuse with CHAR, which is a String.
AdoEnums.DataType. BOOLEAN	Field.getBoolean()	BOOLEAN fields can be placed in a boolean variable.
AdoEnums.DataType. BIGSTR	Field.getString()	BIGSTR fields can be placed in Strings.
AdoEnums.DataType. CHAPTER	Field.getInt()	CHAPTER fields can be placed inside int variables.
AdoEnums.DataType. CHAR	Field.getString()	CHAR fields can be placed in Strings.
AdoEnums.DataType. CURRENCY	Field.getDouble()	Several databases, such as Access, support a currency data type. CURRENCY fields can be placed inside double variables.

ADOEnums. *DataType Value*	*Retrieval Field* *Function*	*Description*
AdoEnums.DataType. DATE	Field.getDouble()	A DATE is a time stamp that is stored as a double. The whole part is the number of days since December 30, 1899, and the fractional part is the fraction of a day.
AdoEnums.DataType. DBDATE	Field.getString()	A DBDATE value is a date field whose value is stored in an YYYYMMDD format.
AdoEnums.DataType. DBTIME	Field.getString()	A DBTIME value is a time field whose value is stored in a HHMMSS format.
AdoEnums.DataType. DBTIMESTAMP	Field.getString()	A DBTIMESTAMP value is a time stamp field whose value is stored in a YYYYMMDDHHMMSSFFFFFF format.
AdoEnums.DataType. DECIMAL	Field.getDouble()	DECIMAL fields can be stored inside double variables.
AdoEnums.DataType. DOUBLE	Field.getDouble()	DOUBLE fields can be stored inside double variables.
AdoEnums.DataType. EMPTY	Field.getClass()	EMPTY fields contain null values.
AdoEnums.DataType. ERROR	Field.getClass()	ERROR fields are used to store database errors. Most databases don't have these, and you probably don't need to trap for these field types.
AdoEnums.DataType. GUID	Field.getClass()	A GUID field contains OLE information. Only Microsoft databases contain these fields, and you probably don't need to worry about them inside your Visual J++ application.
AdoEnums.DataType. IDISPATCH	Field.getClass()	An IDISPATCH interface is used for an OLE IDispatch COM interface, and probably isn't used, especially inside a Visual J++ environment.
AdoEnums.DataType. INTEGER	Field.getInt()	An INTEGER field is a 4-byte signed integer and can be placed inside an INT field.

(continued)

Table 23-4 *(Continued)*

ADOEnums. DataType Value	Retrieval Field Function	Description
AdoEnums.DataType. IUNKNOWN	Field.getClass()	An IUNKNOWN interface is used to indicate an OLE unspecified interface, and probably isn't used, especially inside a Visual J++ environment.
AdoEnums.DataType. LONGVARBINARY	Field.getByteChunk()	LONGVARBINARY fields can be placed in byte arrays. This should not be confused with CHAR, which is a String.
AdoEnums.DataType. LONGVARCHAR	Field.getCharChunk()	LONGVARCHAR fields can be placed in Strings.
AdoEnums.DataType. LONGVARWCHAR	Field.getCharChunk()	LONGVARWCHAR fields can be placed in Strings.
AdoEnums.DataType. NUMERIC	Field.getDouble()	NUMERIC fields can be stored inside double variables.
AdoEnums.DataType. SINGLE	Field.getFloat()	SINGLE fields can be stored inside float variables.
AdoEnums.DataType. SMALLINT	Field.getShort()	A SMALLINT is a 2-byte signed integer. It can be placed in a short variable.
AdoEnums.DataType. TINYINT	Field.getByte()	A TINYINT is a 1-byte signed integer. It can be placed in a byte variable.
AdoEnums.DataType. UNSIGNEDBIGINT	Field.getLong()	Java does not support unsigned data types. An UNSIGNEDBIGINT can be stored inside a long variable, but special twos-complement logic is needed to convert the unsigned long to a signed double.
AdoEnums.DataType. UNSIGNEDINT	Field.getInt()	An UNSIGNEDINT can be stored inside an int variable, but special twos-complement logic is needed to convert the unsigned int to a signed long.
AdoEnums.DataType. UNSIGNEDSMALLINT	Field.getShort()	An UNSIGNEDSMALLINT can be stored inside a short variable, but special twos-complement logic is needed to convert the unsigned short to a signed int.

ADOEnums. DataType Value	Retrieval Field Function	Description
AdoEnums.DataType. UNSIGNEDTINYINT	Field.getByte()	An UNSIGNEDTINYINT is a 1-byte signed integer. It can be placed in a byte variable. The sign usually does not matter when using a byte variable.
AdoEnums.DataType. USERDEFINED	Field.getClass()	Some databases enable the user to define unique field data types. There is no way to trap for these inside a Visual J++ program unless you know exactly how to handle each user-defined data type.
AdoEnums.DataType. VARBINARY	Field.getBytes()	VARBINARY fields can be placed in byte arrays. This should not be confused with CHAR, which is a String.
AdoEnums.DataType. VARCHAR	Field.getString()	VARCHAR fields can be placed in Strings.
AdoEnums.DataType. VARIANT	Field.getClass()	Microsoft databases support Variants. A Variant is a Microsoft data type construct that enables any data type to be placed inside it. VARIANT types can be placed inside a com.ms.com.Variant object.
AdoEnums.DataType. VARWCHAR	Field.getString()	VARWCHAR fields can be placed in Strings.
AdoEnums.DataType. WCHAR	Field.getString()	WCHAR fields can be placed in Strings.

Secret

The getXxx methods shown in Table 23-4 have corresponding setXxx methods that enable you to update fields on the database. For instance, the Field.getString() method returns a String that corresponds to the value in a Field. Similarly, the Field.setString(String newValue) method can set a value in the database. The getXxx and setXxx methods are not used too much with ADO, because data binding (discussed later in this chapter) describes an easier and more elegant way to update Field information.

The following code shows how to use these types in a program:

```
Fields fs_fields = rs_recordset.getFields();
Field fld_first = fs_fields.getItem(0);
int columnType = fld_first.getType( );
boolean b_value;
String s_value;
```

```
int i_value
switch (columnType) {
  case AdoEnums.DataType.BOOLEAN :
    b_value = getBoolean();
    break;
  case AdoEnums.DataType.CHAR:
  case AdoEnums.DataType.VARCHAR:
    s_value = getString();
    break;
  case AdoEnums.DataType.INTEGER:
    i_value = getInt();
    break;
  default:
    MessageBox.show("Cannot handle this data type");
}
```

Field attributes

Field attributes are probably the most nonintuitive part of ADO. Table 23-5 shows the ADO field attributes.

Table 23-5   ADO Field Attributes

Field Attribute	Description
AdoEnums.FieldAttribute.CACHEDEFERRED	Indicates that the provider caches field values; subsequent reads are done from the cache.
AdoEnums.FieldAttribute.FIXED	Indicates that the field contains fixed-length data.
AdoEnums.FieldAttribute.ISNULLABLE	Indicates that the field accepts null values.
AdoEnums.FieldAttribute.LONG	Indicates that the field is a long binary field. It also indicates that you can use the AppendChunk and GetChunk methods.
AdoEnums.FieldAttribute.MAYBENULL	Indicates that you can read null values from the field.
AdoEnums.FieldAttribute.MAYDEFER	Indicates that the field is deferred — that is, the field values are not retrieved from the data source with the whole record, but only when you explicitly access them.
AdoEnums.FieldAttribute.ROWID	Indicates that the field contains a persistent row identifier that cannot be written to and has no meaningful value except to identify the row (such as a record number, unique identifier, and so forth).
AdoEnums.FieldAttribute.ROWVERSION	Indicates that the field contains some kind of time or date stamp used to track updates.
AdoEnums.FieldAttribute.UNKNOWNUPDATABLE	Indicates that the provider cannot determine if you can write to the field.

Field Attribute	Description
AdoEnums.FieldAttribute. UNSPECIFIED	Indicates that an unspecified attribute has been assigned to the field. It's not that useful in Visual J++.
AdoEnums.FieldAttribute. UPDATABLE	Indicates that you can write to the field. This attribute is handy for testing auto-increment fields.

Secret

The integer returned is the sum of all these attributes. Each sum represents a unique combination of attributes. The best way to test for an attribute is to retrieve the attribute with the `Field.getAttributes()` method and then logically bitwise AND? that field with the attribute you want to test. A zero value of the bitwise AND operation indicates that the attribute is not present on the field. For instance, the following code:

```
/*
Use UPDATEABLE bitwise anded with attributes to determine if you can
update a column, or if you cannot. (for example, an autoincrement
field cannot be updated.)
*/
int updatable = AdoEnums.FieldAttribute.UPDATABLE  &
f.getAttributes();
if (updatable == 0) {  //. . . This field is not updatable.  It's
probably autoincrement.
```

tests if a field is updatable or not.

Data binding

Most database packages make you load database values to and from the user window in order for the user to retrieve and update the field. ADO and WFC have simplified this with a process known as data binding. *Data binding* is the act of binding a column to a given WFC Edit or Checkbox so that changes made to the Edit or Checkbox are reflected in the ADO Recordset, and changes in the ADO Recordset are reflected in the Edit or Checkbox. If a new row is made active in a Recordset, the bound controls are updated automatically. When the value of an Edit or Checkbox changes and the Recordset is updated, the values of the bound controls are automatically updated in the database as well.

Data binding saves *a ton* of time when doing database programming. The following code creates a DataBinder and assigns it to a Recordset. It adds binding to update an edit field based on the value of columnName1, and updates a Checkbox based on the value of columnName2:

```
//A DataBinder is used to bind a record set to some WFC columns
//Set the data binder to be linked to the record set
  DataBinder db_binder = new DataBinder(rs_records);
//Bind the ed Edit to columnName1
  db_binder.addBinding( ed, "Text", columnName1);
//Bind the cbx Checkbox to columnName2
  db_binder.addBinding(cbx, "Checked", columnName2);
```

The ADO Class Library

Now you have enough information to build an ADO class library. The goal of this class library is to develop database applications *faster and better* than ever could be developed using the painter. There are three steps to building such a powerful, yet generic, class library:

1. Determine the Labels to use with your database.

2. Determine the Control types to use with your database.

3. Make WFC controls that match your Labels and Edits.

The goal of this class library is to generate, automatically, a WFC panel containing links to an ODBC database and table. The only parameters you want to use are the name of the database and the name of the table. The only lines of code you want to change are the database name and the table name, as shown in boldface in Listing 23-1. (The other boldface area is where the developer declares database fields to be radio buttons.)

Listing 23-1: ADOPanelTest.java

```
import wfc.app.*;
import wfc.core.*;
import wfc.ui.*;
public class ADOPanelTest extends Form {
  public static void main(String args[]) {
    Application.run(new ADOPanelTest());
  }
  public ADOPanelTest() {
  // Now add all the Employee ADOPanel to the form
    String DBName = "EmpDB";
    String tableName = "Employee";
    int numberOfColumns = 2;
  //Make a new ADOPanel with the database, table, and
  //(optionally) the number of columns you want to display.
    ADOPanel adop_employee = new ADOPanel(DBName, tableName,
                  numberOfColumns);
  //Set radio buttons for paytype (optional)
    String s_paytypeDisplay[] = {"Hourly", "Salaried",
        "Not Applicable"};
    String s_paytypeValues[] = {"H", "S", "N"};
    adop_employee.setChoices("Paytype",s_paytypeDisplay,
s_paytypeValues);
  //Now form the ADOPanel
    adop_employee.formPanel();
  //Do the form stuff
    setBackColor(Color.CONTROL);    // set the Form color
    setLocation(new Point(0, 0));   // set the Form location
    setTabIndex(-1);                // Forms don't need a tab stop
    setTabStop(false);              // No need to stop on the form
    setAutoScaleBaseSize(13); // sets the resize formatting
    int width = adop_employee.getSuggestedWidth();
```

```
    int height = adop_employee.getSuggestedHeight();
    setSize (new Point(width+7, height+27));  // Resize
//Set the Windows client area
    setClientSize(new Point(width, height));
    setText ("ADOPanelTest");        // Title
//Add the ADOPanel
    setNewControls(new Control[] {adop_employee});
  }
}
```

Understanding the class library concept

Five main ideas drive class-library development:

- First, it had better be quick. Any developer should be able to make full-featured database applications, when using a database class library, in a fraction of the time it takes to write a database application from scratch or to paint a database application from the Application Wizard.

- A class library should be so simple to use that new developers would actually *want* to use it, while existing Java programmers would be crazy not to.

- A class library should incorporate company standards. If your business always wants certain features on their windows (for example, error-checking, standard menu items, standard button-positioning, radio buttons for choices, and so on), then these ought to be incorporated into the class library so that developers automatically code the way you want them to code.

- A class library should make all database applications function similarly. That way, users trained in one module are close to being trained in all of them. With a painter, every application looks different. A class library, on the other hand, forces all applications to function similarly.

- A class library should be quick and simple by default, but should also provide advanced, well-documented functionality (for example, radio button support) once the developer is familiar with class library development.

Once these benefits are spelled out, it would be crazy to start developing systems in *any language* without first developing a class library.

Binding radio buttons

Radio buttons cannot be bound by traditional binding methods in Visual J++, because radio buttons are a set of controls, rather than a single control. However, you can "trick" the class library into binding the radio button control for you.

Getting the radio button display and database values

First, you write a method (for example, `setChoices`) that accepts a database column name, the displayed values that the user sees, and the internal values for the database. In the following code, a Vector is built that adds the column name and then each bound display/database value. This newly-created Vector is then added to the existing `v_choices` Vector:

```
private Vector v_choices = new Vector();
//...
//Change a column into a radio button with display and DB values.
  public void setChoices(String column, String display[], String
dbValues[]) {
    Vector choicesVect = new Vector();
    choicesVect.addElement(column);
    for (int loop = 0; loop < display.length; loop++){
      choicesVect.addElement(display[loop]);
      choicesVect.addElement(dbValues[loop]);
    }
    i_sizeNeeded += display.length - 1;
    v_choices.addElement(choicesVect);
  }
```

Building the radio buttons

When the Panel is being built, the `v_choices` array is searched for the current column:

```
//Check for Radio buttons
  Field f = fs_fields.getItem(counter);    //Current field
  String columnName = f.getName();    //field name
  boolean b_choices = false;
  Enumeration e = v_choices.elements();
  while (e.hasMoreElements()) {
    Vector v = (Vector) e.nextElement();
    v.trimToSize();
    Enumeration e2 = v.elements();
    String s = (String) e2.nextElement();
    if (s.equals(columnName)) {   //Found the column name
```

After the column name has been found, the slots (which control the number of cells this radio button uses) are adjusted. A new Control array called `radios` is formed that contains the number of slots:

```
// Make controls for group box
  Control radios[] = new Control[(v.size()-1)/2+1];
```

An invisible Edit is then formed and bound to the database. This invisible Edit is added to the `radios` Control array. In addition, if the Edit is changed, the `edChange` method is called:

```
//Make an invisible edit for data binding
  Edit ed = new Edit();
  ed.setVisible(false);
```

```
//When the edit changes, call edChange
  ed.addOnChange(new EventHandler(edChange));
//Add the invisible edit to the group box controls
  radios[0] = (Control) ed;
//Bind the invisible edit to the database
  db_binder.addBinding( ed, "Text", columnName);
```

Then, radio buttons are formed using the display text and added to the radios Control array. If a radio button state is changed, the rbClick method is called:

```
int rbCounter = 1;
while (e2.hasMoreElements()) {
//Go through radio buttons
  RadioButton rb = new RadioButton();
//Set rb text
  rb.setText((String) e2.nextElement());
//retrieve the rb Value fromt the Enumeration
  String rbValue = (String) e2.nextElement();
//Do the rest of the RB stuff
  rb.setBackColor(Color.CONTROL);
  rb.setSize(new Point(fieldSize-10 , 17));
  rb.setLocation(new Point(5, rbCounter * 20));
//When you change the rb, call rbClick
  rb.addOnCheckedChanged(new EventHandler(rbClick));
//Add the RB to the group box controls
  radios[rbCounter++] = (Control) rb;
  }
```

Finally, a GroupBox is formed, and the radios Control array is added to the GroupBox. The GroupBox name is set to the columnName:

```
// New group box
  GroupBox gb = new GroupBox();
//Do the GB stuff
  gb.setText(columnName);
  gb.setSize(new Point(fieldSize, (slots+1)*20+7));
//Add the controls to the group box
  gb.setControls(radios);
```

After this is done, the GroupBox is added to the ADO Panel. The GroupBox contains the invisible Edit (that calls edChange when modified) and the radio buttons (that call rbChange when modified). The GroupBox is shown graphically in Figure 23-4.

Figure 23-4: To bind a database field to radio buttons, add an Invisible Edit to the radio button fields inside a GroupBox.

Binding the radio buttons to the database

After the radio buttons, invisible Edit, and GroupBox have all been created, you need to add the functions that control what happens when any field changes. The invisible Edit is already bound to the database.

Because the Edit is invisible, it can only change when the database changes. When any Edit that is associated with a radio button changes, the edChange method is executed. This method has four steps:

1. Retrieve the Edit from the sender object, the GroupBox from the Edit's parent, the database value from the Edit text, and the database column name from the GroupBox title text:

```
//A Radio Button Edit has changed
private void edChange(Object sender, Event event) {
    Edit ed = (Edit) sender;        //Get the edit box
    GroupBox gb = (GroupBox) ed.getParent();  //get the group box
    String display = null;
    String value = ed.getText();
    String columnName = gb.getText();
```

2. Scroll through the v_choices vector until you reach the database column name:

```
Enumeration e = v_choices.elements();
while (e.hasMoreElements()) {     //Go through RB enumeration
    Vector v = (Vector) e.nextElement();  // retrieve the vector
    Enumeration e2 = v.elements();  //Form an Enumeration
    String s = (String) e2.nextElement();  //get the column name
    if (s.equals(columnName)) {     //is this the right column?
```

3. Once the database column name has been found, find the database value and the associated radio button display value:

```
while (e2.hasMoreElements()) {   //Scroll through all RBs
//Get the display string
    String rbDisplay = (String) e2.nextElement();
//get the value string
    String rbValue = (String) e2.nextElement();
    if (rbValue.equals(value)) {  //The values match up
      display = rbDisplay;  //The display string
      break;        //Inner loop break
    }
}
```

4. Finally, scroll through the controls of the parent GroupBox until you find the right radio button to click:

```
//Search the group box for the right RB to click
    Control[] controls = gb.getControls();
//go through all the controls of the group box
    for (int loop = 0; loop < controls.length; loop++) {
//Find all radio buttons
      if (controls[loop] instanceof RadioButton) {
```

```
        RadioButton rb = (RadioButton) controls[loop];
      //Search for the display string
        if (rb.getText().equals(display)) {
          rb.setChecked(true);    //Found it!
          return;
        }
      }
    }
```

Similarly, when any radio button is clicked, the rbChange method is executed. The rbChange method has four steps:

1. Retrieve the radio button from the sender object, the GroupBox from the radio button's parent, the radio button display value from the radio button text, and the database column name from the GroupBox title text. If the radio button is not clicked, return immediately:

```
//A radio button has been clicked
private void rbClick(Object sender, Event event) {
  RadioButton rb = (RadioButton) sender;  //Get the RB
  if (!rb.getChecked()) {         //Only run this if it's checked
    return;
  }
  GroupBox gb = (GroupBox) rb.getParent();  //Get GB parent
  String display = rb.getText();        //return the text of the RB
  String columnName = gb.getText();     //Return the field name
                                        //from the GB
```

2. Scroll through the v_choices vector until you reach the database column name:

```
Enumeration e = v_choices.elements();
while (e.hasMoreElements()) {      //Go through RB enumeration
  Vector v = (Vector) e.nextElement();  // retrieve the vector
  Enumeration e2 = v.elements();   //Form an Enumeration
  String s = (String) e2.nextElement();  //get the column name
  if (s.equals(columnName)) {       //is this the right column?
```

3. Once the database column name has been found, find the radio button display value and the associated database value:

```
while (e2.hasMoreElements()) {   //Scroll through all RBs
//Get the display string
  String rbDisplay = (String) e2.nextElement();
//get the value string
  String rbValue = (String) e2.nextElement();
  if (rbDisplay.equals(display)) { // This RB is checked
    value = rbValue;
    break;       //Inner loop break
  }
}
```

4. Finally, scroll through the controls of the parent GroupBox until you find what should be the only Edit control. Place the database value in that Edit control:

```
//Search the group box for the only edit
Control[] controls = gb.getControls();
//go through all the controls of the group box
for (int loop = 0; loop < controls.length; loop++) {
  if (controls[loop] instanceof Edit) {     //Did you find the
                                            //edit?
    Edit ed = (Edit) controls[loop];  //Yep
    ed.setText(value);        //Set it the the RB value
    return;
  }
}
```

These functions finish binding a field to a set of radio buttons. Sure, it's a lot of work, but the code is so generic that once you write it, you never need to write it again.

Viewing the ADO class library code

Listing 23-2 is an ADO class library. The ADOPanel class gives a lot of control over a database and includes functions such as binding radio buttons and executing SQL commands. Additionally, the ADOPanel class can automatically format a Panel based on database data types defined in a table or view.

Although the amount of code may seem daunting, developing a class library could be the key to faster development times for everyone, and a standard interface that is easy to debug and train with.

Listing 23-2: ADOPanel.java

```
//import Java packages
import java.util.*;
//import WFC packages
import wfc.app.*;
import wfc.core.*;
import wfc.ui.*;
import wfc.data.*;
import wfc.data.ui.*;
public class ADOPanel extends Panel {
//Vector to add radio button choices
  private Vector v_choices = new Vector();
  private int i_numberFields;  //Fields in SQL statement
  private int i_sizeNeeded;  //Number of "Cells" to display
  private int i_numPanels;//Number of panels columns passed by
  private String s_database;   //Name of the database
  private String s_table;       //Name of the table
  private String s_orderBy;      //Order by column
  private String SQLStatement; //SQLStatement formed for query
  private boolean b_adding = false;//Currently adding a record
  int i_panelWidth = 0;    //Width of each panel
  int i_labelSize = 0;     //Size of the labels
```

```
//ADO and WFC Classes
   private Button bu_update = new Button();  //Update button
   private Button bu_add = new Button();  //Add button
   private Button bu_delete = new Button();  //Delete button
   private Button bu_exit = new Button();  //Exit button
//Data navigator used to move first, previous, next, or last
   private DataNavigator dn_navigator = new DataNavigator();
   private Connection con_dbConnection = null;  //DB connection
   private Recordset rs_records = null;         //DB recordset
//A DataBinder is used to bind a
//record set to some WFC columns
   private DataBinder db_binder = null;     //DB Binder
   private Fields fs_fields = null;         //Fields from query
   public ADOPanel(String db, String table) {
     super();
     afterConstruct(db, table, 1);
   }
   public ADOPanel(String db, String table, int numPanels) {
     super();
     afterConstruct(db, table, numPanels);
   }
   //Set class variables and connect
   //to database to retrieve query
   private void afterConstruct(String db, String table, int numPanels)
{
     s_database = db;
     s_table = table;
     i_numPanels = numPanels;
     ODBCConnect(s_database);
     doSQL();
   }
   public void formClose(Event e) {  //Exit from the database
     Application.exit();
   }
   protected void finalize() {       //Clean up
     try {
       rs_records.close();     //Close the recordset
       con_dbConnection.close();  //Close the DB Connection
     }
     catch (Exception e) {
       handleADOException( e );
     }
   }
//Execute any non-row returning SQL sent by the user.
   public void executeSQL(String SQL) {
     con_dbConnection.execute(SQL);
   }
//Reset the column that the query is ordered by
   public void setOrderBy(String s) {
     s_orderBy = s;
     doSQL();
   }
//Change a column into a radio button
//with display and DB values.
   public void setChoices(String column, String display[],
                          String dbValues[]) {
```

```
      Vector choicesVect = new Vector();
      choicesVect.addElement(column);
      for (int loop = 0; loop < display.length; loop++){
        choicesVect.addElement(display[loop]);
        choicesVect.addElement(dbValues[loop]);
      }
      i_sizeNeeded += display.length - 1;
      v_choices.addElement(choicesVect);
    }
//Return what you think the width should be for this query
  public int getSuggestedWidth() {
    return Math.max(i_numPanels * 250,400);
  }
//Return what you think the height should be for this query
  public int getSuggestedHeight() {
    return i_sizeNeeded * 25 + 40;
  }
//Form the panel using data from the recordset
  public void formPanel() {
    int offset= 0;      //Fields already placed on other panels
    int currentPanel = 0;  //Current panel to fill
    int currentSlot = 0;   //Current cell of the current panel
    int counter;              //Counter for fields
  //Returns the number of cells per panel
    float slotsPerPanel = i_sizeNeeded / i_numPanels;
  //Arrays for panels, fields, and lables
    Control co_labels[][] =
        new Control[i_numPanels][i_numberFields];
    Control co_fields[][] =
        new Control[i_numPanels][i_numberFields];
    Panel fieldPanel[] = new Panel [i_numPanels];
    Panel labelPanel[] = new Panel [i_numPanels];
  //Computer the size of every field/label panel combination
    i_panelWidth = (getSuggestedWidth() - 20) / i_numPanels;
  //Do form stuff
    setBackColor(Color.CONTROL);
    setLocation(new Point(7, 7));
    setSize(new Point(getSuggestedWidth()-10,
            getSuggestedHeight()-10));
    setTabIndex(-1);
    setTabStop(true);
    setText("ADOPanel");
  //Make buttons
    bu_add.setAnchor(ControlAnchor.TOPLEFTRIGHT);
    bu_add.setLocation(new Point(10, 5));
    bu_add.setSize(new Point(59, 20));
    bu_add.setTabIndex(100);
    bu_add.setTabStop(true);
    bu_add.setText("&Add");
    bu_add.addOnClick(new EventHandler(bu_addClick));
    bu_delete.setAnchor(ControlAnchor.TOPLEFTRIGHT);
    bu_delete.setLocation(new Point(70, 5));
    bu_delete.setSize(new Point(59, 20));
    bu_delete.setTabIndex(101);
    bu_delete.setTabStop(true);
    bu_delete.setText("&Delete");
```

```
        bu_delete.addOnClick(new EventHandler(bu_deleteClick));
        bu_update.setAnchor(ControlAnchor.TOPLEFTRIGHT);
        bu_update.setLocation(new Point(130, 5));
        bu_update.setSize(new Point(59, 20));
        bu_update.setTabIndex(102);
        bu_update.setTabStop(true);
        bu_update.setText("&Update");
        bu_update.addOnClick(new EventHandler(bu_updateClick));
        bu_exit.setAnchor(ControlAnchor.TOPLEFTRIGHT);
        bu_exit.setLocation(new Point(190, 5));
        bu_exit.setSize(new Point(59, 20));
        bu_exit.setTabIndex(21);
        bu_exit.setTabStop(true);
        bu_exit.setText("E&xit");
        bu_exit.addOnClick(new EventHandler(bu_exitClick));
    //Make navigator for record movement
        dn_navigator.setAnchor(ControlAnchor.TOPLEFTRIGHT);
        dn_navigator.setLocation(new Point(260, 5));
        dn_navigator.setSize(new Point(120, 20));
        dn_navigator.setTabIndex(17);
        dn_navigator.setTabStop(false);
        dn_navigator.setText("");
    //Allocate panels
        for (counter = 0; counter < i_numPanels; counter++) {
          labelPanel[counter] = new Panel();
          fieldPanel[counter] = new Panel();
        }
    //loop to make the labels
        for (counter = 0; counter < i_numberFields; counter++) {
          Field f = fs_fields.getItem(counter);  //Current field
          String columnName = f.getName();    //field name
          int columnType = f.getType();     //data type
          int displaySize = f.getDefinedSize();  //field size
          String labelName = columnName + ": ";  //label name
          if (columnType == AdoEnums.DataType.BOOLEAN) {
            labelName = "";    //no label name for checkboxes
          }
//Check for current panel
          if (currentSlot >= slotsPerPanel
            && (currentPanel+1) < i_numPanels) {
            currentSlot = 0;
            currentPanel++;
            offset = counter;
          }
        //Now check for radio buttons
          Enumeration e = v_choices.elements();
          while (e.hasMoreElements()) {
            Vector v = (Vector) e.nextElement();
            String s = (String) v.elementAt(0);
            if (s.equals(columnName)) {
              currentSlot += (v.size()-1)/2 + 1;
              labelName = "";    //No labels for radio buttons
            }
          }
          Label lbl = new Label();  // Make new label
        //Do Label stuff
```

```
            lbl.setText(labelName);
            lbl.setAnchor(ControlAnchor.TOPLEFTRIGHT);
            lbl.setBackColor(Color.CONTROL);
            lbl.setLocation(new Point(10, 5 + currentSlot * 20));
            lbl.setTabIndex(2);
            if (displaySize > 255) {   //Check for multiline edits
              lbl.setSize(new Point(100, 59));
              currentSlot += 2;
            }
            else {                //Nope.  It's a single-line
              lbl.setSize(new Point(100, 19));
            }
            int labelSize = lbl.getWidth();  //return label width
            i_labelSize = Math.max(i_labelSize, labelSize);
            currentSlot++;
            co_labels[currentPanel][counter-offset] = (Control) lbl;
          }
      //Now make the fields
        currentSlot = 0;
        offset = 0;
        currentPanel = 0;
        int fieldSize = i_panelWidth - i_labelSize - 8;
        for (counter = 0; counter < i_numberFields; counter++) {
          Field f = fs_fields.getItem(counter);
          String columnName = f.getName();
          int slots = 1;
          int columnType = f.getType();
          int displaySize = f.getDefinedSize();
          if (currentSlot >= slotsPerPanel
            && (currentPanel+1) < i_numPanels) {
            currentSlot = 0;
            currentPanel++;
            offset = counter;
          }
          switch (columnType) {
            case AdoEnums.DataType.BOOLEAN :
              Checkbox cbx = new Checkbox();
              cbx.setText(columnName);
              cbx.setBackColor(Color.CONTROL);
              db_binder.addBinding(cbx, "Checked", columnName);
              co_fields[currentPanel][counter-offset] = (Control) cbx;
              break;
            default :
//Use UPDATEABLE bitwise anded with attributes to
//determine if you can update a column, or if you
//cannot. (For example, an autoincrement field cannot be updated.)
            int updatable = AdoEnums.FieldAttribute.UPDATABLE
                  & f.getAttributes();
              if (updatable == 0) {      //Make it mimic a label
                Edit ed = new Edit();
                ed.setReadOnly(true);
                ed.setBorderStyle(wfc.data.ui.BorderStyle.NONE);
                ed.setBackColor(Color.CONTROL);
                ed.setText("(Autoincrement)");
                db_binder.addBinding( ed, "Text",
                    columnName);
```

```
         co_fields[currentPanel][counter-offset] =
                   (Control) ed;
}
else {
//Check for Radio buttons
  boolean b_choices = false;
  Enumeration e = v_choices.elements();
  while (e.hasMoreElements()) {
    Vector v = (Vector) e.nextElement();
    v.trimToSize();
    Enumeration e2 = v.elements();
    String s = (String) e2.nextElement();
    if (s.equals(columnName)) {
    //This is a radio button.  Adjust cell count
      slots = (v.size()-1)/2;
    // Make controls for group box
      Control radios[] =
           new Control[slots+1];
    //Make an invisible edit for data binding
      Edit ed = new Edit();
      ed.setVisible(false);
    //When the edit changes, call edChange
      ed.addOnChange(new
        EventHandler(edChange));
  //Add the invisible edit to the group box controls
      radios[0] = (Control) ed;
    //Bind the invisible edit to the database
      db_binder.addBinding( ed,
        "Text", columnName);
      int rbCounter = 1;
      while (e2.hasMoreElements()) {
      //Go through radio buttons
        RadioButton rb = new
        RadioButton();
      //Set rb text
        rb.setText((String)
          e2.nextElement());
  //retrieve the rb Value fromt the Enumeration
        String rbValue = (String)
                   e2.nextElement();
      //Do the rest of the RB stuff
        rb.setBackColor(
          Color.CONTROL);
        rb.setSize(new Point(
          fieldSize-10 , 17));
        rb.setLocation(new Point(
          5, rbCounter * 20));
    //When you change the rb, call rbClick
        rb.addOnCheckedChanged(
            new EventHandler(rbClick));
    //Add the RB to the group box controls
        radios[rbCounter++] =
                   (Control) rb;
      }
      b_choices = true;  // This is an RB
    // New group box
```

```
                GroupBox gb = new GroupBox();
             //Do the GB stuff
               gb.setText(columnName);
               gb.setSize(new Point(fieldSize,
                            (slots+1)*20+7));
          //Adjust the cell count appropriately
               slots+=2;
             //Add the controls to the group box
               gb.setControls(radios);
             //Now add the group box to the fields array
               co_fields[currentPanel]
                        [counter-offset] =
                        (Control) gb;
             break;
           }
          }
          if (b_choices == false) {//This is not a group box
            Edit ed = new Edit();   //Make an edit
          //Bind the edit to the column
            db_binder.addBinding( ed, "Text",
                columnName);
          //Set the background color
            ed.setBackColor(Color.WINDOW);
            if (displaySize > 255) {
/*This is a multiline edit.  Make it big and adjust cell count
appropriately */
                ed.setMultiline(true);
                ed.setSize(new Point(fieldSize, 59));
slots = 3;
            }
            else {   //This is a single line edit.
               ed.setSize(new Point(fieldSize, 19));
}
          //Add the edit to the field array
             co_fields[currentPanel][counter-offset]=ed;
          }
        }
        break;
     }
    //Set the control stuff for each field
       co_fields[currentPanel][counter-offset].setAnchor(
            ControlAnchor.TOPLEFTRIGHT);
       co_fields[currentPanel][counter-
offset].setCursor(Cursor.IBEAM);
       co_fields[currentPanel][counter-offset].setLocation(
            new Point(5, 5 + currentSlot * 20));
       co_fields[currentPanel][counter-offset].setTabIndex(counter+1);
       co_fields[currentPanel][counter-offset].setTabStop(true);
       currentSlot += slots;    //Adjust the cell count
    }
  //Add controls to this Panel.
    int numberControls = 5 + (i_numPanels * 2);
    Control controls[] = new Control[numberControls];
    controls[0] = dn_navigator;  //Add navigator
    controls[1] = bu_add;     //Add buttons
    controls[2] = bu_delete;
```

```
        controls[3] = bu_update;
        controls[4] = bu_exit;
        for (int loop = 0; loop < i_numPanels; loop++) {
//set panel attributes
            makePanels(labelPanel[loop], loop, true);
            makePanels(fieldPanel[loop], loop, false);
//initialize number of fields
            int numberFields = i_numberFields;
            for (int loop2 = 0; loop2 < i_numberFields; loop2++) {
//Check for fields on panel
                if (co_fields[loop][loop2] == null) {
                    numberFields = loop2;  //Set the fields on the panel
                    break;      //out of loop
                }
            }
//Make a labels array
            Control labels[] = new Control[numberFields];
//Make a fields array
            Control fields[] = new Control[numberFields];
            for (int loop2 = 0; loop2 < numberFields; loop2++) {
//Assign a labels panel
                labels[loop2] = co_labels[loop][loop2];
//Assign a fields panel
                fields[loop2] = co_fields[loop][loop2];
            }
//Add labels to the panel
            labelPanel[loop].setControls(labels);
//Add fields to the panel
            fieldPanel[loop].setControls(fields);
//Add label panel to controls array
            controls[loop*2+5] = labelPanel[loop];
//Add fields panel to array
            controls[loop*2+6] = fieldPanel[loop];
        }
        setNewControls(controls);  //Add the controls to the form
    }
    //Set all the panel attributes
    private void makePanels(Panel p, int panelNum, boolean isLabel) {
        int x = 5 + panelNum * i_panelWidth;
        int height =  getSuggestedHeight() - 50;
        int width = i_labelSize + 5;
        int y = 30;
        if (!isLabel) {
            x += i_labelSize;
            width = i_panelWidth - i_labelSize;
        }
        p.setAnchor(ControlAnchor.TOPLEFT);
        p.setLocation(new Point(x, y));    //Set panel location
        p.setSize(new Point(width,height));    //Set panel size
        p.setTabIndex(1);          //Allow tabs
        p.setTabStop(true);
    }
    private void rbClick(Object sender, Event event) {
        RadioButton rb = (RadioButton) sender;  //Get the RB
        if (!rb.getChecked()) {    //Only run this if it's checked
            return;
```

```
      }
    GroupBox gb = (GroupBox) rb.getParent();   //Get GB parent
    String display = rb.getText(); //return the text of the RB
//Return the field name from the GB
    String columnName = gb.getText();
    String value = null;            //value is not yet set
    Enumeration e = v_choices.elements();
    while (e.hasMoreElements()) {    //Go through RB enumeration
      Vector v = (Vector) e.nextElement();  //retrieve vector
      Enumeration e2 = v.elements();   //Form an Enumeration
      String s = (String) e2.nextElement();   //get column name
      if (s.equals(columnName)) { //is this the right column?
        while (e2.hasMoreElements()) {   //Scroll through RBs
        //Get the display string
          String rbDisplay = (String) e2.nextElement();
        //get the value string
          String rbValue = (String) e2.nextElement();
          if (rbDisplay.equals(display)) { // RB is checked
            value = rbValue;
            break;      //Inner loop break
          }
        }
        break;           //Outer loop break
      }
    }
    //Search the group box for the only edit
    Control[] controls = gb.getControls();
    //go through all the controls of the group box
    for (int loop = 0; loop < controls.length; loop++) {
      if (controls[loop] instanceof Edit) {//Found the edit?
        Edit ed = (Edit) controls[loop];   //Yep
        ed.setText(value);         //Set it the the RB value
        return;
      }
    }
  }
  //A Radio Button Edit has changed
  private void edChange(Object sender, Event event) {
    Edit ed = (Edit) sender;         //Get the edit box
    GroupBox gb = (GroupBox) ed.getParent();  //get the group box
    String display = null;
    String columnName = gb.getText();
    String value = ed.getText();
    Enumeration e = v_choices.elements();
    while (e.hasMoreElements()) {      //Go through RB enumeration
      Vector v = (Vector) e.nextElement();  //retrieve vector
      Enumeration e2 = v.elements();   //Form an Enumeration
      String s = (String) e2.nextElement();   //get column name
      if (s.equals(columnName)) {   //is this the right column?
        while (e2.hasMoreElements()) {//Scroll through all RBs
        //Get the display string
          String rbDisplay = (String) e2.nextElement();
        //get the value string
          String rbValue = (String) e2.nextElement();
          if (rbValue.equals(value)) {   //The values match up
            display = rbDisplay;   //The display string
```

```
              break;          //Inner loop break
            }
          }
          break;               //Outer loop break
        }
      }
      //Search the group box for the right RB to click
      Control[] controls = gb.getControls();
      //go through all the controls of the group box
      for (int loop = 0; loop < controls.length; loop++) {
        //Find all radio buttons
        if (controls[loop] instanceof RadioButton) {
          RadioButton rb = (RadioButton) controls[loop];
          //Search for the display string
          if (rb.getText().equals(display)) {
            rb.setChecked(true);   //Found it!
            return;
          }
        }
      }
    }
  //Connect to the ADO database
  private void ODBCConnect(String database) {
    try {
//Make a new connection
      con_dbConnection = new Connection();
      //Set the connect string
      con_dbConnection.setConnectionString (
        "Provider=MSDASQL;"+  //Use ODBC connection for OLE DB
        "UID=admin;" +         //Set the user id
        "PWD=;" +              //Set the password
        "DSN=" + database);    //Set the database name
      //Set cursor properties for database client
      con_dbConnection.setCursorLocation (
        AdoEnums.CursorLocation.CLIENT);
      //Open the connection
      con_dbConnection.open();
    }
    catch (Exception e) {
      handleADOException( e );
    }
  }
//Print an error message
  void handleADOException(Exception e) {
    e.printStackTrace();
    MessageBox.show( e.toString());
  }
  public void doSQL() {
    // Default order by is the first column
    if (s_orderBy == null) {
      String statement = "SELECT * FROM " + s_table;
      doSQL(statement);
      Field f = fs_fields.getItem(0);
      s_orderBy = f.getName();
    }
    String statement = "SELECT * FROM " + s_table
```

```
           + " ORDER BY " + s_orderBy;
        doSQL(statement);
      }
    private void doSQL(String SQLStatement) {
      try {
        if (rs_records != null) {
          rs_records.close();   //Release previous records
        }
      //Garbage collect, if necessary
        rs_records = null;
        db_binder = null;
        fs_fields = null;
      //Construct the new record set
        rs_records = new Recordset(); //Construct the record set
      //Attach the record set to the db connection
        rs_records.setActiveConnection(con_dbConnection);
      //Tell the recordset to execute the SQL statement
        rs_records.setSource(SQLStatement);
      //Set the cursor information for the SQL
        rs_records.setCursorType(AdoEnums.CursorType.STATIC);
        rs_records.setCursorLocation( AdoEnums.CursorLocation.CLIENT);
      //Use optimistic locking so others can access the data
        rs_records.setLockType( AdoEnums.LockType.OPTIMISTIC);
      //Now do the query and return the information into the
      //recordset
        rs_records.open();
      //Go to the first record
        rs_records.moveFirst();
      //Set the data navigator to be linked to the recordset
        dn_navigator.setDataSource(rs_records);
      //Set the data binder to be linked to the record set
        db_binder = new DataBinder(rs_records);
      //Get the fields of the record set
        fs_fields = rs_records.getFields();
      //Count the fields
        i_numberFields = fs_fields.getCount();
//Initialize the size needed to reflect the number of columns
        i_sizeNeeded = i_numberFields;
//Adjust size needed for the number of multiline text areas
        for (int counter = 0; counter < i_numberFields; counter++) {
          Field f = fs_fields.getItem(counter);
          if (f.getDefinedSize() > 255) {
            i_sizeNeeded += 2;
          }
        }
      }
      catch (Exception e) {
        handleADOException(e);
      }
    }
    public void bu_addClick(Object sender, Event evt) {
```

```
      try {  //Add was clicked.  Add a new record
        rs_records.addNew(); //insert blank into the record set
        b_adding = true;     //Flag that an add is in progress
        bu_add.setEnabled( false );  //Disable the add button
      }
      catch (Exception e) {
        handleADOException(e);
      }
    }
  public void bu_deleteClick(Object sender, Event evt) {
      try { //Delete was clicked.  Delete the current record
      //Just don't add if an add is in progress
        if( b_adding ) {
          rs_records.cancelUpdate();
          b_adding = false;
        }
        else {     //An add is not in progress
          rs_records.delete(AdoEnums.Affect.CURRENT);
          rs_records.moveNext(); //Go to the next or last record
          if(rs_records.getEOF()) {
            rs_records.moveLast();
          }
        }
      }
      catch (Exception e) {
        handleADOException(e);
      }
//Enable the add button if necessary
      bu_add.setEnabled(true);
    }
  public void bu_updateClick(Object sender, Event evt) {
      try {
/*
 Because the WFC fields have been bound to the record set, all
  you need to update the records from the fields in a
  RecordSet.Update method call.
*/
        rs_records.update();
      }
      catch (Exception e) {
        handleADOException(e);
      }
      b_adding = false;  //If you were adding, you are done now.
//Enable the add button if necessary
      bu_add.setEnabled( true );
    }
  public void bu_exitClick(Object sender, Event evt) {
      Application.exit();     //Bye Bye
    }
}
```

Summary

Microsoft has done wonders with its ADO development environment in Visual J++. While standard, nonpainter WFC control programming is more complicated and less functional than straight Java, ADO programming, in conjunction with WFC, gives Microsoft an edge when it comes to quick, highly functional development.

- ADO is a great tool for database development. ADO comes with functionality that is not found in other Java database products, such as JDBC.

- Although ADO has several different classes, the main classes needed for Visual J++ development are the Connection class, the Recordset class, and the Field class.

- ADO works well in conjunction with WFC when it comes to data binding. In addition, you can manipulate Visual J++ programs to simulate binding in nonstandard fields, such as radio buttons.

- Consider class libraries instead of painting. While painting an application is easy and quick, you end up with non-reusable code, different standards, and, in some cases, slower development times.

Chapter 24

Easy Structured Query Language

■──■

In This Chapter

▶ Mastering the fundamentals of SQL

▶ Examining SQL SELECT statements

▶ Implementing INSERT, UPDATE, and DELETE statements

▶ Using SQL with Java and ADO

■──■

SQL (Structured Query Language) is a language used by most databases. Using SQL, you can manipulate data no matter what the database source. This chapter delves into how to use SQL and the ways you use SQL in a Java program.

Using the SELECT Statement

The SELECT statement is used to pull information from the database. The format for the simplest SELECT statement is as follows:

```
SELECT column1, column2,…
FROM table1, table2
```

For instance, if you have a Microsoft Access database table with the format shown in Figure 24-1, you can SELECT all the rows (or records) from the Employee table by using the following SQL:

```
SELECT  EmployeeID,
Name,
SSN,
Department,
Supervisor,
Paytype,
Probation,
Flextime,
Benefits
FROM Employee
```

The preceding SQL statement retrieves all the rows in the Employee table.

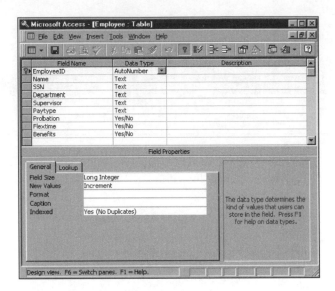

Figure 24-1: Employee Database Table Definition

Understanding the * operative

You can retrieve all the rows and all the columns from a table using the SQL * operative. The following statement selects all the rows and all the columns from the Employee table:

```
SELECT * FROM Employee
```

Secret

The * operative has caused some concern in developer circles. If a database table changes, then every program that relies on the current table configuration becomes invalid. The general rule is only use the * operative when writing a class library.

Using the WHERE clause

Sometimes, you don't want all the rows from a table, but rather you need a subset of all the rows. To combine criteria with a SELECT statement, you need to add a WHERE clause. A SELECT statement using a WHERE clause has the following format:

```
SELECT column1, column2,…
    FROM table1, table2
WHERE column1 = 'value'
```

Consider the following SQL:

```
SELECT  EmployeeID,
Name,
```

```
SSN,
Department,
Supervisor,
Paytype,
Probation,
Flextime,
Benefits
FROM Employee
WHERE Name = 'Fred Flinstone'
```

This SQL statement retrieves all the rows in the Employee table where the Name field contained "Fred Flinstone".

Using the ORDER BY clause

Often, when SELECTing multiple rows, the order in which the rows are retrieved is important. SQL standards claim that all returning rows can be in a random order unless specified by an ORDER BY clause. Consider the following statement:

```
SELECT   EmployeeID,
Name,
SSN,
Department,
Supervisor,
Paytype,
Probation,
Flextime,
Benefits
FROM Employee
ORDER BY Name
```

Now, instead of retrieving Employees at random, the employees are sorted in Name order by the database engine before being retrieved by the program.

Using WHERE and ORDER BY clauses give you several benefits when developing a database program:

- The WHERE clause can limit the number of records you retrieve. This makes database access quicker and reduces network traffic in a client-server environment.

- The ORDER BY clause can handle complex sorting for you so you don't have to worry about it inside a program. Properly done, this not only speeds up development, but also speeds up program execution.

- Indexes are important when using WHERE and ORDER BY clauses. Indexes provide a quick search of certain fields within tables. When a field is specified in a WHERE or ORDER BY clause, the database engine first checks to see if the columns specified are indexed. If so, the index is used to make searches quicker. If you are using WHERE or ORDER BY clauses, be sure to see if you can establish an index on the fields that you are using.

Understanding SQL field functions

In addition to SELECTing fields from a table, you can also perform functions on a field. There are two types of field functions:

- *Granular* functions only consider one row at a time.

- *Aggregate* functions work on a group of rows at a time.

Understanding SQL granular functions

Databases can perform operations with SELECT statements:

```
SELECT purchase_price * (1 + tax_rate) FROM purchases AS total_due
```

The preceding code formats a column called total_due that is equal to the purchase price plus the tax. In addition to straight arithmetic, most databases come with a large set of granular functions that affect the value of a row. For instance, the ABS function is often used to take the absolute value of a number:

```
SELECT ABS(day_due - day_delivered) FROM purchases AS days_off
```

The preceding SQL SELECT statement subtracts the day an item is delivered from the day it is due and takes the absolute value.

Most databases have hundreds of granular functions. Check your database documentation to see which granular functions you have.

Understanding SQL aggregate functions

In addition to the granular functions supported in a database, databases also have a few aggregate functions that consider all the rows or a group of the rows SELECTed. Table 24-1 shows the common SQL aggregate functions.

Table 24-1   SQL Aggregate Functions

SQL Aggregate Function	Description
AVG(columnName)	Returns the average of the column specified
COUNT (*)	Returns the number of rows retrieved
MAX(columnName)	Returns the maximum value of a column
MIN(columnName)	Returns the minimum value of a column
SUM(columnName)	Returns the sum of a column

For instance, the following SQL returns the number of salespeople from the 23rd department and a sum of their sales:

```
SELECT  COUNT(*),
    SUM(salesAmount)
FROM   sales
WHERE departmentID = 23
```

Using the GROUP BY clause

Often, you don't want an aggregation of every row in a SELECT statement, but rather you want to group the rows that are returned by the SELECT statement in some order. This is done using the GROUP BY clause. The GROUP BY clause performs aggregate functions on a series of groups within the rows returned by a SELECT statement. The following statement lists all the rows for all sales by department in order of sales:

```
SELECT   departmentID,
COUNT(*),
    SUM(salesAmount)
FROM    sales
GROUP BY departmentID
ORDER BY 3, 1
```

In the preceding statement, each department has its sales summed separately from every other department. Then the rows that are retrieved are returned in the order of sales and department.

Secret

As you can see by the preceding statement, ORDER BY and GROUP BY statements work well together. In addition, the ORDER BY clause can use either the column name *or* the column order in the SELECT statement. Because the SUM(salesAmount) is the third column selected and department is the first column selected, the preceding ORDER BY sorts by SUM(salesAmount) and then by department.

Using the HAVING clause

One problem with the WHERE clause is that you cannot use aggregate functions inside it. For instance, you *cannot* use WHERE salesAmount > AVG(salesAmount) in a SELECT statement.

To select aggregate conditions, you need to use the HAVING clause in conjunction with the GROUP BY clause. The following code selects those salespeople whose total salesAmount is greater than $50,000:

```
SELECT   salesPersonID,
salesPersonName,
    sum(salesAmount)
FROM    sales
GROUP BY salesPersonID, salesPersonName,
HAVING sum(salesAmount) > 50000
ORDER BY 3, 1
```

Using join operations

So far, all of our SQL examples involve SELECT statements from one table. Often a developer wants to SELECT from several tables at once. To do this, a join is usually used. A join uses more than one table in a SELECT statement.

The following SQL can be used to link two tables, Department and Employee, so that you can see the department name along with all the employees associated with that department:

```
SELECT   Department.name,
Employee.name
FROM     Department,
Employee
WHERE    Employee.departmentID = Department.departmentID
```

In the preceding SQL:

- Two tables (Department and Employee) were joined by their respective `departmentID` fields.

- Because both tables have a name field, the name had to be fully qualified with a *tablename.field* notation rather than using the field as was done before.

Notice how the table name is used to qualify the field name in the preceding SQL. With large SQL statements, this can be quite cumbersome. SQL enables you to assign aliases to tables in a `SELECT` statement to make the chore of writing SQL statements easier:

```
SELECT   d.name,
e.name
FROM     Department d,
Employee e
WHERE    e.departmentID = d.departmentID
```

In the preceding code, I gave the Employee table an alias of e and the Department table an alias of d. The resulting SQL statement was easier to read and shorter.

Using SubSELECT operations

SubSELECTs (also called subqueries) are used when one `SELECT` statement is embedded in another. The following SQL uses a subSELECT to retrieve the name of the salesperson with the highest sales for his or her department:

```
SELECT   s1.Name,
s1.SSN,
s1.Department,
s1.Sales
FROM   Salespeople s1
WHERE   s1.Sales = (SELECT MAX(Sales)
        FROM Salespeople s2
        WHERE s2.Department = s1.Department
```

Secret

Notice that although the same table was used, two different aliases enable you to specify two fields from different declarations of the same table.

Using the DELETE Statement

A DELETE statement removes one or more rows from a database table. The syntax for the DELETE statement is:

```
DELETE FROM tablename
WHERE condition
```

For example, to DELETE all rows from the Employee table with the name "Fred Flinstone", use the following SQL:

```
DELETE FROM employee
WHERE Name = 'Fred Flinstone'
```

Using the UPDATE Command

The UPDATE command changes the values in the columns of the database. The SQL syntax for the UPDATE command is as follows:

```
UPDATE tablename
SET column1 = value1, column2 = value2…
WHERE condition
```

For example, if you want to change the supervisor and department of Fred Flinstone, you use the following SQL syntax:

```
UPDATE employee
SET supervisor = 'Java Man',
        department = 'Coffee Beanery'
WHERE Name = 'Fred Flinstone'
```

Using the INSERT Command

The INSERT command adds a new record to a table in the database. There are two ways to INSERT a record into a database table. For single row entries, a simple INSERT statement is required. For multiple row entries, an INSERT statement combined with a subSELECT statement is required.

Inserting a row

The basic SQL syntax for the INSERT command is as follows:

```
INSERT INTO tablename
      (column1, column2, …)
VALUES
(value1, 'value2', …)
```

To INSERT a new row into the Employee table, use the following SQL syntax:

```
INSERT INTO Employee
    (Name,
SSN,
Department,
Supervisor,
Paytype,
Probation,
Flextime,
Benefits)
VALUES
('Wilma Flinstone',
'000-00-0004',
'NA',
'NA',
'N',
false,
false,
    false)
```

Secret

If a field is defined as autoincrement or a counter, database engine figures out the proper value for the field. It also means that you *cannot* specify its value in an INSERT or UPDATE. Consequently, the EmployeeID, which is autoincrement, is not specified in the INSERT.

Inserting multiple rows using nested SELECT statements

You can INSERT several rows at a time into a table by using nested SELECT statements inside an INSERT statement:

```
INSERT    INTO EmployeeArchive
    (Name,
    SSN,
    Department,
    Supervisor,
    Paytype,
    Probation,
    Flextime,
    Benefits)
  SELECT  Name,
      SSN,
      Department,
      Supervisor,
      Paytype,
      Probation,
      Flextime,
      Benefits
  FROM     Employee
```

Secret

Nested SELECT statements are often used in conjunction with the * operative to archive information. The following statement moves all terminated employees from the Employee table to the EmployeeArchive table:

```
INSERT INTO EmployeeArchive
   SELECT * FROM Employee
WHERE Terminated = TRUE
```

Using SQL with ActiveX Data Objects

You can use SQL inside Visual J++ programs. ADO and JDBC are SQL-driven, and require some SQL to function. Almost any SQL statement can be passed to a database from a JDBC or ADO call. (Chapter 28 discusses JDBC and Chapters 22 and 23 cover ADO.) There are two types of SQL statements: those that return values (SELECT) and those that don't (INSERT, UPDATE, and DELETE). The remainder of this chapter discusses how SQL statements are passed to databases via ADO calls.

When using ADO, INSERT, UPDATE, and DELETE statements all require the Connection.execute(String SQL) method to execute. This involves connecting to a database and then executing the SQL statement:

```
//Build the SQL INSERT statement
   String SQLStatement =  "INSERT INTO EmployeeArchive "
          + "SELECT * FROM Employee "
          + "WHERE Terminated = TRUE"
//Construct the connection
   con_dbConnection = new Connection();  //Make a new connection
//Set the connect string
   con_dbConnection.setConnectionString (
      "Provider=MSDASQL;"+  //Use an ODBC connection for OLE DB
      "UID=admin;" +        //Set the user id
      "PWD=;" +             //Set the password
      "DSN=" + database);      //Set the database name
//Set cursor properties for database client
   con_dbConnection.setCursorLocation (
   AdoEnums.CursorLocation.NONE);
//Open the connection
   con_dbConnection.open();
   con_dbConnection.execute(SQL);
```

SELECT statements are more difficult. They require a Recordset to be built when in use:

```
//Build the SQL SELECT statement
   String SQLStatement =  " SELECT salesPersonID, "
             + "salesPersonName, "
             + "sum(salesAmount) "
             + "FROM sales "
             + "GROUP BY salesPersonID, salesPersonName, "
             + "HAVING sum(salesAmount) > 50000 "
```

```
                    + "ORDER BY 3, 1"
//Construct the new record set
  rs_records = new Recordset();  //Construct the record set
//Attach the record set to the db connection
  rs_records.setActiveConnection(con_dbConnection);
//Tell the recordset to execute the SQL statement
  rs_records.setSource(SQLStatement);
//Set the cursor information for the SQL
  rs_records.setCursorType(AdoEnums.CursorType.STATIC);
  rs_records.setCursorLocation(AdoEnums.CursorLocation.CLIENT);
//Use optimistic locking so others can access the data
  rs_records.setLockType(AdoEnums.LockType.OPTIMISTIC);
//Now do the query and return the information into the recordset
  rs_records.open();
//Go to the first record
  rs_records.moveFirst();
```

As you can see by the preceding code, an ADO Recordset class is used to capture the results of an ADO call. The SQL statement is passed to the Recordset, and the Recordset then executes it using the `Recordset.open` method. The Recordset class has other methods (`moveFirst`, `getField`, and so on, discussed in Chapter 23) that are used to retrieve information once the Recordset has been retrieved.

Summary

This chapter gives Java developers an overview of SQL. To summarize the way SQL statements work:

- `SELECT` statements receive information from the database in a number of formats and configurations.

- `INSERT`, `UPDATE`, and `DELETE` statements change existing data on a database table.

- `INSERT`, `UPDATE`, and `DELETE` statements require a `Connection.execute()` method to execute a SQL command String.

- `SELECT` statements require that a Recordset be built to execute a SQL command String.

Chapter 25

Easy Database Security and Integrity

In This Chapter

▶ Mastering the fundamentals of database security

▶ Adding and removing users and groups

▶ Using Passwords

▶ Examining Microsoft Access-specific security

As a database developer, you need to protect your database from the users (and the users from themselves) to keep your database application up and running correctly. You simply *cannot* write client-server applications without some understanding of database security and database integrity. This chapter transcends specific programming languages (such as Java) and covers concepts that are important to every database developer.

User IDs and Passwords

Every database has a set of users. Users are individuals identified by a user name and a password. User IDs are important for the following reasons:

■ They enable only certain users access to certain tables.

■ They are the mechanism that keeps users from accidentally destroying data they have no right to destroy.

■ They are a way for a database administrator to control security at the database level, rather than the programmer level. This way, the database is protected irrespective of the programmer's skill level.

Secret

Unfortunately, user configurations are not part of standard SQL, and each database implements user security in a different way. Table 25-1 shows a list of user-creation commands that are used by various databases.

Table 25-1 Database User Creations

Database	Objective	Command
Oracle	Creates user with password (SQL*Plus)	CREATE *userid* IDENTIFIED BY *password*
Oracle	Changes password (SQL*Plus)	ALTER *userid* IDENTIFIED BY *password*
Sybase SQL Server	Creates user (stored procedure)	sp_adduser *userid*
Sybase SQL Server	Changes password (stored procedure).	sp_password *oldpassword, newpassword[, user_id]*
Microsoft SQL Server	Creates user (stored procedure)	sp_adduser *userid*
Microsoft SQL Server	Changes password (stored procedure).	sp_password *oldpassword, newpassword[, user_id]*
Sybase SQL Anywhere	Creates user with password (SQL)	GRANT CONNECT TO *userid* IDENTIFIED BY *password*
Microsoft Access	Microsoft Access menu selection.	Tools, Security, User And Group Accounts, *then type in your account information*.

Group User Accounts

Groups are usually considered a special kind of user account. Groups contain users, as shown in Figure 25-1. If you grant several users membership in a group (for example, Web users), you can assign security on a group-by-group basis rather than a row-by-row basis. Going through several groups may be easier than trying to manage several thousand different user accounts.

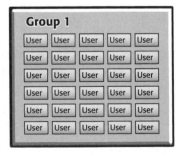 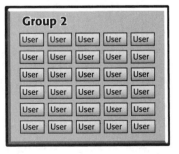

Figure 25-1: A group contains several users.

Every database has group capability. In Microsoft Access, two groups are established when the database is created:

- The Admins group, typically, has access to the entire database.

- The Users group, which, interestingly enough, also has access to the entire database.

Database administrators (DBAs) should start removing permissions from the Users group immediately. Any DBA should belong to the Admins group. For more information about creating users, passwords, and groups in your particular database, consult your user manual.

Get Rid of default security

Every database comes with a set of default security logins that enable the first user to grant other users access to the database. For instance, Access has a default login of Admin with no password. The first thing every database developer should do is to remove the default database security.

Stories abound about how a database was stolen because the administrator forgot to turn off the default security.

Access Security

Many of you are using a Jet database (used by Access and FoxPro databases) for your Web site or local machine. This section discusses how to handle database security within Access using the Access interface as your database administration tool.

Creating an Access workgroup information file

During installation, Access automatically creates a workgroup information file (WIF). The WIF is used to manage Access security. However, the WIF is easy to read, and makes it possible for hackers to create an unauthorized WIF so that they can grant themselves access to your database.

To stop these hackers, you need to create a new WIF and specify a workgroup ID (WID). Only someone who knows the WID can copy the original WIF. To establish a new WIF with a WID, do the following:

1. Exit Microsoft Access.

2. To start the Workgroup Administrator, do one of the following, depending on which operating system you are using:

- If you are using Windows 95, use My Computer or Windows Explorer to open the System subfolder in the Windows folder, and then double-click Wrkgadm.exe, as shown in Figure 25-2.

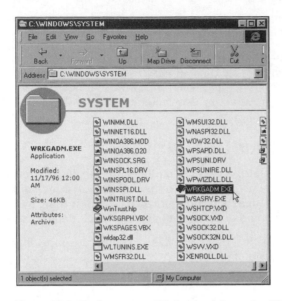

Figure 25-2: To change your Workgroup Information File, run the Workgroup Administrator in your System directory.

- If you are using Windows NT Workstation 4.0, use My Computer or Windows Explorer to open the System32 subfolder in the WinNT folder, and then double-click Wrkgadm.exe.

3. In the Workgroup Administrator dialog box, click Create, as shown in Figure 25-3.

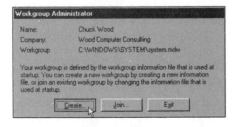

Figure 25-3: The Workgroup Administrator dialog box enables you to join a Workgroup or create a new Workgroup.

4. In the Workgroup Owner Information dialog box, type your Name, Organization, and your Workgroup ID, as shown in Figure 25-4. The WID can be any combination of up to 20 numbers and letters. When you're finished, click OK.

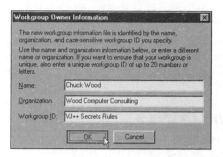

Figure 25-4: The Workgroup Owner Information dialog box enables you to enter your Name, Organization, and a secret Workgroup ID.

Remember to write down the exact Name, Organization, and WID, including uppercase and lowercase. If you need to recreate the WIF, you must supply the three entries again. If you lose or forget your Name, Organization, or WID, you can't recreate them and, therefore, may lose access to your database.

5. Type a new name for the new WIF, and then click OK, as shown in Figure 25-5. (By default, the workgroup information file is saved over the old WIF, and it's OK to replace it if you want to.)

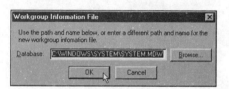

Figure 25-5: The Workgroup Information File dialog box enables you to save your WIF in the window.

6. When you're finished, you see the Confirm Workgroup Information dialog box with your Name, Organization, and Workgroup ID, as shown in Figure 25-6.

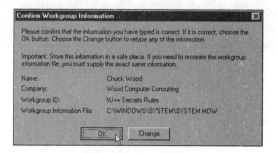

Figure 25-6: The Workgroup Administration File setup is now complete.

The new workgroup information file is used the next time you start Microsoft Access. All user and group accounts or passwords are stored in the new WIF. If another user wants to join your workgroup, they need to copy your WIF and join it.

Managing new users and groups

With any database, it's important to establish new users and new groups for security management. With Access, it's especially important because the use of Access is so prevalent, and many developers know the ins and outs of Access security.

Examining users and groups

To establish security in Access, enter the Access environment and then click Tools, Security, User and Group Accounts (Figure 25-7).

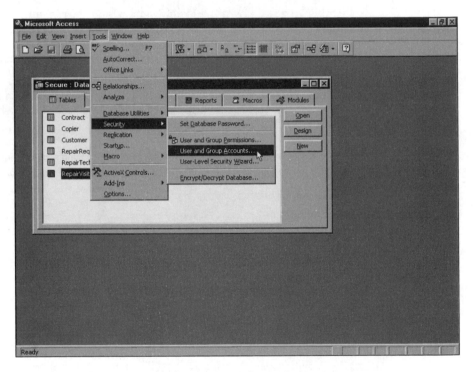

Figure 25-7: Access has easy menu commands for database user management.

The User and Group Accounts dialog box opens. By default, you have two groups (Users and Admins) and one User account (Admin) already set up in your Access database. To create another user, click New, as shown in Figure 25-8.

Figure 25-8: The User and Group Accounts dialog box enables you to add or delete user accounts from an Access database.

This opens the New User/Group dialog box (Figure 25-9). Here, type in the user name that you will log in with, and the Personal ID, which is a description of the user. Now the user appears in the User and Group Accounts dialog box (Figure 25-7). Be sure to add the user to the Admins group.

After the users and groups are created, assign security levels to them.

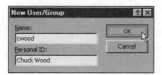

Figure 25-9: The New User/Group dialog box enables you to define a new user name or a new group name.

To force your database to start using login IDs, assign a password to the Admin user. Click the Change Logon Password tab, enter a new password, and then verify it, as shown in Figure 25-10.

Figure 25-10: To implement security, assign a password to the Admin user ID.

Now log in as the new user you just created and change the password as you did for the Admin password.

Using permissions

To grant permissions to a user or group for specific tables, queries, or forms, click Tools, Security, User and Group Permissions, as shown in Figure 25-11.

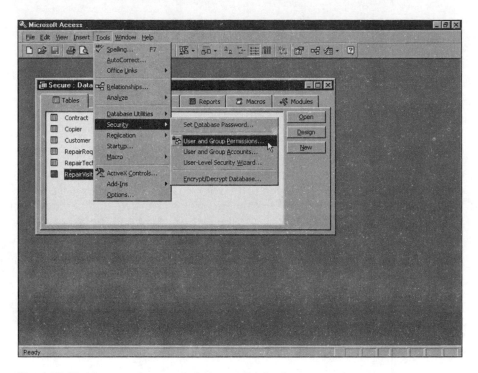

Figure 25-11: It's easy to grant permissions using the Access menu commands.

Secret

This opens the User and Group Permissions dialog box, as seen in Figure 25-12. There are two steps to do immediately:

■ Turn off all default Users group permissions, except perhaps read. That way, no unauthorized users can update your database. (The obvious exception is when you *want* strangers to enter data. In this case, allow Users to Update, Insert, or Delete data when appropriate.)

■ Add all access to the Admins group. That way, any administrator has full access to your database.

You can also change default ownership of a table by using the Change Owner tab of the User and Group Permissions dialog box, as seen in Figure 25-13. By changing all owners from Admin to other users, you disallow much of the Admin access to tables. Instead, the access belongs to the specific user who created the table or the user who needs the access.

Figure 25-12: The User and Group Permissions dialog box enables you to change user and group permissions to database entities.

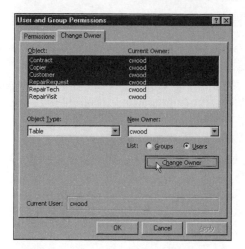

Figure 25-13: The Change Owner tab of the User and Group Permissions dialog box can be used to define new owners for each database table.

Establishing a new Admin

You cannot delete the Admin account. Microsoft Access simply won't let you. Similarly, you can't delete the Admins Group account. However, you shouldn't keep them in their current state. Follow these steps to secure your access database:

1. Add a password to the Admins account.

2. Add the proper security for the Admins group (all security) and the Users group (read-only security, or no security).

3. Add a user, besides Admin, to the Admins group.

4. Log in as the new Admins user.

5. Remove the Admin user from the Admins Account.

6. Change the ownership of all Admins tables to an appropriate owner.

Assigning a WIF to a database

You can assign a workgroup information file (WIF) to a specific database. This process takes several steps:

1. Use the `Wrkgadm.exe` program found in the Windows System folder to create a new WIF, as discussed earlier in this chapter. You end up with something similar to the output shown in Figure 25-14.

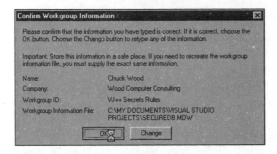

Figure 25-14: Use Wrkgadm.exe to create a new WIF.

2. Click the 32-bit ODBC found in the Windows Control Panel (Figure 25-15) to open the ODBC Data Source Administrator dialog box.

Figure 25-15: The 32-bit ODBC in the Windows Control Panel

3. Click Add to create a new database (Figure 25-16).

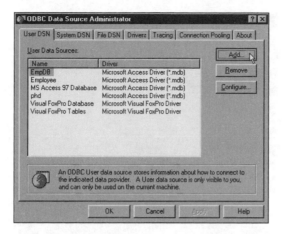

Figure 25-16: The ODBC Data Source Administrator enables you to create, configure, or delete existing ODBC data sources.

Next, the ODBC Administrator prompts you to select the database driver for your new data source. Pick the Microsoft Access driver, as shown in Figure 25-17.

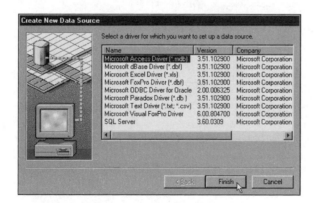

Figure 25-17: You can create a new ODBC data source using any installed ODBC database driver.

This opens the ODBC Microsoft Access 97 Setup dialog box, shown in Figure 25-18. From here, you can create databases, assign existing databases to ODBC, or assign system databases (WIFs) to existing or new databases. Click Create to create a new database, or Select to configure an existing database as an ODBC data source.

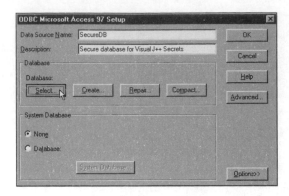

Figure 25-18: The ODBC Microsoft Access 97 Setup dialog box gives the ODBC Access developer an easy way to create or configure Access databases.

Clicking Select or Create enables you to find or declare the physical disk location of your new database in the New Database dialog box (Figure 25-19).

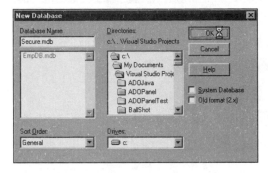

Figure 25-19: Choose the location of your database file in the New Database dialog box.

To assign a WIF to the database you have created, click the Database radio button in the System Database GroupBox in the ODBC Microsoft Access 97 Setup dialog box (Figure 25-18). This enables the System Database command button. Click the System Database button to open the Select System Database dialog box, as seen in Figure 25-20. Here, choose which WIF belongs with your new database.

When you return to the ODBC Data Source Administrator, you see the new database you have created. Furthermore, all security information is stored in the new database.

Figure 25-20: The Select System Database dialog box enables you to select a WIF to be associated with your new database.

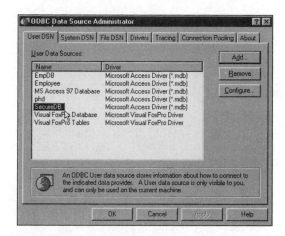

Figure 25-21: The ODBC Data Source Administrator now shows your new database.

Common-Sense Approach to Web Database Security

Security is needed for database development. However, you should be wary of any information on a database that has the potential for literally millions of interactions. There are several ways to protect your data when implementing Web-based database applications:

■ Always disable the default security that comes with the database. Remember, if you have an Access database with an Admin user id and no password, you only have yourself to blame.

■ Back up early and often. After a hacker crashes your database is the wrong time to wonder when the last backup was made.

■ Keep backups for several weeks, months, or even years. A good approach is to keep 60 days of daily backups and save one backup each month for a monthly backup. (Who says you can never go back?)

■ Split your database into two databases — a Web-based database and an internal database. Periodically (for example, every day, every hour) synchronize the two databases so information from the Web-based database is duplicated in the internal database, and information on the internal database is then replicated on the Web. That way, if some hacker trashes your database, you are only a short time away from creating a new, up-to-date database.

■ Only put information on the Web that is needed and used by the Web users. Less information on the Web attracts fewer people trying to scour through data that doesn't belong to them.

Some of these procedures may seem extreme, and hopefully you'll never need them. However, it's your business or your career on the line — so handle it with care.

SQL, ADO, and Security

At this point, ADO doesn't have a way to handle security dynamically. However, DAO and RDO have direct connections to the Jet database engine's User code, where security is handled for Access and FoxPro databases. ADO (as well as JDBC, DAO, and RDO) can execute SQL statements that add users. For instance, if you are attached to an Oracle database and need to execute SQL, you could type in the following Visual J++ code:

```
String s_userSQL = "CREATE userid IDENTIFIED BY password";
Connection con_dbConnection = new Connection();
con_dbConnection.setConnectionString (
        "Provider=MSDASQL;"+    //Use an ODBC connection for OLE DB
        "UID=admin;" +      //Set the user id
        "PWD=;" +         //Set the password
        "DSN=EmpDB");      //Set the database name
con_dbConnection.setCursorLocation (AdoEnums.CursorLocation.CLIENT);
con_dbConnection.open();
con_dbConnection.execute (s_userSQL);
```

The preceding code establishes a database connection using the Admin user ID. Then the `Connection.execute( )` method executes SQL that creates a given user and assigns that user a given password.

Check out your specific database to find out the SQL required for user creation. Then you can use this SQL to create and remove users dynamically during run time.

Summary

You can't be a database developer without a firm understanding of security. This chapter introduces you to some database security issues and delves into the Jet database engine security that's used by Microsoft Access.

- The concept of users and groups is at the heart of database security.

- Disable the default security before you deploy a database.

- When deploying over the Web, back up early and often — it's your best security.

- Every database has a unique way of handling security. If you are going to work with a database, delve into the database documentation to determine the SQL needed to manage your security issues.

Chapter 26

Mastering Data Access Objects

In This Chapter

▶ Starting the Jet database engine

▶ Creating and opening a database using DAO

▶ Creating and modifying tables inside a Jet database using DAO ActiveX calls

▶ Declaring primary keys

▶ Adding or dropping table indexes

▶ Adding, changing, or deleting database information

Microsoft included Data Access Objects (DAO) ActiveX modules with previous versions of Visual J++ to access its Jet database engine. The Jet database engine is used in many other Microsoft products, including Visual Basic and Access.

Secret

DAO has been replaced with ActiveX Data Objects, or ADO, and therefore it isn't included in current versions of Visual J++. However, DAO still needs to be understood to maintain previously developed Visual J++ database applications. If you need to install DAO ActiveX modules, you need to install Visual J++ 1.1 (or earlier), Visual Basic 5.0 (or earlier), or any development environment that contains the DAO ActiveX engine.

Exploring Database Engines

Database engines are programs that run in the background to enable programs to "talk" to the databases. A database engine must be started before you can access or create any database.

This section discusses how to start a database engine and the different methods you can use with a database engine.

Initiation

Database engines are created with the _DBEngine interface. Code similar to the following must appear in every DAO program:

```
import com.ms.com.*;
import dao350.*;
//...
public _DBEngine getDBEngine() throws ComException {
        try {
              if (i_dbEng != null) {
                  return i_dbEng;
              }
              // Create the License Manager object
              ILicenseMgr mgr = new LicenseMgr();
              // Use the License Manager to create the i_dbEngine
              i_dbEng = (_DBEngine) mgr.createWithLic(
                  // The license key for the DAO i_dbEngine
                  "mbmabptebkjcdlgtjmskjwtsdhjbmkmwtrak",
                  // The CLSID for the DAO i_dbEngine
                  "{00000010-0000-0010-8000-00AA006D2EA4}",
                  // The aggregation IUnknown* punkOuter
                  null,
                  // The ctxFlag to create in inproc server
                  ComContext.INPROC_SERVER);
                  i_dbEng.BeginTrans();  // Allow Commits and
                                         // Rollbacks
              return i_dbEng;
        }
        catch(ComException e) {
              // The engine could not be created.  Set i_dbEng to
null.
              ii_error = DATAENGINE_FAILURE;
              i_dbEng = null;
              throw e;
        }
     }
 }
```

The preceding code initiates a database engine. The class ID and the liscense are provided by Microsoft for the DAO library and are available in the DAOSample class that Microsoft included on the Visual J++ installation CD. The steps that you need to access the DAO engine are as follows:

1. Make a new instance of ILicenseMgr, a class included in the com.ms.com package.

2. Start your database engine using the newly created license manager. You need to pass it the license key.

3. Pass the license key ("mbmabptebkjcdlgtjmskjwtsdhjbmkmwtrak") and the Class ID ("{00000010-0000-0010-8000-00AA006D2EA4}") to the createWithLic method to create a server.

Now you have started your database engine.

Secret

DAO can access one database engine per machine, but each database engine can access up to 64 databases per session.

Components

The Jet database engine is made of several components, as shown in Table 26-1 and Figure 26-1.

Table 26-1   Jet Database Engine Components

Engine Component	Description
Engine	The database engine is needed to access a database. Only one engine can be running on a machine at any given time.
Errors	If Jet database errors occur after an engine is started, they are stored in the engine's errors component. The Errors class can be queried to find the error status of the database.
Error	A single error stored in the Errors collection. The Error class can return the error number and description.
Workspaces	Workspaces enable several transactions to run at the same time in the same program. Workspaces are also used to control database security. Although workspaces are not needed to access a database, a default workspace is started when the database engine is started. Any commands that access the database also access this workspace. Workspaces are described in Chapter 14.
Workspace	A Workspace enables you to use transactions and user security.
Databases	Every database that is opened or created in a Workspace is contained in the Database class.
Database	The Database class is used to access tables and fields in your Jet database. Databases are discussed later in this chapter.
Users	The Users collection class contains all the users found in a Workspace or Group. Users are discussed in more detail in Chapter 14.
User	A User class is used to grant access to a Jet database through a Workspace class.
Groups	The Groups class contains all the Groups found in a Workspace or accessed by a user.
Group	A Group class is used to contain several users that have similar access to a database.

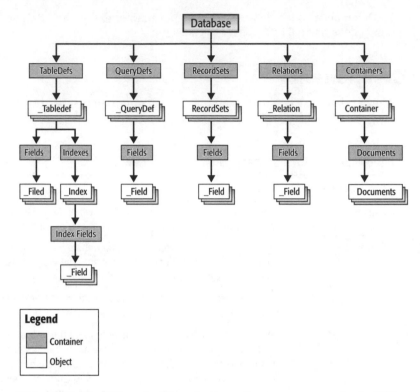

Figure 26-1: The DAO engine hierarchy shows the many components of a DAO database engine.

Transaction commit and rollback

By default, the Jet database engine makes changes to the database permanent. Any `AddNew`, `Edit`, or `Delete` method calls (which are discussed later in this chapter) are not reversable. However, by using *transactions*, you can make temporary changes to a database, and then decide later if you want to save or reverse these changes.

Transactions can be set at the database engine (`_DBEngine`) level, the Workspace level, or the Database level. The Jet database includes three methods (`BeginTrans`, `CommitTrans`, and `Rollback`), described in Table 26-2, that are used to control transactions:

Table 26-2   Transaction Methods

Transaction Method Name	Description
_DBEngine.BeginTrans() Workspace.BeginTrans() Database.BeginTrans()	The BeginTrans method begins a transaction for you. After a BeginTrans method is called, all changes to any database using the database engine are temporary until a CommitTrans or Rollback method is invoked.
_DBEngine.CommitTrans(CommitTransOptionsEnum. dbForceOSFlush)) Workspace.CommitTrans(dbForceOSFlush) Database.CommitTrans(dbForceOSFlush)	The CommitTrans method makes transaction changes. The dbForceOSFlush option forces all cache writes to be written to the database immediately after the commit to ensure that no data is lost. Commits make all changes permanent, *and end the transaction*. To continue transaction processing after a CommitTrans method is called, you must issue another BeginTrans method.
_DBEngine.Rollback() Workspace.Rollback() Database.Rollback()	The Rollback method erases transaction changes *and ends the transaction*. To continue transaction processing after a Rollback method is called, you must issue another BeginTrans method.

Consider the following changes to the getDBEngine method (in boldface):

```
import com.ms.com.*;
import dao350.*;
//...
private static _DBEngine i_dbEng;
//...
public _DBEngine getDBEngine() throws ComException {
    try {
        // Create the License Manager object
        ILicenseMgr mgr = new LicenseMgr();
        // Use the License Manager to create the i_dbEngine
        i_dbEng = (_DBEngine) mgr.createWithLic(
            // The license key for the DAO i_dbEngine
            "mbmabptebkjcdlgtjmskjwtsdhjbmkmwtrak",
            // The CLSID for the DAO i_dbEngine
            "{00000010-0000-0010-8000-00AA006D2EA4}",
            // The aggregation IUnknown* punkOuter
            null,
            // The ctxFlag to create in inproc server
            ComContext.INPROC_SERVER);
        i_dbEng.BeginTrans();  // Allow Commits and Rollbacks
        return i_dbEng;
    }
    catch(ComException e) {
        // The engine could not be created.
        throw e;
```

```
        }
    }
    public void commit() throws ComException {
        try {
            i_dbEng.CommitTrans(CommitTransOptionsEnum.dbForceOSFlush);
            i_dbEng.BeginTrans();
        }
        catch(ComException e) {
            throw e;
        }
    }
    public void rollback() throws ComException {
        try {
            i_dbEng.Rollback();
            i_dbEng.BeginTrans();
        }
        catch(ComException e) {
            throw e;
        }
    }
```

In the preceding code, a local variable, dbEng, is changed to an instance class attribute, i_dbEng. A transaction is started every time the engine is created. Transactions are then controlled by the commit and rollback methods. The commit method uses the CommitTrans method to make transaction changes permanent while the rollback method uses the Rollback method to erase all changes since the last BeginTrans method was called. Both methods then start a new transaction using the BeginTrans method.

The preceding rollback and commit transactions are used later in the chapter when database changes are discussed.

DAO error trapping

You probably noticed in the examples so far that ComException is trapped every time a database function is called. It is important to do this, because every time a database error occurs in DAO, a ComException is thrown. Consider the commit method:

```
public void commit() throws ComException {
    try {
        i_dbEng.CommitTrans(CommitTransOptionsEnum.dbForceOSFlush);
        i_dbEng.BeginTrans();
    }
    catch(ComException e) {
        throw e;
    }
}
```

Here, the `CommitTrans` and `BeginTrans` methods are enclosed within a `try` block. Then `ComException` is caught and immediately rethown to the calling module. This way, if a commit call fails, the calling module can detect it.

Although you have to trap every database error, you don't necessarily need to *handle* each database error at that moment. If your module is not designed or equipped to actually do something about the errors it detects, you could instead rethrow the error to the calling method. I call this *error chaining*. Often, in a database module, no frame or Applet is defined, so there is no easy way to handle errors. Error chaining can be used to pass an error to a module that is more capable of handling the error.

DAO _DBEngine methods

Many `_DBEngine` methods are discussed in this section. Table 26-3 lists all the methods used on a database engine for your reference. Table 26-4 lists StatNum Values.

Secret

Some of these methods are beyond the scope of this book, but can be reviewed using the `DAO.HLP` file available for download from Microsoft (`www.microsoft.com/visualj`) or in the Microsoft Jet Database Engine Programmer's Guide (Microsoft Press, 1996).

Table 26-3   DAO Database Engine Methods

Method	Description
`void CommitTrans(CommitTrans OptionsEnum.dbForceOSFlush);`	Ends a transaction by making temporary transaction changes to a database permanent. Also see the `Rollback` and `BeginTrans` methods.
`void CompactDatabase(String oldDB, String newDB, Variant connectString, Variant encryption, Variant password);`	Copies, compacts, and gives you the option of changing the version, collating order, and encryption of a closed database.
`Database CreateDatabase(String Name, Variant connectString, Variant encryption);`	Creates a database based on a physical file name, a connect string, and the encryption options.
`Workspace CreateWorkspace(String WSName, String user, String password);`	Creates a workspace identified by a name. User and password must also be provided.
`void FreeLocks();`	Releases the locks on a database.
`Errors getErrors();`	Returns the errors that have occurred *on the last database transaction only*.
`String getIniPath();`	Returns the Microsoft Jet database part of the Windows Registry file.

(continued)

Table 26-3   *(Continued)*

Method	Description
`short getLoginTimeout();`	Returns the number of seconds before an error occurs when you attempt to log in to an ODBC database.
`Properties getProperties();`	Returns a list of all properites in a database engine.
`String getSystemDB();`	Returns the path for the current location of the system database file.
`String getVersion();`	Returns the version of the Jet database engine.
`Workspaces getWorkspaces();`	Returns a list of the workspaces that have been implemented in the database engine.
`void Idle(Variant dbFreeLocks);`	Provides the Jet database engine with the opportunity to perform background tasks that may not be current because of intense data processing. This often occurs in multiuser, multitasking environments in which there isn't enough background processing time to keep all records in a Recordset current. Specifying `dbFreeLocks` forces read locks to be released before processing begins.
`int ISAMStats(int StatNum, Variant reset);`	Returns statistics about the database engine. If reset is set to true, the statistics are reset to zero. `StatNum` can be any of the values shown in Table 26-4.
`Database OpenDatabase(String dbName, Variant exclusive, Variant readOnly, Variant databaseSource);`	Opens a database inside the database engine. You can use Boolean Variant arguments to specify exclusive or not, as well as read-only or not. You can also provide a database source string to connect to a database if you're using an external database.
`void putDefaultPassword (String password);`	Sets the default password used by databases created or opened by the Microsoft Jet database engine.
`void putDefaultUser(String user);`	Sets the default user used by databases created or opened by the Microsoft Jet database engine.
`void putIniPath(String);`	Sets the Microsoft Jet database part of the Windows Registry file.

Method	Description
`void putLoginTimeout(short);`	Sets the number of seconds before an error occurs when you attempt to log in to an ODBC database.
`void putSystemDB(String);`	Sets the path for the current location of the system database file.
`void RegisterDatabase(String, String, Boolean, String);`	Enters connection information for an ODBC data source in the ODBC.INI key of the registry file. The ODBC driver needs connection information when the Microsoft Jet database engine opens the data source during a session.
`void RepairDatabase(String);`	Tries to repair a database that has been corrupted, usually by an incomplete write operation. Corruption can occur if an application using the Jet database engine is closed unexpectedly because of a power outage or computer hardware problem.
`void Rollback();`	Ends a transaction by reversing temporary transaction changes to a database. Also see the `CommitTrans` and `BeginTrans` methods.
`void SetDataAccessOption(short option, Variant value);`	Sets the data access for databases not created with DAO 3.5. This won't apply to most Visual J++ applications.
`void SetDefaultWorkspace(String user, String password);`	Sets the default user and password for databases not created with DAO 3.x. In version 3.0, this was changed to the `SetDefaultUser` and `SetDefaultPassword` methods. Consequently, this method won't apply to most Visual J++ applications.

Table 26-4   StatNum Values

Stat Num Value	Statistic returned
0	disk reads
1	disk writes
2	cache reads
3	read-ahead cache reads
4	locks placed
5	release lock calls

Mastering Databases

Of course, you would probably not use a database engine unless you intended to access a database. This section shows how to open, create, and close a database.

Opening databases

Now that you have started your database engine, you can open existing databases inside Visual J++. To open an existing database, you need to use the `OpenDatabase` DAO command:

```
import com.ms.com.*;
import dao350.*;
//...
public Database openDB() throws ComException {
    Database db;
    try {
        // Create Variants for optional parameters
        Variant v1 = new Variant();
        Variant v2 = new Variant();
        Variant v3 = new Variant();
        v1.putBoolean(false);
        v2.putBoolean(false);
        v3.putString("");
        // Open the database for nonexclusive access
        db = i_dbEng.OpenDatabase(i_dbName, v1, v2, v3);
        return db;
    }
    catch(ComException e) {
        // Open existing database failed.
        throw e;
    }
}
```

Secret

A Variant is a class included in the `com.ms.com` package. Often, ActiveX modules are not as strongly typed as Java modules. ActiveX modules can accept different data types as parameters. This can create a problem when calling ActiveX methods from inside Java applications, because Java's strong type checking forces the calling method to specify a type. The Variant class replaces a generic data type and enables you to call ActiveX modules that accept different data types as arguments.

To use the `OpenDatabase` method, first declare three Variants:

1. Boolean (true or false) indicating whether or not the database is to be opened in exclusive mode — that is, whether or not any other user can use the database while it's in use by you

2. Boolean indicating whether or not a database is read-only. By opening a database as read-only, you disallow any changes to that database.

3. The connect string used to connect to the database. For Jet databases, this is usually left blank.

The prototype for the `OpenDatabase` method is as follows:

```
Database OpenDatabase(String Name, Variant Exclusive, Variant
ReadOnly, Variant Connect)
```

Secret

Even though Variants are used to accept certain data types, like Boolean or String, you still can't pass the primative data types if a Variant is called for. In other words, you can't pass a Boolean true or false, but rather must use the `putBoolean` method to set a Variant variable to true or false.

Notice that the COM method is inside a try-catch block. This enables me to create a database if an error occurs while opening a database.

Creating connect strings

Unlike the `OpenDatabase` method, in which no connect string is specified, in the `CreateDatabase` method, a connect stream is useful for determining the language that you want to use in your database. Language support is important because it affects the sort order of your fields within the database. Table 26-5 shows connection strings for some popular languages.

Table 26-5	Create Connection Strings for Different Languages
Language	*Create Connection String*
Arabic	";LANGID=0x0401;CP=1256;COUNTRY=0"
Chinese (Simplified)	";LANGID=0x0804;CP=936;COUNTRY=0"
Chinese (Traditional)	";LANGID=0x0404;CP=950;COUNTRY=0"
Czech	";LANGID=0x0405;CP=1250;COUNTRY=0"
Dutch	";LANGID=0x0413;CP=1252;COUNTRY=0"
General*	";LANGID=0x0409;CP=1252;COUNTRY=0"
Greek	";LANGID=0x0408;CP=1253;COUNTRY=0"
Hebrew	";LANGID=0x040D;CP=1255;COUNTRY=0"
Hungarian	";LANGID=0x040E;CP=1250;COUNTRY=0"
Icelandic	";LANGID=0x040F;CP=1252;COUNTRY=0"
Japanese	";LANGID=0x0411;CP=932;COUNTRY=0"
Korean	";LANGID=0x040C;CP=494;COUNTRY=0"
Nordic (For Jet version 1.0 only)	";LANGID=0x041D;CP=1252;COUNTRY=0"
Norwegian and Danish	";LANGID=0x0414;CP=1252;COUNTRY=0"

(continued)

Table 26-5 *(Continued)*	
Language	*Create Connection String*
Polish	";LANGID=0x0415;CP=1250;COUNTRY=0"
Russian	";LANGID=0x0419;CP=1251;COUNTRY=0"
Spanish	";LANGID=0x040A;CP=1252;COUNTRY=0"
Swedish and Finnish	";LANGID=0x040B;CP=1252;COUNTRY=0"
Thai	";LANGID=0x101E;CP=874;COUNTRY=0"
Turkish	";LANGID=0x041F;CP=1254;COUNTRY=0"

*General is used for English, French, German, Italian, Portuguese, and Spanish

Creating Options

You can also specify different Database options when connecting to your database. In the example earlier in this section, only the `DatabaseTypeEnum.db` Version 3.0 option is used, indicating that this database is to be accessible only from DAO 3.0 and later. The options you can use when creating a database are as follows:

`dbDecrypt`	Decrypts the database during creation.
`dbEncrypt`	Encryptes the database during creation.
`dbVersion10`	Creates a database that uses version 1.0 of Microsoft's Jet Engine.
`dbVersion11`	Creates a database that uses version 1.1 of Microsoft's Jet Engine.
`dbVersion20`	Creates a database that uses version 2.0 of Microsoft's Jet Engine.
`dbVersion30`	Creates a database that uses version 3.0 of Microsoft's Jet Engine.

Secret

You almost always use dbVersion 3.0 when creating a database through DAO. For almost every database function, there is at least a 40 percent decrease in execution time over Version 2.0. With some database functions such as delete, Version 2.0 takes as much as 17 times as long.

Closing databases

Databases can be closed by the `Close` method in the `_Database` class or by assigning the database to null. In many cases, it's a good idea to close a database before trying to open a new database. A typical `closeDB` method would look something like this:

```
import com.ms.com.*;
import dao350.*;
//...
public void closeDB () {
    if (db == null) {
        return;
    }
    try {
        db.Close();
    }
    catch (Exception e) {
        error = CLOSE_FAILURE;
    }
    db = null;
}
```

Implementing database components

A Jet database is made up of several components. The DAO Database hierarchy is shown in Figure 26-2, and is made up of the components shown in Table 26-6.

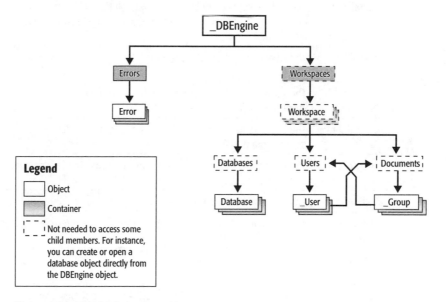

Figure 26-2: The DAO database hierarchy shows the many components of a DAO database.

Table 26-6   DAO Database Components

Database Component	Description
TableDefs	The TableDefs collection object lists all the _TableDefs in a database.
_TableDef	The _TableDef object corresponds to a database table. Using the _TableDef object, you can list all the fields or indexes for a table and retrieve table information, such as table name.
Fields	The Fields collection object lists all the fields for a component. The components that have Fields are _TableDef, _QueryDef, Recordset, Relation, and Index. Using the Fields object, you can list, add, or delete any field in these components.
_Field	The _Field object is a field contained in a _TableDef, _QueryDef, Recordset, Relation, or Index. You can use the Field object to define a new field or to retrieve information about an existing field.
Indexes	The Indexes collection object contains all the indexes used in a table.
_Index	The _Index object lists a single index used in a table.
IndexFields	The IndexFields collection object lists all the fields for an Index. The use of Variants is necessary with the IndexFields class. Indexes are discussed later in this chapter.
QueryDefs	The QueryDefs collection object contains all the QueryDefs used in a database.
_QueryDef	The _QueryDef object is a single _QueryDef. QueryDefs are used to define stored procedures inside a Jet database.
Recordsets	The Recordsets collection object contains all the Recordsets currently defined in a database.
Recordset	The Recordset object enables the programmer to view or update information in the database.
Relations	The Relations collection object contains all the relations in a database.
_Relation	The _Relation object defines the relationship or referential integrity between two tables.
Containers	The Containers collection object lists all the Container objects for a database.
Container	The Container object is a Microsoft Access-specific object that stores macros, reports, and so on. Probably, the Container object is of little use to the Visual J++ developer.
Documents	The Documents collection object lists all the Document objects for a database.
Document	The Document object stores all the Microsoft Access predefined forms. Forms are a handy way to set security inside the Microsoft Access package, but are of little use to the Visual J++ developer.

Examining database methods

The methods in Table 26-7 are defined in the DAO definition for the Database object.

Table 26-7   DAO Database Methods

DAO Method	Description
`void BeginTrans()`	Begins a transaction. Useful for final saves using the `CommitTrans` and `Rollback` methods.
`void Close()`	Closes a database. Use the `Close` method to ensure that database corruption doesn't occur when the database application terminates.
`void CommitTrans(( CommitTrans OptionsEnum.dbForceOSFlush)`	Ends a transaction by making temporary transaction changes to a database permanent. Also see the `Rollback` and `BeginTrans` methods.
`Recordset CreateDynaset(String name, Variant options, Variant inconsistant)`	An obsolete method to create a Dynaset. Probably not useful to those using DAO 3.5 (included with Visual J++) unless accessing an old database.
`Property CreateProperty(Variant name, Variant type, Variant value, Variant DLL)`	Creates a new user-defined property.
`QueryDef CreateQueryDef(Variant name, Variant SQL)`	Creates a new QueryDef object using an SQL command string.
`Relation CreateRelation(Variant name, Variant table, Variant ForeignTable, Variant option)`	Creates a new Relation object between two tables. The option argument is a `long` Variant that must be one of the following Constants: `dbRelationUnique` (relationship is one-to-one) `dbRelationDontEnforce` (relationship isn't enforced — there is no referential integrity) `dbRelationInherited` (relationship exists in a noncurrent database that contains the two attached tables) `dbRelationUpdateCascade` (Updates cascade) `dbRelationDeleteCascade` (Deletes cascade) After defining the relation, you must use the `_Relation.CreateField` method and then the `_Field.putForeignName` method to set the foreign key relationship.

(continued)

Table 26-7   (Continued)

DAO Method	Description
`Recordset CreateSnapshot(String table, Variant options)`	An obsolete method to create a Snapshot. Probably not useful to those using DAO 3.5 (included with Visual J++) unless accessing an old database.
`TableDef CreateTableDef(Variant name, Variant option, Variant sourceTable, Variant connectString`	Creates a Tabledef that can be used to create a table. Source table is the source table in an ODBC connection and is the connect string needed to connect to the remote table if a remote table is used. Options can be one of the following Constants or 0 (none of the following): `dbAttachExclusive` (the table is to be opened for exclusive use — cannot be used for remote tables) `dbAttachSavePWD` (the user ID and password for the remotely attached table are saved with the connection information — this constant can be used on an appended TableDef object for a remote table) `dbSystemObject` (the table is a system table provided by the Jet database engine — this constant can be set on an appended TableDef object only) dbHiddenObject (the table is a hidden table provided by the Jet database engine — this constant can be set on an appended TableDef object) `dbAttachedTable` (the remote table is an attached table from a non-ODBC database, such as a Microsoft Jet or Paradox database) `dbAttachedODBC` (the table is an attached table from an ODBC database, such as Microsoft SQL Server) Remember that you can't change the table structure of a remote attached table.
`void DeleteQueryDef(String name)`	Erases a QueryDef from a database

DAO Method	Description
`void Execute(String SQL, Variant Options)`	Executes a SQL command. SQL is a way to manipulate the database without much knowledge of the DAO objects defined in this chapter. If you know SQL, then you may prefer to do your database programming with it. *You cannot execute SQL SELECT statements in this fashion.* You must use Queries and Recordsets to execute any SQL Select. The following options are available for this method: `dbDenyWrite` (denies write permission to other users) `dbInconsistent` (default that allows inconsistent updates) `dbConsistent` (only allow consistent updates) `dbSQLPassThrough` (causes the SQL statement to be passed to an ODBC database for processing) `dbFailOnError` (rolls back updates if an error occurs and generates a ComException) `dbSeeChanges` (generates a run-time error if another user is changing data you are editing) Because `ExecuteSQL` and `Execute` both work if the SQL is syntactically correct, not if the operation fails, `dbFailOnError` is most often used with the Execute method.
`int ExecuteSQL(String SQL)`	The `ExecuteSQL` method, like the `Execute` method, executes a string of SQL. The ExecuteSQL command returns the number of rows affected.
`int getCollatingOrder()`	Returns the sort order of a database. The valid constants that can be returned are listed in Table 26-8.
`String getConnect()`	Returns the connect string used to connect to the database.
`Containers getContainers()`	Returns the containers found in the database.
`String getDesignMasterID()`	The Design Master in a Jet database is used to contain the database structure of a replicated database. The `getDesignMasterID` is used to retrieve, and then make a copy of, the Design Master.
`String getName()`	Returns the name of the database.

(continued)

Table 26-7 *(Continued)*

DAO Method	*Description*
`Properties getProperties()`	Returns the properties of a database.
`QueryDefs getQueryDefs()`	Returns the QueryDefs contained in a Database object.
`short getQueryTimeout()`	Returns the time limit for a database query.
`int getRecordsAffected()`	Returns the number of records affected by the most recently invoked `Execute` method. This is the same value that is returned by the `ExecuteSQL` command.
`Recordsets getRecordsets()`	Returns the Recordsets object contained in the database.
`Relations getRelations()`	Returns the Relations object contained in the database.
`String getReplicaID()`	Returns a 16-byte, OLE 2 GUID that provides each database replica with a unique identification. A GUID (Globally Unique Identifier/Universally Unique Identifier) is a unique identification string used with remote procedure calls. Every interface and object class uses a GUID for identification. Most of GUID use is hidden from you because the Visual J++ ActiveX implementation is so clean compared to other languages.
`TableDefs getTableDefs()`	Returns the TableDefs container object contained in a database.
`boolean getTransactions()`	Returns true or false depending if transactions are currently in use in the database.
`boolean getUpdatable()`	Returns true or false depending if the database is updateable or read-only
`String getVersion()`	Returns a string containing the version of the DAO database.
`Recordset ListFields(String tableName)`	Obsolete method that returns a Recordset containing the fields in table. This is no longer supported in DAO Version 3.*x*.
`Recordset ListTables()`	Obsolete method that returns a Recordset containing the tables in a database. This is no longer supported in DAO Version 3.*x*.

DAO Method	Description
void MakeReplica(String path, String description, Variant options)	Makes a new replica based on the current replicable database using the supplied path. If you include the dbRepMakeReadOnly constant as the option (value 2), the replicated database is read-only. Otherwise, use a null for the options Variant to allow updates to the new database replica.
void NewPassword(String oldPW, String oldPW)	Replaces the password of the current user in the current database. You need to use Workspaces to change the password of a user.
QueryDef OpenQueryDef(String name)	Opens and returns an existing QueryDef in a database.
Recordset OpenRecordset(String source, Variant type, Variant options)	Creates and returns a Recordset. The source argument can contain a table name, query name, or a SQL statement (usually SELECT) that returns records. The type can be one of the following Constant values: dbOpenTable (table-type Recordset object) dbOpenDynaset (dynaset-type Recordset object) dbOpenSnapshot (snapshot-type Recordset object) The option Variant can be viewed in Table 26-9.
Recordset OpenTable(String, Variant)	Obsolete function that opens and returns a Recordset of an existing table. Not valid in with DAO version 3.x databases.
void putConnect(String connectString)	Resets the connect string used to connect to the database.
void putDesignMasterID(String designID)	The Design Master in a Jet database is used to contain the database structure of a replicated database. The putDesignMasterID method is used to reset the Design Master, probably to an earlier database structure.
void putQueryTimeout(short seconds)	Sets the time limit for a database query.

(continued)

Table 26-7   *(Continued)*

DAO Method	*Description*
void Rollback()	Ends a transaction by reversing temporary transaction changes to a database. Also see the CommitTrans and BeginTrans methods.
void Synchronize(String targetDB, Variant option)	Synchronizes two databases. The type of exchange is controlled by one of the following Constant options: dbRepExportChanges (send changes from database to pathname) dbRepImportChanges (receive changes from pathname) and dbRepImpExpChanges (bidirectional exchange). Design changes are always done first. Both databases must be at the same design level before data can be exchanged, so database changes may be made to the parent database even though dbRepExportChanges is specified so that the database formats agree.

Table 26-8   Database Sort Constants

Constant	*Meaning*
dbSortGeneral	General (English, French, German, Portuguese, Italian, and Modern Spanish)
dbSortArabic	Arabic
dbSortCyrillic	Russian
dbSortCzech	Czech
dbSortDutch	Dutch
dbSortGreek	Greek
dbSortHebrew	Hebrew
dbSortHungarian	Hungarian
dbSortIcelandic	Icelandic
dbSortJapanese	Japanese

Constant	Meaning
dbSortNeutral	Neutral
dbSortNorwdan	Norwegian or Danish
dbSortPDXIntl	Paradox International
dbSortPDXNor	Paradox Norwegian or Danish
dbSortPDXSwe	Paradox Swedish or Finnish
dbSortPolish	Polish
dbSortSpanish	Spanish
dbSortSwedFin	Swedish or Finnish
dbSortTurkish	Turkish
dbSortUndefined	The sort order is undefined or unknown.

Table 26-9   Recordset Open Options

Constant	Description
dbAppendOnly	For a Dynaset-type Recordset, you can append only new records.
dbForwardOnly	The Recordset is a forward-only scrolling snapshot.
dbSQLPassThrough	Causes the SQL statement to be passed to an ODBC database for processing.
dbSeeChanges	A run-time error is generated if another user is changing data you are editing.
dbDenyWrite	Other users can't modify or add records until you destroy the Recordset.
dbDenyRead	For table type recordsets, other users can't view records until you destroy the Recordset.
dbReadOnly	You can't use the Edit, AddNew, or Update methods to modify your Recordset.
dbInconsistent	In a dynaset record type, inconsistent updates are allowed.
dbConsistent	In a dynaset record type, only consistent updates are allowed.

Using Tables and the _TableDef Interface

Tables are the "file cabinets" inside a database that contain records. Each database is almost always made up of several tables.

Creating tables

To create a table, perform the following steps:

1. Get the TableDefs container object from the database using the `Database.getTableDefs` method.

2. Create a _TableDef object by using the `Database.CreateTableDef` method. The `CreateTableDef` method is defined in the Database methods described earlier in this chapter.

3. Create one or more Field objects using the `_TableDef.CreateField` method to add to your table. The Create field is discussed in more detail later in this chapter.

4. Retrieve the Fields container of the table by using the `_TableDef.getFields` method.

5. Append the Field object to the Fields container object using the `Fields.Append` method.

6. Append your newly created _TableDef to the Database TableDefs container by using the `TableDefs.Append` method.

Secret

You can't create a table without any fields.

The following `createTable` method uses the preceding steps to create a table:

```
public void createTable(String tableName) throws ComException{
    try {
    // Get the TableDefs container object
        Variant v1 = new Variant();
        Variant v2 = new Variant();
        Variant v3 = new Variant();
        Variant v4 = new Variant();
        TableDefs tds = idb_db.getTableDefs();
    // Create a _TableDef object
        v1.putString(tableName);
        v2.putInt(0);
        v3.putString("");
        v4.putString("");
        _TableDef td = idb_db.CreateTableDef(v1, v2, v3, v4);
    // Create a Field object
        v1.putString("myfield");
        v2.putInt(DataTypeEnum.dbText);
```

```
            v3.putInt(30);
            Field fld = td.CreateField(v1, v2, v3);
    // Retrieve the Fields container of the table.
            Fields flds = td.getFields();
    // Append the Field object to the Fields container object
            flds.Append(fld);
    // Append your newly created _TableDef to the Database TableDefs
container
            tds.Append(td);
        }
catch (ComException e) { throw e; }
    }
```

Dropping tables

Dropping a table is easier than creating one. All you have to do is retrieve the TableDefs container class and then delete the table using the `TableDefs.Delete(String tablename)` method:

```
public void dropTable(String tableName)  throws ComException {
    try {
        TableDefs tds = idb_db.getTableDefs();
        tds.Delete(tableName);
    }
    catch (ComException e) { throw e; }
}
```

Retrieving an existing table

The _TableDef interface is used to manipulate database tables. To define a _TableDef, you need to perform the following steps:

1. Get the TableDefs container object from the database using the `Database.getTableDefs` method.

2. Get an individual _TableDef by using the `TableDefs.getItem(Variant index)` method.

The following `getTableDef` method can be used to return the _TableDef of a table identified by a table name:

```
public _TableDef getTableDef(String tableName) throws ComException {
    try {
        TableDefs tds = idb_db.getTableDefs();
        _TableDef td = null;
        Variant v1 = new Variant();
        for (int loop = 0; loop < tds.getCount(); loop++) {
            v1.putInt(loop);
            td = tds.getItem(v1);
            if (tableName.equals(td.getName())) {
                break;
```

```
        }
        td = null;
    }
    if (td == null) {
        ComFailException e = new ComFailException ("Table " +
tableName + "does not exist");
        throw e;
    }
    return td;
}
catch (ComException e) { throw e; }
}
```

The following line

```
TableDefs tds = idb_db.getTableDefs();
```

returns a TableDefs object from an instance database variable.

The following section of code defines a Variant and loads it inside a loop with a loop counter. It then loads a _TableDef variable that is indexed by the Variant. If the name of the table (retrieved by the `_TableDef.getName` method) is equal to the `tableName` argument, execution of the loop ends. If the table denoted by the `tableName` argument is not found, `td` is reset by setting it to `null`:

```
Variant v1 = new Variant();
for (int loop = 0; loop < tds.getCount(); loop++) {
    v1.putInt(loop);
    td = tds.getItem(v1);
    if (tableName.equals(td.getName())) {
        break;
    }
    td = null;
}
```

The following code tests if a_TableDef is found. If one is not found, a ComFailException is thrown:

```
if (td == null) {
    ComFailException e = new ComFailException ("Table " +
tableName + "does not exist");
    throw e;
}
    return td;
```

That is how you can retrieve a table using a table name. Now you can use any _TableDef function.

Dissecting table fields

Every table must contain at least one field. Field manipulation using your Java program may be necessary, especially for programmatic updates. This section discusses adding fields, deleting fields, and using indexes.

Adding fields

The CreateField method has the following prototype:

```
CreateField(Variant name, Variant DataTypeEnum, Variant size);
```

The name Variant contains the name of your field, and the size Variant is the number of bytes a field contains. The DataTypeEnum Variant contains one of the data types listed in Table 26-10.

Table 26-10   DataTypeEnum Variant Values

Type Constant	Database Data Type
dbBoolean	Boolean
dbByte	Byte
dbInteger	Integer
dbLong	Long
dbCurrency	Currency
dbSingle	Single
dbDouble	Double
dbDate	Date/Time
dbText	Text
dbLongBinary	Long Binary (OLE Object)
dbMemo	Memo
dbGUID	GUID

The following addField method uses the getTableDef method previously defined in this chapter to add a field to any table in a database. The parameters are the fieldName, a type constant shown in Table 26-10.

```
public void addField(String tableName, String fieldName, short
datatype, int length) throws ComException {
    try {
    // Get the _TableDef
        _TableDef td = getTableDef(tableName);
    // Get all the fields of a table
        Fields flds = td.getFields();
    // Create a database field
        Variant v1 = new Variant();
        Variant v2 = new Variant();
        Variant v3 = new Variant();
        v1.putString(fieldName);
        v2.putInt(datatype);
```

```
    v3.putInt(length);
    Field fld = td.CreateField(v1, v2, v3);
// Append the field to the Fields container
    flds.Append(fld);
    }
    catch (ComException e) { throw e; }
}
```

Deleting fields

Deleting fields is easier than adding them. The following three-line method (plus error trapping) uses the `getTableDef` method to return the _TableDef from a table name, to get the Fields container from the table, and to delete the field name from the Fields container:

```
public void deleteField(String tableName, String fieldName) throws
ComException {
    try {
    // Get the _TableDef
        _TableDef td = getTableDef(tableName);
    // Get all the fields of a table
        Fields flds = td.getFields();
    // Delete the fields from Fields collection
        flds.Delete(fieldName);
    }
    catch (ComException e) { throw e; }
}
```

Searching for fields

There may be times when you want a specific Field object of a table returned. Field objects are returned by using the `getItem` method. The `getItem` method returns a Field based on the value of the field's index — or placement in the database.

The following `getfield` method returns a _Field that corresponds to a field name and a table name by using the `Fields.getItem` method in conjunction with the _Field.getName method. A function such as this can be handy for updating a field in a database using DAO calls:

```
public _Field getField(String tableName, String fieldName) throws
ComException {
    try {
        _TableDef td = getTableDef(tableName);
        Fields flds = td.getFields();
        _Field fld;
        Variant v1 = new Variant();
        for (int loop = 0; loop < flds.getCount(); loop++) {
            v1.putInt(loop);
            fld = flds.getItem(v1);
            if (fieldName.equals(fld.getName())) {
                return fld;
            }
```

```
        }
        ComFailException t = new ComFailException ("Table " +
tableName + "does not exist");
        throw t;
    }
    catch (ComException e) { throw e; }
}
```

Accessing indexes

An index is an important database construct. As tables get larger, searching through them can take a long time. Indexes enable you to streamline the search, usually by incorporating some type of binary or b-tree algorithm. This can reduce the comparisons needed for a search from several thousand or even several million comparisons to often less than 20. When querying on a field like a name or a location, it's often expedient to use an index.

Indexes can also be used to ensure some database integrity. You can define indexes to not allow duplicates. In fact, every database table should have at least one unique index, called a primary key, to differentiate it from other table records. Every table is allowed one primary key, but there can be several unique indexes defined.

Indexes are probably the hardest DAO component to master. To access an index, you must do the following:

1. Get the _TableDef object for the table that needs the index. (Use something similar to the `getTableDef` method defined earlier in this chapter.)

2. Create an Index using the _TableDef.CreateIndex method.

3. Define this index as a primary key, unique, or allows nulls using the Index.putPrimaryKey(boolean), the Index.putUnique(boolean), and the Index.putAllowNulls(boolean) methods. These all default to false.

4. Use the `Index.getFields()` method to get the fields of the newly-defined Index. The tricky part here is that, unlike all other getFields methods used in DAO, the `Index.getFields` method returns a Variant rather than a Fields object.

5. Use the `Variant.getDispatch()` method to return an IndexFields class. The tricky part here is that the Variant dispatch returned is not a Fields object, as you might assume, but rather an IndexFields object. The value returned by the `Variant.getDispatch` method must be cast to an IndexFields method.

Secret

A *dispatch* is a COM interface that is descended from the IDispatch interface. A dispatch can be typecasted into any COM object, but fails at run time if that object is typecasted into an incorrect COM class.

6. Create your Field to put in your index. Note that this Field must be of the same data type and field size as its corresponding _TableDef Field. (You could use the `getFields` method shown earlier in this chapter and then use the `Field.getName`, `Fields.getType`, and `Field.getSize` methods to ensure that they agree.)

7. Append your Field to the IndexFields container object you defined earlier.

8. Because an index can consist of several fields, repeat Steps 6 and 7 until all the fields of the index have been defined.

9. Use the `Variant.putDispatch` method to place the IndexFields object into a Variant object.

10. Use the `Index.putFields` object to place the IndexFields Variant into the index you are defining.

11. Get the Indexes container object using the _TableDef.getIndexes method.

12. Append the newly-created Index object to the Indexes container object by using the `Indexes.Append` method.

Secret

For those of you who know SQL, using the `Database.Execute` or `Database.ExecuteSQL` command to set an index may be easier. SQL is beyond the scope of this chapter, but is covered in a different chapter.

As you can see, setting an Index using DAO is quite complicated. The following function indexes a primary key for the first column in a table when passed a table name and a field name. It uses the getTableDef and `getField` methods that are discussed earlier in this chapter:

```
public void indexPKey(String tableName, String fieldName) throws
ComException {
    try {
    //Get a _TableDef  using the getTableDef method and a table name
        _TableDef td = getTableDef(tableName);
        Variant v1 = new Variant();
        Variant v2 = new Variant();
        Variant v3 = new Variant();
        Variant v4 = new Variant();
    // Create an Index using the CreateIndex method.
        String indexName = tableName + "PKey";
        v1.putString(indexName);
        _Index ndx = td.CreateIndex(v1);
    // Tell DAO if this index is a primary key, unique, or allows
nulls
        ndx.putPrimary(true);
        ndx.putUnique(true);
        ndx.putIgnoreNulls(false);
    // Get the fields of the newly-defined Index
        v4 = ndx.getFields();
    // Get the IndexFields object via dispatch
        IndexFields flds = (IndexFields) v4.getDispatch();
```

```
        // Create your Field that matches the TableDef field to put in
your index
            _Field f = getField(tableName, fieldName);
            v1.putString(f.getName());
            v2.putShort(f.getType());
            v3.putInt(f.getSize());
            Field fld = ndx.CreateField(v1, v2, v3);
        // Append your Field to the IndexFields container object
            flds.Append(fld);
        // Place the IndexFields object into a Variant object
            v1.putDispatch(flds);
        // Place the IndexFields Variant into the index
            ndx.putFields(v1);
        // Get the Indexes container object of the table
            Indexes ndxs = td.getIndexes();
        // Append the index to the TableDef Indexes  object
            ndxs.Append(ndx);
        }
        catch (ComException e) { throw e; }
    }
```

Secret

Although indexes can speed up a search, they tend to slow down inserts and updates to table records. Try not to index every field in a database, or data entry could slow to a crawl.

Making Access Modules

It's probably a good idea to pull all these functions together into one database module. This module could be added to over time, and then imported and used in every Visual J++ database program to make database programming a little easier. The class, DAODatabase (Listing 26-1), combines the methods discussed so far and adds a createOrOpenDB method that opens or creates (if it does not exist) a database. It also adds two constructors if you want to pass a database name or not. In addition, the addField method has been overloaded to enable the creation of a primary key or index at the same time that a field is created. Finally, an indexField module indexes field names contained in a String array.

Notice that the database engine is static. That way, only one database engine is running at any given time. However, several databases can be opened with each instance of DAODatabase using the same database engine.

A finalize destructor method ensures that the database is closed when no longer in use. A getDB method returns the database.

A main method is used for testing only. Most often, DAODatabase is instantiated by another class, rather than run as a stand-alone class, and therefore main is never accessed.

Listing 26-1: DAODatabase.java

```java
import com.ms.com.*;
import dao350.*;

public class DAODatabase {
    public static final int NO_ERROR = 0;
    public static final int DATABASE_CREATED = 1;
    public static final int DATAENGINE_FAILURE = -1;
    public static final int DATABASE_CONNECTION_FAILURE = -2;
    public static final int CLOSE_FAILURE = -3;
    public static final int COMMIT_FAILURE = -4;
    public static final int ROLLBACK_FAILURE = -5;
    public static final int DETERMINE_ERROR_FAILURE = -5;
    public static final int NO_INDEX = 0;
    public static final int UNIQUE_INDEX = 1;
    public static final int NON_UNIQUE_INDEX = 2;
    private static _DBEngine i_dbEng;
    private Database idb_db;
    public int ii_error;
    private String i_dbName;
    public static void main (String args[]) {
        DAODatabase d = new DAODatabase();
        try {
            d.createOrOpenDB("C:\\My Documents\\Visual Studio
Projects\\EmpDB.mdb");
        d.createTable("junk");
            d.addField("junk", "Field1", DataTypeEnum.dbText, 30,
UNIQUE_INDEX, true);
            d.dropTable("junk");
        }
        catch (ComException e) {
      System.out.println(e.getMessage() + d.getErrorMessage());
        }
    }
    public DAODatabase(String a_dbName) throws ComException {
        //This constructor opens a specific database
        try { createOrOpenDB(a_dbName); }
        catch (ComException e) { throw e; }
    }
    public DAODatabase() {
        //This constructor creates an empty  DAODatabase instance
    }
    protected void finalize() throws ComException, Throwable { //
Destructor
        try {
            commit();
            closeDB();
        }
        catch (ComException e) {
            throw e;
        }
        try { super.finalize(); }
        catch (Throwable t) { throw t; }
    }
```

```
    public Database createOrOpenDB(String a_dbName) throws
ComException{
        //Start the database Engine to access DAO
        try {
            i_dbName = a_dbName;
            ii_error = NO_ERROR;
            getDBEngine();
            try { openDB(); }
            catch(ComException e) {
                ii_error = DATABASE_CREATED;
                createDB();
            }
            return idb_db;
        }
        catch (ComException e) {
            idb_db = null;
            throw e;
        }
    }
    public void closeDB () throws ComException {
        if (idb_db == null) {
            return;
        }
        try {
            idb_db.Close();
            idb_db = null;
        }
        catch (ComException e) {
            idb_db = null;
            ii_error = CLOSE_FAILURE;
            throw e;
        }
    }
    public Database openDB() throws ComException {
        try {
            // Create Variants for optional parameters
            Variant v1 = new Variant();
            Variant v2 = new Variant();
            Variant v3 = new Variant();
            closeDB();
            v1.putBoolean(false);
            v2.putBoolean(false);
            v3.putString("");
            // Open the database for nonexclusive access
            idb_db = i_dbEng.OpenDatabase(i_dbName, v1, v2, v3);
            return idb_db;
        }
        catch(ComException e) {
            // Open existing database failed.
            ii_error = DATABASE_CONNECTION_FAILURE;
            idb_db = null;
            throw e;
        }
    }
    public Database createDB () throws ComException {
        try {
```

```
                //Create a variant for arguments
                Variant v1 = new Variant();

                closeDB();
                i_dbEng.Rollback();
                v1.putInt(DatabaseTypeEnum.dbVersion30);
                idb_db = i_dbEng.CreateDatabase(i_dbName,
                    //Use the Constants.General value for USA English.
                    ";LANGID=0x0409;CP=1252;COUNTRY=0",
                    v1);
                i_dbEng.BeginTrans();
        }
        catch(ComException e) {
            // Opening and creating failed.  Set db to null.
            ii_error = DATABASE_CONNECTION_FAILURE;
            idb_db = null;
            throw e;
        }
        return idb_db;
    }
    public Database getDB () {
        return idb_db;
    }
    public _DBEngine getDBEngine() throws ComException {
        try {
            if (i_dbEng != null) {
                return i_dbEng;
            }
            // Create the License Manager object
            ILicenseMgr mgr = new LicenseMgr();
            // Use the License Manager to create the i_dbEngine
            i_dbEng = (_DBEngine) mgr.createWithLic(
                // The license key for the DAO i_dbEngine
                "mbmabptebkjcdlgtjmskjwtsdhjbmkmwtrak",
                // The CLSID for the DAO i_dbEngine
                "{00000010-0000-0010-8000-00AA006D2EA4}",
                // The aggregation IUnknown* punkOuter
                null,
                // The ctxFlag to create in inproc server
                ComContext.INPROC_SERVER);
                i_dbEng.BeginTrans();  // Allow Commits and
                                       // Rollbacks

            return i_dbEng;
        }
        catch(ComException e) {
            // The engine could not be created.  Set i_dbEng to
            // null.
            ii_error = DATAENGINE_FAILURE;
            i_dbEng = null;
            throw e;
        }
    }
    public void commit() throws ComException {
        try {

i_dbEng.CommitTrans(CommitTransOptionsEnum.dbForceOSFlush);
```

```
            i_dbEng.BeginTrans();
        }
        catch(ComException e) {
            ii_error = COMMIT_FAILURE;
            throw e;
        }
    }
    public void rollback() throws ComException {
        try {
            i_dbEng.Rollback();
            i_dbEng.BeginTrans();
        }
        catch(ComException e) {
            ii_error = ROLLBACK_FAILURE;
            throw e;
        }
    }
    public dao350.Error getError() throws ComException {
        try {
            dao350.Error myerror = null;
            Errors errorList = i_dbEng.getErrors();
            int errorCount = errorList.getCount();
            if (errorCount > 0) {
                Variant errorNumber = new Variant();
                errorNumber.putInt(errorCount-1);
                myerror = errorList.getItem(errorNumber);
            }
            return myerror;
        }
        catch(ComException e) {
            ii_error = DETERMINE_ERROR_FAILURE;
            throw e;
        }
    }
    public int getErrorNumber() {
        try {
            dao350.Error error = getError();
            if (error != null) {
                return error.getNumber();
            }
            return 0;
        }
        catch(ComException e) {
            return 0;
        }
    }
    public String getErrorMessage() {
        try {
            dao350.Error error = getError();
            if (error != null) {
                return error.getDescription();
            }
            return "No Database Error Occurred";
        }
        catch(ComException e) {
            return "Error could not be determined.";
```

```
            }
        }
    public void createTable(String tableName) throws ComException{
        try {
        // Get the TableDefs container object
            Variant v1 = new Variant();
            Variant v2 = new Variant();
            Variant v3 = new Variant();
            Variant v4 = new Variant();
            TableDefs tds = idb_db.getTableDefs();
        // Create a _TableDef object
            v1.putString(tableName);
            v2.putInt(0);
            v3.putString("");
            v4.putString("");
            _TableDef td = idb_db.CreateTableDef(v1, v2, v3, v4);
        // Create a Field object
            v1.putString("myfield");
            v2.putInt(DataTypeEnum.dbText);
            v3.putInt(30);
            Field fld = td.CreateField(v1, v2, v3);
        // Retrieve the Fields container of the table.
            Fields flds = td.getFields();
        // Append the Field object to the Fields container object
            flds.Append(fld);
        // Append your newly created _TableDef to the Database
TableDefs container
            tds.Append(td);
        }
        catch (ComException e) { throw e; }
    }
    public void dropTable(String tableName)  throws ComException {
        try {
            TableDefs tds = idb_db.getTableDefs();
            tds.Delete(tableName);
        }
        catch (ComException e) { throw e; }
    }
    public void addField(String tableName, String fieldName, int
datatype, int length) throws ComException {
        try { addField (tableName, fieldName, datatype, length,
NO_INDEX, false); }
        catch (ComException e) { throw e; }
    }
    public void addField(String tableName, String fieldName, int
datatype, int length, int indexType, boolean pkey) throws
ComException {
        try {
        // Get the _TableDef
            _TableDef td = getTableDef(tableName);
        // Get all the fields of a table
            Fields flds = td.getFields();
        // Create a database field
            Variant v1 = new Variant();
            Variant v2 = new Variant();
            Variant v3 = new Variant();
```

```
                v1.putString(fieldName);
                v2.putInt(datatype);
                v3.putInt(length);
                Field fld = td.CreateField(v1, v2, v3);
            // Append the field to the Fields container
                flds.Append(fld);
                String fieldNames[] = new String [1];
                fieldNames[0] = fieldName;
                switch (indexType) {
                    case UNIQUE_INDEX :
                        indexField(tableName, fieldNames, pkey, true);
                        break;
                    case NON_UNIQUE_INDEX :
                        indexField(tableName, fieldNames, false,
                        false);
                        break;
                }
            }
        catch (ComException e) { throw e; }
    }
    public String indexField(String tableName, String fieldNames[],
boolean pkey, boolean unique) throws ComException {
        try {
            Variant v1 = new Variant();
            Variant v2 = new Variant();
            Variant v3 = new Variant();
            Variant v4 = new Variant();
            String indexName = tableName;
        // Get a _TableDef  using the getTableDef method and a table
        // name
            _TableDef td = getTableDef(tableName);
        // Get the Indexes container object of the table
            Indexes ndxs = td.getIndexes();
        // Form an index name that defines this index
            for (int loop = 0; loop < fieldNames.length; loop++) {
                indexName = indexName + fieldNames[loop];
            }
            v1.putString(indexName);
        // Create an Index using the CreateIndex method.
            _Index ndx = td.CreateIndex(v1);
        // Tell DAO if this index is a primary key
            ndx.putPrimary(pkey);
        // Tell DAO if this index is unique or allows nulls
            if (pkey) {
                ndx.putUnique(true);
                ndx.putIgnoreNulls(false);
            }
            else if (unique) {
                ndx.putUnique(true);
                ndx.putIgnoreNulls(true);
            }
            else {
                ndx.putUnique(false);
                ndx.putIgnoreNulls(true);
            }
        // Get the fields of the newly-defined Index
```

```
                v4 = ndx.getFields();
        // Get the IndexFields object via dispatch
            IndexFields flds = (IndexFields) v4.getDispatch();
        // Loop to index all fields in the fieldNames String array
            for (int loop = 0; loop < fieldNames.length; loop++){
        // Make sure the index field info agrees with the table
        // field info
                _Field f = getField(tableName, fieldNames[loop]);
                v1.putString(f.getName());
                v2.putShort(f.getType());
                v3.putInt(f.getSize());
        // Create your Field that matches the TableDef field to put
        // in your index
                Field fld = ndx.CreateField(v1, v2, v3);
        // Append your Field to the IndexFields container object
                flds.Append(fld);
                }
        // Place the IndexFields object into a Variant object
            v1.putDispatch(flds);
        // Place the IndexFields Variant into the index
            ndx.putFields(v1);
        // Append the index to the TableDef Indexes  object
            ndxs.Append(ndx);
        // Return the index name
            return indexName;
        }
        catch (ComException e) { throw e; }
    }
    public void deleteField(String tableName, String fieldName)
throws ComException {
        try {
        // Get the _TableDef
            _TableDef td = getTableDef(tableName);
        // Get all the fields of a table
            Fields flds = td.getFields();
        // Delete the fields from Fields collection
            flds.Delete(fieldName);
        }
        catch (ComException e) { throw e; }
    }
    public _Field getField(String tableName, String fieldName) throws
ComException {
        try {
            _TableDef td = getTableDef(tableName);
            Fields flds = td.getFields();
            _Field fld;
            Variant v1 = new Variant();
            for (int loop = 0; loop < flds.getCount(); loop++) {
                v1.putInt(loop);
                fld = flds.getItem(v1);
                if (fieldName.equals(fld.getName())) {
                    return fld;
                }
            }
            ComFailException t = new ComFailException ("Table " +
tableName + "does not exist");
```

```
                throw t;
            }
        catch (ComException e) { throw e; }
    }
    public _TableDef getTableDef(String tableName) throws
ComException {
        try {
            TableDefs tds = idb_db.getTableDefs();
            _TableDef td = null;
            Variant v1 = new Variant();
            for (int loop = 0; loop < tds.getCount(); loop++) {
                v1.putInt(loop);
                td = tds.getItem(v1);
                if (tableName.equals(td.getName())) {
                    break;
                }
                td = null;
            }
            if (td == null) {
                ComFailException e = new ComFailException ("Table "
+ tableName + "does not exist");
                throw e;
            }
            return td;
        }
        catch (ComException e) { throw e; }
    }
}
```

Using an access module

Database access modules are easy to use. By making some assumptions, you can make accessing your database easier. Assumptions that I've made when creating a database access module are:

■ You don't open a database engine unless you are also going to open a database.

■ If a database is not found, you want to create one.

■ You usually use only one database at a time. (Multiple databases are enabled by multiple instantiation of DAODatabase, but transaction processing is done at the database-engine level rather than the database level.)

■ You usually index on one database column rather than multiple database columns. (Multiple-column indexes are allowed in Listing 26-1, but adding a field and creating an index at the same time is often done.)

■ Probably, the worst assumption I've made is that security is unnecessary. Workspace processing needed for security is not covered in this chapter, but is discussed in Chapter 25.

Of course, any programmer can and will add new code to handle new assumptions and remove some of my assumptions when customizing his or her own DAO application.

For example, if you want to create a program that opens (or creates) a database and then adds fields and indexes, you could then list the database tables and fields, and provide a message box with the results, as shown in Figure 26-3.

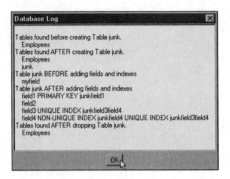

Figure 26-3: An audit trail of database changes (like this one) is often requested by the end user and is useful for troubleshooting software version upgrades.

Listing 26-2 extensively uses the DAODatabase class shown in Listing 26-1. All database manipulations are done through the DAODatabase class. DAOTable (Listing 26-2) uses the DAO sample application database included with Visual J++.

Listing 26-2: DAOTable.java

```java
import dao350.*;
import com.ms.com.*;

public class DAOTable implements IMessageBox {
    private String is_database = ""C:\\My Documents\\Visual Studio
Projects\\EmpDB.mdb"";
    private DAODatabase iDAO_db;
    private Database idb_db;
    private String is_log = "";
    public static void main(String args[]) {
        DAOTable d = null;
        try {
            d = new DAOTable();
            d.doManipulations();
        }
        catch (ComException e) { d.dbErrorMessage(); }
        catch (Throwable t) { d.errorMessage(t); }
    }
    public DAOTable()  throws ComException {
        try {
            iDAO_db = new DAODatabase(is_database);
            idb_db = iDAO_db.getDB();
        }
        catch (ComException e) { throw e; }
        catch (Throwable t) { errorMessage(t); }
```

```
        }
    public void doManipulations() {
        try {
            showTables("Tables found before creating Table junk.");
            iDAO_db.createTable("junk");
            showTables("Tables found AFTER creating Table junk.");
            showFields("Table junk BEFORE adding fields and
            indexes", "junk");
//Add a primary key field
            iDAO_db.addField("junk","field1", DataTypeEnum.dbText,
30, iDAO_db.UNIQUE_INDEX, true);
//Now add two fields
            iDAO_db.addField("junk","field2", DataTypeEnum.dbText,
            30);
            iDAO_db.addField("junk","field3", DataTypeEnum.dbText,
            30);
//Now add a nonunique non-pkey indexed field
            iDAO_db.addField("junk","field4", DataTypeEnum.dbText,
30, iDAO_db.NON_UNIQUE_INDEX, false);
//Now create a multifield nonunique, non-pkey index
            String fieldNames[] = {"field3", "field4"};
            iDAO_db.indexField("junk", fieldNames, false, true);
//Now delete the myfield field created by default when creating the
//table.
            iDAO_db.deleteField("junk","myfield");
            showFields("Table junk AFTER adding fields and indexes",
"junk");
            iDAO_db.dropTable("junk");
            showTables("Tables found AFTER dropping Table junk.");
            showDBLog();
        }
        catch (ComException e) { throw e; }
        catch (Throwable t) { errorMessage(t); }
    }
    public void showMessageBox(String title, String message, int
    type) {
        MessageBox m = new MessageBox (this,  title, message, type);
    }
    public void errorMessage(Throwable t) {
        Class thisclass = t.getClass();
        String message = thisclass.getName() + " -- " +
t.getMessage();
        showMessageBox("An Error Has Occurred", message,
MessageBox.OK);
    }
    public void dbErrorMessage() {
        showMessageBox("Database Error", iDAO_db.getErrorMessage(),
MessageBox.OK);
    }
    public void showDBLog() {
        iDAO_db.commit();
        showMessageBox("Database Log", is_log, MessageBox.OK);
    }
    public void showFields(String message, String tableName) throws
ComException {
        try {
```

```
                _TableDef td = iDAO_db.getTableDef(tableName);
                Fields flds = td.getFields();
                is_log = is_log + "\r\n" + message;
                Variant v1 = new Variant();
                for (int loop = 0; loop < flds.getCount(); loop++) {
                    v1.putInt(loop);
                    _Field fld = flds.getItem(v1);
                    is_log = is_log + "\r\n    " + fld.getName() +
showIndexes(tableName, fld.getName());
                }
            }
        catch (ComException e) { throw e; }
        catch (Throwable t) { errorMessage(t); }
    }
    private String showIndexes(String tableName, String fieldName)
throws ComException {
        String myString = "";
        try {
            Variant v1 = new Variant();
            _TableDef td = iDAO_db.getTableDef(tableName);
            Indexes ndxs = td.getIndexes();
            for (int ndxLoop = 0; ndxLoop < ndxs.getCount();
ndxLoop++) {
                v1.putInt(ndxLoop);
                _Index ndx = ndxs.getItem(v1);
                v1 = ndx.getFields();
                IndexFields flds = (IndexFields) v1.getDispatch();
                for (int fldLoop = 0; fldLoop < flds.getCount();
fldLoop++) {
                    v1.putInt(fldLoop);
                    v1 = flds.getItem(v1);
                    _Field fld = (_Field) v1.getDispatch();
                    if (fieldName.equals(fld.getName())) {
                        if (ndx.getPrimary()) {
                            myString = myString + " PRIMARY KEY ";
                        }
                        else if (ndx.getUnique()) {
                            myString = myString + " UNIQUE INDEX "
;
                        }
                        else {
                            myString = myString + " NON-UNIQUE
INDEX " ;
                        }
                        myString = myString + ndx.getName();
                    }
                }
            }
        }
        catch (ComException e) { throw e; }
        return myString;
    }
    public void showTables(String message)  throws ComException {
        String errorString;
        try {
            TableDefs tds = idb_db.getTableDefs();
```

```
            Variant v1 = new Variant();
            is_log = is_log + "\r\n" + message;
            for (int loop = 0; loop < tds.getCount(); loop++) {
                v1.putInt(loop);
                _TableDef td = tds.getItem(v1);
                String name = td.getName();
                // Ignore system tables
                if (!name.startsWith("MSys")) {
                    is_log = is_log + "\r\n    " + name;
                }
            }
        }
        catch (ComException e) { throw e; }
        catch (Throwable t) { errorMessage(t); }
    }
    public void answer(int ans) {
        System.exit(0);
    }
}
```

Table 26-11 shows the methods defined in Listing 26-2.

Table 26-11	Methods Defined in Listing 26-2
Method Name	**Description**
main	The `main` method instantiates the `DAOTable` class and calls the `doManipulations` method.
DAOTable	The `DAOTable` constructor instantiates `DAODatabase` and loads the class `Database` variable for any `Database` methods that need to be called.
doManipulations	The `doManipulations` method is the main function in the `DAOTable` class. It calls methods that add and drop tables from the database and fields from the database tables. It also calls methods that return and display information about the current status of the database.
showMessageBox	`DAOTable` implements `IMessageBox`. This enables `DAOTable` to display a message box containing any string. The `showMessageBox` method is used to instantiate a `MessageBox` class and display information. The `MessageBox` class calls the `answer` method when a button is pressed.
errorMessage	The `errorMessage` formats a message from an exception and calls the `showMessageBox` method to display it.
dbErrorMessage	The `dbErrorMessage` retrieves a database error and calls the `showMessageBox` method to display it.

(continued)

Table 26-11 *(Continued)*

Method Name	Description
showDBLog	If the showDBLog method is called, it means that all functions worked perfectly. A commit is issued to the database to make the changes permanent, and the showMessageBox method is called to display the database log of changes.
showFields	The showFields method lists all the fields in a database and calls showIndexes to see if each field is indexed and how.
showIndexes	The showIndexes method identifies the index name and type associated with a field.
showTables	The showTables method lists the tables in a database.
answer	The answer method is called by the MessageBox class through the IMessageBox interface.

Getting information from a database

Listing 26-2 has three new methods (showFields, showIndexes, and showTables) that return information about the database. This is slightly different than previous methods that were used to create or alter the current database.

Getting table information

The showTables method, listed here, adds all the table names in a database to the is_log String class attribute. Tables are listed by looping through the TableDefs container object, returning each table indexed by the _TableDef.getItem method, and returning the table name using the _TableDef.getName method. If a table begins with MSys, then it is a system table, and should not be listed:

```
public void showTables(String message)   throws ComException {
    String errorString;
    try {
        TableDefs tds = idb_db.getTableDefs();
        Variant v1 = new Variant();
        is_log = is_log + "\r\n" + message;
        for (int loop = 0; loop < tds.getCount(); loop++) {
            v1.putInt(loop);
            _TableDef td = tds.getItem(v1);
            String name = td.getName();
            // Ignore system tables
            if (!name.startsWith("MSys")) {
                is_log = is_log + "\r\n     " + name;
            }
        }
```

```
        }
        catch (ComException e) { throw e; }
        catch (Throwable t) { errorMessage(t); }
    }
```

Getting field information

The `showFields` method lists all the fields in a table. First, the
`DAODatabase.getTableDef` method is used to return the _TableDef of the table
that corresponds to a `tableName`. Then the Fields container of the database
is returned using the `_TableDef.getFields` method.

Retrieving each field name is similar to retrieving each table name. Each field
is retrieved using the `Fields.getItem` method, and the field name is
appended using the `flds.getName` method. In addition, index information is
added by calling the `showIndexes` method. The `showFields` method is listed
here:

```
public void showFields(String message, String tableName) throws
ComException {
    try {
        _TableDef td = iDAO_db.getTableDef(tableName);
        Fields flds = td.getFields();
        is_log = is_log + "\r\n" + message;
        Variant v1 = new Variant();
        for (int loop = 0; loop < flds.getCount(); loop++) {
            v1.putInt(loop);
            _Field fld = flds.getItem(v1);
            is_log = is_log + "\r\n      " + fld.getName() +
showIndexes(tableName, fld.getName());
        }
    }
    catch (ComException e) { throw e; }
    catch (Throwable t) errorMessage(t);
}
```

Manipulating Tables with Recordsets

As with ADO, DAO Recordsets are important in manipulating data inside a
Jet database. This section describes how to manipulate records inside a
database.

Opening a Recordset

To open a Recordset, you must use the `Database.OpenRecordset` method.
(This method is described in the Database Methods section earlier in this
chapter.) This is typically done in the `init` method or the `start` method in
an Applet.

The following `start` method retrieves the current database and opens a Recordset. After this is done, the module creates a form, moves to the first record in the table, and uses a `showData` method, which displays the data of the current record on the form.

```
public void start() {
        try {
            iDAO_db = new DAODatabase(is_database);
            idb_db = iDAO_db.getDB();
            Variant v4 = new Variant();
            Variant v5 = new Variant();
            Variant v6 = new Variant();
            v4.putShort(RecordsetTypeEnum.dbOpenTable);
            v5.putInt(RecordsetOptionEnum.dbSeeChanges);
            v6.putInt(LockTypeEnum.dbOptimistic);
            irs_recordset = idb_db.OpenRecordset(is_table, v4, v5,
            v6);
            // Create and display the form from a recordset
            if_form = new DAOForm(irs_recordset);
            add("Center", if_form);
            irs_recordset.MoveFirst();
            if_form.showData();
        }
        catch (ComException e) databaseError();
}
```

Retrieving information

Retrieving information from a database consists of two steps:

1. Querying the database for desired information

2. Displaying the information from the query

Querying the database

Five main methods are used to position records in a Recordset. They are listed in Table 26-12.

Table 26-12   Recordset Positioning Commands

Method	*Description*
`Recordset.MoveFirst()`	Moves the current record to the first record in a Recordset.
`Recordset.MoveLast(int async)`	Moves the current record to the last record in a Recordset. You can specify dbAsyncronous and use the `stillExecuting` method to enable your program to continue.
`Recordset.MoveNext()`	Moves the current record to the next record in a Recordset.

Method	Description
Recordset.MovePrev()	Moves the current record to the previous record in a Recordset.
Recordset.Move(int numRows, Variant startBookmark)	Moves the current record a specific number of rows. The numRows argument enables you to move down (positive number) or up (negative number). You can also start from a bookmark rather than the current position.

Secret

Although bookmarks are not used here, they are a great way to find the current record, especially if the database changes a lot. To get a bookmark for the current record, use code similar to the following line:

```
Safearray bookmark = irs_recordset.getBookmark();
```

This bookmark can then be used with a Move() to return to the previous position even if other records have been added to the table. This enables you to keep track of your current position even in a multiuser environment.

The following code segment from the handleEvent method tests which button the user pressed and uses the MoveFirst, MovePrev, MoveNext, and MoveLast methods to scroll through a table on the database:

```
else if (evt.target == icb_first){
    before_move();
    irs_recordset.MoveFirst();
}
else if (evt.target == icb_prev){
    getNextChosen = false;
    before_move();
    irs_recordset.MovePrevious();
    if (irs_recordset.getPercentPosition() < 0.0) {
        showStatus("Last record on table");
        irs_recordset.MoveFirst();
    }
}
else if (evt.target == icb_next){
    before_move();
    irs_recordset.MoveNext();
    if (irs_recordset.getNoMatch()) {
        showStatus("Last record on table");
        irs_recordset.MoveLast(0);
    }
}
else if (evt.target == icb_last){
    before_move();
    irs_recordset.MoveLast(0);
}
```

If an error is encountered, some error recovery is attempted. Rather than simply display an error if the next record or previous record does not exist (error number 3021), the error is trapped. The code is then modified to display the first or last record and then show a status message:

```
catch (ComException e) {
    int errorNum = iDAO_db.getErrorNumber();
    if (errorNum == 3021) { //No current record
        try {
            if (getNextChosen) {
                irs_recordset.MoveLast(0);
                if_form.showData();
                showStatus("There are no more records");
            }
            else {
                irs_recordset.MoveFirst();
                if_form.showData();
                showStatus("There are no previous
                records");
            }
        }
        catch (ComException e2) databaseError();
    }
    else {
        databaseError();
    }
```

Displaying the current record

To display a field, first retrieve it using a getItem method. Then you can use the Field.getName() method to return the name of the field, the getSize method to return the size of a field, and the getType method to return the data type of the field.

The following loop scrolls through the fields in a table and develops a form based on the data type of each field:

```
switch (f.getType()) {
                case (DataTypeEnum.dbBoolean) :
                    icm_field[loop] = new
Checkbox(fieldLabel.getText());
                    fieldLabel.setText("");
                    break;
                case (DataTypeEnum.dbDate) :
                    icm_field[loop] = new TextField(10);
                    break;
                case (DataTypeEnum.dbLong) :
                    if ((f.getAttributes() &
FieldAttributeEnum.dbAutoIncrField) != 0) {
                        icm_field[loop] = new Label("");
                    }
                    else {
                        icm_field[loop] = new
TextField(Math.min(fieldSize,60));
```

```
                }
                break;
            case (DataTypeEnum.dbInteger) :
            case (DataTypeEnum.dbSingle) :
            case (DataTypeEnum.dbDouble) :
            case (DataTypeEnum.dbByte) :
            case (DataTypeEnum.dbCurrency) :
            case (DataTypeEnum.dbText) :
                icm_field[loop] = new
TextField(Math.min(fieldSize,60));
                break;
            case (DataTypeEnum.dbLongBinary) :
            case (DataTypeEnum.dbMemo) :
            case (DataTypeEnum.dbGUID) :
                labelY = 8.0;
                icm_field[loop] = new TextArea(3, 60);
                break;
        }
```

Secret

A `GridBagLayout` is probably the best way to generate automatic forms. A GridBagLayout gives you a grid with different row or column widths, like your Excel spreadsheet.

Then the `scrollThroughData` method is called. It also scrolls through fields using the `Field.getValue` method to store the field value in a Variant. The data type is then tested to determine the display method (`setState` for boolean CheckBoxes, `setText` for other fields).

```
private boolean scrollThroughData(boolean doUpdates) throws
ComException {
        try {
            boolean updates_made = false;
            // Loop through to get field names and types
            for (int loop = 0; loop < ii_numberOfFields; loop++) {
                Variant v1 = new Variant();
                v1.putInt(loop);
                _Field f = iflds_fields.getItem(v1);
                v1 = f.getValue();
                short fieldType = f.getType();
                if (fieldType == DataTypeEnum.dbBoolean) {
                    Checkbox cbxHolder;
                    cbxHolder = (Checkbox) icm_field[loop];
                    if (v1.getvt() <= v1.VariantNull) { //Check if
                    //   a variant type is there
                        if (doUpdates) {
                            if (cbxHolder.getState() == true) {
                                updates_made = true;
                                v1.putBoolean(true);
                                f.putValue(v1);
                            }
                        }
                        else {
                            cbxHolder.setState(false);
                        }
```

```
                                        }
                                        else {      //Set to value in db
                                            if (doUpdates) {
                                                if (cbxHolder.getState() !=
v1.getBoolean()) {

                                                    updates_made = true;

v1.putBoolean(cbxHolder.getState());
                                                    f.putValue(v1);
                                                }
                                            }
                                            else {
                                                cbxHolder.setState(v1.getBoolean());
                                            }
                                        }
                                    }
                                    else if ((fieldType == DataTypeEnum.dbLong)
                                        && ((f.getAttributes() &
FieldAttributeEnum.dbAutoIncrField) != 0)) {
                                        Label lbHolder;
                                        lbHolder = (Label) icm_field[loop];
                                        if (v1.getvt() <= v1.VariantNull) { //Check if
// a variant type is there
                                            lbHolder.setText("");
                                        }
                                        else {      //Set to value in db
                                            lbHolder.setText(v1.toString());
                                        }
                                    }
                                    else{
                                        TextComponent tcHolder;
                                        tcHolder = (TextComponent) icm_field[loop];
                                        String compare = tcHolder.getText();
                                        if (v1.getvt() <= v1.VariantNull) { //Check if
// a variant type is there
                                            if (doUpdates) {
                                                if (!compare.equals("")) {
                                                    updates_made = true;
                                                    v1.putString(compare);
                                                    f.putValue(v1);
                                                }
                                            }
                                            else {
                                                tcHolder.setText("");
                                            }
                                        }
                                        else {      //Set to value in db
                                            if (doUpdates) {
                                                if (!compare.equals(v1.toString())) {
                                                    updates_made = true;
                                                    v1.putString(compare);
                                                    f.putValue(v1);
                                                }
```

```
                    }
                    else {
                        tcHolder.setText(v1.toString());
                    }
                }
            }
        }
        v1 = null; //Deallocate
        f = null;
    }
    return updates_made;
}
catch (ComException e) { throw e; }
}
```

Inserting and updating rows

To insert a row into a table, use the `Recordset.AddNew` method, as shown:

```
before_move();
ib_addingRecord = true;
irs_recordset.AddNew();
```

This places the Recordset in `add` mode. Similarly, you can place the current row in a table by using the `Recordset.Edit` method to place the database in edit mode. Before any movement of the current row in a database, the `before_move` method places `irs_recordset` into edit mode unless it is already in add mode. Then it calls `DAOForm.checkForUpdate` to see if any fields have been updated. If any records have been updated, the `Recordset.Update` method is called to make the add or edit permanent. If no fields have been changed, the edit or add is canceled using the `Recordset.CancelUpdate` method.

Secret

The `Recordset.Update` method results in an error unless preceded by a `Recordset.AddNew` method or a `Recordset.Edit` method. After the `Recordset.Update` method successfully executes, the Recordset is no longer in add or edit mode. An update is shown in the `before_move()` method shown below:

```
public boolean before_move() throws ComException{
  showStatus("");
  try {
    if (irs_recordset.getUpdatable() == false) {
      showStatus("Recordset is not updatable");
    }
    else {
      if (!ib_addingRecord) {
        irs_recordset.Edit();
      }
      if (if_form.checkForUpdate()) {
        ib_changes_made = true;
        showStatus("Changes Made");
        irs_recordset.Update();
```

```
      if (ib_addingRecord) {
        irs_recordset.MoveLast(0);
        ib_addingRecord = false;
      }
      return true;
    }
    irs_recordset.CancelUpdate();
  }
  ib_addingRecord = false;
}
catch (ComException e) {
  ib_addingRecord = false;
  throw e;
}
return false;
}
```

Then the `scrollThroughData` method is called. If the field is being updated, the window field value is compared to the database field value; if they are different, the `Field.putValue` method is called to set the field to the window value, as shown in this snippet of code:

```
TextComponent tcHolder;
tcHolder = (TextComponent) icm_field[loop];
String compare = tcHolder.getText();
if (v1.getvt() <= v1.VariantNull) { //Check if a variant type is
there
  if (doUpdates) {
    if (!compare.equals("")) {
      updates_made = true;
      v1.putString(compare);
      f.putValue(v1);
    }
  }
  else {
    tcHolder.setText("");
  }
}
else {   //Set to value in db
  if (doUpdates) {
    if (!compare.equals(v1.toString())) {
      updates_made = true;
      v1.putString(compare);
      f.putValue(v1);
    }
  }
  else {
    tcHolder.setText(v1.toString());
  }
}
```

Deleting rows

Deleting rows is rather easy. The `Recordset.Delete()` method deletes the current row. A call to the `MoveNext()` method is made to move to the next record. (Error trapping enables the last record to be deleted. The last record then becomes the current record.) This is shown by the following two lines of code:

```
irs_recordset.Delete();
irs_recordset.MoveNext();
```

Making a DAO form

The `DAOFrame` class shown in Listing 26-3 and the `DAOForm` class shown in Listing 26-4 are used together to enable you to display, modify, and update *any* database. These two classes detect the fields in a database table and format a frame window appropriately, as shown in Figure 26-4.

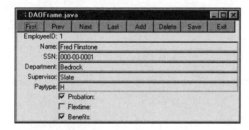

Figure 26-4: `DAOFrame` and the `DAOForm` class can automatically format any database table for data entry and viewing.

To change the display, change your database or change the constant values that point to the `is_database` and `is_table` at the top of the `DAOFrame` class. The `DAOFrame` and `DAOForm` classes automatically format a data entry window for your table.

Listing 26-3: DAOFrame.java

```java
import java.awt.*;
import dao350.*;
import com.ms.com.*;

public class DAOFrame extends Frame implements IMessageBox {
    private String is_database = "C:\\My Documents\\Visual Studio
Projects\\EmpDB.mdb";
    private String is_table = "Employee";
    boolean ib_addingRecord = false;
    boolean ib_changes_made = false;
    private Panel ip_toolbar;
```

```
            private Button icb_first;
            private Button icb_prev;
            private Button icb_next;
            private Button icb_last;
            private Button icb_add;
            private Button icb_delete;
            private Button icb_save;
            private Button icb_exit;
            private DAOForm if_form;      // Data Entry Form
            private DAODatabase iDAO_db;
            private Database idb_db;
            private Recordset irs_recordset;
            public static void main(String args[]){
            DAOFrame d = new DAOFrame();
            d.init();
            d.start();
            d.setTitle("DAOFrame.java");
                d.show();
        }
        public void showStatus(String message){
        MessageBox mb = new MessageBox(this, "DAO Error", message,
MessageBox.OK);
        }
        public void init(){
        //Database stuff—Create the database engine using the license
key
            ip_toolbar = new Panel();
            ip_toolbar.setLayout(new GridLayout(1, 8));
            ip_toolbar.add(icb_first = new Button("First"));
            ip_toolbar.add(icb_prev = new Button("Prev"));
            ip_toolbar.add(icb_next = new Button("Next"));
            ip_toolbar.add(icb_last = new Button("Last"));
            ip_toolbar.add(icb_add = new Button("Add"));
            ip_toolbar.add(icb_delete = new Button("Delete"));
            ip_toolbar.add(icb_save = new Button("Save"));
            ip_toolbar.add(icb_exit = new Button("Exit"));
            add("North", ip_toolbar);
            resize(320, 400);
        }
        public void start() {
            try {
                iDAO_db = new DAODatabase(is_database);
                idb_db = iDAO_db.getDB();
                Variant v4 = new Variant();
                Variant v5 = new Variant();
                Variant v6 = new Variant();
                v4.putInt(RecordsetTypeEnum.dbOpenTable);
                v5.putInt(RecordsetOptionEnum.dbSeeChanges);
                v6.putInt(LockTypeEnum.dbOptimistic);
                irs_recordset = idb_db.OpenRecordset(is_table, v4, v5,
v6);
                // Create and display the form from a recordset
                if_form = new DAOForm(irs_recordset);
                add("Center", if_form);
                irs_recordset.MoveFirst();
```

```
                if_form.showData();
            }
        catch (ComException e) { databaseError("Connection error in
start method"); }

    }
    protected void finalize(){
        try {
            irs_recordset.Close();      // Close the recordset
            irs_recordset = null;
            remove(if_form);            // Remove the form
            if_form = null;
        }
        catch (ComException e) { databaseError("Close error in
finalize method"); }
    }
    public void answer(int ans){ // Needed for IMessageBox Interface
        switch (ans) {
            case MessageBox.YES :
                iDAO_db.commit();
            case MessageBox.NO : // Continue from YES
                closeProgram();
        }
    }
    public void closeProgram(){
        iDAO_db.rollback();
        finalize();
        System.exit(0);
    }
    public boolean action(Event evt, Object what){
        boolean getNextChosen = true;
        // See which button was pushed
        try {
            if (evt.target == icb_exit) {
                before_move();
                if (ib_changes_made) {
                    MessageBox m = new MessageBox(this,
                        "Changes Have Been Made!!",
                        "Changes have been made.  Do you wish to
                        save?",
                        MessageBox.YES_NO_CANCEL);
                }
                else {
                    closeProgram();
                }
            }
            else if (evt.target == icb_first){
                before_move();
                irs_recordset.MoveFirst();
            }
            else if (evt.target == icb_prev){
                getNextChosen = false;
                before_move();
                irs_recordset.MovePrevious();
                if (irs_recordset.getPercentPosition() < 0.0) {
```

```
                        showStatus("Last record on table");
                        irs_recordset.MoveFirst();
                    }
                }
                else if (evt.target == icb_next){
                    before_move();
                    irs_recordset.MoveNext();
                    if (irs_recordset.getNoMatch()) {
                        showStatus("Last record on table");
                        irs_recordset.MoveLast(0);
                    }
                }
                else if (evt.target == icb_last){
                    before_move();
                    irs_recordset.MoveLast(0);
                }
                else if (evt.target == icb_add){
                    before_move();
                    ib_addingRecord = true;
                    irs_recordset.AddNew();
                }
                else if (evt.target == icb_delete){
                    irs_recordset.Delete();
                    irs_recordset.MoveNext();
                }
                else if (evt.target == icb_save){
                    before_move();
                    iDAO_db.commit();
                    ib_changes_made = false;
                }
                else {     // No button was pushed
                    return super.action(evt, what);
                }
                if_form.showData();    // Show the record
            }
        catch (ComException e) {
            int errorNum = iDAO_db.getErrorNumber();
            if (errorNum == 3021) { //No current record
                try {
                    if (getNextChosen) {
                        irs_recordset.MoveLast(0);
                        if_form.showData();
                        showStatus("There are no more records");
                    }
                    else {
                        irs_recordset.MoveFirst();
                        if_form.showData();
                        showStatus("There are no previous
                        records");
                    }
                }
            catch (ComException e2) { databaseError("Action error in
moving first or last"); }
            }
            else {
```

```
                    databaseError("Action error");
                }
            }
        return true;
        }
        public boolean handleEvent(Event  evt){
            if (evt.id == Event.WINDOW_DESTROY || evt.target ==
icb_exit) {
        evt.target = (Object) icb_exit;
        action (evt, (Object) icb_exit);
            }
            else {      // No button was pushed
                return super.handleEvent(evt);
            }
        return true;
        }
        public void databaseError(String message){
            MessageBox mb = new MessageBox(this, "Database Error",
              message + "\n"
             + "Database error #"
                        + Integer.toString(iDAO_db.getErrorNumber())
                        + " -- "
                        + iDAO_db.getErrorMessage(),
              MessageBox.OK);
        }
      public boolean before_move() throws ComException{
          showStatus("");
          try {
              if (irs_recordset.getUpdatable() == false) {
                  showStatus("Recordset is not updatable");
              }
              else {
                  if (!ib_addingRecord) {
                      irs_recordset.Edit();
                  }
                  if (if_form.checkForUpdate()) {
                      ib_changes_made = true;
                      showStatus("Changes Made");
                      irs_recordset.Update(0, false);
                      if (ib_addingRecord) {
                          irs_recordset.MoveLast(0);
                          ib_addingRecord = false;
                      }
                      return true;
                  }
                  irs_recordset.CancelUpdate(0);
              }
              ib_addingRecord = false;
          }
          catch (ComException e) {
              ib_addingRecord = false;
              throw e;
          }
          return false;
      }
}
```

The DAOForm class shown in Listing 26-4 builds a Java Component based on the contents of a database table. This Component is placed on DAOFrame for displaying.

Listing 26-4: DAOForm.java

```java
import java.awt.*;
import dao350.*;
import com.ms.com.*;
public class DAOForm extends Panel{  // Data Entry Form
    protected GridBagLayout igbl_layout = new GridBagLayout();
    protected GridBagConstraints  igbc_constraints = new
GridBagConstraints();
    private Recordset irs_recordset;
    private int ii_numberOfFields = 255;
    private Component icm_field[] = new Component[ii_numberOfFields];
    private Fields iflds_fields;
    // Create the form
    DAOForm(Recordset r) throws ComException{
        try {
            irs_recordset = r;
            // Set the recordset
            iflds_fields = irs_recordset.getFields();
            makeForm();
        }
        catch (ComException e) { throw e; }
    }
    private void makeForm() throws ComException {
        // Loop through to get field names and types
        try {
        // Set form to a grid bag layout
        setLayout(igbl_layout);
        ii_numberOfFields = iflds_fields.getCount();
        igbc_constraints.fill = GridBagConstraints.BOTH;
        for (int loop = 0; loop < ii_numberOfFields; loop++) {
            Variant v1 = new Variant();
            v1.putInt(loop);
            _Field f = iflds_fields.getItem(v1);
            Label fieldLabel = new Label(f.getName() + ":",
Label.RIGHT);
            int fieldSize = f.getSize();
            double labelY = 1.0;
            switch (f.getType()) {
                case (DataTypeEnum.dbBoolean) :
                    icm_field[loop] = new
Checkbox(fieldLabel.getText());
                    fieldLabel.setText("");
                    break;
                case (DataTypeEnum.dbDate) :
                    icm_field[loop] = new TextField(10);
                    break;
                case (DataTypeEnum.dbLong) :
                    if ((f.getAttributes() &
FieldAttributeEnum.dbAutoIncrField) != 0) {
                        icm_field[loop] = new Label("");
                    }
```

```
                        else {
                            icm_field[loop] = new
TextField(Math.min(fieldSize,60));
                        }
                        break;
                case (DataTypeEnum.dbInteger) :
                case (DataTypeEnum.dbSingle) :
                case (DataTypeEnum.dbDouble) :
                case (DataTypeEnum.dbByte) :
                case (DataTypeEnum.dbCurrency) :
                case (DataTypeEnum.dbText) :
                    icm_field[loop] = new
TextField(Math.min(fieldSize,60));
                    break;
                case (DataTypeEnum.dbLongBinary) :
                case (DataTypeEnum.dbMemo) :
                case (DataTypeEnum.dbGUID) :
                    labelY = 8.0;
                    icm_field[loop] = new TextArea(3, 60);
                    break;
            }
            igbc_constraints.gridwidth  =  1;    // Reset
            igbc_constraints.weightx = 1.0;
            igbc_constraints.weighty = labelY;
            igbl_layout.setConstraints(fieldLabel,
igbc_constraints);
            add(fieldLabel);
            igbc_constraints.weightx = 3.0;
            igbc_constraints.gridwidth =
GridBagConstraints.REMAINDER;
            igbl_layout.setConstraints(icm_field[loop],
igbc_constraints);
            add(icm_field[loop]);
            v1 = null;              //Deallocate
            fieldLabel = null;
            f = null;
        }    //Loop ends
        }    //try ends
        catch ( ComException e) { throw e; }
    }
    public boolean checkForUpdate() throws ComException {
        try { return scrollThroughData(true); }
        catch (ComException e) { throw e; }
    }
    public void showData() throws ComException {
        try { scrollThroughData(false); }
        catch (ComException e) {  throw e; }
    }
    private boolean scrollThroughData(boolean doUpdates) throws
ComException {
        try {
            boolean updates_made = false;
            // Loop through to get field names and types
            for (int loop = 0; loop < ii_numberOfFields; loop++) {
                Variant v1 = new Variant();
                v1.putInt(loop);
```

```
                    _Field f = iflds_fields.getItem(v1);
                    v1 = f.getValue();
                    short fieldType = f.getType();
                    if (fieldType == DataTypeEnum.dbBoolean) {
                        Checkbox cbxHolder;
                        cbxHolder = (Checkbox) icm_field[loop];
                        if (v1.getvt() <= v1.VariantNull) { //Check if
                        // a variant type is there
                            if (doUpdates) {
                                if (cbxHolder.getState() == true) {
                                    updates_made = true;
                                    v1.putBoolean(true);
                                    f.putValue(v1);
                                }
                            }
                            else {
                                cbxHolder.setState(false);
                            }
                        }
                        else {      //Set to value in db
                            if (doUpdates) {
                                if (cbxHolder.getState() !=
v1.getBoolean()) {

                                    updates_made = true;

v1.putBoolean(cbxHolder.getState());
                                    f.putValue(v1);
                                }
                            }
                            else {
                                cbxHolder.setState(v1.getBoolean());
                            }
                        }
                    }
                    else if ((fieldType == DataTypeEnum.dbLong)
                        && ((f.getAttributes() &
FieldAttributeEnum.dbAutoIncrField) != 0)) {
                        Label lbHolder;
                        lbHolder = (Label) icm_field[loop];
                        if (v1.getvt() <= v1.VariantNull) { //Check if
                        // a variant type is there
                            lbHolder.setText("");
                        }
                        else {      //Set to value in db
                            lbHolder.setText(v1.toString());
                        }
                    }
                    else{
                        TextComponent tcHolder;
                        tcHolder = (TextComponent) icm_field[loop];
                        String compare = tcHolder.getText();
                        if (v1.getvt() <= v1.VariantNull) { //Check if
                        // a variant type is there
                            if (doUpdates) {
                                if (!compare.equals("")) {
                                    updates_made = true;
```

```
                                    v1.putString(compare);
                                    f.putValue(v1);
                                }
                            }
                            else {
                                tcHolder.setText("");
                            }
                        }
                        else {     //Set to value in db
                            if (doUpdates) {
                                if (!compare.equals(v1.toString())) {
                                    updates_made = true;
                                    v1.putString(compare);
                                    f.putValue(v1);
                                }
                            }
                            else {
                                tcHolder.setText(v1.toString());
                            }
                        }
                    }
                    v1 = null; //Deallocate
                    f = null;
                }
                return updates_made;
            }
        catch (ComException e) { throw e; }
    }
}
```

Summary

Microsoft made Java a viable tool for corporate and Web development when it first developed DAO. Although DAO code and DAO developers still exist, now DAO has been replaced with ADO.

- DAO uses the Jet database engine to access database tables.

- DAO uses ActiveX to create and modify tables inside a Jet database.

- DAO can manipulate primary keys and table indexes.

- You can SELECT information from a Jet database using DAO Recordsets.

- You can add, change, or delete database information using the ExecuteSQL DAO command.

Chapter 27

Mastering Remote Data Objects

The OLE DB access used in ADO adds an additional layer to ODBC access. Instead of using ADO to access your ODBC object, you can use Remote Data Objects (RDO).

Secret

RDO accesses ODBC data sources faster than ADO. This is why RDO is still considered a viable development option, at least until more OLE DB native sources are available. Still, ADO is easier to use and faster if used with an OLE DB data source. With this in mind, it may be wise to use ADO, instead of RDO, so that future revisions of your software are up-to-date and fast.

Examining RDO

Visual J++ programs access ODBC data using RDO. RDO uses ActiveX controls to manipulate ODBC databases. This is different from DAO, which does not use ODBC, but rather uses a Jet database engine. It's also different from ADO, which uses an OLE DB engine to access ODBC data.

RDO is installed automatically when you install Visual J++, unless you choose a customized installation and specifically remove RDO from the installation list. (If you do this, run Setup to install it for this chapter.)

Mastering RDO Connections

RDO applications are driven by an ODBC connection. The connection enables your Java program to access your ODBC database.

Connections are established with a *connect string*. The connect string is built with the user ID, password, and ODBC data source name:

```
String connectString =
  "UID=cwood;PWD=secret;DSN=Sample Database";
```

A database connection can be made using UID, PWD, and DSN string arguments to build a connect string:

```
String UID, PWD, DSN;
//Processing and determine values for UID, PWD, and DSN
String connectString =
     "UID=" + UID + ';'
   + "PWD=" + PWD + ';'
  + "DSN=" + DSN + ';';
```

You only need to provide a data source name to establish a connection; however, other connection options are available, as shown in Table 27-1.

Table 27-1   Connect String Options

Option	Sample Use	Description
DSN	DSN=Sample Database;	The DSN is your ODBC data source name. This is the name you assigned to your ODBC connection when you created it.
UID	UID=Chuck;	If you have permissions assigned to your database, the UID enables you to pass a user ID.
PWD	PWD=Secret;	This is the password associated with the UID.
DRIVER	DRIVER=WOD50T;	The Driver is the path of the database driver you are using. Note that brackets are required for driver names that include spaces.
DATABASE	DATABASE=EmpDB;	The Database is the file name of the database you wish to connect to.
SERVER	SERVER=DBServer;	This enables you to name the remote server containing your database.
WSID	WSID=WS23;	This is your workstation ID used by the network.
APP	APP=Employee;	This is the Application name. At run time, this is your EXE name.

Secret

A DSN-less connection is a connection with no DSN. Database connections are made specifically to a database using other ODBC connect string parameters. If an empty DSN is specified when establishing a DSN-less connection, DSN must be the last argument.

After building a connect string, connect to the database by using `putConnect` to place the connect string into the RDO driver and then using `EstablishConnection`:

```
import msrdo20.*;
//Get a new connection object
RDOc_connection = (_RDOConnection) new RDOConnection();
//Connect using the connect string
RDOc_connection.putConnect(connectString);
//Prompt for any missing connection information
v1.putInt(PromptConstants.rdDriverComplete);
v2.putBoolean(false);  //Readonly is false
v3.putInt(0);  //Synchronous operations
RDOc_connection.EstablishConnection(v1, v2, v3);
```

The syntax for the `EstablishConnection` method is as follows:

```
EstablishConnection(Prompt, Readonly, Option);
```

`EstablishConnection` uses Variants for arguments. The `Readonly` argument can be zero for update access or any other integer Variant for read-only access. The prompt argument is used to control the user prompt. Table 27-2 shows the prompts that can be used when establishing a connection.

Table 27-2   Prompts for Establishing a Connection

Prompt	Description
PromptConstants. rdDriverPrompt	Always prompt the user for connection information.
PromptConstants. rdDriverNoPrompt	Use the connection information provided and provide a trappable error if the connection fails.
PromptConstants. rdDriverComplete	Use the connection information provided and display a prompt if the connection fails.
PromptConstants. rdDriverCompleteRequired	Use the connection information provided and provide a prompt with only enough information to secure a connection if the connection fails.

The option argument controls how SQL statements are executed when using this connection. Table 27-3 lists the options for the `EstablishConnection` method.

Table 27-3   Options for Establishing a Connection

Option	Description
0	No options are desired.
OptionConstants.rdAsyncEnable	Executes the operation asynchronously. You can use the getStillConnecting method, which returns a Boolean to check if the connection is finished or not.
OptionConstants.rdExecDirect	Uses the ODBC SQLExecDirect function to execute all SQL statements.

Commit and rollback transactions

As with ADO and DAO, you can use transactions with RDO. If you have an error, transaction processing enables you to roll back your work to a given point. For instance, if you are updating five tables and your SQL returns an error on the third table, perhaps you don't want any of the updates to be applied to the tables. To handle this, you can start a transaction at the beginning of the update, and then if one of the updates fails, you can issue a rollback to bring the database back to the state it was in before any of the updates occurred. If there are no errors, after the updates are complete, you issue a commit.

Transactions are necessary for database integrity, and should be used whenever a *logical* unit of work (for example, five tables need to be updated) is different from the *physical* unit of work needed to accomplish it (issuing an update on a database). Using transactions, you can group your work logically and avoid corruption of your database in the event of errors. To begin a transaction, use the BeginTrans() method:

```
public boolean startTrans() {
  try {
  RDOc_connection.BeginTrans();
  return true;
}
catch (ComException ce) {
  doError();
  return false;
}
}
```

Then, if you need to reverse all changes since the beginning of the transaction, do a rollback using the RollbackTrans() method:

```
public boolean rollback() {
  try {
    RDOc_connection.RollbackTrans();
```

```
    startTrans();
    return true;
  }
  catch (ComException ce) {
    doError();
    return false;
  }
}
```

To make your changes permanent, commit the changes using the
CommitTrans() method:

```
public boolean commit() {
  try {
    RDOc_connection.CommitTrans();
    startTrans();
    return true;
  }
  catch (ComException ce) {
    doError();
    return false;
  }
}
```

Secret

Transactions are part of the SQL standard, and almost all databases support
them in some form. Their implementation, however, can vary from one
database to another.

For instance, Sybase SQL Anywhere automatically commits transactions
when you disconnect. Microsoft Access, on the other hand, requires you to
issue the commit when you are using transactions or all changes are rolled
back. It's a good idea to put transaction support in your RDOLibrary and
include the following:

■ Starts using transactions automatically. Your programs can commit or
roll back anytime that it is needed.

■ Begins a new transaction after each commit or rollback. A transaction is
always in place to handle commits and rollbacks, and the developer
doesn't have to worry about starting a new transaction. To begin a new
transaction, simply commit or roll back.

■ Automatically commits in the finalize() method. The work is
committed if the program closes.

Error processing

Error processing is vital when doing database calls. Typically, the database
engines generate errors but don't handle them. Error handling is left for you,
the developer. It's a good idea to place error handling in your RDOLibrary.
To facilitate error handling, the RDOLibrary is extended from Frame. This
Frame is only displayed if an error occurs.

Errors are tracked in ODBC at the database engine level. Database engines are important since they contain the environments that contain all the transactions, as shown in Figure 27-1.

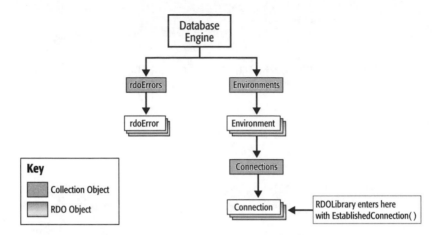

Figure 27-1: You can see how errors and connections relate to each other through the database engine and environment.

Use the getOwner() and GetOwner() methods to retrieve the engine and environment of the RDO:

```
//Get the environment and engine for error processing
RDOv_environment = RDOc_connection.getOwner();
RDOe_engine = RDOv_environment.GetOwner();
```

Secret

Notice how the connection getOwner and environment GetOwner methods have different cases. You might think that Microsoft is being inconsistent, but in actuality, the environment GetOwner method is an actual RDO function, while getOwner is an RDO connection property. Visual J++ can't access ActiveX properties the way Visual Basic can. Microsoft wrote routines prefaced with "get" (for example, getOwner, getCount, getItem) that return properties (such as Owner, Count, Item, and so on). Remember to keep the connection getOwner() method lowercase and keep the environment GetOwner() method uppercase.

To trap RDO errors, do the following:

1. Retrieve the RDOErrors collection object by using the getRDOErrors engine method.

2. Use a for loop to scroll through each RDOError and add its description to an errorText string.

3. Retrieve the first error, and then display the error number, SQLState, and source in text fields.

This is shown in the doError() method:

```
public void doError() {
  Variant v = new Variant();
  RDOErrors errs = RDOe_engine.getRDOErrors();
  int numErrors = errs.getCount();
  RDOError err;
  String errorText = "";
  for (int errorNum=0; errorNum < numErrors; rrorNum++) {
    v.putInt(errorNum);
    err = errs.getItem(v);
    errorText += err.getDescription();
  }
  if (numErrors > 0) {
    v.putInt(0);
    err = errs.getItem(v);
    ta_error_message.setText(errorText);
    tf_SQLCode.setText (Integer.toString(err.getNumber()));
    tf_SQLState.setText(err.getSQLState());
    ta_error_syntax.setText(err.getSource());
  }
  show();
}
```

Now use a try-catch construct to test each RDO call. If an error occurs, call the doError method, as follows:

```
try {
  //database processing
}
catch (ComException ce) {
  doError();
}
```

Getting Table Information

A listing of tables in a database can be retrieved from an RDO connection. Figure 27-2 shows how tables are related to a connection.

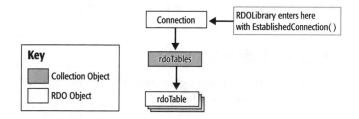

Figure 27-2: You can access a database's tables through the database connection.

The following code returns a String array containing all of the tables in a database:

```
public String[] getTables() {
  String tables[];
  Variant v;

  try {
    RDOTables rts = RDOc_connection.getRDOTables();
    int numTables = rts.getCount();
    tables = new String[numTables];
    v = new Variant();

    for (int tableNum = 0;
         tableNum < numTables;
         tableNum++) {
      v.putInt(tableNum);
      RDOTable rt = rts.getItem(v);
      tables[tableNum] = rt.getName();
    }
    return tables;
  }
  catch (ComException ce) {
    doError();
  }
  return (String[]) null;
}
```

In the preceding code, the following steps are used:

1. The `_RDOConnection.getRDOTables()` method is used to return the RDOTables collection object from the connection.

2. The `RDOTables.getCount()` method is used to determine the number of tables.

3. Inside a `for` loop, the `RDOTables.getItem()` method is used to retrieve each RDOTable construct found in RDOTables.

4. The `RDOTable.getName()` method is used to retrieve the name of each table to build the `tableNames` String array.

5. If an error occurs, the `doError()` method is called and a null is returned.

Using RDO Result Sets

Like DAO, RDO uses result set objects to handle multiple return values from database operations, such as SELECT statements.

Using SQL commands

RDO uses SQL to provide much of its functionality. There are two types of SQL statements:

- Those that update database data or settings (for example, INSERT, UPDATE, or DELETE)

- Those that return a list of values based on the data in the database (such as Select)

The doSQL method receives one SQL parameter and tests for a SELECT statement at the beginning of the statement. If a SELECT statement is present, the RDOLibrary.SelectSQL method is called and the Panel is initialized. Otherwise, the RDOLibrary.executeSQL method is called, as shown by this code:

```
public void doSQL(String SQL) {
  //Execute a select statement
  //Decide what type of SQL was sent
  String query = SQL.trim().substring(0,6).toLowerCase();
  if (query.equals("select")) {
    RDO.SelectSQL(SQL);
    i_rows = RDO.getRowCount();
    init();
  }
  else {
    RDO.executeSQL(SQL);
  }
}
```

Tip

The RDOLibrary methods executeSQL and SelectSQL are discussed later in this section.

When the doSQL() method is called, an entire table is displayed by forming a SELECT statement using the table name:

```
public void doTable(String table) {
  doSQL("Select * FROM " + table);
}
```

SQL commands with no result sets

If a SQL command returns zero rows, such as with UPDATE or INSERT commands, you can execute the SQL statement with the _RDOConnection. Execute() method. This is shown in the RDOLibrary.executeSQL method found in Listing 27-1, later in this chapter:

```
public boolean executeSQL(String SQL) {
  Variant v = new Variant();

  try {
    v.putInt(OptionConstants.rdExecDirect);
```

```
        RDOc_connection.Execute(SQL, v);
        return true;
    }
    catch (ComException ce) {
        doError();
    }
    return false;
}
```

The preceding `Execute` method is equivalent to the EXECUTE IMMEDIATE SQL command. The `rdExecDirect` option enables you to execute SQL with one RDO `execute` call instead of an RDO `prepare` call and a separate RDO `execute` call.

SQL selects with result sets

RDO processing often involves retrieving columns and rows from a query. A result set is formed by passing a SELECT SQL statement to the `_RDOConnection.OpenResultset()` method:

```
public boolean SelectSQL(String query) {
    //Setup Variants for optional parameters
    Variant v1 = new Variant();
    Variant v2 = new Variant();
    Variant v3 = new Variant();

    //Set optional parameters
    //Type of cursor
    v1.putInt(ResultsetTypeConstants.RDOpenKeyset);
    //Locking is optimistic concurrency
    v2.putInt(LockTypeConstants.rdConcurRowVer);
    //No other options
    v3.putInt(0);
    try {
        RDOr_resultSet = (_RDOResultset)
        RDOc_connection.OpenResultset (query,v1,v2,v3);
    }
    catch (ComException ce) {
        doError();
        return false;
    }
    setColumnNames();
    //Get the first row in the result set
    return true;
}
```

The `OpenResultset()` method shown in the preceding section of code returns a result set using a SQL SELECT statement. The syntax for the `OpenResultset()` method is as follows:

```
_RDOConnection.OpenResultset
    (query, cursor type, lock type, options)
```

The OpenResultset() call returns an RDO result set. The query variable is a String containing a Select SQL statement.

The cursor type is a Variant that is set to one of the following constants:

ResultsetTypeConstants Constant	*Description*
RDOpenForwardOnly	Opens an updatable forward-only-type RDOResultset object. This type of cursor can only access data once – from beginning to end.
RDOpenKeyset	Opens an updatable keyset-type RDOResultset object. Changes made to the underlying tables by other users are not detected by this cursor type, but the data access is faster than RDOpenDynamic.
RDOpenDynamic	Opens an updatable dynamic-type RDOResultset object. Changes made to the underlying tables by other users are detected by this cursor type.
RDOpenStatic	Opens a read-only, static-type RDOResultset object. Changes made by other users are not detected by this data type.

The lock type is a Variant whose value controls the type of access other users have to data found in your cursor. The following constants are available for lock type:

LockTypeConstants Constants	*Description*
rdConcurReadOnly	Other users have read-only access.
rdConcurLock	This value establishes pessimistic concurrency. Pessimistic concurrency allows no updates of the data until the current row is released.
rdConcurRowVer	This value establishes optimistic concurrency based on row ID. Optimistic concurrency locks the data during the SELECT and when an UPDATE is issued, but leaves the data open for update at all other times.
rdConcurValues	This value establishes optimistic concurrency based on row values. Original values are checked during update.
rdConcurBatch	This value establishes optimistic concurrency based on bulk updates. This is handy for updating many records simultaneously.

The valid Options for `OpenResultset` are the same as those listed in Table 27-3 (none (0), `OptionConstants.rdAsyncEnable,` or `OptionConstants.rdExecDirect`).

Evaluating column information

In a result set, you can determine the name of the columns that are available, their data type, and whether or not each column is updatable. This involves calling RDO methods to inquire about the columns.

An `RDOColumns` container object is contained in every result set. The `RDOColumns` container object contains several column objects, as shown in Figure 27-3.

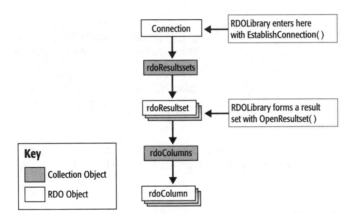

Figure 27-3: Every result set has columns.

The `getRDOColumns()` method is used to retrieve the `RDOColumns` container object:

```
RDOcol_columns = RDOr_resultSet.getRDOColumns();
```

Then a loop is executed that scrolls through the columns to retrieve the `RDOColumn` variables from the `RDOColumns` container class. The `RDOColumns.getCount` method returns the number of columns in the `RDOColumns` container, and the `RDOColumns.getItem` method returns each column. The `RDOColumn.getName` method is used to return the name of the column into a column name class variable array:

```
Variant v = new Variant();
i_columnCount = RDOcol_columns.getCount();
for (int column = 0; column < i_columnCount; column++) {
  v.putInt(column);
  _RDOColumn c = RDOcol_columns.getItem(v);
  sa_columnNames[column] = c.getName();
```

A column can have several attributes, but you only care if the column is updatable. The `RDOColumn.getAttributes` method retrieves all the attributes of a column. The resulting integer is then logically ANDed with the `AttributeConstants.rdUpdatableColumn` and compared to zero to see if a column is updatable or not. The results are stored in a boolean class variable array:

```
int attribute = c.getAttributes();
if ((attribute & AttributeConstants.rdUpdatableColumn)>0) {
  ba_updatable[column] = true;
}
else {
  ba_updatable[column] = false;
}
```

The `RDOColumn.getType` method can retrieve the data type of each column. The return value can be tested against the `DataTypeConstants` variables to determine what data type is returned:

```
switch(c.getType()) {
   case DataTypeConstants.rdTypeBIT :
    sh_datatypes[column] = BOOLEAN;
    break;
   case DataTypeConstants.rdTypeTINYINT :
    sh_datatypes[column] = BYTE;
    break;
   case DataTypeConstants.rdTypeSMALLINT :
    sh_datatypes[column] = SHORT;
    break;
   case DataTypeConstants.rdTypeINTEGER :
   case DataTypeConstants.rdTypeBIGINT :
    sh_datatypes[column] = INT;
    break;
   case DataTypeConstants.rdTypeREAL :
    sh_datatypes[column] = FLOAT;
    break;
   case DataTypeConstants.rdTypeFLOAT :
   case DataTypeConstants.rdTypeNUMERIC :
   case DataTypeConstants.rdTypeDECIMAL :
   case DataTypeConstants.rdTypeDOUBLE :
    sh_datatypes[column] = DOUBLE;
    break;
   case DataTypeConstants.rdTypeCHAR :
   case DataTypeConstants.rdTypeVARCHAR :
   case DataTypeConstants.rdTypeLONGVARCHAR :
   case DataTypeConstants.rdTypeBINARY :
   case DataTypeConstants.rdTypeVARBINARY:
   case DataTypeConstants.rdTypeLONGVARBINARY :
    sh_datatypes[column] = STRING;
    break;
   case DataTypeConstants.rdTypeDATE :
   case DataTypeConstants.rdTypeTIME :
   case DataTypeConstants.rdTypeTIMESTAMP:
```

```
        sh_datatypes[column] = TIMESTAMP;
        break;
}
```

The `RDOTableChanges` program, shown in Listing 27-2, retrieves these `RDOLibrary` variables to build a Panel containing all the columns. Nonupdatable columns are changed to Labels and boolean variables are changed to Checkboxes and their Labels are deleted in the `init` method:

```
//Set the labels and fields
short dataTypes[] = RDO.getDataTypes();
String columnNames[] = RDO.getColumnNames();

co_fields = new Component[dataTypes.length];
for (int columnNum = 0; columnNum < dataTypes.length; columnNum++) {
  if (dataTypes[columnNum] == RDO.BOOLEAN) {
    //Skip this grid cell
    p_labels.add(new Label(""));
    Checkbox cbx = new Checkbox(columnNames[columnNum]);
    co_fields[columnNum] = (Component) cbx;
  }
  else {
    //  Create the label and add it into the form
    p_labels.add(new Label(columnNames[columnNum]));
    //  Create the field and add it into the form
    if (!RDO.getUpdatable(columnNum)) {
      Label lb = new Label();
      co_fields[columnNum] = (Component) lb;
    }
    else {
      TextField tf = new TextField(25);
      co_fields[columnNum] = (Component) tf;
    }
  }
  p_fields.add(co_fields[columnNum]);
}
```

Analyzing movement within a result set

Result sets contain rows of data produced by the SQL statement used to create the result set. When you first open a result set, column information is available, but you can't retrieve row information until you tell RDO what row you want to view. Do this using the RDO `move` methods shown in Table 27-4.

Table 27-4   RDO Move Methods

Move Method	*Description*
`MoveFirst()`	Moves the row pointer to the first row in the database.
`MoveLast()`	Moves the row pointer to the last row in the database.

Move Method	Description
MovePrevious()	Moves the row pointer to the row immediately preceding the current row. If no row precedes the current row, the _resultSet.getBOF() returns true. Otherwise, _resultSet.getBOF() returns false.
MoveNext()	Moves the row pointer to the row immediately following the current row. If no row follows the current row, the _resultSet.getEOF() returns true. Otherwise, _resultSet.getEOF() returns false.
Move(int row, Variant start)	The move method moves the row pointer to a specific row relative to a start position. The start position is actually a bookmark retrieved by the getBookmark() method.

The following code shows how to use the movePrevious method in a Visual J++ program:

```
public boolean movePrevious() {
  try {
    RDOr_resultSet.MovePrevious();
    //Make sure we don't move before BOF
    if (RDOr_resultSet.getBOF()) {
      moveFirst();
      return false;
    }
    fillColumns();
    return true;
  }
  catch (ComException ce) {
    doError();
  }
  return false;
}
```

Retrieving data from a result set

Once a current row has been established, each RDOColumn contains data that can be retrieved by the RDOColumn.getvalue method. The fillColumns method in Listing 27-1 shows how a Variant array is filled with values from the current row of a result set:

```
_RDOColumn c;
for (column = 0; column < va_columns.length; column++) {
  va_columns[column] = null;
  v.putInt(column);
  c = RDOcol_columns.getItem(v);
  va_columns[column] = c.getValue();
}
```

The following `showData` method retrieves the Variant columns value array built in the `RDOLibrary`. It then displays each column based on data type and if the column is updateable or not:

```
void showData() {
  //Create a Variant to get the value of each column
  Variant columns[] = RDO.getColumns();
  short dataTypes[] = RDO.getDataTypes();
  for (int column = 0; column < columns.length; column++) {
    //Set the field in the form
    if (dataTypes[column] == RDO.BOOLEAN) {
      Checkbox cbx = (Checkbox) co_fields[column];
      if (columns[column].getvt() != Variant.VariantBoolean) {
        cbx.setState(false);
      }
      else { //False or null
        cbx.setState (columns[column].getBoolean());
      }
    }
    else if (!RDO.getUpdatable(column)) {
      Label lb = (Label) co_fields[column];
      lb.setText(columns[column].toString());
    }
    else {
      TextField tf = (TextField) co_fields[column];
      tf.setText(columns[column].toString());
    }
  }
}
```

Deleting rows

To delete the current row from a record set, call the `_RDOResultset.Delete()` method:

```
public boolean delete() {
  try {
    RDOr_resultSet.Delete();
    return true;
  }
  catch (ComException ce) {
    doError();
  }
  return false;
}
```

Secret

The Delete method deletes the current row, but then you aren't attached to any valid row. A `move` method should be called after a delete to reposition the row pointer.

Inserting and updating rows

Result sets can be updated with the _RDOResultset.Update() method. The method applies changes made to a result set to the source database. The steps for updating a database are as follows:

1. Place the result set in *Addnew* mode or in *Edit* mode. Result sets have three possible update modes: none, Addnew, or Edit. A result set needs to be in Addnew or Edit mode for a database update to occur.

Secret

The _RDOResultset.Addnew() method actually adds a new row to the result set and changes the row pointer to the newly added blank row. The same calls that retrieve data can be used to retrieve nulls or blanks from the new row and to display them on the screen.

2. Apply changes to the result set by using the _RDOColumn.putValue() method. (The argument to this method is a Variant.)

3. Use the _RDOResultSet.Update() method to save changes to the database.

4. If a transaction is used, commit or roll back when appropriate.

5. Make sure that all errors are trapped because more database errors occur during inserting and updating rows than during any other database transaction.

If the Add button is pressed in the RDOTableChanged class, the RDOLibrary.add method is called which in turn calls the _RDOResultSet.AddNew() method and fills the columns:

```
public boolean add() {
  try {
    RDOr_resultSet.AddNew();
    fillColumns();
    return true;
  }
  catch (ComException ce) {
    doError();
  }
  return false;
}
```

When the Save button is pressed, the TableChanges.saveInfo() method is called (Listing 27-2). The saveInfo method tests if an update was made and then fills a fields Variant array with the proper values entered by the user from the window. The data types are tested to see what data type to place inside the Variant:

```
if (b_updateMade) {
  Variant fields[] = new Variant[co_fields.length];
  short dataTypes[] = RDO.getDataTypes();
  for (int column = 0;
    column < co_fields.length;
```

```
        column++) {
        fields[column] = new Variant();
        if (dataTypes[column] == RDOLibrary.BOOLEAN) {
          Checkbox c = (Checkbox) co_fields[column];
          fields[column].putBoolean(c.getState());
          break;
        }
        else {
          String s;
          if (!RDO.getUpdatable(column)) {
            Label l = (Label) co_fields[column];
            s = l.getText();
          }
          else {
            TextField t = (TextField)co_fields[column];
            s = t.getText();
          }
          switch(dataTypes[column]) {
            case RDOLibrary.STRING:
              fields[column].putString(s);
              break;
            case RDOLibrary.BYTE:
              if (s.length() > 0) {
                fields[column].putByte((byte) s.charAt(1));
              }
              else {
                fields[column].putNull();
              }
              break;
            case RDOLibrary.INT:
              fields[column].putInt (Integer.parseInt(s));
              break;
            case RDOLibrary.SHORT:
              fields[column].putShort((short) Integer.parseInt(s));
              break;
            case RDOLibrary.FLOAT:
              fields[column].putFloat (Float.valueOf(s).floatValue());
              break;
            case RDOLibrary.DOUBLE:
              fields[column].putDouble
(Double.valueOf(s).doubleValue());
              break;
            case RDOLibrary.TIMESTAMP:
              fields[column].putString(s);
              double d = fields[column].toDate();
              fields[column].putDate(d);
              break;
          }
        }
      }
  if (RDO.save(fields)) {
    showStatus("Update Successful!");
    b_updateMade = false;   //reset update flag
```

```
  }
  else {
    showStatus("Update failed!");
  }
}
else {
  showStatus("No updates needed");
}
```

The final lines of the RDOTableChanges.saveInfo() method call the RDOLibrary.save() method (Listing 27-1), passing the fields Variant array containing the new field values. The RDOLibrary.save method performs three tasks:

1. Checks the result set's Edit mode. If there is no current Edit mode, the save method assumes that an update is occurring and places the result set in Edit mode.

2. Traverses the fields Variant array, placing each Variant into the appropriate column.

3. Calls the _RDOResultset.Update() method to update the database with the new columns.

This is shown in this section of the RDOLibrary.save() method:

```
Variant v = new Variant();
_RDOColumn c;
int edMode = RDOr_resultSet.getEditMode();
if (edMode == EditModeConstants.rdEditNone) {
  RDOr_resultSet.Edit();
}
for (int column = 0; column < fields.length; column++) {
  if (ba_updatable[column]) {
    v.putInt(column);
    c = RDOcol_columns.getItem(v);
    c.putValue(fields[column]);
  }
}
RDOr_resultSet.Update();
```

Writing an RDO Class Library

As with DAO, an RDO class library simplifies database access for you and all developers at your site. The code shown in Listing 27-1 is a functional RDO class library developed using techniques described in this section.

Listing 27-1 RDOLibrary.java

```
import java.awt.*;
import java.awt.event.*;
import com.ms.com.*;
import msrdo20.*;
```

```
public class RDOLibrary extends Frame implements ActionListener,
WindowListener{
  public static final short BOOLEAN = 1;
  public static final short BYTE = 2;
  public static final short INT = 3;
  public static final short SHORT = 4;
  public static final short FLOAT = 5;
  public static final short DOUBLE = 6;
  public static final short STRING = 7;
  public static final short TIMESTAMP = 8;
  private _rdoConnection rdoc_connection;
  private _rdoResultset rdor_resultSet;
  private rdoColumns rdocol_columns;
  private _rdoEngine rdoe_engine;
  private _rdoEnvironment rdov_environment;
  private int i_columnCount;
  private int i_rowCount;
  private String sa_columnNames[];
  private Variant va_columns[];
  private short sh_datatypes[];
  private boolean ba_updatable[];
  private TextArea ta_error_message;
  private TextField tf_SQLCode;
  private TextField tf_SQLState;
  private TextArea ta_error_syntax;
  private Button bu_OK = new Button("OK");

  public RDOLibrary (String DSN) {
    this(DSN, "", "");
  }
  public RDOLibrary (String DSN, String UID, String PWD){
    addWindowListener(this);
    bu_OK.addActionListener(this);
    buildErrorFrame();
    buildConnection(DSN, UID, PWD);
  }
  public void buildConnection(String DSN, String UID, String PWD){
    //Build connection
    Variant v1 = new Variant();
    Variant v2 = new Variant();
    Variant v3 = new Variant();
    String connectString =
        "UID=" + UID + ';'
      + "PWD=" + PWD + ';'
      + "DSN=" + DSN + ';';
    try {
      //Get a new connection object
      rdoc_connection = (_rdoConnection) new rdoConnection();
      //Get the environment and engine for error processing
      rdov_environment = rdoc_connection.getOwner();
      rdoe_engine = rdov_environment.GetOwner();
      //Connect using the connect string
      rdoc_connection.putConnect(connectString);
      //Prompt for any missing connection information
      v1.putInt(PromptConstants.rdDriverComplete);
      v2.putBoolean(false);   //Readonly is false
```

```
        v3.putInt(0);   //Synchronous operations
        rdoc_connection.EstablishConnection(v1, v2, v3);
        startTrans();
      }
    catch (ComException ce) {
      doError();
      }
  }
  public void buildErrorFrame(){
    //Add error processing stuff
    Panel north = new Panel();
    Panel center = new Panel();
    Panel south = new Panel();
    setLayout(new BorderLayout());
    north.setLayout(new FlowLayout());
    center.setLayout(new GridLayout(2,2));
    south.setLayout(new FlowLayout());
    north.add (new Label("SQL Code:"));
    north.add (tf_SQLCode = new TextField("   "));
    north.add (new Label("SQL State:"));
    north.add (tf_SQLState = new TextField("   "));
    center.add (new Label("Error:"));
    center.add (ta_error_message = new TextArea());
    center.add (new Label("Syntax:"));
    center.add (ta_error_syntax = new TextArea());
    south.add (bu_OK);
    add ("North", north);
    add ("Center", center);
    add ("South", south);
    setSize (500, 400);
  }
  public void finalize() {
    try {
      //Close the resultset, if active
      if (rdor_resultSet != null) {
        rdor_resultSet.Close();
        rdor_resultSet = null;
      }
      commit();
    }
    catch (ComException ce) {
      doError();
    }
  }
  public boolean startTrans() {
    try {
      rdoc_connection.BeginTrans();
      return true;
    }
    catch (ComException ce) {
      doError();
      return false;
    }
  }
  public boolean commit() {
    try {
```

```
              rdoc_connection.CommitTrans();
              startTrans();
              return true;
            }
          catch (ComException ce) {
            doError();
            return false;
          }
        }
      public boolean rollback() {
          try {
            rdoc_connection.RollbackTrans();
            startTrans();
            return true;
          }
          catch (ComException ce) {
            doError();
            return false;
          }
        }
      public void doError() {
          Variant v = new Variant();
          rdoErrors errs = rdoe_engine.getrdoErrors();
          int numErrors = errs.getCount();
          rdoError err;
          String errorText = "";
          for (int errorNum = 0; errorNum < numErrors; errorNum++) {
            v.putInt(errorNum);
            err = errs.getItem(v);
            errorText += err.getDescription();
          }
          if (numErrors > 0) {
            v.putInt(0);
            err = errs.getItem(v);
            ta_error_message.setText(errorText);
            tf_SQLCode.setText(Integer.toString(err.getNumber()));
            tf_SQLState.setText(err.getSQLState());
            ta_error_syntax.setText(err.getSource());
          }
          show();
        }
      public boolean SelectSQL(String query) {
          //Setup Variants for optional parameters
          Variant v1 = new Variant();
          Variant v2 = new Variant();
          Variant v3 = new Variant();

          //Set optional parameters
          //Type of cursor
          v1.putInt(ResultsetTypeConstants.rdOpenKeyset);
          //Locking is optimistic concurrency
          v2.putInt(LockTypeConstants.rdConcurRowVer);
          //No other options
          v3.putInt(0);
          try {
            rdor_resultSet = (_rdoResultset)
```

```java
      rdoc_connection.OpenResultset (query,v1,v2,v3);
    }
    catch (ComException ce) {
      doError();
      return false;
    }
    setColumnNames();
    //Get the first row in the resultset
    return true;
  }
  public void fillColumns() {
    //Create a Variant to get the value of each column
    Variant v = new Variant();
    _rdoColumn c;
    int column;

    try {
      for (column = 0; column < va_columns.length; column++) {
        va_columns[column] = null;
        v.putInt(column);
        c = rdocol_columns.getItem(v);
        va_columns[column] = c.getValue();
      }
    }
    catch (ComException ce) {
      doError();
    }
  }
  public void setColumnNames() {
    Variant v = new Variant();

    try {
      rdocol_columns = rdor_resultSet.getrdoColumns();
      i_columnCount = rdocol_columns.getCount();
      va_columns = null;
      sa_columnNames = null;
      sh_datatypes = null;
      va_columns = new Variant[i_columnCount];
      sa_columnNames = new String[i_columnCount];
      sh_datatypes = new short[i_columnCount];
      ba_updatable = new boolean[i_columnCount];
      for (int column = 0; column < i_columnCount; column++) {
        v.putInt(column);
        _rdoColumn c = rdocol_columns.getItem(v);
        sa_columnNames[column] = c.getName();
        int attribute = c.getAttributes();
        if ((attribute & AttributeConstants.rdUpdatableColumn) > 0)
{
          ba_updatable[column] = true;
        }
        else {
          ba_updatable[column] = false;
        }
        switch(c.getType()) {
          case DataTypeConstants.rdTypeBIT :
          sh_datatypes[column] = BOOLEAN;
```

```
            break;
          case DataTypeConstants.rdTypeTINYINT :
            sh_datatypes[column] = BYTE;
            break;
          case DataTypeConstants.rdTypeSMALLINT :
            sh_datatypes[column] = SHORT;
            break;
          case DataTypeConstants.rdTypeINTEGER :
          case DataTypeConstants.rdTypeBIGINT :
            sh_datatypes[column] = INT;
            break;
          case DataTypeConstants.rdTypeREAL :
            sh_datatypes[column] = FLOAT;
            break;
          case DataTypeConstants.rdTypeFLOAT :
          case DataTypeConstants.rdTypeNUMERIC :
          case DataTypeConstants.rdTypeDECIMAL :
          case DataTypeConstants.rdTypeDOUBLE :
            sh_datatypes[column] = DOUBLE;
            break;
          case DataTypeConstants.rdTypeCHAR :
          case DataTypeConstants.rdTypeVARCHAR :
           case DataTypeConstants.rdTypeLONGVARCHAR :
          case DataTypeConstants.rdTypeBINARY :
          case DataTypeConstants.rdTypeVARBINARY:
          case DataTypeConstants.rdTypeLONGVARBINARY :
            sh_datatypes[column] = STRING;
            break;
          case DataTypeConstants.rdTypeDATE :
          case DataTypeConstants.rdTypeTIME :
          case DataTypeConstants.rdTypeTIMESTAMP:
            sh_datatypes[column] = TIMESTAMP;
            break;
          }
        }
      }
      catch (ComException ce) {
        doError();
      }
  }
  public boolean add() {
    try {
      rdor_resultSet.AddNew();
      fillColumns();
      return true;
    }
    catch (ComException ce) {
      doError();
    }
    return false;
  }
  public boolean save(Variant[] fields) {
    Variant v = new Variant();
    _rdoColumn c;
    try {
      int edMode = rdor_resultSet.getEditMode();
```

```java
      if (edMode == EditModeConstants.rdEditNone) {
        rdor_resultSet.Edit();
      }
      for (int column = 0; column < fields.length; column++) {
        if (ba_updatable[column]) {
          v.putInt(column);
          c = rdocol_columns.getItem(v);
          c.putValue(fields[column]);
        }
      }
      rdor_resultSet.Update();
      return true;
    }
    catch (ComException ce) {
      doError();
    }
    return false;
  }
  public boolean delete() {
    try {
      rdor_resultSet.Delete();
      return true;
    }
    catch (ComException ce) {
      doError();
    }
    return false;
  }
  public int getColumnCount() {
    return i_columnCount;
  }
  public int getRow() {
    return rdor_resultSet.getAbsolutePosition();
  }
  public int getRowCount() {
    Variant v = rdor_resultSet.getBookmark();
    try {
      moveLast();
      i_rowCount = rdor_resultSet.getAbsolutePosition();
      rdor_resultSet.putBookmark(v);
      return i_rowCount;
    }
    catch (ComException ce) {
      doError();
    }
    return -1;
  }
  public boolean moveFirst() {
    try {
      rdor_resultSet.MoveFirst();
      fillColumns();
      return true;
    }
    catch (ComException ce) {
      doError();
    }
```

```
      return false;
    }
    public boolean moveNext() {
      try {
        rdor_resultSet.MoveNext();
        //Make sure we don't move before EOF
        if (rdor_resultSet.getEOF()) {
          moveLast();
          return false;
        }
        fillColumns();
        return true;
      }
      catch (ComException ce) {
        doError();
      }
      return false;
    }
    public boolean movePrevious() {
      try {
        rdor_resultSet.MovePrevious();
        //Make sure we don't move before BOF
        if (rdor_resultSet.getBOF()) {
          moveFirst();
          return false;
        }
        fillColumns();
        return true;
      }
      catch (ComException ce) {
        doError();
      }
      return false;
    }
    public boolean moveLast() {
      Variant v = new Variant();
      try {
        v.putInt(0);   //Synchronous operations
        rdor_resultSet.MoveLast(v);
        fillColumns();
        return true;
      }
      catch (ComException ce) {
        doError();
      }
      return false;
    }
    public boolean executeSQL(String SQL) {
      Variant v = new Variant();

      try {
        v.putInt(OptionConstants.rdExecDirect);
        rdoc_connection.Execute(SQL, v);
        return true;
      }
      catch (ComException ce) {
```

```
        doError();
      }
      return false;
  }
  public _rdoConnection getConnection() {
    return rdoc_connection;
  }
  public _rdoResultset getResultSet() {
    return rdor_resultSet;
  }
  public Variant[] getColumns() {
    return va_columns;
  }
  public boolean getUpdatable(int columnNum) {
    return ba_updatable[columnNum];
  }
  public String[] getColumnNames() {
    return sa_columnNames;
  }
  public String[] getTables() {
    String tables[];
    Variant v;

    try {
      rdoTables rts = rdoc_connection.getrdoTables();
      int numTables = rts.getCount();
      tables = new String[numTables];
      v = new Variant();

      for (int tableNum = 0; tableNum < numTables; tableNum++) {
        v.putInt(tableNum);
        rdoTable rt = rts.getItem(v);
        tables[tableNum] = rt.getName();
      }
      return tables;
    }
    catch (ComException ce) {
      doError();
    }
    return (String[]) null;
  }
  public short[] getDataTypes() {
    return sh_datatypes;
  }
//The actionPerformed method is required by the ActionListener
interface
  public void actionPerformed(ActionEvent event) {   //bu_OK was
clicked
    setVisible(false);
  }
//The following methods are required by the WindowListener interface
  public void windowClosing(WindowEvent e) {   //User closed window
    setVisible(false);
  }
  public void windowActivated(WindowEvent e) { }   //Window got focus
```

```
  public void windowDeactivated(WindowEvent e) { }  //Window lost
focus
  public void windowDeiconified(WindowEvent e) { }  //Window expanded
  public void windowClosed(WindowEvent e) { }  //Window is done
closing
  public void windowIconified(WindowEvent e) { }  //Window is turned
into an icon
  public void windowOpened(WindowEvent e) { }  //Window is first
opened
}
```

Writing an RDO Resultset Library

Listing 27-2 shows how to make a Panel that formats an RDO database by using the RDOLibrary class library.

Listing 27-2: RDOTableChanges.java

```
import java.awt.event.*;
import java.awt.*;
import java.util.*;
import com.ms.com.*;

public class RDOTableChanges extends Panel implements ActionListener,
MouseListener {
  //Call the RDOLibrary class shown after
  //the cwRDO class in this listing
  private RDOLibrary RDO;

  //Form Panels
  Panel p_labels;
  Panel p_fields;
  //Form components
  Component co_fields[];
  int i_rows;

  //Checks for adding records and updates made
  boolean b_updateMade = false;

  //Toolbar
  Button bu_first = new Button("First");
  Button bu_prev = new Button("Prev");
  Button bu_next = new Button("Next");
  Button bu_last = new Button("Last");
  Button bu_add = new Button("Add");
  Button bu_delete = new Button("Delete");
  Button bu_save = new Button("Save");

  //Status label at the bottom
  Label l_status = new Label();

  public RDOTableChanges(String database, String table) {
    super();
    //Create Panels for the toolbar and form
```

```
    Panel form = new Panel();
    Panel toolbar = new Panel();
    //Create form Panels for labels and fields
    p_labels = new Panel();
    p_fields = new Panel();

    //Open a connection to the data source
    RDO = new RDOLibrary(database);
    setLayout(new BorderLayout());
    toolbar.add(bu_first);
    toolbar.add(bu_prev);
    toolbar.add(bu_next);
    toolbar.add(bu_last);
    toolbar.add(bu_add);
    toolbar.add(bu_delete);
    toolbar.add(bu_save);
    bu_first.addActionListener(this);
    bu_prev.addActionListener(this);
    bu_next.addActionListener(this);
    bu_last.addActionListener(this);
    bu_add.addActionListener(this);
    bu_delete.addActionListener(this);
    bu_save.addActionListener(this);
    add("North", toolbar);
    //Set those Panels as a grid, one or two columns wide
    form.setLayout(new GridLayout(0, 2));
    p_labels.setLayout(new GridLayout(0, 1));
    p_fields.setLayout(new GridLayout(0, 1));
    //Set the form as labels to the left, fields to the right
    p_labels.add(new Label("Please select a table or enter an SQL
command."));
    p_fields.add(new Label(" "));
    form.add(p_labels);
    form.add(p_fields);
    l_status.setText("");
    add("South", l_status);
    add("Center", form);
    doTable(table);
  }
  public void doTable(String table) {
    doSQL("Select * FROM " + table);
  }
  public void doSQL(String SQL) {
    //Execute a select statement
    //Decide what type of SQL was sent
    String query = SQL.trim().substring(0,6).toLowerCase();
    if (query.equals("select")) {
      RDO.SelectSQL(SQL);
      i_rows = RDO.getRowCount();
      init();
    }
    else {
      RDO.executeSQL(SQL);
    }
  }
  public void finalize() {
```

```java
        if (RDO != null) {
          RDO = null;
        }
    }
    public void showRowCount(String message) {
      String msg;
      int row = RDO.getRow();

      if (row < 0) {
        row = i_rows;
      }
      if (message == null || message.length() == 0) {
        msg = "";
      }
      else {
        msg = message + " -- ";
      }
      showStatus(msg + "Row "
           + String.valueOf(row)
           + " of "
           + String.valueOf(i_rows) );
    }
    public void init() {
      //Set the labels and fields
      short dataTypes[] = RDO.getDataTypes();
      String columnNames[] = RDO.getColumnNames();

      p_labels.removeAll();
      p_fields.removeAll();
      co_fields = null;
      co_fields = new Component[dataTypes.length];
      for (int columnNum = 0; columnNum < dataTypes.length;
columnNum++) {
          if (dataTypes[columnNum] == RDO.BOOLEAN) {
            p_labels.add(new Label("")); //Skip this grid cell
            Checkbox cbx = new Checkbox(columnNames[columnNum]);
            co_fields[columnNum] = (Component) cbx;
            cbx.addMouseListener(this);
          }
        else {
    //  Create the label and add it into the form
          p_labels.add(new Label(columnNames[columnNum]));
    //  Create the field and add it into the form
          if (!RDO.getUpdatable(columnNum)) {
            Label lb = new Label();
            co_fields[columnNum] = (Component) lb;
          }
          else {
            TextField tf = new TextField(25);
            co_fields[columnNum] = (Component) tf;
            tf.addActionListener(this);
          }
        }
        p_fields.add(co_fields[columnNum]);
      }
      RDO.moveFirst();
```

```
      showData();
    }
void showData() {
  //Create a Variant to get the value of each column
  Variant columns[] = RDO.getColumns();
  short dataTypes[] = RDO.getDataTypes();
  for (int column = 0; column < columns.length; column++) {
    //Set the field in the form
    if (dataTypes[column] == RDO.BOOLEAN) {
      Checkbox cbx = (Checkbox) co_fields[column];
      if (columns[column].getvt() != Variant.VariantBoolean) {
        cbx.setState(false);
      }
      else { //False or null
        cbx.setState(columns[column].getBoolean());
      }
    }
    else if (!RDO.getUpdatable(column)) {
      Label lb = (Label) co_fields[column];
      lb.setText(columns[column].toString());
    }
    else {
      TextField tf = (TextField) co_fields[column];
      tf.setText(columns[column].toString());
    }
  }
}
public void showStatus(String error) {
  l_status.setText(error);
}
public void saveInfo() {
  if (b_updateMade) {
    Variant fields[] = new Variant[co_fields.length];
    short dataTypes[] = RDO.getDataTypes();
    for (int column = 0; column < co_fields.length; column++) {
      fields[column] = new Variant();
      if (dataTypes[column] == RDOLibrary.BOOLEAN) {
        Checkbox c = (Checkbox) co_fields[column];
        fields[column].putBoolean(c.getState());
        break;
      }
      else {
        String s;
        if (!RDO.getUpdatable(column)) {
          Label l = (Label) co_fields[column];
          s = l.getText();
        }
        else {
          TextField t = (TextField) co_fields[column];
          s - t.getText();
        }
        switch(dataTypes[column]) {
          case RDOLibrary.STRING:
            fields[column].putString(s);
            break;
          case RDOLibrary.BYTE:
```

```
                if (s.length() > 0) {
                  fields[column].putByte((byte)
                    s.charAt(1));
                }
                else {
                  fields[column].putNull();
                }
                break;
            case RDOLibrary.INT:
              fields[column].putInt(Integer.parseInt(s));
              break;
            case RDOLibrary.SHORT:
              fields[column].putShort((short)
                Integer.parseInt(s));
              break;
            case RDOLibrary.FLOAT:
              fields[column].putFloat(
                Float.valueOf(s).floatValue());
              break;
            case RDOLibrary.DOUBLE:
              fields[column].putDouble(
                Double.valueOf(s).doubleValue());
              break;
            case RDOLibrary.TIMESTAMP:
              fields[column].putString(s);
              double d = fields[column].toDate();
              fields[column].putDate(d);
              break;
          }
        }
      }
      if (RDO.save(fields)) {
        showStatus("Update Successful!");
        b_updateMade = false;  //reset update flag
      }
      else {
        showStatus("Update failed!");
      }
    }
    else {
      showStatus("No updates needed");
    }
  }
// Mouse methods required by the MouseListener interface
  public void mouseClicked(MouseEvent e) {
      b_updateMade = true;   //A Checkbox has been clicked
  }
  public void mousePressed(MouseEvent e) { }
  public void mouseReleased(MouseEvent e) { }
  public void mouseEntered(MouseEvent e) { }
  public void mouseExited(MouseEvent e) { }
//The actionPerformed method is required by the ActionListener
interface
  public void actionPerformed(ActionEvent event) {   //bu_OK was
clicked
    if (i_rows < 1) {
```

```java
      showStatus("There are no rows currently selected from the
database.");
      return;   // No need to display
    }
    // Get the text of the button
    String buttonText = event.getActionCommand();
  //Test for buttons
    if (buttonText.equals("First")) {
      RDO.moveFirst();
      showRowCount ("Getting first record");
    }
    else if (buttonText.equals("Prev")) {
      if (RDO.movePrevious() == false) {
        showRowCount("First record has been reached");
      }
      else {
        showRowCount("Getting previous record");
      }
    }
    else if (buttonText.equals("Next")) {
      if (RDO.moveNext() == false) {
        showRowCount ("Last record has been reached");
      }
      else {
        showRowCount("Getting next record");
      }
    }
    else if (buttonText.equals("Last")) {
      RDO.moveLast();
      showRowCount ("Getting last record");
    }
    else if (buttonText.equals("Delete")) {
      RDO.delete();
      i_rows --;
      if (RDO.moveNext() == false) {
        RDO.moveLast();
        if (RDO.moveNext() == false) {
          showRowCount ("Getting last record");
        }
        else {
          showRowCount ("No more records");
        }
      }
      else {
        showRowCount("Getting next record");
      }
      showRowCount("Record deleted");
    }
    else if (buttonText.equals("Save")) {
      saveInfo();
      return;   //No need to redisplay
    }
    else if (buttonText.equals("Add")) {
      RDO.add();
      i_rows ++;
      showRowCount("Record ready to add");
```

```
          }
       else {
          b_updateMade = true;  //An update has been made
          return;  //No need to redisplay
       }
       showData(); //Show the current row
    }
}
```

Figure 27-4 shows the results of Listing 27-2.

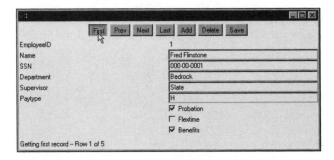

Figure 27-4: This is how a program looks with the `RDOTableChanges` Panel added to the center Panel.

Summary

Although ADO and OLE DB are in line to replace RDO and ODBC as database standards, RDO is still a viable way to access ODBC data sources. To summarize:

- The RDO hierarchy consists of result sets, tables, and fields, and is similar to ADO and DAO.

- RDO edges out ADO in ODBC database access.

- You may be better off using ADO for your ODBC access rather than RDO.

- ADO edges out RDO in general database access and ease of use. If your database has an OLE DB driver available, use it instead of the ODBC driver.

Chapter 28

Pure Java with JDBC

In This Chapter

▶ Mastering JDBC

▶ Using JDBC Connections

▶ Developing JDBC ResultSets

▶ Making JDBC SQL commands

▶ Writing a JDBC class library

JDBC is the standard for Java database access. Although Microsoft is pushing ADO as the database solution for Java developers, using ADO ties you *and your users* to Microsoft operating systems, and forces you to ignore Unix, Macintosh, and VMS users that are still prevalent. JDBC, on the other hand, delivers on the promise of "write once, run anywhere" that Sun is pushing for Java.

Secret

This whole chapter can be considered a secret. Microsoft wants you to use ADO for your database access and does not document JDBC well. Other Visual J++ books have followed suit and have not discussed JDBC. If you want JDBC access inside Visual J++, this book is the one for you!

Understanding JDBC

JDBC is a product purchased by Sun Microsystems to add to their Java offering. JDBC allows database connections to a myriad of databases, including ODBC databases. Many database vendors, such as Oracle, Sybase, and even Microsoft, have JDBC drivers available for their databases. Figure 28-1 shows how JDBC is implemented in a Java environment.

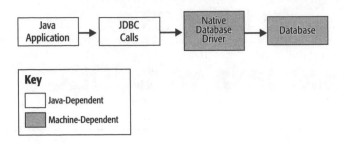

Figure 28-1: JDBC calls reside in the Java environment. These JDBC calls access database drivers that exist in the machine's native environment.

JDBC database development follows these steps:

1. Establish a JDBC Connection

2. Issue a specific SQL command

3. Make a ResultSet to hold the results (if applicable)

4. Scroll through the ResultSet (if applicable) to display the results

5. Check for database errors

JDBC is the simplest way (other than painters such as the Visual J++ Application Wizard) for developers to access a database.

Connecting to a JDBC Database

Although it's never necessary to declare an `import` command in a Java program, the following `import` command can dramatically reduce the amount you need to type:

```
import java.sql.*;
```

After you decide what JDBC driver to use, execute it. This can be difficult, because drivers are typically machine-dependent and not written in Java. Therefore, database drivers have no class structure and no way to call the constructor to start executing. This problem is resolved using the `Class.forName` method. The `Class.forName` method always executes the constructor of any class. Use it to start your JDBC driver:

```
Class.forName("com.ms.jdbc.odbc.JdbcOdbcDriver");
```

The preceding command executes Microsoft's JDBC/ODBC driver.

What's in a forName — Microsoft's Versus Sun's JDBC Driver

In Sun's Java 1.1 specification, database driver names are not explicitly specified. Sun's JDBC/ODBC driver, therefore, has a different name than Microsoft's JDBC/ODBC driver. Microsoft, of course, does not document this *anywhere* because they would much rather you use ADO than JDBC. (That's why you bought this book, right?)

Microsoft's JDBC connection is:

```
Class.forName("com.ms.jdbc.odbc.JdbcOdbcDriver");
```

Sun's JDBC/ODBC connection is different:

```
Class.forName("sun.jdbc.odbc.JdbcOdbcDriver");
```

If you try to connect to one JDBC driver from a Java Virtual Machine that supports the other, you receive a null-pointer exception and you cannot connect.

Of course, this introduces an interesting problem. How are you going to achieve the Java promise of "write-once, run-anywhere" when the ODBC default connection classes are different? You have two solutions:

1. Don't use the ODBC drivers that come with Sun JDK or Microsoft Visual J++. This isn't as big a sacrifice as it first appears. Most database vendors have more efficient drivers that don't require client-side ODBC setup. In other words, for efficient client-server development, you need to switch engines eventually, anyway.

2. Detect the Java Virtual Machine vendor and use the proper forName call for the virtual machine you're using. This is done easily by using a System.getProperty call:

```
//Visual J++ users
if (System.getProperty("java.vendor").equals("Microsoft
Corp.")) {
  Class.forName("com.ms.jdbc.odbc.JdbcOdbcDriver");
}
else {     // Non-Visual J++ Users
  Class.forName("sun.jdbc.odbc.JdbcOdbcDriver");
}
```

The preceding code detects which Java vendor you are using. If you detect "Microsoft Corp.", that means that you are using a Microsoft-approved Java VM. If not, that means your machine is probably Sun-compliant.

Using these methods, you can use the proper JDBC/ODBC driver no matter what machine you're using. (You can also use the same technique to choose between ADO and JDBC, if you like.)

After connecting the database engine, declare a connection. The `java.sql.Connection` class can use the `java.sql.DriverManager` class to declare a connection. You can also pass a user ID and a password:

```
String url = "jdbc:odbc:EmpDB";
Connection con = DriverManager.getConnection(url, "user",
"password");
```

In the preceding case, an ODBC database named Employee is declared on the local machine. Using JDBC, Java programs can access databases. Other proprietary databases are supported, and are documented by the individual database vendors.

The `getConnection` method throws a `SQLException` if there's an error, so catch this error in your code, or you receive a compiler error.

In Java, you need to create a `Statement` variable to hold your SQL statement:

```
Statement selectStatement = con.createStatement();
```

Use your `Statement` class to execute your SQL statement using the `executeQuery` method. The results are stored in a `ResultSet` class:

```
String SQL = "SELECT EmployeeID, Name, SSN, Department, Supervisor, "
+
            "Paytype, Probation, Flextime, Benefits" +
                " FROM Employee";
ResultSet result = selectStatement.executeQuery(SQL);
```

Using a ResultSet

Usually, a SELECT statement executed by the `executeQuery` method returns more than one row of data. To handle multiple rows returned from a single SELECT, the `ResultSet` class is used. Every JDBC program then needs to traverse the ResultSet to retrieve the information from the database.

After every SELECT, the current row pointer is positioned at row zero. It needs to be moved to row one before any information can be retrieved. The `next()` method of the ResultSet class moves the row pointer to the next row:

```
result.next()
```

Usually the `next()` method is used in conjunction with an `if` clause to test for the presence of a next row:

```
if [PGC5](result.next( )) {
    displayResult( );
}
```

After you position the row pointer, retrieve the results using one of the "get" methods (`getInt`, `getString`, getBoolean, and so on). The following code shows how to retrieve Strings from a JDBC database:

```
tf_name.setText(String.toString(result.getInt(1)));
tf_name.setText(result.getString(2));
tf_ssn.setText(result.getString(3));
tf_department.setText(result.getString(4));
tf_supervisor.setText(result.getString(5));
String paytype = result.getString(6);
if (paytype.equals("H")) {
cbx_hourly.setState(true);
}
else {
    cbx_salaried.setState(true);
}
cbx_probation.setState(result.getBoolean(7));
cbx_flextime.setState(result.getBoolean(8));
cbx_benefits.setState(result.getBoolean(9));
```

When this is finished, you can process the data you have SELECTed.

Using ExecuteUpdate

Every time you update your database, use the `executeUpdate` method rather than the `executeQuery` method.

```
SQLStatement.executeUpdate(String SQL);
```

The `executeQuery` method returns a ResultSet, but the `executeUpdate` method does not. The following code can execute SQL to either INSERT or UPDATE a record based on a boolean variable named `b_adding`:

```
String SQL = null;
if (b_adding == true) {
SQL = "INSERT INTO employee (" +
"(Name, " +
"SSN, " +
"Department, " +
"Supervisor, " +
"Paytype, " +
"Probation, " +
"Flextime, " +
"Benefits)" +
"VALUES (" +
" 'Wilma Flinstone', " +
" '000-00-0010', " +
" 'NA', " +
" 'NA', " +
" 'N', " +
"false, " +
"false, " +
"false)";
        }
        else {
```

```
            SQL = "UPDATE employee SET " +
"Name = 'Wilma Flinstone', " +
"SSN =  '000-00-0010', " +
"Department = 'NA', " +
"Supervisor = 'NA', " +
"Paytype = 'N', " +
"Probation = false, " +
"Flextime = false, " +
"Benefits = false) " +
" WHERE EmployeeID = 4";
    }
}
SQLStatement.executeUpdate(SQL);
```

The preceding code either adds or updates a row in the Employee table.

Building a Simple Database Program

You might want code that can scroll through the Employee table in a form that looks like Figure 28-2.

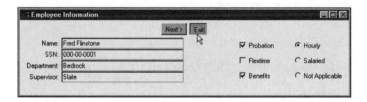

Figure 28-2: Employee Information window

Using what you've learned so far in this chapter, the code for this is seen in Listing 28-1.

Listing 28-1: JDBCEmp.java

```
import java.awt.event.*;
import java.awt.*;
import java.util.*;
import java.sql.*;

public class JDBCEmp extends Frame implements ActionListener,
WindowListener{
// Define the Label components
    private Label lb_name = new Label("Name: ", Label.RIGHT);
    private Label lb_ssn = new Label("SSN: ", Label.RIGHT);
    private Label lb_department = new Label("Department: ",
Label.RIGHT);
    private Label lb_supervisor = new Label("Supervisor: ",
Label.RIGHT);
    private Label lb_status = new Label("", Label.CENTER);

// Define the TextField components for data entry
```

```java
    private TextField tf_name = new TextField();
    private TextField tf_ssn = new TextField();
    private TextField tf_department = new TextField();
    private TextField tf_supervisor = new TextField();

// Define the CheckBox and RadioButton components for data entry
    private Checkbox cbx_probation = new Checkbox("Probation");
    private Checkbox cbx_flextime = new Checkbox("Flextime");
    private Checkbox cbx_benefits = new Checkbox("Benefits");
    private CheckboxGroup cbxg_paytype = new CheckboxGroup();
    private Checkbox cbx_hourly = new Checkbox("Hourly",
cbxg_paytype, false);
    private Checkbox cbx_salaried = new Checkbox("Salaried",
cbxg_paytype, true);
    private Checkbox cbx_na = new Checkbox("Not Applicable",
cbxg_paytype, true);
// Define what buttons are used
    private Button bu_next = new Button("Next >");
    private Button bu_exit = new Button("Exit");

//JDBC url and ResultSet
    static String url = "jdbc:odbc:EmpDB";
    private ResultSet result;

    public static void main(String[] args) {
        JDBCEmp a = new JDBCEmp();          // Construct JDBCEmp
    }
    public JDBCEmp() {
// Define Panels
        Panel labels = new Panel();
        Panel fields = new Panel();
        Panel checkboxes = new Panel();
        Panel radioButtons = new Panel();
        Panel toolbar = new Panel();
        Panel eastPanel = new Panel();
        setTitle("Employee Information");
// Set Layouts
        setLayout(new BorderLayout());
        labels.setLayout(new GridLayout(0,1));
        fields.setLayout(new GridLayout(0,1));
        checkboxes.setLayout(new GridLayout(0,1));
        radioButtons.setLayout(new GridLayout(0,1));
        eastPanel.setLayout(new GridLayout(1,3));
    // Add lablels to the frame
        eastPanel.add(new Label());
        labels.add(lb_name);
        labels.add(lb_ssn);
        labels.add(lb_department);
        labels.add(lb_supervisor);
        add("West", labels);
    //Add fields to the frame
        fields.add(tf_name);
        fields.add(tf_ssn);
        fields.add(tf_department);
        fields.add(tf_supervisor);
        add("Center", fields);
```

```java
    //Add checkboxes to the frame
        checkboxes.add(cbx_probation);
        checkboxes.add(cbx_flextime);
        checkboxes.add(cbx_benefits);
        eastPanel.add(checkboxes);
    //Make radio button panel and add it to the east panel
        radioButtons.add(cbx_hourly);
        radioButtons.add(cbx_salaried);
        radioButtons.add(cbx_na);
        eastPanel.add(radioButtons);
        add("East", eastPanel);
    //Make toolbar
        toolbar.setLayout(new FlowLayout());
        toolbar.add(bu_next);
        toolbar.add(bu_exit);
    //Add listeners
        addWindowListener(this);
        bu_exit.addActionListener(this);
        bu_next.addActionListener(this);
// Add Panels to the Frame, show the frame, and do the database
// stuff
        add("North", toolbar);
        lb_status.setForeground(Color.red);
        add("South", lb_status);
        setSize (600, 160);
        show();
        doDatabase();
    }
    public void doDatabase() {
        // Non-Visual J++ Users:
Class.forName("sun.jdbc.odbc.JdbcOdbcDriver");
        try {
// Run database driver
    // Visual J++ Users
    if (System.getProperty("java.vendor").equals("Microsoft Corp."))
{
        Class.forName("com.ms.jdbc.odbc.JdbcOdbcDriver");
    }
    else {          // Non-Visual J++ Users
        Class.forName("sun.jdbc.odbc.JdbcOdbcDriver");
    }
// Connect to the database
            Connection con = DriverManager.getConnection(url, "",
"");
// Define an SQL statement
            Statement selectStatement = con.createStatement();
            String SQL = "SELECT Name, SSN, Department, Supervisor,
" +
            "Paytype, Probation, Flextime, Benefits" +
                " FROM Employee";
//Get the result set and point to the first row
            result = selectStatement.executeQuery(SQL);
            if (result.next()) {
                displayResult();
            }
        }
```

```
        //Catch any Exceptions
            catch (Exception e2) {
                lb_status.setText("Could not select.");
                return;
            }
        }
// Retrieve information from the ResultSet and display it on the
Frame components
    public void displayResult() {
        try {
            tf_name.setText(result.getString(1));
            tf_ssn.setText(result.getString(2));
            tf_department.setText(result.getString(3));
            tf_supervisor.setText(result.getString(4));
            String paytype = result.getString(5);
            if (paytype.equals("H")) {
                cbx_hourly.setState(true);
            }
            else {
                cbx_salaried.setState(true);
            }
            cbx_probation.setState(result.getBoolean(6));
            cbx_flextime.setState(result.getBoolean(7));
            cbx_benefits.setState(result.getBoolean(8));
        }
        catch (Exception e2) {
            lb_status.setText("Could not display results.");
            return;
        }
    }
//The actionPerformed method is required by the ActionListener
//,interface
    public void actionPerformed(ActionEvent event) {
        // Get the text of the button
        String buttonText = event.getActionCommand();
        //Test for buttons
        if (buttonText.equals("Next >")) {
            try {displayResult();}
            catch (Exception e) {
                lb_status.setText("Could not get next record.");
            }
        }
        else if (buttonText.equals("Exit")) {
            dispose();
            System.exit(0);
        }
    }
// The following are required by the WindowListener interface
    public void windowClosing(WindowEvent e) {      //User closed
                                                    //window
        dispose();
        System.exit(0);
    }
    public void windowActivated(WindowEvent e) { }     //Window got
                                                       // focus
```

```
    public void windowDeactivated(WindowEvent e) { }   //Window
                                                       //lost focus
    public void windowDeiconified(WindowEvent e) { }   //Window
                                                       //expanded
    public void windowClosed(WindowEvent e) { }    //Window is done
                                                   // closing
    public void windowIconified(WindowEvent e) { }     //Window is
                                                   //turned into
//an icon
    public void windowOpened(WindowEvent e) { }      //Window is first
                                                     //opened
}
```

Mastering JDBC Class Libraries

When you think of object-oriented development, you usually think of
reusable code. However, nothing about the code in Listing 28-1 is reusable.
You need to develop a class library that reuses code for any database.

As you can tell, components are easier to place in a pure Java program than
in a WFC program, but database access is easier and more powerful with ADO
than with JDBC. If you want to do JDBC development, you can either develop
a JDBC class library or spend literally *months* for each development effort.
Similar to the ADO class library, a JDBC class library can be developed that
can generate the Employee database shown in Figure 28-3 quickly.

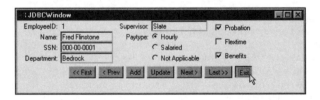

Figure 28-3: Database Frame generated by a class library

Listing 28-2 shows the code used to generate Figure 28-3. The JDBCWindow
program calls JDBCPanel, a class library, to format the window
automatically. The only variables passed to the class library are the name of
the database, the name of the table, and any radio buttons that are used (as
shown in boldface).

Listing 28-2: JDBCWindow.java

```
import java.awt.*;
import java.awt.event.*;
import java.util.*;
import java.sql.*;

public class JDBCWindow extends Frame implements WindowListener,
IJDBCPanel {
```

```
// The database class library is invoked by constructing the JDBCPanel
// class
    private JDBCPanel JDBCP_panel;

// The IJDBCPanel interface requires that you have a showStatus method.
// This method sets the lb_status text to a given message.
    private Label lb_status = new Label("", Label.CENTER);

    public static void main(String[] args) {
        JDBCWindow a = new JDBCWindow();       // Construct JDBCWindow
    }
    public JDBCWindow() {
        addWindowListener(this);
        setTitle("JDBCWindow");
        setLayout(new BorderLayout());
// Add message
        lb_status.setForeground(Color.red);
        add("South", lb_status);
// Catch all database errors
        try {
// Add a panel for the Employee table in the EmpDB ODBC database
// Pass the name of the database, the table name, and the number of
// panels to format the columns
            JDBCP_panel = new JDBCPanel(this, "EmpDB", "Employee", 3);
// Before forming the database panel,tell JDBCP_panel know about any
// radio buttons that need to be formatted
            String s_paytypeDisplay[] = {"Hourly",
                          "Salaried",
                          "Not Applicable"};
            String s_paytypeValues[] = {"H", "S", "N"};
            JDBCP_panel.setChoices("Paytype",
                          s_paytypeDisplay,
                          s_paytypeValues);
// Call the formPanel method to actually put database information on the
// Panel
            JDBCP_panel.formPanel();
            add("Center", JDBCP_panel);
        }
        catch (Exception e) {
            showStatus("JDBCPanel error: " + e.getMessage());
        }
        setSize (JDBCP_panel.getSuggestedWidth(),
JDBCP_panel.getSuggestedHeight());
        show();
    }

//Required by the IJDBCPanel interface
    public void showStatus(String message) {
        lb_status.setText(message);
    }
// The following are required by the WindowListener interface
    public void windowClosing(WindowEvent e) {     //User closed window
        dispose();
        System.exit(0);
    }
    public void windowActivated(WindowEvent e) { }     //Window got focus
```

```
public void windowDeactivated(WindowEvent e) { }    //Window lost
                                                    // focus
public void windowDeiconified(WindowEvent e) { }    //Window expanded
public void windowClosed(WindowEvent e) { }    //Window is done
                                               // closing
public void windowIconified(WindowEvent e) { }    //Window is turned
                                                  // into an icon
public void windowOpened(WindowEvent e) { }    //Window is first
                                               // opened
}
```

Once more, class libraries show their importance. By simply passing the database name and the table name, you can generate complex programs automatically.

Understanding the need for new components

The WFC components are harder to place on a window than Java components. Java components can use layouts that control their positioning. Once you are familiar with using Layouts, specifying a specific position on the window for a control seems overly complicated.

However, except for positioning, WFC components have more built-in functionality. For instance, WFC multiline Edits wrap, as do WFC Labels. By contrast, Java Labels truncate and TextArea Components scroll. This is quite annoying, especially when trying to display database information.

Java's answer to this — build your own components. Listing 28-3 shows you how to inherit TextArea to make a wrapping text area component.

Listing 28-3: WrappingText4Area.java

```
import java.awt.*;
Public class WrappingTextArea extends TextArea {
    String s_textBeforeWrap = null;
    // Reset the text
    public void addNotify() {
        super.addNotify();
        setText(s_textBeforeWrap);
    }
    // Override the setText method
    public void setText(String s) {
        s_textBeforeWrap = s;
        String newString = "";
        String s_holder = null;
        int width = size().width - 25;    //Width - Borders
        int startingPoint = 0;
        int lastSpace = 0;
        int sLength = s.length();

        if (s == null) {
            super.setText("");
            return;
```

```
            }
            if (width <= 0) {
                super.setText(s);
                return;
            }
            FontMetrics fm = getFontMetrics(getFont());
            if (fm.stringWidth(s) <= width) {
                super.setText(s);
                return;
            }
        while (startingPoint < sLength) {   // Start a new line
        s_holder = s.substring(startingPoint);
        String newlineCharacter = "";
        while (fm.stringWidth(s_holder) > width) {   // Truncate each
                                                     // line
            lastSpace = s_holder.lastIndexOf(' ');
            int lastNewLine = s_holder.lastIndexOf('\n');
            if (lastNewLine > 0 && lastNewLine < lastSpace) {
              lastSpace = lastNewLine;
            }
            if (lastSpace <= 0) {
              lastSpace = s_holder.length();
              break;
            }
            if (lastSpace == lastNewLine) {
              newlineCharacter = ""; // Hard return ('\n')
            }
            else {
              newlineCharacter = "\015"; // Soft return
            }
            s_holder = s_holder.substring(0, lastSpace);
          }
          newString = newString + s_holder + newlineCharacter;
          startingPoint += lastSpace + 1;
        }
      super.setText(newString);
    }
  // Override the getText method
  public String getText() {
//     return s_textBeforeWrap;
      String s = super.getText();
      //Replace soft returns with empty strings
      int lastSpace = s.lastIndexOf('\015');
      while (lastSpace > 0) {
        s = s.substring(0, lastSpace) + s.substring(lastSpace + 1);
        lastSpace = s.lastIndexOf('\015');
      }
      return s;
    }
}
```

In Listing 28-3, only three methods in the WrappingTextArea class override
the TextArea methods:

1. The `setText` method adds "soft return" characters to split the line and make it wrap.

2. The `getText` method removes the soft returns.

3. When the user types something, `addNotify` is called so that the text can be wrapped while the typing changes the `WrappingTextArea`.

Understanding ResultSetMetaData

Often, you want to retrieve information about your result set. To do this, use the ResultSetMetaData class. This class retrieves information about the result set and columns within the result set.

To form a ResultSetMetaData class, use the `ResultSet.getMetaData` method:

`ResultSetMetaData rsmd_results = result.getMetaData();`

After forming the result set, you can retrieve information about the columns in the result set.

Getting column information

The ResultSetMetaData class contains several methods that can be used to retrieve column information. Table 28-1 shows these methods.

Table 28-1   ResultSetMetaData Class Methods to Retrieve Column Information

ResultSetMetaData Method	*Description*
`ResultSetMetaData .getColumnCount()`	Returns an integer containing the number of columns in a ResultSet.
`ResultSetMetaData .getColumnName(column)`	Returns a String containing the column name. Column is an integer whose value is from one through `getColumnCount()`.
`ResultSetMetaData .getColumnType(column)`	Returns an integer containing the column data type. Data types are discussed in more detail later in this section. Column is an integer whose value is from one through `getColumnCount()`.
`ResultSetMetaData .getColumnDisplaySize(column)`	Returns an integer containing the size of a column. Column is an integer whose value is from one through `getColumnCount()`.
`ResultSetMetaData .isAutoIncrement(column)`	Returns a boolean true if a field is an auto increment field and a false otherwise. Column is an integer whose value is from one through `getColumnCount()`.

Using data types

The `ResetSetMetaData.getColumnType(int column)` method returns the data type of a specific column in a record set. Table 28-2 shows the valid types.

Table 28-2   JDBC Data Types

Types constant returned from getColumnType()	Description
Types.BIGINT	A BIGINT type indicates that the column should be placed in a long variable.
Types.BINARY	A BINARY type indicates that the column should be placed in a byte array. Byte arrays use ASCII instead of Unicode, which is used by String types.
Types.BIT	A BIT type indicates that the column should be placed in a boolean variable.
Types.CHAR	A CHAR type indicates that the column should be placed in a String variable.
Types.DATE	DATE columns use a long containing a specific day. Each database implements date variables somewhat differently, but usually they take the form of the number of days from a given day.
Types.DECIMAL	A DECIMAL type indicates that the column should be placed in a double variable.
Types.DOUBLE	A DOUBLE type indicates that the column should be placed in a double variable.
Types.FLOAT	A FLOAT type indicates that the column should be placed in a float variable.
Types.INTEGER	An INTEGER type indicates that the column should be placed in an int variable.
Types.LONGVARBINARY	A LONGVARBINARY type indicates that the column should be placed in a byte array. Byte arrays use ASCII instead of Unicode, which is used by String types.
Types.LONGVARCHAR	A LONGVARCHAR type indicates that the column should be placed in a String variable.
Types.NULL	A NULL type indicates that the column returns a null value. Note that a column can contain nulls but still be a valid data type.
Types.NUMERIC	A NUMERIC type indicates that the column should be placed in a double variable.

(continued)

Table 28-2 *(Continued)*

Types constant returned from getColumnType()	*Description*
Types.OTHER	An OTHER type indicates that the column's data type is database-specific. You need to use the getObject and setObject commands to retrieve an OTHER type.
Types.REAL	A REAL type indicates that the column should be placed in a double variable.
Types.SMALLINT	A SMALLINT type indicates that the column should be placed in a short variable.
Types.TIME	TIME columns use a long containing a specific time. Each database implements time variables somewhat differently, but usually they take the form of the number of milliseconds or billionths of seconds since the beginning of the day.
Types.TIMESTAMP	TIMESTAMP columns use a long or double containing a specific date and time. Each database implements timestamp variables somewhat differently, but usually they take the form of the number of days from a given date for the mantissa of the ordinate, and number of milliseconds or billionths of seconds since the beginning of the day for the ordinate of the double.
Types.TINYINT	A TINYINT type indicates that the column should be placed in a byte variable.
Types.VARBINARY	A VARBINARY type indicates that the column should be placed in a byte array. Byte arrays use ASCII instead of Unicode, which is used by String types.
Types.VARCHAR	A VARCHAR type indicates that the column should be placed in a String variable.

To test data types, a switch statement works well. The following getDBValue method retrieves columns from a database and formats them to a String:

```
//Get the current value of a column number
  public String getDBValue(int column) throws Exception {
    String value = null;
    switch (rsmd_results.getColumnType(column)) {
      case Types.BIT :        //boolean
        value = String.valueOf(result.getBoolean(column));
        break;
      case Types.CHAR :       //Strings
      case Types.LONGVARCHAR :
      case Types.VARCHAR :
        value = result.getString(column);
```

```
        break;
      case Types.REAL :        //Float
        value = String.valueOf(result.getFloat(column));
        break;
      case Types.DOUBLE :        //Double
      case Types.FLOAT :
        value = String.valueOf(result.getDouble(column));
        break;
      case Types.INTEGER :      //Integer
        value = String.valueOf(result.getInt(column));
        break;
      case Types.SMALLINT :      //Short
        value = String.valueOf(result.getShort(column));
        break;
      case Types.BIGINT :        //Long
        value = String.valueOf(result.getLong(column));
        break;
      case Types.BINARY :        //Byte Array
      case Types.LONGVARBINARY :
      case Types.VARBINARY :
        value = new String (result.getBytes(column));
      case Types.TINYINT :      //Byte
        byte byteArray[] = new byte[1];
        byteArray[0] = result.getByte(column);
        value = new String (byteArray);
        break;
      case Types.DATE :        //Date
      case Types.TIME :        //Time
      case Types.TIMESTAMP :    //TimeStamp
      case Types.DECIMAL :     //java.math.BigDecimal
      case Types.NUMERIC :     //java.math.BigDecimal
      default :
        throw new SQLException(
          "JDBCPanel can't handle a column's datatype");
    }
    if (value == null) {
      return "";
    }
    return value;
  }
```

Writing a JDBC library

Using the methods and procedures discussed earlier, a class library can be written to format a window with database columns automatically or to access databases. Listing 28-4 and the interface shown in Listing 28-5 provide the capability to detect the columns used, to format them appropriately, and to perform all the database functions needed for a database program. Simply by changing the name of the database and sending any necessary radio button information, you can have another working database program. By using updateable views or queries instead of tables, you can even update multiple tables.

Listing 28-4: JDBCPanel.java

```java
import java.awt.*;
import java.awt.event.*;
import java.util.*;
import java.sql.*;
class JDBCPanel extends Panel implements ActionListener {
  //Vector for components
  private Vector v_components = new Vector();
  //Vector for radio buttons
  private Vector v_choices = new Vector();
  private int i_columns;          //Number of fields
  private int i_components;        //Number of components
  private int i_numPanels;        //Number of panels
  private String s_database;       //Database name
  private String s_table;          //Table name
  private String s_orderBy;        //Order by
  private Connection dbConnection;    //Connection to DB
  private Statement SQLStatement;     //Statement to be executed
  private ResultSet result;          //Result set to store the statement
  private ResultSetMetaData rsmd_results;  //Information about the
result set
//Add buttons
  private Button bu_first = new Button("<< First");
  private Button bu_prev = new Button("< Prev");
  private Button bu_update = new Button("Update");
  private Button bu_clear = new Button("Add");
  private Button bu_next = new Button("Next >");
  private Button bu_last = new Button("Last >>");
  private Button bu_exit = new Button("Exit");
//Currently adding a record
  private boolean b_adding = false;
//The class that called me
  private IJDBCPanel iJDBC_callingClass;
//Not a stand alone program
  public static void main (String Args[]) {
    System.out.println("You must call JDBCPanel from another
program");
  }
//Constructors
  public JDBCPanel(IJDBCPanel i, String db, String table) throws
Exception {
    super();
    afterConstruct(i, db, table, 1);
  }
  public JDBCPanel(IJDBCPanel i, String db, String table, int
numPanels) throws Exception {
    super();
    afterConstruct(i, db, table, numPanels);
  }
//Set up Panel
  private void afterConstruct(IJDBCPanel i, String db, String table,
int numPanels) throws Exception {
    s_database = db;
    s_table = table;
    i_numPanels = numPanels;
```

```
        ODBCConnect(s_database);
        iJDBC_callingClass = i;
        selectSQL();
    }
//Sort records
    public void setOrderBy(String s) throws SQLException {
        s_orderBy = s;
        selectSQL();
    }
//Add a radio button
    public void setChoices(String column, String display[], String
values[]) throws Exception {
        Vector choicesVect = new Vector();
        choicesVect.addElement(column);
        for (int loop = 0; loop < display.length; loop++){
            choicesVect.addElement(display[loop]);
            choicesVect.addElement(values[loop]);
        }
        i_components += display.length - 1;
        v_choices.addElement(choicesVect);
    }
    public int getSuggestedWidth() {   //Return suggested width
        return Math.max(i_numPanels * 250,400);
    }
    public int getSuggestedHeight() {   //Return suggested height
        if (i_components < i_columns) {
            return 480;
        }
        return 50 + i_components / i_numPanels * 35;
    }
//Form the panel from the columns
    public void formPanel() throws Exception {
        int currentPanel;
        int counter;
        float componentsPerPanel;
        int radioButtons = 0;
        Component co_holder = null;
    //Make panels
        Panel pa_panels[] = new Panel [i_numPanels];
        Panel labelPanel[] = new Panel [i_numPanels];
        Panel fieldPanel[] = new Panel [i_numPanels];
        Panel normalFields = new Panel();
        Panel memos = new Panel();
        Panel toolbar = new Panel();
    //Set layouts
        normalFields.setLayout(new GridLayout(1, i_numPanels));
        memos.setLayout(new GridLayout(0, 1));
        setLayout(new BorderLayout());
        toolbar.setLayout(new FlowLayout());
    //Build toolbar
        toolbar.add(bu_first);
        toolbar.add(bu_prev);
        toolbar.add(bu_clear);
        toolbar.add(bu_update);
        toolbar.add(bu_next);
        toolbar.add(bu_last);
```

```
      toolbar.add(bu_exit);
   //Add action listeners for toolbar
      bu_first.addActionListener(this);
      bu_prev.addActionListener(this);
      bu_clear.addActionListener(this);
      bu_update.addActionListener(this);
      bu_next.addActionListener(this);
      bu_last.addActionListener(this);
      bu_exit.addActionListener(this);
      if (i_components < i_columns) {
        add("North", normalFields);
        add("Center", memos);
      }
      else {
        add("Center", normalFields);
      }
      add("South", toolbar);
      componentsPerPanel = (float) i_components / (float) i_numPanels;
      currentPanel = 0;
      for (counter = 0; counter < i_numPanels; counter++) {
      //Make big panel
        pa_panels[counter] = new Panel();
        pa_panels[counter].setLayout(new BorderLayout());
        normalFields.add(pa_panels[counter]);
      //Make label panel and put it on big panel
        labelPanel[counter] = new Panel();
        labelPanel[counter].setLayout(new GridLayout(0,1));
        pa_panels[counter].add("West", labelPanel[counter]);
      //Make field panel and put it on big panel
        fieldPanel[counter] = new Panel();
        fieldPanel[counter].setLayout(new GridLayout(0,1));
        pa_panels[counter].add("Center", fieldPanel[counter]);
      }
   //Scroll through the fields
      for (counter = 0; counter < i_columns; counter++) {
      //Make sure you're on the right panel
        if (counter + radioButtons >=
((currentPanel+1)*componentsPerPanel)
          && (currentPanel+1) < i_numPanels) {
          currentPanel++;
        }
    //Get column info from the record set meta data
      String columnName = rsmd_results.getColumnName(counter+1);
      int columnType = rsmd_results.getColumnType(counter+1);
      int displaySize = rsmd_results.getColumnDisplaySize(counter+1);
      String labelName = columnName + ": ";
    //Adjust component appropriate to column type
      switch (columnType) {
        case Types.BIT :  //Boolean
          co_holder = (Component) new Checkbox(columnName);
          labelName = "";
          break;
        default :
          if (rsmd_results.isAutoIncrement(counter+1)) {
            co_holder = (Component) new
                Label("(Autoincrement)");
```

```
              }
              else {
              //Scroll through radio buttons
                boolean b_choices = false;
                Enumeration e = v_choices.elements();
              //More RBs to check?
                while (e.hasMoreElements()) {
                  Vector v = (Vector) e.nextElement();
                  String s = (String) v.elementAt(0);
                //This is a radio button
                  if (s.equals(columnName)) {
                    CheckboxGroup cbg =
                      new CheckboxGroup();
                    Enumeration e2 = v.elements();
                    e2.nextElement();
                  //Add displays
                    while (e2.hasMoreElements()) {
if (b_choices) {
                        radioButtons++;
                      }
                    co_holder = (Component)
                      new Checkbox(
                       (String)
e2.nextElement(),                            cbg, !b_choices);
                    // Don't display values
                      e2.nextElement();
                      v_components.addElement(
                        co_holder);
                    fieldPanel[currentPanel].add(
                      co_holder);
                    labelPanel[currentPanel].add(
new Label(                             labelName,
                        Label.RIGHT));
                      labelName = "";
                      b_choices = true;
                    }
                    co_holder = null;
                    break;
                  }
                }
                if (b_choices == false) {   //Not a radio button
                  if (displaySize < 256) {   //Single-line
                    co_holder = (Component)
                        new TextField();
                  }
                  else {            //Multiline
                    co_holder = (Component)
                        new WrappingTextArea();
                  }
                }
              }
            break;
          }
        if (co_holder != null) {   //A component has been added
          v_components.addElement(co_holder);
          if (displaySize < 256) {   //Single line
```

```
                fieldPanel[currentPanel].add(co_holder);
                labelPanel[currentPanel].add(new Label(
                    labelName, Label.RIGHT));
            }
            else {                    //Multi line
                Panel p = new Panel();
                p.setLayout(new BorderLayout());
                p.add("North",new Label(labelName));
                p.add("Center",co_holder);
                memos.add(p);
            }
        }
    }
    getNextRow();   //Go to first row
}
//Connect to an ODBC database
  private void ODBCConnect(String database) throws Exception {
    // Visual J++ Users
    if (System.getProperty("java.vendor").equals("Microsoft Corp."))
{
        Class.forName("com.ms.jdbc.odbc.JdbcOdbcDriver");
    }
    else {      // Non-Visual J++ Users
        Class.forName("sun.jdbc.odbc.JdbcOdbcDriver");
    }
  //Connect to the ODBC database
    dbConnection = DriverManager.getConnection("jdbc:odbc:" +
database, "", "");
  //Create a statement for the ODBC database
    SQLStatement = dbConnection.createStatement();
}
//Method for SELECTing records via the default SELECT
  public void selectSQL() throws SQLException {
    // Default order by is the first column
    if (s_orderBy == null) {
        String statement = "SELECT * FROM " + s_table;
        selectSQL(statement);
        s_orderBy = rsmd_results.getColumnName(1);
    }
    String statement = "SELECT * FROM " + s_table
        + " ORDER BY " + s_orderBy;
    selectSQL(statement);   //Execute the statement
}
//Method for SELECTing records via an SQL statement
  private void selectSQL(String statement) throws SQLException {
  //Get the result set
    result = SQLStatement.executeQuery(statement);
  //Get the result set information and properties
    rsmd_results = result.getMetaData();
  //Get the number of columns
    i_columns = rsmd_results.getColumnCount();
  //Initialize the number of components
    i_components = i_columns;
  //Scroll through the components and subtract memos out. They
  //are handled differently in another panel
    for (int counter = 0; counter < i_columns; counter++) {
```

```java
          if (rsmd_results.getColumnDisplaySize(counter+1) > 255) {
            i_components--;
          }
        }
      }
//Add record
    public void clearPanel() throws Exception {
      b_adding = true;
      Component co_holder = null;
      // Go backwards for the CheckboxGroups.
      for (int counter = v_components.size()-1; counter >= 0; counter-
-) {
        co_holder = (Component) v_components.elementAt(counter);
        if (co_holder instanceof Label) {  //Autoincrement
          Label lb = (Label) co_holder;
          lb.setText("(Autoincrement)");
        }
        else if (co_holder instanceof Checkbox) {   //Boolean
          Checkbox cb = (Checkbox) co_holder;
          cb.setState(true);
        }
        else if (co_holder instanceof TextComponent) {   //Other
          TextComponent tc = (TextComponent) co_holder;
          tc.setText("");
        }
      }
    }
//This method executes updatable SQL and the resets the display
    public void executeSQL(String SQL) throws Exception {
      SQLStatement.executeUpdate(SQL);
      SQL = "SELECT * FROM " + s_table
        + " WHERE " + s_orderBy + " >= " + getSQLKey()
        + " ORDER BY " + s_orderBy;
      selectSQL(SQL);
      if (getSQLKey().equals("(Autoincrement)")) {
        getLastRow();
      }
      if (result.next()) {
        displayResult();
      }
      else {
        getFirstRow();
      }
    }
// Delete a record
    public void deleteDB() throws Exception {
      String SQLKey = getSQLKey();
      String SQL = "DELETE FROM " + s_table
        + " WHERE " + s_orderBy + " = " + SQLKey;
      executeSQL(SQL);
    }
// Update or finish adding a record
    public void updateDB() throws Exception {
      String SQL = null;
      int counter;
      if (b_adding) {
```

```
        boolean b_pastFirstColumn = false;
        String columns = "";
        String values = "";
        for (counter = 0; counter < i_columns; counter++) {
          if (rsmd_results.isAutoIncrement(counter+1)) {
            continue;
          }
          if (b_pastFirstColumn) {
            columns += ", ";
            values += ", ";
          }
          columns += rsmd_results.getColumnName(counter+1);
          values += getSQLScreenValue(counter);
          b_pastFirstColumn = true;
        }
        SQL = "INSERT INTO " + s_table + " ("
          + columns + ") VALUES (" + values + ")";
      }
      else {
        SQL = "UPDATE " + s_table + " SET ";
        boolean b_pastFirstColumn = false;
        for (counter = 0; counter < i_columns; counter++) {
          if (rsmd_results.isAutoIncrement(counter+1)) {
            continue;
          }
          if (b_pastFirstColumn) {
            SQL += ", ";
          }
          SQL += rsmd_results.getColumnName(counter+1);
          SQL += " = " + getSQLScreenValue(counter);
          b_pastFirstColumn = true;
        }
        SQL += " WHERE " + s_orderBy + " = " + getSQLKey();
      }
      executeSQL(SQL);
    }
//get the SQL key from the window
  private String getSQLKey() throws Exception {
    return getSQLScreenValue(result.findColumn(s_orderBy) - 1);
  }
//Get the SQL key from the window and put quotes on it
  private String getSQLScreenValue(int column) throws Exception {
    return putQuotesOnString(getScreenValue(column), column+1);
  }
//Get a column's value from the window
  private String getScreenValue(int column) throws Exception{
    Component co_holder;
    Enumeration e = v_components.elements();
  //Scroll through columns.
    for (int counter = 0; counter <= column; counter++) {
      String columnName = rsmd_results.getColumnName(counter+1);
      int columnType = rsmd_results.getColumnType(counter+1);
      int displaySize = rsmd_results.getColumnDisplaySize(counter+1);

      co_holder = (Component) e.nextElement();
      int vectSize = v_choices.size();
```

```java
          for (int loop = 0; loop < vectSize; loop++) {
            Vector v = (Vector) v_choices.elementAt(loop);
            String s = (String) v.elementAt(0);
            if (s.equals(columnName)) {   //Is this a radio button?
              for (int loop2 = 2; loop2 < v.size(); loop2+=2) {
                Checkbox cb;
                if (loop2 > 2) {
                  cb = (Checkbox) e.nextElement();
                }
                else {
                  cb = (Checkbox) co_holder;
                }
                if (cb.getState() && counter == column) {
                  return (String) v.elementAt(loop2);
                }
              }
            }
          }
          if (rsmd_results.isAutoIncrement(counter+1)   //AutoIncrement
              && counter == column) {
            Label lb = (Label) co_holder;
            return lb.getText();
          }
          else if (columnType == Types.BIT   //Boolean
              && counter == column) {
            Checkbox c = (Checkbox) co_holder;
            if (c.getState()) {
              return "true";
            }
            else {
              return "false";
            }
          }
          else if (counter == column) {   //Other
            TextComponent tc = (TextComponent) co_holder;
            return tc.getText();
          }
        }
      throw new SQLException("Cound not get value");
    }
  private String putQuotesOnString(String s, int column) throws
SQLException{
      String value = s.toString();
      switch (rsmd_results.getColumnType(column)) {
      //Strings
        case Types.CHAR :
        case Types.LONGVARCHAR :
        case Types.VARCHAR :
      //Byte Arrays
        case Types.BINARY :
        case Types.LONGVARBINARY :
        case Types.VARBINARY :
      //Byte
        case Types.TINYINT :
          value = "'" + value + "'";
          break;
```

```
      }
      return value;
    }
//JDBC doesn't handle previous rows well. Do it for them.
  public void getPrevRow() throws Exception {
    String value = getSQLKey();
    String screenValue = value;
  //Statement to get the previous key
    String statement = "SELECT MAX(" + s_orderBy +
      ") FROM " + s_table
      + " WHERE " + s_orderBy + " < " + value;
    selectSQL(statement);
    if (result.next()) {   //Get the results
      value = getDBValue(1);
      value = putQuotesOnString(value, 1);
    //Now reinitialize query starting from the previous value
      statement = "SELECT * FROM " + s_table
        + " WHERE " + s_orderBy + " >= " + value
        + " ORDER BY " + s_orderBy;
      selectSQL(statement);
      getNextRow();
      if (screenValue.equals(getSQLKey())) {
        throw new Exception("First record reached");
      }
    }
    else {
      selectSQL();
      throw new Exception("First record reached");
    }
  }
  public void getFirstRow() throws Exception {
    selectSQL();   //Reinitialize SQL
    if (result.next()) {   //get next
      displayResult();   //Display
    }
    else {
      throw new Exception("No records found");
    }
  }
  public void getLastRow() throws Exception {   //Get last row
  //Select the last row
    String statement = "SELECT * FROM " + s_table
        + " WHERE " + s_orderBy + " = ("
          + "SELECT MAX(" + s_orderBy + ") "
          + "FROM " + s_table + ")"
        + " ORDER BY " + s_orderBy;
    selectSQL(statement);
    if (result.next()) {
      do {
        displayResult();
      } while (result.next());
    }
    else {
      throw new Exception("No records found");
    }
  }
```

```java
    public void getNextRow() throws Exception {
  //Next rows are kinda easy
    if (result.next()) {
      displayResult();
    }
    else {
      throw new Exception("Last record reached");
    }
  }
//Go through columns and display components
  public void displayResult() throws Exception {
    b_adding = false;
    Enumeration e = v_components.elements();
    Component co_holder;
    for (int counter = 0; counter < i_columns; counter++) {
      co_holder = (Component) e.nextElement();
      int columnType = rsmd_results.getColumnType(counter+1);
      int displaySize = rsmd_results.getColumnDisplaySize(counter+1);
      String columnName = rsmd_results.getColumnName(counter+1);

      if (rsmd_results.isAutoIncrement(counter+1)) {
        Label lb = (Label) co_holder;
        lb.setText(getDBValue(counter+1));
      }
      else if (columnType == Types.BIT) {   //Boolean
        Checkbox c = (Checkbox) co_holder;
        boolean b = result.getBoolean(counter+1);
        c.setState(b);
      }
      else {
        String dbValue = getDBValue(counter+1);
        boolean b_choices = false;
        Enumeration e2 = v_choices.elements();
        while (e2.hasMoreElements()) {
          Vector v = (Vector) e2.nextElement();
          String s = (String) v.elementAt(0);
          if (s.equals(columnName)) {   //Radio Button?
            for (int loop2 = 2; loop2 < v.size(); loop2+=2) {
              String value = (String) v.elementAt(loop2);
              Checkbox cb;
              if (loop2 > 2) {
                cb = (Checkbox) e.nextElement();
              }
              else {
                cb = (Checkbox) co_holder;
              }
              if (value.equals(dbValue)) {
                cb.setState(true);
              }
            }
            b_choices = true;
            break;
          }
        }
        if (b_choices == false) {   //Text area
          TextComponent tc = (TextComponent) co_holder;
```

```
                tc.setText(dbValue);
              }
           }
        }
      }
//Get the current value of a column name
   public String getDBValue(String column) throws Exception {
     return getDBValue(result.findColumn(column));
   }
//Get the current value of a column number
   public String getDBValue(int column) throws Exception {
     String value = null;
     switch (rsmd_results.getColumnType(column)) {
       case Types.CHAR :        //Strings
       case Types.LONGVARCHAR :
       case Types.VARCHAR :
         value = result.getString(column);
         break;
       case Types.REAL :        //Float
         value = String.valueOf(result.getFloat(column));
         break;
       case Types.DOUBLE :        //Double
       case Types.FLOAT :
         value = String.valueOf(result.getDouble(column));
         break;
       case Types.INTEGER :     //Integer
         value = String.valueOf(result.getInt(column));
         break;
       case Types.SMALLINT :     //Short
         value = String.valueOf(result.getShort(column));
         break;
       case Types.BIGINT :        //Long
         value = String.valueOf(result.getLong(column));
         break;
       case Types.BINARY :        //Byte Array
       case Types.LONGVARBINARY :
       case Types.VARBINARY :
         value = new String (result.getBytes(column));
       case Types.TINYINT :     //Byte
         byte byteArray[] = new byte[1];
         byteArray[0] = result.getByte(column);
         value = new String (byteArray);
         break;
       case Types.DATE :        //Date
       case Types.TIME :        //Time
       case Types.TIMESTAMP :     //TimeStamp
       case Types.DECIMAL :     //java.math.BigDecimal
       case Types.NUMERIC :     //java.math.BigDecimal
       default :
         throw new SQLException(
           "JDBCPanel can't handle a column's datatype");
```

```
      }
      if (value == null) {
        return "";
      }
      return value;
    }
//The actionPerformed method is required by the ActionListener
interface
    public void actionPerformed(ActionEvent event) {
      try {
      // Get the text of the button
        iJDBC_callingClass.showStatus("");
        String buttonText = event.getActionCommand();
      //Test for buttons
        if (buttonText.equals("<< First")) {
          getFirstRow();
        }
        else if (buttonText.equals("< Prev")) {
          getPrevRow();
        }
        else if (buttonText.equals("Update")) {
          updateDB();
        }
        else if (buttonText.equals("Add")) {
          clearPanel();
        }
        else if (buttonText.equals("Next >")) {
          getNextRow();
        }
        else if (buttonText.equals("Last >>")) {
          getLastRow();
        }
        else if (buttonText.equals("Exit")) {
          System.exit(0);
        }
      }
      catch (Exception e) {
        iJDBC_callingClass.showStatus("JDBCPanel error: " +
e.getMessage());
      }
    }
}
```

The IJDBCPanel **interface is used to enable the** JDBCPanel **class to "talk to" the calling class. This is shown in Listing 28-5.**

Listing 28-5: IJDBCPanel.java

```
public interface IJDBCPanel {
public void showStatus(String message);
}
```

Summary

Although not as full-featured as ADO, JDBC is easier to learn and understand, and enables you to run your database applications from any Java-compliant machine, rather than Microsoft-only machines.

- Class libraries help with Java development, especially with JDBC.

- If you want Java database connections that run anywhere, JDBC is your only choice.

- Remember, when executing the `forName` method, Visual J++ machines are different from Java machines and need different parameters.

Java Operators and Language

This appendix contains tables that describe the Java language.

Table A-1 describes Java's comments.

Table A-1 Comments	
Comment	***Description***
`// Comment`	`//` is used as a Single line comment. All text on the same line following `//` is treated as comments and ignored by the compiler.
`/* Mutliline Comment */`	`/*` and `*/` are used to enclose multiline comments. All text between the `/*` and the `*/` is treated as comments and is ignored by the compiler.
`//* Multiline documentation */`	`//*` and `*/` are used to enclose multiline documentation. This documentation is treated as comments by the compiler and is converted to HTML to implement as HTML documentation using the JavaDoc utility or equivalent.

A single line comment appears as follows:

```
//This is a single line comment
```

whereas a multiple-line comment appears as follows:

```
/*
This is a multiple
line comment
*/
```

Table A-2 describes Java Data Types.

Table A-2	Java Data Types		
Data Type	**Default**	**Size***	**Description**
boolean	false	1 bit**	boolean can be true or false.
char	null	2 bytes	char defines a Unicode character. For details, see Appendix C.
byte	null	1 byte	byte defines an ASCII character.
short	0	2 bytes	short is a signed integer ranging from –32,768 to 32,767.
int	0	4 bytes	int is a signed integer ranging from –2,147,483,648 to 2,147,483,647.
long	0	8 bytes	long is an extremely long, signed integer ranging from –9,223,372,036,854,775,808 to 9,223,372,036,854,775,807.
float	0.0	4 bytes	float is a floating-point (also called decimal) number that ranges from +/–1.40239846E-45 (.00000...014 with 44 zeros between the decimal point and the 1) and +/–3.40282347E+38 (3400...0 with 37 zeros at the end). Although numbers can get rather large or small with a float, there are, at most, nine significant digits in a float. When numbers get very large or very small, some rounding or truncating occurs.
double	0.0	8 bytes	double is a floating-point decimal that ranges from +/–4.94065645841246544E-324 (.000...494 with 323 zeros between the decimal and the 4) to +/–1.79769313486231570E+308 (17900...000 with 306 zeros at the end). As with float, the numbers in a double can get very large, but there are only, at most, eight significant digits in a double. Very large or very small numbers are rounded or truncated.
String	null	Varies	String is a class data type. A *class data type* is not a true data type, but rather a prewritten class that is included with Visual J++. String is used to manipulate strings in a Visual J++ program. Because it is a class data type, it is capitalized.

*1 byte equals 8 bits.
**Visual J++ actually dedicates up to an entire byte to a boolean variable but still allows only *true* and *false* values.

To declare an integer in Java and initialize it to 1, you would use a line of Java code like the following:

```
int my_number = 1;
```

Table A-3 lists binary arithmetic operators.

Table A-3   Binary Arithmetic Operators

Operator	Example	Description
*	a * b	* is used for multiplication. a * b returns the product of a multiplied by b.
/	a / b	/ is used for division. a / b returns the quotient of a divided by b.
%	a % b	% is the modulus operator (also called the remainder operator). a % b returns the remainder when a is divided by b.
+	a + b	+ is used for addition as well as string concatenation. If a and b are numbers, a + b returns the sum of a and b. If a and b are strings, a + b returns the concatenation of the two strings.
-	a - b	- is used for subtraction. a - b returns the difference between a and b.
=	a = b	= is used for assignment. a = b copies the value of b into a.

Table A-4 lists bitwise operators.

Table A-4   Bitwise Operators

Operator	Example	Description
~	~a	The bitwise complement (~) is used to reverse the sign on a bit.
&	a & b	The bitwise AND (&) performs an AND operation on two variables. This sets the result to 1 if both variables are 1; otherwise, it sets the result to 0.
^	a ^ b	The bitwise XOR (exclusive OR) operator (^) returns true if one and only one of the two variables tested are true. If both variables are true or both variables are false, a false value is returned.
|	a | b	The bitwise OR operator (also known as the inclusive OR operator) returns a true if either of the two variables tested are true. Otherwise, a false value is returned.

(continued)

Table A-4	*(Continued)*	
Operator	*Example*	*Description*
<<	a << b	<< is the left-shift operator. << left-shifts all bits in one variable. In this example, the bits in *a* are left-shifted *b* times. The leftmost bits are discarded, and the rightmost bits are set to 0. Each shift has the effect of multiplying an integer by 2.
>	a > b	> is the right-shift with sign preserve operator. > right-shifts all bits in a variable. In this example, the bits in *a* are right-shifted left *b* times. The rightmost bit is discarded, and the leftmost bit is set to preserve the sign of the original value. Each shift has the effect of dividing an integer by 2.
>>	a >> b	>> is the right-shift operator. >> shifts all bits to the right, just like the > operator, except the sign is not preserved. The rightmost bit is discarded, and the leftmost bit is set to zero. Sometimes, each shift has the effect of dividing an integer by 2, but the results vary depending on the original sign bit.

Table A-5 lists results from logical operations.

Table A-5	Results from Logical Operations				
a	*b*	*~a*	*a & b*	*a ^ b*	*a | b*
0	0	1	0	0	0
0	1	1	0	1	1
1	0	0	0	1	1
1	1	0	1	0	1

Table A-6 lists combination assignment operators.

Table A-6	Combination Assignment Operators	
Operator	*Example*	*Equivalent Expression*
*=	a *= b	a = a * b
/=	a /= b	a = a / b
%=	a %= b	a = a % b
+=	a += b	a = a + b

Operator	Example	Equivalent Expression
-=	a -= b	a = a - b
&=	a &= b	a = a & b
^=	a ^= b	a = a ^ b
|=	a |= b	a = a | b
>=	a >= b	a = a > b
<<=	a <<= b	a = a << b
>>=	a >>= b	a = a >> b

Table A-7 lists unary arithmetic operators.

Table A-7   Unary Arithmetic Operators

Operator	Example	Description
+	+a	+ serves as a unary plus. A unary plus has no effect on an equation, but can be used for emphasis. For example, instead of typing a * b, you could type +a * b and retrieve the same result.
-	-a	- serves as a unary minus. A unary minus takes the opposite sign of a variable before an operation. -a * b returns the same result as (-1) * (a * b).

++	++a
	a++
		++ is used to increment a variable. When ++ is placed before a variable, that variable is incremented before the rest of the operation occurs. For example,
		`c = ++a * b;`
		
		is the equivalent of
		`a = a + 1;`
		`c = a * b;`
		
		Similarly,
		`c = a++ * b;`
		
		is the equivalent of
		`c = a * b;`
		`a = a + 1;`

(continued)

Table A-7   *(Continued)*

Operator	*Example*	*Description*

`- -`	`--a`
	`a—`
		`--` is used to decrement a variable. When `--` is placed before a variable, that variable is decremented before the rest of the operation occurs. When `--` is placed after a variable, that variable is incremented after the operation occurs. For example,
		`c = --a * b;`
		
		is the equivalent of
		`a = a - 1;`
		`c = a * b;`
		
		On the other hand,
		`c = a-- * b;`
		
		is the equivalent of
		`c = a * b;`
		`a = a - 1;`

`(data type)`	`(String) a`	A data type in parentheses is called a casting operator because it casts a variable to a new type for an operation. (String) a returns a casted as a string.

Table A-8 lists logical operators.

Table A-8   **Logical Operators**

Operator	*Example*	*Description*
`==`	`if (a == b)...`	`==` is the logical equals operator. `==` tests whether two expressions have the same value. If `==` is used on a class, it tests whether the two classes refer to the same object.
`!=`	`if (a != b)...`	`!=` is the logical not-equals operator. `!=` returns true if two expressions contain different values. If `!=` is used on a class, it tests whether the two classes refer to different objects.
`!`	`if (!bool_var)`	`!` is the logical not operator. `!` tests a boolean expression. If the boolean expression is true, !boolean returns false. Otherwise, it returns true.
`<`	`if (a < b) {...`	`<` is the less-than operator. It tests whether one value is less than another.
`>`	`if (a > b) {...`	`>` is the greater-than operator. It tests whether one value is greater than another.

Operator	Example	Description
<=	if (a <= b) {...	<= is the less-than-or-equal operator. It tests whether one value is less than or equal to another.
>=	if (a >= b) {...	>= is the greater-than operator. It tests whether one value is greater than or equal to another.
&&	if (bool1 && bool2)...	&& is the logical conditional AND operator. It evaluates two boolean expressions until one evaluates to false. It then returns true if all boolean expressions are true, and returns false if any are false.
||	if (bool1 || bool2)...	|| is the logical conditional OR operator. It evaluates two boolean expressions until one evaluates to true. It then returns true if any boolean expressions are true, and returns false if all are false.
&	if (bool1 & bool2)...	& is the logical AND operator. It evaluates two boolean expressions *entirely*. It then returns true if all boolean expressions are true, and returns false if any are false. Usually, & is inefficient because *all* expressions are evaluated before a true or false is returned. && should usually be used instead unless all expressions need to be processed.
| ^	if (bool1 | bool2) {... if (bool1 ^ bool2) {...	| and ^ are logical OR operators. They evaluate two boolean expressions *entirely*. They then return true if any boolean expressions are true and false if all are false. Usually, | and ^ are inefficient because *all* expressions are evaluated before a true or false is returned. || should usually be used instead unless all expressions need to be processed.
?:	a = (bool ? if_true : if_false);	? and : are known as the conditional operator. The conditional operator is used to test a boolean expression and then return one value if the boolean expression is true or another value if the boolean expression is false. Although an if...else... statement could achieve the same effect, ? and : can be used for simple assignments; this operator is a great space saver. It may also be marginally more efficient than an if...else... statement.

Table A-9 lists miscellaneous operators.

Table A-9　Miscellaneous Operators

Operator	Example	Description
[ ]	new int[5]	The array operator ([ ]) is used to declare and reference arrays.
.	import java.awt.*	The period operator (.) indicates that a variable or method is a member of a class.
:	case 23 :	The colon operator (:) is used after a case statement in a switch construct.
,	int a, b;	The comma operator (,) allows the multiple listing of variables in a declaration or multiple statements into a single statement.
instanceof	if (var instanceof Class) {...	The instanceof variable returns a true or false depending on whether a variable is an instance of a class. This instanceof operator is often used with inheritance.

Table A-10 lists the order of operations.

Table A-10　Order of Operations

Step	Operations in This Step
1	() [] .
2	++ − ! [~] instanceof + (unary) - (unary)
3	* / %
4	+(binary) -(binary)
5	<< > >>
6	& (bitwise)
7	^ (bitwise)
8	| (bitwise)
9	?:
10	< > <= >= == !=
11	& (logical)

Step	Operations in This Step
12	^ (logical)
13	| (logical)
14	&&
15	||
16	= *= /= %= += -= <<= >= >>= &= ^= |=
17	,

The equation

```
my_number = 3 + 4 * 5
```

sets `my_number` to 23. The multiplication is performed first (4*5 = 20) and then the addition (20 + 3 = 23). Conversely, the equation

```
my_number = (3 + 4) * 5
```

sets `my_number` to 35 because the equation in parentheses, the addition, is performed first (3 + 4 = 7) and then the result is multiplied by 5 (7 * 5 = 35).

Table A-11 lists character literals.

Table A-11   Character Literals

Character Literal	Symbol
Continuation	\
New Line (NL or CR/LF)	\n
Horizontal Tab (HT)	\t
Backspace (BS)	\b
Carriage Return (CR)	\r
Form Feed (FF)	\f
Backslash (\)	\\
Single Quote (')	\'
Double Quote (")	\"
Octal Bit Pattern (0###)	\###
Hexadecimal Bit Pattern (0x##)	\x##
Unicode Character (0x####)	\u####

If you want to format a string to look like this:

```
When Abe said, "Four score and seven years ago," he meant 87 years.
```

use the following:

```
String my_quote = "When Abe said, " +
 "\"Four score and seven years ago,\" he meant 87 years.";
```

In many languages, it is difficult to put a quote inside a quoted string, but using character literals in Java makes it easy.

Appendix B

Reserved Words in Visual J++

Visual J++ has many reserved words that you are not allowed to use in your programs except to perform the functions that Java and Visual J++ have intended. This appendix lists these reserved words.

Reserved Word	Description
abstract	Declares that a class cannot be instantiated; only its descendants can be. It also is used to declare virtual methods in an ancestor class.
boolean	Used to declare a boolean data type inside a class or method. A boolean data type has two values: true and false. (Note: *Boolean* with a capital *B* is not a reserved word.)
break	Used to break out of a loop or switch block. When breaking out of a loop, it is usually contained within an if statement. It is usually the last line of each case in a switch block.
byte	Used to declare an 8-bit, single-character data type inside a class or method. A byte variable can be used to store ASCII characters. (Note: *Byte* with a capital *B* is not a reserved word.)
case	A keyword that is used in a switch statement. A switch statement is used to execute one of several sections of code depending on the value of a variable.
catch	Used to trap errors within a try block.
char	Used to declare a 16-bit-single-character data type inside a class or method. A char variable can be used to store Unicode characters.
class	Used to declare a class inside a Visual J++ module.
const	The const keyword is not currently used in Visual J++, but may be implemented by Java and Visual J++ in future releases.
continue	Used to skip all following statements in a loop and continue with the next iteration of the loop. continue is usually embedded within an if or switch block. (Note: *Continue* with a capital *C* is not a reserved word.)
default	Used to execute statements in a switch block if all cases within the switch block are false. It is the functional equivalent to an else statement in an if[el]else if[el] else block.
delegate	Used in Visual J++ only to pass the address of a method.
do	Used with the while keyword to form a post-test loop.

(continued)

Reserved Word	Description
double	Used to declare a double-precision floating-point number inside a class or method.
else	Used within an `if` statement structure to execute a block of statements if the condition tested in the `if` statement fails.
extends	Used for inheritance. When one class (Class1) `extends` another class (Class2), then Class1 is inherited from Class2.
false	A constant used to test for a false condition or to assign a false value to a boolean variable.
final	This keyword is a modifier. When a class is declared `final`, then that class cannot be inherited. When a method is declared `final`, then that method can never be overridden by subclasses. When an attribute or variable is declared `final`, then that variable is to be initialized immediately, used as a constant, and never modified.
finally	This keyword is run at the end of a `try[el]catch` block. It is not often used except to clean up memory and databases left after a `try` block.
float	Used to declare a single-precision floating-point number inside a class or method.
for	Used to set up a loop with initialization, condition testing, and a statement to be run during each iteration of the loop. It is similar to the C/C++ `for` statement.
goto	This is not currently used in Visual J++, but may be implemented by Java and Visual J++ in future releases.
if	Used to test a condition and then execute a set of code if that condition is true.
implements	Used to implement an interface inside a class.
import	Used to automatically reference a package or class outside the current module.
instanceof	Tests whether a variable is an instance of a particular class. This is useful when you have a class array of inherited classes; `instanceof` can be used to test each class instance to see what subclass it belongs to.
int	Used to declare an integer number inside a class or method. (Note: *Int* with a capital *I* is not a reserved word.)
interface	Used to set up Java interfaces. Interfaces are not classes, but contain methods that are grouped together. Interfaces can be thought of as method prototypes that must be defined in a class.
long	Used to declare a long integer number inside a class or method.
multicast	Used only in Visual J++ to pass the same pointer to multiple recipients.

Reserved Word	*Description*
native	Used to declare a function as external to Visual J++. This is often used with external C++ functions that a Visual J++ program can execute.
new	Used to instantiate a class. new sets up memory, runs any constructors, and returns a pointer to the new class.
null	A constant. All instances of classes are initialized to null until set up with a new command or until assigned to an existing class.
package	Used to group classes together. Although Visual J++ projects have made packages somewhat obsolete, packages are still used in older Java modules ported to Visual J++, and the Java class structure uses packages. Packages can also be used to share scope among different classes, but this violates encapsulation and is usually indicative of bad program design.
private	A scope modifier for attributes and methods. A private attribute or method is accessible (visible) only within the same class as the private attribute or method is declared.
private protected	A scope modifier for attributes and methods. Although actually two keywords, the keyword functionality changes when private and protected are combined. A private protected attribute or method is accessible (visible) only within the same class as the private attribute or method is declared a descendant (subclass) of the class. Unlike protected classes, private protected classes are not accessible to other classes in the same package.
protected	A scope modifier for attributes and methods. A protected attribute or method is accessible (visible) only within the same class as the private attribute or method is declared, descendants (subclasses) of the class, and other classes in the same package, if applicable.
public	A scope modifier for classes, attributes, and methods. A public class, attribute, or method is accessible (visible) to any other method, even those methods in other classes.
return	Used to send control back from a called method to the calling method or function. If there was no calling method, control is passed back to the operating system. The return keyword is also used to pass variables back from the called method to the calling method or function.
short	Used to declare a small integer number inside a class or method.
static	A modifier for methods and attributes. When an attribute is declared static, memory is immediately set up for that attribute, and only one attribute exists for every instance of that attribute. A static attribute can also be accessed from any class that has access to the class, even without instantiating the class. Static methods can be called without instantiating a class.

(continued)

Reserved Word	Description
super	Used to call the ancestor constructor as the first line of your descendent constructor. It's also used to access ancestor attributes that have been overridden by descendent attributes.
switch	Used to execute one of several sections of code depending on the value of a variable.
synchronized	Used as a method modifier and a statement. A synchronized static method modifier locks the class to make sure no other threads can modify the class concurrently. A synchronized nonstatic modifier locks the instance of the class to make sure that no other threads can modify the class instance concurrently. As a statement, synchronized is used to lock an object or array before executing a block of code.
this	Refers to the current instance of a class. this is often used for a class to pass itself to an outside method or to call a constructor from another constructor.
throw	Used to force an error signal to occur.
throws	Used when a method is declared to indicate that this method can cause the thrown exception or error.
transient	An attribute modifier that indicates a variable is used for a class "scratch" variable, and therefore does not need to be saved to disk when the class is saved or cloned to other instances of a class.
true	A constant used to test for a true condition or to assign a true value to a boolean variable.
try	Used to set up an error-catching block. Any errors caught are processed by catch and finally blocks.
void	Used in method declarations. A void method indicates that the method does not return any value to the calling method.
volatile	Used in attribute declarations. Specifying that an attribute is volatile indicates that the attribute may be changed asynchronously. This usually means that the variable is part of the hardware configuration and the value may change from time to time without any action of any class method. Therefore, no optimizations should be performed on a volatile attribute.
while	Used to form a pretest loop. while can also be used in conjunction with the do statement to form a post-test loop.

Appendix C

HTML Reference

As programming tools go, HTML is a nice tool for quick development — but it's not exactly a programming language. Rather, HTML formatting codes and links are similar to those found in old Word and WordPerfect documents or in old RunOff editors.

HTML Structure and Syntax

Before programming in a language like Visual J++, you should ask yourself whether the same task could be accomplished using HTML. You may find that your programs are shorter and easier to maintain, and your development time decreases.

Remember, HTML and Visual J++ often work in conjunction with each other. It would be a mistake to avoid the easy-to-use HTML simply because you have a powerful programming language like Visual J++.

Consider the Web page in Figure C-1. In traditional programming languages, the home page in Figure C-1 would take a long time to program. If you use HTML, however, the process is quite simple.

Figure C-1: IDG's home page can be found at www.idgbooks.com.

An HTML document is simply a text file containing text and codes. The script of Figure C-1 uses the following codes:

- All HTML code is placed between ‹HTML› and ‹/HTML› symbols at the top and the bottom of the HTML script.

- All beginning information (such as titles) is placed between ‹HEAD› and ‹/HEAD› symbols.

- The title, enclosed by ‹TITLE› and ‹/TITLE›, is used to display the title of the HTML document in the toolbar (refer to Figure C-1). The title must be placed in the ‹HEAD› section.

- ‹BODY› and ‹/BODY› are used to define the body of the HTML.

- ‹H1›, ‹H2›, and so on (up to ‹H6›) are used to emphasize text to a lesser and lesser degree for each heading level. Similarly, ‹EM› and ‹STRONG› are used for emphasis by usually italics and bold, respectively. ‹CENTER›, ‹LEFT›, and ‹RIGHT› can be used to position text on the window.

- ‹IMG[el]› is used to define an image on your Web page. The picture file, the alignment (top, middle, or bottom), and the width and height must all be defined.

- ‹P› and ‹/P› are used to signify the start and end of a paragraph. There's usually a double space between paragraphs. ‹BR› is used for a line break to return to the next line.

- ‹HR› is used to draw a horizontal line across the Web page.

- ‹A› and ‹/A› are used to establish links to other addresses.

There are other HTML commands, but as you can see, you can do most of what you want using the preceding commands.

Secret

You can not include a ‹, ›, &, or " as text in your document because HTML looks at these as commands. To display a character, you must use *escape sequences*. Table C-1 shows some valid HTML escape sequences.

Table C-1   Escape Sequences in HTML

Escape Sequence	Description
&lt	Less-than sign
&gt	Greater-than sign
&amp	Ampersand
&quot	Quote
	En space
	Em space

Escape Sequence	Description
	No break space
&endash	En Dash
&emdash	Em Dash
&reg	Register mark
&copy	Copyright mark

HTML and Java

When coding Visual J++, you need to use the <PPLET> HTML tag to embed your Visual J++ class into your HTML document. Listing C-1 shows the HTML code needed to run a HelloWorld Java program.

Listing C-1: HTML to Show a HelloWorld Java Class Program

```
<html>
<head>
<title>Hello World</title>
</head>
<body>
<applet CODE="HelloWorld.class" WIDTH=150 HEIGHT=25></applet>
</body>
</html>
```

This simple HTML code in Listing C-1 embeds the HelloWorld class inside an HTML document. Browsers that are Java- and Visual J++- aware run the HelloWorld class whenever the HTML is loaded.

In the following example:

```
<applet code=Sounds.class width=200 height=200>
<param name=sounds value="sounds.au">
```

the <APPLET> key is immediately followed by the <PARAM> key. This enables your HTML to pass parameters to your applet. In this case, the Sounds class runs, and the sounds.au file name is passed as a parameter.

HTML Reference

Because Internet Explorer and Netscape are constantly adding or replacing tags in their products, some tags only work with one of the two browsers. For example, there's talk of an <EMBED> tag replacing or supplementing the <APPLET> tag that would enable multiple language support — rather than just Java and Visual J++ support.

Table C-2 shows a list of most of the available HTML tags.

Table C-2 HTML Reference

HTML Tag	Tag Name	Description
`<!-- >`	Comment	Used to comment your code.
`<A>`	Anchor	Used to anchor or link your site to another Web site in the `<BODY>` section of your HTML document.
`<ABBREV>`	Abbreviation	Displays normal text, and enables Web browsers to index your Web site.
`<ACRONYM>`	Acronym	Displays normal text, and enables Web browsers to index your Web site.
`<ADDRESS>`	Address	Used to display address or contact information, slightly indented and usually in italics.
`<APP>`	Applet (Java alpha)	Enables you to embed Java alpha classes. Since Java 1.0 went into production, this tag is obsolete.
`<APPLET>`	Applet	Enables you to embed Java and Visual J++ classes.
`<AREA>`	Area	Enables you to define hot spots within an image.
`<AU>`	Author	Same as `<AUTHOR>`.
`<AUTHOR>`	Author	Displays the author of the text or Web page. This is picked up by browser indexers.
`<B>`	Bold	Defines text that should be displayed in a boldface font.
`<BANNER>`	Banner	Defines text that does not scroll with the rest of the document.
`<BASE>`	Base	Defines the URL address of the current Web site. This is typically used to allow you to change the location of the Web site without changing the links to figures, Visual J++ classes, and so on.
`<BASEFONT>`	BaseFont	Defines the font that relative font changes are based on.
`<BGSOUND>`	Background Sound	Defines a .WAV, .AU, or .MID resource that is played when the page is opened.
`<BIG>`	Big Text	Displays text in a larger font than usual.
`<BLOCKQUOTE>`	Block Quote	The block quote tag defines text that is quoted from somewhere else.
`<BODY>`	Body	Defines the body of the document.
` `	LineBreak	Starts any additional text on the next line.
`<BQ>`	Block Quote	Same as `<BLOCKQUOTE>`.

HTML Tag	Tag Name	Description
`<CAPTION>`	Caption	Defines the caption of a figure or table and is used within <FIG> or <TABLE> tags.
`<CENTER>`	Center	Centers text until the current paragraph ends or the next paragraph begins. Note: The HTML 3.0 construct, `<P ALIGN=CENTER>text</P>`, should be used instead of the `<CENTER>` tag because the `<CENTER>` tag is not part of the HTML standard — it is part of Netscape's and Internet Explorer's valid tags.
`<CITE>`	Citation	Defines text that cites a book or other work.
`<CODE>`	Code	Defines text that is displayed in a proportional (fixed width) font.
`<CREDIT>`	Credit	Defines text that credits a figure or quote. `<CREDIT>` is used in <FIG> or <BQ> tags.
DD>	Definition (in a list)	Defines a definition that's part of a definition list.
`<DEL>`	Deleted Text	Marks text that has been deleted. This is useful in a group environment where the rest of the team needs to be aware of deletions from a document.
`<DFN>`	Definition	Defines text that may define a term.
`<DIR>`	Directory List	Lists items (see `<LI>`) that do not have a bullet or number in front of them.
`<DIV>`	Division	Divides a document into sections.
`<DL>`	Definition List	Begins a definition list.
`<DT>`	Definition Term	Defines terms inside a definition list.
`<EM>`	Emphasized	Emphasizes text—most browsers display this as italics.
`<FIG>`	Figure	Defines a figure to be displayed in your HTML document.
`<FN>`	Footnote	Defines footnote text, which is often displayed in a pop-up window.
`<FONT>`	Font	Defines a font that differs from the base font in size or color.
`<FORM>`	Form	Defines a form that is made up of input elements such as checkboxes, radio buttons, and data entry fields.
`<H1>`	Heading 1	The first-level heading in a body.
`<H2>`	Heading 2	The second-level heading in a body.
`<H3>`	Heading 3	The third-level heading in a body.
`<H4>`	Heading 4	The fourth-level heading in a body.

(continued)

Table C-2 *(Continued)*

HTML Tag	Tag Name	Description
`<H5>`	Heading 5	The fifth-level heading in a body.
`<H6>`	Heading 6	The sixth-level heading in a body.
`<HEAD>`	Head	Head defines the heading part of your HTML document. This differs from the <H1> through <H6> tags in that the <HEAD> tag identifies a section in your HTML where the heading, author, and web title that appears on the web browser title bar can be added. <H1> through <H6> are merely formatting directives.
`<HR>`	Horizontal Rule	Draws a horizontal line across your Web page. This is often used to separate sections of your Web pages.
`<HTML>`	HTML	`<HTML>` and `</HTML>` are used to enclose all your HTML statements in a Web page.
`<I>`	Italic	Displays text as italic.
`<IMG>`	Inline Image	Displays an image (JPG or GIF picture) in your HTML document. (The `<FIG>` tag is an improvement over the `<IMG>` tag.)
`<INPUT>`	Form Input	Using `<INPUT>`, you can define checkboxes, files, images, passwords, radio buttons, ranges, resets, scribbles, or text.
`<INS>`	Inserted Text	Marks inserted text. This is useful in a group environment where the rest of the team needs to be aware of what is inserted into a document.
`<ISINDEX>`	Is Index	Declares that the current HTML document is a searchable index. This tag is only valid in the `<HEAD>` section.
`<KBD>`	Keyboard	Defines text that should be shown in a proportional (fixed width) font.
`<LANG>`	Language	Used to alter the language used for a block of text.
`<LH>`	List Heading	Used to define a heading for an ordered (`<OL>`), unordered (`<UL>`), or directory (`<DIR>`) list.
`<LI>`	List Item	Used to define an entry for an ordered (`<OL>`), unordered (`<UL>`), menu (`<MENU>`), or directory (`<DIR>`) list.
`<LINK>`	Link	Establishes a link to another URL in the `<HEAD>` section.
`<LISTING>`	Listing	Defines a program listing. `<LISTING>` is obsolete — use `<PRE>` instead..

HTML Tag	*Tag Name*	*Description*
`<MAP>`	Map	Defines `<AREA>` tags over an inline image.
`<MARQUEE>`	Marquee	Defines a moving piece of text, like a marquee.
`<MATH>`	Math	Defines a formula or equation.
`<MENU>`	Menu List	Allows you to define a list (`<LI>`) to act as a menu.
`<META>`	Meta	Declares that HTTP Meta name-value pairs are used for this Web page.
`<NOBR>`	No Break	Indicates that no lines implement line breaks except those explicitly coded with a ` ` tag.
`<NOTE>`	Note	Displays text in note format.
`<OPTION>`	Form Select Option	Allows you to specify options for your HTML document.
`<OL>`	Ordered List	Displays a list with numbered items.
`<OVERLAY>`	Overlay	Speeds up image rendering by drawing small changes over a base figure. However, `<OVERLAY>` can cause a maintenance headache with your Web pages.
`<P>`	Paragraph	Defines a block of text to be displayed in paragraph form. It also allows you to specify formatting characteristics (such as `<CENTER>`) to a block of text.
`<PERSON>`	Person	Defines a person in your document. `<PERSON>` displays like normal text, but is used by indexers to make persons on your Web page accessible by Web browsers.
`<PRE>`	Preformatted	Defines text that should be shown in a proportional (fixed width) font with the line breaks and other white space specified. There is no need to use ` `, `<TAB>`, and so on with `<PRE>` because the formatting is defined by the source.
`<Q>`	Quote	Displays text with quotes around it. You can also use the &quot escape character to display a quote.
`<RANGE>`	Range	Defines a range within a document.
`<S>`	Strike through	Displays text with strike through font.
`<SAMP>`	Sample	Defines text that should be shown as literal characters in a proportional (fixed width) font.
`<SELECT>`	Form Select	Defines a form in your HTML document.
`<SMALL>`	Small Text	Displays text in a smaller font than usual.
`<SPOT>`	Spot	Used to specify a location in a document where there is no tag.

(continued)

Table C-2 *(Continued)*

HTML Tag	Tag Name	Description
`<STRONG>`	Strong	Used to emphasize text, usually displayed as boldface.
`<SUB>`	Subscript	Displays text as a subscript, which is a little smaller and below the line of normal text.
`<SUP>`	Superscript	Displays text as a superscript, which is a little smaller and above the line of normal text.
`<TAB>`	Horizontal Tab	Used to place a horizontal tab inside your HTML document.
`<TABLE>`	Table	Initiates a table in your HTML document.
`<TD>`	Table Data	Defines table data for a table row in a table in your HTML document. `<TD>` can only be used within a `<TR>` description.
`<TEXTAREA>`	Form Text Area	Defines a text area in your HTML form.
`<TH>`	Table Header	Defines a header for a table in your HTML document.
`<TITLE>`	Title	Defines a title for your HTML Web page. This is usually displayed in the title bar of your browser.
`<TR>`	Table Row	Defines a row in a table in your HTML document.
`<TT>`	Teletype	Defines text in proportional (fixed width) font.
`<U>`	Underlined	Defines text to be underlined.
`<UL>`	Unordered List	Displays a list with bulleted items.
`<VAR>`	Variable	Displays text as a variable. Most browsers display `variable`-defined text in italics.
`<WBR>`	Word Break	Identifies a place where a word can be broken, or where a line can be broken inside a `<NOBR>` block.
`<XMP>`	Example	Defines example text. <XMP> is obsolete. See `<PRE>` and `<SAMP>` for other alternatives.

Secret

HTML documentation is available on the Internet. To find detailed lists of up-to-date HTML tags, search for "HTML and tags" using your Internet World Wide Web browser. You should also see the World Wide Web Consortium's Web page at `www.w3c.org`.

Comparing Visual J++ with C++

This appendix is for C++ developers who want to learn Java. This should be an easy transition because Java's syntax is derived from C++. Those who are already familiar with Java, but not Visual J++, may derive some benefit from the Visual J++ discussion.

Before beginning to write Java programs and Applets, you must first understand the programming structure. This section covers some fundamental Java concepts targeted toward C++ programmers designed to bring them up to speed in Java.

You write two simple Visual J++ programs: a stand-alone application that displays a string that is passed as a parameter to the program, and an HTML page-based Java Applet.

Java Language Structure

The Java language structure is unique among languages. Many facets of the language, from how it compiles to bytecodes and its directory-based structure aren't found in other languages. This section deals with how to structure a Java program.

The Java Virtual Machine

Java programs compile into a CLASS file rather than an EXE file. The CLASS files need a Java Virtual Machine (VM) to run. Java VMs are available on almost all UNIX, Macintosh, mainframe (VM, CICS, etc.), and DOS/Windows machines, making any Java code you *compile* quite portable. Because Java programs run on a Virtual Machine rather than a physical machine, you, in theory, no longer have to worry about individual machine or operating system idiosyncrasies. This is why Java has become so popular so quickly.

For Visual J++ developers, the best Java VMs to use are JVIEW for stand-alone applications and Internet Explorer 3.0 for Web Applets. This is because Microsoft has added many classes and ActiveX support to the original Java language specification, and Microsoft Java VMs support these additions, whereas other Java class viewers and Web browsers do not.

ActiveX and the Internet

Some say that Microsoft has muddied the Java waters by introducing ActiveX capabilities to their Java VM contained in Internet Explorer 3.0 and later. By doing this, currently only Windows applications that run Internet Explorer can run Java Applets containing ActiveX calls. Even Netscape has not yet added ActiveX support.

However, Microsoft is trying to establish an open standard, and has licensed the ActiveX technology to other companies that can develop cross-platform ActiveX capabilities. Furthermore, ActiveX support can enhance a Web page with available ActiveX controls from Microsoft (such as Microsoft Word and PowerPoint displays).

Hopefully, other browsers can "keep up" with Internet Explorer, and provide ActiveX capabilities in all Web browsers and all Java VMs. Furthermore, Visual J++ classes still run standard Java classes on those machines that don't support ActiveX.

Visual J++ can add ActiveX support to any of your Java applications, unlike other Java compilers. This, too, may change in the near future as market pressures force many Java compilers to provide ActiveX support.

Classes, packages, and directories

Like in C++, Java supports the class construct. `DisplayString` is a class that encapsulates all fields and methods by declaring itself a class:

```
public class DisplayString extends java.awt.Frame {
```

In C++, the same class has the following prototype:

```
class DisplayString : public Frame {
  public :
```

As you can see, class declarations in C++ and Java are similar. The `public` keyword indicates that this class is accessible to all, like in C++. The `extends Frame` clause implies that the `DisplayString` class is inherited from a Frame class.

Frames are child windows of the browser or Java viewer that you're running. Frames easily give your program a graphical appearance. However, notice in the preceding C++ example, you inherited from a Frame class. The Java example did the same, except the prefix `java.awt.` indicates that Frame is part of a larger collection of classes. This collection of classes is called a *package*. The Frame class itself is part of the Abstract Window Toolkit (AWT) defined by Java in the `java.awt` package. (Hence, the Frame class is referred to as `java.awt.Frame`, as shown).

A package indicates that several CLASS files are contained in a directory *relative to the current directory* (or to a directory specified in the class path in your registry) named `java/awt/`. Furthermore, a class file is compiled called `java/awt/Frame.class`.

As you can see by Figure D-1, the Java language contains a set of standard libraries that are part of the Java language specification. As with C++, there is a kernel of C++-like commands that are used as the actual Java language, whereas much of the Java language consists of predefined classes and methods (functions) that are provided as part of the standard Java language specification.

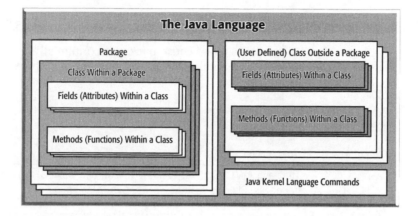

Figure D-1: The Java language consists of a kernel of C++-like commands and classes defined inside and outside of packages.

A function in C++ is called a *method* in Java.

Visual J++ does not allow global methods or variables. In fact, no variables (called *fields* or *attributes*) or functions (called *methods*) can exist outside a class. A *class* is an object-oriented construct that groups fields and methods together. Unlike in C++, there can be only one public class per file. If you want to use another public class, you must open a new file to do so. In Visual J++, this is done through the project workspace, which is covered in Chapter 1.

You can define your own packages with the `package` statement. The following statement:

```
package mypack;
```

places your class file in the `mypack` subdirectory. From there, it is compiled with other classes contained in the `mypack` directory. The `package` statement must be the first line in your Java program.

Although packages are often used in commercial development, each class in a package, by default, automatically has access to all class variables declared in other packages. Packages, then, enable a type of global access to your class variables, unless those class variables are specifically protected with the `private` keyword.

Although Visual J++ supports packages, Visual J++ development typically involves Solutions and Projects to group classes together. While packages detract from encapsulation and hurt the maintainability of code, projects encapsulate every class and provide easy access to public class variables. To group classes together in a project or a solution, use the Project Explorer described in Chapter 1.

Packages Included with Java and Visual J++

Java comes with several packages. These packages contain all the methods that are defined to the Java specification. Eight of the most popular packages are described in Table D-1.

Table D-1	Java Packages
Package	**Description**
java.awt	The Java AWT (Abstract Window Toolkit) defines all of the graphical interfaces. Classes such as `Frame`, `Graphics`, and `Button` are defined in the `java.awt` package.
java.lang	Much of the Java language specification is contained within the `java.lang` package — classes such as `String`, `Math`, and `Thread`.
java.io	Contains those classes whose methods affect disk or stream I/O.
java.net	Contains classes whose methods affect communication with the network and with URLs.
java.util	Contains miscellaneous useful utility classes like `Date`, `Random`, and `Vector`.
java.awt.image	Although the `Image` class is actually contained in the java.awt package, `java.awt.image` contains classes that are used to track and produce images.
java.awt.peer	Contains interfaces that are used to define other windows toolkits.
java.applet	Contains only one class: `Applet`. The `Applet` class is used as a parent to any class that wants to communicate through a Web browser.

To enhance Java in its Visual J++ environment, Microsoft added ActiveX support and a Developer Studio environment for development and debugging.

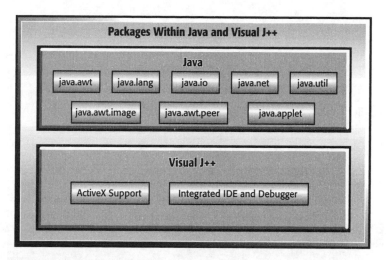

Figure D-2: Visual J++ consists of eight Java packages and additional support for ActiveX and debugging.

Methods

Methods in Visual J++ are almost identical to C++ functions. Methods are executed when a Visual J++ program runs. If you want to write a stand-alone class that displays any strings that are passed to it, you would make a class declaration containing methods to display the string parameter, similar to that in Listing D-1.

Listing D-1: DisplayString.java

```
import java.awt.*;        // Search java.awt package for classes
public class DisplayString extends Frame {  // Inherit java.awt.Frame
for this class
   private String s_display;     // Declare a String to display
// Entry point for a Java Application
   public static void main (String args[]) {
// Construct a new DisplayString object
     Frame f = new DisplayString(args);
   }
// Constructor for DisplayString
   public DisplayString(String args[]) {
// The super class (ancestor) constructor may need calling if
// the sub class uses different parameters in its constructor.
     super();        // Call the Frame constructor
     s_display = "";         // Initialize String
// For loop to go through arguments
     for (int loop = 0; loop < args.length; loop++) {
// Add the argument to the display string and add a space
       s_display = s_display + args[loop]+ " ";
     }
```

```
      if (s_display.length() == 0) {     // Check for arguments
        s_display = "No arguments to be displayed";
      }
      setTitle("Display String Frame"); //Set title of the Frame
      setSize(300,200);        // Resize the frame
      show();           // Show the frame
  }
// The paint method is called whenever a Frame is painted or
resized.
  public void paint(Graphics g) {
// Write the display string on the Frame.
    g.drawString(s_display, 50, 50);
  }
}
```

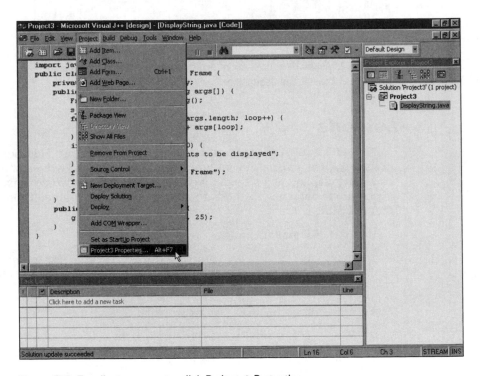

Figure D-3: To adjust arguments, click Project ⇨ Properties.

With Visual J++, you can specify default arguments for a project to be used in development. You can click Project, Properties (Figure D-3) to set arguments for a stand-alone application. In Figure D-4, the arguments `Send Invoice to Lance Tillman for $4,200` were added to the command line. This resulted in the Frame shown in Figure D-5.

Figure D-4: To adjust arguments, click Project ➪ Properties.

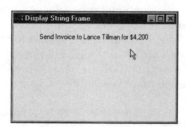

Figure D-5: Frames are used to develop stand-alone Windows applications in Java.

The DisplayString class contains three methods. The main method is executed every time a stand-alone Visual J++ program runs, like the main function is executed at the beginning of a C++ program, or the WinMain function is executed at the start of a Windows C++ program. The main method passes the argument list to the DisplayString constructor. The DisplayString constructor formats command line arguments into a String array called s_display. Then a new frame is created, the title and size are set, and the frame is shown.

Tip

As with C++, case is important in Java and Visual J++. A String (with a capital S) is a class that's included with Java to handle all string manipulation. When referring to classes, such as a String array, always use an initial capital letter.

The paint method in Listing D-1 is called from the Frame ancestor when the Frame window first is painted. The paint method is called whenever a graphical component, like a frame, is drawn on a monitor. In the paint method in Listing D-1, you take the graphical representation of a text string and place it on the graphical part of the Frame.

Fields

Fields in Java are almost identical to fields in C++. In Listing D-1, a String named s_display is declared to be a Java class variable:

```
public class DisplayString extends Frame {
  private static String s_display;
```

In C++, the same declaration appears as follows:

```
class DisplayString : public Frame {
 private :
     static char *s_display;
  public :
```

The only difference in the declarations is that in C++, strings must be pointers to null-terminated character arrays, whereas in Java, pointers are hidden, and a String is a predefined class.

Modifiers

Modifiers in Java are similar to C++. Although methods, classes, and fields aren't required on every declaration, almost all classes, methods, and fields use them. Modifiers, like private, public, and static, are placed in front of the class, method, or field declaration, and are used to define the scope, accessibility, or memory usage of a class, method, or field. Table D-2 shows a list of all modifiers that affect the scope of a class, method, or variable.

Table D-2   Java Scope Modifiers

Modifier	How Used	Description
public	class	A public class modifier indicates that the class can be instantiated by any other class. Each Java program file can have only one public class.
	method	A public method can be called from any other Java method.
	field	A public field can be accessed from any other Java method.
private	method	A private method can be called only by those methods within the same class.
	field	A private field can be accessed only by those methods within the same class.
protected	method	A protected method can be called by any method within the same class or package, or by any method in a descendent class.
	field	A protected field can be accessed by any method within the same class or package, or by any method in a descendent class.

Modifier	How Used	Description
private protected	method	A private protected method can be called by any method within the same class or by any method in a descendent class.
	field	A private protected method can be accessed by any method within the same class or by any method in a descendent class.
(no modifiers)	class	If no modifiers are given to a class, then that class can be instantiated by any method within the same package.
	method	If no modifiers are given to a method, then that method can be called by any method within the same package.
	field	If no modifiers are given to a field, then that field can be accessed by any method within the same package.

If a modifier description is not listed for a class, method, or field in Table D-2 or Table D-3, then that modifier cannot be used by that class, method, or field. For instance, you can't have a private class or a native field.

Table D-3 shows modifiers that affect or describe the memory usage, inheritance, and location of a class, method, or field.

Table D-3   Nonscope Java Modifiers

Modifier	How Used	Description
abstract	class	This class contains some abstract methods with no body that need to be defined by a descendent class.
	interface	An interface is a special kind of abstract class. Interfaces are described in detail in Chapter 6. Interfaces are always abstract whether or not they are explicitly defined to be abstract.
	method	This class contains no body, but rather is defined in a child class. This way, if a parent class calls the abstract method, the descendent method is called. All nonabstract descendents must define a body for each abstract method declared in a parent class, and only abstract parent classes can contain abstract methods.
final	class	A final class may not be inherited from.
	method	A final method may not be overshadowed by a descendant method of the same name.
	field	A final field is constant. The value of a final field must be defined when it is declared.

(continued)

Table D-3	(Continued)	
Modifier	*How Used*	*Description*
static	method	A static method can be called without instantiating the class. Static methods can only call other static methods unless they instantiate a class and call that class's methods. Static methods only have access to static fields or fields within instantiated classes.
	field	A static field is allocated at runtime and can be accessed without instantiating a class.
native	method	A native method is available as a C++ compiled executable or DLL. This method is machine-dependent and exists outside of the Java Virtual Machine. Native methods are declared in Java, but the body of a native method is always omitted. Native methods should probably be replaced with ActiveX modules when possible, because ActiveX modules have better type checking.
synchronized	method	With multithreaded programs, the synchronized modifier prevents any class variables from being changed while the synchronized method is running. The synchronized modifier is covered in more detail in Chapter 21: Advanced Threads.
transient	field	The transient modifer is not currently used. In future specifications of Java, transient will be used to define fields that can be deallocated after class methods are finished running. Although transient currently has no effect, be extremely careful using this modifier. Future versions of your programs may have intermittent errors if you use it.
volatile	field	The value of a volatile field changes *asynchronously*, or is changed by other programs outside of the Java VM. The volatile keyword tells Java not to store the contents of the field in a register, and to re-retrieve the field's value from memory every time the field is used.

Java Similarities with C++

Because Java was based on C++, there are strong similarities between the two languages. This section describes those similarities.

Operators

Java operators are almost identical to C++, including the test equals operator (==) used in conditional statements, the conditional operator (?:), and the increment and decrement operators (++ and --). The only differences are as follows:

- \>> and the equivalent combination operator >>= are used as right shifts that preserve the sign bit of a variable. Of course, bitwise operators are not often used by Java programmers, and sign-preserving bitwise operators will probably be used even less, because dividing by two and truncating would produce the same results and be easier to understand.

- &, ^, and | can all be used as logical operators that evaluate an entire expression before returning a result. These are less efficient than the equivalent && and || variables that return a result as soon as possible, but you can use &, ^, and | if you are evaluating the result of a function that must be executed.

- delete is considered an operator in C++, but is not supported in Java. All memory deallocation is handled by the Java VM garbage collection, and you don't have to mess with it anymore.

- new is considered a keyword in Java rather than an operator in C++. The only difference is that the new keyword must be followed by a constructor method call. Therefore, parentheses are required during construction, as seen by the new call in Listing D-1:

```
Frame f = new DisplayString();
```

- Java includes an instanceof logical operator. This operator is used to test if a variable that is declared as an ancestor or an interface is an "instance of" a particular subclass. For example, in the main function, you defined a Frame variable as a new DisplayString. The following expression would test true:

```
if (f instanceof DisplayString) . . .
```

- There is no sizeof operator. Arrays can use the length parameter, as seen in Listing D-1, to determine the size of an array. Strings can use the String.length() function to return the length of a string.

- The : (colon) operator is only applicable when using the case statement inside a switch construct. Inheritance typically implied by the : operator is replaced by the extends Java keyword to indicate inheritance.

- The C++ :: (double colon) operator is not used in Java. All Java methods are defined within the class declaration, and cannot be defined outside of the class declaration. Therefore, :: is not needed during method declaration to determine what class a method belongs to.

There is no need for scope resolution using :: as is done in C++. There are no external global functions allowed, and to call an ancestor function, you use the super keyword. The following statement returns the value returned by the myfunction method found in the ancestor class:

```
return super.myfunction();
```

- The , (comma) operator is implemented in Java, as in C++, except for evaluations in if, while, and for constructs. To simulate the comma, use an && between sections. In a for loop, you can still use a comma operator in the initialization and increment sections, but not in the evaluation section as in C++.

Looping and decision statements

The if, switch, do, while, and for statements are the same in Java as they are in C++. However, in C++ zero (0) and NULL are equivalent to false. In Java, false is a reserved word that is different from both zero (0) and null. Also, as was mentioned before, the comma operator can be used in the evaluation part of a for loop:

```
for (initialization; evaluation; increment) { . . .
```

However, in Java, you cannot use the comma operator in the evaluation of a loop and must instead use the && operator to achieve the same effect. (Often, the && operator is used in the evaluation section of a for loop anyway, so this may not affect many C++ developers.)

The continue and break statements work the same in C++ as they do in Java. However, Java allows labeled break and continue statements in for, while, do, and switch statements:

```
int max = array.length;
int last_checked;
outer: for (loop1=0; loop1 < array.length ; loop1++) {
  last_checked = 0;
  for (loop2=0; loop2 < array.length - loop1; loop2++) {
    if (loop2 > max) {
      if (last_checked == 0) {
        break outer;
      }
      continue outer;
    }
    if (array[loop2] < array[loop2+1]) {
      last_checked = loop2;
      int holder = array[loop2];
      array[loop2] = array[loop2+1];
      array[loop2+1] = holder;
    }
  }
  max = last_checked;
}
```

When the preceding bubble sort executes, it keeps track of how far it should process (with max) and if any more sorting is necessary. If the inner sort is finished, a `continue` statement executes that breaks out of the inner loop and continues the outer loop. If the entire array is sorted, the outer loop is broken out of from a `break` statement inside the inner loop.

Secret

Although `goto` is a reserved word, it currently is not in use. Java has no `goto` statement, making the use of `break` and `continue` important.

The `do-while` and the `while` statements behave the same in Java as they do in C++. The `do` loop:

```
do {
  // loop statements go here
} while (test_condition == true);
```

tests a condition after executing the statements inside the loop at least once. This is called a post-test loop, because the testing occurs after the execution of a loop. The `while` statement:

```
while (test_condition == true) {
  // loop statements go here
}
```

tests conditions before a loop executes, and does not execute the loop at all if the test_condition is not true, as in C++.

The `switch` statement evaluates one variable against a series of constants, and has not changed from C++. The following `switch` statement tests a status code and assigns a `status_string` based on the code. If the status code is invalid, an error_message method is called:

```
switch (status) {
  case 'I' :
    status_string = "Inactive";
    break;
  case 'A' :
    status_string = "Active";
    break;
  default :
    error_message("Invalid Status");
} // End switch month
```

The main method

As with C++, Java programs always start with a main method. However, there are some differences in implementation:

- The main method in C++ must always be a standalone function; in Java, main must be contained within every standalone application's starting class.

■ The prototype for a main function in C++ is either:

```
void main();
```

or:

```
void main(int argc, char * argv[]);
```

depending on whether or not you want to check for arguments passed to the program. In this prototype, argc is the number of arguments and argv is a pointer to a string array containing those arguments. Conversely, in Java the main method within a class must always be defined as:

```
public static void main (String args[]) {
```

In Java, args is a String array that contains all the parameters passed to a Java program. To find the number of parameters, you query args.length.

Secret

The .length attribute can be used on any array defined in Java, as seen in the for loop in Listing D-1:

```
for (int loop = 0; loop < args.length; loop++) {
```

Secret

C++/Windows developers don't use a main function, but rather a WinMain function. The differences between a C++ main function used in non-Windows development and a WinMain function used in C++ windows development are quite significant. A main function in C++ has the following function prototype:

```
void main();
```

Alternatively, if you intend to pass command-line arguments to your non-Windows program, you would use the following main function prototype:

```
void main(int argc, char * argv[]);
```

where argc? is the number of arguments passed and argv is a pointer to a string array containing each of the arguments.

Windows developers, on the other hand, use a WinMain function as the entry point into their Windows C++ program with the following prototype:

```
int PASCAL WinMain(HINSTANCE hCurrInstance,
    HINSTANCE hPrevInstance,
    LPSTR lpCmdLine, int nCmdShow);
```

Because Java originated from the Unix world where Windows does not exist (much), the main function was adopted rather than the WinMain function. (It's a good thing, too. The main function is much easier to understand, and most C++ developers were annoyed at the additional complication needed using the WinMain function for the Windows environment.)

Method overloading

Just as in C++, you can overload methods in Java. Overloaded methods are quite prevalent in the Java language specifications. For instance, the Java prototype for the write method in the `java.io.BufferedOutputStream` **class** can be used to write a single byte (as follows):

```
public synchronized void write(int b);
```

or can be used to write an entire byte array:

```
public synchronized void write(byte buffer[ ], int offset, int len);
```

A call using the following syntax

```
java.io.BufferedOutputStream.write((int) 'A');
```

calls a method different from the one called by this next syntax:

```
java.io.BufferedOutputStream.write(myarray, 0, myarray.length);
```

Overloaded methods are a great way to simplify your method names and to simplify maintenance and development in your projects.

Arrays

Array processing and declaration is similar in Java and C++. Brackets are used to indicate an array, and array numbering starts at zero. There are some important differences, however:

- In C++, arrays are pointers. This is not the case in Java. Although you might not notice the difference, some array processing has changed because of this. In C++, the following array declaration is valid:

  ```
  int array[ ]; // Valid C++, but invalid Java syntax
  ```

- This syntax is not valid in Java. All array sizes must be declared immediately. However, you can declare a variable length array using the following syntax:

  ```
  int array[ ] = new int[variable_length];
  ```

  variable_length is a variable containing the length of the array.

- All arrays in Java have a `.length` attribute. This enables you to test the number of possible elements in any array:

  ```
  for (int loop = 0; loop < array.length; loop++) {
  ```

  This is handy. In C++, you need to use the `sizeof` operator and divide by the number of bytes contained in the array data type. Java's `.length` attribute simplifies this greatly.

Keywords

There are three remaining keywords in Java that have not been discussed that are similar to C++:

■ `void` declares that a method doesn't return a variable. The main method uses void in this manner:

```
public static void main (String args[]) {
```

Unlike C++, `void` cannot be used to describe a method with no parameters. Instead, an empty parenthesis is used for that. (C++ can, of course, optionally use empty parentheses instead of `void` as well.)

■ `return` still ends a method and returns control to the calling method. The following line of code returns with no arguments for a void method:

```
return;
```

Note that a `return` in the main method terminates the program. The following line of code returns a variable from a method.

```
return variable;
```

■ `this` is used to pass the current class to another method, as in C++. An example of `this` usage is as follows, where the current object is passed to the otherMethod method in the OtherClass class:

```
OtherClass.otherMethod(this);
```

Java Differences with C++

Although Java has many syntactical similarities with C++, it is its own language and not a C++ subset as I've seen written in several magazines. This section describes some of the differences between Java and C++.

No C++ directives

C++ programs go through a preprocessor which converts directives — specifically #include and #define, although other C++ directives exist — into C++ code to be compiled. Java has no preprocessor and no directives. While there is no real substitute for the #IFDEF directive, this section shows Java's substitute for #include and #define.

The import statement versus the #include metacommand

Java's import statement is used in the first line in Listing D-1:

```
import java.awt.*;
```

The import command is often confused with the #include metacommand in C++. However, they have little in common. Java does not support header files (also known as included files, copybooks, and so on). The import statement enables a type of shorthand in your Java program. Instead of typing java.awt.Frame in the following class declaration:

```
public class DisplayString extends java.awt.Frame {
```

you can use an import statement, as done in Listing D-1 with import java.awt.*; you can type **Frame**, and the Visual J++ compiler knows what you're talking about.

```
import java.awt.*;
public class DisplayString extends Frame {
```

The import statement is more of a redirection than a code-copier. When the Visual J++ compiler sees extends Frame, it first looks for a Frame.class file in the current directory, then in the class path, then it looks for a Frame class prefixed by all the clauses defined by the import statement. In fact, what you import doesn't even have to exist, and you receive no error unless you write code that assumes it's there. This is vastly different from the C++ #include metacommand, which copies source code directly into your C++ program before compiling.

Tip
It's true that a Java program has no way to copy source from another program. Although copying code may be useful in some situations, for the most part, copying code is unnecessary. Typical C++ header files contain the class definition and function prototypes, neither of which are supported in Java.

The final Modifier versus the #define Metacommand

The #define metacommand in C++ is used to efficiently declare inline functions and constants. Java uses the final modifier for the same purpose. To declare a constant in Java, you place the final modifier before the constant declaration:

```
public final int only_one = 1;
```

In the preceding example, one is assigned to the only_one constant. The Visual J++ compiler then tries to optimize the use of only_one by replacing only_one with the number 1 throughout your class.

Although true inline functions are not supported in Java, you can declare a method to be final:

```
public final myMethod() { ...
```

or a class to be final:

```
public final class MyClass { ...
```

Typically, Java developers declare methods and classes final to prevent them from being inherited. However, because of some situations involving subclasses, the Java Virtual Machine cannot load a method into cache or register memory unless the method is determined to be final. Hence, if you will never inherit a class or method, be sure to declare the class or method final.

Pointers, garbage collection versus free() and delete

Remember all those memory leaks you had in C++, and how much time it took you to track them down? As part of security, Java does not support any type of pointer. This not only makes for a more secure system, but also makes programming in Java easier to learn, do, and maintain than in C++.

Also, Java does its own garbage collection, so you no longer have to worry about this. There is neither a `free()` method, nor a delete operator. Java determines when a section of memory is no longer in use and automatically deallocates it.

Data types

Here are some comparisons and contrasts between C++ data types and Java data types:

- Java supports short, int, long, float, and double, just like C++.

- Unlike C++, Java supports a boolean data type.

- Java's char data type is two bytes instead of one and is based on Unicode instead of ASCII. (Unicode is described in Appendix E.) For a single-byte data type, Java has provided the byte data type.

- Several different data types, defined as classes, are included in the Java language specification. These data types include String and Date, as well as "object wrappers" for most of the primitive data types (Float, Integer, Long, Double, and so on). Date is defined in the `java.util` package, and the rest of the object wrappers are defined in the `java.lang` package.

Strings

Although character arrays and byte arrays are still supported, the `String` class (defined in the java.lang package) makes string processing much easier than it is in C++. The strings in Java are slightly different from strings in C++:

- Unicode is the basis for strings in Java, rather than ASCII in C++. Therefore, when reading or writing strings, you must be careful to convert to bytes.

■ The `String` class supports + and = operators. Statements like:

```
string1 = string2 + string3;
```

are valid in Java.

■ The test for equality *still* has to be done by function, as it is done in C++. The `compareTo` method in the `String` class replaces the `strcmp` function in C++. The following `compareTo` call:

```
int results = string1.compareTo(string2)
```

sets results to 1 if `string1` is greater than `string2`, 0 if `string1` and `string2` are equal, and -1 if `string1` is less than `string2`. The equals method is often simpler to use (but not as versatile), because the equals method returns only a true if two strings are equal and a false if they're not. The following statement can be used to compare two strings:

```
if (string1.equals(string2)) {
  // Strings are equal
}
else {
  // Strings are not equal
}
```

NULL and null

In the Java language specification, null is a reserved word. It specifically means that the value for a variable is unknown. This is different from C++, where NULL is equal to zero (0). Furthermore, primitive data types (boolean, float, int, short, long, double, and char) cannot be set to null in Java. C++ has no such restriction.

Java exceptions

Java has a unique method of error trapping. With Java, you can trap any errors you want using a construct known as a try-catch-finally block. You can also trigger an error using a throw statement. Finally, in addition to the system errors that can occur, or are already defined for you, you can define your own errors that function like the system errors.

Understanding Visual J++ errors and exceptions

As shown in Figure D-6, Java contains two classes of errors. Errors descended from an Error class are called *Errors* (with a capitol E). Errors usually indicate a serious problem, such as `out of memory`, or the `Java Virtual Machine` is not responding. *Exceptions*, on the other hand, are usually situational and probably due to a programming situation rather than a system problem. Examples of Exceptions include end of file errors, divide by zero, and so on.

The Java Error Class Structure

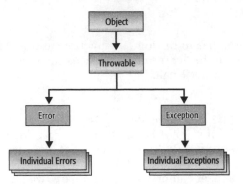

Figure D-6: The Visual J++ error structure has two categories of errors: Error and Exception.

All Errors and Exceptions are descended from a Throwable class. The Throwable class enables the user to use a class to both trigger and catch. You learn more about the Throwable class in the section "Creating Your Own Errors and Exceptions and the throw statement" later in this appendix.

Using error-handling statements

Java's error-handling statements enable you to effectively trap and trigger errors. The try-catch-finally block enables you to trap errors that may occur; the throw statement enables you to trigger an error.

Exceptions and sometimes Errors often need to be trapped for processing. Consider the following code:

```
public static double myPower (double a, double b) {
  double answer = Math.pow(a, b);
  return answer;
}
```

You know that the pow method sometimes throws an ArithmeticException, and you want to catch it, and perhaps give an error message that is understood by the user. ArithmeticException is a predefined Visual J++ Exception. You could use a try-catch-finally block to clean up any conditions set up in the try block. The following code could accomplish this:

```
public static double myPower (double a, double b) {
  try {
    double answer = Math.pow(a, b);
    return answer;
  }
```

```
catch (ArithmeticException e) {
  errorMessage(Double.toString + " raised to the "
      + Double.toString+ "!!! " +
      "ArithmeticException occurs."
      + e.getMessage());
  return 0.0;
}
finally {
        errorMessage (Double.toString + " raised to the "
              + Double.toString
              + "!!!   An unknown error has occurred.   "
              + e.getMessage());
        return 0.0;
    }
}
```

Now, looking at the preceding code, instead of executing a method, first `try` a method. If an error occurs that you expected, you can use the `catch` keyword to catch the error. The `finally` keyword is used to catch any errors not anticipated. (Note that the `finally` keyword is normally executed no matter what errors have been caught. However, the `return` at the end of the `try-catch` blocks enables this `finally` clause to `catch` any errors that were not caught previously.)

Creating your own errors and exceptions

Unfortunately, you can't catch all the errors you want to. For example, if you take a negative number to a negative power, Visual J++ could give you a `NaN` as an answer. (In the Double and Float classes, `NaN` means that the number is 'Not a Number'.) You may need to create your own statements to handle this. Consider the following code:

```
class myException extends Exception {
  public myException () {
    super ();  // Run the parent constructor.
  }
  public myException (String s) {
    super (s);  // Run the parent constructor.
  }
}

public static double myPower (double a, double b)
              throws myException {
  try {
    double answer = Math.pow(a, b);
    // Test for Not a Number
    if (Double.isNaN(answer)) {
      throw new myException(
  "Can't take a fractional power of a negative number");
```

```
    }
      return answer;
    }
  catch (ArithmeticException e) {
    errorMessage(Double.toString
      + " raised to the " + Double.toString+ "!!! "
      + "ArithmeticException occurs."
      + e.getMessage());
    return 0.0;
  }
  catch (myException e) {
    errorMessage(Double.toString
      + " raised to the " + Double.toString
      + "myException occurs."
      + e.getMessage());
    return 0.0;
  }
  finally {
        errorMessage (Double.toString
          + " raised to the " + Double.toString
          + "!!!  An unknown error has occurred.   "
          + e.getMessage());
        return 0.0;
    }
}
```

The first class inherits from the Exception class. In this class, you are
defining a new exception for use in a system.

In the `myPower` method declaration in the preceding code, the `throws`
keyword is used. The `throws` keyword indicates that an error is thrown
during the execution of this function. Then, in the middle of the code, you
use the `throw` keyword to trigger `myException`. Then a `catch` keyword is used
to execute code if `myException` is thrown.

The Importance of Error Trapping

If a method throws an error, the error *must* be caught every time the method is called by another
method, or a syntax error results. Often, you see lines of code like the following:

```
try { fis = new FileInputStream(selectedFile); }
catch (FileNotFoundException e) { }
catch (IOException e) { }
```

Although the code works, you have disabled and ignored any errors that might result from opening a
`FileInputStream`. (File I/O is covered in Chapter 17.)

Ignoring errors is sometimes expedient; testing for every thrown error is often not necessary.
However, by ignoring errors that occur, you may make debugging and run-time error trapping more
difficult.

Although it may seem like a bit of work, exception handling in Java is easy to understand and maintain. It's also much more versatile than error and exception handling in other languages.

Miscellaneous

There are some miscellaneous differences between C++ and Java. The following is a list of specific differences between the two languages:

- There is no enum (Enumerated Data Types) statement in Java, like there is in C++. The enum keyword is not often used, except to define constants that are required as parameters to functions, so this functionality must be hard-coded into each function by the developer. Perhaps future Java language specifications will contain an enum keyword.

- There is no struct statement in Java, like there is in C++. In C++, struct can be replaced in its entirety by class. The class construct in Java can do anything the C++ struct can do. Therefore, struct is not needed in Java.

- There is no union statement in Java, like there is in C++. Java did not put a union clause in the language for security reasons, because redefining data types with other data types introduced a type of possible memory overrun into the Java language. However, I think a union clause can possibly be implemented and may be implemented in future Java language specifications.

- Global variables and global methods are not allowed in Java. Every variable must be defined within a class or method, and every method must be contained within a class.

- Function prototyping is not allowed or necessary in Java. Java supports forward reference checking with methods, so prototypes aren't needed. The one possible exception to this is using an abstract method, which then must be overshadowed (with the same method heading) in every descendent class.

- There is no typedef statement in Java as there is in C++. However, just as C++ no longer needs a typedef as it was needed in C, Java doesn't need a typedef either.

- In C++, you can define a function with a variable number of arguments by using ellipses (...) in the function prototype and function definition, as shown by the following printf function prototype:

```
int printf(const char *format, ...)
```

Forms of the popular printf command carried most C programmers through all their input and output routines. Even in C++, where redirection to streams is often used, the printf function still has its place.

Java does not support weak type checking. You can "kinda" simulate weak type checking with several method overloads, but you never get true variable argument lists. (Nor is this likely to change in the future.)

Programming in Java

You have already written a standalone application in Java with the DisplayString program. In this section, you see how to write a Web Applet and how to make a class both standalone and run in an HTML page.

Developing a Web applet

Web programs are tiny because large programs take too long to download over a modem to be usable. The bulk of the run-time library code for a Java program resides in the Java virtual machine and the classes.zip library that comes with all Java enabled browsers. Java applets consist of calls to the library that already exists on the local machine.

You're not quite done with the DisplayString program yet. Listing D-2 and Figure D-4 show the text for the DisplayStringApplet, which is almost identical to the DisplayString program except that it runs as a Web Applet rather than a stand-alone program.

Listing D-2: DisplayStringApplet.java

```
import java.awt.*;          // Search java.awt package for classes
import java.applet.*;        // Search java.applet package for
classes
// Inherit java.applet.Applet for this class
public class DisplayStringApplet extends Applet {
  private String s_display;       // Declare a String to display
// The init method is the first method called in an applet.
  public void init () {
    s_display = getParameter("Display");    // Get the parameter
    if (s_display == null || s_display.length() == 0) {  // Check
                                                         // for
                                                         // arguments

      s_display = "No arguments to be displayed";
    }
  }
// The paint method is called whenever a Applet is painted or
// resized.
  public void paint(Graphics g) {
    g.drawString(s_display, 50, 50);    // Write the display string
on the Web page.
  }
}
```

In Listing D-2, you can see that java.applet.* is imported. This gives us shorthand access to the java.applet package:

```
import java.applet.*;
```

The next difference between DisplayString in Listing D-1 and DisplayStringApplet in Listing D-2 is that DisplayStringApplet is inherited from the `java.applet.Applet` class rather than the `java.awt.Frame` class, as you can see by the `extends` Applet phrase in the class declaration:

```
public class DisplayStringApplet extends Applet {
```

Applet is a special class that sets up your program to run in a Web browser. Even the window setup and resizing isn't necessary. Web Applets have no constructor. This is because they are not instantiated in the normal sense as stand-alone classes are. However, the `init()` method can be used to define class fields or any other initialization. The `init()` method is inherited from the Applet class. The `paint` method is called by the Applet class when the applet first starts running. Then you can paint your string onto your Web page using the same techniques you did with your Frame program.

Using HTML to run an applet

Every Java Applet needs to be placed inside an HTML Web page. The HTML "language" is more of a format specification than a language, much like early WordPerfect or Runoff documents. The HTML language is covered in some detail in Appendix A. Listing D-3 shows the HTML code used to run the DisplayStringApplet program.

Listing D-3: HTML code to run DisplayStringApplet

```
<html>
<head>
<title>Display String Applet</title>
</head>
<body>
<hr>
<applet
code=DisplayStringApplet
width=400
height=75>
<param
name=Display
value="Send invoice to Lance Tillman for $4,200">
</applet>
<hr>
</body>
</html>
```

Two tags are used to run Java Applets. One is the <APPLET> tag. This tag is used to define which Java Applet you're running and how much Web page space the program needs:

```
<applet
code=DisplayStringApplet
width=400
height=75>
```

In listing D-2, the `java.applet.Applet.getParameter` method is used to get the string associated with the "Display" parameter:

```
s_display = getParameter("Display");
```

This parameter must be defined within the HTML Web page using the <PARAM> tag:

```
<param
name=Display
value="Send invoice to Lance Tillman for $4,200">
```

After the `param` keyword, you then declare a name for your parameter and a value for your parameter. In the preceding example, the name of the parameter is Display and the value of the Display parameter is `"Send invoice to Lance Tillman for $4,200"`. As you can see, HTML coding is not hard and is part of the reason why the World Wide Web became so pervasive in such a short time. Because Web pages are easy to write, many programmers and nonprogrammers have become proficient at Web page development. The Web page defined in Listing D-3, containing the DisplayStringApplet Java program, can be viewed in Figure D-7.

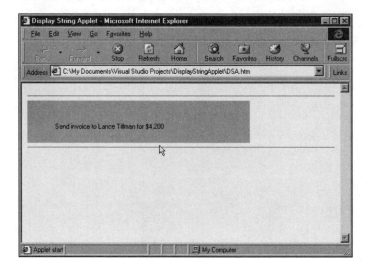

Figure D-7: The DisplayStringApplet can run on a Web page on the Internet.

Although there's a little more to running Applets, there's not much. Applets are easily developed with Java and Visual J++. This is why Java became such a hit so quickly.

Appendix E

Unicode

The ASCII standard has long fallen short in several areas, including international support, mathematical and technical writings, and symbols. The Unicode Worldwide Character Standard (or just *Unicode*) is Java's answer to this dilemma. Unicode is a character coding system designed to support multiple languages, both modern and ancient, as well as technical writings.

Why Unicode?

The secret to Unicode's versatility is that Unicode uses two bytes for storage rather than ASCII's one byte. ASCII only allows 256 unique characters, whereas Unicode allows 65,534 unique characters.

You can specify a Unicode symbol in a string by the formatting command "\u*xxxx*", where *xxxx* is a number that corresponds to the proper Unicode number. Unicode is broken into several categories, which are listed in Table E-1.

The Unicode Standard

The Unicode Standard is copyrighted by the Unicode Consortium, and Unicode is a trademark of the Unicode Consortium.

Because of the huge size of Unicode, listing the entire Unicode is impractical for this appendix. There are two books on the entire Unicode standard:

- *The Unicode Standard, Worldwide Character Encoding, Version 1.0*, Volume 1, Addison-Wesley, 1990 (ISBN 0-201-56788-1)

- *The Unicode Standard, Worldwide Character Encoding, Version 1.0*, Volume 2, Addison-Wesley, 1992 (ISBN 0-201-60845-6)

Table E-1   Unicode Categories

Hexadecimal Range	Unicode Category
0000 – 1FFF	Alphabets
2000 – 2FFF	Symbols and Punctuation
3000 – 4DFF	Chinese, Japanese, and Korean Auxiliary and Unified "Ideographs"
A000 – DFFF	Reserved for Future Assignment
E000 – FFFD	Restricted Use
FFFE – FFFF	Excluded from the Unicode Standard

Secret

Note that FFFE and FFFF are two characters that are excluded from Unicode. This enables you to flag invalid strings in your Unicode-based languages. (In other words, high values are not valid for Unicode characters.)

Alphabets

The Unicode alphabets are derived from 24 supported scripts. These characters cover the major written languages of the world. Table E-2 describes alphabets that are supported in Unicode.

Table E-2   Alphabets Supported in Unicode

Hexadecimal Range	Alphabet Supported in Unicode
0020 – 007E	Basic Latin (The graphic part of US-ASCII)
00A0 – 00FF	Latin Supplement (Extended ASCII)
0100 – 017F	Latin Extended-A
0180 – 024F	Latin Extended-B
0250 – 02AF	IPA Extensions
02B0 – 02FF	Spacing Modifier Letters
0300 – 036F	Combining Diacritical Marks
0370 – 03CF	Basic Greek
03D0 – 03FF	Greek Symbols and Coptic
0400 – 04FF	Cyrillic

Hexadecimal Range	Alphabet Supported in Unicode
0500 – 052F	Unassigned
0530 – 058F	Armenian
0590 – 05CF	Hebrew Extended-A
05D0 – 05EA	Basic Hebrew
05EB – 05FF	Hebrew Extended-B
0600 – 0652	Basic Arabic
0653 – 06FF	Arabic Extended
0700 – 08FF	Ethiopic (still under construction)
0900 – 097F	Devanagari
0980 – 09FF	Bengali
0A00 – 0A7F	Gurmukhi
0A80 – 0AFF	Gujarati
0B00 – 0B7F	Oriya
0B80 – 0BFF	Tamil
0C00 – 0C7F	Telugu
0C80 – 0CFF	Kannada
0D00 – 0D7F	Malayalam
0D80 – 0DFF	Sinhalese (still under construction)
0E00 – 0E7F	Thai
0E80 – 0EFF	Lao
0F00 – 0F7F	Burmese (still under construction)
0F80 – 0FDF	Khmer (still under construction)
1000 – 105F	Tibetan (still under construction)
1060 – 109F	Mongolian (still under construction)
10A0 – 10CF	Georgian Extended
10D0 – 10FF	Basic Georgian
1100 – 11FF	Hangul Jamo
1200 – 125F	Ethiopian (still under construction)
1E00 – 1EFF	Latin Extended Additional
1F00 – 1FFF	Greek Extended

Unsupported Languages

Some modern written languages are not yet supported, or are only partially supported, in Unicode 1.1 due to the need for further research into how to encode certain scripts. The following languages have not yet been finalized in the Unicode standard (and are listed as still under construction in Table E-2):

- Burmese
- Ethiopian
- Ethiopic (Amharic, Geez)
- Sinhalese (Sri Lankan)
- Khmer (Cambodian)
- Tibetan
- Mongolian

The following languages have filed a petition for Unicode support:

- Cherokee
- Cree
- Maldivian (Dihevi)
- Moso (Naxi)
- Pahawh Hmong
- Rong (Lepcha)
- Tai Lu
- Tai Mau
- Tifinagh
- Yi (Lolo)

Secret

Of the languages that have applied for Unicode support, Cherokee seems to be the furthest along by having their own graphical character font defined in the computer. They may soon get Unicode support in the next version of Unicode.

The ASCII Codes

Regular ASCII (0-127) and Extended ASCII (128-255) codes make up the first 1-256 characters of Unicode. They're also used in HTML to help format screens. Table E-3 lists the first 127 characters. This table can be used for String sort order in your English-based programs.

Table E-3   ASCII Chart (Character Codes 0 – 127)

000 blank (Null)	016 right triangle	032 space	048 0	064 @	080 P	096 [ag]	112 p
001 happy face	017 left triangle	033 !	049 1	065 A	081 Q	097 a	113 q
002 inverted happy face	018 up/down arrow	034 "	050 2	066 B	082 R	098 b	114 r
003 heart	019 double	035 #	051 3	067 C	083 S	099 c	115 s
004 diamond	020 paragraph sign	036 $	052 4	068 D	084 T	100 d	116 t
005 club	021 section sign	037 %	053 5	069 E	085 U	101 e	117 u
006 spade	022 rectangle	038 &	054 6	070 F	086 V	102 f	118 v
007 bullet	023 up/down to line	039 '	055 7	071 G	087 W	103 g	119 w
008 inverted bullet	024 up arrow	040 (	056 8	072 H	088 X	104 h	120 x
009 circle	025 down arrow	041)	057 9	073 I	089 Y	105 i	121 y
010 inverted	026 right arrow	042 *	058 :	074 J	090 Z	106 j	122 z
011 male sign	027 left arrow	043 +	059 ;	075 K	091 [	107 k	123 {
012 female sign	028 lower left box	044 ,	060 <	076 L	092 \	108 l	124 [vb]
013 single note	029 left/right arrow	045 [ms]	061 =	077 M	093]	109 m	125 }
014 double note	030 up triangle triangle	046 .	062 >	078 N	094 [td]	110 n	126 [td]
015 sun	031 down triangle	047 /	063 ?	079 O	095 _	111 o	127 house

Symbols and Punctuation

Symbols and punctuation are often similar in several languages. Unicode codes 2000 – 27BF are used to specify punctuation, as shown in Table E-4.

Table E-4	Symbols and Punctuation Supported in Unicode
Hexadecimal Range	**Symbol or Punctuation Supported in Unicode**
2000 – 206F	General punctuation
2070 – 209F	Superscripts and subscripts
20A0 – 20CF	Currency symbols
20D0 – 20FF	Combining diacritical marks for symbols
2100 – 214F	Letter-like symbols
2150 – 218F	Number forms
2190 – 21FF	Arrows
2200 – 22FF	Mathematical operators
2300 – 23FF	Miscellaneous technical
2400 – 243F	Control pictures
2440 – 245F	Optical Character Recognition
2460 – 24FF	Enclosed alphanumerics
2500 – 257F	Box drawings
2580 – 259F	Block elements
25A0 – 25FF	Geometric shapes
2600 – 26FF	Miscellaneous symbols
2700 – 27BF	Dingbats

Chinese, Japanese, and Korean Auxiliary and Unified Ideographs

Some languages don't use an alphabet paradigm in their written work. Languages such as Chinese, Japanese, and Korean (CJK) use word-based alphabets. As these countries represent a large portion of the world's population and the world's technical base, they cannot be ignored by any multilingual support. Consequently, these languages require special consideration from Unicode. Table E-5 shows how Unicode categorizes the CJK languages.

Table E-5	CJK Auxiliary and Unified Ideographs Supported in Unicode
Hexadecimal Range	**Alphabet Supported in Unicode**
3000 – 303F	CJK Symbols and Punctuation
3040 – 309F	Hiragana
30A0 – 30FF	Katakana
3100 – 312F	Bopomofo
3130 – 318F	Hangul Compatibility Jamo
3190 – 319F	CJK Miscellaneous (Kaeriten)
3200 – 32FF	Enclosed CJK Letters and Months
3300 – 33FF	CJK Compatibility
3400 – 3D2D	Hangul
3D2E – 44B7	Hangul Supplementary-A
44B8 – 4DFF	Hangul Supplementary-B
4E00 – 9FFF	CJK Unified Ideographs

Restricted Use

Restricted use codes are codes that are used for compatibility, combination characters, and form variants. Table E-6 lists the Unicode restricted use codes.

Table E-6	Unicode Restricted Use Codes
Hexadecimal Range	**Restricted Use Breakdown in Unicode**
E000 – F8FF	Private Use Area
F900 – FAFF	CJK Compatibility Ideographs
FB00 – FB4F	Alphabetic Presentation Forms
FB50 – FDFF	Arabic Presentation Forms-A
FE20 – FE2F	Combinint Half Marks
FE30 – FE4F	CJK Compatibility Forms (verticals and overlines)
FE50 – FE6F	Small Form Variants
FE70 – FEFE	Arabic Presentation Forms-B
FF00 – FFEF	Half-width and Full-width Forms
FFF0 – FFFD	Specials

Unicode and ASCII Conversion

Often, the data you read into your English-based programs is in ASCII format. ASCII characters use one byte instead of two, so some conversion is necessary. Java and Visual J++ provide a Universal Translation Format (UTF-8) with the `java.io.DataInputStream.readUTF()` and `java.io.DataOutputStream.writeUTF()` methods. These methods automatically convert Unicode into ASCII-based information found in Table E-7.

Table E-7   Unicode to ASCII Conversion

Unicode Start	Unicode End	UTF-8 size
'\u0000' (0)	'\u007F' (255)	8 bits (ASCII 0 – 255)
'\u0080' (256)	'\u07FF' (2047)	11 bits
'\u0800' (2048)	'\uFFFF' (65535)	16 bits

As you can see, UTF-8 encoding can be used to convert Unicode to ASCII, because ASCII is all contained in the eight-bit (one-byte) size of the UTF-8 standard.

Appendix F

What's on the CD-ROM

The CD-ROM bundled with this book contains a whole bunch of tools that can help you develop, test, and deploy your applications. Table F-1 describes the tools that you can find on the CD-ROM. Some of these tools have uses beyond strict Visual J++ development.

Table F-1   CD-ROM Contents

Item or Package	Description
This Book	The entire text of *Visual J++ 6 Secrets* is on the CD-ROM in PDF format. This enables you to search through the book's content.
Adobe Acrobat Reader	This utility from Adobe lets you read and print electronic documents saved as .PDF files. You can not only read the book on-screen, but also print out (for your own use) topics of special interest.
Source Code Examples from the Book	This book is just chock-full of source code. Every program in any listing in the book is also placed on the CD. (Note that each program is in its own directory, listed by program name.)
Sun JDK (Version 1.1.6)	Sometimes, you may not be sure how Sun's standard Java environment will react to your Visual J++ code. Sun's JDK is included so you can test your Visual J++ code and classes against the Sun standard.
Internet Explorer 4	Have you ever tried to download IE 4 from Microsoft's Web site? I used to start it before I went to bed at night, and it usually finished sometime the next morning. Fortunately, we have IE 4 on the CD.
Paint Shop Pro	This image creation and manipulation program is easy to use and is very functional. This software is an evaluation version; the user *must* purchase the registered copy after the evaluation period or remove the evaluation version from his/her system.
WinZip	Microsoft can deploy in ZIP format, and WinZip can help you manage your ZIP files. However, far from being a Visual J++-only tool, WinZip can be used to compress any files easily and quickly.
WS_FTP	Microsoft can automatically deploy your solution to a remote server. WS_FTP allows you to view all the files on your server and transfer files from your Web server to your local machine, and from your local machine to your Web server.

Index

(continued)

(continued)

X

Y

Z

IDG BOOKS WORLDWIDE, INC.
END-USER LICENSE AGREEMENT

4. **Restrictions on Use of Individual Programs.** You must follow the individual requirements and restrictions detailed for each individual program in Appendix F of this Book. These limitations are also contained in the individual license agreements recorded on the Software Media. These limitations may include a requirement that after using the program for a specified period of time, the user must pay a registration fee or discontinue use. By opening the Software packet, you will be agreeing to abide by the licenses and restrictions for these individual programs that are detailed in Appendix F and on the Software Media. None of the material on this Software Media or listed in this Book may ever be redistributed, in original or modified form, for commercial purposes.

5. **Limited Warranty.**

   (a) IDGB warrants that the Software and Software Media are free from defects in materials and workmanship under normal use for a period of sixty (60) days from the date of purchase of this Book. If IDGB receives notification within the warranty period of defects in materials or workmanship, IDGB will replace the defective Software Media.

   (b) **IDGB AND THE AUTHOR OF THE BOOK DISCLAIM ALL OTHER WARRANTIES, EXPRESS OR IMPLIED, INCLUDING WITHOUT LIMITATION IMPLIED WARRANTIES OF MERCHANTABILITY AND FITNESS FOR A PARTICULAR PURPOSE, WITH RESPECT TO THE SOFTWARE, THE PROGRAMS, THE SOURCE CODE CONTAINED THEREIN, AND/OR THE TECHNIQUES DESCRIBED IN THIS BOOK. IDGB DOES NOT WARRANT THAT THE FUNCTIONS CONTAINED IN THE SOFTWARE WILL MEET YOUR REQUIREMENTS OR THAT THE OPERATION OF THE SOFTWARE WILL BE ERROR-FREE.**

   (c) This limited warranty gives you specific legal rights, and you may have other rights that vary from jurisdiction to jurisdiction.

6. **Remedies.**

   (a) IDGB's entire liability and your exclusive remedy for defects in materials and workmanship shall be limited to replacement of the Software Media, which may be returned to IDGB with a copy of your receipt at the following address: Software Media Fulfillment Department, Attn.: *Visual J++ 6 Secrets*, IDG Books Worldwide, Inc., 7260 Shadeland Station, Ste. 100, Indianapolis, IN 46256, or call 1-800-762-2974. Please allow three to four weeks for delivery. This Limited Warranty is void if failure of the Software Media has resulted from accident, abuse, or misapplication. Any replacement Software Media will be warranted for the remainder of the original warranty period or thirty (30) days, whichever is longer.

(b) In no event shall IDGB or the author be liable for any damages whatsoever (including without limitation damages for loss of business profits, business interruption, loss of business information, or any other pecuniary loss) arising from the use of or inability to use the Book or the Software, even if IDGB has been advised of the possibility of such damages.

(c) Because some jurisdictions do not allow the exclusion or limitation of liability for consequential or incidental damages, the above limitation or exclusion may not apply to you.

7. **U.S. Government Restricted Rights.** Use, duplication, or disclosure of the Software by the U.S. Government is subject to restrictions stated in paragraph (c)(1)(ii) of the Rights in Technical Data and Computer Software clause of DFARS 252.227-7013, and in subparagraphs (a) through (d) of the Commercial Computer - Restricted Rights clause at FAR 52.227-19, and in similar clauses in the NASA FAR supplement, when applicable.

8. **General.** This Agreement constitutes the entire understanding of the parties and revokes and supersedes all prior agreements, oral or written, between them and may not be modified or amended except in a writing signed by both parties hereto that specifically refers to this Agreement. This Agreement shall take precedence over any other documents that may be in conflict herewith. If any one or more provisions contained in this Agreement are held by any court or tribunal to be invalid, illegal, or otherwise unenforceable, each and every other provision shall remain in full force and effect.

Java™ Developer's Kit Version 1.1.6, Binary Code License

This binary code license ("License") contains rights and restrictions associated with use of the accompanying software and documentation ("Software"). Read the License carefully before installing the Software. By installing the Software you agree to the terms and conditions of this License.

1. **Limited License Grant.** Sun grants to you ("Licensee") a non-exclusive, non-transferable limited license to use the Software without fee for evaluation of the Software and for development of Java™-compatible applets and applications. Licensee may make one archival copy of the Software and may re-distribute complete, unmodified copies of the Software to software developers within Licensee's organization to avoid unnecessary download time, provided that this License conspicuously appear with all copies of the Software. Except for the foregoing, Licensee may not re-distribute the Software in whole or in part, either separately or included with a product. Refer to the Java Runtime Environment Version 1.1.6 binary code license (http://java.sun.com/products/JDK/1.1/index.html) for the availability of runtime code which may be distributed with Java compatible applets and applications.

2. **Java Platform Interface.** Licensee may not modify the Java Platform Interface ("JPI", identified as classes contained within the "java" package or any subpackages of the "java" package), by creating additional classes within the JPI or otherwise causing the addition to or modification of the classes in the JPI. In the event that Licensee creates any Java-related API and distributes such API to others for applet or application development, Licensee must promptly publish an accurate specification for such API for free use by all developers of Java-based software.

3. **Restrictions.** Software is confidential copyrighted information of Sun and title to all copies is retained by Sun and/or its licensors. Licensee shall not modify, decompile, disassemble, decrypt, extract, or otherwise reverse engineer Software. Software may not be leased, assigned, or sublicensed, in whole or in part. Software is not designed or intended for use in on-line control of aircraft, air traffic, aircraft navigation or aircraft communications; or in the design, construction, operation or maintenance of any nuclear facility. Licensee warrants that it will not use or redistribute the Software for such purposes.

4. **Trademarks and Logos.** This License does not authorize Licensee to use any Sun name, trademark or logo. Licensee acknowledges that Sun owns the Java trademark and all Java-related trademarks, logos and icons including the Coffee Cup and Duke ("Java Marks") and agrees to: (i) to comply with the Java Trademark Guidelines at http://java.sun.com/trademarks.html; (ii) not do anything harmful to or inconsistent with Sun's rights in the Java Marks; and (iii) assist Sun in protecting those rights, including assigning to Sun any rights acquired by Licensee in any Java Mark.

5. **Disclaimer of Warranty.** Software is provided "AS IS," without a warranty of any kind. ALL EXPRESS OR IMPLIED REPRESENTATIONS AND WARRANTIES, INCLUDING ANY IMPLIED WARRANTY OF MERCHANTABILITY, FITNESS FOR A PARTICULAR PURPOSE OR NON-INFRINGEMENT, ARE HEREBY EXCLUDED.

6. **Limitation of Liability.** SUN AND ITS LICENSORS SHALL NOT BE LIABLE FOR ANY DAMAGES SUFFERED BY LICENSEE OR ANY THIRD PARTY AS A RESULT OF USING OR DISTRIBUTING SOFTWARE. IN NO EVENT WILL SUN OR ITS LICENSORS BE LIABLE FOR ANY LOST REVENUE, PROFIT OR DATA, OR FOR DIRECT, INDIRECT, SPECIAL, CONSEQUENTIAL, INCIDENTAL OR PUNITIVE DAMAGES, HOWEVER CAUSED AND REGARDLESS OF THE THEORY OF LIABILITY, ARISING OUT OF THE USE OF OR INABILITY TO USE SOFTWARE, EVEN IF SUN HAS BEEN ADVISED OF THE POSSIBILITY OF SUCH DAMAGES.

7. **Termination.** Licensee may terminate this License at any time by destroying all copies of Software. This License will terminate immediately without notice from Sun if Licensee fails to comply with any provision of this License. Upon such termination, Licensee must destroy all copies of Software.

8. **Export Regulations.** Software, including technical data, is subject to U.S. export control laws, including the U.S. Export Administration Act and its associated regulations, and may be subject to export or import regulations in other countries. Licensee agrees to comply strictly with all such regulations and acknowledges that it has the responsibility to obtain licenses to export, re-export, or import Software. Software may not be downloaded, or otherwise exported or re-exported (i) into, or to a national or resident of, Cuba, Iraq, Iran, North Korea, Libya, Sudan, Syria or any country to which the U.S. has embargoed goods; or (ii) to anyone on the U.S. Treasury Department's list of Specially Designated Nations or the U.S. Commerce Department's Table of Denial Orders.

9. **Restricted Rights.** Use, duplication or disclosure by the United States government is subject to the restrictions as set forth in the Rights in Technical Data and Computer Software Clauses in DFARS 252.227-7013(c) (1) (ii) and FAR 52.227-19(c) (2) as applicable.

10. **Governing Law.** Any action related to this License will be governed by California law and controlling U.S. federal law. No choice of law rules of any jurisdiction will apply.

11. **Severability.** If any of the above provisions are held to be in violation of applicable law, void, or unenforceable in any jurisdiction, then such provisions are herewith waived to the extent necessary for the License to be otherwise enforceable in such jurisdiction. However, if in Sun's opinion deletion of any provisions of the License by operation of this paragraph unreasonably compromises the rights or increase the liabilities of Sun or its licensors, Sun reserves the right to terminate the License and refund the fee paid by Licensee, if any, as Licensee's sole and exclusive remedy.

CD-ROM Installation Instructions

1. Insert the *Visual J++ 6 Secrets CD-ROM* into your CD-ROM drive.

2. Click the Start button, followed by Programs, and then Windows Explorer. In the left-hand Explorer Window, select the CD-ROM drive (for example, **D:**).

3. Explorer displays the contents of the disc. All program listings from the book are grouped by program name rather than by chapter number. This facilitates easier searching for code examples.

4. If the directory contains a program that must be installed on your hard disk before you use it, there will be a key executable file (one whose name ends in .EXE) that you must launch to initiate the setup process.

Please see Appendix F for a complete listing of the CD-ROM contents.